CLYMER®

YAMAHA

YZF-R1 • 1998-2003

The world's finest publisher of mechanical how-to manuals

CLYMER®

P.O. Box 12901, Overland Park, Kansas 66282-2901

Copyright ©2004 Penton Business Media, Inc.

FIRST EDITION
First Printing September, 2004
Second Printing July, 2008

Printed in U.S.A.

CLYMER and colophon are registered trademarks of Penton Business Media, Inc.

ISBN-10: 0-89287-892-4

ISBN-13: 978-0-89287-892-5

Library of Congress: 2004112262

AUTHOR: Ed Scott.

TECHNICAL PHOTOGRAPHY: Ed Scott. Special thanks to Curt Jordan of Jordan Engineering, Carlsbad, CA.

TECHNICAL ILLUSTRATIONS: Mitzi McCarthy.

WIRING DIAGRAMS: Bob Meyer and Lee Buell.

EDITOR: James Grooms.

PRODUCTION: Darin Watson.

TOOLS AND EQUIPMENT: K & L Supply Co. at www.klsupply.com.

COVER: Mark Clifford Photography at www.markclifford.com. 2001 R1 courtesy of John Shin.

CLYMER®

Publisher Shawn Etheridge

EDITORIAL

Editorial Director
James Grooms

Editor
Steven Thomas

Associate Editor
Rick Arens

Authors
Jay Bogart
Michael Morlan
George Parise
Mark Rolling
Ed Scott
Ron Wright

Technical Illustrators
Steve Amos
Errol McCarthy
Mitzi McCarthy
Bob Meyer

Group Production Manager
Dylan Goodwin

Production Manager
Greg Araujo

Senior Production Editor
Darin Watson

Production Editors
Holly McComas
Adriane Roberts
Taylor Wright

Production Designer
Jason Hale

MARKETING/SALES AND ADMINISTRATION

Sales Managers
Justin Henton
Matt Tusken

Marketing and Sales Representative
Erin Gribbin

Director, Operations–Books
Ron Rogers

Customer Service Manager
Terri Cannon

Customer Service Account Specialist
Courtney Hollars

Customer Service Representatives
Dinah Bunnell
April LeBlond

Warehouse & Inventory Manager
Leah Hicks

Penton Media

P.O. Box 12901, Overland Park, KS 66282-2901 • 800-262-1954 • 913-967-1719

More information available at *clymer.com*

CONTENTS

QUICK REFERENCE DATA

MOTORCYCLE INFORMATION

MODEL:_____ YEAR:_____

VIN NUMBER:_____

ENGINE SERIAL NUMBER:_____

CARBURETOR SERIAL NUMBER OR I.D. MARK:_____

TIRE AND WHEEL SPECIFICATIONS

Item	Front	Rear
Tire type	Tubeless	Tubeless
Size		
1998-2001 models	120/70 ZR17 (58W)	180/55 ZR17 (73W)
2002-2003 models	120/70 ZR17 (58W)	190/55 ZR17 M/C (73W)
Manufacturer		
1998-1999 models	D207FN (Dunlop)	D207L (Dunlop)
2000-2001 models	MEZ3Y (Metzeler) or D207FQ (Dunlop)	MEZ3Y (Metzeler) or D207N (Dunlop)
2002-2003 models	Pilot Sport E (Michelin) D2008FL (Dunlop)	Pilot Sport (Michelin) D208L (Dunlop)
Minimum tread depth		
1998-1999 models	1.6 mm (0.06 in.)	1.6 mm (0.06 in.)
2000-2001 models	0.8 mm (0.03 in.)	0.8 mm (0.03 in.)
2002-2003 models	1.6 mm (0.06 in.)	1.6 mm (0.06 in.)
Inflation pressure (cold)[1]	250 kPa (36 psi)	250 kPa (36 psi) 290 kPa (42 psi)[2]

1. Tire inflation pressure is for original equipment tires. Aftermarket tires may require different inflation pressure. The use of tires other than those specified by Yamaha may cause instability.
2. Tire pressure for maximum load of 90 kg (198 lbs.).

RECOMMENDED LUBRICANTS AND FLUIDS AND CAPACITIES

Brake fluid	DOT 4
Cooling system	
Coolant type	High quality ethylene-glycol
Coolant capacity	
1998-2001 models	
Radiator and engine	2.55 L (2.7 U.S. qt.)
Reserve tank	0.45 L (0.48 U.S. qt.)
2002-2003 models	
Radiator and engine	2.45 L (2.6 U.S. qt.)
Reserve tank	0.24 L (0.25 U.S. qt.)
Drive chain	Engine oil or chain lubricant suitable for O-ring type chains

(continued)

RECOMMENDED LUBRICANTS AND FLUIDS AND CAPACITIES (continued)

Engine oil	
Grade	Yamalube 4, API SE or SF (non-friction modified)
Viscosity	SAE 10W/30 or 10W/40
Capacity	
1998-2001 models	
Oil change only	2.7 L (2.9 U.S. qt.)
Oil and filter change	2.9 L (3.1 U.S. qt.)
After disassembly (engine dry)	3.6 L (3.8 U.S. qt.)
2002-2003 models	
Oil change only	2.9 L (3.07 U.S. qt.)
Oil and filter change	3.1 L (3.28 U.S. qt.)
After disassembly (engine dry)	3.8 L (4.02 U.S. qt.)
Fuel	
Type	Unleaded
Octane	Pump research octane of 86 or higher
Fuel tank	
Capacity, including reserve	
1998-2001 models	18.0 L (4.75 U.S. gal.)
2002-2003 models	17.0 L (4.49 U.S. gal.)
Reserve only	
1998-2001 models	5.5 L (1.45 U.S. gal.)

MAINTENANCE AND TUNE-UP SPECIFICATIONS

Brake pedal height	
Top of brake pedal below footrest bracket	
1998-2001 models	35-40 mm (1.38-1.57 in.)
2002-2003 models	38-42 mm (1.50-1.65 in.)
Carburetor synchronizing level difference (maximum)	
1998-2001 models	1.33 kPa/10 mm Hg (0.4 in. Hg)
Clutch lever free play	10-15 mm (0.39-0.59 in.)
Compression pressure @ 400 rpm	
(at sea level)	1450 kPa (210 psi)
Drive chain free play	40-50 mm (1.57-1.97 in.)
EXUP cable free play	1.5 mm (0.059 in.)
Gearshift pedal	
1998-2001 models (distance between pivot points)	305 mm (12.0 in.)
2002-2003 models	38-43 mm (1.50-1.69 in.)
Idle speed	
1998-1999 models	1050-1150 rpm
2000-2003 models	1000-1100 rpm
Spark plug type	
1998-2001 models	CR9E (NGK) or U27ESR-N (Denso)
2002-2003 models	CR9EIA-9 (NGK) or IU27D (Denso)
Spark plug gap	
1998-2001 models	0.7-0.8 mm (0.028-0.031 in.)
2002-2003 models	0.8-0.9 mm (0.032-0.035 in.)
Throttle body synchronizing level difference (maximum)	
2002-2003 models	1.33 kPa (0.4 in. Hg)
Throttle cable free play	3-5 mm (0.12-0.20 in.)
Valve clearance (cold)	
1998-2001 models	
Intake	0.11-0.20 mm (0.0043-0.0079 in.)
Exhaust	0.21-0.30 mm (0.0083-0.0118 in.)
2002-2003 models	
Intake	0.11-0.20 mm (0.0043-0.0079 in.)
Exhaust	0.21-0.27 mm (0.0083-0.0106 in.)

MAINTENANCE AND TUNE UP TORQUE SPECIFICATIONS

Item	N•m	in.-lb.	ft.-lb.
Brake hose banjo bolt	30	–	22
Cylinder head cover bolt	12	106	–
Drive sprocket nut	85	–	61
Driven sprocket nuts			
1998-2001 models	69	–	50
2002-2003 models	100	–	72
Front axle (1998-2001 models)	72	–	52
Front axle bolt (2002-2003 models)	90	–	65
Front axle pinch bolt			
1998-2001 models	28	–	17
2002-on models	18	–	13
Oil drain bolt	43	–	31
Oil filter cartridge	17	–	12
Oil gallery plug			
1998-2001 models	20	–	14
2002-2003 models	10	88	–
Timing mark inspection cap	15	–	11
Rear axle nut	150	–	110
Spark plug	13	115	–

CHAPTER ONE

GENERAL INFORMATION

This detailed and comprehensive manual covers the Yamaha YZF-R1 models from 1998-2003. The text provides complete information on maintenance, tune-up, repair and overhaul. Hundreds of photos and drawings guide the reader through every job.

All procedures are in step-by-step form and designed for the reader who may be working on the motorcycle for the first time.

MANUAL ORGANIZATION

A shop manual is a tool and as in all Clymer manuals, the chapters are thumb tabbed for easy reference. Main headings are listed in the table of contents and the index. Frequently used specifications and capacities from the tables at the end of each individual chapter are listed in the *Quick Reference Data* section at the front of the manual. Specifications and capacities are provided in metric and U.S standard units of measure.

During some of the procedures there will be references to headings in other chapters or sections of the manual. When a specific heading is called out it in a step it will be *italicized* as it appears in the manual. If a sub-heading is indicated as being "in this section" it is located within the same main heading. For example, the sub-heading *Handling Gasoline Safely* is located within the main heading **SAFETY**.

This chapter provides general information on shop safety, tools and their usage, service fundamentals and shop supplies. General motorcycle specifications and useful workshop data are in **Tables 1-9** at the end of the chapter.

Chapter Two provides methods for quick and accurate diagnosis of problems. Troubleshooting procedures present typical symptoms and logical methods to pinpoint and repair the problem.

Chapter Three explains all routine maintenance necessary to keep the motorcycle running well. Chapter Three also includes recommended tune-up procedures, eliminating the need to constantly consult the chapters on the various assemblies.

Subsequent chapters describe specific systems such as engine, transmission, clutch, drive system, fuel and exhaust systems, suspension and brakes.

WARNINGS, CAUTIONS AND NOTES

The terms, WARNING, CAUTION and NOTE have specific meanings in this manual.

A WARNING emphasizes areas where injury or even death could result from negligence. Mechanical damage may also occur. WARNINGS *are to be taken seriously.*

A CAUTION emphasizes areas where equipment damage could result. Disregarding a CAUTION could cause permanent mechanical damage, though injury is unlikely.

A NOTE provides additional information to make a step or procedure easier or clearer. Disregarding a NOTE could cause inconvenience, but would not cause equipment damage or personal injury.

SAFETY

Professional mechanics can work for years and never sustain a serious injury or mishap. Follow these guidelines and practice common sense to safely service the motorcycle.

1. Do not operate the motorcycle in an enclosed area. The exhaust gasses contain carbon monoxide, an odorless, colorless, and tasteless poisonous gas. Carbon monoxide levels build quickly in small enclosed areas and can cause unconsciousness and death in a short time. Make sure the work area is properly ventilated or operate the motorcycle outside.

2. *Never* use gasoline or any extremely flammable liquid to clean parts. Refer to *Cleaning Parts* and *Handling Gasoline Safely* in this chapter.

3. *Never* smoke or use a torch in the vicinity of flammable liquids, such as gasoline or cleaning solvent.

4. If welding or brazing on the motorcycle, remove the fuel tank, carburetor and shocks to a safe distance at least 50 ft. (15 m) away.

5. Use the correct type and size of tools to avoid damaging fasteners.

6. Keep tools clean and in good condition. Replace or repair worn or damaged equipment.

7. When loosening a tight fastener, be guided by what would happen if the tool slips.

8. When replacing fasteners, make sure the new fasteners are of the same size and strength as the original ones.

9. Keep the work area clean and organized.

10. Wear eye protection *anytime* the safety of the eyes is in question. This includes procedures involving drilling, grinding, hammering, compressed air and chemicals.

11. Wear the correct clothing for the job. Tie up or cover long hair so it can not get caught in moving equipment.

12. Do not carry sharp tools in clothing pockets.

13. Always have an approved fire extinguisher available. Make sure it is rated for gasoline (Class B) and electrical (Class C) fires.

14. Do not use compressed air to clean clothes, the motorcycle or the work area. Debris may be blown into the eyes or skin. *Never* direct compressed air at anyone. Do not allow children to use or play with any compressed air equipment.

15. When using compressed air to dry rotating parts, hold the part so it can not rotate. Do not allow the force of the air to spin the part. The air jet is capable of rotating parts at extreme speed. The part may be damaged or disintegrate, causing serious injury.

16. Do not inhale the dust created by brake pad and clutch wear. These particles may contain asbestos. In addition, some types of insulating materials and gaskets may contain asbestos. Inhaling asbestos particles is hazardous to health.

17. Never work on the motorcycle while someone is working under it.

18. When placing the motorcycle on a stand, make sure it is secure before walking away.

Handling Gasoline Safely

Gasoline is a volatile flammable liquid and is one of the most dangerous items in the shop. Because gasoline is used so often, many people forget that it is hazardous. Only use gasoline as fuel for gasoline internal combustion engines. Keep in mind, when working on a motorcycle, gasoline is always present in the fuel tank, fuel line and carburetor. To avoid a disastrous accident when working around the fuel system, carefully observe the following precautions:

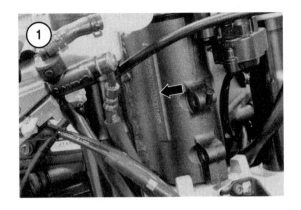

1. *Never* use gasoline to clean parts. See *Cleaning Parts* in this section.

2. When working on the fuel system, work outside or in a well-ventilated area.

3. Do not add fuel to the fuel tank or service the fuel system while the motorcycle is near open flames, sparks or where someone is smoking. Gasoline vapor is heavier than air; it collects in low areas and is more easily ignited than liquid gasoline.

4. Allow the engine to cool completely before working on any fuel system component.

5. On carburetted models, when draining the carburetor, catch the fuel in a plastic container and then pour it into an approved gasoline storage devise.

6. Do not store gasoline in glass containers. If the glass breaks, a serious explosion or fire may occur.

7. Immediately wipe up spilled gasoline with rags. Store the rags in a metal container with a lid until they can be properly disposed of, or place them outside in a safe place for the fuel to evaporate.

8. Do not pour water onto a gasoline fire. Water spreads the fire and makes it more difficult to put out. Use a class B, BC or ABC fire extinguisher to extinguish the fire.

9. Always turn off the engine before refueling. Do not spill fuel onto the engine or exhaust system. Do not overfill the fuel tank. Leave an air space at the top of the tank to allow room for the fuel to expand due to temperature fluctuations.

Cleaning Parts

Cleaning parts is one of the more tedious and difficult service jobs performed in the home garage. There are many types of chemical cleaners and solvents available for shop use. Most are poisonous and extremely flammable. To prevent chemical exposure, vapor buildup, fire and serious injury, observe each product warning label and note the following:

1. Read and observe the entire product label before using any chemical. Always know what type of chemical is being used and whether it is poisonous and/or flammable.

2. Do not use more than one type of cleaning solvent at a time. If mixing chemicals is called for, measure the proper amounts according to the manufacturer.

3. Work in a well-ventilated area.

4. Wear chemical-resistant gloves.

5. Wear safety glasses.

6. Wear a vapor respirator if the instructions call for it.

7. Wash hands and arms thoroughly after cleaning parts.

8. Keep chemical products away from children and pets.

9. Thoroughly clean all oil, grease and cleaner residue from any part that must be heated.

10. Use a nylon brush when cleaning parts. Metal brushes may cause a spark.

11. When using a parts washer, only use the solvent recommended by the manufacturer. Make sure the parts washer is equipped with a metal lid that will lower in case of fire.

Warning Labels

Most manufacturers attach information and warning labels to the motorcycle. These labels contain instructions important to personal safety when operating, servicing, transporting and storing the motorcycle. Refer to the owner's manual for the description and location of labels. Order replacement labels from the manufacturer if they are missing or damaged.

SERIAL NUMBERS

Serial numbers are stamped on various locations on the frame, engine, transmission and carburetor. Record these numbers in the *Quick Reference Data* section at the front of the manual. Have these numbers available when ordering parts.

The frame serial number (**Figure 1**) is stamped on the right side of the steering head.

The VIN number label (**Figure 2**) is located on the right side of the frame adjacent to the steering head.

The engine serial number is stamped on a pad at the right side surface of the upper crankcase (**Figure 3**).

The carburetor serial number (**Figure 4**) is located on the side of the carburetor body above the float bowl.

The fuel injection throttle body serial number (**Figure 5**) is located on the left intake side of the throttle body.

FASTENERS

Proper fastener selection and installation is important to ensure that the motorcycle operates as designed and can be serviced efficiently. The choice of original equipment fasteners is not arrived at by chance. Make sure replacement fasteners meet all the same requirements as the originals.

Threaded Fasteners

Threaded fasteners secure most of the components on the motorcycle. Most are tightened by turning them clockwise (right-hand threads). If the normal rotation of the component being tightened would loosen the fastener, it may have left-hand threads. If a left-hand threaded fastener is used, it is noted in the text.

Two dimensions are required to match the thread size of the fastener: the number of threads in a given distance and the outside diameter of the threads.

Two systems are currently used to specify threaded fastener dimensions: the U.S. Standard system and the metric system (**Figure 6**). Pay particular attention when working with unidentified fasteners; mismatching thread types can damage threads.

> *CAUTION*
> *To ensure that the fastener threads are not mismatched or cross-threaded, start all fasteners by hand. If a fastener is hard to start or turn, determine the cause before tightening with a wrench.*

The length (L, **Figure 7**), diameter (D) and distance between thread crests (pitch) (T) classify metric screws and bolts. A typical bolt may be identified by the numbers, 8—1.25 × 130. This indicates the bolt has diameter of 8 mm, the distance between thread crests is 1.25 mm and the length is 130 mm. Always measure bolt length as shown in L, **Figure 7** to avoid purchasing replacements of the wrong length.

The numbers located on the top of the fastener (**Figure 7**) indicate the strength of metric screws and bolts. The higher the number, the stronger the fastener is. Typically, unnumbered fasteners are the weakest.

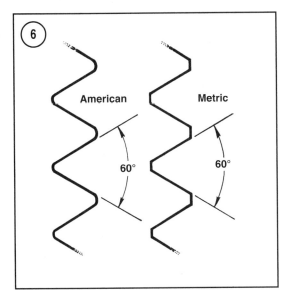

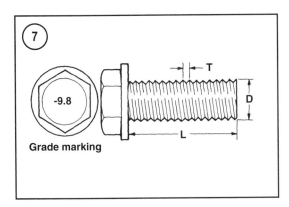

Grade marking

Many screws, bolts and studs are combined with nuts to secure particular components. To indicate the size of a nut, manufacturers specify the internal diameter and the thread pitch.

The measurement across two flats on a nut or bolt indicates the wrench size.

WARNING
Do not install fasteners with a strength classification lower than what was originally installed by the manufacturer. Doing so may cause equipment failure and/or damage.

Torque Specifications

The materials used in the manufacture of the motorcycle may be subjected to uneven stresses if the fasteners of the various subassemblies are not installed and tightened correctly. Fasteners that are improperly installed or work loose can cause extensive damage. It is essential to use an accurate torque wrench, described in this chapter, with the torque specifications in this manual.

Specifications for torque are provided in Newton-meters (N•m), foot-pounds (ft.-lb.) and inch-pounds (in.-lb.). Refer to **Table 5** for general torque specifications. To use **Table 5**, first determine the size of the fastener as described in *Fasteners* in this chapter. Torque specifications for specific components are at the end of the appropriate chapters. Torque wrenches are covered in the *Basic Tools* section.

Self-Locking Fasteners

Several types of bolts, screws and nuts incorporate a system that creates interference between the two fasteners. Interference is achieved in various ways. The most common type is the nylon insert nut and a dry adhesive coating on the threads of a bolt.

Self-locking fasteners offer greater holding strength than standard fasteners, which improves their resistance to vibration. All self-locking fasteners cannot be reused. The materials used to form the lock become distorted after the initial installation and removal. It is a good practice to discard and replace self-locking fasteners after their removal. Do not replace self-locking fasteners with standard fasteners.

Washers

There are two basic types of washers: flat washers and lockwashers. Flat washers are simple discs with a hole to fit a screw or bolt. Lockwashers are used to prevent a fastener from working loose.

Washers can be used as spacers and seals, or to help distribute fastener load and to prevent the fastener from damaging the component.

As with fasteners, make sure replacement washers are of the same design and quality as the originals.

Cotter Pins

A cotter pin is a split metal pin inserted into a hole or slot to prevent a fastener from loosening. In certain applications, such as the rear axle on an ATV or motorcycle, the fastener must be secured in this way. For these applications, a cotter pin and castellated (slotted) nut is used.

To use a cotter pin, first make sure the diameter is correct for the hole in the fastener. After correctly tightening the fastener and aligning the holes, insert the cotter pin through the hole and bend the ends over the fastener (**Figure 8**). Unless instructed to do so, never loosen a tightened fastener to align the holes. If the holes do not align, tighten the fastener just enough to achieve alignment.

Cotter pins are available in various diameters and lengths. Measure length from the bottom of the head to the tip of the shortest pin.

Snap Rings and E-clips

Snap rings (**Figure 9**) are circular-shaped metal retaining clips. They are required to secure parts and gears in place on parts such as shafts, pins or rods. External type snap rings are used to retain items on shafts. Internal type snap rings secure parts within housing bores. In some applications, in addition to securing the component(s), snap rings of varying thickness also determine endplay. These are usually called selective snap rings.

Two basic types of snap rings are used: machined and stamped snap rings. Machined snap rings (**Figure 10**) can be installed in either direction, since both faces have sharp edges. Stamped snap rings (**Figure 11**) are manufactured with a sharp edge and a round edge. When installing a stamped snap ring in a thrust application, install the sharp edge facing away from the part producing the thrust.

E-clips are used when it is not practical to use a snap ring. Remove E-clips with a flat blade screwdriver by prying between the shaft and E-clip. To in-

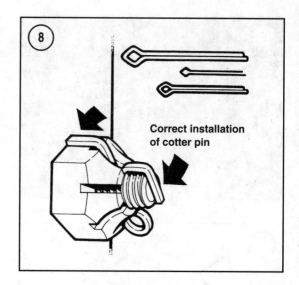

Correct installation of cotter pin

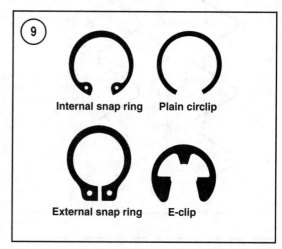

Internal snap ring   Plain circlip

External snap ring   E-clip

stall an E-clip, center it over the shaft groove and push or tap it into place.

Observe the following when installing snap rings:

1. Remove and install snap rings with snap ring pliers. Refer to *Snap Ring Pliers* in this chapter.

2. In some applications, it may be necessary to replace snap rings after removing them.

3. Compress or expand snap rings only enough to install them. If overly expanded, they lose their retaining ability.

4. After installing a snap ring, make sure it seats completely.

5. Wear eye protection when removing and installing snap rings.

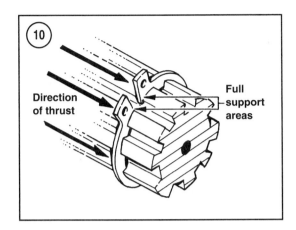

Direction of thrust

Full support areas

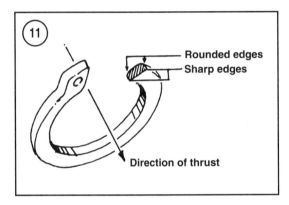

Rounded edges
Sharp edges

Direction of thrust

SHOP SUPPLIES

Lubricants and Fluids

Periodic lubrication helps ensure a long service life for any type of equipment. Using the correct type of lubricant is as important as performing the lubrication service, although in an emergency the wrong type is better than not using one. The following section describes the types of lubricants most often required. Make sure to follow the manufacturer's recommendations for lubricant types.

Engine oils

Engine oil is classified by two standards: the American Petroleum Institute (API) service classification and the Society of Automotive Engineers (SAE) viscosity rating. This information is on the oil container label. Two letters indicate the API service classification. The number or sequence of numbers and letter (10W-40 for example) is the oil's viscosity rating. The API service classification and the SAE viscosity index are not indications of oil quality.

The service classification, *SE* for example, indicates that the oil meets specific lubrication standards. The first letter in the classification *S* indicates that the oil is for gasoline engines. The second letter indicates the standard the oil satisfies. Do not use oil labeled ENERGY CONSERVING; it is specifically designed for automotive applications.

Always use an oil with a classification recommended by the manufacturer. Using an oil with a different classification can cause engine damage.

Viscosity is an indication of the oil's thickness. Thin oils have a lower number while thick oils have a higher number. Engine oils fall into the 5- to 50-weight range for single-grade oils.

Most manufacturers recommend multi-grade oil. These oils perform efficiently across a wide range of operating conditions. Multi-grade oils are identified by a *W* after the first number, which indicates the low-temperature viscosity.

Engine oils are most commonly mineral (petroleum) based; however, synthetic and semi-synthetic types are used more frequently. When selecting engine oil, follow the manufacturer's recommendation for type, classification and viscosity when selecting engine oil.

Greases

Grease is lubricating oil with thickening agents added to it. The National Lubricating Grease Institute (NLGI) grades grease. Grades range from No. 000 to No. 6, with No. 6 being the thickest. Typical multipurpose grease is NLGI No. 2. For specific applications, manufacturers may recommend water-resistant type grease or one with an additive such as molybdenum disulfide (MoS_2).

Brake fluid

Brake fluid is the hydraulic fluid used to transmit hydraulic pressure (force) to the wheel brakes. Brake fluid is classified by the Department of Transportation (DOT). Current designations for brake fluid are DOT 3, DOT 4 and DOT 5. This classification appears on the fluid container.

Each type of brake fluid has its own definite characteristics. Do not intermix different types of brake fluid as this may cause brake system failure. DOT 5 brake fluid is silicone based. DOT 5 is not compatible with other brake fluids or in systems for which it was not designed. Mixing DOT 5 fluid with other fluids may cause brake system failure. When adding brake fluid, *only* use the fluid recommended by the manufacturer.

Brake fluid will damage any plastic, painted or plated surface it contacts. Use extreme care when working with brake fluid and remove any spills immediately with soap and water.

Hydraulic brake systems require clean and moisture free brake fluid. Never reuse brake fluid. Keep containers and reservoirs properly sealed.

> *WARNING*
> *Never put a mineral-based (petroleum) oil into the brake system. Mineral oil will cause rubber parts in the system to swell and break apart, resulting in complete brake failure.*

Coolant

Coolant is a mixture of water and antifreeze used to dissipate engine heat. Ethylene glycol is the most common form of antifreeze used. Check the motorcycle manufacturer's recommendations when selecting antifreeze, most require one specifically designed for use in aluminum engines. These types of antifreeze have additives that inhibit corrosion.

Only mix distilled water with antifreeze. Impurities in tap water may damage internal cooling system passages.

Drive chain lubricant

There are many types of chain lubricants available. Which type of drive chain lubricant to use depends on the type of chain.

On O-ring (sealed) chains, the lubricant keeps the O-rings pliable and prevents corrosion. The actual chain lubricant is enclosed in the chain by the O-rings. Recommended types include aerosol sprays specifically designed for O-ring chains, and conventional engine and gear oils. When using a spray lubricant, make sure it is suitable for O-ring chains.

Do not use a high-pressure washer, solvents or gasoline to clean an O-ring chain; they should only be cleaned with kerosene.

Cleaners, Degreasers and Solvents

Many chemicals are available to remove oil, grease and other residue from the motorcycle. Before using cleaning solvents, consider how they will be used and disposed of, particularly if they are not water-soluble. Local ordinances may require special procedures for the disposal of many types of cleaning chemicals. Refer to *Safety and Cleaning Parts* in this chapter for more information on their use.

Use brake parts cleaner to clean brake system components when contact with petroleum-based products will damage seals. Brake parts cleaner leaves no residue. Use electrical contact cleaner to clean electrical connections and components without leaving any residue. Carburetor cleaner is a powerful solvent used to remove fuel deposits and varnish from fuel system components. Use this cleaner carefully, as it may damage finishes.

Generally, degreasers are strong cleaners used to remove heavy accumulations of grease from engine and frame components.

Most solvents are designed to be used with a parts washing cabinet for individual component cleaning. For safety, use only nonflammable or high flash point solvents.

Gasket Sealant

Sealants are used in combination with a gasket or seal and are occasionally alone. Follow the manufacturer's recommendation when using sealants. Use extreme care when choosing a sealant different from the type originally recommended. Choose sealants based on their resistance to heat, various fluids and their sealing capabilities.

One of the most common sealants is room temperature vulcanizing (RTV) sealant. This sealant cures at room temperature over a specific time period. This allows the repositioning of components without damaging gaskets.

Moisture in the air causes the RTV sealant to cure. Always install the tube cap as soon as possible after applying RTV sealant. RTV sealant has a limited shelf life and will not cure properly if the shelf life has expired. Keep partial tubes sealed and discard them if they have surpassed the expiration date.

Applying RTV sealant

Clean all old gasket residue from the mating surfaces. Remove all gasket material from blind threaded holes; it can cause inaccurate bolt torque. Spray the mating surfaces with aerosol parts cleaner and then wipe with a lint-free cloth. The area must be clean for the sealant to adhere.

Apply RTV sealant in a continuous bead 2-3 mm (0.08-0.12 in.) thick. Circle all the fastener holes unless otherwise specified. Do not allow any sealant to enter these holes. Assemble and tighten the fasteners to the specified torque within the time frame recommended by the RTV sealant manufacturer.

Gasket Remover

Aerosol gasket remover can help remove stubborn gaskets. This product can speed up the removal process and prevent damage to the mating surface that may be caused by using a scraping tool. Most of these types of products are very caustic. Follow the gasket remover manufacturer's instructions for use.

Threadlocking Compound

A threadlocking compound is a fluid applied to the threads of fasteners. After tightening the fastener, the fluid dries and becomes a solid filler between the threads. This makes it difficult for the fastener to work loose from vibration, or heat expansion and contraction. Some threadlocking compounds also provide a seal against fluid leakage.

Before applying threadlocking compound, remove any old compound from both thread areas and clean them with aerosol parts cleaner. Use the compound sparingly. Excess fluid can run into adjoining parts.

> *CAUTION*
> *Threadlocking compounds are anaerobic and will stress, crack and attack most plastic parts and surfaces. Use caution when using these products in areas where plastic components are located.*

Threadlocking compounds are available in different strengths. Follow the particular manufacturer's recommendations regarding compound selection. Two manufacturers of threadlocking compound are ThreeBond and Loctite. They both offer a wide range of compounds for various strength, temperature and repair applications.

BASIC TOOLS

Most of the procedures in this manual can be carried out with simple hand tools and test equipment familiar to the home mechanic. Always use the correct tools for the job at hand. Keep tools organized and clean. Store them in a tool chest with related tools organized together.

Quality tools are essential. The best are constructed of high-strength alloy steel. These tools are light, easy to use and resistant to wear. Their working surface is devoid of sharp edges and the tool is carefully polished. They have an easy-to-clean finish and are comfortable to use. Quality tools are a good investment.

Some of the procedures in this manual specify special tools. In many cases the tool is illustrated in use. Those with a large tool kit may be able to use a suitable substitute or fabricate a suitable replacement. However, in some cases, the specialized equipment or expertise may make it impractical for the home mechanic to attempt the procedure. When necessary, such operations come with the recommendation to have a dealership or specialist perform the task. It may be less expensive to have a professional perform these jobs, especially when considering the cost of equipment.

If special tools are required, make sure to order them well in advance of starting the procedures to ensure they are on hand.

When purchasing tools to perform the procedures covered in this manual, consider the tool's potential frequency of use. If just starting a tool kit, consider purchasing a basic tool set from a quality tool supplier. These sets are available in many tool combinations and offer substantial savings when compared to individually purchased tools. As work experience grows and tasks become more complicated, specialized tools can be added.

Screwdrivers

Screwdrivers of various lengths and types are mandatory for the simplest tool kit. The two basic types are the slotted tip (flat blade) and the Phillips tip. These are available in sets that often include an assortment of tip sizes and shaft lengths.

As with all tools, use a screwdriver designed for the job. Make sure the size of the tip conforms to the size and shape of the fastener. Use them only for driving screws. Never use a screwdriver for prying or chiseling metal. Repair or replace worn or damaged screwdrivers. A worn tip may damage the fastener, making it difficult to remove.

Phillips-head screws are often damaged by incorrectly fitting screwdrivers. Quality Phillips screwdrivers are manufactured with their crosshead tip machined to Phillips Screw Company specifications. Poor quality or damaged Phillips screwdrivers can back out and round over the screw head, resulting in a condition known as camout. Compounding the problem of using poor quality screwdrivers are Phillips-head screws made from weak or soft materials and screws initially installed with air tools.

The best type of screwdriver to use on Phillips screws is the ACR Phillips II screwdriver, patented by the Phillips Screw Company. ACR stands for the horizontal anti-camout ribs found on the driving faces or flutes of the screwdrivers tip. ACR Phillips II screwdrivers were designed as part of a manufacturing drive system to be used with ACR Phillips II screws, but they work well on all common Phillips screws. A number of tool companies offer ACR Phillips II screwdrivers in different tip sizes and interchangeable bits to fit screwdriver bit holders.

NOTE
Another way to prevent camout and to increase the grip of a Phillips screwdriver is to apply valve grinding compound or Permatex Screw & Socket Gripper to the screwdriver tip. After loosening or tightening the screw, clean the screw recess to prevent engine oil contamination.

Wrenches

Open-end, box-end and combination wrenches (**Figure 12**) are available in a variety of types and sizes.

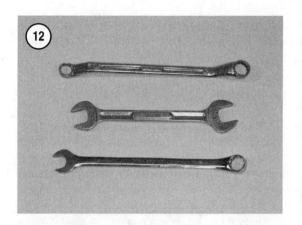

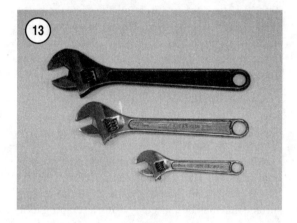

The number stamped on the wrench refers to the distance between the work areas. This size must match the size of the fastener head.

The box-end wrench is an excellent tool because it grips the fastener on all sides. This reduces the chance of the tool slipping. The box-end wrench is designed with either a 6 or 12-point opening. For stubborn or damaged fasteners, the 6-point provides superior holding ability by contacting the fastener across a wider area at all six edges. For general use, the 12-point works well. It allows the wrench to be removed and reinstalled without moving the handle over such a wide arc.

An open-end wrench is fast and works best in areas with limited overhead access. It contacts the fastener at only two points, and is subject to slipping under heavy force, or if the tool or fastener is worn. A box-end wrench is preferred in most instances, especially when breaking loose and applying the final tightness to a fastener.

The combination wrench has a box-end on one end, and an open-end on the other. This combination makes it a very convenient tool.

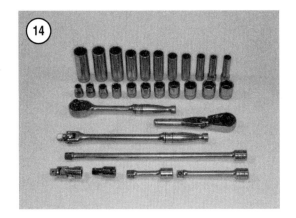

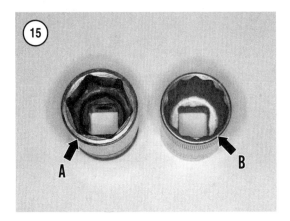

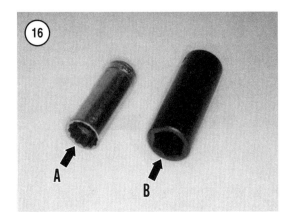

Adjustable Wrenches

An adjustable wrench or Crescent wrench (**Figure 13**) can fit nearly any nut or bolt head that has clear access around its entire perimeter. Adjustable wrenches are best used as a backup wrench to keep a large nut or bolt from turning while the other end is being loosened or tightened with a box-end or socket wrench.

Adjustable wrenches contact the fastener at only two points, which makes them more subject to slipping off the fastener. The fact that one jaw is adjustable and may loosen only aggravates this shortcoming. Make certain the solid jaw is the one transmitting the force.

Socket Wrenches, Ratchets and Handles

Sockets that attach to a ratchet handle (**Figure 14**) are available with 6-point (A, **Figure 15**) or 12-point (B) openings and different drive sizes. The drive size indicates the size of the square hole that accepts the ratchet handle. The number stamped on the socket is the size of the work area and must match the fastener head.

As with wrenches, a 6-point socket provides superior-holding ability, while a 12-point socket needs to be moved only half as far to reposition it on the fastener.

Sockets are designated for either hand or impact use. Impact sockets are made of thicker material for more durability. Compare the size and wall thickness of a 19-mm hand socket (A, **Figure 16**) and the 19-mm impact socket (B). Use impact sockets when using an impact driver or air tools. Use hand sockets with hand-driven attachments.

> *WARNING*
> *Do not use hand sockets with air or impact tools, as they may shatter and cause injury. Always wear eye protection when using impact or air tools.*

Various handles are available for sockets. The speed handle is used for fast operation. Flexible ratchet heads in varying lengths allow the socket to be turned with varying force, and at odd angles. Extension bars allow the socket setup to reach difficult areas. The ratchet is the most versatile. It allows the user to install or remove the nut without removing the socket.

Sockets combined with any number of drivers make them undoubtedly the fastest, safest and most convenient tool for fastener removal and installation.

Impact Driver

An impact driver provides extra force for removing fasteners, by converting the impact of a hammer into a turning motion. This makes it possible to remove stubborn fasteners without damaging them. Impact drivers and interchangeable bits (**Figure 17**) are available from most tool suppliers. When using a socket with an impact driver make sure the socket is designed for impact use. Refer to *Socket Wrenches, Ratchets and Handles* in this section.

> *WARNING*
> *Do not use hand sockets with air or impact tools as they may shatter and cause injury. Always wear eye protection when using impact or air tools.*

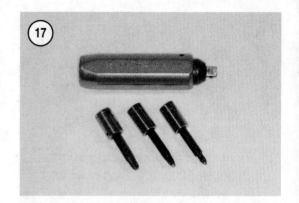

Allen Wrenches

Allen or setscrew wrenches (**Figure 18**) are used on fasteners with hexagonal recesses in the fastener head. These wrenches are available in L-shaped bar, socket and T-handle types. A metric set is required when working on most motorcycles. Allen bolts are sometimes called socket bolts.

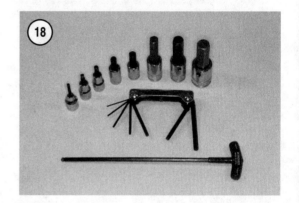

Torque Wrenches

A torque wrench is used with a socket, torque adapter or similar extension to tighten a fastener to a measured torque. Torque wrenches come in several drive sizes (1/4, 3/8, 1/2 and 3/4) and have various methods of reading the torque value. The drive size indicates the size of the square drive that accepts the socket, adapter or extension. Common methods of reading the torque value are the deflecting beam, the dial indicator and the audible click (**Figure 19**).

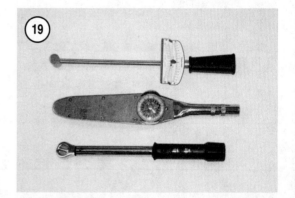

When choosing a torque wrench, consider the torque range, drive size and accuracy. The torque specifications in this manual provide an indication of the range required. A torque wrench is a precision tool that must be properly cared for to remain accurate. Store torque wrenches in cases or separate padded drawers within a toolbox. Follow the manufacturer's instructions for their care and calibration.

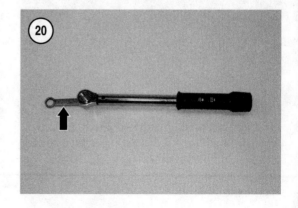

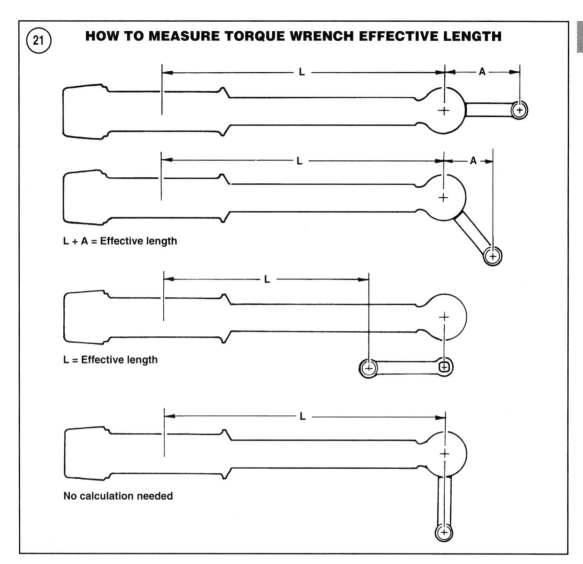

HOW TO MEASURE TORQUE WRENCH EFFECTIVE LENGTH

L + A = Effective length

L = Effective length

No calculation needed

Torque Adapters

Torque adapters or extensions extend or reduce the reach of a torque wrench. The torque adapter shown in **Figure 20** is used to tighten a fastener that cannot be reached due to the size of the torque wrench head, drive, and socket. If a torque adapter changes the effective lever length (**Figure 21**), the torque reading on the wrench will not equal the actual torque applied to the fastener. It is necessary to recalibrate the torque setting on the wrench to compensate for the change of lever length. When a torque adapter is used at a right angle to the drive head, calibration is not required, since the effective length has not changed.

To recalculate a torque reading when using a torque adapter, use the following formula, and refer to **Figure 21**.

$$TW = \frac{TA \times L}{L + A}$$

TW is the torque setting or dial reading on the wrench.

TA is the torque specification and the actual amount of torque applied to the fastener.

A is the amount that the adapter increases (or in some cases reduces) the effective lever length as measured along the centerline of the torque wrench (**Figure 21**).

L is the lever length of the wrench as measured from the center of the drive to the center of the grip.

The effective length is the sum of L and A (**Figure 21**).

Example:

TA = 20 ft.-lb.

A = 3 in.

L = 14 in.

$$TW = \frac{20 \times 14}{14 + 3} = \frac{280}{17} = 16.5 \text{ ft. lb.}$$

In this example, the torque wrench would be set to the recalculated torque value (TW = 16.5 ft.-lb.). When using a beam-type wrench, tighten the fastener until the pointer aligns with 16.5 ft.-lb. In this example, although the torque wrench is pre set to 16.5 ft.-lb., the actual torque is 20 ft.-lb.

Pliers

Pliers come in a wide range of types and sizes. Pliers are useful for holding, cutting, bending, and crimping. Do not use them to turn fasteners. **Figure 22** and **Figure 23** show several types of useful pliers. Each design has a specialized function. Slip-joint pliers are general-purpose pliers used for gripping and bending. Diagonal cutting pliers are needed to cut wire and can be used to remove cotter pins. Needlenose pliers are used to hold or bend small objects. Locking pliers (**Figure 23**), sometimes called Vise-grips, are used to hold objects very tightly. They have many uses ranging from holding two parts together, to gripping the end of a broken stud. Use caution when using locking pliers, as the sharp jaws will damage the objects they hold.

Snap Ring Pliers

Snap ring pliers are specialized pliers with tips that fit into the ends of snap rings to remove and install them.

Snap ring pliers are available with a fixed action (either internal or external) or convertible (one tool works on both internal and external snap rings). They may have fixed tips or interchangeable ones of various sizes and angles. For general use, select a convertible type of pliers with interchangeable tips.

WARNING
Snap rings can slip and fly off when removing and installing them. Also,

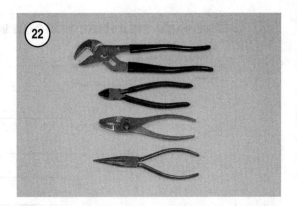

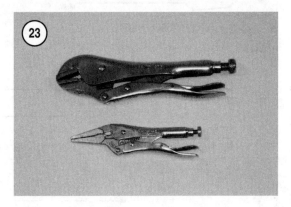

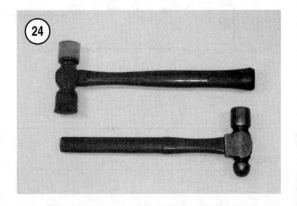

the snap ring plier's tips may break. Always wear eye protection when using snap ring pliers.

Hammers

Various types of hammers (**Figure 24**) are available to fit a number of applications. A ball-peen hammer is used to strike another tool, such as a punch or chisel. Soft-faced hammers are required when a metal object must be struck without damag-

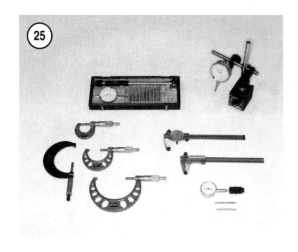

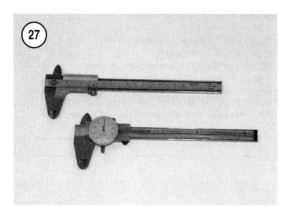

ing it. *Never* use a metal-faced hammer on engine and suspension components, as damage will occur in most cases.

Always wear eye protection when using hammers. Make sure the hammer face is in good condition and the handle is not cracked. Select the correct hammer for the job and make sure to strike the object squarely. Do not use the handle or the side of the hammer to strike an object.

PRECISION MEASURING TOOLS

The ability to accurately measure components is essential to successfully rebuild an engine. Equipment is manufactured to close tolerances and obtaining consistently accurate measurements is essential to determining which components require replacement or further service.

Each type of measuring instrument is designed to measure a dimension with a certain degree of accuracy and within a certain range. When selecting the measuring tool, make sure it is applicable to the task. Refer to **Figure 25** for a comprehensive measuring set.

As with all tools, measuring tools provide the best results if cared for properly. Improper use can damage the tool and result in inaccurate results. If any measurement is questionable, verify the measurement using another tool. A standard gauge is usually provided with measuring tools to check accuracy and calibrate the tool if necessary.

Precision measurements can vary according to the experience of the person performing the procedure. Accurate results are only possible if the mechanic possesses a feel for using the tool. Heavy-handed use of measuring tools will produce less accurate results. Hold the tool gently by the fingertips so the point at which the tool contacts the object is easily felt. This feel for the equipment will produce more accurate measurements and reduce the risk of damaging the tool or component. Refer to the following sections for specific measuring tools.

Feeler Gauge

The feeler or thickness gauge (**Figure 26**) is used for measuring the distance between two surfaces.

A feeler gauge set consists of an assortment of steel strips of graduated thickness. Each blade is marked with its thickness. Blades can be of various lengths and angles for different procedures.

A common use for a feeler gauge is to measure valve clearance. Wire (round) type gauges are used to measure spark plug gap.

Calipers

Calipers (**Figure 27**) are excellent tools for obtaining inside, outside and depth measurements. Although not as precise as a micrometer, they allow reasonable

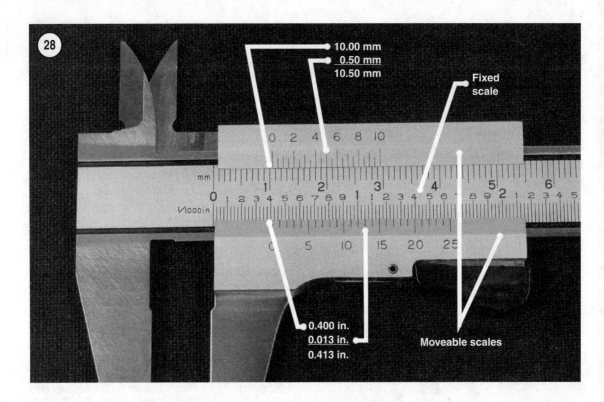

10.00 mm
 0.50 mm
10.50 mm

Fixed scale

0.400 in.
0.013 in.
0.413 in.

Moveable scales

DECIMAL PLACE VALUES*

0.1	Indicates 1/10 (one tenth of an inch or millimeter)
0.010	Indicates 1/100 (one one-hundreth of an inch or millimeter)
0.001	Indicates 1/1,000 (one one-thousandth of an inch or millimeter)

*This chart represents the values of figures placed to the right of the decimal point. Use it when reading decimals from one-tenth to one one-thousandth of an inch or millimeter. It is not a conversion chart (for example: 0.001 in. is not equal to 0.001 mm).

---

precision, typically to within 0.05 mm (0.001 in.). Most calipers have a range up to 150 mm (6 in.).

Calipers are available in dial, vernier or digital versions. Dial calipers have a dial readout that provides convenient reading. Vernier calipers have marked scales that must be compared to determine the measurement. The digital caliper uses a LCD to show the measurement.

Properly maintain the measuring surfaces of the caliper. There must not be any dirt or burrs between the tool and the object being measured. Never force

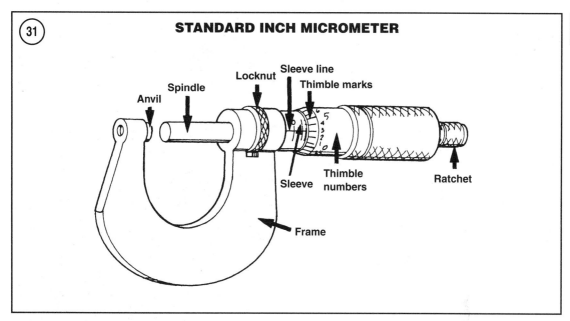

STANDARD INCH MICROMETER

the caliper closed around an object; close the caliper around the highest point so it can be removed with a slight drag. Some calipers require calibration. Always refer to the manufacturer's instructions when using a new or unfamiliar caliper.

To read a vernier caliper refer to **Figure 28**. The fixed scale is marked in 1 mm increments. Ten individual lines on the fixed scale equal 1 cm. The moveable scale is marked in 0.05 mm (hundredth) increments. To obtain a reading, establish the first number by the location of the 0 line on the movable scale in relation to the first line to the left on the fixed scale. In this example, the number is 10 mm. To determine the next number, note which of the lines on the movable scale align with a mark on the fixed scale. A number of lines will seem close, but only one will align exactly. In this case, 0.50 mm is the reading to add to the first number. The result of adding 10 mm and 0.50 mm is a measurement of 10.50 mm.

Micrometers

A micrometer is an instrument designed for linear measurement using the decimal divisions of the inch or meter (**Figure 29**). While there are many types and styles of micrometers, most of the procedures in this manual call for an outside micrometer. The outside micrometer is used to measure the out-side diameter of cylindrical forms and the thickness of materials.

A micrometer's size indicates the minimum and maximum size of a part it can measure. The usual sizes (**Figure 30**) are 0-1 in. (0-25 mm), 1-2 in. (25-50 mm), 2-3 in. (50-75 mm) and 3-4 in. (75-100 mm).

Micrometers that cover a wider range of measurements are available. These use a large frame with interchangeable anvils of various lengths. This type of micrometer offers a cost savings; however, its overall size may make it less convenient.

When reading a micrometer, numbers are taken from different scales and added together. The following sections describe how to read the measurements of various types of outside micrometers.

For accurate results, properly maintain the measuring surfaces of the micrometer. There cannot be any dirt or burrs between the tool and the measured object. Never force the micrometer closed around an object. Close the micrometer around the highest point so it can be removed with a slight drag. **Figure 31** shows the markings and parts of a standard inch micrometer. Be familiar with these terms before using a micrometer in the follow sections.

Standard inch micrometer

The standard inch micrometer is accurate to one-thousandth of an inch or 0.001. The sleeve is marked in 0.025 in. increments. Every fourth sleeve mark is numbered 1, 2, 3, 4, 5, 6, 7, 8, 9. These numbers indicate 0.100, 0.200, 0.300, and so on.

The tapered end of the thimble has twenty-five lines marked around it. Each mark equals 0.001 in. One complete turn of the thimble will align its zero mark with the first mark on the sleeve or 0.025 in.

When reading a standard inch micrometer, perform the following steps while referring to **Figure 32**.

1. Read the sleeve and find the largest number visible. Each sleeve number equals 0.100 in.

2. Count the number of lines between the numbered sleeve mark and the edge of the thimble. Each sleeve mark equals 0.025 in.

3. Read the thimble mark that aligns with the sleeve line. Each thimble mark equals 0.001 in.

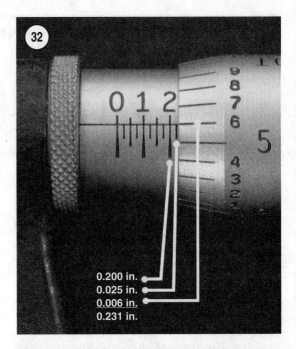

0.200 in.
0.025 in.
0.006 in.
0.231 in.

NOTE
If a thimble mark does not align exactly with the sleeve line, estimate the amount between the lines. For accurate readings in ten-thousandths of an inch (0.0001 in.), use a vernier inch micrometer.

4. Add the readings from Steps 1-3.

Metric micrometer

The standard metric micrometer is accurate to one one-hundredth of a millimeter (0.01-mm). The sleeve line is graduated in millimeter and half millimeter increments. The marks on the upper half of the sleeve line equal 1.00 mm. Each fifth mark above the sleeve line is identified with a number. The number sequence depends on the size of the micrometer. A 0-25 mm micrometer, for example, will have sleeve marks numbered 0 through 25 in 5 mm increments. This numbering sequence continues with larger micrometers. On all metric micrometers, each mark on the lower half of the sleeve equals 0.50 mm.

The tapered end of the thimble has fifty lines marked around it. Each mark equals 0.01 mm. One complete turn of the thimble aligns its 0 mark with the first line on the lower half of the sleeve line or 0.50 mm.

When reading a metric micrometer, add the number of millimeters and half-millimeters on the sleeve line to the number of one one-hundredth mil-

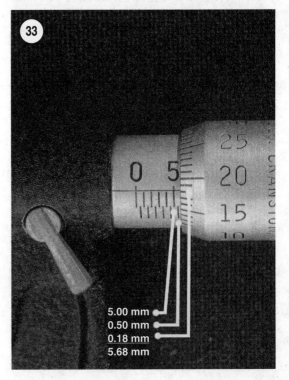

5.00 mm
0.50 mm
0.18 mm
5.68 mm

limeters on the thimble. Perform the following steps while referring to **Figure 33**.

1. Read the upper half of the sleeve line and count the number of lines visible. Each upper line equals 1 mm.

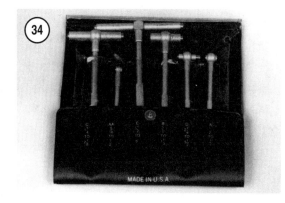

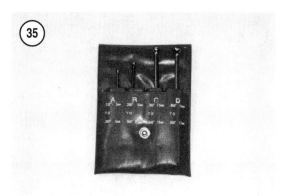

it to ensure that the proper amount of pressure is applied.

   b. If the adjustment is correct, the 0 mark on the thimble will align exactly with the 0 mark on the sleeve line. If the marks do not align, the micrometer is out of adjustment.

   c. Follow the manufacturer's instructions to adjust the micrometer.

2B. To check a micrometer larger than 1 in. or 25 mm use the standard gauge supplied by the manufacturer. A standard gauge is a steel block, disc or rod machined to an exact size.

   a. Place the standard gauge between the spindle and anvil and measure its outside diameter or length. If the micrometer has a ratchet stop, use it to ensure the proper amount of pressure is applied.

   b. If the adjustment is correct, the 0 mark on the thimble will align exactly with the 0 mark on the sleeve line. If the marks do not align, the micrometer is out of adjustment.

   c. Follow the manufacturer's instructions to adjust the micrometer.

Care

Micrometers are precision instruments. They must be used and maintained with great care. Note the following:

1. Store micrometers in protective cases or separate padded drawers in a toolbox.

2. When in storage, make sure the spindle and anvil faces do not contact each other or another object. If they do, temperature changes and corrosion may damage the contact faces.

3. Do not clean a micrometer with compressed air. Dirt forced into the tool will cause wear.

4. Lubricate micrometers with WD-40 to prevent corrosion.

Telescoping and Small Bore Gauges

Use telescoping gauges (**Figure 34**) and small bore gauges (**Figure 35**) to measure bores. Neither gauge has a scale for direct readings. An outside micrometer must be used to determine the reading.

To use a telescoping gauge, select the correct size gauge for the bore. Compress the movable post and carefully insert the gauge into the bore. Carefully move the gauge in the bore to make sure it is cen-

2. See if the half-millimeter line is visible on the lower sleeve line. If so, add 0.50 mm to the reading in Step 1.

3. Read the thimble mark that aligns with the sleeve line. Each thimble mark equals 0.01 mm.

NOTE
If a thimble mark does not align exactly with the sleeve line, estimate the amount between the lines. For accurate readings in two-thousandths of a millimeter (0.002 mm), use a metric vernier micrometer.

4. Add the readings from Steps 1-3.

Adjustment

Before using a micrometer, check its adjustment as follows.

1. Clean the anvil and spindle faces.

2A. To check a 0-1 in. or 0-25 mm micrometer:

   a. Turn the thimble until the spindle contacts the anvil. If the micrometer has a ratchet stop, use

tered. Tighten the knurled end of the gauge to hold the movable post in position. Remove the gauge and measure the length of the posts. Telescoping gauges are typically used to measure cylinder bores.

To use a small-bore gauge, select the correct size gauge for the bore. Carefully insert the gauge into the bore. Tighten the knurled end of the gauge to carefully expand the gauge fingers to the limit within the bore. Do not overtighten the gauge, as there is no built-in release. Excessive tightening can damage the bore surface and damage the tool. Remove the gauge and measure the outside dimension (**Figure 36**). Small bore gauges are typically used to measure valve guides.

Dial Indicator

A dial indicator (A, **Figure 37**) is a gauge with a dial face and needle used to measure variations in dimensions and movements. Measuring brake rotor runout is a typical use for a dial indicator.

Dial indicators are available in various ranges and graduations and with three basic types of mounting bases: magnetic, clamp, or screw-in stud. When purchasing a dial indicator, select the magnetic stand (B, **Figure 37**) type with a continuous dial.

Cylinder Bore Gauge

A cylinder bore gauge is similar to a dial indicator. The gauge set shown in **Figure 38** consists of a dial indicator, handle, and different length adapters (anvils) to fit the gauge to various bore sizes. The bore gauge is used to measure bore size, taper and out-of-round. When using a bore gauge, follow the manufacturer's instructions.

Compression Gauge

A compression gauge (**Figure 39**) measures combustion chamber (cylinder) pressure, usually in psi or kg/cm^2. The gauge adapter is either inserted or screwed into the spark plug hole to obtain the reading. Disable the engine so it will not start and hold the throttle in the wide-open position when performing a compression test. An engine that does not have adequate compression cannot be properly tuned. Refer to Chapter Three.

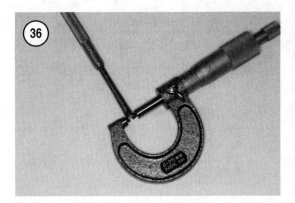

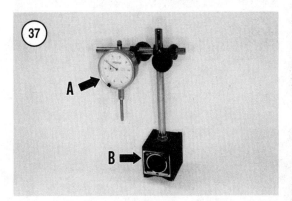

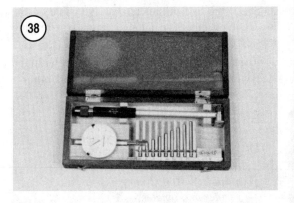

Multimeter

A multimeter (**Figure 40**) is an essential tool for electrical system diagnosis. The voltage function indicates the voltage applied or available to various electrical components. The ohmmeter function tests circuits for continuity or lack of continuity and measures the resistance of a circuit.

Some manufacturers' specifications for electrical components are based on results using a specific test meter. Results may vary if using a meter not rec-

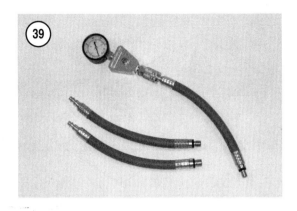

ommend by the manufacturer is used. Such requirements are noted when applicable.

Ohmmeter (analog) calibration

Each time an analog ohmmeter is used or if the scale is changed, the ohmmeter must be calibrated.

Digital ohmmeters do not require calibration.

1. Make sure the meter battery is in good condition.
2. Make sure the meter probes are in good condition.
3. Touch the two probes together and observe the needle location on the ohms scale.

The needle must align with the 0 mark to obtain accurate measurements.

4. If necessary, rotate the meter ohms adjust knob until the needle and 0 mark align.

ELECTRICAL SYSTEM FUNDAMENTALS

A thorough study of the many types of electrical systems used in today's motorcycles is beyond the scope of this manual. However, an understanding of electrical basics is necessary to perform simple diagnostic tests.

Refer to Chapter Two for typical electrical troubleshooting procedures and Chapter Ten for specific component testing.

Voltage

Voltage is the electrical potential or pressure in an electrical circuit and is expressed in volts. The more pressure (voltage) in a circuit, the more work can be performed.

Direct current (DC) voltage means the electricity flows in one direction. All circuits powered by a battery are DC circuits.

Alternating current (AC) means the electricity flows in one direction momentarily, then switches to the opposite direction. Alternator output is an example of AC voltage. This voltage must be changed or rectified to direct current to operate in a battery powered system.

Resistance

Resistance is the opposition to the flow of electricity within a circuit or component and is measured in ohms. Resistance causes a reduction in available current and voltage.

Resistance is measured in an inactive circuit with an ohmmeter. The ohmmeter sends a small amount of current into the circuit and measures how difficult it is to push the current through the circuit.

An ohmmeter, although useful, is not always a good indicator of a circuit's actual ability under operating conditions. This is due to the low voltage (6-9 volts) that the meter uses to test the circuit. The voltage in an ignition coil secondary winding can be several thousand volts. Such high voltage can cause the coil to malfunction, even though it tests acceptable during a resistance test.

Resistance generally increases with temperature. Perform all testing with the component or circuit at room temperature. Resistance tests performed at high temperatures may indicate high resistance readings and result in the unnecessary replacement of a component.

Amperage

Amperage is the unit of measure for the amount of current within a circuit. Current is the actual flow of electricity. The higher the current, the more work that can be performed up to a given point. If the current flow exceeds the circuit or component capacity, the system will be damaged.

BASIC SERVICE METHODS

Most of the procedures in this manual are straightforward and can be performed by anyone reasonably competent with tools. However, consider personal capabilities carefully before attempting any operation involving major disassembly of the engine.

1. Front, in this manual, refers to the front of the motorcycle. The front of any component is the end closest to the front of the motorcycle. The left and right sides refer to the position of the parts as viewed by the rider sitting on the seat facing forward.

2. Whenever servicing an engine or suspension component, secure the motorcycle in a safe manner.

3. Tag all similar parts for location and mark all mating parts for position. Record the number and thickness of any shims as they are removed. Identify parts by placing them in sealed and labeled plastic sandwich bags.

4. Tag disconnected wires and connectors with masking tape and a marking pen. Do not rely on memory alone.

5. Protect finished surfaces from physical damage or corrosion. Keep gasoline and other chemicals off painted surfaces.

6. Use penetrating oil on frozen or tight bolts. Avoid using heat where possible. Heat can warp, melt or affect the temper of parts. Heat also damages the finish of paint and plastics.

7. When a part is a press fit or requires a special tool for removal, the information or type of tool is identified in the text. Otherwise, if a part is difficult to remove or install, determine the cause before proceeding.

8. To prevent objects or debris from falling into the engine, cover all openings.

9. Read each procedure thoroughly and compare the illustrations to the actual components before

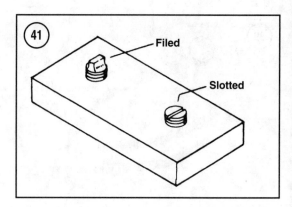

starting the procedure. Perform the procedure in sequence.

10. Recommendations are occasionally made to refer service to a dealership or specialist. In these cases, the work can be performed more economically by the specialist, than by the home mechanic.

11. The term *replace* means to discard a defective part and replace it with a new part. *Overhaul* means to remove, disassemble, inspect, measure, repair and/or replace parts as required to recondition an assembly.

12. Some operations require the use of a hydraulic press. If a press is not available, have these operations performed by a shop equipped with the necessary equipment. Do not use makeshift equipment that may damage the motorcycle.

13. Repairs are much faster and easier if the motorcycle is clean before starting work. Degrease the motorcycle with a commercial degreaser; follow the directions on the container for the best results. Clean all parts with cleaning solvent as they are removed.

CAUTION
Do not direct high-pressure water at steering bearings, carburetor hoses, wheel bearings, suspension and electrical components. The water will force the grease out of the bearings and possibly damage the seals.

14. If special tools are required, have them available before starting the procedure. When special tools are required, they will be described at the beginning of the procedure.

15. Make diagrams of similar-appearing parts. For instance, crankcase bolts are often not the same lengths. Do not rely on memory alone. It is possible that carefully laid out parts will become disturbed,

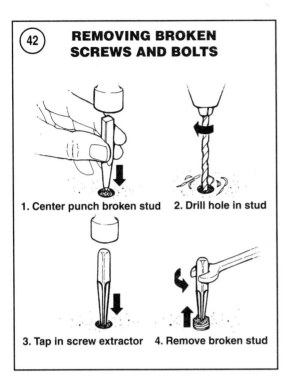

REMOVING BROKEN SCREWS AND BOLTS

1. Center punch broken stud
2. Drill hole in stud
3. Tap in screw extractor
4. Remove broken stud

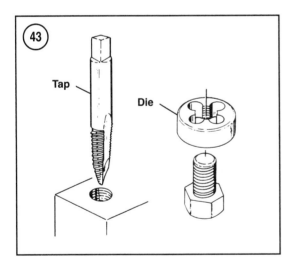

Tap

Die

20. Use grease to hold small parts in place if they tend to fall out during assembly. Do not apply grease to electrical or brake components.

Removing Frozen Fasteners

If a fastener cannot be removed, several methods may be used to loosen it. First, apply penetrating oil such as Liquid Wrench or WD-40. Apply it liberally and let it penetrate for 10-15 minutes. Rap the fastener several times with a small hammer. Do not hit it hard enough to cause damage. Reapply the penetrating oil if necessary.

For frozen screws, apply penetrating oil as described, then insert a screwdriver in the slot and rap the top of the screwdriver with a hammer. This loosens the rust so the screw can be removed in the normal way. If the screw head is too damaged to use this method, grip the head with locking pliers and twist the screw out.

Avoid applying heat unless specifically instructed, as it may melt, warp or remove the temper from parts.

Removing Broken Fasteners

If the head breaks off a screw or bolt, several methods are available for removing the remaining portion. If a large portion of the remainder projects out, try gripping it with locking pliers. If the projecting portion is too small, file it to fit a wrench or cut a slot in it to fit a screwdriver (**Figure 41**).

If the head breaks off flush, use a screw extractor. To do this, centerpunch the exact center of the remaining portion of the screw or bolt. Drill a small hole in the screw and tap the extractor into the hole. Back the screw out with a wrench on the extractor (**Figure 42**).

Repairing Damaged Threads

Occasionally, threads are stripped through carelessness or impact damage. Often the threads can be repaired by running a tap (for internal threads on nuts) or die (for external threads on bolts) through the threads (**Figure 43**). To clean or repair spark plug threads, use a spark plug tap.

If an internal thread is damaged, it may be necessary to install a Helicoil or some other type of thread

making it difficult to reassemble the components correctly without a diagram.

16. Make sure all shims and washers are reinstalled in the same location and position.

17. Whenever rotating parts contact a stationary part, look for a shim or washer.

18. Use new gaskets if there is any doubt about the condition of old ones.

19. If self-locking fasteners are used, replace them with new ones. Do not install standard fasteners in place of self-locking ones.

insert. Follow the manufacturer's instructions when installing their insert.

If it is necessary to drill and tap a hole, refer to **Table 8** for metric tap and drill sizes.

Stud Removal/Installation

A stud removal tool (**Figure 44**) is available from most tool suppliers. This tool makes the removal and installation of studs easier. If one is not available, thread two nuts onto the stud and tighten them against each other. Remove the stud by turning the lower nut (**Figure 45**).

1. Measure the height of the stud above the surface.
2. Thread the stud removal tool onto the stud and tighten it, or thread two nuts onto the stud.
3. Remove the stud by turning the stud remover or the lower nut.
4. Remove any threadlocking compound from the threaded hole. Clean the threads with an aerosol parts cleaner.
5. Install the stud removal tool onto the new stud or thread two nuts onto the stud.
6. Apply threadlocking compound to the threads of the stud.
7. Install the stud and tighten with the stud removal tool or the top nut.
8. Install the stud to the height noted in Step 1 or its torque specification.
9. Remove the stud removal tool or the two nuts.

Removing Hoses

When removing stubborn hoses, do not exert excessive force on the hose or fitting. Remove the hose clamp and carefully insert a small screwdriver or pick tool between the fitting and hose. Apply a spray lubricant under the hose and carefully twist the hose off the fitting. Clean the fitting of any corrosion or rubber hose material with a wire brush. Clean the inside of the hose thoroughly. Do not use any lubricant when installing the hose (new or old). The lubricant may allow the hose to come off the fitting, even with the clamp secure.

Bearings

Bearings are used in the engine and transmission assembly to reduce power loss, heat and noise resulting from friction. Because bearings are preci-

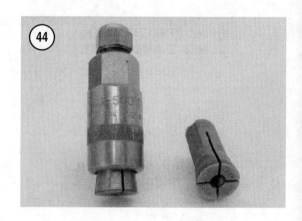

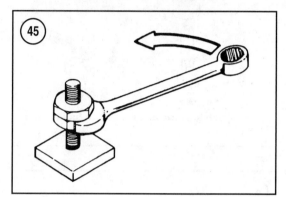

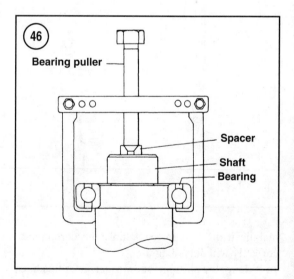

sion parts, they must be maintained with proper lubrication and maintenance. If a bearing is damaged, replace it immediately. When installing a new bearing, take care to prevent damaging it. Bearing replacement procedures are included in the individual chapters where applicable; however, use the following sections as a guideline.

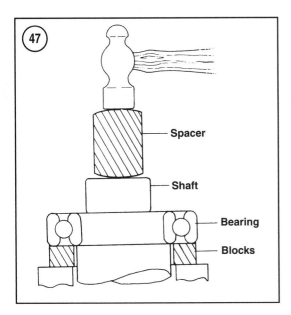

47

Spacer

Shaft

Bearing

Blocks

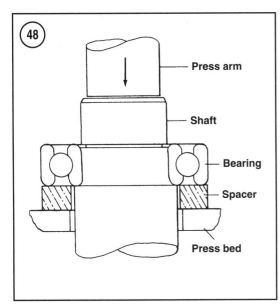

48

Press arm

Shaft

Bearing

Spacer

Press bed

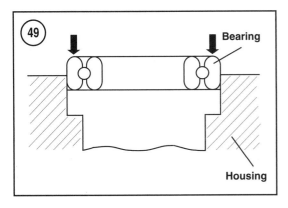

49

Bearing

Housing

NOTE
Unless otherwise specified, install bearings with the manufacturer's mark or number facing outward.

Removal

While bearings are normally removed only when damaged, there may be times when it is necessary to remove a bearing that is in good condition. However, improper bearing removal will damage the bearing and maybe the shaft or case half. Note the following when removing bearings.

1. When using a puller to remove a bearing from a shaft, take care that the shaft is not damaged. Always place a piece of metal between the end of the shaft and the puller screw. In addition, place the puller arms next to the inner bearing race. See **Figure 46**.

2. When using a hammer to remove a bearing from a shaft, do not strike the hammer directly against the shaft. Instead, use a brass or aluminum rod between the hammer and shaft (**Figure 47**) and make sure to support both bearing races with wooden blocks as shown.

3. The ideal method of bearing removal is with a hydraulic press. Note the following when using a press:

  a. Always support the inner and outer bearing races with a suitable size wooden or aluminum ring (**Figure 48**). If only the outer race is supported, pressure applied against the balls and/or the inner race will damage them.

  b. Always make sure the press arm (**Figure 48**) aligns with the center of the shaft. If the arm is not centered, it may damage the bearing and/or shaft.

  c. The moment the shaft is free of the bearing, it will drop to the floor. Secure or hold the shaft to prevent it from falling.

Installation

1. When installing a bearing in a housing, apply pressure to the *outer* bearing race (**Figure 49**). When installing a bearing on a shaft, apply pressure to the *inner* bearing race (**Figure 50**).

2. When installing a bearing as described in Step 1, some type of driver is required. Never strike the bearing directly with a hammer or the bearing will

be damaged. When installing a bearing, use a piece of pipe or a driver with a diameter that matches the bearing inner race. **Figure 51** shows the correct way to use a driver and hammer to install a bearing.

3. Step 1 describes how to install a bearing in a case half or over a shaft. However, when installing a bearing over a shaft and into the housing at the same time, a tight fit will be required for both outer and inner bearing races. In this situation, install a spacer underneath the driver tool so pressure is applied evenly across both races. If the outer race is not supported as shown in **Figure 52**, the balls will push against the outer bearing race and damage it.

Interference fit

1. Follow this procedure when installing a bearing over a shaft. When a tight fit is required, the bearing inside diameter will be smaller than the shaft. In this case, driving the bearing on the shaft using normal methods may cause bearing damage. Instead, heat the bearing before installation. Note the following:

    a. Secure the shaft so it is ready for bearing installation.

    b. Clean all residues from the bearing surface of the shaft. Remove burrs with a file or sandpaper.

    c. Fill a suitable pot or beaker with clean mineral oil. Place a thermometer rated above 120° C (248° F) in the oil. Support the thermometer so that it does not rest on the bottom or side of the pot.

    d. Remove the bearing from its wrapper and secure it with a piece of heavy wire bent to hold it in the pot. Hang the bearing in the pot so it does not touch the bottom or sides of the pot.

    e. Turn the heat on and monitor the thermometer. When the oil temperature rises to approximately 120° C (248° F), remove the bearing from the pot and quickly install it. If necessary, place a socket on the inner bearing race and tap the bearing into place. As the bearing chills, it will tighten on the shaft, so installation must be done quickly. Make sure the bearing is installed completely.

2. Follow this step when installing a bearing in a housing. Bearings are generally installed in a housing with a slight interference fit. Driving the bearing into the housing using normal methods may damage

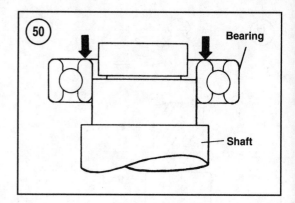

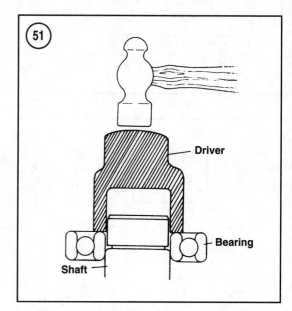

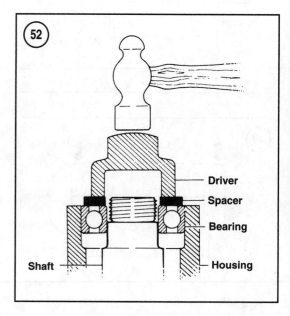

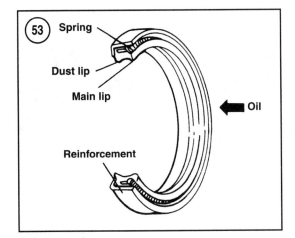

or housing. The direct heat will destroy the case hardening of the bearing and will likely warp the housing.

b. Remove the housing from the oven or hot plate, and hold onto the housing with a kitchen potholder, heavy gloves or heavy shop cloth. It is hot!

NOTE
Remove and install the bearings with a suitable size socket and extension.

c. Hold the housing with the bearing side down and tap the bearing out. Repeat for all bearings in the housing.

d. Before heating the bearing housing, place the new bearing in a freezer if possible. Chilling a bearing slightly reduces its outside diameter while the heated bearing housing assembly is slightly larger due to heat expansion. This will make bearing installation easier.

NOTE
Always install bearings with the manufacturer's mark or number facing outward.

e. While the housing is still hot, install the new bearing(s) into the housing. Install the bearings by hand, if possible. If necessary, lightly tap the bearing(s) into the housing with a socket placed on the outer bearing race (**Figure 49**). Do not install new bearings by driving on the inner-bearing race. Install the bearing(s) until it seats completely.

Seal Replacement

Seals (**Figure 53**) are used to contain oil, water, grease or combustion gasses in a housing or shaft. Improper removal of a seal can damage the housing or shaft. Improper installation of the seal can damage the seal. Note the following:

1. Prying is generally the easiest and most effective method of removing a seal from the housing. However, always place a rag underneath the pry tool (**Figure 54**) to prevent damage to the housing.

2. Pack waterproof grease in the seal lips before the seal is installed.

the housing or cause bearing damage. Instead, heat the housing before the bearing is installed. Note the following:

CAUTION
Before heating the housing in this procedure, wash the housing thoroughly with detergent and water. Rinse and rewash the cases as required to remove all traces of oil and other chemical deposits.

a. Heat the housing to approximately 100° C (212° F) in an oven or on a hot plate. An easy way to check that it is the proper temperature is to place tiny drops of water on the housing; if they sizzle and evaporate immediately, the temperature is correct. Heat only one housing at a time.

CAUTION
Do not heat the housing with a propane or acetylene torch. Never bring a flame into contact with the bearing

3. In most cases, install seals with the manufacturer's numbers or marks face out.

4. Install seals with a socket placed on the outside of the seal as shown in **Figure 55**. Drive the seal squarely into the housing until it is flush (**Figure 56**). Never install a seal by hitting against the top of the seal with a hammer.

STORAGE

Several months of non-use can cause a general deterioration of the motorcycle. This is especially true in areas of extreme temperature variations. This deterioration can be minimized with careful preparation for storage. A properly stored motorcycle will be much easier to return to service.

Storage Area Selection

When selecting a storage area, consider the following:

1. The storage area must be dry. A heated area is best, but not necessary. It should be insulated to minimize extreme temperature variations.

2. If the building has large window areas, mask them to keep sunlight off the motorcycle.

3. Avoid buildings in industrial areas where corrosive emissions may be present. Avoid areas close to saltwater.

Preparing the Motorcycle for Storage

The amount of preparation a motorcycle should undergo before storage depends on the expected length of non-use, storage area conditions and personal preference. Consider the following list the minimum requirement:

1. Wash the motorcycle thoroughly. Make sure all dirt, mud and road debris are removed.

2. Start the engine and allow it to reach operating temperature. Drain the engine oil, and transmission oil, regardless of the riding time since the last service. Fill the engine and transmission with the recommended type of oil.

3A. On carbureted models, drain the fuel from the carburetors as follows:

   a. Turn the fuel shutoff valve (**Figure 57**) off.

   b. Disconnect the fuel pump electrical connector.

   c. Open the drain screws and thoroughly drain the fuel from the float bowls into a suitable container.

   d. Move the choke lever to the full open position.

   e. Operate the start button and try to start the engine. This will draw out all remaining fuel from the jets.

3B. On fuel injected models, fill the fuel tank completely. There is no need to try to empty the fuel rail or the fuel delivery or return lines since they are not vented to the atmosphere.

4. Remove the spark plugs and pour a teaspoon of engine oil into the cylinders. Place a rag over the openings and slowly turn the engine over to distribute the oil. Reinstall the spark plugs.

5. Remove the battery. Store the battery in a cool and dry location.

6. Cover the exhaust and intake openings.

7. Reduce the normal tire pressure by 20%.

8. Apply a protective substance to the plastic and rubber components. Make sure to follow the manu-

facturer's instructions for each type of product being used.

9. Place the motorcycle on a stand or wooden blocks, so the wheels are off the ground. If this is not possible, place a piece of plywood between the tires and the ground. Inflate the tires to the recommended pressure if the motorcycle can not be elevated.

10. Cover the motorcycle with old bed sheets or something similar. Do not cover it with any plastic material that will trap moisture.

Returning the Motorcycle to Service

The amount of service required when returning a motorcycle to service after storage depends on the length of non-use and storage conditions. In addition to performing the reverse of the above procedure, make sure the brakes, clutch, throttle and engine stop switch work properly before operating the motorcycle. Refer to Chapter Three and evaluate the service intervals to determine which areas require service.

Table 1 SERIAL NUMBERS (U.S. MODELS)

Year/model	VIN number	Model code
1998		
YZF-R1K (49-state)	N/A	N/A
YZF-R1K C (CA)	N/A	N/A
1999		
YZF-R1L (49-state)	N/A	N/A
YZF-R1LC (CA)	N/A	N/A
2000		
YZF-R1M (U.S.A)	JYARN05E-YA000009-2003	5JJ4
YZFR1MC (CA)	JYARN05Y-YA000003-2003	5JJ5
2001		
YZF-R1N (U.S.A)	JYARN05E-1A005825-2003	5JJC
YZFR1NC (CA)	JYARN05Y-YA000983-2003	5JJD
2002		
YZF-R1P (49-state)	JYARN010E-2A000007-2003	5PW4
YZF-R1PC (CA)	JYARN010Y-2A000005-2003	5PW5
2003		
YZF-R1P (49-state)	N/A	N/A
YZF-R1PC (CA)	N/A	N/A

Table 2 MOTORCYCLE DIMENSIONS

Overall length	2035 mm (80.1 in.)
Overall width	695 mm (27.4 in.)
Overall height	1095 mm (43.1 in.)
Wheel base	1395 mm (54.9 in.)
Seat height	815 mm (32.1 in.)
Ground clearance	140 mm (5.51 in.)
Minimum turning radius	3400 mm (134 in.)

Table 3 MOTORCYCLE WEIGHT

Dry weight	
49 states and Canada	
1998-1999 models	177 kg (390 lbs.)
2000-2003 models	175 kg (386 lbs.)
California	
1998-1999 models	178 kg (392 lbs.)
2001-2003 models	175 kg (386 lbs.)
Curb weight	
49 states and Canada	
1998-1999 models	198 kg (437 lbs.)
2000-2003 models	199 kg (439 lbs.)
California	
1998-1999 models	194 kg (428 lbs.)
2000-2003 models	195 kg (430 lbs.)
Maximum weight capacity	
49 states and Canada	
1998-1999 models	197 kg (434 lbs.)
2000-2003 models	201 kg (443 lbs.)
California	
1998-1999 models	196 kg (432 lbs.)
2000-2003 models	200 kg (441 lbs.)

Table 4 FUEL TANK CAPACITY

1998-2001 models	
Total (including reserve)	18.0 liters (4.75 U.S. gal.)
Reserve	5.5 liters (1.45 U.S. gal.)
2002-2003 models	
Total (including reserve)	17.0 liters (4.49 U.S. gal.)
Reserve	3.3 liters (0.87 U.S. gal.)

Table 5 GENERAL TORQUE SPECIFICATIONS

Fastener size or type	N•m	in.-lb.	ft.-lb.
5 mm screw	4	35	–
5 mm bolt and nut	5	44	–
6 mm screw	9	80	–
6 mm bolt and nut	10	88	–
6 mm flange bolt (8 mm head, small flange)	9	80	–
6 mm flange bolt (10 mm head) and nut	12	106	–
8 mm bolt and nut	22	–	16
8 mm flange bolt and nut	27	–	20
10 mm bolt and nut	35	–	26
10 mm flange bolt and nut	40	–	29
12 mm bolt and nut	55	–	41

Table 6 CONVERSION FORMULAS

Multiply:	By:	To get the equivalent of:
Length		
Inches	25.4	Millimeter
Inches	2.54	Centimeter
Miles	1.609	Kilometer
Feet	0.3048	Meter
Millimeter	0.03937	Inches
Centimeter	0.3937	Inches
Kilometer	0.6214	Mile
Meter	0.0006214	Mile
Fluid volume		
U.S. quarts	0.9463	Liters
U.S. gallons	3.785	Liters
U.S. ounces	29.573529	Milliliters
Imperial gallons	4.54609	Liters
Imperial quarts	1.1365	Liters
Liters	0.2641721	U.S. gallons
Liters	1.0566882	U.S. quarts
Liters	33.814023	U.S. ounces
Liters	0.22	Imperial gallons
Liters	0.8799	Imperial quarts
Milliliters	0.033814	U.S. ounces
Milliliters	1.0	Cubic centimeters
Milliliters	0.001	Liters
Torque		
Foot-pounds	1.3558	Newton-meters
Foot-pounds	0.138255	Meters-kilograms
Inch-pounds	0.11299	Newton-meters
Newton-meters	0.7375622	Foot-pounds
Newton-meters	8.8507	Inch-pounds
Meters-kilograms	7.2330139	Foot-pounds
Volume		
Cubic inches	16.387064	Cubic centimeters
Cubic centimeters	0.0610237	Cubic inches
Temperature		
Fahrenheit	$(F - 32°) \times 0.556$	Centigrade
Centigrade	$(C \times 1.8) + 32$	Fahrenheit
Weight		
Ounces	28.3495	Grams
Pounds	0.4535924	Kilograms
Grams	0.035274	Ounces
Kilograms	2.2046224	Pounds
Pressure		
Pounds per square inch	0.070307	Kilograms per square centimeter
Kilograms per square centimeter	14.223343	Pounds per square inch
Kilopascals	0.1450	Pounds per square inch
Pounds per square inch	6.895	Kilopascals
Speed		
Miles per hour	1.609344	Kilometers per hour
Kilometers per hour	0.6213712	Miles per hour

1

Table 7 TECHNICAL ABBREVIATIONS

ABDC	After bottom dead center
AP	Atmospheric pressure
ATDC	After top dead center
BBDC	Before bottom dead center
BDC	Bottom dead center
BTDC	Before top dead center
C	Celsius (Centigrade)
cc	Cubic centimeters
cid	Cubic inch displacement
CDI	Capacitor discharge ignition
CP	Crankshaft position
CT	Coolant temperature
cu. in.	Cubic inches
ECT	Engine coolant temperature
ECU	Engine control unit
EVAP	Evaporative emission control system
EXUP	Exhaust Ultimate Power Valve
F	Fahrenheit
ft.	Feet
ft.-lb.	Foot-pounds
gal.	Gallons
H/A	High altitude
hp	Horsepower
IAP	Intake air pressure
IAT	Intake air temperature
in.	Inches
in.-lb.	Inch-pounds
I.D.	Inside diameter
kg	Kilograms
kgm	Kilogram meters
km	Kilometer
kPa	Kilopascals
L	Liter
m	Meter
MAG	Magneto
ml	Milliliter
mm	Millimeter
N•m	Newton-meters
O.D.	Outside diameter
oz.	Ounces
psi	Pounds per square inch
PTO	Power take off
pt.	Pint
qt.	Quart
rpm	Revolutions per minute
RTV	Room temperature vulcanizing
TP	Throttle position

Table 8 METRIC TAP AND DRILL SIZES

Metric size	Drill equivalent	Decimal fraction	Nearest fraction
3 × 0.50	No. 39	0.0995	3/32
3 × 0.60	3/32	0.0937	3/32
4 × 0.70	No. 30	0.1285	1/8
4 × 0.75	1/8	0.125	1/8

(continued)

Table 8 METRIC TAP AND DRILL SIZES (continued)

Metric size	Drill equivalent	Decimal fraction	Nearest fraction
5 × 0.80	No. 19	0.166	11/64
5 × 0.90	No. 20	0.161	5/32
6 × 1.00	No. 9	0.196	13/64
7 × 1.00	16/64	0.234	15/64
8 × 1.00	J	0.277	9/32
8 × 1.25	17/64	0.265	17/64
9 × 1.00	5/16	0.3125	5/16
9 × 1.25	5/16	0.3125	5/16
10 × 1.25	11/32	0.3437	11/32
10 × 1.50	R	0.339	11/32
11 × 1.50	3/8	0.375	3/8
12 × 1.50	13/32	0.406	13/32
12 × 1.75	13/32	0.406	13/32

Table 9 METRIC, INCH AND FRACTIONAL EQUIVALENTS

mm	in.	Nearest fraction	mm	in.	Nearest fraction
1	0.0394	1/32	26	1.0236	1 1/32
2	0.0787	3/32	27	1.0630	1 1/16
3	0.1181	1/8	28	1.1024	1 3/32
4	0.1575	5/32	29	1.1417	1 5/32
5	0.1969	3/16	30	1.1811	1 3/16
6	0.2362	1/4	31	1.2205	1 7/32
7	0.2756	9/32	32	1.2598	1 1/4
8	0.3150	5/16	33	1.2992	1 5/16
9	0.3543	11/32	34	1.3386	1 11/32
10	0.3937	13/32	35	1.3780	1 3/8
11	0.4331	7/16	36	1.4173	1 13/32
12	0.4724	15/32	37	1.4567	1 15/32
13	0.5118	1/2	38	1.4961	1 1/2
14	0.5512	9/16	39	1.5354	1 17/32
15	0.5906	19/32	40	1.5748	1 9/16
16	0.6299	5/8	41	1.6142	1 5/8
17	0.6693	21/32	42	1.6535	1 21/32
18	0.7087	23/32	43	1.6929	1 11/16
19	0.7480	3/4	44	1.7323	1 23/32
20	0.7874	25/32	45	1.7717	1 25/32
21	0.8268	13/16	46	1.8110	1 13/16
22	0.8661	7/8	47	1.8504	1 27/32
23	0.9055	29/32	48	1.8898	1 7/8
24	0.9449	15/16	49	1.9291	1 15/16
25	0.9843	31/32	50	1.9685	1 31/32

CHAPTER TWO

TROUBLESHOOTING

The troubleshooting procedures described in this chapter provide typical symptoms and logical methods for isolating the cause(s). There may be several ways to solve a problem, but only a systematic approach will be successful in avoiding wasted time and possibly unnecessary parts replacement.

Gather as much information as possible to aid in diagnosis. Never assume anything and do not overlook the obvious. Make sure the start switch is in the run position and there is fuel in the tank. Learning to recognize symptoms will make troubleshooting easier. In most cases, expensive and complicated test equipment is not needed to determine whether repairs can be performed at home. On the other hand, be realistic and do not start procedures that are beyond the experience and equipment available. Many service departments will not take work that involves the re-assembly of damaged or abused equipment; if they do, expect the cost to be high. If the motorcycle does require the attention of a professional, describe symptoms and conditions accurately and fully. The more information a technician

has available, the easier it will be to diagnose the problem.

Proper lubrication and maintenance reduces the chance that problems will occur. However, even with the best of care, the motorcycle may require troubleshooting.

OPERATING REQUIREMENTS

An engine needs three basics to run properly: correct air/fuel mixture, compression and a spark at the right time. If one basic requirement is missing, the engine will not run. Four-stroke engine operating principles are shown in **Figure 1**.

If the motorcycle has not been used for any length of time and refuses to start, check and clean the spark plugs. If the plugs are not fouled, inspect the fuel system. This includes the fuel tank, fuel and vacuum hoses, fuel pump, and the carburetor assembly or fuel injection system. Gasoline tends to lose its potency after standing for long periods; as it

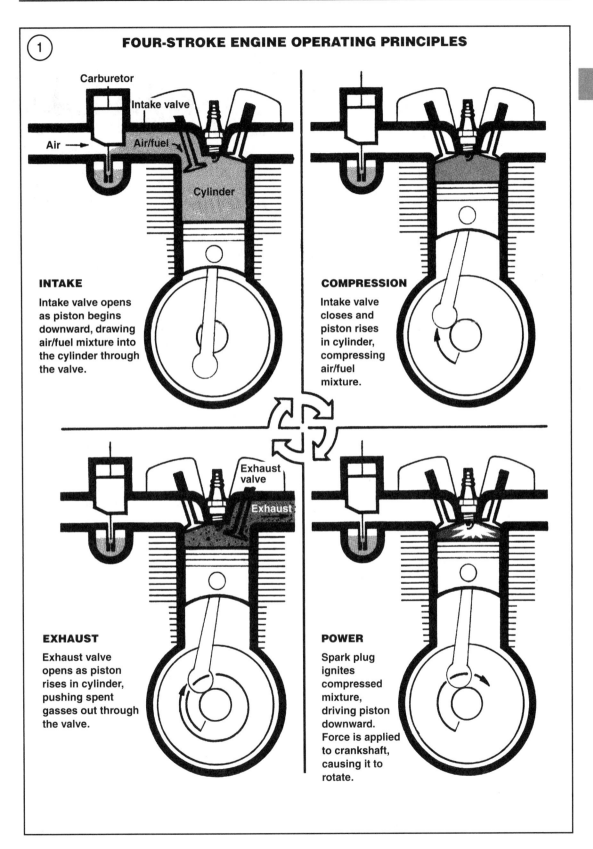

FOUR-STROKE ENGINE OPERATING PRINCIPLES

INTAKE

Intake valve opens as piston begins downward, drawing air/fuel mixture into the cylinder through the valve.

COMPRESSION

Intake valve closes and piston rises in cylinder, compressing air/fuel mixture.

EXHAUST

Exhaust valve opens as piston rises in cylinder, pushing spent gasses out through the valve.

POWER

Spark plug ignites compressed mixture, driving piston downward. Force is applied to crankshaft, causing it to rotate.

evaporates, the mixture becomes richer. Condensation may contaminate gasoline with water. Drain the old gas and try starting with a fresh tankful.

STARTING THE ENGINE (CARBURETED MODELS)

When experiencing engine starting troubles, it is easy to work out of sequence and forget basic engine starting procedures. The following sections list recommended starting procedures for carbureted models at the various ambient temperatures and engine conditions.

Starting Notes

1. All models are equipped with a sidestand ignition cut-off system. The position of the sidestand will affect engine starting. Note the following:
   a. The engine cannot start when the sidestand is down and the transmission is in gear.
   b. The engine can start when the sidestand is down and the transmission is in neutral. The engine will stop if the transmission is put in gear with the sidestand down.
   c. The engine can be started when the sidestand is up and the transmission is in neutral or in gear with the clutch lever pulled in.

2. Before starting the engine, shift the transmission into neutral and place the engine stop switch in the RUN position.

3. Turn the ignition switch on and confirm the following:
   a. The neutral indicator light is on (when the transmission is in neutral).
   b. The oil level and coolant temperature warning lights are on.

4. The engine is now ready to start. Refer to the starting procedure that best describes the conditions.

5. If the engine idle speed is high for more than five minutes and/or the throttle is snapped on and off repeatedly at normal air temperature, the exhaust pipe may discolor.

6. Excessive choke can cause an excessively rich fuel mixture. This condition can wash oil off of the pistons and cylinder walls, causing piston and cylinder scuffing.

CAUTION
Once the engine starts, the oil level warning light should go off in a few seconds. If the light stays on longer than a few seconds, stop the engine immediately. Check the oil level as described in Chapter Three. If the oil level is good, the oil filter or oil cooler may be plugged, the oil pressure may be too low, or the oil pressure switch may be shorted. Check the lubrication system and correct the problem before restarting the engine. If the oil level switch is good, some type of stoppage has occurred in the lubrication system and oil is not being delivered to engine components. Severe engine damage will occur if the engine is run with low oil pressure. Refer to **Engine Lubrication** *in this chapter.*

CAUTION
Do not operate the starter for more than five seconds at a time. Wait for approximately 10 seconds between starting attempts.

Starting Procedures

Engine cold with air temperature between 10-35° C (50-95° F)

1. Review the *Starting Notes* section.
2. Turn the ignition switch on.
3. Place the engine stop switch in the RUN position.
4. Pull the choke lever to the fully on position (**Figure 2**).
5. Operate the starter button and start the engine. Do not open the throttle.

NOTE
When the engine is started with the throttle open and the choke on, a lean mixture will result and cause hard starting.

6. With the engine running, operate the choke lever as required to keep the engine idle between 1500-2500 rpm.

7. After approximately 30 seconds, push the choke lever to the fully off position (**Figure 3**). If the idle is rough, open the throttle slightly until the engine warms up.

Cold engine with air temperature of 10° C (50° F) or lower

1. Review the *Starting Notes* section.
2. Turn the ignition switch on.
3. Place the engine stop switch in the RUN position.
4. Pull the choke lever to the fully on position (**Figure 2**).
5. Operate the starter button and start the engine. Do not open the throttle when pressing the starter button.
6. Once the engine is running, open the throttle slightly to help warm the engine. Operate the engine until the choke can be turned to the fully off position (**Figure 3**) and the engine responds to the throttle smoothly.

Warm engine and/or air temperature 35° C (95° F) or higher

1. Review the *Starting Notes* section.
2. Turn the ignition switch on.

3. Place the engine stop switch in the RUN position.
4. Open the throttle slightly and push the starter button. Do not operate the choke.

Engine flooded

If the engine will not start after a few attempts, it may be flooded. If a gasoline smell is present after attempting to start the engine and the engine will not start, the engine is probably flooded. To start a flooded engine, perform the following:

1. Turn the ignition switch on.
2. Turn the engine stop switch to the OFF position.
3. Push the choke lever to the off position (**Figure 3**).
4. Open the throttle completely and operate the starter for five seconds.
5. Wait 10 seconds, then continue with Step 6.
6. Place the engine stop switch in the RUN position.
7. Open the throttle slightly and push the starter button to start the engine. Do not use the choke.

STARTING THE ENGINE (FUEL INJECTED MODELS)

When experiencing engine-starting troubles, it is easy to work out of sequence and forget basic starting procedures. The following sections describe the recommended starting procedures for fuel injected models.

Starting Notes

1. All models are equipped with a sidestand ignition cut-off system. The position of the sidestand will affect engine starting. Note the following:
   a. The engine cannot start when the sidestand is down and the transmission is in gear.
   b. The engine can start when the sidestand is down and the transmission is in neutral. The engine will stop if the transmission is put in gear with the sidestand down.
   c. The engine can be started when the sidestand is up and the transmission is in neutral or in gear with the clutch lever pulled in.
2. Before starting the engine, shift the transmission into neutral and confirm that the engine stop switch is in the RUN position.

3. Turn the ignition switch on and confirm that the following warning lights are on:

   a. The neutral indicator light (when the transmission is in neutral).

   b. The oil level warning light.

   c. Coolant temperature warning light.

   d. Engine speed indicator light.

   e. Engine trouble warning light.

4. The engine is now ready to start. The motorcycle's fuel injection system is fitted with an automatic fast idle system. Refer to the following starting procedures.

> *CAUTION*
> *Once the engine starts, the oil level warning light should go off in a few seconds. If the light stays on longer than a few seconds, stop the engine immediately. Check the oil level as described in Chapter Three. If the oil level is good, the oil filter or oil cooler may be plugged, the oil pressure may be too low, or the oil pressure switch may be shorted. Check the lubrication system and correct the problem before restarting the engine. If the oil level switch is good, some type of stoppage has occurred in the lubrication system and oil is not being delivered to engine components. Severe engine damage will occur if the engine is run with low oil pressure. Refer to **Engine Lubrication** in this chapter.*

> *NOTE*
> *The fuel injected models are equipped with a lean angle sensor system that turns the engine and fuel pump off if the motorcycle falls over on its side with the engine running. After such an event, and the motorcycle is returned to the upright position, the ignition switch must be turned off, then turned back on before the engine will restart.*

Starting Procedure

All ambient and engine temperatures

1. Review the *Starting Notes* section.

2. Turn the ignition switch on.

3. Place the engine stop switch in the RUN position.

4. Depress the starter button and start the engine. Do not open the throttle when pressing the starter button.

> *NOTE*
> *To prevent the engine from starting with the throttle in the wide-open position, the ECU interrupts the fuel supply if the throttle is in this position while the engine is cranking. The only time it would be necessary to open the throttle all the way is when attempting to start a flooded engine. Refer to **Engine flooded** in this section.*

Engine flooded

If the engine will not start after a few attempts, it may be flooded. If a gasoline smell is present after attempting to start the engine, the engine is probably flooded. To start a flooded engine:

1. Turn the engine stop switch to the OFF position.

2. Open the throttle fully.

3. Turn the ignition switch on and operate the starter button for five seconds.

4. Follow the *All ambient and engine temperatures* starting procedure. Note the following:

   a. If the engine starts but idles roughly, vary the throttle position slightly until the engine idles and responds smoothly.

   b. If the engine does not start, turn the ignition switch off and wait approximately 10 seconds. Then repeat Steps 1-3. If the engine still will not start, refer to *Starting Difficulties* in this chapter.

STARTING DIFFICULTIES

If the engine does not start, perform the following procedure in sequence while remembering the *Operating Requirements* described in this chapter. If the engine fails to start after performing these checks, refer to the troubleshooting procedures indicated in the steps.

1. Refer to *Starting the Engine* in this chapter to make sure all switches and starting procedures are correct.

2. If the starter does not operate, refer to *Starting System* in this chapter.

3. If the starter operates, and the engine seems flooded, refer to *Engine flooded* in this chapter. If the engine is not flooded, continue with Step 4.

4. On fuel injected models, turn the ignition switch on and check the fuel level. If the fuel level warning light is on, the fuel level in the tank is low. The amount of fuel remaining in the tank when the fuel level light comes on is less than one gallon (0.87 U.S. gal./3.3 liters).

5. If there is sufficient fuel in the fuel tank, remove one of the spark plugs immediately after attempting to start the engine. The plug's insulator should be wet, indicating that fuel is reaching the engine. If the plug tip is dry, fuel is not reaching the engine. Confirm this condition by checking another spark plug. A faulty fuel pump or a clogged fuel filter (carbureted models) can cause this condition. Refer to *Fuel System* in this chapter. If there is fuel on the spark plug and the engine will not start, the engine may not have adequate spark. Continue with Step 6.

6. Make sure each spark plug wire is secure. On fuel injected models, remove the fuel tank (Chapter Nine) and push on the 2-pin electrical connector (**Figure 4**) on the top of each direct ignition coil. If necessary, carefully push and slightly rotate the direct ignition coil on the top of the spark plug(s). If the engine does not start, continue with Step 7.

7. Perform the *Spark Test* described in this section. If there is a strong spark, perform Step 8. If there is no spark or if the spark is very weak, refer to *Ignition System* in this chapter.

8. Check cylinder compression as described in Chapter Three.

Spark Test

Perform a spark test to determine if the ignition system is producing adequate spark. This test can be performed with a spark plug or a spark tester. A spark tester is used as a substitute for the spark plug and allows the spark to be more easily observed between the adjustable air gap. The tool shown is available from Motion Pro (part No. 08-0122). If a spark tester is not available, always use a *new* spark plug.

> *WARNING*
> *Step 1 must be performed to disable the fuel system. Otherwise, fuel will enter into the cylinders when the engine is turned over during the spark test, flooding the cylinders and creating explosive fuel vapors.*

1. Remove the fuel tank and air filter housing as described in Chapter Eight or Chapter Nine.

2. Remove the spark plugs as described in Chapter Three.

3. Connect each spark plug wire and connector to a new spark plug (**Figure 5**) or tester (**Figure 6**) and touch each spark plug base or tester to a good en-

gine ground. Position the spark plugs or tester so the electrodes are visible.

WARNING
Mount the spark plugs, or spark tester, away from the spark plug holes in the cylinder head so the spark plugs or tester cannot ignite the gasoline vapors in the cylinder. If the engine is flooded, do not perform this test. The firing of the spark plugs or spark tester can ignite fuel that is ejected through the spark plug holes.

4. Shift the transmission to neutral, turn the ignition switch on and place the engine stop switch in the RUN position.

WARNING
Do not hold the spark plugs, tester, wire or connector, or a serious electrical shock may result.

5. Operate the starter button to turn the engine over. A fat blue spark must be evident across the spark plug electrodes or between the tester terminals. Repeat for each cylinder.

6. If the spark is good at each spark plug, the ignition system is functioning properly. Check for one or more of the following possible malfunctions:

    a. Faulty fuel system component. Refer to *Fuel System* in this chapter.

    b. Engine damage (low compression).

    c. Engine flooded.

7. If the spark was weak or if there was no spark at one or more plugs, note the following:

    a. If there is no spark on all of the plugs, check for a problem on the input side of the ignition system at the ICM (1998-2001) or the ECU (2002-2003), as described in *Ignition System* in this chapter.

    b. If there is no spark at one spark plug only, the spark plug is probably faulty or there is a problem with the spark plug wire or plug cap. Retest with a spark tester, or use a new spark plug. If there is still no spark at that one plug, make sure the spark plug cap is installed correctly.

    c. If there is no spark, the ignition coil is faulty.

    d. Troubleshoot the ignition system as described under *Ignition System* in this chapter.

8. Install the spark plugs as described in Chapter Three.

9. Install the air filter housing and fuel tank as described in Chapter Eight or Chapter Nine.

Engine is Difficult to Start

1. After attempting to start the engine, remove one of the spark plugs as described in Chapter Three and check for the presence of fuel on the plug tip. Note the following:

    a. If there is no fuel visible on the plug, remove another spark plug. If there is no fuel on this plug, perform Step 2.

    b. If there is fuel present on the plug tip, go to Step 5.

    c. If there is an excessive amount of fuel on the plug, check for a clogged or plugged air filter, incorrect choke operation and adjustment (carbureted models) or incorrect throttle valve operation (stuck open) (fuel injected models).

2. Refer to *Fuel Pump* in Chapter Eight or Chapter Nine. Note the following:

    a. If the fuel pump operation is correct, go to Step 4.

    b. If the fuel pump operation is faulty, replace the fuel pump and retest the fuel system.

3A. On carbureted models, perform the *Fuel Flow Test* in Chapter Eight. Note the following:

    a. If the fuel flow is normal, go to Step 5.

    b. If there is no fuel flow, replace the fuel pump as described in Chapter Eight.

    c. If there is fuel flow but the volume is less than specified, check for a clogged fuel line.

3B. On fuel injected models, perform the *Fuel Flow Test* in Chapter Nine. Note the following:

    a. If the fuel flow is normal, go to Step 5.

    b. If there is no fuel flow, check the pressure regulator as described in Chapter Nine. Replace if necessary.

    c. If there is fuel flow but the volume is less than specified, check for a clogged fuel tube and fuel return tube. Then check for a damaged pressure regulator or damaged fuel pump.

4. On fuel injected models, inspect the fuel injectors as described in Chapter Nine.

5. Perform the spark test as described in this chapter. Note the following:

a. If the spark is weak or if there is no spark, go to Step 6.

b. If the spark is good, go to Step 7.

6. If the spark is weak or if there is no spark, check the following:

a. Fouled spark plug(s).

b. Damaged spark plug(s).

c. Loose or damaged spark plug wire(s).

d. Loose or damaged spark plug cap(s).

e. Damaged ICM (1998-2001) or ECU (2002-2003).

f. Damaged ignition timing coil.

g. Damaged ignition coil(s).

h. Damaged engine stop switch.

i. Damaged ignition switch.

j. Dirty or loose-fitting connectors.

7. If the engine turns over but does not start, the engine compression is probably low. Check for the following possible malfunctions:

a. Leaking cylinder head gasket.

b. Valve clearance too tight.

c. Bent or stuck valve(s).

d. Incorrect valve timing. Worn cylinders and/or pistons rings.

8. If the spark is good, try starting the engine by following normal starting procedures. If the engine starts but then stops, check for the following conditions:

a. Incorrect choke operation on carbureted models.

b. Leaking or damaged intake manifold.

c. Contaminated fuel.

d. Incorrect ignition timing due to a damaged ignition coil(s) or ignition pickup coil.

Engine Will Not Crank

If the engine will not turn over, check for one or more of the following possible malfunctions:

1. Blown main fuse.

2. Discharged battery.

3. Defective starter or starter relay switch.

4. Seized piston(s).

5. Seized crankshaft bearings.

6. Broken connecting rod(s).

7. Locked-up transmission or clutch assembly.

8. Defective starter clutch.

ENGINE PERFORMANCE

If the engine runs, but performance is unsatisfactory, refer to the following procedure(s) that best describes the symptom(s).

NOTE
The ignition timing is not adjustable. If incorrect ignition timing is suspected as being the cause of a malfunction, check the timing as described in Chapter Three. If the timing is incorrect, a defective ignition system component is indicated. Refer to **Ignition System** *in this chapter.*

Engine Will Not Idle

1. Clogged air filter element.

2. Poor fuel flow.

3A. On carbureted models, incorrect carburetor synchronization.

3B. On fuel injected models, incorrect throttle body synchronization.

4. Fouled or improperly gapped spark plug(s).

5. Leaking head gasket or vacuum leak.

6. Leaking or damaged intake manifold(s).

7. Incorrect ignition timing: Damaged ICM (1998-2001) or ECU (2002-2003), or ignition timing coil.

8. Obstructed or defective carburetor(s) or fuel injector(s).

9. Low engine compression.

Poor Overall Performance

1. Support the motorcycle with the rear wheel off the ground, then spin the rear wheel by hand. If the wheel spins freely, perform Step 2. If the wheel does not spin freely, check for the following conditions:

a. Dragging rear brake.

b. Damaged rear axle/bearing holder assembly.

c. Damaged drive chain (swollen O-rings).

2. Check the clutch adjustment and operation. If the clutch slips, refer to *Clutch* in this chapter.

3. If Step 1 and Step 2 did not locate the problem, test ride the motorcycle and accelerate lightly. If the engine speed increased according to throttle position, perform Step 4. If the engine speed did not in-

crease, check for one or more of the following problems:

   a. Clogged air filter.
   b. Restricted fuel flow.
   c. Pinched fuel tank breather hose.
   d. Clogged or damaged muffler and/or EXUP valve assembly.

4. Check for one or more of the following problems:

   a. Low engine compression.
   b. Worn spark plugs.
   c. Fouled spark plug(s).
   d. Incorrect spark plug heat range.
   e. Clogged or defective fuel injector(s).
   f. Incorrect ignition timing: Damaged ICM (1998-2001) or ECU (2002-2003), or ignition timing coil.
   g. Incorrect oil level (too high or too low).
   h. Contaminated oil.
   i. Worn or damaged valve train assembly.
   j. Engine overheating. Refer to *Engine Overheating* in this section.

5. If the engine knocks when it is accelerated or when running at high speed, check for one or more of the following possible malfunctions:

   a. Incorrect type of fuel.
   b. Lean fuel mixture.
   c. Advanced ignition timing: Damaged ICM (1998-2001) or ECU (2002-2003), or ignition timing coil.
   d. Excessive carbon buildup in combustion chamber.
   e. Worn pistons and/or cylinder bores.

Poor Idle or Low Speed Performance

1. Check the starter valve synchronization (Chapter Three).
2. Check for damaged intake manifolds or loose throttle body and air filter housing hose clamps.
3. Check the fuel flow and the carburetors or fuel injectors (Chapter Eight or Chapter Nine).
4. Perform the spark test in this section. Note the following:

   a. If the spark is good, go to Step 5.
   b. If the spark is weak, test the ignition system as described in this chapter.

5. Check the ignition timing as described in Chapter Three. Note the following:

   a. If the ignition timing is incorrect, the ICM (1998-2001) or ECU (2002-2003) is probably defective.
   b. If the ignition timing is correct, recheck the fuel system.

Poor High Speed Performance

1. Check the fuel flow and the carburetors or the fuel injectors (Chapters Eight or Chapter Nine).
2. Check ignition timing as described in Chapter Three. If ignition timing is correct, perform Step 3.
3. If the timing is incorrect, test the following ignition system components as described in Chapter Ten:

   a. ICM (1998-2001) or ECU (2002-2003).
   b. Ignition timing coil.
   c. Ignition coils.

4. Check the valve clearance as described in Chapter Three. Note the following:

   a. If the valve clearance is correct, perform Step 5.
   b. If the clearance is incorrect, readjust the valves.

5. Incorrect valve timing and worn or damaged valve springs can cause poor high-speed performance. If the camshafts were timed just prior to the motorcycle experiencing this type of problem, the cam timing may be incorrect. If the cam timing was not set or changed, and all of the other inspection procedures in this section failed to locate the problem, remove the cylinder heads and inspect the camshafts and valve assembly.

Running Rich

Fuel injected engines are sensitive to correct fuel pressure. If the motorcycle is running rich, it may be due to a kinked or blocked low-pressure return hose attached to the base of the fuel pump. This type of blockage can cause the fuel to backup in the fuel distribution pipe and create a rich running engine.

If this problem exists, partially raise the rear of the fuel tank and check to make sure the low-pressure hose is positioned correctly within the fuel tank and air filter housing area. When installing the fuel tank make sure the fuel low-pressure hose is routed correctly with no sharp bends or where it may become crimping or blocking.

Engine Overheating

Cooling system malfunction

1. Low coolant level.
2. Air in cooling system.
3. Clogged radiator, hose or engine coolant passages.
4. Thermostat stuck closed.
5. Clogged or damaged oil cooler.
6. Worn or damaged radiator cap.
7. Damaged water pump.
8. Damaged fan motor switch.
9. Damaged fan motor.
10. Damaged temperature gauge.
11. Damaged coolant temperature sensor.

Other causes

1. Incorrect carburetor jet selection or throttle body adjustment.
2. Improper spark plug heat range.
3. Low oil level.
4. Oil not circulating properly.
5. Valves leaking.
6. Heavy engine carbon deposits in combustion chamber.
7. Dragging brake(s).
8. Clutch slipping.

Engine Not Reaching Operating Temperature

1. Thermostat stuck open.
2. Defective fan motor switch.
3. Inaccurate temperature gauge.
4. Defective coolant temperature sensor.

Engine Backfires

1. Incorrect ignition timing (due to loose or defective ignition system component).
2. Incorrect carburetor jet selection or throttle body adjustment.

Engine Misfires During Acceleration

1. Incorrect ignition timing (due to loose or defective ignition system component).
2. Incorrect carburetor jet selection or throttle body adjustment.

ENGINE NOISES

Unusual noises are often the first indication of a developing problem. Investigate any new noises as soon as possible. Something that may be a minor problem, if corrected, could prevent the possibility of more extensive damage.

Use a special mechanic's stethoscope or a small section of hose held near the ear (not directly on the ear) with the other end close to the source of the noise to isolate the location. Determining the exact cause of a noise can be difficult. If this is the case, consult with a professional mechanic to determine the cause. Do not disassemble major components until all other possibilities have been eliminated.

Consider the following when troubleshooting engine noises:

1. A knocking or pinging during acceleration is typically caused by using a lower octane fuel than recommended. May also be caused by poor fuel. Pinging can also be caused by an incorrect spark plug heat range or carbon build-up in the combustion chamber. Refer to *Spark Plugs* and *Compression Test* in Chapter Three.
2. Slapping or rattling noises at low speed or during acceleration may be caused by excessive piston-to-cylinder wall clearance (piston slap).

NOTE
Piston slap is easier to detect when the engine is cold and before the pistons have expanded. Once the engine has warmed up, piston expansion reduces piston-to-cylinder clearance.

3. A knocking or rapping while decelerating is usually caused by excessive rod bearing clearance.
4. A persistent knocking and vibration occurring every crankshaft rotation is usually caused by worn rod or main bearing(s). Can also be caused by broken piston rings or damaged piston pins.
5. A rapid on-off squeal may indicate a compression leak around the cylinder head gasket or spark plug(s).
6. Check for the following if there is excessive valve train noise:
   a. Valve clearance excessive.
   b. Worn or damaged camshaft.
   c. Damaged camshaft, camshaft drive chain and guides.
   d. Worn or damaged valve lifters and/or shims.
   e. Damaged valve lifter bore(s).

f. Valve sticking in guide(s).

g. Broken valve spring(s).

h. Low oil pressure.

i. Clogged cylinder oil hole or oil passage.

ENGINE LUBRICATION

An improperly operating engine lubrication system will quickly lead to engine seizure. Check the engine oil level before each ride, and top off as described in Chapter Three. Oil pump service is described in Chapter Five.

High Oil Consumption or Excessive Exhaust Smoke

1. Worn valve guides.
2. Worn or damaged piston rings.

Oil Leaks

1. Clogged air filter housing breather hose.
2. Loose engine parts.
3. Damaged gasket sealing surfaces.

High Oil Pressure

1. Clogged oil filter.
2. Clogged oil cooler.
3. Clogged oil gallery or metering orifices.
4. Incorrect type of engine oil.

Low Oil Pressure

1. Low oil level.
2. Worn or damaged oil pump.
3. Clogged oil strainer screen.
4. Clogged oil filter.
5. Clogged oil cooler.
6. Internal oil leakage.
7. Incorrect type of engine oil.

No Oil Pressure

1. Damaged oil pump.
2. Low oil level.
3. Damaged oil pump drive shaft.
4. Damaged oil pump drive sprocket.
5. Incorrect oil pump installation.

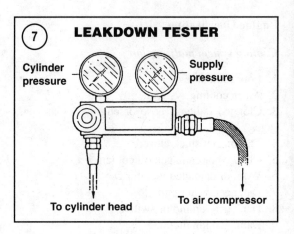

Oil Level Warning Light Stays On

1. Low oil level.
2. Damaged oil level switch and/or relay.
3. Short circuit in warning light circuit.

Oil Level Too Low

1. Oil level not maintained at correct level.
2. Worn piston rings.
3. Worn cylinder(s).
4. Worn valve guides.
5. Worn valve stem seals.
6. Piston rings incorrectly installed during engine overhaul.
7. External oil leakage.
8. Oil leaking into the cooling system.

Oil Contamination

1. Blown head gasket allowing coolant to leak into the engine.
2. Water contamination.
3. Oil and filter not changed at specified intervals or when operating conditions demand more frequent changes.

CYLINDER LEAKDOWN TEST

A cylinder leakdown test can locate engine problems from leaking valves, blown head gasket or broken, worn or stuck piston rings. To perform this test, apply compressed air to the cylinder and then measuring the percent of leakage. Use a cylinder leakdown tester (**Figure 7**) and an air compressor to perform this test.

Follow the manufacturer's directions along with the following information when performing a cylinder leakdown test.

1. Start and run the engine until it is warm. Turn off the engine.

2. Remove the fuel tank and air filter housing as described in Chapter Eight or Chapter Nine.

3. Remove the No. 1 cylinder spark plug as described in Chapter Three.

4. Set the No. 1 piston to TDC on its compression stroke as described under *Valve Clearance* in Chapter Three.

> *WARNING*
> *The crankshaft may rotate when compressed air is applied to the cylinder. Remove any tools that may be attached to the end of the crankshaft.*

> *NOTE*
> *To prevent the engine from turning over as compressed air is applied to the cylinder, shift the transmission into sixth gear and then have an assistant apply the rear brake.*

5. Thread the 10-mm test adapter into the No. 1 spark plug hole and make the hose connections following the manufacturer's instructions.

6. Apply compressed air to the leakdown tester and make a cylinder leakage test following the manufacturer's instructions. Read the percent of leakage on the gauge, following the manufacturer's instructions. Note the following:

   a. For a new or rebuilt engine, a leakage rate of 0 to 5 percent per cylinder is desired. A leakage rate of 6 to 14 percent is acceptable and means the engine is in good condition.

   b. When testing a used engine, the critical rate is not the percent of leakage for each cylinder, but instead, the difference between the cylinders. On a used engine, a leakage rate of 10 percent or less between cylinders is satisfactory.

   c. A leakage rate exceeding 10 percent between cylinders points to an engine in poor condition and requires further inspection and possible repair.

7. After checking the percent of leakage, and with air pressure still applied to the combustion chamber, listen for air escaping from the following areas. If necessary, use a mechanic's stethoscope to pinpoint the source.

   a. Air leaking through the exhaust pipe indicates a leaking exhaust valve.

   b. Air leaking through the carburetors or the throttle body indicates a leaking intake valve.

   c. Air leaking through the crankcase breather tube suggests worn piston rings or a worn cylinder bore.

   d. Air leaking into the cooling system will cause the coolant to bubble in the radiator or coolant reserve tank. When this condition is indicated, check for a damaged cylinder head gasket and warped cylinder head or cylinder block surfaces.

8. Remove the leakdown tester and repeat these steps for each cylinder.

9. After testing each cylinder, reverse Step 2 and Step 3 to complete installation.

CLUTCH

Excessive Clutch Lever Operation

If the clutch lever is too hard to pull in, check the following:

1. Dry and/or dirty clutch cable.

2. Kinked or damaged clutch cable.

3. Damaged clutch lifter bearing.

Rough Clutch Operation

This condition can be caused by excessively worn, grooved or damaged clutch housing slots.

Clutch Slips

If the engine speed increases without an increase in motorcycle speed, the clutch is probably slipping. The main causes of clutch slip are:

1. Worn clutch plates.

2. Weak clutch diaphragm plate.

3. Insufficient clutch lever free play.

4. Damaged clutch lifter piece.

5. Clutch plates contaminated by engine oil additive.

Clutch Drags

If the clutch will not disengage or if the motorcycle creeps with the transmission in gear and the clutch disengaged, the clutch is dragging. Some main causes of clutch drag are:
1. Excessive clutch lever free play.
2. Warped clutch plates.
3. Damaged clutch lifter assembly.
4. Loose clutch housing locknut.
5. Engine oil level too high.
6. Incorrect oil viscosity.
7. Engine oil additive being used.
8. Damaged clutch hub and clutch housing splines.

GEARSHIFT LINKAGE

The gearshift linkage assembly connects the gearshift pedal (external shift mechanism) to the shift drum (internal shift mechanism).

The external shift mechanism can be examined after removing the clutch assembly. The internal shift mechanism can be examined after disassembling the crankcase.

Transmission Jumps Out of Gear

1. Loose stopper arm mounting bolt.
2. Damaged stopper arm.
3. Weak or damaged stopper arm spring.
4. Loose or damaged shift drum.
5. Loose stopper plate bolt.
6. Bent shift fork shaft.
7. Bent or damaged shift fork(s).
8. Worn gear dogs or slots.
9. Damaged shift drum grooves.
10. Weak or damaged gearshift linkage springs.

Difficult Shifting

1. Incorrect clutch operation.
2. Incorrect engine oil viscosity.
3. Loose or damaged stopper arm assembly.
4. Loose stopper plate bolt.
5. Loose stopper plate and pin.
6. Bent shift fork shaft.
7. Bent or damaged shift fork(s).
8. Worn gear dogs or slots.
9. Damaged shift drum grooves.
10. Weak or damaged gearshift linkage springs.

11. Incorrect gearshift linkage installation.

Shift Pedal Does Not Return

1. Bent shift shaft.
2. Weak or damaged shift shaft spindle return spring.
3. Shift shaft incorrectly installed (return spring incorrectly indexed around pin).

TRANSMISSION

Transmission symptoms are sometimes hard to distinguish from clutch symptoms. Prior to working on the transmission, make sure the clutch and gearshift linkage assemblies are not causing the problem.

Difficult Shifting

1. Incorrect clutch operation.
2. Bent shift fork(s).
3. Damaged shift fork guide pin(s).
4. Bent shift fork shaft.
5. Bent shift spindle.
6. Damaged shift drum grooves.

Jumps Out of Gear

1. Loose or damaged shift drum stopper arm.
2. Bent or damaged shift fork(s).
3. Bent shift fork shaft.
4. Damaged shift drum grooves.
5. Worn gear dogs or slots.
6. Broken shift shaft return springs.

Incorrect Shift Lever Operation

1. Bent shift pedal or linkage.
2. Stripped shift pedal splines.
3. Damaged shift pedal linkage.

Excessive Gear Noise

1. Worn or damaged transmission bearings.
2. Worn or damaged gears.
3. Excessive gear backlash.

FUEL SYSTEM
(CARBURETED MODELS)

Many riders automatically assume the carburetors are at fault when the engine does not run properly. While fuel system problems are not uncommon, carburetor adjustment is seldom the answer. In many cases, adjusting will only compound the problem by making the engine run worse.

Isolate fuel system problems to the fuel tank, fuel shutoff valve and filter, fuel pump, fuel hoses, external fuel filter or the carburetors. Make sure that the ignition system is working properly.

Most fuel system problems result from an empty fuel tank, a plugged fuel filter or fuel valve, sour fuel, a dirty air filter or clogged carburetor jets.

Identifying Carburetor Conditions

Refer to the following conditions to identify whether the engine is running lean or rich.

Rich

1. Fouled spark plugs.
2. Engine misfires and runs rough under load.
3. Excessive exhaust smoke as the throttle is increased.
4. An extreme rich condition results in a choked or dull sound from the exhaust and an inability to clear the exhaust with the throttle held wide open.

Lean

1. Blistered or very white spark plug electrodes.
2. Engine overheats.
3. Slow acceleration, engine power is reduced.
4. Flat spots on acceleration that are similar in feel to when the engine starts to run out of gas.
5. Engine speed fluctuates at full throttle.

Fuel Level System

Proper carburetor operation depends on a constant and correct carburetor fuel level. As fuel is drawn from the float bowl during engine operation, the float level in the bowl drops. As the float drops, the fuel valve moves away from its seat and allows fuel to flow through the seat into the float bowl. Fuel entering the float bowl will cause the float to rise and push against the fuel valve. When the fuel level reaches a predetermined level, the fuel valve is pushed against the seat to prevent the float bowl from overfilling.

If the fuel valve fails to close, the engine will run too rich or flood with fuel. Symptoms of this problem are rough running, excessive black smoke and poor acceleration. This condition will sometimes clear up when the engine is run at wide-open throttle, as the fuel is being drawn into the engine before the float bowl can overfill. As the engine speed is reduced, however, the rich running condition returns.

Several things can cause fuel overflow. In most instances, it can be as simple as a small piece of dirt trapped between the fuel valve and seat or an incorrect float level.

Starter (Choke) System

A cold engine requires a rich mixture to start and run properly. A cable-actuated starter (choke) lever located on the left side handlebar and the valve on each carburetor are used for cold starting.

If the engine is difficult to start when cold, check the starter (choke) cable operation. If necessary, lubricate the cable assembly as described in Chapter Three.

FUEL SYSTEM
(FUEL INJECTION MODELS)

The following section isolates common fuel system problems under specific complaints.

Engine Will Not Start

If the engine will not start and the electrical and mechanical systems are operating correctly, check the following:
1. Intake air leak at the intake manifold, air filter or throttle body assembly.
2. Contaminated or old fuel.
3. Clogged fuel tube.
4. Clogged fuel injector filter.
5. Sticking or damaged fuel injector needle.
6. Damaged fuel pump.
7. Faulty fuel pump system.

Engine Starts but Idles and Runs Poorly or Stalls

An engine that idles roughly or stalls may have one or more of the following problems:
1. Intake air leak at the intake manifold, air filter or throttle body assembly.
2. Contaminated or old fuel.
3. Clogged fuel tube.
4. Clogged fuel injector filter.
5. Sticking or damaged fuel injector needle.
6. Incorrect idle speed.
7. Incorrect starter valve synchronization.

Poor Fuel Mileage and Engine Performance

1. Infrequent tune-ups. Compare the service records with the recommended service intervals in Chapter Three.
2. Clogged air filter.
3. Clogged fuel system.
4. Damaged pressure regulator.

Engine Backfires or Misfires During Acceleration

1. Lean fuel mixture.
2. Incorrect throttle body adjustment.
3. Ignition system malfunction.
4. Ignition is intermittently stopped by ECU rpm limiter circuit.
5. Faulty vacuum hoses.
6. Vacuum leaks at the throttle body and/or intake manifold(s).
7. Fouled spark plug(s).

ELECTRICAL SYSTEM

This section describes electrical test equipment and typical test procedures.

Electrical troubleshooting can be very time-consuming and frustrating without proper knowledge and a suitable plan. Refer to the wiring diagrams at the end of the manual for component and connector identification. Use the wiring diagrams to help determine how the circuit works by tracing the current paths from the power source through the circuit components to ground. Also check any circuits that share the same fuse, ground or switch. If the other circuits work properly and the shared wiring is in

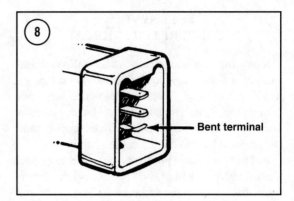

Bent terminal

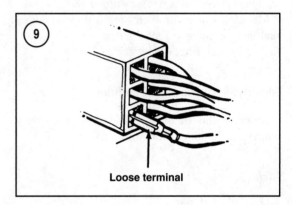

Loose terminal

good condition, the cause must be in the wiring used only by the suspect circuit. If all related circuits are faulty at the same time, the probable cause is a poor ground connection or a blown fuse(s).

As with all troubleshooting procedures, analyze typical symptoms in a systematic process. Never assume anything and do not overlook the obvious like a blown fuse or an electrical connector that has separated. Test the simplest and most obvious cause first and try to make tests at easily accessible points on the motorcycle.

Preliminary Checks and Precautions

Prior to starting any electrical troubleshooting procedure, perform the following:

1. Check the main fuse (Chapter Ten). If the fuse is blown, replace it.

2. Check the individual fuses mounted in the fuse box (Chapter Ten). Remove the suspected fuse and replace if blown.

3. Inspect the battery. Make sure it is fully charged, and that the battery leads are clean and securely at-

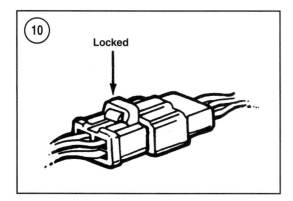

Locked

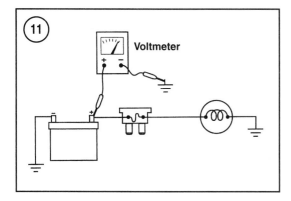

Voltmeter

tached to the battery terminals. Refer to *Battery* in Chapter Ten.

> *NOTE*
> *Always consider electrical connectors the weak link in the electrical system. Dirty, loose fitting and corroded connectors cause numerous electrical related problems, especially on high-mileage motorcycles. When troubleshooting an electrical problem, carefully inspect the connectors and wiring harness.*

4. Disconnect each electrical connector in the suspect circuit and check that there are no bent metal terminals (male or female) inside the connectors (**Figure 8**). Bent terminals will not connect, causing an open circuit.

5. Make sure the metal terminals on the end of each wire (**Figure 9**) are pushed all the way into the plastic connector. If not, carefully push them in with a narrow blade screwdriver.

6. Check the wires where they enter the individual connectors.

7. Make sure all electrical terminals within the connector are clean and free of corrosion. Clean, if necessary, and pack the connectors with dielectric grease.

> *NOTE*
> *Dielectric grease is used as an insulator on electrical components such as connectors and battery connections. Dielectric grease can be purchased at automotive part stores.*

8. Push the connectors together and make sure they are fully engaged and locked together (**Figure 10**).

9. Never pull on the electrical wires when disconnecting an electrical connector—pull only on the connector plastic housing.

10. Never use a self-powered test light on circuits that contain solid-state devices. The solid-state devices may be damaged.

Test Equipment

Test light or voltmeter

A test light can be constructed of a 12-volt light bulb with a pair of test leads carefully soldered to the bulb. To check for battery voltage (12 volts) in a circuit, attach one lead to ground and the other lead to various points along the circuit. Where battery voltage is present, the light bulb will light.

A voltmeter is used in the same manner as the test light to determine if battery voltage is present in any given circuit. The voltmeter, unlike the test light, will also indicate how much voltage is present at each test point. When using a voltmeter, attach the positive lead to the component or wire to be checked and the negative lead to a good ground (**Figure 11**).

Self-powered test light

A self-powered test light can be constructed of a 12-volt light bulb, a pair of test leads and a 12-volt battery. When the test leads are touched together, the light bulb illuminates.

Use a self-powered test light as follows:

1. Touch the test leads together to make sure the light bulb goes on. If not, correct the problem prior to using it in a test procedure.

2. Disconnect the motorcycle's battery or remove the fuse(s) that protects the circuit to be tested. Refer to Chapter Ten.

3. Select two points within the circuit that should have continuity.

4. Attach one lead of the self-powered test light to each point.

5. If there is continuity, the self-powered test light bulb will come on.

6. If there is no continuity, the self-powered test light bulb will not come on. This indicates an open circuit.

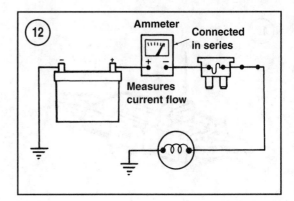

Ammeter

An ammeter measures the flow of current (amps) in a circuit (**Figure 12**). When connected in series in the circuit, the ammeter determines whether current is flowing in the circuit, and whether the current flow is excessive because of a short in the circuit. This current flow is usually referred to as current draw. Comparing actual current draw in the circuit or component to the manufacturer's specified current draw rating provides useful diagnostic information.

Ohmmeter

The ohmmeter reads resistance in ohms. Like the self-powered test light, an ohmmeter contains its own power source and should not be connected to a live circuit.

Ohmmeters may be an analog type (needle scale) or a digital type (LCD or LED readout). Both types of ohmmeters have a switch that allows the selection of different ranges of resistance for accurate readings. The analog ohmmeter also has a set-adjust control that is used to zero or calibrate the meter needle for accurate adjustments. Digital ohmmeters do not require calibration.

An ohmmeter is used by connecting its test leads to the terminals or leads of the circuit or component being tested (**Figure 13**). If an analog meter is used, it should be calibrated by crossing the test leads and adjusting the meter needle until it reads zero. When the leads are uncrossed, the needle should move to the other end of the scale, indicating infinite resistance.

The infinite reading indicates an open in the circuit or component; a reading of zero indicates conti-

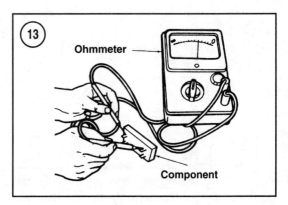

nuity. If the meter needle falls between these two points on the scale, it indicates the actual resistance to current flow that is present. To determine the resistance, multiply the meter reading by the ohmmeter scale. For example, a meter reading of 5 ohms multiplied by the R × 1000 scale is 5000 ohms of resistance.

> *CAUTION*
> *Never connect an ohmmeter to a circuit that has power applied to it. Always disconnect the negative battery cable before using the ohmmeter.*

Jumper wire

When using a jumper wire, always install an inline fuse/fuse holder (available at most auto supply stores or electronic supply stores) to the jumper wire. Never use a jumper wire across any load (a component that is connected and turned on). This would result in a direct short and will blow the fuse(s).

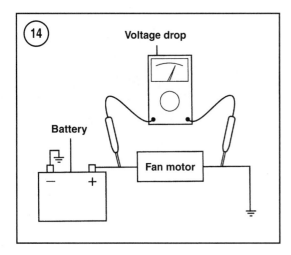

Test Procedures

Voltage testing

Unless otherwise specified, all voltage tests are made with the electrical connectors still connected. Insert the test leads into the backside of the connector. Make sure the test lead touches the wire or metal terminal within the connector. If the test lead only touches the wire insulation, a false reading will result.

Always check both sides of the connector, as one side may be loose or corroded. This prevents electrical flow through the connector. This type of test can be performed with a test light or a voltmeter. A voltmeter gives the best results.

> *NOTE*
> *If using a test lamp, it does not make any difference which test lead is attached to ground.*

1. Attach the negative test lead (if using a voltmeter) to a good ground (bare metal). Make sure the part used for ground is not insulated with a rubber gasket or rubber grommet.

2. Attach the positive test lead (if using a voltmeter) to the point being checked.

3. Turn the ignition switch on. If using a test light, the test light will come on if voltage is present. If using a voltmeter, note the voltage reading. The reading should be within 1 volt of battery voltage. If the voltage is less, there is a problem in the circuit.

Voltage drop test

Resistance causes voltage to drop. This resistance can be measured in an active circuit by using a voltmeter to perform a voltage drop test. A voltage drop test compares the difference between the voltage available from the start of a circuit to the voltage at the end of the circuit while the circuit is operational. If the circuit has no resistance, there will be no voltage drop. The greater the resistance, the greater the voltage drop will be. A voltage drop of one volt or more indicates excessive resistance in the circuit. It is important to remember that a 0 reading on a voltage drop test is good; a battery voltage reading indicates an open circuit. A voltage drop test is an excellent way to check the condition of relays, battery cables and other high-current electrical loads.

1. Connect the positive meter test lead to the electrical source (where electricity is coming from).

2. Connect the negative meter test lead to the electrical load (where electricity is going). See **Figure 14**.

3. If necessary, activate the component(s) in the circuit.

4. A voltage reading of 1 volt or more indicates excessive resistance in the circuit. A reading equal to battery voltage indicates an open circuit.

Continuity test

A continuity test is made to determine if the circuit is complete with no opens in either the electrical wires or components within that circuit.

Unless otherwise specified, all continuity tests are made with the electrical connector still connected. Insert the test leads into the backside of the connector. Make sure the test lead touches the wire or metal terminal within the connector. If the test lead only touches the wire insulation, a false reading will result. Always check both sides of the connectors as one side may be loose or corroded. This prevents electrical flow through the connector.

This type of test can be performed with a self-powered test light or an ohmmeter. An ohmmeter will give the best results. If using an analog ohmmeter, calibrate the meter by touching the leads together and turning the ohm calibration knob until the meter reads zero.

1. Disconnect the negative battery cable.

2. Attach one test lead, the test light or ohmmeter, to one end of the part of the circuit to be tested.

3. Attach the other test lead to the other end of the part of the circuit to be tested.

4. If the circuit has continuity, a self-powered test lamp will illuminate and an ohmmeter will indicate low or no resistance. If the circuit is open, a self-powered test lamp will not illuminate and an ohmmeter will indicate infinite resistance.

Testing for a short with a self-powered test light or ohmmeter

This test can be performed with either a self-powered test light or an ohmmeter.

1. Disconnect the battery negative lead from the battery.

2. Remove the blown fuse from the fuse panel.

3. Connect one test lead of the test light or ohmmeter to the load side or battery side of the fuse terminal in the fuse panel.

4. Connect the other test lead to a good ground (bare metal). Make sure the part used for a ground is not insulated with a rubber gasket or rubber grommet.

5. With the self-powered test light or ohmmeter attached to the fuse terminal and ground, wiggle the wiring harness relating to the suspect circuit at 6 in. (15.2 cm) intervals. Start next to the fuse panel and work away from the fuse panel. Watch the self-powered test light or ohmmeter while moving along the harness.

6. If the test light blinks or the needle on the ohmmeter moves, there is a short-to-ground at that point in the harness.

Testing for a short with a test light or voltmeter

1. Remove the blown fuse from the fuse panel.

2. Connect the test light or voltmeter across the fuse terminals in the fuse panel. Turn the ignition switch on and check for battery voltage.

3. With the test light or voltmeter attached to the fuse terminals, wiggle the wiring harness relating to the suspect circuit at 15.2 cm (6 in.) intervals. Start next to the fuse panel and work away from the fuse panel. Watch the test light or voltmeter while moving along the harness.

4. If the test light blinks or the needle on the voltmeter moves, there is a short-to-ground at that point in the harness.

LIGHTING SYSTEM

If bulbs burn out frequently, the cause may be excessive vibration, loose connections that permit sudden current surges or the installation of the wrong type of bulb. Most light and ignition problems are caused by loose or corroded ground connections. Check these prior to replacing a bulb or electrical component.

CHARGING SYSTEM

The charging system consists of the battery, alternator and a voltage regulator/rectifier. A 30 amp (1998-2001) or 50 amp (2002-2003) main fuse protects the circuit.

Alternating current generated by the alternator is rectified to direct current. The voltage regulator maintains the voltage to the battery and additional electrical loads at a constant voltage regardless of variations in engine speed and load.

Battery Discharging

Before testing the charging system, the battery must be fully charged. If necessary, inspect and charge the battery as described in Chapter Ten.

1. Check all of the connections. Make sure they are tight and free of corrosion.

2. Perform the *Regulated Voltage Test* in Chapter Ten.

    a. If the voltage reading is 14.0-14.8 volts at 5000 rpm, continue at Step 3.

    b. If the voltage reading is incorrect, go to Step 5.

    c. If the regulated voltage exceeds 15.5 volts, refer to *Battery Overcharging* in this section.

3. Perform the *Current Leakage (Draw) Test* as described in Chapter Ten.

   a. If the current draw is 1.2 mA or less, continue at Step 6.

   b. If the current draw exceeds 1.2 mA, continue at Step 4.

4. Disconnect the regulator/rectifier connector(s) and repeat Step 3. Refer to **Figure 15** for 1998-2001 models or **Figure 16** for 2002-2003 models.

   a. If the current draw reading is correct (1.2 mA or less), the regulator/rectifier is defective. Replace the regulator/rectifier (Chapter Ten) and retest.

   b. Moisture or electrolyte on the top of the battery can create a path for current to flow from the battery. Clean the top of the battery and repeat the current draw test. If the drain is still excessive, check the wiring harness for a short circuit. If the wiring harness is in good condition, test the ignition switch as described in Chapter Ten. If the ignition switch is in good condition, the battery is probably defective. Test the battery as described in Chapter Ten.

5. Perform the *Stator Coil Resistance Test* as described in Chapter Ten.

   a. If the stator resistance is not as specified, replace the stator coil and retest.

   b. If the resistance is correct, check for an open circuit, loose or corroded connections or damaged wiring and repair or replace the harness as required.

Battery Overcharging

If the regulated voltage exceeds 15.5 volts at 5000 rpm, perform the following test. Prior to test-

ing, make sure the battery is in serviceable condition.

1. Check all connections for loose or corroded connections.

2. Perform the *Regulated Voltage Test* in Chapter Ten.

   a. If the voltage reading is correct, the battery is damaged. Replace the battery.

   b. If the regulated voltage exceeds the 15.5 volts, perform Step 3.

3. Check for dirty or loose-fitting terminals, including ground wires and terminals. Check for an open circuit in the wiring harness. Inspect the regulator/rectifier connector for dirty or loose-fitting terminals. If the battery continues to overcharge after cleaning or repairing these connectors, the regulator/rectifier is defective. Replace it and retest.

IGNITION SYSTEM

All models are equipped with a transistorized ignition system. Because of the solid state design, problems with the transistorized system are rare. If a problem occurs, it generally causes a weak spark or no spark at all. An ignition system with a weak spark or no spark is relatively easy to troubleshoot. It is difficult, however, to troubleshoot an ignition system that only malfunctions when the engine is hot or under load.

Ignition System Precautions

Protect the ignition system as follows:

1. Never disconnect any of the electrical connectors while the engine is running.

2. Apply dielectric grease to all electrical connectors prior to reconnecting them. This will help seal out moisture.

3. Make sure all electrical connectors are free of corrosion and are completely coupled to each other.

4. The ICM (1998-2001) or ECU (2002-on) must always be mounted securely to the top of the rear fender under the seat.

Troubleshooting Preparation

1. Refer to the wiring diagrams at the end of this manual for the specific model.

2. Check the wiring harness for visible signs of damage.

3. Make sure all connectors are properly attached to each other and locked in place.

4. Check all electrical components for a good ground to the engine or frame.

5. Check all wiring for short circuits or open circuits.

6. Remove the seat as described in Chapter Sixteen.

7. Make sure the fuel tank has an adequate supply of fresh gasoline.

8. Check the spark plug cable routing and their connections at the spark plugs. If there is no spark or only a weak one, repeat the test with new spark plugs. If the condition remains the same with new spark plugs and if all external wiring connections are good, the problem is most likely in the ignition system. If a strong spark is present, the problem is probably not in the ignition system. Check the fuel system.

9. Remove the spark plugs and examine them as described in Chapter Three.

ICM (1998-2001 Models) or ECU (2002-2003 Models) Testing and Replacement

There are no test procedures for the ICM (1998-2001). There are no direct test procedures for the ECU (2002-2003). Refer to *Ignition System* in Chapter Ten. If the unit is suspect, have a Yamaha dealership check it out or by installing one of their test units to ensure the suspect unit is faulty. Make sure nothing has been overlooked before purchasing a new ICM/ECU. Most parts suppliers will not accept the returns of an electrical component.

Ignition Coil Cables and Caps Inspection (1998-2001 Models)

All 1998-2001 models are equipped with resistor- or suppression-type spark plug cables. These cables reduce radio interference. The cable's conductor consists of a carbon-impregnated fabric core material instead of solid wire.

If a plug cable becomes damaged, either due to corrosion or conductor breaks, its resistance increases. Excessive cable resistance will cause engine misfire and other ignition or drivability problems.

When troubleshooting the ignition system, inspect the spark plug cables (**Figure 17**) for:

1. Corroded or damaged connector ends.

2. Breaks in the cable insulation that could allow arcing.

3. Split or damaged plug caps that could allow arcing to the cylinder head.

4. Replace damaged or questionable spark plug cable assembly.

STARTING SYSTEM

The starting system consists of the starter, starter gears, starter relay switch, starter switch button, ignition switch, engine stop switch, starting system cutoff relay, clutch switch, clutch diode, neutral switch, side stand switch, main and auxiliary fuses and battery.

When the starter switch button (**Figure 18**) is pressed, it allows current to flow through the starter relay switch coil. This will cause the coil contacts to close, allowing electricity to flow from the battery to the starter.

> *CAUTION*
> *Do not operate the starter for more than five seconds at a time. Wait approximately 10 seconds between starting attempts.*

The starter should turn when the starter switch button is depressed and the transmission is in neutral and/or the clutch lever pulled in. If the starter does not operate properly, perform the following preliminary checks.

1. Check the battery to make sure it is fully charged. Refer to Chapter Ten for battery service.

2. Check the starter cable and ground wire for loose or damaged connections.

3. Check the battery cables for loose or damaged connections. Then check the battery state of charge as described under *Battery* in Chapter Ten.

4. If the starter does not operate correctly after making these checks, perform the test procedure that best describes the starting malfunction.

Starter Inoperative

1. Check for a blown main fuse or sub-fuse (Chapter Ten). If the fuses are good, continue with Step 2.

2. Check the starter cable for an open circuit or dirty or loose-fitting terminals.

3. Check the starter relay switch connectors for dirty or loose-fitting terminals. Clean and repair as required.

4. Check the starter relay switch (**Figure 19**, typical) as follows. Turn the ignition switch on and depress the starter switch button. When the starter switch button is depressed, the starter relay switch should click once.

   a. If the relay clicks, continue with Step 5.

   b. If the relay does not click, go to Step 6.

> *CAUTION*
> *Because of the large amount of current that flows from the battery to the starter in Step 5, use large diameter cables when making the connection.*

5. Remove the starter from the motorcycle as described in Chapter Ten. Using an auxiliary battery and cables, apply battery voltage directly to the starter. The starter should turn when battery voltage is applied directly.

   a. If the starter did not turn, disassemble and inspect the starter as described in Chapter Ten. Test the starter components and replace worn or damaged parts as required.

   b. If the starter turned, check for loose or damaged starter cables. If the cables are good, check the starter relay switch as described in Chapter Ten. Replace the starter relay switch if necessary.

6. Check the starter relay switch (**Figure 19**, typical) ground circuit as described under *Starter Relay Switch* in Chapter Ten.

   a. If there is continuity, continue with Step 7.

   b. If there is no continuity reading (high resistance), check for a loose or damaged connector or an open circuit in the wiring harness. If these items are in good condition, test the neutral switch, sidestand switch and clutch diode as described in Chapter Ten.

   c. Reconnect the starter relay switch electrical connector (**Figure 19**, typical).

7. Check the starter relay voltage as described under *Starter Relay Switch* in Chapter Ten.

   a. If battery voltage is indicated, continue with Step 8.

   b. If there is no battery voltage reading, check for a blown main or sub-fuse in Chapter Ten. If the fuses are good, check for an open circuit in the wiring harness or for dirty or loose-fitting terminals. If the wiring and connectors are in good condition, check for a defective ignition and/or starter switch in Chapter Ten.

8. Perform the starter relay switch operational check as described under *Starter Relay Switch* in Chapter Ten.

   a. If the starter relay switch is normal, check for dirty or loose-fitting terminals in its connector block.

b. If the starter relay switch is defective, replace it and retest.

Starter Operates Slowly

If the starter turns slowly and all engine components and systems are normal, perform the following:

1. Test the battery as described in Chapter Ten.
2. Check for the following:
   a. Loose or corroded battery terminals.
   b. Loose or corroded battery ground cable.
   c. Loose starter cable and ground lead.
3. Remove and bench test the starter.
4. Check the starter for binding during operation. Disassemble the starter and check the armature shafts for bending or damage. Also check the starter clutch as described in Chapter Six.

Starter Operates but Engine Does Not Turn Over

1. If the starter is running backward and the starter was just reassembled, or if the starter cables were disconnected and then reconnected to the starter:
   a. The starter is reassembled incorrectly.
   b. The starter cables are incorrectly installed.
2. Check for a damaged starter clutch in Chapter Ten.
3. Check for a damaged or faulty starter drive gears in Chapter Ten.

Starter Relay Switch Clicks but Engine Does Not Turn

Crankshaft cannot turn because of mechanical failure.

Starter Operates With the Transmission in Neutral but Does Not With the Transmission in Gear With the Clutch Lever Pulled In and the Sidestand Up

1. Turn the ignition switch on and move the sidestand up and down while watching the sidestand switch indicator light.
   a. If the indicator light works properly, perform Step 2.

b. If the indicator light does not work, check for a blown bulb, damaged sidestand switch (Chapter Ten) or an open circuit in the wiring harness.
2. Test the clutch switch as described in Chapter Ten. Note the following:
   a. If the clutch switch is good, perform Step 3.
   b. If the clutch switch is defective, replace the switch and retest.
3. Test the sidestand switch as described in Chapter Ten. Note the following:
   a. If the sidestand switch is good, perform Step 4.
   b. If the sidestand switch is defective, replace switch and retest.
4. Check for an open circuit in the wiring harness. Check for a loose or damaged electrical connector.

WARNING
Before riding the motorcycle, make sure the sidestand switch and its indicator light work properly. Riding the motorcycle with the sidestand down can cause loss of control.

FRONT SUSPENSION AND STEERING

Steering is Sluggish

1. Incorrect steering stem adjustment (too tight).
2. Damaged steering head bearings.
3. Tire pressure too low.

Steers to One Side

1. Bent axle.
2. Bent frame.
3. Worn or damaged wheel bearings.
4. Worn or damaged swing arm pivot bearings.
5. Damaged steering head bearings.
6. Bent swing arm.
7. Incorrectly installed wheels.
8. Front and rear wheels are not aligned.
9. Front fork legs positioned unevenly in steering stem.
10. Incorrect drive chain adjustment.

Front Suspension Noise

1. Loose mounting fasteners.
2. Damaged fork(s) or rear shock absorber.
3. Low fork oil capacity.
4. Loose or damaged fairing mounts.

Front Wheel Wobble/Vibration

1. Loose front wheel axle.
2. Loose or damaged wheel bearing(s).
3. Damaged wheel rim(s).
4. Damaged tire(s).
5. Unbalanced tire and wheel assembly.

Hard Suspension (Front Fork)

1. Incorrectly adjusted fork.
2. Excessive tire pressure.
3. Damaged steering head bearings.
4. Incorrect steering head bearing adjustment.
5. Bent fork tubes.
6. Binding slider.
7. Incorrect weight fork oil.
8. Plugged fork oil passage.

Hard Suspension (Rear Shock Absorber)

1. Incorrectly adjusted rear shock.
2. Excessive rear tire pressure.
3. Shock incorrectly adjusted.
4. Damaged shock linkage components.
5. Damaged shock absorber collar(s).
6. Damaged shock absorber bearing.
7. Damaged swing arm pivot bearings.

Soft Suspension (Front Fork)

1. Incorrectly adjusted fork.
2. Insufficient tire pressure.
3. Insufficient fork oil level or fluid capacity.
4. Incorrect fork oil viscosity.
5. Weak or damaged fork springs.

Soft Suspension (Rear Shock Absorber)

1. Incorrectly adjusted rear shock.
2. Insufficient rear tire pressure.
3. Weak or damaged shock absorber spring.
4. Damaged shock absorber.
5. Incorrect shock absorber adjustment.
6. Leaking damper unit.

BRAKE SYSTEM

The front and rear brake units are critical to riding performance and safety. Inspect the front and rear brakes frequently; repair any problem immediately. When replacing or refilling the disc brake fluid, use only DOT 4 brake fluid from a closed container. Refer to Chapter Fifteen for additional information on brake fluid selection and disc brake service.

When checking brake pad wear, check that the brake pads in each caliper contact the disc squarely. If one of the brake pads is wearing unevenly, suspect a warped or bent brake disc or damaged caliper.

Always check the brake operation before riding the motorcycle.

Soft or Spongy Brake Lever or Pedal

When the front brake lever or rear brake pedal travel increases, the brake system is not capable of producing sufficient brake force. When an increase in lever/pedal travel is noticed or when the brake feels soft or spongy, check the following possible causes:

1. Air in system.

NOTE
If the brake level in the reservoir drops too low, air can enter the hydraulic system through the master cylinder. Air can also enter the system from loose or damaged hose fittings. Air in the hydraulic system results in a soft or spongy brake lever or pedal action. This condition is noticeable and reduces brake performance. When it is suspected that air has entered the hydraulic system, flush the brake system and bleed the

brakes as described in Chapter Fifteen.

2. Low brake fluid level.

NOTE
As the brake pads wear, the brake fluid level in the master cylinder reservoir drops. Whenever adding brake fluid to the reservoirs, visually check the brake pads for wear. If there does not appear to be an increase in pad wear, check the brake hoses and banjo bolts for leaks.

3. Leak in the brake system.
4. Contaminated brake fluid.
5. Plugged brake fluid passages.
6. Damaged brake lever or pedal assembly.
7. Worn or damaged brake pads.
8. Worn or damaged brake disc.
9. Warped brake disc.
10. Contaminated brake pads and disc.

NOTE
A leaking fork seal can allow oil to contaminate the brake pads and disc.

11. Worn or damaged master cylinder cups and/or cylinder bore.
12. Worn or damaged brake caliper piston seals.
13. Contaminated master cylinder assembly.
14. Contaminated brake caliper assembly.
15. Brake caliper not sliding correctly on slide pins.
16. Sticking master cylinder piston assembly.
17. Sticking brake caliper pistons.

Brake Drag

When the brakes drag, the brake pads are not capable of moving away from the brake disc when the brake lever or pedal is released. Any of the following causes, if they occur, would prevent correct brake pad movement and cause brake drag.
1. Warped or damaged brake disc.
2. Brake caliper not sliding correctly on slide pins.
3. Sticking or damaged brake caliper pistons.
4. Contaminated brake pads and disc.
5. Plugged master cylinder port.

6. Contaminated brake fluid and hydraulic passages.
7. Restricted brake hose joint.
8. Loose brake disc mounting bolts.
9. Damaged or misaligned wheel.
10. Incorrect wheel alignment.
11. Incorrectly installed brake caliper.

Hard Brake Lever or Pedal Operation

When the brakes are applied and there is sufficient brake performance but the operation of brake lever or pedal feels excessively hard, check for the following possible causes:
1. Clogged brake hydraulic system.
2. Sticking caliper piston.
3. Sticking master cylinder piston.
4. Glazed or worn brake pads.
5. Mismatched brake pads.
6. Damaged front brake lever.
7. Damaged rear brake pedal.
8. Brake caliper not sliding correctly on slide pins.
9. Worn or damaged brake caliper seals.

Brakes Grab

1. Damaged brake pad pin bolt. Look for steps or cracks along the pad pin bolt surface.
2. Contaminated brake pads and disc.
3. Incorrect wheel alignment.
4. Warped brake disc.
5. Loose brake disc mounting bolts.
6. Brake caliper not sliding correctly on slide pins.
7. Mismatched brake pads.
8. Damaged wheel bearings.

Brake Squeal or Chatter

1. Contaminated brake pads and disc.
2. Incorrectly installed brake caliper.
3. Warped brake disc.
4. Incorrect wheel alignment.
5. Mismatched brake pads.
6. Incorrectly installed brake pads.

Leaking Brake Caliper

1. Damaged dust and piston seals.
2. Damaged cylinder bore.
3. Loose caliper body bolts.
4. Loose banjo bolt.
5. Damaged banjo bolt washers.
6. Damaged banjo bolt threads in caliper body.

Leaking Master Cylinder

1. Damaged piston secondary seal.
2. Damaged piston snap ring/snap ring groove.
3. Worn or damaged master cylinder bore.
4. Loose banjo bolt.
5. Damaged banjo bolt washers.
6. Damaged banjo bolt threads in master cylinder body.
7. Loose or damaged reservoir cap.

2

CHAPTER THREE

LUBRICATION, MAINTENANCE AND TUNE-UP

This chapter describes lubrication, maintenance and tune-up procedures. Procedures that require more than minor disassembly or adjustment are covered in the appropriate subsequent chapter. Specifications are listed at the end of the chapter.

To maximize the service life of the motorcycle and gain the utmost in safety and performance, it is necessary to perform periodic inspections and maintenance. Minor problems found during routine service can be corrected before they develop into major ones. A neglected motorcycle will be unreliable and may be dangerous to ride. **Figure 1** and **Figure 2** show the location of various components relating to service procedures.

Table 1 lists the recommended lubrication, maintenance and tune-up intervals. If the motorcycle is operated in extreme conditions, it may be appropriate to reduce the interval between some maintenance items.

Before servicing the motorcycle, make sure the procedures and the required skills are thoroughly understood. If experience and equipment are lim-

ited, start by performing basic procedures, and perform more involved tasks as further experience is gained and the necessary tools are acquired.

FUEL TYPE

All models covered in this manual require fuel with a pump octane number of 86 or higher. Using fuel with a lower octane number can cause pinging or spark knock and lead to engine damage.

When choosing gasoline and filling the fuel tank, note the following:

1. When filling the tank, do not overfill it. There should be no fuel in the filler neck (tube located between the fuel cap and tank).

2. Oxygenated fuels can damage plastic and paint. Make sure not to spill fuel on the fuel tank during filling. If using oxygenated fuel, make sure it meets the minimum octane requirements.

3. Ethanol (ethyl or grain alcohol) fuels that contain more than 10 percent ethanol by volume may cause engine starting and performance related problems.

3

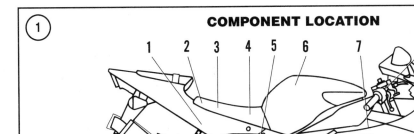

① COMPONENT LOCATION

1. Fuse panel
   (1998-2001 models)
2. Ignition control
   module (1998-2001
   models); Engine
   control unit
   (2002-2003 models)

3. Fuel injection main
   fuse (2002-2003
   models)
4. Battery
5. Rear brake reservoir
6. Air filter element

7. Radiator cap
8. Front brake light
   switch
9. Rear brake light
   switch
10. Rear brake pedal

11. Engine oil filler cap
12. Engine oil level
    check window
13. Coolant reservoir
14. Radiator
15. Oil filter cartridge
16. Front fork oil seal

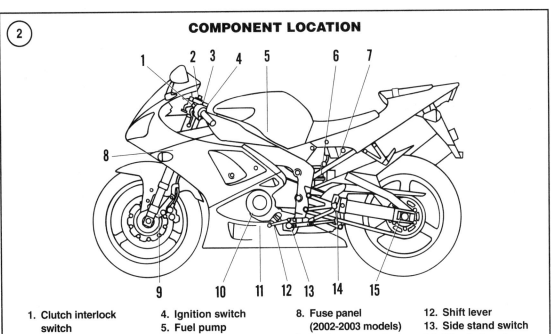

② COMPONENT LOCATION

1. Clutch interlock
   switch
2. Fork rebound and
   spring preload
   adjusters
3. Clutch lever

4. Ignition switch
5. Fuel pump
6. Shock absorber
   damping adjuster
7. Starter relay

8. Fuse panel
   (2002-2003 models)
9. Fork compression
   damping adjuster
10. Alternator
11. Oil drain plug

12. Shift lever
13. Side stand switch
14. Shock absorber
    adjust point
15. Drive chain
    adjuster

4. Methanol (methyl or wood alcohol) fuels that contain more than 5 percent methanol by volume may cause engine starting and performance related problems. Fuel that contains methanol must have corrosion inhibitors to protect the metal, plastic and rubber parts in the fuel system from damage.

TUNE-UP PROCEDURES

A complete tune-up restores performance lost due to normal wear and deterioration of engine parts. Perform the individual items that comprise a tune-up at the intervals specified in **Table 1**. More frequent service may be required if the motorcycle is operated primarily in stop-and-go traffic or in areas where there is a large amount of blowing dirt and dust.

The Vehicle Emission Control Information labels are attached to the inside of the pillion seat storage compartment. Refer to **Table 4** for tune-up specifications.

NOTE
*If the specifications on the Vehicle Emission Control Information label differ from those in **Table 4**, use those on the label.*

To perform a tune-up, service the following as described in this chapter:
1. Air filter.
2. Spark plugs.
3. Engine compression.
4. Ignition timing inspection.
5. Valve clearance and adjustment.
6A. Carburetor synchronization (carbureted models).
6B. Throttle body synchronization (fuel injected models).
7. Engine oil and filter.
8. Drive chain.
9. Brake system.
10. Tires.
11. Suspension components.
12. Fasteners.

AIR FILTER

Replacement

The air filter removes dust and abrasive particles from the air before the air enters the engine.

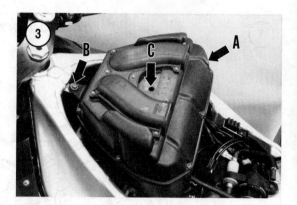

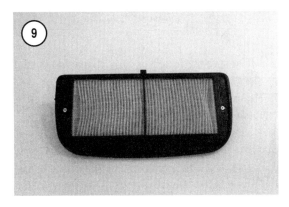

A clogged air filter element will decrease the efficiency and life of the engine. With a damaged air filter, very fine particles could enter the engine and cause rapid wear of the piston rings, cylinder and bearings. Never run the motorcycle without the air filter element installed. Replace the air filter element at the service intervals specified in **Table 1**.

CAUTION
*Follow the service intervals specified in **Table 1** with general use. Service*

the air filter more often if dusty areas are frequently encountered.

1. Remove the rider's seat as described in Chapter Sixteen.
2. Remove the fuel tank as described in Chapter Eight or Chapter Nine.
3A. On carbureted models, perform the following:
   a. Remove the air filter housing cover screws and lift the cover (A, **Figure 3**) off the housing. Do not forget the front (B, **Figure 3**) and center (C) bolts.
   b. Lift the air filter element (**Figure 4**) out of the housing.
   c. Cover the exposed carburetor inlets to prevent objects from entering the carburetors.
3B. On fuel injected models, perform the following:
   a. Remove the air filter housing cover screws and lift the cover (**Figure 5**) off the housing. Do not forget the center screw and the front screw (**Figure 6**).
   b. Lift the air filter element (**Figure 7**) out of the housing.
   c. Cover the exposed throttle body air funnels to prevent objects from entering the throttle bodies.
4. Check the element for damage or dirt buildup. Replace the element if necessary or if the mileage interval has been reached.

CAUTION
On carbureted models in Step 5A, do not direct compressed air directly toward the inside surface of the element. This forces the dirt and dust into the pores of the element, thus restricting air flow.

5A. On carbureted models only, perform the following:
   a. Gently tap the air filter element to loosen the dust.
   b. Apply compressed air at an angle toward the *outside surface* of the element (**Figure 8**) to remove all loosened dirt and dust.
5B. On fuel injected models, visually inspect the viscous type air filter element (**Figure 9**) for contamination or damage. Do *not* apply compressed air to the air filter element as it will be damaged.

6. Check the inside of the air filter air box (**Figure 10**) and cover for dirt and debris.

7. Wipe out the interior of the air box with a damp cloth. Remove any debris that may have passed through a broken element.

8. Remove the covering installed in Step 5.

9A. On 1998-2001 models, install the air filter element into the housing (**Figure 4**). Push it down until it is correctly seated.

9B. On 2002-2003 models, position the air filter element with the FRONT mark (**Figure 11**) facing toward the front of the motorcycle and install it (**Figure 7**). Push it down until it is correctly seated.

10. Install the air filter housing cover and its screws; tighten the screws securely. Make sure the housing cover is seated around the lower housing.

11. Install the fuel tank as described in Chapter Eight or Chapter Nine.

ENGINE COMPRESSION TEST

A cranking compression test is one of the quickest ways to check the internal condition of the engine (piston rings, pistons, head gasket, valves and cylinders). There is no recommended interval to check the compression. However, it is a good idea to perform a test at each tune-up, record it in the maintenance log at the back of the manual, and compare it with subsequent readings.

Use the spark plug tool included in the motorcycle's tool kit and a screw-in type compression gauge with a flexible adapter (**Figure 12**). Before using the gauge, check that the rubber gasket on the end of the adapter is not cracked or damaged; this gasket seals the cylinder to ensure accurate compression readings.

> *NOTE*
> *The compression gauge in Figure 12 is made by Motion Pro and includes flexible adapters for different spark plug thread size.*

> *NOTE*
> *Make sure the socket used to remove the spark plugs is equipped with a rubber insert that secures the spark plug. This type of socket is included in the standard tool kit and is necessary for both removal and installation, since the spark plugs are located in the cylinder head receptacles. It is not*

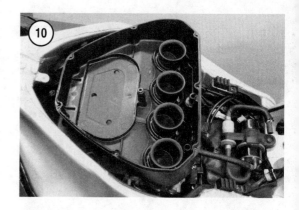

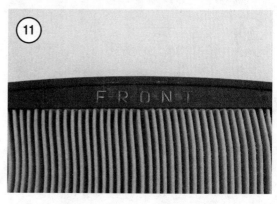

possible to remove or install the spark plugs by hand.

1. Make sure the battery is fully charged to ensure proper engine cranking speed.

2. Run the engine until it reaches normal operating temperature, then turn it off.

3. Remove the rider's seat as described in Chapter Sixteen.

4. Remove the fuel tank as described in Chapter Eight or Chapter Nine.

5. Remove the spark plugs as described under *Spark Plugs* in this chapter.

> *WARNING*
> *Step 6 must be performed to disable the fuel system. Otherwise, fuel will enter the cylinders when the engine is turned over during the compression test, flooding the cylinders and creating explosive fuel vapors.*

6. On 1998-2001 models, disconnect the fuel pump black 2-pin electrical connector containing one black/blue and one black wire.

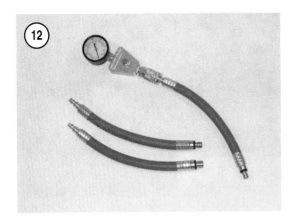

7. Lubricate the threads of the compression gauge adapter with a *small* amount of antiseize compound and carefully thread the gauge into one of the spark plug holes.

CAUTION
Do not crank the engine more than is absolutely necessary. When the spark plug direct ignition coil leads are disconnected, the ignition system will produce the highest voltage possible and the coils may overheat and be damaged.

8. Move the engine stop switch to the RUN position, then turn the ignition switch on. Open the throttle completely and using the starter, crank the engine over until there is no further rise in pressure. Maximum pressure is usually reached within 4-7 seconds of engine cranking. Record the reading and the cylinder number. The number one cylinder is on the left side.
9. Repeat Step 7 and Step 8 for the other cylinders.
10. Standard compression pressure is specified in **Table 4**. Low compression indicates worn or broken rings, leaky or sticky valves, blown head gasket or a combination of all three. Also note any difference between the cylinders.
   a. If the compression readings are near the specification and do not differ between cylinders by more than 10 percent, the rings and valves are in good condition.
   b. If a low reading, or a significant difference (10 percent or more) between cylinders is obtained, it indicates valve or piston ring trouble. To determine which, pour about a teaspoon of engine oil into the spark plug hole

of the cylinder(s) with the low reading. Turn the engine over once to distribute the oil, then take another compression test and record the reading. If the compression increases significantly, the valves are good but the rings and/or cylinder bore are defective on that cylinder. If compression does not increase, the valves require servicing.

NOTE
If the compression is low, the engine cannot be tuned to maximum performance.

11. On 1998-2001 models, connect the fuel pump 2-pin electrical connector.
12. Install the spark plugs as described under *Spark Plugs* in this chapter.
13. Install the fuel tank as described in Chapter Eight or Chapter Nine.
14. Install the rider's seat as described in Chapter Sixteen.

SPARK PLUGS

Inspect and replace the spark plugs at the service intervals specified in **Table 1**.

Removal

When properly read, a spark plug can reveal the operating condition of its cylinder. As each spark plug is removed, label it with its cylinder number. The number one cylinder is on the left side. Use the spark plug tools included in the motorcycle's tool kit.

NOTE
Make sure the socket used to remove the spark plugs is equipped with a rubber insert that secures the spark plug. This type of socket is included in the standard tool kit and is necessary for both removal and installation. The spark plugs are located deep within the cylinder head receptacles and cannot be reached by hand.

1. Remove the rider's seat as described in Chapter Sixteen.

2. Remove the fuel tank and air filter housing as described in Chapter Eight or Chapter Nine.

NOTE
*Refer to **Quick Release Trim Clips** in Chapter Sixteen for the correct procedure for releasing and installing the clips.*

3A. On 1998-2001 models, perform the following:

a. Disconnect the ignition coil 3-pin electrical connector (**Figure 13**).

b. Remove the two trim clips (A, **Figure 14**) securing the ignition coil plate.

c. Partially pull up on the ignition coil plate, then grasp the spark plug lead as near the spark plug as possible and pull the lead off the plug.

d. Disconnect all spark plug leads, then remove the ignition coil plate (B, **Figure 14**).

e. Reinstall the trim clips onto the ignition coil plate to avoid misplacing them.

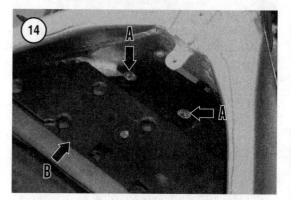

3B. On 2002-2003 models, perform the following:

a. Remove the three trim clips securing the ignition coil plates and remove both plates (**Figure 15**). Reinstall the trim clips onto the ignition coil plates to avoid misplacing them.

b. Carefully disconnect the 2-pin electrical connector (**Figure 16**) from the top of each direct ignition coil.

c. Carefully pull straight up on the direct ignition coil and disengage it from the top of the spark plug. Remove it from the cylinder head cover and spark plug.

4. Clean the cylinder head cover and frame surfaces with compressed air. Check for and remove all loose debris or small parts that could fall into the spark plug receptacles in the cylinder head cover.

CAUTION
Whenever the spark plugs are removed, dirt around them can fall into the spark plug hole. This can cause serious engine damage.

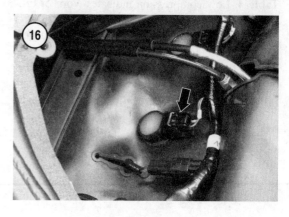

5. Install the spark plug socket onto the spark plug (**Figure 17**). Make sure it is correctly seated, then loosen and remove the spark plug. Mark the spark plug as to which cylinder it was removed from.

6. Repeat Step 5 for the remaining spark plugs.

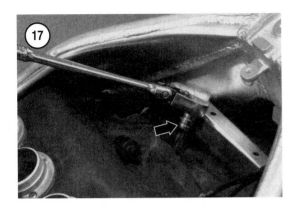

7. Inspect the spark plugs carefully as described in this section.

8. On 2002-2003 models, also inspect the spark plug direct ignition coil for external wear or damage. Inspect the 2-pin electrical connector for corrosion or damage. To service the spark plug direct ignition coils, refer to *Direct Ignition Coil* in Chapter Ten.

3

Gap

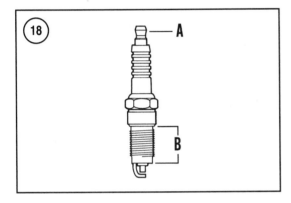

Carefully gap new plugs to ensure a reliable, consistent spark. To do this, use a spark plug gapping tool with a wire gauge. Refer to **Table 4**.

1. Remove the new plugs from the box. If installed, unscrew the terminal nut (A, **Figure 18**) from the end of the spark plug. It is not used with this ignition system.

2. Insert a round feeler gauge between the center and the side electrode of the plug (**Figure 19**). If the gap is correct, a slight drag should be felt as the gauge is pulled through. If there is no drag, or if the gauge will not pass through, bend the side electrode with the gapping tool (**Figure 20**) to set the gap.

3. Repeat for all four spark plugs.

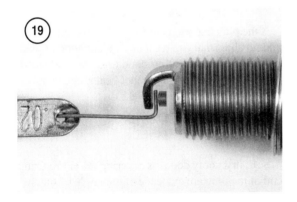

Installation

1. Apply a *light* coat of antiseize compound onto the threads (B, **Figure 18**) of the spark plug before installing it. Remove any compound that contacts the plug's firing tip. Do not apply engine oil on the plug threads.

CAUTION
The cylinder head is aluminum. If the spark plug is cross-threaded into the cylinder head, the threads will be damaged.

2. The spark plugs are recessed into the cylinder head and cannot be started by hand. Install the spark plug into the spark plug socket. Make sure it is properly seated in the socket so it will not fall out during installation. Carefully screw the spark plug in by hand until it seats. Very little effort is required. If force is necessary, the plug may be cross-threaded. Unscrew it and try again.

3. Tighten the spark plug to 13 N•m (115 in.-lb.). If a torque wrench is not available, tighten it 1/2 turn after the gasket contacts the head.

CAUTION
Do not overtighten the spark plug. This will crush the gasket and destroy its sealing ability. It may also damage the spark plug threads in the cylinder head.

4A. On 1998-2001 models, perform the following:
  a. Connect all spark plug leads and push them down until they are completely seated. Repeat for each spark plug.
  b. Install the ignition coil plate (B, **Figure 14**) and secure it with the two trim clips (A).
  c. Connect the ignition coil 3-pin electrical connector (**Figure 13**).
4B. On 2002-2003 models, perform the following:
  a. Carefully push straight down on the direct ignition coil and engage it onto the top of the spark plug. Push it down until it seats completely on the spark plug and the cylinder head cover. Repeat for each spark plug.
  b. Carefully connect the 2-pin electrical connector onto the top of each direct ignition coil.
  c. Install both ignition coil plates (**Figure 15**) and secure it with the three trim clips.
5. Install the fuel tank and air filter housing as described in Chapter Eight or Chapter Nine.
6. Install the rider's seat as described in Chapter Sixteen.

Heat Range

Spark plugs are available in various heat ranges, hotter or colder than the plugs originally installed by the manufacturer.

Select a plug with a heat range designed for the loads and conditions under which the motorcycle will be operated. A plug with an incorrect heat range can foul, overheat and cause piston damage.

In general, use a hot plug for low speeds and low temperatures. Use a cold plug for high speeds, high engine loads and high temperatures. The plug should operate hot enough to burn off unwanted deposits, but not so hot that it is damaged or causes preignition. To determine if plug heat range is correct, remove each spark plug and examine the insulator.

Do not change the spark plug heat range to compensate for adverse engine or air/fuel mixture conditions. Compare the insulator to those in **Figure 21** (typical) when reading plugs.

When replacing plugs, make sure the reach (B, **Figure 18**) is correct. A longer than standard plug could interfere with the piston, causing engine damage. Refer to **Table 4** for recommended spark plugs.

Inspection

Inspecting or reading the spark plugs can provide a significant amount of information regarding engine performance. Reading plugs that have been in use will give an indication of spark plug operation, air/fuel mixture composition and engine conditions (such as oil consumption or piston wear). Before checking new spark plugs, operate the motorcycle under a medium load for approximately 6 miles (10 km). Avoid prolonged idling before shutting off the engine. Remove the spark plugs as described in this chapter. Examine each plug and compare it to those in **Figure 21** (typical).

Normal condition

If the plug has a light tan- or gray-colored deposit and no abnormal gap wear or erosion, good engine, fuel system and ignition conditions are indicated. The plug in use is of the proper heat range and may be serviced and returned to use.

Carbon-fouled

Soft, dry, sooty deposits covering the entire firing end of the plug are evidence of incomplete combustion. Even though the firing end of the plug is dry, the plug's insulation decreases when in this condition. The carbon forms an electrical path that bypasses the spark plug electrodes, resulting in a misfire condition. One or more of the following can cause carbon fouling:
1. Rich fuel mixture.
2. Cold spark plug heat range.
3. Clogged air filter.
4. Improperly operating ignition component.
5. Ignition component failure.
6. Low engine compression.
7. Prolonged idling.

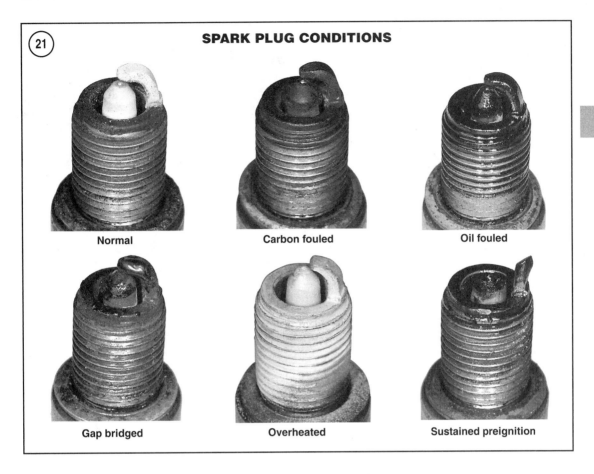

SPARK PLUG CONDITIONS

Normal   Carbon fouled   Oil fouled

Gap bridged   Overheated   Sustained preignition

Oil-fouled

The tip of an oil-fouled plug has a black insulator tip, a damp oily film over the firing end and a carbon layer over the entire nose. The electrodes are not worn. Oil fouled spark plugs may be cleaned in an emergency, but it is better to replace them. It is important to correct the cause of the fouling before the engine is returned to service. Common causes for this condition are:

1. Incorrect air/fuel mixture.

2. Faulty fuel injection system (fuel injected models).

3. Low idle speed or prolonged idling.

4. Ignition component failure.

5. Cold spark plug heat range.

6. Engine still being broken in.

7. Valve guides worn.

8. Piston rings worn or broken.

Gap bridging

Plugs with this condition exhibit gaps shorted out by combustion deposits between the electrodes. If this condition is encountered, check for excessive carbon or oil in the combustion chamber. Be sure to locate and correct the cause of this condition.

Overheating

Badly worn electrodes and premature gap wear are signs of overheating, along with a gray or white blistered porcelain insulator surface. The most common cause for this condition is using a spark plug of the wrong heat range (too hot). If the spark plug is in the correct heat range and is overheating, consider the following causes:

1. Lean air/fuel mixture.

2. Faulty fuel injection operation (fuel injected models).

3. Improperly operating ignition component.

4. Cooling system malfunction.

5. Engine lubrication system malfunction.

6. Engine air leak.

7. Improper spark plug installation.

8. No spark plug gasket.

Worn out

Corrosive gases formed by combustion and high voltage sparks have eroded the electrodes. A spark plug in this condition requires more voltage to fire under hard acceleration. Replace with a new spark plug.

Preignition

If the electrodes are melted, preignition is almost certainly the cause. Check for intake air leaks at the manifolds and carburetors, or throttle bodies, and advanced ignition timing. It is also possible that a plug of the wrong heat range (too hot) is being used. Find the cause of the preignition before returning the engine into service.

IGNITION TIMING INSPECTION

NOTE
The manufacturer does not provide a service procedure for checking the ignition timing on 2002-2003 models. If there is a problem with one or more ignition system components; refer to ***Ignition System*** *in Chapter Two.*

The engine is equipped with a non-adjustable transistorized ignition system. However, periodically check the timing to make sure all ignition components are operating correctly. Incorrect ignition timing can cause a drastic loss of engine performance. It may also cause overheating, detonation and engine damage.

Before starting this procedure, check all electrical connections related to the ignition system. Make sure all connections are tight and free of corrosion. Refer to *Ignition System* in Chapter Ten.

WARNING
Do not start and run the motorcycle in an enclosed area. The exhaust gasses contain carbon monoxide, a colorless, odorless, poisonous gas. The carbon monoxide levels build quickly in an enclosed area and can cause unconsciousness and death in a short time.

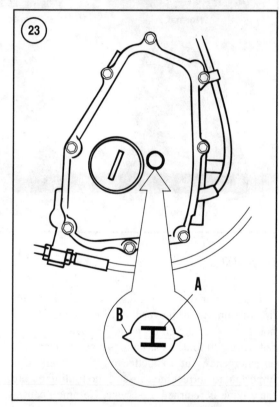

1. Remove the right side fairing and the bottom cowl as described in Chapter Sixteen.

2. Start the engine and let it reach normal operating temperature. Shut off the engine.

3. Remove the rider's seat as described in Chapter Sixteen.

4. Remove the fuel tank and air cleaner housing as described in Chapter Eight.

5. Remove the timing mark inspection cap (**Figure 22**) and it's sealing washer on the timing coil rotor cover.

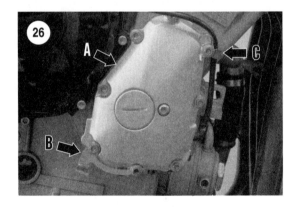

9. Re-start the engine and set the idle speed as described in this chapter.

10. Aim the timing light at the timing hole and pull the trigger.

11. The ignition timing is correct if the index line on the timing coil rotor (A, **Figure 23**) aligns with the index notch on the cover (B).

12. Turn off the engine.

13. If the timing is incorrect, there is a problem with one or more ignition system components; refer to *Ignition System* in Chapter Two. There is no method of adjusting ignition timing.

14. Remove the fuel tank.

15. Disconnect the timing light from the No. 1 spark plug wire.

16. Move the ignition coil plate back into position and secure it with the two quick disconnect fasteners (A, **Figure 14**).

17. Install the timing mark inspection cap and sealing washer (**Figure 24**) onto the timing coil rotor cover. Tighten the cap to 15 N•m (11 ft.-lb.).

18. Install the air cleaner housing and fuel tank as described in Chapter Eight.

19. Install the rider's seat (Chapter Sixteen).

20. Install the right side fairing and the bottom cowl as described in Chapter Sixteen.

VALVE CLEARANCE

Valve clearance specification is listed in **Table 4**.

Measurement

NOTE
Valve clearance measurement and adjustment must be performed with the engine temperature below 35° C (95° F).

1. Remove the cylinder head cover as described in Chapter Four.

2. Remove the right side fairing as described in Chapter Sixteen.

3. Disconnect the clutch cable (**Figure 25**) from the timing coil cover.

4. Place a drain pan under the timing coil cover as some oil may drain out.

5. Remove the screws securing the timing coil cover (A, **Figure 26**) and remove the cover and gasket. Do not lose the locating dowels. Note the loca-

6. Remove the two trim clips (A, **Figure 14**) securing the ignition coil plate. Lift up on the ignition coil plate (B, **Figure 14**) to gain access to the spark plug wires.

7. Connect the timing light to the No. 1 spark plug wire, following the manufacturer's instructions.

8. Temporarily install the fuel tank.

CAUTION
Do no allow any debris to fall into the carburetor while performing this test.

tion of the clutch cable bracket (B, **Figure 26**) and the electrical cable locating tab (C).

6. Remove all of the spark plugs as described in this chapter. This will make it easier to turn the engine by hand.

7. Refer to **Figure 27** for cylinder number locations. Measure the valve clearance's in the following cylinder sequence: No. 1, No. 2, No. 4 and No. 3.

8. Correctly position the engine for measuring valve clearances:

   a. Using a wrench on the timing coil rotor bolt (**Figure 28**), rotate the engine *clockwise*, as viewed from the right side of the motorcycle, until the timing coil rotor T mark (A, **Figure 29**) aligns with the crankcase mating surface (B).

   b. The camshaft lobes on the No. 1 cylinder must be pointing away from each other (**Figure 30**).

> *NOTE*
> *If the camshaft lobes point toward each other, the engine is positioned incorrectly. If this condition exists, rotate the engine clockwise, as viewed from the right side of the motorcycle, 360° (one full turn) and realign the timing coil rotor mark (A, **Figure 29**) with the crankcase mating surface (B).*

9. Measure the clearance of the No. 1 cylinder's intake and exhaust valves by inserting a flat feeler gauge between the cam and the valve lifter surface. When the clearance is correct, there will be a slight drag on the feeler gauge when it is inserted and withdrawn (**Figure 31**). Record the clearance and cylinder number and whether it is an intake or exhaust valve. The clearance dimensions will be used during the adjustment procedure if valve adjustment is necessary.

> *NOTE*
> *Refer to **Figure 32** for the correct amount of **clockwise** crankshaft rotation for the remainder of this procedure. Each step describes a rotation of 180°.*

10. Rotate the crankshaft *clockwise* 180° (1/2 turn) until the timing coil rotor I mark (A, **Figure 33**) aligns with the crankcase mating surface (B). With

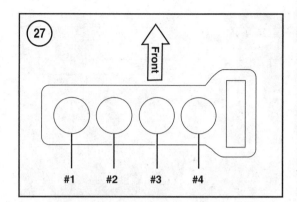

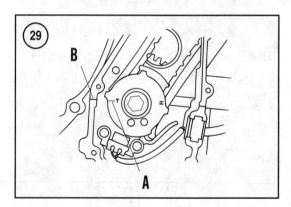

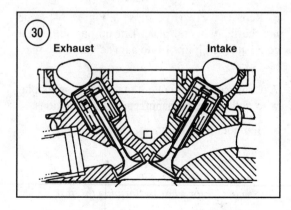

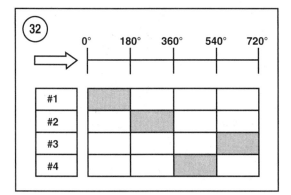

	0°	180°	360°	540°	720°
#1					
#2					
#3					
#4					

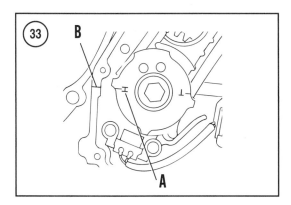

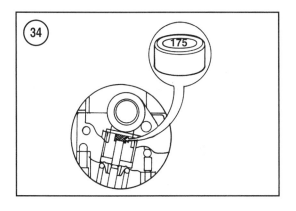

the engine in this position, measure the clearance of the No. 2 cylinders' intake and exhaust valves as described in Step 9.

11. Rotate the crankshaft *clockwise* 180° (1/2 turn) until the timing coil rotor T mark (A, **Figure 29**) aligns with the crankcase mating surface (B). With the engine in this position, measure the clearance of the No. 4 cylinders' intake and exhaust valves as described in Step 9.

12. Rotate the crankshaft *clockwise* 180° (1/2 turn) until the timing coil rotor I mark (A, **Figure 33**) aligns with the crankcase mating surface (B). With the engine in this position, measure the clearance of the No. 3 cylinders' intake and exhaust valves as described in Step 9.

13. If any of the valve clearance measurements are incorrect, replace the pad installed under the valve lifter with a pad of a different thickness. The pads are available from a Yamaha dealership in 0.025 mm thickness increments that range from 1.20 to 2.40 mm. The thickness is marked on the top of the pad (**Figure 34**). To adjust the valve clearance, refer to *Adjustment* in this section.

14. If all of the valve clearances are correct, continue with Step 15.

15. Reinstall the spark plugs as described in this chapter.

16. Install the cylinder head cover as described in Chapter Four.

17. If removed, install the locating dowels (A, **Figure 35**), then install the *new* gasket (B) and the timing coil cover (A, **Figure 26**). Install the clutch cable bracket (B, **Figure 26**) and the electrical cable locating tab (C) in the correct locations and tighten the screws securely.

Adjustment

1. Remove the camshafts as described under *Camshaft Removal* in Chapter Four.

2. When removing the valve lifters and shims, note the following:

    a. Identify and store valve lifters and shims so they can be installed in their original locations. This step is critical to ensure correct valve clearance adjustment and assembly.

    b. The shims are located under the valve lifters and may stick to the valve lifters when the lifter is removed. Remove the lifter carefully to avoid dropping the shim into the crankcase. Use a magnet to remove the lifter. The shims can be removed with a magnet or tweezers.

    c. Clean the valve lifters and shims in solvent and dry with compressed air.

3. Remove the valve lifter (**Figure 36**) and shim (**Figure 37**) for each valve to be adjusted. Label and store each lifter and shim assembly in the marked container.

> *NOTE*
> *Always measure the thickness of the old shim with a micrometer to make sure of the exact thickness of the shim. If the shim is worn to less than the indicated thickness marked on it (**Figure 38**, typical), the calculations for a new shim will be inaccurate. Measure the new shim to make sure it is marked correctly and not worn.*

4. Measure the thickness of the old shim with a micrometer (**Figure 39**).

5. Using the recorded valve clearance, the specified valve clearance and the old shim thickness, determine the new shim thickness with the following equation:

    $a = (b - c) + d$

    where:

    a is the new shim thickness.

    b is the measured valve clearance.

    c is the specified valve clearance.

    d is the old shim thickness.

6. Refer to the following as an *example*:

    a. If the measured intake valve clearance is 0.26 mm, the old shim thickness is 1.870 mm and the specified valve clearance is 0.15 mm (midpoint of specification).

    b. Then $a = (0.26 - 0.15) + 1.870$, $a = 1.980$.

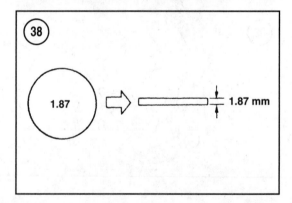

1.87 → 1.87 mm

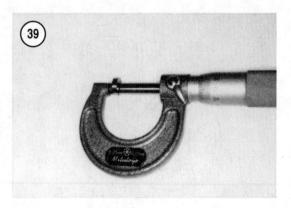

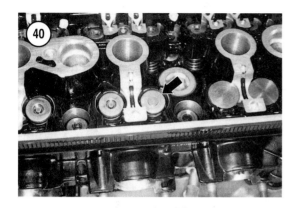

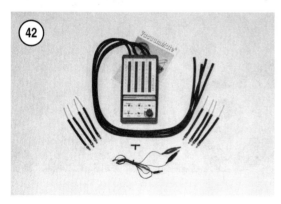

c. The new indicated shim thickness in this *example* is 1.980.

NOTE
If the required shim thickness exceeds 2.400 mm, the valve seat is heavily carboned and must be cleaned or refaced.

7. Apply clean engine oil to both sides of the new shim.

8. Install the new shim (**Figure 37**) and make sure it is correctly seated in the valve retainer (**Figure 40**). Install the valve lifter (**Figure 41**).

9. Repeat for each valve to be adjusted.

10. Install the camshafts as described under *Camshaft Installation* in Chapter Four.

11. Rotate the crankshaft clockwise several times to turn the camshafts and seat the new shims.

12. Recheck the valve clearances as described in the preceding procedure. Repeat this procedure until all valve clearances are correct.

13. Reinstall the spark plugs as described in this chapter.

14. Install the cylinder head cover as described in Chapter Four.

15. If removed, install the locating dowels (A, **Figure 35**), then install the *new* gasket (B) and the timing coil rotor cover (A, **Figure 26**). Install the clutch cable bracket (B, **Figure 26**) and the electrical cable locating tab (C) in the correct locations and tighten the screws securely.

CARBURETOR SYNCHRONIZATION (1998-2001 MODELS)

WARNING
Do not start and run the motorcycle in an enclosed area. The exhaust gasses contain carbon monoxide, a colorless, tasteless, poisonous gas. Carbon monoxide levels build quickly in a small enclosed area and can cause unconsciousness and death in a short time.

Correct carburetor synchronization ensures that each cylinder receives the same air/fuel mixture by synchronizing the vacuum in each carburetor. When the synchronization is correct, the engine warms up faster and throttle response, performance and mileage are improved.

Prior to synchronizing the carburetors, make sure the air filter element is clean and that the valve clearances are correct. Also ensure the ignition system is operating correctly by checking the ignition timing.

A vacuum gauge set (**Figure 42**) that can measure the vacuum in each cylinder simultaneously is required to synchronize the carburetors.

1. Start the engine and let it reach normal operating temperature.

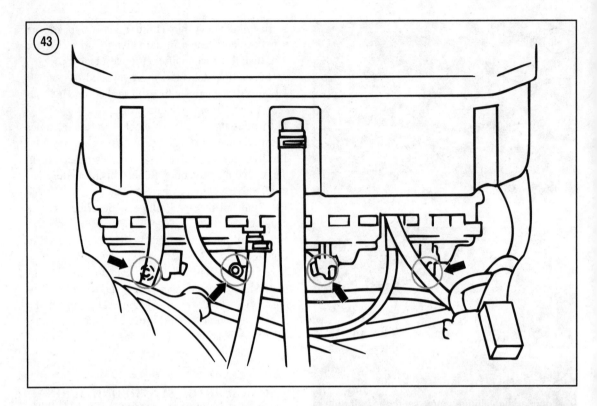

2. Install the portable tachometer, following the manufacturer's instructions.

3. Make sure the idle speed is within the range specified in **Table 4**. If necessary, adjust the idle speed as described in this chapter. Shut off the engine.

4. Remove the rider's seat as described in Chapter Sixteen.

5. Remove the fuel tank as described in Chapter Eight.

WARNING
When using an auxiliary fuel tank, make sure the tank is secure and all fuel lines are tight to prevent leaks.

NOTE
Fuel tanks from small displacement motorcycles, ATV's and lawn mowers make excellent auxiliary fuel tanks. Make sure the tank is mounted securely and positioned so that the connecting fuel hose is not kinked or obstructed.

6. Install an auxiliary fuel tank onto the motorcycle, and attach its fuel hose to the carburetor assembly.

7A. On 1998-1999 models, unscrew and remove the small screws and copper washers (**Figure 43**) from all four carburetors.

7B. On 2000-2001 models, perform the following:
    a. Release the clamp and disconnect the Air Induction System hose from the No. 1 cylinder carburetor fitting.
    b. Unscrew and remove the small screws and copper washers (**Figure 43**) from the remaining three carburetors.

8. Balance the vacuum gauge set, following the manufacturer's instructions, prior to using it in this procedure.

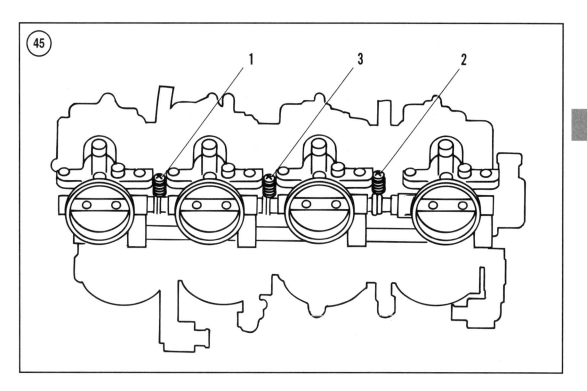

3

9. Connect the vacuum gauge set to the bolt hole in each carburetor, following the manufacturer's instructions.

10. Start the engine and let it idle.

11. If the carburetors are correctly balanced, the vacuum gauges will all be at the same level. The vacuum pressure difference between two carburetors should not exceed 1.33 kPa/10 mm Hg (0.4 in. Hg).

> *NOTE*
> *The No. 4 carburetor is the base carburetor. It has no synchronizing screw. The other three carburetors must be synchronized to the No. 4 carburetor.*

> *NOTE*
> *Snap the throttle a few times and recheck the synchronization readings after each adjustment. Readjust synchronization if required.*

12. Use a short screwdriver (**Figure 44**), turn the synchronizing screw (1, **Figure 45**) in either direction and adjust the No. 1 carburetor to the No. 2 carburetor.

13. Next, turn the synchronizing screw (2, **Figure 45**) in either direction and adjust the No. 3 carburetor to the No. 4 carburetor.

14. Next, turn the synchronizing screw (3, **Figure 45**) in either direction and adjust the No. 2 carburetor to the No. 3 carburetor.

15. Snap the throttle a few times and recheck the synchronization readings after all four carburetors have been adjusted. Readjust synchronization if required.

16. If necessary, adjust the idle speed to the specification in **Table 4**.

17. Shut off the engine.

18. Disconnect the auxiliary fuel tank and the vacuum gauge set from the carburetors.

19. Disconnect the vacuum gauge set from each carburetor.

20. Screw and the four small screws and copper washers (**Figure 43**) into the carburetors and tighten securely.

21. Install the fuel tank as described in Chapter Eight.

22. Install the rider's seat as described in Chapter Sixteen.

23. Restart the engine and check the engine idle speed.

24. Adjust the throttle cable free play as described in this chapter.

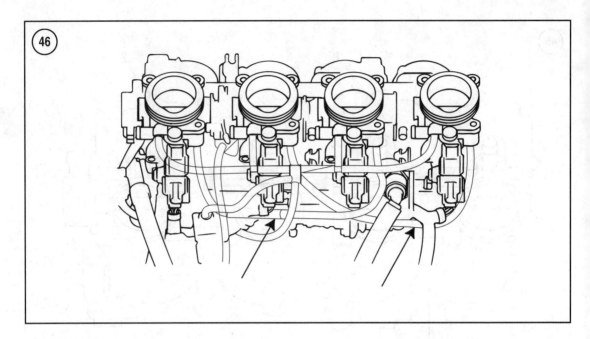

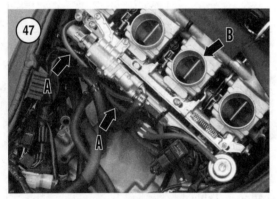

FUEL INJECTION STARTER VALVE
SYNCHRONIZATION (2002-2003 MODELS)

WARNING
Do not start and run the motorcycle in
an enclosed area. The exhaust gasses
contain carbon monoxide, a colorless,
tasteless, poisonous gas. Carbon mon-
oxide levels build quickly in a small
enclosed area and can cause uncon-
sciousness and death in a short time.

Correct starter valve synchronization ensures that
each cylinder receives the same air/fuel mixture by
synchronizing the vacuum in each throttle intake
port. When the synchronization is correct, the engine warms up faster and throttle response, performance and mileage are improved.

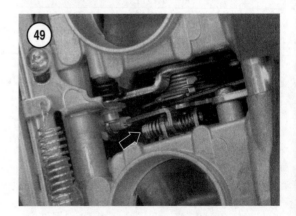

Prior to synchronizing the starter valves, make
sure the air filter element is clean and the valve clearances are correct. Also ensure the ignition system is
operating correctly by checking the ignition timing.

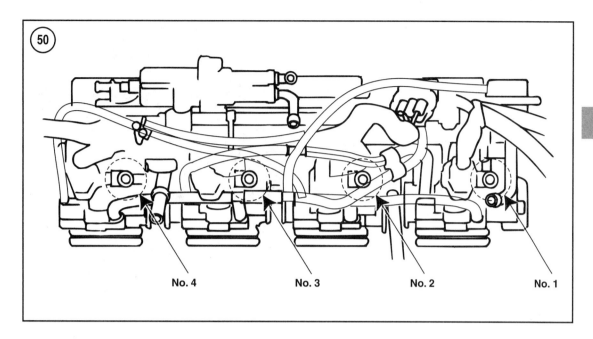

No. 4   No. 3   No. 2   No. 1

A vacuum gauge set (**Figure 42**) that can measure the vacuum in each cylinder simultaneously is required to synchronize the starter valves.

1. Start the engine and let it reach normal operating temperature.

2. Install the portable tachometer following the manufacturer's instructions.

3. Make sure the idle speed is within the range specified in **Table 4**. If necessary, adjust the idle speed as described in this chapter. Shut off the engine.

4. Remove the rider's seat as described in Chapter Sixteen.

5. Remove the fuel tank as described in Chapter Nine.

WARNING
When using an auxiliary fuel tank, make sure the tank is secure and that all fuel lines are tight to prevent leaks.

NOTE
Fuel tanks from small displacement motorcycles, ATV's and lawn mowers make excellent auxiliary fuel tanks. Make sure the tank is mounted securely and positioned so that the connecting fuel hose is not kinked or obstructed.

6. Install an auxiliary fuel tank onto the motorcycle, and attach its fuel hose to the throttle body assembly.

7. Disconnect the four synchronizing hoses (**Figure 46**) from the two interconnecting hose (A, **Figure 47**) small black fittings. Leave each of the four short hoses attached to the throttle body fittings. Do not misplace the two small black fittings.

8. Connect the four hoses from the vacuum gauge to the four short hoses (**Figure 48**) connected to the throttle bodies, following the manufacturer's instructions.

9. Balance the vacuum gauge set, following its manufacturer's instructions, prior to using it in this procedure.

10. Start the engine and let it idle at the speed specified in **Table 4**. If necessary, adjust the idle speed as described in this chapter.

11. If the throttle bodies are correctly balanced, the vacuum gauges will all be at the same level or within 10 mm (0.40 in.) Hg of the No. 3 (base) throttle body.

NOTE
*The No. 3 throttle body (B, **Figure 47**) is the base throttle body and has no synchronization screw, the other three throttle bodies must be synchronized to it.*

12. Use a short screwdriver and turn the adjust screw (**Figure 49**) and adjust the No. 1, No. 2 and No. 4 (**Figure 50**) until they have the same gauge readings as the No. 3 throttle body.

13. Snap the throttle a few times and recheck the synchronization readings. The vacuum gauges must all be at the same level or within 10 mm (0.39 in.) Hg of the No. 3 throttle body. Readjust the idle speed and synchronization if required. Repeat until all adjustments remain the same.

14. Disconnect the vacuum gauge set.

15. Disconnect the auxiliary fuel tank.

16. Reconnect the four synchronizing hoses as follows:

    a. Install a fitting onto the No. 1 hose, then connect the No. 1 and No. 3 throttle body short hoses together.

    b. Install a fitting onto the No. 2 hose, then connect the No. 2 and No. 4 throttle body short hoses together.

17. Make sure the short hoses are securely connected to the two fittings to avoid a vacuum leak.

18. Install the fuel tank as described in Chapter Nine.

19. Restart the engine and reset the engine idle speed, if necessary.

20. Shut off the engine.

IDLE SPEED ADJUSTMENT (ALL MODELS)

Check and, if necessary, adjust the idle speed at the intervals in **Table 1**. Prior to adjusting the idle speed, make sure the air filter element is clean, the valve clearances are correct and the carburetors or fuel injector throttle bodies are synchronized.

1. Make sure the throttle cable free play is adjusted correctly. Check and adjust as described in this chapter.

2. Start the engine and warm it to its normal operating temperature.

3. Remove the left side fairing panel as described in Chapter Sixteen.

> *NOTE*
> *The engine must be at normal operating temperature for the idle speed adjustment to be accurate.*

4. On the left side, turn the idle speed knob (**Figure 51**) in or out to adjust the idle speed. The correct idle speed is listed in **Table 4**.

5. Open and close the throttle a couple of times and check for variations in idle speed. Readjust if necessary.

> *WARNING*
> *With the engine running at idle speed, move the handlebars from side to side. If the idle speed increases during this movement, either the throttle cables need adjusting or they may be incorrectly routed through the frame. Correct this problem immediately. Do not ride the motorcycle in this unsafe condition.*

6. Install the left side fairing panel as described in Chapter Sixteen.

FUEL HOSE INSPECTION

Inspect the fuel hoses at the intervals specified in **Table 1**.

1. Raise and support the fuel tank as described in Chapter Eight or Chapter Nine.

2. Inspect the fuel hose(s) (**Figure 52**) for leaks, hardness, age deterioration or other damage.

3. On fuel injected models, make sure the fuel supply hose is attached correctly and that the retaining clip (**Figure 53**) is in place.

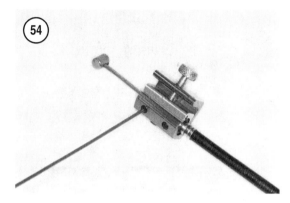

4. Replace damaged fuel hose(s) as described in Chapter Eight or Chapter Nine.

5. Lower and secure the fuel tank.

CONTROL CABLE LUBRICATION (NON-NYLON LINED CABLES ONLY)

Lubricate the non-nylon lined control cables with a cable lubricant and cable lubricator (**Figure 54**) during cable adjustment or if they become stiff or sluggish. The main cause of cable breakage or stiffness is improper lubrication. Periodic lubrication ensures a long service life. Inspect the cables for fraying, and check the sheath for chafing. Replace any defective cables.

CAUTION
When servicing nylon-lined and other aftermarket cables, follow the cable manufacturer's instructions.

1. Disconnect each throttle cable as described under *Throttle Cable Replacement* in Chapter Eight or Chapter Nine.

2. On carbureted models, disconnect the choke cable at both ends as described under *Starter (Choke) Cable Replacement* in Chapter Eight.

3. Disconnect the clutch cable as described under *Clutch Cable Replacement* in Chapter Six.

4. Disconnect the EXUP cables as described under *EXUP Cable Replacement* in Chapter Eight or Chapter Nine.

5. Attach a cable lubricator (**Figure 54**) to each cable, following the manufacturer's instructions.

6. Insert the nozzle of the lubricant can into the lubricator, press the button on the can and hold it down until the lubricant begins to flow out of the other end of the cable. If the lubricant flows out from the cable lubricator, the lubricator is not installed properly onto the end of the cable. The lubricator may have to be installed a few times to get it to seal properly. Place a shop cloth at the end of the cable(s) to catch all excess lubricant that flows out.

NOTE
If lubricant does not flow out the end of the cable, check the entire cable for fraying, bending or other damage.

7. Remove the lubricator and wipe off all excess lubricant from the cable. Place a dab of grease onto the cable barrel before reconnecting it.

8. Reverse Step 1 and Step 2 to install the cables.

9. Adjust the throttle cables and clutch cable as described in this chapter. There is no adjustment procedure for the choke cable.

10. Adjust the EXUP cables as described in this chapter.

THROTTLE CABLES

Throttle Operation Inspection

Check the throttle operation at the intervals specified in **Table 1**.

Check for smooth throttle operation from the fully closed to fully open positions. Check at various steering positions. The throttle lever must return to the fully closed position without any hesitation.

Check the throttle cables for damage, wear or deterioration. Make sure the throttle cables are not kinked at any place.

If the throttle lever does not return to the fully closed position smoothly and the cables do not appear to be damaged, lubricate the throttle cables as described in this chapter. At the same time, clean and lubricate the throttle grip housing with a lightweight oil. If the throttle still does not return properly, the cables are probably kinked or routed incorrectly. Replace the throttle cables as described in Chapter Eight or Chapter Nine.

Check free play at the throttle grip flange (**Figure 55**). The free play specification is 3-5 mm (0.12-0.20 in.). If adjustment is required, perform the following procedure.

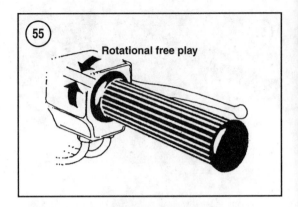

Throttle Cable Adjustment (Carbureted Models)

All models are equipped with two throttle cables. The decelerator (or push) cable is located at the bottom of the throttle cable bracket (A, **Figure 56**). The accelerator (or pull) cable is located at the top of the throttle cable bracket (B, **Figure 56**). The carburetor assembly shown in this figure has been removed and is placed upside down to better illustrate the steps.

> *WARNING*
> *If idle speed increases when the handlebar is turned, check the throttle cable routing. Correct this problem immediately. Do not ride the motorcycle in this unsafe condition.*

1. Remove the rider's seat as described in Chapter Sixteen.
2. Remove the right side fairing panel as described in Chapter Sixteen.
3. Remove the fuel tank and air filter housing as described in Chapter Eight.
4. Remove the ignition coil plate as described in Chapter Ten.
5. Carefully pull the rubber dam (**Figure 57**) forward and off the carburetor assembly to expose the throttle cable ends (**Figure 58**).
6. At the carburetor end of the throttle cables, perform the following:
    a. Loosen the locknut (A, **Figure 59**) on the decelerator cable, then turn the adjuster (B) in either direction to eliminate any slack in the cable. Tighten the locknut.
    b. Loosen the locknut (C, **Figure 59**) on the accelerator cable, then turn the adjuster (D) in

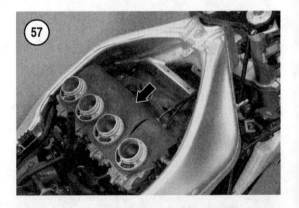

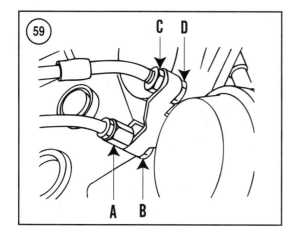

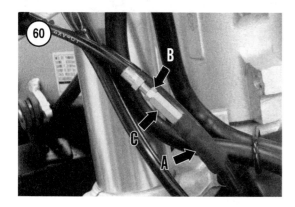

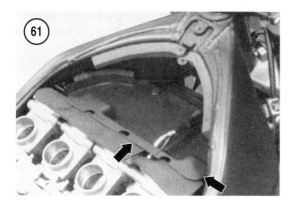

a. On the right side of the steering stem, slide back the rubber boot (A, **Figure 60**) on the in-line adjuster.

b. Loosen the locknut (B, **Figure 60**) and turn the adjuster (C) in either direction until the correct amount of free play is obtained. Tighten the locknut.

8. Operate the throttle a few times. The throttle grip should now be adjusted correctly. If not, the throttle cables may have stretched. Replace cables in this condition.

9. Carefully pull the rubber dam (**Figure 57**) rearward and over the carburetor assembly (**Figure 58**).

10. Install the ignition coil plate (Chapter Ten).

11. Install the air filter housing and fuel tank as described in Chapter Eight.

12. Install the right side fairing (Chapter Sixteen).

13. Install the rider's seat (Chapter Sixteen).

14. Sit on the seat and start the engine with the transmission in neutral. Turn the handlebars from lock to lock to check for idle speed variances due to improper cable routing or damage.

WARNING
If idle speed increases when the handlebar is turned, check the throttle cable routing. Do not ride the motorcycle in this unsafe condition.

15. Test ride the motorcycle, slowly at first, to make sure the throttle cables are operating correctly. Readjust if necessary.

Throttle Cable Adjustment (Fuel Injected Models)

WARNING
If idle speed increases when the handlebar is turned, check the throttle cable routing. Correct this problem immediately. Do not ride the motorcycle in this unsafe condition.

1. Remove the rider's seat (Chapter Sixteen).

2. Remove the right side fairing panel as described in Chapter Sixteen.

3. Remove the fuel tank and air filter housing as described in Chapter Eight.

4. Remove the three trim clips securing the ignition coil plates and remove both plates (**Figure 61**). Reinstall the trim clips to avoid misplacing them.

either direction until the correct amount of free play is obtained. Tighten the locknut.

c. Operate the throttle a few times. The throttle grip should now be adjusted correctly. If not, the throttle cables may have stretched. Replace cables in this condition.

7. If the correct amount of free play cannot be achieved at the carburetor end of the throttle cables, perform the following at the throttle in-line cable adjuster:

5. Carefully pull the rubber dam (A, **Figure 62**) forward and off the throttle body assembly to expose the throttle cable ends (B).

6. At the throttle body end of the throttle cables, perform the following:

   a. Loosen the locknut (A, **Figure 59**) on the decelerator cable, then turn the adjuster (B) in either direction to eliminate any slack in the cable. Tighten the locknut.

   b. Loosen the locknut (C, **Figure 59**) on the accelerator cable, then turn the adjuster (D) in either direction until the correct amount of free play is obtained. Tighten the locknut.

   c. Operate the throttle a few times. The throttle grip should now be adjusted correctly. If not, the throttle cables may have stretched. Replace cables in this condition.

7. If the correct amount of free play cannot be achieved at the throttle body end of the throttle cables, perform the following at the throttle in-line cable adjuster:

   a. On the right side of the steering stem, slide back the rubber boot (A, **Figure 63**) on the in-line adjuster.

   b. Loosen the locknut (B, **Figure 63**) and turn the adjuster (C) in either direction until the correct amount of free play is obtained. Tighten the locknut.

8. Operate the throttle a few times. The throttle grip should now be adjusted correctly. If not, the throttle cables may have stretched. Replace cables in this condition.

9. Carefully pull the rubber dam (A, **Figure 62**) rearward and over the throttle body assembly.

10. Install the filter housing and fuel tank as described in Chapter Nine.

11. Install the right side fairing as described in Chapter Sixteen.

12. Install the rider's seat as described in Chapter Sixteen.

13. Sit on the seat and start the engine with the transmission in neutral. Turn the handlebars from lock to lock to check for idle speed variances due to improper cable routing or damage.

> *WARNING*
> *If idle speed increases when the handlebar is turned, check the throttle cable routing. Do not ride the motorcycle in this unsafe condition.*

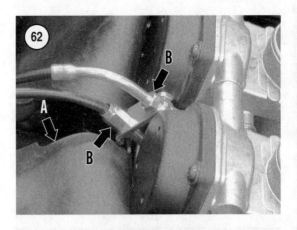

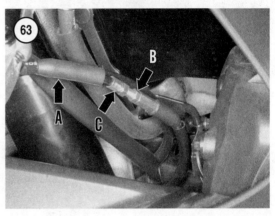

14. Test ride the motorcycle, slowly at first, to make sure the throttle cables are operating correctly. Readjust if necessary.

STARTER (CHOKE) CABLE

Inspect the starter (choke) cable (carbureted models only) at both ends for fraying or other damage.

The lever mounted on the left handlebar should move smoothly between its fully open and fully closed positions. If the lever moves roughly, lubricate the cable as described in this section. Then check the cable for any kinks or other damage.

There is no adjustment procedure for the starter (choke) cable.

CLUTCH CABLE ADJUSTMENT

Check the clutch adjustment frequently and adjust it, if necessary, to compensate for clutch cable stretch and clutch plate wear. Excessive clutch lever

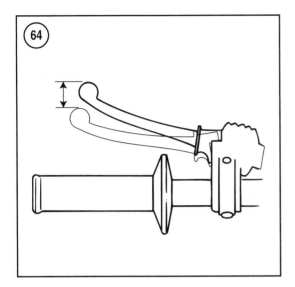

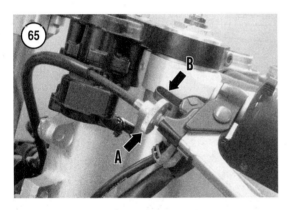

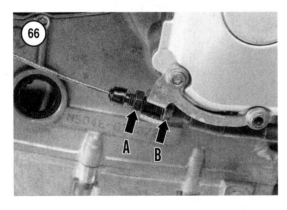

1. With the engine turned off, pull the clutch lever toward the handlebar until resistance is felt, then stop and measure the free play at the end of the clutch lever (**Figure 64**).

2. Minor adjustments can be made at the clutch hand lever adjuster. Turn the clutch cable adjuster dial (A, **Figure 65**) in either direction to obtain the correct amount of free play. Make sure the spring detent (B, **Figure 65**) is pressed securely against the dial to prevent accidental rotation.

NOTE
If sufficient free play cannot be obtained at the clutch hand lever, additional adjustment must be made at the opposite end of the clutch cable.

3. If the proper amount of free play cannot be achieved at the clutch hand lever adjuster, perform the following:
   a. Remove the right side faring panel as described in Chapter Sixteen.
   b. At the clutch cable inline adjuster on the right side, loosen the locknut (A, **Figure 66**) and turn the adjust nut (B) until the correct amount of free play is achieved at the clutch lever on the handlebar.
   c. Hold onto the adjust nut (B, **Figure 66**) and securely tighten the locknut (A).
   d. If necessary, fine-tune the adjustment at the clutch hand lever adjuster.

4. Make sure the locknut (A, **Figure 66**) is tight.

5. Start the engine and make sure the clutch operates correctly.

6. If removed, install the right side faring panel as described in Chapter Sixteen.

7. If the proper amount of free play cannot be achieved by using this adjustment procedure, either the cable has stretched to the point that it needs to be replaced or the friction discs inside the clutch assembly are worn and need replacing. Refer to Chapter Six for clutch cable and clutch component service.

GEARSHIFT PEDAL ADJUSTMENT

Adjust the gearshift pedal by loosening the locknuts at each end and rotating the shift rod in either direction to obtain the correct adjustment.

1. On 1998-2001 models, perform the following:

play prevents the clutch from disengaging and causes clutch drag. Too little or no clutch lever free play does not allow the clutch to fully engage, resulting in clutch slippage. Both conditions cause unnecessary clutch wear.

The specified clutch lever free play is 10-15 mm (0.39-0.59 in.).

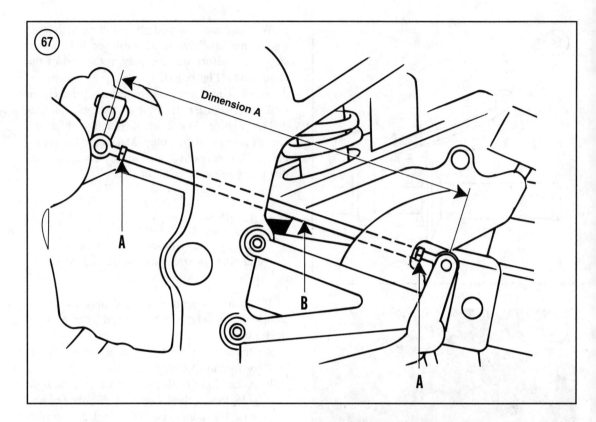

a. Loosen the locknuts (A, **Figure 67**) and rotate
the shift rod (B) in either direction until the
distance between the shift rod pivot points is
305 mm (12.0 in.).

b. Hold onto the shift rod joint with a wrench
(A, **Figure 68**), tighten the locknut (B) at
each end securely and recheck the dimension.
Readjust if necessary.

2. On 2002-2003 models, perform the following:

NOTE
Only one of the locknuts is visible in
Step 2a, loosen the locknut at each
end of the shift rod.

a. Loosen the locknut (A, **Figure 69**) at each
end and rotate the shift rod (B) in either direction until the top of the shift pedal is 38-43
mm (1.50-1.69 in.) below the bottom of the
riders footrest bracket.

b. Hold onto the shift rod joint with a wrench
(A, **Figure 68**) and tighten the locknut (B) at
each end securely and recheck the dimension.
Readjust if necessary.

3. After the pedal height is correctly adjusted,
make sure the shift rod joints at the end of the shaft

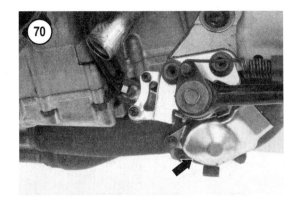

are correctly aligned to each other. If they are out of alignment, the shift shaft will bind and prevent correct gear engagement. If necessary, repeat sub-step 1a or 2a and correctly align both shift rod joints.

EXUP SYSTEM

On 1998-2001 models, the EXUP servomotor is located under the fuel tank on the left side of the frame and the EXUP pulley and related mechanism is located on the left side of the exhaust pipe assembly.

On 2002-2003 models, the EXUP servomotor is located on the frame behind the right side of the engine and the EXUP pulley and related mechanism is located on the right side of the exhaust pipe assembly.

EXUP system service, other than the following check and cable adjustment, is covered in Chapter Eight or Chapter Nine.

3

Check and Cable Adjustment (1998-2001 Models)

1. Remove the fuel tank (Chapter Eight).
2. Remove the bottom cowl (Chapter Sixteen).

NOTE
The EXUP cover is subjected to road debris, heat and moisture that will cause corrosion. If necessary, apply WD-40 or Liquid Wrench to the cover bolts in order to loosen them in the next step. It may also be necessary to use an impact driver to loosen the bolts.

3. On the left side of the exhaust system, remove the bolts securing the EXUP cover (**Figure 70**) and remove the cover.
4. Start the engine and increase engine speed. As engine speed increases past 2000 rpm, the servomotor should start to turn and the pulley on the exhaust should start to rotate. Turn off the engine.
5. If the servomotor does not rotate, proceed with Step 6.
6. On the right side of the area under the fuel tank, pull back the rubber boot (A, **Figure 71**), follow the wires (B), locate the EXUP servomotor 4-pin electrical connector and disconnect it.
7. Pull the servomotor up and out of the frame mounting tab and set it on its side.

CAUTION
In Step 8, do not leave the battery leads connected to the terminals for more than 2-3 seconds. If attached longer, the servomotor will be damaged.

8. Connect a fully charged 12-volt battery to the servomotor side of the electrical connector as follows:
   a. Positive battery lead: black/yellow terminal.
   b. Negative battery lead: black/red terminal.
9. The servomotor pulley should rotate (A, **Figure 72**) and operate the cables (B). If the pulley does not

rotate, the servomotor is faulty and should be replaced.

10. If the servomotor rotates, but the cables and exhaust pulley does not operate correctly, the control cables may be damaged or corroded. Disconnect the cables from the servomotor and lubricate the cables as described under *Control Cable Lubrication* in this chapter. Reconnect the cables.

11. After the cables have been lubricated, repeat Step 8 and Step 9 to make sure the cables are moving correctly and the exhaust pulley is rotating correctly. If the pulley moves but moves erratically, the EXUP valve and internal components may be corroded and require service. If necessary, refer to Chapter Eight for service procedures.

12. Install the servomotor back onto the frame mounting tab. Press it down until it is positioned correctly.

13. Reconnect the servomotor electrical connector and pull the rubber boot back into place.

14. At the exhaust pipe, push on both EXUP cables and check for free play as shown in **Figure 73**. The maximum amount of free play is 1.5 mm (0.059 in.).

15. If necessary, adjust the cables as follows:

   a. Loosen both locknuts (A, **Figure 74**).

   b. To lock the pulley in place, insert a 4-mm long pin through the notch in the EXUP pulley and into the hole in the EXUP valve cover (**Figure 75**).

   c. Turn both adjusting nuts (B, **Figure 74**) *counterclockwise* until there is no cable free play.

   d. Turn both adjusting nuts (B, **Figure 74**) *clockwise* 1/2 turn.

   e. Tighten both locknuts (A, **Figure 74**) securely.

   f. Make sure the free play in both cables is equal and does not exceed the maximum free play.

   g. Remove the 4-mm pin from the EXUP pulley and cover (**Figure 75**).

16. Apply a liberal coat of WD-40, or an equivalent, to the pulley and control cable ends prior to installing the cover.

17. Install the EXUP cover (**Figure 70**) and tighten the bolts securely.

18. Install the bottom cowl as described in Chapter Sixteen.

19. Install the fuel tank as described in Chapter Eight.

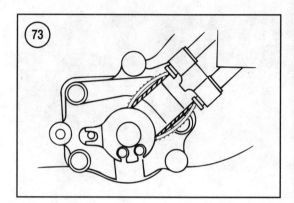

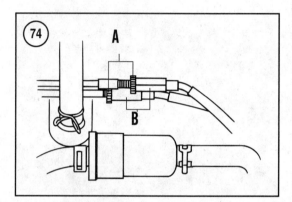

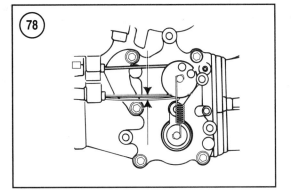

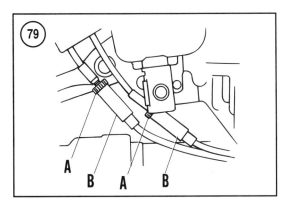

Check and Cable Adjustment (2002-2003 Models)

1. Remove the bottom cowl as described in Chapter Sixteen.

NOTE
The EXUP cover is subjected to road debris, heat and moisture that will cause corrosion. If necessary, apply WD-40 or Liquid Wrench to the bolts in order to loosen them in the next step. It may also be necessary to use an impact driver to loosen the bolts.

2. On the right side of the exhaust system, remove the bolts securing the EXUP cover (**Figure 76**) and remove the cover.

3. On the right side of the frame, remove the bolts securing the EXUP servomotor cover (**Figure 77**) and remove the cover.

4. Start the engine and increase engine speed. As engine speed increases past 2000 rpm, the servomotor should start to turn and the pulley should start to rotate.

5. If the servo does not rotate and operate the servomotor cables, the servo may be faulty. Refer to Chapter Nine for troubleshooting procedures.

6. If the servomotor rotates, but the cables and pulley do not operate correctly, the control cables may be corroded and may require lubrication.

7. If necessary, disconnect the cables from the servomotor and lubricate the cables as described under *Control Cable Lubrication* in this chapter.

8. After the cables have been lubricated, repeat Step 6 and Step 7 to make sure the cables are moving correctly and the pulley is rotating correctly. If the pulley moves but moves erratically, the valve and internal components may be corroded and require service. If necessary, refer to Chapter Nine for service procedures.

9. Push on both EXUP cables and check for free play as shown in **Figure 78**. The maximum amount of free play is 1.5 mm (0.059 in.).

10. If necessary, adjust the cables as follows:
    a. Loosen both locknuts (A, **Figure 79**).
    b. To lock the pulley in place, insert a 4-mm long pin, or punch (A, **Figure 80**) through the notch in the EXUP pulley and into the hole in the EXUP valve cover (B).
    c. Turn both adjusting nuts (B, **Figure 79**) *counterclockwise* until there is no cable free play.

d. Turn both adjusting nuts (B, **Figure 79**) *clockwise* 1/2 turn.

e. Tighten both locknuts (A, **Figure 79**) securely.

f. Make sure the free play in both cables is equal and does not exceed the maximum free play.

g. Remove the 4-mm pin, or punch, from the EXUP pulley.

11. Apply a liberal coat of WD-40, or an equivalent, to the pulley and control cable ends prior to installing the cover.

12. Install the EXUP cover (**Figure 76**) and tighten the bolts securely.

13. Install the EXUP servomotor cover (**Figure 77**) and tighten the bolts securely.

14. Install the bottom cowl as described in Chapter Sixteen.

ENGINE OIL AND FILTER

Engine Oil Level Check

Check the engine oil level at the oil level gauge located on the bottom right side of the crankcase.

1. Park the motorcycle on level ground on the sidestand.

2. Start the engine and let it idle for 2-3 minutes.

3. Shut the engine off and let the oil settle for 3 minutes.

> *CAUTION*
> *Do not check the oil level with the motorcycle on its sidestand; the oil will flow away from the oil level gauge and result in a false reading.*

4. Support the motorcycle upright on a level surface.

5. Check the engine oil level on the oil level gauge (**Figure 81**). The oil level must be between the MAXIMUM and the MINIMUM level lines (**Figure 82**).

6. If the oil level is low, remove the oil fill cap (**Figure 83**). Add the recommended oil (**Table 3**) to correct the level. Add oil slowly to avoid overfilling.

> *NOTE*
> *Refer to **Engine Oil and Filter Change** in this section for additional information on oil selection.*

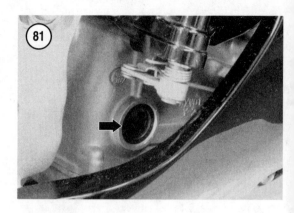

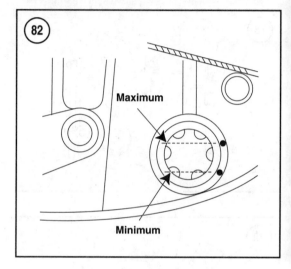

7. Inspect the O-ring on the oil fill cap. Replace it if it is starting to deteriorate or harden.

8. Install the oil fill cap and tighten securely.

9. If the oil level is too high, perform the following:

a. Remove the oil fill cap and draw out the excess oil, using a syringe or suitable pump.

b. Recheck the oil level and adjust if necessary.

c. Install the oil fill cap and tighten securely.

Engine Oil and Filter Change

Regular oil and filter changes contribute more to engine longevity than any other maintenance. The recommended oil and filter change interval is listed in **Table 1**. This assumes the motorcycle is operated in moderate climates. If the motorcycle is not operated on a regular basis, consider using a time interval for oil changes. Combustion acids, formed by gasoline and water vapor, contaminate the oil even if the motorcycle is not run for several months. If a

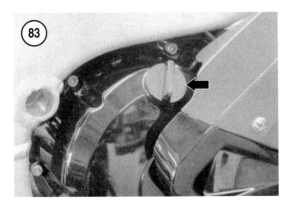

3

motorcycle is operated under dusty conditions, the oil gets dirty more quickly and should be changed more frequently than recommended.

Use only high-quality oil with an API classification of SE or higher. The classification is printed on the container. Try to use the same brand of oil at each oil change. Yamaha recommends Yamalube 4 SAE 10W-30 oil under normal conditions.

CAUTION
Only use oils with an API classification of SE or higher. Oils which con-

tain friction modifiers to reduce frictional losses on engine components are specifically designed for automotive engines. These oils, labeled *ENERGY CONSERVING, can damage motorcycle engines and clutches.*

NOTE
A socket-type oil filter wrench must be used when removing the oil filter because of the small working area between the oil filter and exhaust pipes.

NOTE
Never dispose of oil in the trash, on the ground or down a storm drain. Many service stations and oil retailers will accept used oil and filters for recycling. Do not combine other fluids with engine oil to be recycled. To locate a recycler, contact the American Petroleum Institute (API) at www.recycleoil.org.

NOTE
Warming the engine allows the oil to heat up; thus it flows freely and carries more contamination and sludge out with it.

1. Start the engine and run it until it is at normal operating temperature, then turn it off.
2. Remove the lower cowl (Chapter Sixteen).
3. Support the motorcycle on level ground on the sidestand when draining the engine oil. This ensures complete draining.

WARNING
The engine, exhaust pipes and oil are hot! Work quickly and carefully when removing the oil drain bolt and oil filter to avoid contacting the oil.

4. Clean the area around the oil drain bolt and oil filter.
5. Place a clean drip pan under the crankcase and remove the oil drain bolt (**Figure 84**) and washer.
6. Remove the oil filler cap (**Figure 83**), as this helps speed up the flow of oil.
7. Allow the oil to drain completely.
8. To replace the oil filter, perform the following:
   a. Temporarily install the oil drain bolt (**Figure 84**) and washer and tighten finger-tight. Then move the drain pan underneath the oil filter (**Figure 85**).

b. Place a large piece of aluminum foil over the exhaust pipe and EXUP housing to keep the oil off them during the next steps.

c. Install a socket-type oil filter wrench squarely onto the oil filter and turn the filter counter-clockwise until oil begins to run out, then un-screw and remove the oil filter.

d. Hold the filter over the drain pan and pour out any remaining oil, then place the old filter in a plastic bag, seal it and discard it properly.

e. Carefully clean the sealing surface on the crankcase for the oil filter. Do not allow any dirt or other debris to enter the engine.

f. Lubricate the rubber seal on the new filter with engine oil.

g. Install the new oil filter onto the threaded fit-ting on the crankcase.

h. Tighten the filter by hand until it contacts the crankcase. Then tighten it an additional 3/4 turn. If using the oil filter socket, tighten to 17 N•m (13 ft.-lb.).

CAUTION
Overtightening the filter will cause it to leak.

9. Move the drain pan back underneath the oil drain bolt, then remove the bolt and its washer. Al-low any remaining oil to drain into the pan.

10. Inspect the oil drain bolt gasket. Install a new gasket at every other oil change.

11. Install the oil drain bolt (**Figure 84**) and its gas-ket and tighten to 43 N•m (32 ft.-lb.).

12. Use a funnel and fill the engine with the correct weight and quantity of oil (**Table 3**).

13. Remove the funnel and install the oil filler cap (**Figure 83**) and its O-ring. Tighten it securely.

14. Remove the aluminum foil and clean off any residual oil that may have come in contact with the exhaust system prior to starting the engine.

15. Start the engine and allow it to idle.

CAUTION
The oil pressure warning light should go out within 1-3 seconds. If it stays on, shut off the engine immediately and locate the problem. Do not run the engine with the oil pressure warn-ing light on.

16. Check the oil filter and drain bolt for leaks.

17. Turn the engine off after 2-3 minutes and check the oil level as described in this chapter. Adjust the oil level if necessary.

WARNING
Prolonged contact with oil may cause skin cancer. Wash hands thoroughly with soap and water after contacting engine oil.

18. Install the lower cowl (Chapter Sixteen).

Engine Oil Flow Check

There is no oil pressure switch or oil pressure warning light. If an oil circulation problem is sus-pected, check the oil flow.

1. Park the motorcycle on level ground on the sidestand.

2. Start the engine and run it until it is at normal op-erating temperature, then turn it off.

3. Make sure the oil level is correct; add oil if nec-essary.

4. Remove the right side fairing panel as described in Chapter Sixteen.

8B. If oil seeps from around the oil gallery plug, the lubrication system is operating correctly. Shut the engine off.

9. Tighten the oil gallery plug (**Figure 87**) to the following:

    a. On 1998-2001 models: 20 N•m (14 ft.-lb.).

    b. On 2002-2003 models: 10 N•m (88 in.-lb.)

10. Start the engine and check for leaks.

11. Install the right side fairing panel as described in Chapter Sixteen.

COOLING SYSTEM

Check, inspect and service the cooling system at the intervals specified in **Table 1**.

> *WARNING*
> *When performing any service work on the engine or cooling system, never remove the radiator cap, coolant drain bolt or disconnect any coolant hose while the engine and radiator are hot. Scalding fluid and steam may be blown out under pressure and cause serious injury.*

5. Place a drain pan underneath the oil gallery plug (**Figure 86**) on the front right side of the cylinder head.

> *NOTE*
> *Figure 87 is shown with the cylinder head removed to better illustrate the step.*

6. Loosen, but do not remove, the oil gallery plug (**Figure 87**).

7. Start the engine and allow it to idle.

8A. Oil should start to seep from around the oil gallery plug within one minute. If no oil comes out after one minute, shut off the engine and check the following:

    a. Make sure the oil level is correct.

    b. Check for a clogged oil filter cartridge.

    c. Check for a clogged oil pump timing screen.

    d. Check for oil pump damage (excessive clearance).

    e. Check for clogged or damaged oil galleries.

    f. Check for a faulty oil pressure relief valve (stuck in the open position).

    g. Excessive crankshaft bearing oil clearance.

Coolant Type

If adding coolant to the cooling system, use a high-quality ethylene-glycol coolant containing corrosion inhibitors for aluminum engines. Mix antifreeze and water, use a 50:50 mixture of distilled water. Use only soft or distilled water. Never use tap water, as this will damage engine parts. Distilled, or purified, water can be purchased at supermarkets or drug stores in gallon containers. Never use a alcohol-based antifreeze.

Coolant Test

> *WARNING*
> *Do not remove the radiator cap when the engine is hot.*

1. Remove the screw(s) securing the right side fairing inner panel (**Figure 88**) and remove the panel.

2. Remove the radiator cap (**Figure 89**).

3. Test the specific gravity of the coolant with an antifreeze tester to ensure adequate temperature and corrosion protection. A 50:50 mixture is recommended.

Never allow the mixture to become less than 40 percent antifreeze. See *Coolant Type* in this section.

4. Reinstall the radiator cap (**Figure 89**) and tighten securely.

5. Install the right side fairing inner panel and tighten the screws securely.

Coolant Level

NOTE
*The coolant level can be checked with the right side fairing in place as shown in **Figure 90**. If the coolant level must be adjusted, the right side fairing panel must be removed as described in Chapter Sixteen.*

1. Park the motorcycle on level ground.

2. Start the engine and allow it to idle until it reaches normal operating temperature. Shut off the engine.

3A. On 1998-2001 models, perform the following:
   a. On the right side, check the coolant level in the reserve tank. It should be between the UPPER and LOWER level marks (**Figure 91**).
   b. If necessary, remove the coolant reserve tank cap (**Figure 92**) and add coolant into the reserve tank (not the radiator) to bring the level to the upper mark. See *Coolant Type* in this section.
   c. Reinstall the reserve tank cap.

3B. On 2002-2003 models, perform the following:
   a. On the right side, check the coolant level in the reserve tank. It should be between the UPPER and LOWER level marks (**Figure 93**).
   b. If necessary, remove the coolant reserve tank cap (**Figure 94**) and add coolant into the reserve tank (not the radiator) to bring the level to the upper mark. See *Coolant Type* in this section.
   c. Reinstall the reserve tank cap.

4. If removed, install the right side fairing panel as described in Chapter Sixteen.

Cooling System Inspection

1. Remove the lower cowl and both side fairing panels as described in Chapter Sixteen.

2. Check all cooling system hoses for damage or deterioration. Replace any hose that is questionable. Make sure all hose clamps are tight.

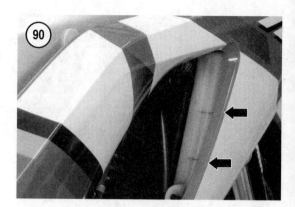

3. Carefully clean any dirt and debris from the radiator core. Use a whiskbroom, compressed air or low-pressure water. If an object has hit the radiator, carefully straighten the fins with a small screwdriver.

Pressure test

A cooling system tester is required to make the following tests.

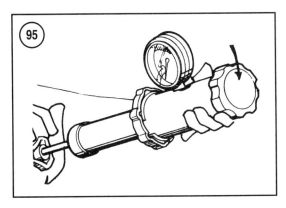

WARNING
Do not remove the radiator cap when the engine is hot.

1. Park the motorcycle on level ground.

2. Remove the screw(s) securing the right side fairing inner panel (**Figure 88**) and remove the panel.

3. Remove the radiator cap (**Figure 89**).

4. Pressure test the radiator cap (**Figure 95**, typical) using a cooling system tester. Refer to the manufacturer's instructions when making the tests. The specified radiator cap pressure is 95-125 kPa

(13.7-18.1 psi). Replace the radiator cap if it does not hold pressure or if the relief pressure is too high or too low.

NOTE
The manufacturer does not recommend pressure testing the cooling system.

5. Reinstall the radiator cap (**Figure 89**).

6. Install the right side fairing panel and tighten the screws securely.

Coolant Change and Air Bleeding

Drain and refill the cooling system at the intervals listed in **Table 1**.

It is sometimes necessary to drain the cooling system when performing a service on some part of the engine. If the coolant is still in good condition, the coolant can be reused if it is not contaminated. Drain the coolant into a clean pan and pour the coolant into a clean container for storage.

WARNING
Waste antifreeze is toxic and may never be discharged into storm sewers, septic systems, waterways, or onto the ground. Place used antifreeze in the original container and dispose of it according to local regulations. Do not store coolant where it is accessible to children or pets.

WARNING
Do not remove the radiator cap (Figure 89) if the engine is hot. The coolant is very hot and is under pressure. Severe scalding will result if hot coolant contacts skin.

CAUTION
Be careful not to spill antifreeze on painted surfaces, as it will damage the surface. Wash immediately with soapy water and rinse thoroughly.

Perform the following procedure when the engine is cold.

1. Park the motorcycle on level ground.

2. Remove the lower cowl and both side fairings as described in Chapter Sixteen.

3. At the front of the engine, place a drain pan under the oil filter area.

4. Remove the drain bolt (**Figure 96**) and sealing washer from the water pump outlet pipe. Allow the coolant to drain into the pan.

> *NOTE*
> *When the radiator cap is removed in the next step, the coolant will spray from the drain bolt hole (**Figure 96**) with considerable force. Hold the drain pan near directly under the outlet pipe, then have an assistant loosen and remove the radiator cap.*

5. Slowly remove the radiator cap (**Figure 89**) and allow the coolant to drain completely through the drain hole. Reinstall the drain bolt and sealing washer on the water pump outlet pipe (**Figure 96**). Replace the sealing washer if it is leaking or damaged. Tighten the coolant drain bolt securely.

6. Move the drain pan under the alternator cover area.

7. On the left side, loosen the camp band screw (A, **Figure 97**) and disconnect the radiator lower hose (B) from the water pump inlet pipe. Drain the radiator completely.

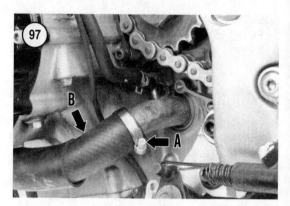

8. Reinstall the hose onto the water pump inlet pipe and tighten the clamp screw securely.

9. Drain the coolant reserve tank as follows:
   a. Remove the reserve tank cap (**Figure 92**).
   b. Disconnect the breather hose (A, **Figure 98**, typical) from the reserve tank.
   c. Remove the reserve tank mounting bolts (B, **Figure 98**, typical).
   d. Drain the coolant from the reserve tank into the drain pan.
   e. Rinse the inside of the coolant reserve tank with water and allow to drain.
   f. Install the mounting bolts and tighten securely.
   g. Connect the breather hose onto the reserve tank.
   h. Install the tank cap.

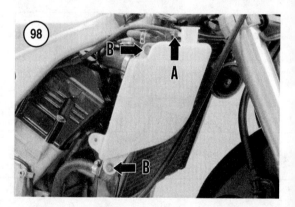

> *CAUTION*
> *Do not use a higher percentage of antifreeze-to-water solution than is recommended under **Coolant Type** in this section. A higher concentration of coolant will actually decrease the performance of the cooling system.*

10. Place a funnel in the radiator filler neck and slowly refill the radiator and engine with a mixture of 50 percent antifreeze and 50 percent distilled water. Add the mixture slowly so it will expel as much air as possible from the cooling system. Refer to *Coolant Type* in this section before purchasing and mixing coolant. **Table 3** lists engine coolant capacity.

11. Sit on the motorcycle and slowly rock it from side to side to help expel air bubbles from the engine, radiator and coolant hoses.

12. Fill the coolant reserve tank to the UPPER level line. On the right side, check the coolant level in the

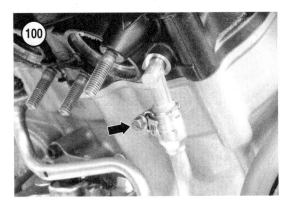

reserve tank. It should be between the UPPER and LOWER level marks (**Figure 93**, typical).

> *WARNING*
> *Do not start and run the motorcycle in an enclosed area. The exhaust gasses contain carbon monoxide, a colorless, odorless, poisonous gas. Carbon monoxide levels build quickly in a small enclosed area and can cause unconsciousness and death in a short time.*

13. After filling the radiator, leave the radiator cap off and bleed the cooling system as follows:

    a. Start the engine and allow it to idle for two to three minutes.

    b. Snap the throttle a few times to bleed air from the cooling system. When the coolant level drops in the radiator, add coolant to bring the level to the bottom of the filler neck.

    c. When the radiator coolant level has stabilized, perform Step 14.

14. Install the radiator cap (**Figure 89**). Turn the radiator cap clockwise to the first stop. Then push the cap down and turn it clockwise until it stops.

15. Start the engine and let it run at idle speed until the engine reaches normal operating temperature. Make sure there are no air bubbles in the coolant and the coolant level in the coolant reserve tank stabilizes at the correct level. Add coolant to the coolant reserve tank, as necessary.

16. Install both side fairings and lower cowl as described in Chapter Sixteen.

17. Test ride the motorcycle and readjust the coolant level in the reserve tank as required.

EMISSION CONTROL SYSTEMS

Air Induction System (AIS) Inspection

All 2000-2003 models are equipped with an Air Induction System (AIS) that assists in burning unburned exhaust gasses. The system injects fresh air into the cylinder exhaust ports, thus reducing the emission of hydrocarbons. Check all AIS hoses (**Figure 99**) for deterioration, damage or loose connections. Replace any parts or hoses as required.

Check the tightness of the fitting clamps at the cylinder head (**Figure 100**). Tighten if necessary. Refer to the emission control sections in Chapter Eight for additional information for both the carbureted and fuel injected models.

Evaporative Emission Control System Inspection (California Models Only)

All models sold in California are equipped with the evaporative emission control system. A vacuum hose routing diagram label (**Figure 101**) is attached to the rear fender under the passenger's seat. At the intervals specified in **Table 1**, check all emission control hoses for deterioration, damage or loose connections. Also check the charcoal canister housing for damage. Replace any parts or hoses as required. Refer to the emission control sections in Chapter Eight for additional information for both carbureted and fuel injected models.

BATTERY

The original equipment battery is a maintenance-free type. Maintenance-free batteries do not require periodic electrolyte inspection and water cannot be added. Refer to *Battery Service* in Chapter Ten for service, testing and replacement procedures.

TIRES AND WHEELS

Tire Inspection

1. Check and adjust the tire pressure (**Table 2**) to maintain the tire profile (**Figure 102**), good traction and handling and to get the maximum life out of the tire. Check tire pressure when the tires are cold. Never release air pressure from a warm or hot tire to match the recommended tire pressure; doing so causes the tire to be under-inflated. Use an accurate tire pressure gauge and reinstall the air valve cap (A, **Figure 103**).
2. Periodically inspect the tires for the following:
   a. Deep cuts and imbedded objects, such as nails and stones. If a nail or other object is in a tire, mark its location with a light crayon prior to removing it. This helps to locate the hole for repair. Refer to Chapter Twelve for tire changing and repair information.
   b. Flat spots.
   c. Cracks.
   d. Separating plies.
   e. Sidewall damage.

> *WARNING*
> *If a small object has punctured the tire, air leakage may be very slow due to the tendency of tubeless tires to self-seal when punctured. Check the tires carefully.*

Tire Wear Analysis

Analyze abnormal tire wear to determine the cause. Common causes are:

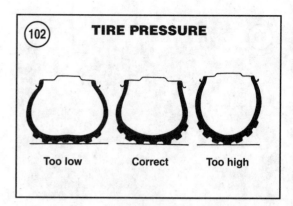

TIRE PRESSURE

Too low   Correct   Too high

1. Incorrect tire pressure. Check the tire pressure and examine the tire tread as follows:
   a. Measure the tread depth (**Figure 104**) in the center of the tire using a small ruler or a tread depth gauge. Yamaha recommends replacing the original equipment tires before the center tread depth has worn to the minimum tread depth listed in **Table 2**.
   b. Compare the wear in the center of the contact patch with the wear at the edge of the contact patch.
   c. If the tire shows excessive wear at the edge of the contact patch, but the wear at the center of the contact patch is normal, the tire has been under-inflated. Under-inflated tires result in higher tire temperatures, hard or imprecise steering and abnormal wear.
   d. If the tire shows excessive wear in the center of the contact patch, but wear at the edge of the contact patch is normal, the tire has been over-inflated. Over-inflated tires result in a hard ride and abnormal wear.
   e. The tires are also designed with tread wear indicators that appear when the tires are worn

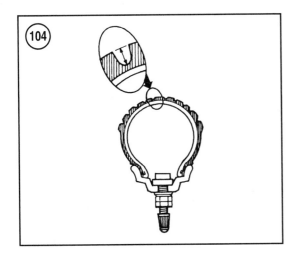

out. When these are visible, the tires are no longer safe and must be replaced.

2. Overloading.

3. Incorrect wheel alignment.

4. Incorrect wheel balance. Balance the tire/wheel assembly when installing a new tire, and then rebalance each time the tire is removed.

5. Worn or damaged wheel bearings.

Wheel Inspection

Frequently inspect the wheel (B, **Figure 103**) for cracks, warp or dents. A damaged wheel may cause an air leak or steering vibration.

Wheel rim runout is the amount of wobble a wheel shows as it rotates. Check runout with the wheels on the motorcycle. Refer to *Wheel Runout and Balance* in Chapter Twelve for service procedures.

FRONT FORK OIL CHANGE

All models are equipped with cartridge forks. This type of fork must be partially disassembled for fork oil replacement and oil level adjustment. Refer to *Front Fork Disassembly and Assembly* in Chapter Thirteen.

DRIVE CHAIN

Drive Chain Lubrication

Lubricate the drive chain at the interval indicated in **Table 1**. A properly maintained drive chain will provide maximum service life and reliability. Yamaha recommends SAE 10W-30 engine oil or Yamaha Chain and Cable Lube designed for O-ring chains.

> *CAUTION*
> *Not all commercial chain lubricants are recommended for use on O-ring drive chains. Read the product label to be sure it is formulated for O-ring chains.*

> *NOTE*
> *On an O-ring type drive chain, the chain lubrication described in this procedure is used mainly to keep the O-rings pliable and to prevent the side plates and rollers from rusting. The actual chain lubrication is enclosed within the chain by the O-rings.*

1. Ride the motorcycle a few miles to warm the drive chain. A warm chain increases lubricant penetration.

2. Park the motorcycle on level ground. Support the motorcycle securely on a swing arm stand with the rear wheel off the ground.

3. Oil the bottom chain run. Concentrate on getting the oil down between the side plates on both sides of the chain. Do not over-lubricate.

4. Rotate the chain and continue lubricating until the entire chain has been lubricated.

5. Turn the rear wheel slowly and wipe off excess oil from the chain with a shop cloth. Also wipe off lubricant from the rear hub, wheel and tire.

6. Remove the auxiliary stand.

Drive Chain Cleaning

Clean the drive chain after riding in dusty or sandy conditions. A properly maintained chain provides maximum service life and reliability.

Because all models are equipped with an endless drive chain, it is not practical to break the chain in order to clean it. This section describes how to clean the drive chain while it is mounted on both sprockets.

> *WARNING*
> *To avoid catching fingers and rag between the chain and sprocket, do not rotate the rear wheel when cleaning the chain.*

> *CAUTION*
> *All models are equipped with an O-ring drive chain. Clean the chain*

with kerosene only. Solvents and gasoline cause the rubber O-rings to swell. The drive chain then becomes so stiff it cannot move or flex. If this happens, the drive chain must be replaced. High pressure washers and steam cleaning can also damage the O-rings.

1. Ride the motorcycle a few miles to warm the drive chain. A warm chain increases lubricant penetration.

2. Park the motorcycle on level ground. Support the motorcycle securely on a swing arm stand with the rear wheel off the ground.

3. Place some stiff cardboard and a drain pan underneath the drive chain.

> *NOTE*
> *Do not splash the kerosene when cleaning the drive chain in the following steps. Make sure to keep the kerosene off of the rear tire and other parts as much as possible.*

4. Wear rubber gloves and soak a thick rag in kerosene, then wipe it against the section of chain that is exposed on the lower chain run. When this section of the chain is clean, turn the rear wheel to expose the next section and clean it. Repeat until all of the chain is clean. To remove stubborn dirt, scrub the rollers and side plates with a soft brush. Clean one section of the chain at a time.

5. Turn the rear wheel slowly and wipe the drive chain dry with a thick shop cloth.

> *WARNING*
> *Clean the rear swing arm, driven sprocket, chain guard, wheel and tire of all kerosene residue.*

6. Lubricate the drive chain as previously described in this section.

Drive Chain and Sprocket Inspection

Frequently check the chain and both sprockets for excessive wear and damage.

1. Clean the drive chain as described in this chapter.

2. Park the motorcycle on level ground. Support the motorcycle securely on a swing arm stand with the rear wheel off the ground.

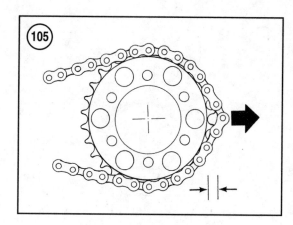

3. Turn the rear wheel and inspect both sides of the chain for missing or damaged O-rings.

4. At the rear sprocket, pull one of the links away from the driven sprocket. If the link pulls away more than 1/2 the height of the sprocket tooth (**Figure 105**), the chain is excessively worn.

5. Inspect the inner plate chain faces (**Figure 106**). They should be polished on both sides. If they show considerable uneven wear on one side, the sprockets are not aligned properly. Severe wear requires replacement of not only the drive chain but also the drive and driven sprockets.

6. Inspect the drive and driven sprockets (**Figure 107**) for the following defects:

    a. Undercutting or sharp teeth (**Figure 108**).

    b. Broken teeth.

7. Check the drive sprocket nut and the driven sprocket nuts for looseness. If loose, tighten to the following:

    a. Drive sprocket nut: 85 N•m (63 ft.-lb.).

    b. Driven sprocket nuts: 1998-2001 models, 69 N•m (51 ft.-lb.); 2002-2003 models, 100 N•m (74 ft.-lb.).

8. If excessive chain or sprocket wear is evident, replace the drive chain and both sprockets as a complete set. If only the drive chain is replaced, the worn sprockets will cause rapid chain wear.

Drive Chain Adjustment

Check and adjust the drive chain at the intervals specified in **Table 1**. If the motorcycle is operated at sustained high speeds or if it is repeatedly accelerated very hard, inspect the drive chain adjustment more often. A properly lubricated and adjusted drive chain will provide maximum service life and

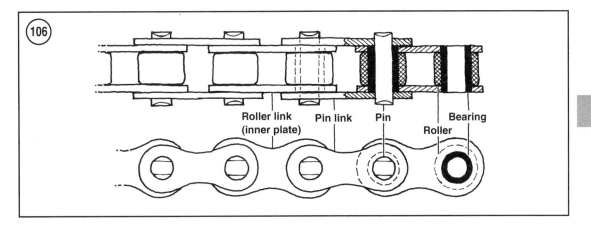

Roller link (inner plate)   Pin link   Pin   Bearing   Roller

3

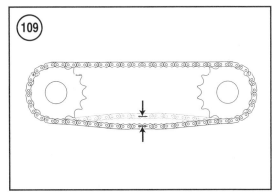

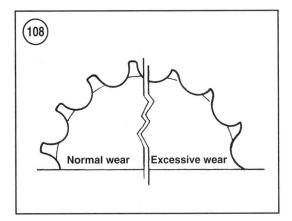

Normal wear   Excessive wear

reliability. The correct amount of drive chain free play (**Figure 109**), when pushed up midway on the lower chain run, is listed in **Table 4**.

When adjusting the chain, check the free play at several places along its length by rotating the rear wheel. The chain will rarely wear uniformly and as a result will be tighter at some places than others. Measure the chain free play halfway between the sprockets (**Figure 109**). Make sure the chain free

play at the tightest place on the chain is not less than the specification in **Table 4**.

1. Turn the engine off and shift the transmission into neutral.

2. Park the motorcycle on level ground. Support the motorcycle securely on a swing arm stand with the rear wheel off the ground.

CAUTION
As the drive chain stretches and wears, the chain will become tighter at one point. The chain must be checked and adjusted at this point.

3. Turn the rear wheel slowly, then stop it and check the chain tightness. Continue until the tightest point is located. Mark this spot with chalk and turn the wheel so that the mark is located on the lower chain run, midway between both drive sprockets. Check and adjust the drive chain as follows.

CAUTION
If the drive chain is kinked or feels tight, it may require cleaning and lu-

brication. Clean and lubricate the drive chain as described in this chapter.

4. Lower the motorcycle so the rear wheel is on the ground, then support it on its sidestand.

5. Loosen the rear axle nut. Refer to **Figure 110** for 1998-2001 models or **Figure 111** for 2002-2003 models. Loosen both adjuster locknuts (A, **Figure 112**) and turn both adjuster bolts (B) an equal number of turns to obtain the correct drive chain free play. Check that the same adjuster marks on both the right and left side are aligned with the same index mark on the swing arm (**Figure 113**).

6. Recheck chain free play.

7. To verify the swing arm adjuster marks, remove the drive chain guard and check rear wheel alignment by sighting along the drive chain as it runs over the rear driven sprocket. It should leave the driven sprocket in a straight line as shown in A, **Figure 114**. If it is cocked to one side or the other (B or C, **Figure 114**), perform the following:

   a. Check that the adjusters are set to the same index mark position on the swing arm.

   b. If not, readjust the drive chain to achieve the same position on both sides as well as maintaining the correct free play.

8. Tighten the rear axle nut to 150 N•m (111 ft.-lb.).

Swing Arm Slider Inspection

A slider is installed on the left side of the swing arm (**Figure 115**) to protect the swing arm from chain damage. Inspect the slider frequently for advanced wear or damage that would allow the chain to contact and damage the swing arm. Replace the slider (**Figure 116**) if it is worn to the limit line. Replace the slider after removing the swing arm as described under *Swing Arm Removal/Installation* in Chapter Fourteen.

BRAKE SYSTEM

Check the brake fluid in each brake master cylinder at the intervals listed in **Table 1**. At the same time, inspect the brake pads for wear. Brake bleeding, servicing the brake components and brake pad replacement are covered in Chapter Fifteen.

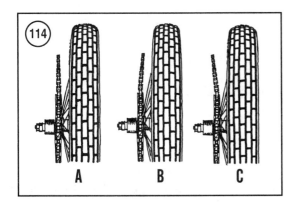

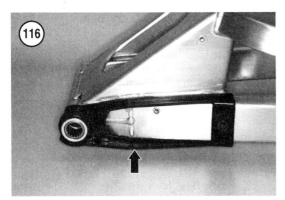

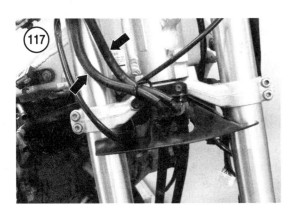

Brake Hose Inspection

Check the brake hoses between the front (**Figure 117**, typical) and rear master (**Figure 118**, typical) cylinders and the brake calipers. If there is any leakage, tighten the banjo bolt (30 N•m [22 ft.-lb.]) or hose and then bleed the brake as described in Chapter Fifteen. If this does not stop the leak or if a brake line is obviously damaged, cracked or chafed, replace the brake hose and bleed the system.

Brake Fluid Type

Use DOT 4 brake fluid in the front and rear master cylinder reservoirs.

> *WARNING*
> *Use brake fluid clearly marked DOT 4. Others may cause brake failure. Do not intermix different brands or types of brake fluid, as they may not be compatible. Do not intermix silicone-based (DOT 5) brake fluid, as it can cause brake component damage, leading to brake system failure.*

> *CAUTION*
> *Handle brake fluid carefully. Do not spill it on painted or plastic surfaces, as it will damage the surface. Wash the area immediately with soap and water and thoroughly rinse it off.*

Brake Fluid Change

Every time the reservoir cap is removed, a small amount of dirt and moisture enters the brake fluid. The same thing happens if a leak occurs or when a brake hose is loosened. Dirt can clog the system and cause unnecessary wear. Water in the brake fluid will vaporize at high brake system temperatures, impairing the hydraulic action and reducing the brake's stopping ability. To maintain peak performance, change the brake fluid at the interval in **Table 1** or whenever the caliper or master cylinder is overhauled. To change brake fluid, follow the brake bleeding procedure in Chapter Fifteen.

Front Brake Fluid Level Inspection

1. Move the handlebar so the front master cylinder is level.
2. The brake fluid level must be above the lower level line (A, **Figure 119**) on the reservoir housing. If the brake fluid level is at or below the lower level line, continue with Step 3.

> *WARNING*
> *If the reservoir is empty, air has probably entered the brake system. Bleed the front brakes as described in Chapter Fifteen.*

3. Wipe the master cylinder cap clean. Loosen the screw and release the cap stopper (B, **Figure 119**).
4. Unscrew the cap (C, **Figure 119**) and remove the diaphragm holder and diaphragm.
5. Add fresh DOT 4 brake fluid to fill the reservoir housing to the upper level mark on the reservoir housing.
6. Install the diaphragm and the diaphragm holder. Screw on the master cylinder cap (C, **Figure 119**) and tighten securely.
7. Move the cap stopper (B, **Figure 119**) into position and tighten the screw securely.
8. If the brake fluid level was low, check the brake pads for excessive wear as described in this section.

> *NOTE*
> *A low brake fluid level usually indicates brake pad wear. As the pads wear and become thinner, the brake caliper pistons automatically extend farther out of their bores. As the caliper pistons move outward, the brake fluid level drops in the system. However, if the brake fluid level is low and the brake pads are not worn excessively, check all of the brake hoses for leaks.*

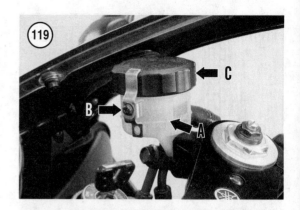

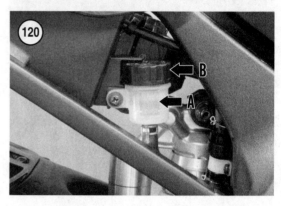

Rear Brake Fluid Level Inspection

1. Park the motorcycle on level ground. Support the motorcycle securely on a swing arm stand to set the motorcycle in a level position.

> *WARNING*
> *Do not check the rear brake fluid level with the motorcycle resting on its sidestand. A false reading will result.*

2. The brake fluid level must be above the lower level line (A, **Figure 120**) on the reservoir housing. If the brake fluid level is at or below the lower level line, continue with Step 3.

> *NOTE*
> *If the reservoir is empty, air has probably entered the brake system. Bleed the rear brake as described in Chapter Thirteen.*

3. Wipe the master cylinder cap clean.
4. On 1998-1999 models, remove the bolt securing the reservoir and cap stopper to the frame. Remove the cap stopper.

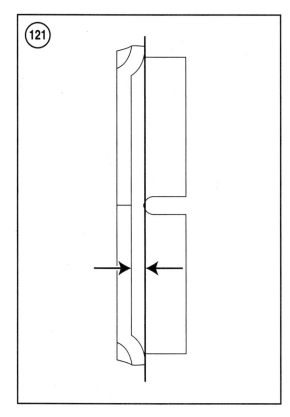

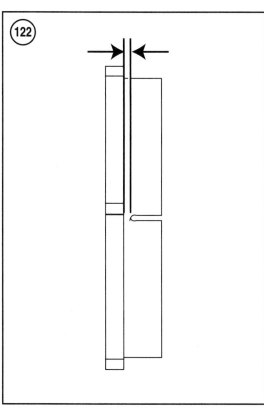

5. Unscrew the cap (B, **Figure 120**) and remove the diaphragm holder and diaphragm.

6. Add fresh DOT 4 brake fluid to fill the reservoir housing to the upper level mark on the reservoir housing.

7. Install the diaphragm and the diaphragm holder. Screw on the master cylinder cap (B, **Figure 120**) and tighten securely.

8. On 1998-1999 models, perform the following:

    a. Reposition the reservoir onto the frame, then install the cap stopper onto the cap.

    b. Install the bolt securing the reservoir and cap stopper to the frame and tighten securely.

9. If the brake fluid level was low, check the brake pads for excessive wear as described in this section.

> *NOTE*
> *A low brake fluid level usually indicates brake pad wear. As the pads wear and become thinner, the brake caliper pistons automatically extend farther out of their bores. As the caliper pistons move outward, the brake fluid level drops in the system. However, if the brake fluid level is low and the brake pads are not worn excessively, check all of the brake hoses and lines for leaks.*

Brake Pad Wear Inspection

Inspect the brake pads for wear at the intervals specified in **Table 1**.

1. Remove the caliper assembly as described in Chapter Fifteen.

2. Inspect the front and rear brake pads for uneven wear, scoring, oil contamination or other damage. If there is no visible brake pad damage or contamination, perform Step 3.

3. Replace the brake pads as a set if either pad is worn to the bottom of the wear groove. Refer to **Figure 121** for the front brake pads on all years and for the rear brake pads on 1998-2001 models. Refer to **Figure 122** for the rear brake pads for 2002-2003 models.

4. If either set of pads is worn to the wear groove, the pads must be replaced as described in Chapter Fifteen.

Rear Brake Pedal Height Adjustment

Adjust the rear brake pedal height so the top surface of the pedal is 35-40 mm (1.38-1.57 in.) below the bottom surface of the rider's footrest bracket (**Figure 123**).

1. At the rear brake master cylinder, loosen the locknut (A, **Figure 124**) and turn the pushrod (B) until the correct pedal height is achieved.

2. Tighten the locknut (A, **Figure 124**) and recheck the adjustment.

3. Park the motorcycle on level ground. Support the motorcycle securely on a swing arm stand with the rear wheel off the ground.

4. Spin the rear wheel by hand and apply the rear brake several times. Make sure the rear wheel turns without any brake drag and that the rear brake works correctly.

Front Brake Light Switch Adjustment

There is no adjustment for the front brake light switch.

Rear Brake Light Switch Adjustment

Periodically check the rear brake light switch adjustment.

1. Turn the ignition switch on.

2. Depress the brake pedal. The brake light must come on just before the brake begins to work.

3. If the brake light comes on too late, perform the following:

   a. Hold the brake light switch body (A, **Figure 125**).

   b. Turn the adjuster nut (B, **Figure 125**) as required to make the brake light come on earlier.

NOTE
Do not turn the switch body when adjusting the rear brake light switch.

   c. Recheck the rear brake light switch adjustment.

4. Turn the ignition switch off.

HEADLIGHT AIM INSPECTION

Check the headlight aim at the intervals specified in **Table 1**. Refer to *Headlight* in Chapter Ten.

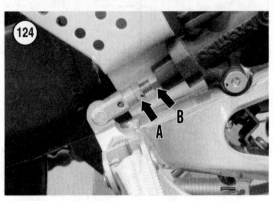

SIDESTAND AND IGNITION CUT-OFF SWITCH INSPECTION

Check the sidestand and the ignition cut-off system operation at the intervals specified in **Table 1**.

1. Park the motorcycle on level ground. Support the motorcycle securely on a swing arm stand with the rear wheel off the ground.

2. Operate the sidestand and check its movement and spring tension. Replace the spring if it is weak or damaged.

3. Lubricate the sidestand pivot bolt (**Figure 126**) if necessary.

4. Check the sidestand ignition cut-off system as follows:

   a. Park the motorcycle so both wheels are on the ground.

   b. Sit on the motorcycle and raise the sidestand.

   c. Shift the transmission into neutral.

   d. Start the engine, then squeeze the clutch lever and shift the transmission into gear.

   e. Move the sidestand down. When doing so, the engine should stop.

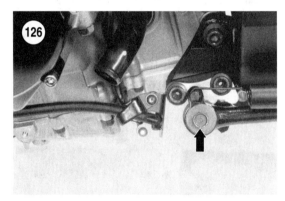

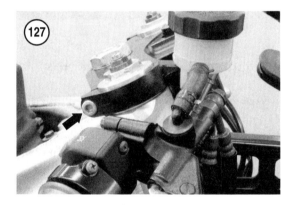

f. If the engine did not stop as the sidestand was lowered, inspect the sidestand switch as described under *Switches* in Chapter Ten.

STEERING BEARING INSPECTION

Inspect the steering head adjustment at the intervals specified in **Table 1**.

1. Support the motorcycle on a stand with the front wheel off the ground.

NOTE
When performing Step 2, make sure the control cables do not interfere with handlebar movement.

2. Hold onto the handlebars and move them from side to side. Note any binding or roughness.
3. Support the motorcycle so that both wheels are on the ground.
4. Sit on the motorcycle and hold on to the handlebars. Apply the front brake lever and try to push the front fork forward. Try to detect any movement in the steering head area. If so, the bearing adjustment is loose and requires adjustment.
5. If any roughness, binding or looseness was detected when performing Step 2 or Step 4, service the steering bearings as described in Chapter Thirteen.

FRONT SUSPENSION INSPECTION

Inspect the front suspension at the intervals specified in **Table 1**.

1. Use a soft wet cloth to wipe the fork tubes to remove any dirt and debris. As this debris passes against the fork seals, it will eventually damage the seals and cause an oil leak.
2. Check the fork sliders for any oil seal leaks or damage.
3. Apply the front brake and pump the fork up and down as vigorously as possible. Check for smooth operation.
4. Make sure the upper (**Figure 127**) and lower (**Figure 128**) fork tube pinch bolts are tight.
5. Check that the handlebar mounting bolts are tight.
6A. On 1998-2001 models, make sure the front axle is tightened to 72 N•m (53 ft.-lb.).
6B. On 2002-2003 models, make sure the front axle bolt is tightened to 90 N•m (66 ft.-lb.).
7. Make sure the front axle pinch bolt(s) are tightened to the following:
    a. 1998-2001 models: 28 N•m (21 ft.-lb.).
    b. 2002-2003 models: 18 N•m (13 ft.-lb.).
8. To adjust the front fork settings, refer to Chapter Thirteen.

WARNING
If any of the previously mentioned fasteners are loose, refer to Chapter Thirteen for procedures and torque specifications.

REAR SUSPENSION INSPECTION

Inspect the rear suspension at the intervals specified in **Table 1**.

1. With both wheels on the ground, check the shock absorber by bouncing on the seat several times.

2. Park the motorcycle on level ground. Support the motorcycle securely on a swing arm stand with the rear wheel off the ground.

3. With an assistant steadying the motorcycle, push hard on the rear wheel (sideways) to check for side play in the rear swing arm bearings.

4. Check the shock absorber for signs of oil leakage, loose mounting fasteners or other damage.

5. Check for loose or missing suspension fasteners.

6. Make sure the rear axle nut (**Figure 129**) is tightened to 150 N•m (111 ft.-lb.).

7. Check the drive chain guard for loose or missing fasteners.

8. To adjust the rear shock absorber settings, refer to Chapter Fourteen.

> *WARNING*
> *If any of the previously mentioned fasteners are loose, refer to Chapter Fourteen for procedures and torque specifications.*

FASTENER INSPECTION

Constant vibration can loosen many fasteners on a motorcycle.

1. Check the tightness of all exposed fasteners. Refer to the appropriate chapter for torque specifications.

2. Check that all hose clamps, cable stays and safety clips are properly installed. Replace missing or damaged items.

WHEEL BEARING INSPECTION

Inspect the wheel bearings at the interval specified in **Table 1**. Check the wheel bearings whenever the wheels are removed or whenever there is the likelihood of water or other contamination. Refer to Chapter Twelve for service procedures.

LIGHTS AND HORN INSPECTION

With the engine running, check the following.

1. Pull the front brake lever and check that the brake light comes on.

2. Push the rear brake pedal and check that the brake light comes on.

3. Move the dimmer switch up and down between the high and low positions and check to see that both headlight elements are working.

4. Move the turn signal switch to the left position and then to the right position and check that all four turn signal lights are working.

5. Operate the horn button and make sure that the horn sounds loudly.

6. If the horn or any light failed to work properly, refer to Chapter Ten.

Table 1 MAINTENANCE SCHEDULE*

Every 500 miles (800 km)
  Lubricate drive chain
  Check drive chain tension and adjust if necessary
  Check tire inflation pressure

Initial 600 miles (1000 km) or 1 month
  Change engine oil and replace oil filter
  Check the idle speed
  Check the carburetor synchronization (1998-2001 models)
  Check the throttle body synchronization (2002-2003 models)
  Check the brake system
  Check the clutch operation
  Check sidestand switch operation; clean if necessary
  Check steering play
  Lubricate the control cables
  Lubricate clutch and brake lever pivot shafts
  Check and tighten fasteners

Every 4000 miles (6400 km) or every 6 months
  Change the engine oil
  Check spark plugs. Clean and adjust gap if necessary
  Check and adjust the engine idle speed
  Clean and Inspect the air filter (1998-2001 models); replace if necessary
  Inspect the air filter (2002-2003 models); replace if necessary
  Check the carburetor synchronization (1998-2001 models); adjust as necessary
  Check the throttle body synchronization (2002-2003 models); adjust as necessary
  Check all fuel and vacuum lines for cracks or leaks
  Check the air induction system. Check the air cut-off valve, reed valves and hose for
    leakage and damage (2000-2003 models)
  Check the exhaust system for leaks and damage
  Check and adjust engine coolant level
  Check the cooling system hoses for cracks or damage
  Check brake pad wear. Replace the pads as necessary
  Lubricate the rear brake pedal pivot with engine oil
  Check and adjust the clutch cable
  Check the crankcase ventilation system for cracks or damage
  Lubricate the control cables with cable lube or engine oil
  Lubricate the clutch and brake lever pivot shafts with engine oil
  Check front and rear suspension operation and inspect for leaks
  Check the tires and wheels; inspect wheel bearings for looseness
  Check the steering head bearings and adjustment
  Check and lubricate side stand pivot
  Check sidestand and sidestand switch for proper operation; clean if necessary
  Check and tighten all fasteners
  Check and adjust the headlight aim

Every 8000 miles (12,800 km) or 12 months
  Perform the 4000 miles (6400 km) service checks
  Change the engine oil and replace oil filter
  Replace spark plugs
  Lubricate swing arm pivot bearings
  Check rear suspension linkage, lubricate if necessary

Every 12,000 miles (19,000 km) or 18 months
  Perform the 4000 miles (6400 km) service checks
  On California models, check the evaporative emission control system for damage; replace as necessary

Every 16,000 miles (25,000 km) or 24 months
  Perform the 4000 miles (6400 km) service checks
  Replace the fuel filter (1998-2001 models)
  Inspect entire cooling system for leaks or damage

(continued)

Table 1 MAINTENANCE SCHEDULE (continued)*

Every 16,000 miles (25,000 km) or 24 months (continued)
  Replace coolant
  Clean, inspect and repack swing arm pivot bearings
  Clean, inspect and repack steering head bearings
Every 20,000 miles (31,000 km) or 30 months
  Replace the fuel filter (1998-2001 models)
Every 26,600 miles (42,000 km)
  Perform valve adjustment
Every 2 years
  Change the brake fluid

*Consider this maintenance schedule as a guide to general maintenance and lubrication intervals. Harder than normal use and exposure to mud and high humidity will require more frequent attention to most maintenance items.

Table 2 TIRE AND WHEEL SPECIFICATIONS

Item	Front	Rear
Tire type	Tubeless	Tubeless
Size		
1998-2001 models	120/70 ZR17 (58W)	180/55 ZR17 (73W)
2002-2003 models	120/70 ZR17 (58W)	190/55 ZR17 M/C (73W)
Manufacturer		
1998-1999 models	D207FN (Dunlop)	D207L (Dunlop)
2000-2001 models	MEZ3Y (Metzeler) or D207FQ (Dunlop)	MEZ3Y (Metzeler) or D207N (Dunlop)
2002-2003 models	Pilot Sport E (Michelin) or D2008FL (Dunlop)	Pilot Sport (Michelin) or D208L (Dunlop)
Minimum tread depth		
1998-1999 models	1.6 mm (0.06 in.)	1.6 mm (0.06 in.)
2000-2001 models	0.8 mm (0.03 in.)	0.8 mm (0.03 in.)
2002-2003 models	1.6 mm (0.06 in.)	1.6 mm (0.06 in.)
Inflation pressure (cold)[1]	250 kPa (36 psi)	250 kPa (36 psi) 290 kPa (42 psi)[2]

1. Tire inflation pressure is for original equipment tires. Aftermarket tires may require different inflation pressure. The use of tires other than those specified by Yamaha may cause instability.
2. Tire pressure for maximum load of 198 lbs. (90 kg).

Table 3 RECOMMENDED LUBRICANTS AND FLUIDS AND CAPACITIES

Brake fluid	DOT 4
Cooling system	
Coolant type	High quality ethylene -glycol
Coolant capacity	
1998-2001 models	
Radiator and engine	2.55 L (2.7 U.S. qt.)
Reserve tank	0.45 L (0.48 U.S. qt.)
2002-2003 models	
Radiator and engine	2.45 L (2.6 U.S. qt.)
Reserve tank	0.24 L (0.25 U.S. qt.)
Drive chain	Engine oil or chain lubricant suitable for O-ring type chains

(continued)

Table 3 RECOMMENDED LUBRICANTS AND FLUIDS AND CAPACITIES (continued)

Engine oil	
Grade	Yamalube 4, API SE or higher (non-friction modified)*
Viscosity	SAE 10W/30 or 10W/40
Capacity	
1998-2001 models	
Oil change only	2.7 L (2.9 U.S. qt.)
Oil and filter change	2.9 L (3.1 U.S. qt.)
After disassembly (engine dry)	3.6 L (3.8 U.S. qt.)
2002-2003 models	
Oil change only	2.9 L (3.07 U.S. qt.)
Oil and filter change	3.1 L (3.28 U.S. qt.)
After disassembly (engine dry)	3.8 L (4.02 U.S. qt.)
Fuel	
Type	Unleaded
Octane	Pump research octane of 86 or higher
Fuel tank	
Capacity, including reserve	
1998-2001 models	18.0 L (4.75 U.S. gal.)
2002-2003 models	17.0 L (4.49 U.S. gal.)
Reserve only	
1998-2001 models	5.5 L (1.45 U.S. gal.)

*Refer to text for additional information.

Table 4 MAINTENANCE AND TUNE-UP SPECIFICATIONS

Brake pedal height	
Top of brake pedal below footrest bracket	
1998-2001 models	35-40 mm (1.38-1.57 in.)
2002-2003 models	38-42 mm (1.50-1.65 in.)
Carburetor synchronizing level difference (maximum)	
1998-2001 models	1.33 kPa/10 mm Hg (0.4 in. Hg)
Clutch lever free play	10-15 mm (0.39-0.59 in.)
Compression pressure @ 400 rpm	
(at sea level)	1450 kPa (210 psi)
Drive chain free play	40-50 mm (1.57-1.97 in.)
EXUP cable free play	1.5 mm (0.059 in.)
Gearshift pedal	
1998-2001 models (distance between pivot points)	305 mm (12.0 in.)
2002-2003 models	38-43 mm (1.50-1.69 in.)
Idle speed	
1998-1999 models	1050-1150 rpm
2000-2003 models	1000-1100 rpm
Spark plug type	
1998-2001 models	CR9E (NGK) or U27ESR-N (Denso)
2002-2003 models	CR9EIA-9 (NGK) or IU27D (Denso)
Spark plug gap	
1998-2001 models	0.7-0.8 mm (0.028-0.031 in.)
2002-2003 models	0.8-0.9 mm (0.032-0.035 in.)
Throttle body synchronizing level difference (maximum)	
2002-2003 models	1.33 kPa/10 mm Hg (0.4 in. Hg)
Throttle cable free play	3-5 mm (0.12-0.20 in.)
Valve clearance (cold)	
1998-2001 models	
Intake	0.11-0.20 mm (0.0043-0.0079 in.)
Exhaust	0.21-0.30 mm (0.0083-0.0118 in.)
2002-2003 models	
Intake	0.11-0.20 mm (0.0043-0.0079 in.)
Exhaust	0.21-0.27 mm (0.0083-0.0106 in.)

Table 5 MAINTENANCE AND TUNE UP TORQUE SPECIFICATIONS

Item	N•m	in.-lb.	ft.-lb.
Brake hose banjo bolt	30	–	22
Cylinder head cover bolt	12	106	–
Drive sprocket nut	85	–	63
Driven sprocket nuts			
1998-2001 models	69	–	51
2002-2003 models	100	–	74
Front axle (1998-2001 models)	72	–	53
Front axle bolt (2002-2003 models)	90	–	66
Front axle pinch bolt			
1998-2001 models	28	–	21
2002-2003 models	18	–	13
Oil drain bolt	43	–	32
Oil filter cartridge	17	–	13
Oil gallery plug			
1998-2001 models	20	–	15
2002-2003 models	10	88	–
Timing mark inspection cap	15	–	11
Rear axle nut	150	–	111
Spark plug	13	115	–

CHAPTER FOUR

ENGINE TOP END

This chapter provides complete service and overhaul procedures for the engine top end. The lower end of the engine is covered in Chapter Five, while clutch procedures are in Chapter Six and the transmission procedures are in Chapter Seven.

Engine specifications are in **Tables 1-3** at the end of the chapter.

The YZF-R1 is a liquid-cooled inline four-cylinder engine with double overhead camshafts. The crankshaft is supported by five main bearings and the camshafts are chain driven by the timing sprocket on the crankshaft. The camshafts operate directly on top of the valve lifters. Shims under the valve lifters determine valve clearance.

The cylinders are an integral part of the upper crankcase, which is referred to in this manual as the upper crankcase/cylinder block and is covered in Chapter Five.

The lubrication system is a wet sump type with the oil supply housed in the lower crankcase. The chain-driven oil pump delivers oil directly to the oil cooler. These components are also covered in Chapter Five.

ENGINE SERVICE NOTES

An important part of successful engine service is preparation. Before servicing the engine, note the following:

1. Review the information in Chapter One, especially the *Basic Service Methods* and *Precision Measuring Tools* sections. Accurate measurements are critical to a successful engine rebuild.

2. Clean the entire engine and frame with a commercial degreaser before removing engine components. A clean motorcycle is easier to work on and this will help prevent the possibility of dirt and debris falling into the open engine.

3. Cover the O-ring chain before degreasing the engine. The chemicals in the degreaser will cause the O-rings to swell, permanently damaging the chain.

4. Have all the necessary tools and parts on hand before starting the procedure(s). Store parts in boxes, plastic bags and containers. Use masking tape and a permanent, waterproof marking pen to label parts. Record the location, position and thickness of all shims and washers as they are removed.

5. Use a box of assorted size and color vacuum hose identifiers (Lisle part No. 74600) for identifying hoses and fittings during engine services.

6. Throughout the text there are references to the left and right side of the engine. This refers to the engine as it is mounted in the frame, not how it may sit on the workbench.

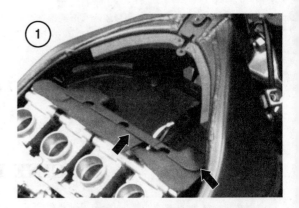

7. When inspecting components described in this chapter, compare the measurements to the service specifications listed in **Table 2**. Replace any part that is out of specification, worn to the service limit or damaged.

8. Always replace worn or damaged fasteners with those of the same size, type and torque requirements. If a specific torque value is not listed in the text or in **Table 3**, refer to the general torque specification table in Chapter One.

9. Use a vise with protective jaws to hold parts.

10. Use a press or special tools when force is required to remove and install parts. Do not try to pry, hammer or otherwise force them on or off.

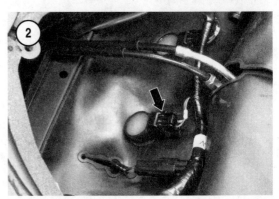

11. Replace all O-rings and seals with *new* ones during assembly. Set aside old seals and O-rings so they can be compared with the new ones if necessary. Apply a small amount of grease to the inner lips of each new oil seal to prevent damage when the engine is first started.

CYLINDER HEAD COVER

The cylinder head cover can be removed with the engine mounted in the frame. This procedure is shown with the engine removed to better illustrate the steps.

Removal

1. Park the motorcycle on level ground. Support the motorcycle securely on a swing arm stand with the rear wheel off the ground.

2. Remove both side fairing panels (Chapter Sixteen).

3. Drain the cooling system as described under *Coolant Change* in Chapter Three.

> *NOTE*
> *Refer to **Body Panel Fasteners** in Chapter Sixteen for the correct procedure for releasing and installing the trim clips.*

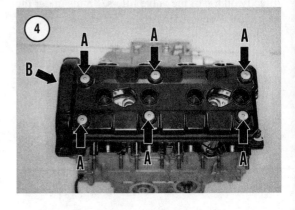

4A. On 1998-2001 models, perform the following:
   a. Remove the carburetor assembly as described in Chapter Eight.
   b. Remove the ignition coil plate assembly as described in Chapter Ten.

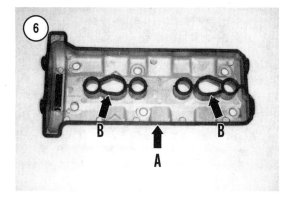

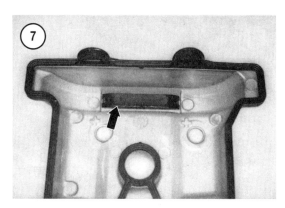

4B. On 2002-2003 models, perform the following:

   a. Remove the throttle body assembly as described in Chapter Nine.

   b. Remove the three trim clips securing the ignition coil plates and remove both plates (**Figure 1**). Install the trim clips onto the plates to avoid misplacing them.

   c. Carefully disconnect the 2-pin electrical connector (**Figure 2**) from the top of each direct ignition coil.

   d. Carefully pull straight up on the direct ignition coil and disengage it from the top of the spark plug. Remove it from the cylinder head cover and the spark plugs.

5. Remove the radiator assembly and thermostat housing assembly as described in Chapter Eleven.

6. Use compressed air to clean debris from the area above and around the cylinder head cover to prevent dirt from falling into the cylinder head after removing the cylinder head cover.

7. On 2002-2003 models, disconnect the electrical connector from the cylinder identification sensor (**Figure 3**).

8. Remove the cylinder head cover bolts and rubber seals (A, **Figure 4**).

9. Lift up on the cylinder head cover and pull it toward the rear to clear the frame cross bracket.

10. Remove the cylinder head cover (B, **Figure 4**) and gasket.

11. Inspect the cylinder head cover as described in this section.

Installation

1. Apply a light coat of gasket sealer to the semi-circular cutouts (**Figure 5**) on the right side of the cylinder head to provide a leak-free seal, following the sealant manufacturer's instructions.

2. Install the cylinder head cover (B, **Figure 4**) onto the cylinder head while noting the following:

   a. Make sure the cylinder head cover gasket is correctly positioned around the perimeter (A, **Figure 6**) and around each spark plug hole and coolant inlet (B).

   b. Check that the timing chain top guide (**Figure 7**) is in place.

   c. Carefully install the cylinder head cover into position on the cylinder head (**Figure 8**). Push it down until it seats.

d. Confirm that the gasket seats squarely into the cylinder head semi-circular cutouts.

3. If removed, install the rubber seals (**Figure 9**) onto each bolt.

4. Install the cylinder head cover bolts (A, **Figure 4**) and tighten to 12 N•m (106 in.-lb.).

5. On 2002-2003 models, reconnect the electrical connector onto the cylinder identification sensor (**Figure 3**).

6. Install the thermostat housing assembly and the radiator assembly as described in Chapter Eleven.

7A. On 1998-2001 models, perform the following:

a. Install the ignition coil plate assembly as described in Chapter Ten.

b. Install the carburetor assembly as described in Chapter Eight.

7B. On 2002-2003 models, perform the following:

a. Carefully push straight down on the direct ignition coil and engage it onto the top of the spark plug. Push it down until it bottoms. Repeat for each spark plug.

b. Connect the 2-pin electrical connector (**Figure 2**) to the top of each direct ignition coil.

c. Install both ignition coil plates (**Figure 1**) and secure them with the three trim clips.

d. Install the throttle body assembly as described in Chapter Nine.

8. Install both side fairing panels as described in Chapter Sixteen.

Inspection

1. Clean the cover in solvent and dry with compressed air.

2. Inspect the rubber gasket assembly around the perimeter of the cylinder head cover (A, **Figure 6**) and each spark plug hole and coolant inlet (B). Replace the gasket if it is starting to deteriorate or harden.

3. If necessary, replace the cylinder head cover gasket or reinstall the original gasket as follows:

a. Remove the old gasket and thoroughly clean any debris or oil residue from the gasket groove around the perimeter of the cover and around the spark plug holes.

b. Clean the grooves with solvent and dry with compressed air.

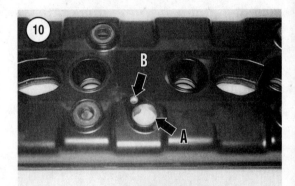

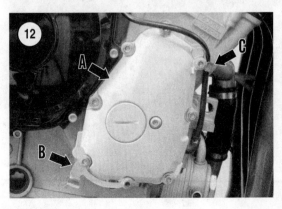

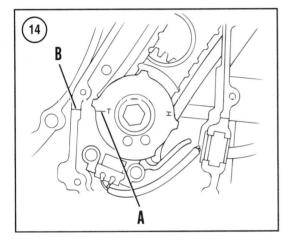

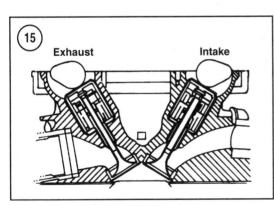

NOTE
Yamaha does not recommend the use of any type of gasket sealer to secure the gasket in place on the cylinder head cover.

c. Install the gasket into the grooves in the cylinder head cover.

4. Check the timing chain top guide (**Figure 7**) for wear or damage. Replace if necessary.

5. On 2002-2003 models, if removed, inspect the cylinder identification sensor receptacle (A, **Figure 10**) for wear or elongation. Check the threads (B, **Figure 10**) for the mounting screw.

CAMSHAFTS

The camshafts can be serviced with the engine installed in the frame. They are shown with the engine removed to better illustrate the steps.

Camshaft Removal

1. Remove the cylinder head cover as described in this chapter.
2. Remove the spark plugs as described in Chapter Three. This makes it easier to rotate the engine.
3. Disconnect the clutch cable from the cable holder.
4. Place a clean drain pan underneath the timing coil rotor cover on the right side.

NOTE
Some engine oil will drain when the timing coil rotor cover is removed.

5. Disconnect the clutch cable (**Figure 11**) from the cable bracket on the timing coil cover.
6. Place a drain pan under the timing coil rotor cover as some oil may drain out.
7. Remove the screws securing the timing coil rotor cover (A, **Figure 12**) and remove the cover and gasket. Do not lose the locating dowels. Note the location of the clutch cable bracket (B, **Figure 12**) and the electrical cable locating tab (C).
8. Correctly position the engine so the No. 1 cylinder is at top dead center (TDC) on the compression stroke as follows:
   a. Using a wrench on the timing coil rotor bolt (**Figure 13**), rotate the engine *clockwise*, as viewed from the right side of the motorcycle, until the timing coil rotor T mark (A, **Figure 14**) aligns with the crankcase mating surface (B).
   b. The camshaft lobes on the No. 1 cylinder must be pointing away from each other (**Figure 15**).

NOTE
If the camshaft lobes point toward each other, the engine is positioned

*incorrectly. If this condition exists, rotate the engine clockwise, as viewed from the right side of the motorcycle, 360° (one full turn) and realign the timing coil rotor T mark (A, **Figure 14**) with the crankcase mating surface (B).*

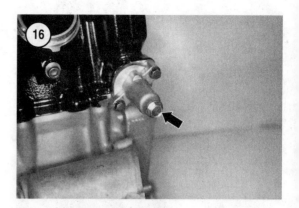

9. Remove the cap bolt and washer (**Figure 16**) from the end of the camshaft drive chain tensioner.

10. Insert a small flat blade screwdriver into the opening, rotate the tensioner lifter shaft *clockwise* to the fully retracted position.

11A. On 1998-2001 models, remove the bolts securing the camshaft drive chain tensioner and the float chamber air vent hose holder. Remove the holder and the tensioner assembly and gasket.

11B. On 2002-2003 models, remove the bolts (A, **Figure 17**) securing the camshaft drive chain tensioner (B). Remove the tensioner assembly and gasket.

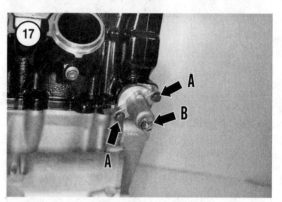

12. Refer to **Figure 18** and identify the camshaft holders as to exhaust (E) or intake (I), and right (R) or left (L). The exhaust camshaft holders have four bolts and the intake camshaft holders have eight bolts.

> *CAUTION*
> *Due to the valve spring pressure applied against the camshaft holders, failure to loosen the camshaft holder bolts as described in Step 13 may cause the camshaft holders to distort or break. Because the camshaft holders and cylinder head are matched units, a broken camshaft holder(s) also requires replacement of the cylinder head.*

13. Loosen the camshaft holder bolts gradually and in a crisscross pattern in two to three stages working from the outside in. Do not forget the four bolts on the two end holders (**Figure 18**). Continue until all the bolts are loose, and then remove the bolts and the camshaft holders (**Figure 18**). Do not lose the twelve locating dowels installed between the six camshaft holders and the cylinder head.

14. Disengage the camshaft chain from the sprockets and remove the intake (A, **Figure 19**) and exhaust (B) camshafts. Insert a scribe through the

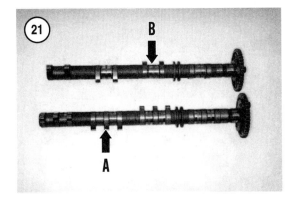

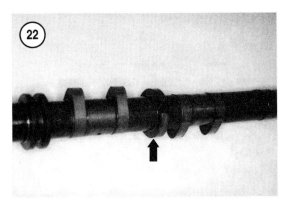

camshaft chain to the prevent it from falling into the engine.

15. Remove the camshaft chain guide (exhaust side) (**Figure 20**) from the engine.

16. Inspect the camshafts as described in this chapter.

Camshaft Installation

1. If removed, install the valve shims and lifters into the cylinder head as described in this chapter.

> *NOTE*
> *In the following steps, rotate the engine with a socket on the timing coil bolt (**Figure 13**).*

2. Using the bolt on the timing coil rotor (**Figure 13**), rotate the engine *clockwise*, as viewed from the right side of the motorcycle, until the timing coil rotor T mark (A, **Figure 14**) aligns with the crankcase mating surface (B). Verify that the No. 1 piston is at TDC.

3. Apply molybdenum disulfide grease to the six camshaft holders and cylinder head camshaft bearing journals.

4. The camshafts are identified for correct placement in the cylinder head as follows:

    a. Intake camshaft: three lobes per cylinder (A, **Figure 21**).

    b. Exhaust camshaft: two lobes per cylinder (B, **Figure 21**).

> *NOTE*
> *The exhaust camshaft on 2002-2003 models has an additional boss with a notch (**Figure 22**) used to trigger the cylinder identification sensor. Do not install this camshaft into a 1998-2001 model engine.*

5. Install the camshaft chain guide (exhaust side) (**Figure 20**) down through the cylinder head, cylinder block and into the locating groove in the lower crankcase (**Figure 23**). Press the guide down until it bottoms.

6. Install the exhaust camshaft as follows:

    a. Position the exhaust camshaft with the index punch mark facing straight up.

b. Install the exhaust camshaft into the cylinder head and mesh it with the camshaft chain (**Figure 24**).

c. Temporarily install the right side camshaft holder and check the alignment of the index punch mark on the camshaft with the index line on the camshaft holder (**Figure 25**).

d. If necessary, disengage the camshaft chain and slightly rotate the camshaft until alignment is achieved. Mesh the camshaft with the chain.

7. Install the intake camshaft as follows:

a. Position the intake camshaft with the index punch mark facing straight up.

b. Install the intake camshaft (A, **Figure 26**) into the cylinder head and mesh it with the camshaft chain.

c. Temporarily install the left side camshaft holder and check the alignment of the index punch mark on the camshaft with the index line on the camshaft holder (B, **Figure 26**).

d. If necessary, disengage the camshaft chain and slightly rotate the camshaft until alignment is achieved. Mesh the camshaft with the chain.

8. Recheck the alignment of the index punch mark on both camshafts with the index line on both camshaft holders. Remove both camshaft holders.

9. Make sure both camshafts are correctly seated in the cylinder head bearing surfaces (**Figure 27**).

10. If removed, install the locating dowels (**Figure 28**) into the camshaft holders or cylinder head.

11. Install the camshaft bearing holders in the correct locations as shown in **Figure 18**. Also check that the directional arrow (**Figure 29**) on the top surface is pointing toward the right side of the engine.

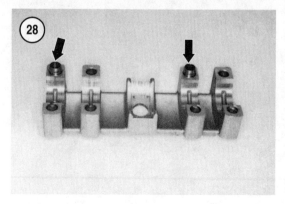

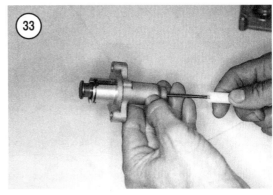

12. Install the mounting bolts (**Figure 30**) and tighten finger-tight.

13. Tighten the camshaft holder bolts gradually and in a crisscross pattern in two to three stages working from the inside out. Do not forget the four bolts on the two end holders (**Figure 18**). Continue until all the bolts are tightened to 10 N•m (88 in.-lb.).

14. To ensure that camshaft timing is correct, perform the following:

   a. Insert a finger into the camshaft chain tensioner hole in the cylinder and apply pressure against the chain.

   b. Recheck the alignment of the index punch mark on both camshafts with the index line on both camshaft holders. Refer to **Figure 31** for the intake camshaft and **Figure 32** for the exhaust camshaft.

   c. Also make sure the timing coil rotor T mark (A, **Figure 14**) is still aligned with the crankcase mating surface (B).

CAUTION
The index lines must be aligned correctly at this time; otherwise, camshaft timing will be incorrect. Do not proceed if the camshaft sprocket index lines are positioned incorrectly. Readjust the camshafts at this time if necessary.

15. Push the end camshaft chain drive tensioner and using a small flat blade screwdriver through the opening, rotate the lifter shaft *counterclockwise* to the fully retracted position (**Figure 33**). Hold the screwdriver in this position and install the camshaft drive chain tensioner (**Figure 34**) and *new* gasket. Make sure the UP mark is facing up.

16A. On 1998-2001 models, install the float chamber air vent hose holder, then install the bolts securing the camshaft drive chain tensioner. Tighten the bolts to 10 N•m (88 in.-lb.).

16B. On 2002-2003 models, install the bolts (A, **Figure 17**) securing the camshaft drive chain tensioner (B). Tighten the bolts (A, **Figure 17**) to 10 N•m (88 in.-lb.).

17. Remove the screwdriver and make sure the rod releases.

18. Install the cap bolt (**Figure 16**) and washer, and tighten to the following:

    a. 1998-2001 models: 10 N•m (88 in.-lb.).

    b. 2002-2003 models: 7 N•m (62 in.-lb.).

19. If removed, install the locating dowels (A, **Figure 35**), then install the *new* gasket (B) and the timing coil rotor cover (A, **Figure 12**). Install the clutch cable bracket (B, **Figure 12**) and the electrical cable locating tab (C) in the correct locations and tighten the screws securely.

20. Connect the clutch cable from the cable holder.

21. Measure the valve clearance as described in Chapter Three.

22. Install the spark plugs as described in Chapter Three.

23. Install the cylinder head cover as described in this chapter.

24. Check the engine oil level as described in Chapter Three and add oil as required.

25. Adjust the clutch cable as described in Chapter Three.

Camshaft Inspection

When measuring the camshafts, compare the measurements to the specifications in **Table 2**. Replace worn or damaged parts as described in this section.

1. Clean the camshafts in solvent and dry thoroughly before inspecting and measuring them.

2. Check the camshaft lobes (A, **Figure 36**) for wear. The lobes should not be scored and the edges should be square. Replace the camshaft if the lobes are scored, worn or damaged.

3. Check the camshaft bearing journals (B, **Figure 36**) for wear or scoring. Replace the camshaft if the journals are scored, worn or damaged.

NOTE
If the camshaft lobes and journals exhibit lack of lubrication wear, check

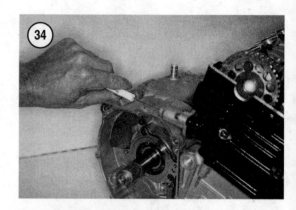

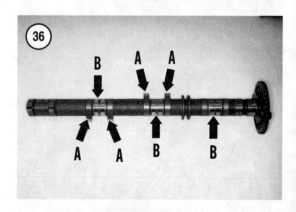

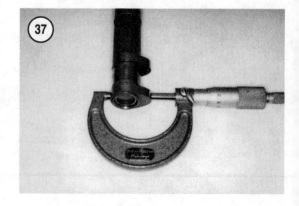

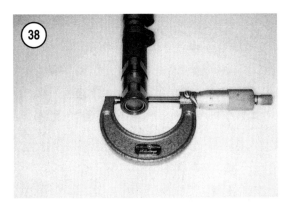

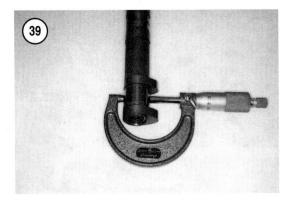

the camshaft holder oil passages for contamination.

4. Measure each camshaft lobe height (**Figure 37**) and width (**Figure 38**) with a micrometer.

5. Measure each camshaft journal outside diameter (**Figure 39**) with a micrometer.

6. Make sure all oil holes (**Figure 40**) are clear. Clean out with solvent and compressed air if necessary.

7. Inspect the camshaft bearing surface (**Figure 41**) for wear or damage.

8. Support the camshaft journals on a set of V-blocks or crankshaft truing stand and measure runout with a dial indicator.

NOTE
Do not remove the camshaft sprockets from the camshafts to inspect them.

9. Inspect the camshaft sprockets (A, **Figure 42**).
   a. Damaged gear teeth.
   b. Excessive wear.

NOTE
If the camshaft sprockets are worn, also check the camshaft chain, chain guides and chain tensioner for wear or damage.

10. Check the tightness of the sprocket mounting bolts (B, **Figure 42**). If loose, remove the bolt(s), apply a medium strength threadlocking compound to the threads and tighten to 24 N•m (18 ft.-lb.).

Camshaft Holder Inspection

1. Before cleaning the camshaft holders, inspect the oil lubrication holes for contamination. Small passages and holes in the camshaft holder provide

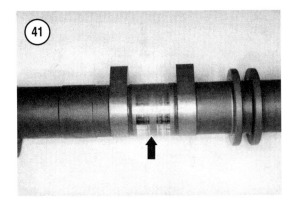

pressure lubrication for the camshaft journals. Make sure these passages and holes are clean and open.

> *NOTE*
> *Infrequent oil and filter changes may be indicated if the camshaft holders passages are dirty. Contaminated oil passages can result in camshaft failure.*

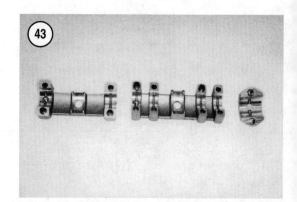

2. Thoroughly clean the camshaft holders (**Figure 43**) in solvent and dry with compressed air.

3. Check the camshaft holders (**Figure 43**) for stress cracks and other damage.

4. Inspect the bearing surfaces in the cylinder head (**Figure 44**) and bearing holders (**Figure 45**) for wear and scoring. If damage is present, the cylinder head and camshaft holders must be replaced as a set. To determine operational clearance, perform the *Camshaft Journal Oil Clearance Measurement* procedure in this section.

5. Check the camshaft holders mounting bolts for hex-head or thread damage.

Camshaft Journal Oil Clearance Measurement

This section describes how to measure the bearing clearance between the camshaft, the camshaft holders and cylinder head journal using Plastigage. Plastigage, available in different clearance ranges, is a material that flattens when pressure is applied to it. The marked bands on the envelope are then used to measure the width of the flattened Plastigage.

1. Wipe all oil residue from each camshaft bearing journal on the camshafts, the camshaft holder and the cylinder head.

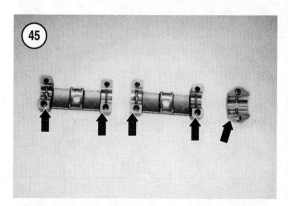

2. The camshafts are identified for correct placement in the cylinder head as follows:

    a. Intake camshaft: three lobes per cylinder (A, **Figure 46**).

    b. Exhaust camshaft: two lobes per cylinder (B, **Figure 46**).

> *NOTE*
> *The exhaust camshaft on 2002-2003 models has an additional boss with a notch (**Figure 47**) used to trigger the cylinder identification sensor. Do not install this camshaft into a 1998-2001 model engine.*

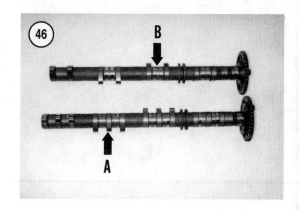

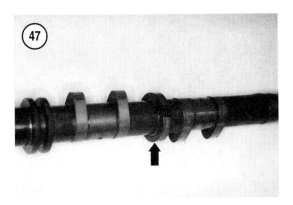

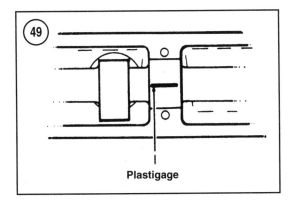

Plastigage

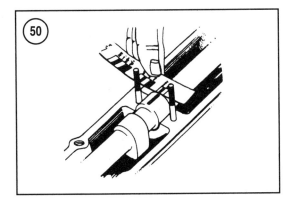

NOTE
It is not necessary to install the cam-shaft chain onto the sprockets for this procedure even though it is shown in place in Step 3.

3. Install the intake (A, **Figure 48**) and exhaust (B) camshafts into the cylinder head. Position the camshaft lobes so the majority of the valves will not be pressed open when the camshaft is installed. Refer to *Camshaft Installation* in this section.

4. Wipe all oil from the camshaft bearing journals before applying the Plastigage material.

5. Place a strip of Plastigage material on the top of each camshaft bearing journal (**Figure 49**), parallel to the camshaft.

6. Install and tighten the camshaft holder as described under *Camshaft Installation* in this section.

CAUTION
Do not rotate the camshafts with the Plastigage in place.

CAUTION
Loosen the camshaft holder bolts as described or the camshaft holder may be damaged.

7. Loosen and remove the camshaft holder mounting bolts as described under *Camshaft Removal* in this section.

8. Remove the camshaft holder carefully, making sure the camshafts do not rotate.

9. Measure the width of the flattened Plastigage (**Figure 50**, typical) according to the manufacturer's instructions and compare to the camshaft journal oil clearance specification in **Table 2**. Note the following:

    a. If all the measurements are within specification, the cylinder head, camshaft and camshaft holder can be reused.

    b. If any measurement exceeds the service limit, replace the camshaft(s) and recheck the oil clearance.

    c. If the new measurement exceeds the service limit with the new camshaft, replace the camshaft holder and the cylinder head as a set.

10. Remove all Plastigage material from the camshafts, the camshaft holders and the cylinder head.

CAMSHAFT CHAIN TENSIONER

Removal/Installation

1. Park the motorcycle on level ground. Support the motorcycle securely on a swing arm stand with the rear wheel off the ground.

2A. On 1998-2001 models, remove the carburetor assembly as described in Chapter Eight.

2B. On 2002-2003 models, remove the throttle body assembly as described in Chapter Nine.

3. Remove the cap bolt and washer (**Figure 51**) from the camshaft drive chain tensioner.

4. Insert a small flat blade screwdriver into the opening, rotate the tensioner lifter shaft *clockwise* to the fully retracted position.

5A. On 1998-2001 models, remove the bolts securing the camshaft drive chain tensioner and the float chamber air vent hose holder. Remove the holder and the tensioner assembly and gasket.

5B. On 2002-2003 models, remove the bolts (A, **Figure 52**) securing the camshaft drive chain tensioner (B). Remove the tensioner assembly and gasket.

6. Inspect the tensioner assembly as described in this chapter.

7. Push the end camshaft chain drive tensioner and using a small flat blade screwdriver through the opening, rotate the lifter shaft *counterclockwise* to the fully retracted position (**Figure 53**). Hold the screwdriver in this position and install the camshaft drive chain tensioner (**Figure 54**) and *new* gasket.

8A. On 1998-2001 models, install the float chamber air vent hose holder, then install the bolts securing the camshaft drive chain tensioner. Tighten the bolts to 10 N•m (88 in.-lb.).

8B. On 2002-2003 models, install the bolts (A, **Figure 52**) securing the camshaft drive chain tensioner (B). Tighten the bolts (A, **Figure 52**) to 10 N•m (88 in.-lb.).

9. Install the cap bolt (**Figure 51**) and washer, and tighten to the following:

   a. 1998-2001 models: 10 N•m (88 in.-lb.).

   b. 2002-on models: 7 N•m (62 in.-lb.).

10A. On 1998-2001 models, install the carburetor assembly as described in Chapter Eight.

10B. On 2002-2003 models, install the throttle body assembly as described in Chapter Nine.

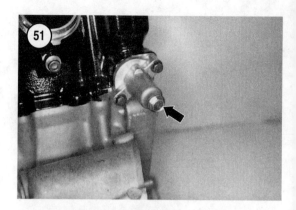

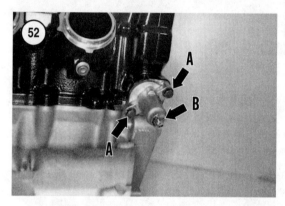

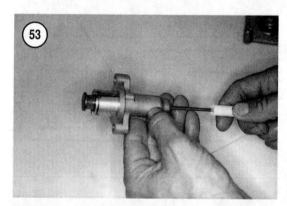

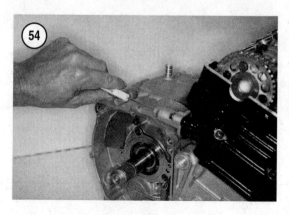

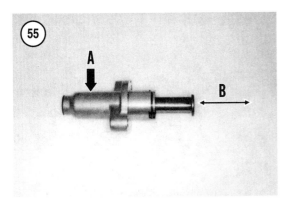

Inspection

The camshaft chain tensioner (A, **Figure 55**) cannot be rebuilt or serviced.

1. Move the tensioner pushrod (B, **Figure 55**) in and out by hand. The pushrod must move smoothly with no roughness or binding.

2. Inspect the end of the pushrod (**Figure 56**) for wear or damage.

3. Remove all gasket residue from the tensioner housing.

4. Replace the camshaft chain tensioner if necessary.

CAMSHAFT CHAIN, TIMING SPROCKET AND CHAIN GUIDE

Removal

1. Remove the cylinder head as described in this chapter.

2. Remove the pin (A, **Figure 57**) securing the camshaft chain tensioner guide (B). Withdraw the guide up through the cylinder block (**Figure 58**).

3. Remove the right crankcase cover and ignition timing coil rotor as described under *Timing Coil Rotor Removal/Installation* in Chapter Ten.

4. Disengage the camshaft chain (A, **Figure 59**) from the timing sprocket and remove the chain.

5. Slide the timing sprocket (**Figure 60**) off the locating pin and the end of the crankshaft.

6. Remove the locating pin (**Figure 61**) the end of the crankshaft.

7. Inspect the components as described in this section.

Installation

1. Install the locating pin (**Figure 61**) into the end of the crankshaft and push it on until it bottoms.

> *CAUTION*
> *The timing sprocket is not symmetrical and must be installed onto the crankshaft in the correct direction.*

2. Align the timing sprocket narrow shoulder side (A, **Figure 62**) going on first.

3. Align the timing sprocket hole (B, **Figure 62**) with the locating pin (C) and install the timing sprocket (**Figure 60**). Push it on until it bottoms.

4. Install the chain down through the chain cavity (A, **Figure 59**) in the cylinder block and mesh it with the timing sprocket (B).

5. Install the right crankcase cover and ignition timing coil rotor as described in Chapter Ten.

6. Install the camshaft chain tensioner guide down through the cylinder block (**Figure 58**).

7. Install the pin (A, **Figure 57**) securing the camshaft tensioner guide (B).

8. Install the cylinder head (this chapter).

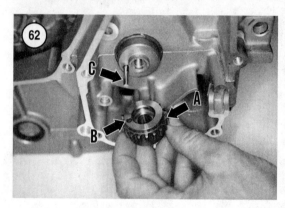

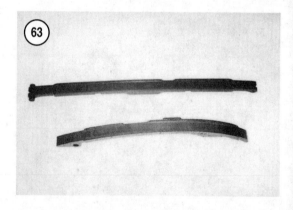

Inspection

1. Wash all parts in solvent. Dry with compressed air.

2. Inspect the guides (**Figure 63**) for wear, chipping or other damage.

3. Inspect the timing sprocket (**Figure 64**) for wear or damage. If damaged, check the camshaft chain and camshaft sprockets for wear. Refer to *Camshaft Inspection* in this chapter.

4. Inspect the chain (**Figure 65**) for wear or damage. If damaged, check the camshaft sprockets for wear. Refer to *Camshaft Inspection* in this chapter.

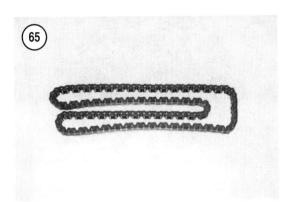

4

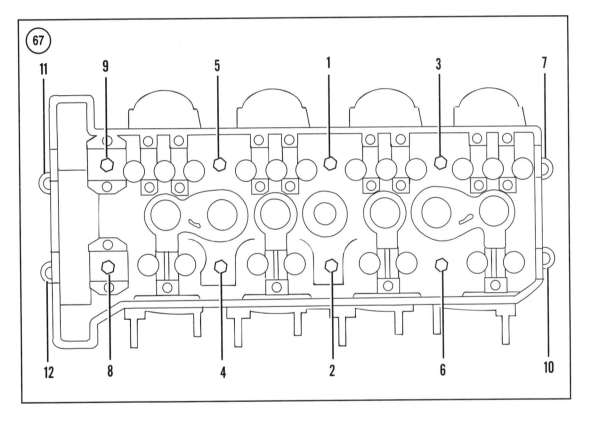

CYLINDER HEAD

Removal

1. Remove the engine from the frame as described in Chapter Five.

2. On 2000-2003 models, loosen the Air Induction System (AIS) fitting clamps at the cylinder head (**Figure 66**) and disconnect the fittings.

3. Remove the cylinder head cover and camshafts as described in this chapter.

4. Remove the camshaft chain tensioner as described in this chapter.

5. Remove the camshaft chain, timing sprocket and chain guides as described in this chapter.

> *CAUTION*
> *Do not remove the cylinder head mounting bolts or remove the cylinder head when the engine is hot. Doing so could cause the cylinder head to warp, requiring its replacement.*

6. Using the reverse of the torque pattern in **Figure 67**, loosen all bolts and nuts 1/2 turn at a time in two to three steps.

7. Remove the two 6-mm Allen bolts (**Figure 68**) from the right side of the cylinder head.

8. Remove the cap nuts and washers (**Figure 69**) from the left side of the cylinder head.

NOTE
*The three sleeve nuts No. 1, 3 and 5 and five shoulder nuts No. 2, 4, 6, 8 and 9 in **Figure 67** must be installed in the correct location during assembly. Note their locations at this time.*

9. Remove the three sleeve nuts and washers (**Figure 70**) from the intake side of the cylinder head. Use a magnetic tool to remove the washers from the cylinder head receptacles.

10. Remove the remaining five shoulder nuts and washers from the cylinder head.

11. Loosen the cylinder head by tapping around the perimeter with a rubber or plastic mallet.

12. When the cylinder head is free, pull it up and off the crankcase/cylinder block assembly.

13. Place the cylinder head on wooden blocks to avoid damaging the gasket surfaces.

14. Remove the cylinder head gasket and locating dowels.

NOTE
After removing the cylinder head, check the top and bottom gasket surfaces for any indications of coolant leakage. Also check the head gasket for signs of leakage. A blown gasket could indicate a warped cylinder head or other damage.

15. If the cylinder head is not going to be serviced, place it in a strong cardboard box and cover it to keep the valve lifters in place and keep the cylinder head clean.

16. If necessary, remove the camshaft chain and guides as described in this chapter.

17. If necessary, remove the valve lifters and shims as described in this chapter.

Installation

1. If removed, install the camshaft chain and guides as described in this chapter.

2. If removed, install the valve lifters and shims as described in this chapter.

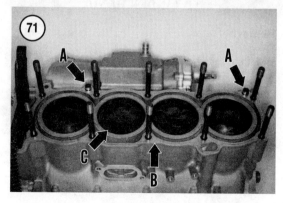

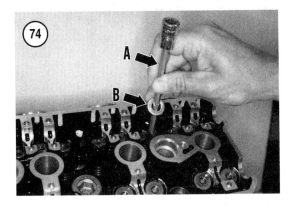

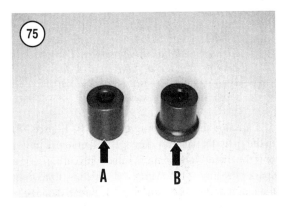

3. Clean the cylinder head and cylinder gasket surfaces of all gasket residue.

4. If removed, install the two dowel pins (A, **Figure 71**).

5. Install a *new* cylinder head gasket (**Figure 72**) over the dowel pins and seat it against the cylinder block. Feed the camshaft chain through the gasket opening.

6. Feed the camshaft chain through the opening in the cylinder head, then position the cylinder head over the cylinder block and both dowel pins, seating it against the gasket (**Figure 73**). Check that the cylinder head is sitting flush against the head gasket around the entire perimeter.

NOTE
Do not lubricate the 6-mm Allen bolt threads.

7. Lubricate the cylinder head bolt threads and washer seating surfaces with molybdenum oil or clean engine oil.

8. Place a screwdriver or socket extension over the bolt head (A, **Figure 74**) and slide the *new* washer (B) down onto the bolt. Install all eight washers.

9. Install the cap nuts and washers (**Figure 69**) onto the left side of the cylinder head.

10. Install the two 6-mm Allen bolts (**Figure 68**) onto the right side of the cylinder head.

NOTE
*The three sleeve nuts (A, **Figure 75**) No. 1, 3 and 5 in **Figure 67** and five shoulder nuts (B, **Figure 75**) No. 2, 4, 6, 8 and 9 in **Figure 67** must be installed in the correct location as noted during removal.*

11. Install the three sleeve nuts and washers (**Figure 70**) onto the bolts on the intake side of the cylinder head.

12. Install the remaining five shoulder nuts and washers onto the cylinder head bolts.

13. Tighten all bolts and nuts securely, but not to the torque specifications.

14A. On 1998-2001 models, using the torque pattern in **Figure 67**, tighten the following bolts and nuts in two steps:

    a. Three sleeve nuts and five shoulder nuts: 50 N•m (37 ft.-lb.).

    b. Two cap nuts: 50 N•m (37 ft.-lb.).

14B. On 2002-2003 models, using the torque pattern in **Figure 67**, tighten the following bolts and nuts in two steps:

    a. Three sleeve nuts and five shoulder nuts: preliminary stage 20 N•m (15 ft.-lb.), final stage 50 N•m (37 ft.-lb.).

    b. Two cap nuts: preliminary stage 20 N•m (15 ft.-lb.), final stage 65 N•m (48 ft.-lb.).

15. Tighten the two 6-mm Allen bolts to 12 N•m (106 in.-lb.).

16. Install the camshaft chain, timing sprocket and chain guides as described in this chapter.

17. Install the camshaft chain tensioner as described in this chapter.

18. Install the camshafts and cylinder head cover as described in this chapter.

19. On 2000-2003 models, perform the following:

    a. Install a *new* muffler gasket into each AIS cylinder head fittings.

    b. Connect the AIS tubes onto the cylinder head and tighten the fitting clamps (**Figure 66**) securely.

20. Install the engine into the frame as described in Chapter Five.

21. Start the engine and check for leaks.

Solvent Test for Valve Seat Seal

Before removing the valves from the cylinder head, perform a solvent test to check the valve face-to-valve seat seal.

1. Remove the cylinder head as described in this chapter.

2. Support the cylinder head with the exhaust ports facing up (**Figure 76**). Then pour solvent or kerosene into the ports. Immediately check the combustion chambers for fluid leaking past the exhaust valves.

3. Repeat Step 2 for the intake valves.

4. If there is fluid leakage around one or both sets of valves, the valve(s) is not seating correctly. The following conditions will cause poor valve seating:

    a. A bent valve stem.

    b. A worn or damaged valve seat.

    c. A worn or damaged valve face.

    d. A crack in the combustion chamber.

Inspection

1. Perform the solvent test before cleaning or servicing the cylinder head.

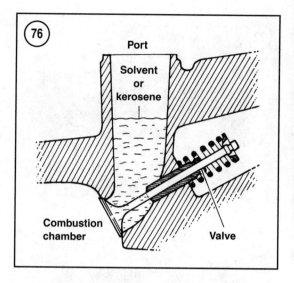

2. Remove all traces of gasket residue from the cylinder head (**Figure 77**) and cylinder block (B, **Figure 71**) surfaces. Do not scratch the gasket surface.

3. Before removing the valves, remove all carbon deposits from the combustion chambers (A, **Figure 78**) with a wire brush or wooden scraper. Take care not to damage the head, valves or spark plug threads.

> *CAUTION*
> *If the combustion chambers are cleaned with the valves removed, it is easy to damage a valve seat. A damaged or even slightly scratched valve seat causes poor valve sealing.*

4. Examine the spark plug threads (B, **Figure 78**) in the cylinder head for damage. If damage is minor or if the threads are contaminated with carbon, use a spark plug thread tap to clean the threads, following the manufacturer's instructions. If thread damage is

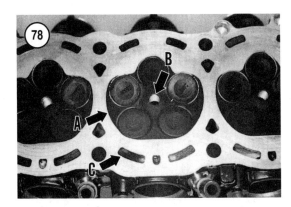

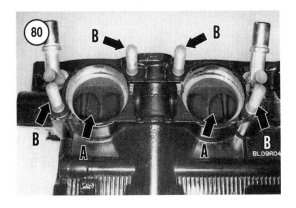

head and are hard to access. To prevent galling, apply an antiseize compound on the plug threads before installation and do not overtighten. Do not lubricate the spark plug threads with engine oil.

NOTE
When using a tap to clean spark plug threads, lubricate the tap with aluminum tap cutting fluid or kerosene.

5. Make sure the coolant passages (C, **Figure 78**) are clear. Clean out with low air pressure if necessary.

6. Clean the entire head in solvent and dry with compressed air.

CAUTION
If the cylinder head was bead-blasted, make sure to clean the head thoroughly with solvent. Residual grit seats in small crevices and other areas and can be hard to remove. Chase each exposed thread with a tap to remove grit from the threads. Residual grit left in the engine will cause premature piston, ring and bearing wear.

7. Check for cracks in the combustion chamber, intake ports (**Figure 79**) and exhaust ports (A, **Figure 80**). A cracked head must be replaced.

8. Examine the piston crowns (C, **Figure 71**). The crowns should show no signs of wear or damage. If the crown appears pecked or spongy-looking, check the spark plug, valves and combustion chamber for aluminum deposits. If these deposits are found, the cylinder is overheating due to a lean fuel mixture or preignition.

CAUTION
Do not clean the piston crowns while the pistons are installed in the cylinder block. Carbon scraped from the tops of the pistons will fall between the cylinder wall and piston and onto the piston rings. Because carbon grit is very abrasive, premature cylinder, piston and ring wear will occur. If the piston crowns have heavy deposits of carbon, remove the pistons as described in Chapter Five and clean them. Excessive carbon buildup on the piston crowns reduces piston cool-

severe, repair the head by installing a steel thread insert. Purchase thread insert kits at an automotive supply store, or have the inserts installed by a Yamaha dealership or machine shop.

CAUTION
Aluminum spark plug threads are commonly damaged due to galling, cross-threading and overtightening. It is easy to cross thread spark plugs on this engine because the plug holes are recessed deep within the cylinder

ing, raises engine compression and causes overheating.

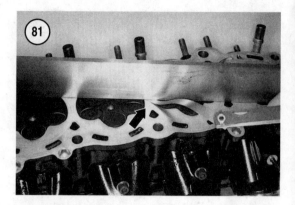

9. Place a straightedge across the gasket surface at several points. Measure warp by inserting a feeler gauge between the straightedge and cylinder head at each location (**Figure 81**). The service limit for warp is listed in **Table 2**. If warp exceeds this limit, the cylinder head must be resurfaced or replaced. Distortion or nicks in the cylinder head surface could cause an air leak and result in overheating.

10. Check the exhaust pipe studs (B, **Figure 80**) for looseness or thread damage. Slight thread damage can be repaired with a thread file or die. If thread damage is severe, replace the damaged stud(s) as described in Chapter One.

11. On 2000-2003 models, inspect the AIS fittings (**Figure 82**) for looseness or damage.

12. Check the valves and valve guides as described under *Valves and Valve Components* in this chapter.

13. Inspect the valve lifters and valve lifter bores in the cylinder head as described under *Valve Lifters and Shims* in this chapter.

VALVE LIFTERS AND SHIMS

Removal

1. Remove the cylinder head cover and camshafts as described in this chapter.

2. Before removing the valve lifters and shims, note the following:

  a. Temporarily install the spark plugs to close off the openings into the cylinder block.

  b. Use a divided container to store the valve lifters and shims so they will be installed in their original mounting positions. This will make valve clearance adjustment much easier after the cylinder head and camshaft have been installed.

  c. The shims may stick to the bottom of the valve lifter. Remove the valve lifters carefully to prevent a shim from falling into the engine.

  d. Remove the valve lifters carefully to avoid damaging the lifter bores in the cylinder head.

3. Remove one of the valve lifters (**Figure 83**) and its respective shim (**Figure 84**) and place both of them in the correct location in the holder.

4. Repeat Step 3 for all of the valve lifters and shims.

1. Lubricate the valve lifters and shims with clean engine oil.

2. Install a shim into the valve retainer bore (**Figure 84**) with its thickness number facing down. Make sure it is seated correctly.

3. Install the valve lifter (**Figure 85**) over the shim and into the cylinder head bore. Push the lifter down until it seats against the shim.

4. Repeat for each shim and valve lifter.

4

Inspection

Maintain the correct alignment of the valve lifters and shims when inspecting them.

1. Inspect the valve lifters and shims for wear and damage.

2. Check each valve lifter (**Figure 86**) for any scoring or other damage. The lifter must operate in its cylinder head bore with no binding or chatter. If the side of a lifter is damaged, replace it.

3. Check the valve lifter bores (**Figure 87**) in the cylinder head for any scoring or damage. These surfaces must be smooth.

4. Check the shims for stress cracks and other damage.

VALVES AND VALVE COMPONENTS

Due to the number of special tools and the skills required to use them, it is general practice for those who perform their own service to remove the cylinder head and entrust valve service to a Yamaha dealership or machine shop. The following procedures describe how to check for valve component wear and to determine what type of service is required.

Installation

The shims and valve lifters must be installed in their original operating positions as noted during removal.

> *NOTE*
> *If the shims and valve lifters were not stored in a marked divided container, the valve clearance will be more time consuming after installing the camshafts and camshaft holder.*

Valve Service Tools

To remove and install the valves in this section, the following tools are required:

1. Valve spring compressor.

2. Valve lifter bore protector. This tool is used to protect the valve lifter bore when removing and installing the valves. This tool can be made from a 35 mm film container cut to the dimensions shown in **Figure 88**.

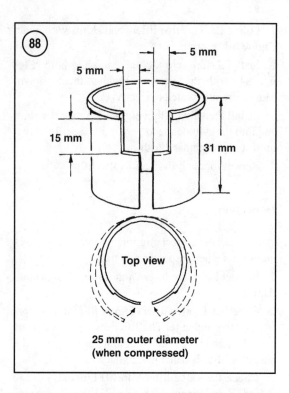

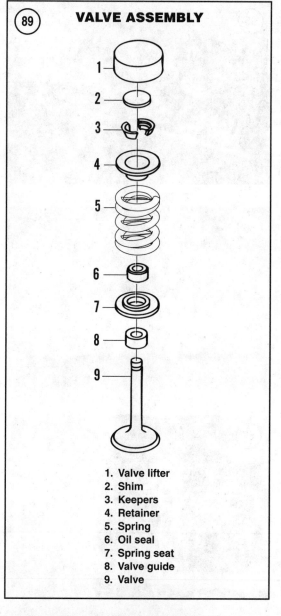

VALVE ASSEMBLY

1. Valve lifter
2. Shim
3. Keepers
4. Retainer
5. Spring
6. Oil seal
7. Spring seat
8. Valve guide
9. Valve

Valve Removal

Refer to **Figure 89**.

1. Remove the camshafts, valve lifters and shims as described in this chapter.

2. Remove the cylinder head as described in this chapter.

3. Install the protector into the valve lifter bore (**Figure 90**) of the valve being removed.

4. Install a valve spring compressor squarely over the upper retainer with the other end of the tool placed against the valve head (**Figure 91**).

5. Tighten the valve spring compressor until the valve keepers separate. Lift the valve keepers out through the valve spring compressor with needlenose pliers or tweezers (**Figure 92**).

6. Gradually loosen the valve spring compressor and remove it from the head.

7. Remove the protector from the valve lifter bore.

8. Remove the spring retainer (**Figure 93**).

9. Remove the valve spring (**Figure 94**).

> *CAUTION*
> *Remove any burrs from the valve stem grooves (**Figure 95**) before removing the valve; otherwise, the valve guides will be damaged.*

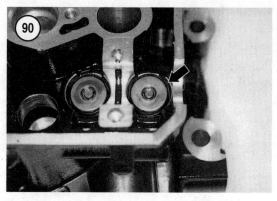

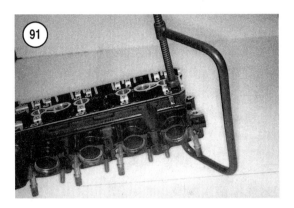

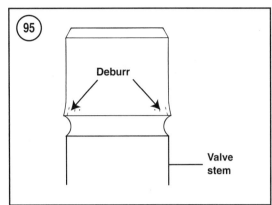

Deburr

Valve
stem

4

10. Turn the cylinder head over and remove the valve (**Figure 96**).

NOTE
If a valve is difficult to remove, it may be bent, causing it to stick in its valve guide. This condition will require valve and valve guide replacement.

11. Pull the oil seal (**Figure 97**) off of the valve guide and discard it.

12. Remove the spring seat (**Figure 98**).

> *NOTE*
> *All components of each valve assembly must be kept together (**Figure 99**). Place each set in a plastic bag, a divided carton or into separate small boxes. Label the sets as to which cylinder and either intake or exhaust valves. This will keep them from getting mixed up and will make installation simpler. Do not intermix components from the valves, or excessive wear may result.*

13. Mark all parts as they are removed so that they will be installed in their same locations.

14. Repeat for the remaining intake and exhaust valves as necessary.

> *NOTE*
> *Do not remove the valve guides unless they require replacement.*

Valve Installation

Refer to **Figure 89**.

Following the reference marks made during removal, install the valves in their original locations. Refer to the identification marks on each valve head (**Figure 100**).

1. Install the spring seat (**Figure 101**) and make sure it is seated squarely on the cylinder head surface (**Figure 98**).

> *NOTE*
> *The intake and exhaust valve seals are **not** identical. Do not intermix the seals during installation.*

2. Lubricate the inside of a *new* oil seal with engine oil. Install the oil seal (**Figure 102**). Then push the seal straight down the valve guide until it snaps into the groove in the top of the guide (**Figure 97**). Check that the oil seal is centered and seats squarely on top of the guide. If the seal is cocked to one side, oil will leak past the seal during engine operation.

> *NOTE*
> *The oil seals must be replaced whenever the valves are removed. Also, if*

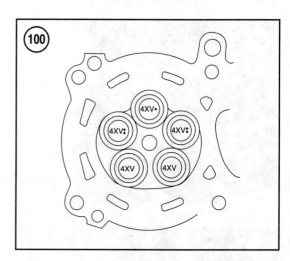

the new seal was installed and then removed, do not reuse it.

3. Install the valve as follows:
   a. Turn the cylinder head over.
   b. Coat a valve stem with molybdenum disulfide oil.
   c. Install the valve partway into its guide (**Figure 96**); then, slowly turn the valve as it en-

4

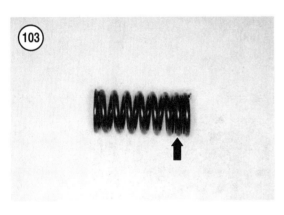

ters the valve stem seal and continue turning it until the valve is installed all the way. To avoid damage, rotate and push the valve through its valve guide.

4. Position the valve springs with the tightly wound spring coils (**Figure 103**) of the spring facing the combustion chamber.

5. Install the valve spring (**Figure 104**). Make sure the spring is seated correctly (**Figure 94**).

6. Install the retainer (**Figure 105**) on top of the valve spring. Make sure the retainer is seated correctly (**Figure 93**).

7. Install the protector, used during removal, into the valve lifter bore.

> *CAUTION*
> *To avoid loss of spring tension, do not compress the spring(s) any more than necessary when installing the valve keepers.*

8. Compress the valve spring with a valve spring compressor tool (**Figure 91**) and install the valve keepers (**Figure 106**). Make sure the keepers fit

into the rounded groove in the valve stem (**Figure 107**).

9. Remove the valve spring compressor tool.

> *CAUTION*
> *If Step 10 is not performed, the valve keepers may pop out of the valve stem groove after the cylinder head has been installed and the engine is started. This may result in engine damage.*

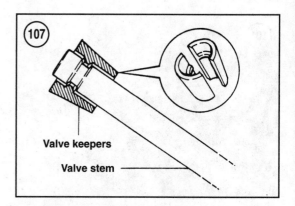

Valve keepers

Valve stem

10. Place a drift onto the top of the valve stem (**Figure 108**) and tap on the end with a hammer (**Figure 109**) to ensure the keepers are seated correctly. If the keepers are not installed correctly, they will pop out at this time.

11. Repeat Steps 1-10 for the remaining valves.

12. Install the cylinder head as described in this chapter.

13. Install the shims, the valve lifters and the camshafts as described under *Camshaft Installation* in this chapter.

14. After installing the cylinder head, camshafts and camshaft holder on the engine, check and adjust the valve clearance as described in Chapter Three.

Valve Component Inspection

When measuring the valve components, compare the actual measurements to the specifications in **Table 2**. Replace parts that are damaged or out of specification as described in this section.

1. Clean the valve components in solvent. Do not damage the valve seating surface.

2. Inspect the valve face (**Figure 110**) for burning, pitting or other signs of wear. Unevenness of the valve face is an indication that the valve is not serviceable. If the wear on a valve is too extensive to be corrected by hand-lapping the valve into its seat, replace the valve. The face on the valve cannot be ground. Replace the valve if defective.

3. Inspect the valve stems for wear and roughness. Check the valve keeper grooves for damage.

4. Measure each valve stem outside diameter with a micrometer (**Figure 111**). Note the following:

   a. If a valve stem is out of specification, discard the valve.

   b. If a valve stem is within specification, record the measurement so it can be used to deter-

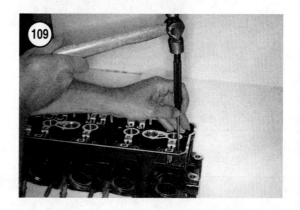

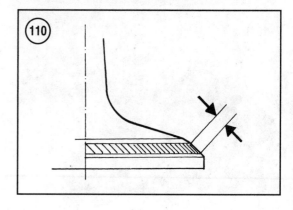

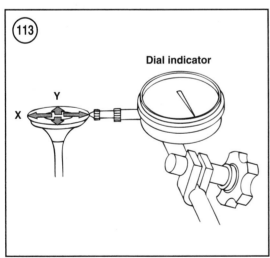

Dial indicator

mine the valve stem-to-guide clearance in Step 7.

5. Place the valve stem on two V-blocks and measure the runout with a dial indicator (**Figure 112**).

NOTE
Yamaha recommends reaming the valve guides to remove any carbon

buildup before checking and measuring the guides in the following steps. For the home mechanic it is more practical to remove carbon and varnish from the valve guides with a stiff spiral wire brush. Then clean the valve guides with solvent to wash out all debris. Dry with compressed air.

6. Insert each valve into its respective valve guide and move it up and down by hand. The valve should move smoothly.

7. Measure each valve guide inside diameter with a small bore gauge and record the measurements. Note the following:

NOTE
Because valve guides wear unevenly (oval shape), measure each guide at different positions. Use the largest bore diameter measurement when determining its size.

  a. If a valve guide is out of specification, replace it as described in this section.
  b. If a valve guide is within specification, record the measurement so it can be used to determine the valve stem-to-guide clearance in Step 7.

8. Subtract the measurement made in Step 4 from the measurement made in Step 7 to determine the valve stem-to-guide clearance. Note the following:

  a. If the clearance is out of specification, determine if a new guide would bring the clearance within specification.
  b. If the clearance would be out of specification with a new guide, replace the valve and valve guide as a set.

9. If a small bore gauge and inside micrometer are not available, insert each valve into it guide. Hold the valve just slightly off its seat and rock it sideways or use a dial indicator with its plunger against the valve head (**Figure 113**). If the valve rocks more than slightly, the guide is probably worn and should be replaced. As a final check, take the cylinder head and valve assemblies to a Yamaha dealership or machine shop and have the valve guides accurately measured.

10. Inspect the valve springs as follows:

  a. Inspect each spring for any cracks, distortion or other damage.

b. Measure the free length of each valve spring with a vernier caliper (**Figure 114**).

c. Replace the defective spring(s).

11. Check the upper retainer and valve keepers. If they are in good condition, they may be reused; replace in pairs as necessary.

12. Inspect the valve seats as described under *Valve Seat Inspection* in this chapter.

Valve Guide Replacement

Special tools and considerable experience are required to properly replace the valve guides in the cylinder head. If these tools are unavailable, have a Yamaha dealership or machine shop perform this procedure. Removing the cylinder head, then taking it to a dealership or machine shop to have the valves guides replaced, can save a considerable amount of money. The following procedure is provided for those who choose to perform this task. When a valve guide is replaced, also replace the valve.

Tools

The following Yamaha special tools, or equivalents, are required for this procedure:

1. Intake valve guide remover (4.0 mm): 90890-04111.

2. Exhaust valve guide remover (4.5 mm): YM-04116 (U.S.), 90890-04116 (U.K.).

3. Intake valve guide installer (4.0 mm): 90890-04112.

4. Exhaust valve guide installer (4.5 mm): YM-04117 (U.S.), 90890-04117 (U.K.).

5. Intake valve guide reamer: 90890-04113.

6. Exhaust valve guide reamer: YM-04118 (U.S.), 90890-04118 (U.K.).

Procedure

1. If still in place, remove the securing screws and remove all four intake manifolds from the cylinder head.

2. Place the new valve guides in a freezer for approximately one hour prior to heating the cylinder head. Chilling them will slightly reduce the outside diameter, while the hot cylinder head is slightly larger due to heat expansion. This will make valve guide installation much easier.

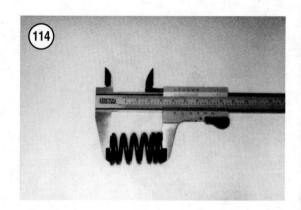

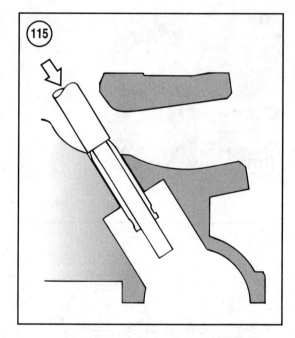

NOTE
To monitor the cylinder head temperature when heating it in Step 4, use heat indicator sticks, available at welding supply stores. Follow the manufacturer's directions when using the sticks.

3. The valve guides are installed with a slight interference fit. Heat the cylinder head in a shop oven or on a hot plate. Heat the cylinder head to a temperature of 100-150° C (212-300° F).

WARNING
Wear insulated or welding gloves when performing the following procedure. The cylinder head will be very hot.

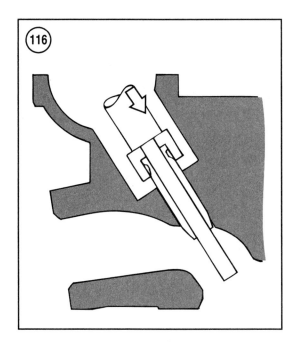

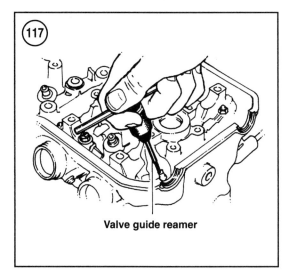

Valve guide reamer

CAUTION
Do not heat the cylinder head with a torch (propane or acetylene); never bring a flame into contact with the cylinder head or valve guide. The direct heat will destroy the case hardening of the valve guide and may warp the cylinder head.

4. Remove the cylinder head from the oven or hot plate. Place it on wooden blocks with the combustion chambers facing up. Make sure the cylinder head is properly supported on the wooden blocks.

CAUTION
Do not attempt to remove the valve guides if the head is not hot enough. Doing so may damage the valve guide bore.

5. From the combustion side of the cylinder head, drive out the old valve guide with a hammer and the Yamaha valve guide remover, or an equivalent (**Figure 115**). Discard the valve guides after removing them. Never reinstall a valve guide that has been removed, as it is no longer within tolerances.

6. Reheat the cylinder head as described in Step 4, then remove it from the heat source and install it onto the wooden blocks with the valve spring side facing up.

7. Remove a new valve guide from the freezer.

8. Using the valve guide driver tool, from the top-side (valve spring side) of the cylinder head, drive in the valve guide (**Figure 116**) until the tool bottoms on the cylinder head surface.

9. Repeat for each valve guide.

10. After the cylinder head has cooled to room temperature, ream the new valve guide as follows:

   a. Use the Yamaha valve guide reamer and a tap wrench.

   b. Apply cutting oil to both the new valve guide and the valve guide reamer.

CAUTION
Always rotate the reamer clockwise when installing and removing it in the valve guides. If the reamer is rotated counterclockwise, it will dull its cutting surfaces and damage the guide.

   c. Insert the reamer from the valve spring side and rotate it clockwise through the valve guide (**Figure 117**). Continue to rotate the reamer and work it down through the entire length of the new valve guide. Apply additional cutting oil during this procedure.

   d. While rotating the reamer clockwise, withdraw the reamer from the valve guide.

11. If necessary, repeat for any other valve guide.

12. Thoroughly clean the cylinder head and valve guides with solvent to remove all metal particles. Clean the cylinder head with hot soapy water, rinse the cylinder head completely and thoroughly dry it with compressed air.

13. Measure the valve guide inside diameter with a small bore gauge. This measurement must be within the specification listed in **Table 2**.

14. Lubricate the valve guides with engine oil.

15. Recondition the valve seats as described in this chapter.

16. Install the intake manifolds in their original locations on the cylinder head.

Valve Seat Inspection

The most accurate method for checking the valve seat surface is to use a marking compound (machinist's dye), available from auto parts and tool stores. Marking compound is used to locate high or irregular spots when checking or making close fits. Follow the manufacturer's directions.

> *NOTE*
> *Because of the close operating tolerances within the valve assembly, the valve stem and guide must be within tolerance; otherwise, the inspection results will be inaccurate.*

1. Remove the valves as described in this chapter.

2. Clean the valve seat in the cylinder head and valve mating areas with contact cleaner.

3. Thoroughly clean all carbon deposits from the valve face with solvent and dry thoroughly.

4. Spread a thin layer of marking compound evenly on the valve face.

5. Slowly insert the valve into its guide.

6. Support the valve with two fingers (**Figure 118**) and tap the valve up and down in the cylinder head. Do not rotate the valve or a false reading will result.

7. Remove the valve and examine the impression left by the marking compound. If the impression on the valve or in the cylinder head is not even and continuous and the valve seat width (**Figure 119**) is not within the specified tolerance listed in **Table 2**, the valve seat in the cylinder head must be reconditioned.

8. Closely examine the valve seat in the cylinder head (**Figure 120**). It should be smooth and even with a polished seating surface.

9. If the valve seat is not in good condition, recondition the valve seat as described in this chapter.

10. Repeat for the other valves.

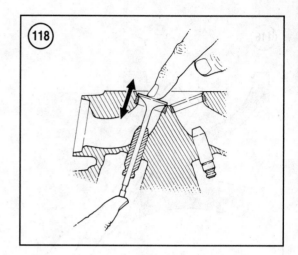

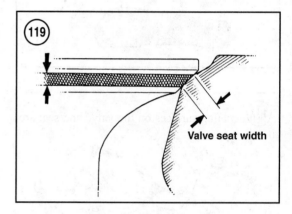

Valve seat width

Valve Seat Reconditioning

Special valve cutters and considerable experience are required to properly recondition the valve seats in the cylinder head. If these tools are unavailable, have a Yamaha dealership or machine shop perform this procedure. Removing the cylinder head, then taking it to a dealership or machine shop to have the valve seats reconditioned, can save a considerable amount of money. The manufacturer does not provide service information for valve seat reconditioning.

Valve Lapping

Valve lapping is a simple operation that can restore the valve seat without machining if the amount of wear or distortion is not too great.

This procedure should only be performed after determining that the valve seat width is within specifications.

1. Smear a light coating of fine grade valve lapping compound on the valve face seating surface.
2. Insert the valve into the head.
3. Wet the suction cup of the lapping stick and stick it onto the head of the valve. Spin the tool in both directions while pressing it against the valve seat, and lap the valve to the seat. Every 5 to 10 seconds, lift and rotate the valve 180° in the valve seat. Continue until the mating surfaces on the valve and seat are smooth and equal in size.
4. Closely examine the valve seat in the cylinder head (**Figure 120**). It should be smooth and even with a smooth, polished seating ring.
5. Repeat Steps 1-4 for the other valves.

6. Thoroughly clean the valves and cylinder head in solvent and then with hot soapy water to remove all valve grinding compound. Dry thoroughly.

CAUTION
Any compound left on the valves or in the cylinder head causes excessive wear to the engine components.

7. Install the valve assemblies as described in this chapter.
8. After the lapping is completed and the valves are reinstalled in the head, perform the *Solvent Test* described in this chapter. There should be no leakage past the seat. If leakage occurs, the combustion chamber appears wet. If fluid leaks past any of the seats, disassemble that valve assembly and repeat the lapping procedure until there is no leakage.

NOTE
This solvent test does not ensure long-term durability or maximum power. It merely ensures maximum compression will be available on initial start-up after assembly.

9. If the cylinder head and valve components are cleaned in detergent and hot water, apply a light coat of engine oil to all bare metal surfaces to prevent rust formation.

Table 1 GENERAL ENGINE SPECIFICATIONS

Item	Specification
Cylinder arrangement	In-line four-cylinder inclined from vertical
Engine type	Four-stroke, DOHC, five valve head
Bore × stroke	74 × 58 mm (2.91 × 2.28 in.)
Displacement	998 cc (60.8 cu. in.)
Compression ratio	11.8:1
Compression pressure @350 rpm	
(at sea level)	1450 kPa (210 psi)
Ignition type	Electronic (fully transistorized)
Ignition timing	
1998-2001 models	5° BTDC @ 1100 rpm
2002-2003 models	5° BTDC @ 1050 rpm
Advanced timing	
1998-2001 models	55° BTDC @ 5000 rpm
2002-2003 models	N/A
Cooling system	Liquid cooled
Lubrication system	
Type	Wet sump, forced pressure
Oil pump	Trochoid
Oil pressure (at oil pressure switch)	
at 80° C (176° F)	45 kPa (6.4 psi) @ 1100 rpm

Table 2 ENGINE TOP END SPECIFICATIONS

Item	Standard mm (in.)	Service limit mm (in.)
Camshaft		
Cam lobe height		
Intake	32.50-32.60 (1.2795-1.2835)	32.40 (1.2756)
Exhaust	32.95-33.05 (1.2972-1.3012)	32.85 (1.2933)
Cam lobe width		
Intake	24.95-25.05 (0.9823-0.9862)	24.85 (0.9783)
Exhaust	24.95-25.05 (0.9823-0.9862)	24.85 (0.9783)
Cam cap inside diameter	24.500-24.521 (0.9647-0.9654)	–
Cam journal outside diameter		
1998-1999 models	24.437-24.450 (0.9621-0.9626)	–
2000-2003 models	24.459-24.472 (0.9630-0.9635)	–
Journal oil clearance		
(bearing clearance)		
1998-1999 models	0.050-0.084 (0.0020-0.0033)	–
2000-2003 models	0.028-0.062 (0.0011-0.0024)	–
Camshaft runout	–	0.03 (0.0012)
Cylinder head warp	–	0.10 (0.004)
Valves		
Valve clearance (cold)		
1998-2001 models		
Intake	0.11-0.20 (0.0043-0.0079)	–
Exhaust	0.21-0.30 (0.0083-0.0118)	–
2002-2003 models		
Intake	0.11-0.20 (0.0043-0.0079)	–
Exhaust	0.21-0.27 (0.0083-0.0106)	–
Valve stem outside diameter		
Intake	3.975-3.900 (0.1565-0.1535)	3.945 (0.1553)
Exhaust		
1998-1999 models	4.460-4.475 (0.1756-0.1762)	4.43 (0.1744)
2000-2003 models	4.465-4.480 (0.1758-0.1764)	4.43 (0.1744)
Valve stem runout	–	0.01 (0.0004)
Valve guide inside diameter		
Intake	4.000-4.012 (0.1575-0.1580)	4.05 (0.1594)
Exhaust	4.500-4.512 (0.1772-0.1776)	4.55 (0.1791)
Valve stem-to-guide clearance		
Intake	0.010-0.037 (0.0004-0.0015)	0.08 (0.0031)
Exhaust		
1998-1999 models	0.025-0.052 (0.0010-0.0020)	0.08 (0.0031)
2000-2003 models	0.020-0.047 (0.0008-0.0019)	0.085 (0.0033)
Valve face width		
Intake and exhaust	1.76-2.90 (0.0693-0.1142)	–
Valve seat width		
Intake and exhaust	0.90-1.10 (0.035-0.043)	
Valve springs		
Valve spring free length		
Intake	38.9 (1.53)	–
Exhaust	40.67 (1.60)	–

Table 3 ENGINE TOP END TORQUE SPECIFICATIONS

Item	N•m	in.-lb.	ft.-lb.
Camshaft chain tensioner			
Mounting bolts	10	88	–

(continued)

Table 3 ENGINE TOP END TORQUE SPECIFICATIONS (continued)

Item	N•m	in.-lb.	ft.-lb.
Camshaft chain tensioner (continued)			
Cap bolt			
1998-2001 models	10	88	–
2002-2003 models	7	62	–
Camshaft holder bolts	10	88	–
Camshaft sprocket bolts	24	–	18
Cylinder head cover bolts	12	106	–
Cylinder head			
Allen bolts	12	106	–
Sleeve/shoulder nuts			
and cap nuts			
1998-2001 models	50	–	37
Sleeve and shoulder nuts			
2002-2003 models			
Preliminary	20	–	15
Final	50	–	37
Cap nuts			
2002-2003 models			
Preliminary	20	–	15
Final	65	–	48
Spark plug	13	115	–

4

CHAPTER FIVE

ENGINE LOWER END

This chapter describes service procedures for lower end engine components. Engine removal and installation procedures are also described. Specifications and bearing selection tables are in **Tables 1-5** at the end of the chapter.

SERVICING ENGINE IN FRAME

The following components can be serviced while the engine is installed in the frame:
1. Camshafts.
2. Clutch.
3. Exterior gearshift mechanism.
4. Alternator.
5. Timing coil and rotor.
6. Starter.
7. Carburetor assembly or throttle body assembly.
8. Oil cooler.

ENGINE SERVICE NOTES

Before removing and installing the engine in the frame, note the following:
1. Park the motorcycle on level ground. Support the motorcycle securely on a swing arm stand with the rear wheel off the ground.
2. A hydraulic floor jack is required to support the engine.
3. Due to the weight and size of the engine, it is essential that a minimum of two, preferably three, people perform engine removal and installation.
4. Cover the O-ring drive chain before degreasing the engine. The chemicals in the degreaser will cause the O-rings to swell, permanently damaging the chain.
5. Label all electrical connectors and hoses with tape and a permanent pen prior to disconnecting them.

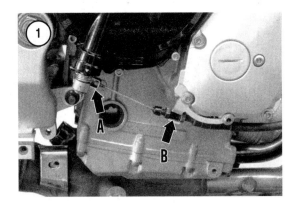

ENGINE

Removal

1. Support the motorcycle on a swing arm safety stand. Block the front wheel so the motorcycle will not roll in either direction while on the safety stand.
2. Remove the following as described in Chapter Sixteen:
   a. Both seats.
   b. Front fairing.
   c. Both side fairings.
   d. Bottom and rear cowls.
3. Disconnect the negative battery cable as described in Chapter Ten.
4. Remove the following as described in Chapter Eight or Chapter Nine:
   a. Fuel tank.
   b. Air filter housing assembly.
   c. Carburetor assembly or throttle body assembly.

> *CAUTION*
> *Plug the cylinder head intake openings with rubber plugs or clean shop rags.*

5. Drain the cooling system as described in Chapter Three.
6. Remove the radiator, coolant hoses and pipes as described in Chapter Eleven.
7. Remove the muffler and exhaust pipe as described in Chapter Eight or Chapter Nine.
8. On California models, remove the EVAP canister and EVAP purge control valve as described in Chapter Eight.
9. Drain the engine oil as described in Chapter Three.

10. Remove the oil filter as described in Chapter Three.
11. Remove the oil cooler as described in this chapter.
12. Remove the drive sprocket as described in this chapter.

> *NOTE*
> *After removing the drive sprocket, pull the drive chain back onto the driven sprocket to take out the slack and move the loose end of the chain out of the way. Use a tie-wrap and secure the loop of chain together on the driven sprocket.*

13. On 1998-2001 models, remove the ignition coil plate assembly as described in Chapter Ten. Do not remove the spark plugs from the cylinder head.
14. Disconnect the air induction system assembly from the front of the cylinder block as described in Chapter Eight.
15. Remove the thermostat housing as described in Chapter Eleven.
16. Disconnect the clutch cable from the clutch arm (A, **Figure 1**) and the cable bracket (B) on the timing coil cover.
17. Remove the starter as described in Chapter Ten.
18. Label and disconnect the following electrical connectors:
   a. Timing coil 2-pin electrical connector.
   b. Speed sensor 3-pin black electrical connector.
   c. Oil level switch wire connector.
   d. Alternator stator 3-pin electrical connector.
   e. Sidestand 2-pin electrical connector.
   f. Neutral switch wire connector.
   g. On 2002-2003 models, the cylinder identification sensor 3-pin electrical connector.
19. Remove the camshaft chain tensioner as described in Chapter Four.
20. If the engine is going to be disassembled, remove the following parts while the engine is still in the frame.
   a. Clutch assembly (Chapter Six).
   b. Alternator stator and flywheel (Chapter Ten).
   c. External gearshift linkage assembly (Chapter Six).
21. Secure the engine with a hydraulic jack. Place a wooden block between the engine and jack support. Operate the jack to place tension against the engine and to help with engine mounting bolt removal.

5

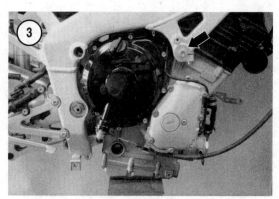

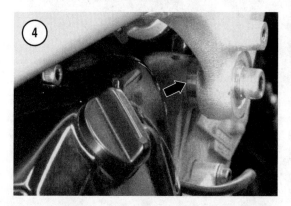

22. Check the engine to make sure all electrical connectors and hoses are disconnected and will not interfere with engine removal.

> *CAUTION*
> *Continually adjust the jack height during engine removal and installation to prevent damage to the mounting bolt threads and hardware. Ideally, the jack should support the engine so its mounting bolts can be easily removed or installed.*

23A. On 1998-2001 models, on the right side, perform the following:
    a. Loosen the pinch bolt (**Figure 2**) on the right side front upper mounting bolt.
    b. Remove the front upper mounting bolt (**Figure 3**) and washer. Remove the collar (**Figure 4**) located between the frame and the engine.

23B. On 2002-2003 models, on the right side, perform the following:
    a. Loosen both pinch bolts (A, **Figure 5**) on the right side front upper mounting bolts.
    b. Remove the primary front upper mounting bolt (B, **Figure 5**), washer and collar.
    c. Remove the secondary front upper mounting bolt (C, **Figure 5**), washer and collar.

24A. On 1998-2001 models, on the left side, remove the two front upper mounting bolts and washers (A, **Figure 6**).

24B. On 2002-2003 models, on the left side, remove the two front upper mounting bolts and washers (A, **Figure 7**).

25. On the right side, remove the self-locking nuts on the rear upper (**Figure 8**) and rear lower (**Figure 9**) through bolts.

26A. On 1998-2001 models, on the left side, remove the lower through bolt (**Figure 10**).

5

26B. On 2002-2003 models, on the left side, re-move the lower through bolt (**Figure 11**). Do not lose the spacer located on the right side between the frame and engine mounting boss.

> *NOTE*
> *Have an assistant steady the engine on the jack when removing the last bolt.*

27A. On 1998-2001 models, on the right side re-move the upper rear through bolt (B, **Figure 6**). Do not lose the spacer located on the right side between the frame and engine mounting boss.

27B. On 2002-2003 models, on the right side re-move the upper rear through bolt (B, **Figure 7**). Do not lose the spacer located on the right side between the frame and engine mounting boss.

> *WARNING*
> *The following steps require the aid of an assistant to safely remove the en-gine assembly from the frame. Due to the weight of the engine, it is sug-gested that at least one helper, prefer-ably two, assist in engine removal.*

28. Gradually lower the engine assembly to clear the frame and maneuver the engine down and out of the frame. The engine can be removed through ei-ther side of the frame. Take the engine to a work-bench or engine stand for further disassembly.

29. Refer to *Cleaning and Inspection* in this section.

Installation

1. Check the coolant hoses, vacuum hoses and fuel lines, spark plug cables and electrical wires and

connectors throughout the frame. If necessary, reposition them so that they will not interfere or be damaged when installing the engine.

WARNING
The following steps require the aid of a helper, preferably two, to safely install the engine in the frame.

2. With one or more assistants, carefully transfer the engine from the workbench or engine stand to the floor directly below the frame. Install the engine on a floor jack and steady the engine by hand.

3. Slowly maneuver the engine and center it between the sides of the frame.

CAUTION
Before installing the mounting bolts that pass through the frame and engine, make sure the engine is square and level with the frame. Attempting to install the bolts with the engine misaligned can damage the various fasteners.

CAUTION
Do not thoroughly tighten the engine mounting bolts and nuts until all have been installed and the thread engagement is correct.

4. At the upper rear mounting bolt area, perform the following:
  a. Position the spacer with the flange side facing the engine mounting boss and install the spacer between the frame and the engine mounting boss and frame.
  b. Install the upper through bolt from the left side through the frame, engine mounting bosses, the spacer and the frame. Refer to B, **Figure 6** for 1998-2001 models or B, **Figure 7** for 2002-2003 models. Push the bolt in until it bottoms.
  c. On the right side, install a *new* self-locking nut (**Figure 8**) and tighten securely.

5. In the lower mounting bolt area, perform the following:
  a. On 2002-2003 models, position the spacer with the flange side facing the engine mounting boss and install the spacer between the frame and the engine mounting boss and frame.

  b. Install the lower through bolt (**Figure 11**) from the left side through the frame, engine mounting bosses, the spacer (2002-2003 models) and the frame. Push the bolt in until it bottoms.
  c. On the right side, install a *new* self-locking nut (**Figure 9**) and tighten securely.

6A. On 1998-2001 models, on the left side, install the front upper mounting bolts and washers (A, **Figure 6**).

6B. On 2002-2003 models, on the left side, install the front upper mounting bolts and washers (A, **Figure 7**).

7A. On 1998-2001 models, on the right side, position the collar (**Figure 4**) between the frame and the cylinder head, then install the front upper mounting bolt (**Figure 3**). Tighten securely.

7B. On 2002-2003 models, on the right side, perform the following:
  a. Install the secondary front upper mounting bolt (C, **Figure 5**), washer and collar.
  b. Install the primary front upper mounting bolt (B, **Figure 5**), washer and collar.

8A. On 1998-2001 models, tighten the bolts and nuts to the following:
  a. Left side, upper front mounting bolts: 40 N•m (30 ft.-lb.).
  b. Right side, upper front mounting bolts: 55 N•m (41 ft.-lb.).
  c. Right side, upper pinch bolt: 24 N•m (18 ft.-lb.).
  d. Lower rear through bolt nut: 55 N•m (41 ft.-lb.).
  e. Upper rear through bolt nut: 55 N•m (41 ft.-lb.).

8B. On 2002-2003 models, tighten the bolts and nuts to the following:
  a. Left side, upper front mounting bolts: 45 N•m (33 ft.-lb.).
  b. Right side, primary upper front mounting bolt: 45 N•m (33 ft.-lb.).
  c. Right side, secondary upper front mounting bolt: 45 N•m (33 ft.-lb.).
  d. Right side, upper front mounting bolts pinch bolts: 24 N•m (18 ft.-lb.).
  e. Lower rear through bolt nut: 50 N•m (37 ft.-lb.).
  f. Upper rear through bolt nut: 50 N•m (37 ft.-lb.).

9. If the engine was disassembled, install the following parts:

    a. Clutch assembly (Chapter Six).

    b. Alternator stator and flywheel (Chapter Ten).

    c. External gearshift linkage assembly (Chapter Six).

10. Install the camshaft chain tensioner as described in Chapter Four.

11. Connect the following electrical connectors:

    a. Timing coil 2-pin electrical connector.

    b. Speed sensor 3-pin black electrical connector.

    c. Oil level switch wire connector.

    d. Alternator stator 3-pin electrical connector.

    e. Sidestand 2-pin electrical connector.

    f. Neutral switch wire connector.

    g. On 2002-2003 models, the cylinder identification sensor 3-pin electrical connector.

12. Install the starter as described in Chapter Ten.

13. Connect the clutch cable to the cable bracket (B, **Figure 1**) and on the timing coil cover and onto the clutch arm (A).

14. Install the thermostat housing as described in Chapter Eleven.

15. Install the ignition coil assemblies as described in Chapter Ten.

16. Install the air induction system assembly onto the front of the cylinder block as described in Chapter Eight.

17. Install the drive sprocket as described in this chapter.

18. Install the oil cooler as described in this chapter.

19. Install the oil filter as described in Chapter Three.

20. Refill the engine oil as described in Chapter Three.

21. On California models, install the EVAP canister and EVAP purge control valve as described in Chapter Eight.

22. Install the muffler and exhaust pipe as described in Chapter Eight or Chapter Nine.

23. Install the radiator, coolant hoses and pipes as described in Chapter Eleven.

24. Refill the cooling system as described in Chapter Three.

25. Install the following as described in Chapter Eight or Chapter Nine:

    a. Carburetor assembly or throttle body assembly.

    b. Air filter housing assembly.

    c. Fuel tank.

26. Connect the negative battery cable as described in Chapter Ten.

> *NOTE*
> *Do not install the fairing assembly until after starting the engine and checking for leaks.*

27. Start the engine and check for oil and coolant leaks. At the same time the engine is running, bleed the cooling system as described in Chapter Three.

28. Install the following as described in Chapter Sixteen:

    a. Bottom and rear cowls.

    b. Both side fairings.

    c. Front fairing.

    d. Seat.

29. Operate the clutch lever, making sure there is resistance at the lever when operated. If necessary, adjust the clutch as described in Chapter Three.

30. Shift the transmission into gear and check clutch and transmission operation.

31. Slowly test-ride the motorcycle to ensure all systems are operating correctly.

Cleaning and Inspection

1. Remove any corrosion from the engine mount bolts with a wire wheel.

2. Clean and dry the engine mount bolts, nuts adjust bolts, locknuts and collars.

3. Replace damaged fasteners.

4. Check the coolant hoses for cracks, leakage or other damage. Replace if necessary.

5. Check the wire harness routing in the frame. Check the harness cover and wires for chafing or other damage. Replace harness cable guides and clips as required.

6. Clean the electrical connectors with contact cleaner.

OIL PAN, OIL STRAINER AND PRESSURE RELIEF VALVE

The oil pan can be removed with the engine installed in the frame. The following procedure is shown with the engine removed to better illustrate the steps.

Oil Pan Removal/Installation

1. Support the motorcycle on a swing arm safety stand.

2. Block the front wheel so the motorcycle will not roll in either direction while on the safety stand.

3. Remove both side fairing panels and bottom cowl as described in Chapter Sixteen.

4. Remove the exhaust system as described in Chapter Eight or Chapter Nine.

5. Drain the engine oil as described in Chapter Three.

6. Thoroughly clean the exterior of the oil pan and lower crankcase of all dirt and debris.

7. If compressed air is available, clean dirt and debris off the oil pan, frame and other parts to prevent particles from entering the exposed engine crankcase.

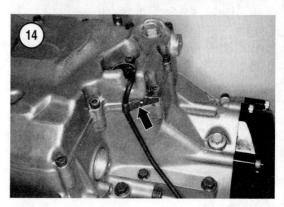

> *NOTE*
> *Place an empty oil drain pan underneath the engine when performing Step 8.*

> *NOTE*
> *These two bolts (**Figure 12**) have a threadlocking compound on the threads. If necessary, use an impact driver and Allen wrench to loosen them.*

8. Using a crisscross pattern, loosen the bolts securing the oil pan (**Figure 13**) to the lower crankcase; allow residual oil to drain into the drain pan. If the oil pan is stuck to the crankcase, tap it with a plastic mallet; do not pry the oil pan away from the crankcase.

9. Remove the oil pan mounting bolts and remove the oil pan. Note the location of the oil level sensor

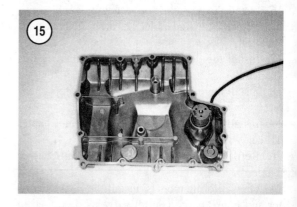

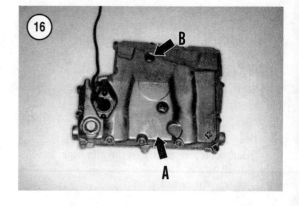

5

electrical wire bracket (**Figure 14**) under the one bolt.

10. Remove the gasket and the locating dowels if loose.

11. Check the inside of the oil pan (**Figure 15**) for aluminum or metal debris, which indicates engine, clutch or transmission damage.

12. Remove any gasket residue from the oil pan and lower crankcase mating surfaces.

13. Thoroughly clean the oil pan in solvent and then dry with compressed air. Remove any oil sludge left in the pan.

14. Inspect the bottom surface of the oil pan (A, **Figure 16**) for cracks or damage from road debris.

15. Make sure the water pump drain hole (B, **Figure 16**) in the base of the oil pan is clear. Clean out if necessary.

16. Make sure the oil strainer (A, **Figure 17**) and pressure relief valve (B) are properly installed; refer to the appropriate procedure in this section.

17. Make sure the drain pipe (A, **Figure 18**) is installed and the O-ring (B) is in place. Apply clean engine oil to the O-ring.

18. If removed, install the locating dowels. Refer to **Figure 19** and **Figure 20**.

19. Install a *new* gasket (**Figure 21**) onto the lower crankcase.

20. Install the oil pan onto the lower crankcase. Align the oil pan drain hole post (A, **Figure 22**) with the drain pipe (B) and install the oil pan.

21. Align the holes in the oil pan with the threaded holes in the lower crankcase.

22. Apply a low strength threadlocking compound onto only these two bolts (**Figure 12**).

23. Install the oil level sensor electrical wire bracket (**Figure 14**) under the one bolt.

24. Install the bolts finger-tight to seat the oil pan against the crankcase sealing surface. Tighten all of the bolts securely in a crisscross pattern and in two or three steps to 10 N•m (88 in.-lb.).

25. Fill the engine with the correct type and quantity of oil as described in Chapter Three.

26. Install the exhaust system as described in Chapter Eight or Chapter Nine.

27. Start the engine and check the oil pan for leaks.

28. Install both side fairing panels and bottom cowl as described in Chapter Sixteen.

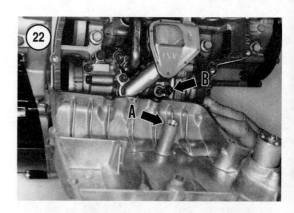

Oil Strainer, Drain Pipe and Oil Pipe Removal/Installation

1. Remove the oil pan as described in this chapter.

2. Remove the drain pipe (A, **Figure 18**) from the water pump. Do not lose the two O-rings.

> *NOTE*
> *The two bolts securing the oil strainer have a threadlocking compound on the threads. If necessary, use an impact driver and Allen wrench to loosen them.*

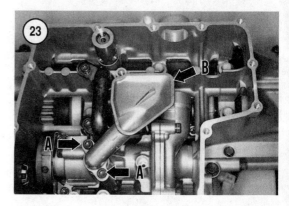

3. Remove the two bolts (A, **Figure 23**) securing the oil strainer (B) and remove the oil strainer from the oil pump.

4. Remove the bolts (A, **Figure 24**) securing the oil pipe (B) and remove the oil pipe. Do not lose the O-rings.

5. Check the oil strainer screen (**Figure 25**) for clogging or damage. If the screen is clogged, remove it and clean it (**Figure 26**) in solvent and thoroughly dry. If the screen cannot be cleaned or if it is damaged, replace the oil strainer assembly.

6. Make sure both the drain pipe and oil pipe are clear. Clean out if necessary.

7. Install *new* O-rings (**Figure 27**) onto the oil pipe and install the oil pipe (B, **Figure 24**). Tighten the bolts (A, **Figure 24**) to 10 N•m (88 in.-lb.).

8. Install oil strainer (B, **Figure 23**) onto the oil pump.

9. Apply a low strength threadlocking compound onto the two bolts and install the bolts (A, **Figure 23**). Tighten the bolts to 10 N•m (88 in.-lb.).

10. Install *new* O-rings (**Figure 28**) onto the water pump drain pipe and install the drain pipe. Push the drain pipe into position on the water pump and push it down until it bottoms.

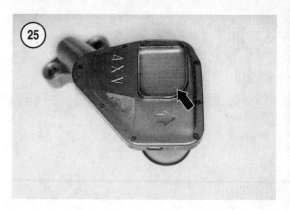

11. Install the oil pan as described in this section.

**Oil Pressure Relief Valve
Removal/Inspection/Installation**

1. Remove the oil pan and gasket as described in this chapter.

2. Pull straight up and remove the oil pressure relief valve (**Figure 29**) from the lower crankcase and place it on a clean, lint-free cloth. If the valve is not going to be serviced, store it in a sealed plastic bag until it is installed.

CAUTION
Handle the oil pressure relief valve carefully to prevent dirt from entering the valve and scoring the piston and cylinder.

3. Remove the O-ring seal from the body and discard it.

4. Service the oil pressure relief valve as follows:
   a. Remove the snap ring from the end of the valve (**Figure 30**). Then remove the washer, spring and piston.
   b. Clean and dry all parts.
   c. Check the piston and piston pin for scoring, scratches or other damage.
   d. Inspect the spring for cracks, stretched coils or other damage.
   e. If any part shows severe wear or damage, replace the pressure relief valve assembly.

CAUTION
The relief valve spring tension helps control oil pressure. A weak or damaged spring can reduce oil pressure and cause engine damage. The piston will be forced open at a lower oil pres-

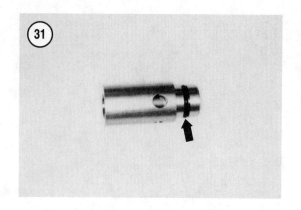

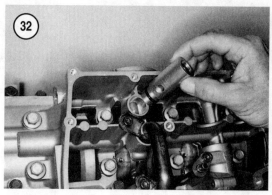

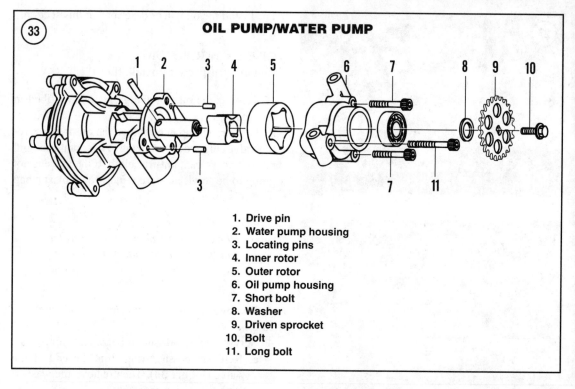

OIL PUMP/WATER PUMP

1. Drive pin
2. Water pump housing
3. Locating pins
4. Inner rotor
5. Outer rotor
6. Oil pump housing
7. Short bolt
8. Washer
9. Driven sprocket
10. Bolt
11. Long bolt

sure, reducing the amount of oil the engine receives. Likewise, a damaged or stuck piston can reduce oil pressure.

f. Reverse these steps to assemble the pressure relief valve assembly. Make sure the piston seats against the stop pin. Install a new snap ring with its flat side facing out. Make sure the snap ring seats in the groove completely (**Figure 30**).

5. Install a *new* O-ring seal (**Figure 31**) into the relief valve groove.

6. Install and push the pressure relief valve into the crankcase until it bottoms (**Figure 32**).

7. Install the oil pan as described in this chapter.

OIL PUMP/WATER PUMP

The oil pump/water pump assembly (**Figure 33**) is mounted in the lower crankcase. The oil pump is an integral part of the water pump and is removed as an assembly. The disassembly/assembly and inspection procedures in this section cover the oil pump specific portion of the assembly. The water pump is covered in Chapter Eleven.

5

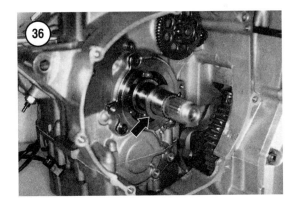

This procedure is shown with the engine removed and partially disassembled to better illustrate these steps. It is not necessary to remove the engine for this procedure.

Removal

1. Remove the clutch assembly as described under *Clutch* in Chapter Six.

2. Remove the bolts (**Figure 34**) securing the oil pump/water pump drive chain guide and remove the guide.

3. On 2002-2003 models, if still in place slide the washer off the transmission shaft.

4. Slide the drive sprocket (A, **Figure 35**) and drive chain (B) off the transmission shaft.

5. Remove the washer (**Figure 36**) from the transmission shaft.

6. If the engine is removed from the frame, turn it over on the workbench.

7. If still in place, remove the oil filter (**Figure 37**).

8. Remove the bolt (**Figure 38**) securing the water pump outlet pipe assembly and withdraw the assembly (**Figure 39**) from the lower crankcase.

9. Remove the oil strainer, drain pipe and oil pipe as described in this chapter.

10. Remove the bolt (A, **Figure 40**) securing the oil delivery pipe (B) and remove the pipe.

11. Remove the bolts (A, **Figure 41**) securing the drive chain and cover (B) and remove the cover.

12. Remove the single long flange bolt (**Figure 42**) securing the oil pump to the lower crankcase.

13. Remove the long locating dowel pin (**Figure 43**) from the bolt hole.

14. Move the oil pump/water pump assembly toward the right side and out of the lower crankcase receptacle on the left side (**Figure 44**).

15. Lift up on the left side of the assembly and disengage the drive chain from the sprocket (**Figure 45**).

16. Pull straight up and remove the oil pump/water pump assembly from the lower crankcase.

17. If necessary, inspect the oil pump as described in this chapter.

18. Inspect the oil pump drive sprocket assembly as described in Chapter Six.

19. Rotate the driven sprocket (**Figure 46**) and drive shaft by hand. If there is any binding or roughness, service the oil pump as described in this chapter.

20. If the oil pump/water pump assembly is not going to be disassembled, place it in a clean plastic bag until it is installed.

Installation

1. Apply clean engine oil to the *new* O-ring (**Figure 47**) in the crankcase.

2. Pull up on the drive chain (**Figure 48**), partially install the oil pump/water pump assembly into the

5

lower crankcase and mesh the chain with the driven sprocket (**Figure 45**).

3. Lower the oil pump/water pump assembly into the lower crankcase (**Figure 49**).

4. Move the oil pump/water pump assembly toward the left side and into the lower crankcase receptacle (**Figure 44**). Push the assembly toward the left side until it bottoms (**Figure 50**).

5. Install the long locating dowel pin (**Figure 43**) and push it in until it bottoms (**Figure 51**).

6. Install the single long flange bolt (**Figure 42**) securing the oil pump to the lower crankcase.

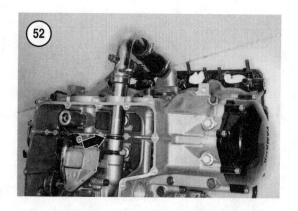

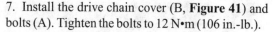

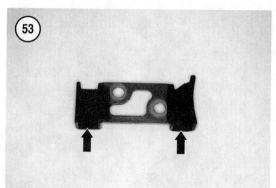

7. Install the drive chain cover (B, **Figure 41**) and bolts (A). Tighten the bolts to 12 N•m (106 in.-lb.).

8. Install the oil delivery pipe (B, **Figure 40**) and bolt (A). Tighten the bolt to 10 N•m (88 in.-lb.).

9. Install the oil pipe, drain pipe and oil strainer as described in this chapter.

10. Apply clean engine oil to the *new* O-ring (**Figure 52**) and install the water pump outlet pipe assembly (**Figure 39**) into the lower crankcase. Push it in until it bottoms in the water pump portion of the assembly.

11. Apply a medium-strength threadlocking compound onto the bolt (**Figure 38**). Tighten the bolt to 10 N•m (88 in.-lb.).

12. Install the oil filter (**Figure 37**).

13. If the engine is removed, turn it over on the workbench.

14. Install the washer (**Figure 36**) onto the transmission shaft.

15. Slide the drive sprocket (A, **Figure 35**) and drive chain (B) onto the transmission shaft.

16. On 2002-2003 models, install the washer onto the transmission shaft.

17. Install the oil pump/water pump drive chain guide. Apply a low strength threadlocking compound onto the bolts (**Figure 34**). Tighten the bolt to 12 N•m (106 in.-lb.).

18. Install the clutch assembly as described under *Clutch (External Components)* in Chapter Six.

Inspection

1. Inspect the drive chain guide (**Figure 53**) where the drive chain runs for wear or damage. Replace if necessary.

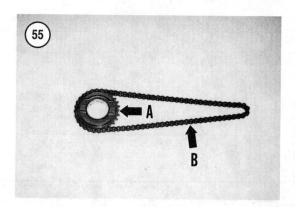

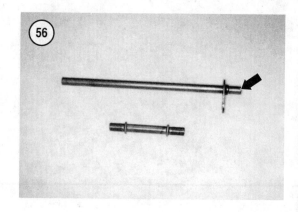

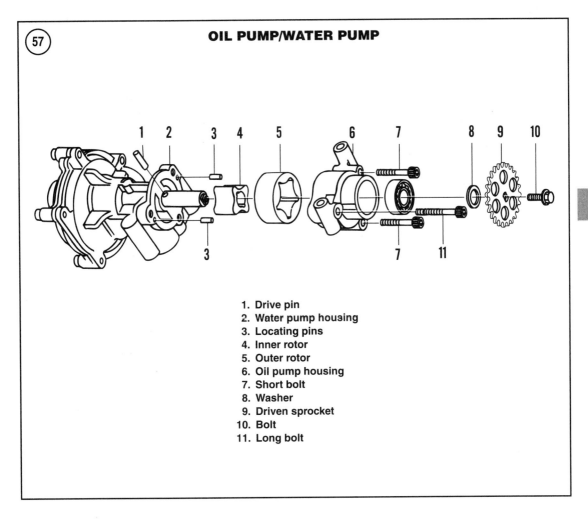

OIL PUMP/WATER PUMP

1. Drive pin
2. Water pump housing
3. Locating pins
4. Inner rotor
5. Outer rotor
6. Oil pump housing
7. Short bolt
8. Washer
9. Driven sprocket
10. Bolt
11. Long bolt

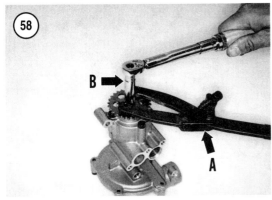

2. Inspect the inner bearing surface (**Figure 54**) of the driven sprocket for wear or damage. Replace the driven sprocket if necessary.

3. Inspect the driven sprocket teeth (A, **Figure 55**) for chipped or missing teeth. If damaged also check

the drive chain (B, **Figure 55**) for damage. Replace as necessary.

4. Make sure the oil delivery pipe (**Figure 56**) is clear. Clean out with solvent and air pressure if necessary.

Disassembly

Refer to **Figure 57**.

NOTE
When disassembling the oil pump, place the parts on a clean, lint-free cloth or towel.

1. Remove the oil pump/water pump assembly as described in this chapter.

2. Hold the driven sprocket with a flywheel holder (A, **Figure 58**) and loosen the bolt (B). Re-

move the bolt and the driven sprocket (**Figure 59**).

3. Remove the washer (**Figure 60**) from the bearing.

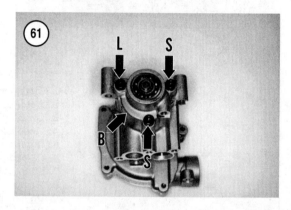

> *NOTE*
> *Two different length bolts (one long one and two short ones) secure the oil pump housing.*

4. Remove the long bolt (L, **Figure 61**) and two short bolts (S) securing the oil pump housing and remove the housing (B).

> *CAUTION*
> *Prior to removing the rotors, check for a punch mark on the outer surface. If there is no mark, make one with a scribe or punch. The rotors must be reinstalled into the body in the same direction.*

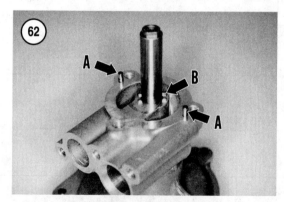

5. Remove the outer and inner rotors.

6. If still in place, remove the locating dowels (A, **Figure 62**).

7. Remove the drive pin (B, **Figure 62**) from the impeller shaft.

8. Further disassembly is not necessary unless the impeller shaft (**Figure 63**) requires replacement. To replace the impeller shaft, refer to *Water Pump* in Chapter Eleven.

9. Inspect the components as described in this section.

Assembly

1. Lubricate all components with clean engine oil.

2. If removed, install the water pump impeller shaft as described in Chapter Eleven.

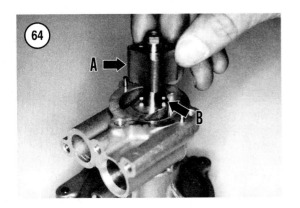

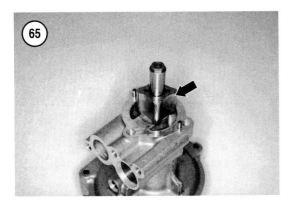

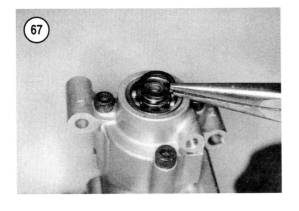

3. Install the locating dowels (A, **Figure 62**).

4. Install the drive pin (B, **Figure 62**) through the impeller shaft and center it.

CAUTION
Refer to the punch mark or scribe mark indicating the direction of the rotors. The rotors must be reinstalled in the same direction.

5. Install the inner rotor (A, **Figure 64**) onto the impeller shaft and seat it onto the drive pin (B). Push it down and ensure it is properly indexed onto the drive pin (**Figure 65**).

6. Install the outer rotor (**Figure 66**) onto the inner rotor and push it down until it is correctly seated.

7. Install the oil pump housing (B, **Figure 61**).

8. Install the long bolt (L, **Figure 61**) and two short bolts (S) securing the oil pump housing. Tighten the bolts to 10 N•m (88 in.-lb.).

9. Install the washer (**Figure 67**) onto the bearing.

10. Install the drive sprocket (**Figure 68**) and rotate it by hand. If there is any binding or roughness, disassemble the oil pump and check the parts for correct alignment.

11. Apply a medium-strength threadlocking compound onto the drive sprocket mounting bolt and install the (**Figure 59**).

12. Hold the driven sprocket with a flywheel holder (A, **Figure 58**) and tighten the bolt (B) to 15 N•m (133 in.-lb.).

13. Install the oil pump/water pump assembly as described in this chapter.

Inspection (Internal Components)

When measuring the oil pump components, compare the actual measurements to the specifications in **Table 1**. If either the outer or inner rotor is out of specification, they must be replaced as a set.

1. Clean all parts in solvent and dry with compressed air.

2. Inspect the inner surface of the housing (**Figure 69**) and the inner and outer rotor set (**Figure 70**) for wear, cracks or other damage.

3. Inspect the bearing (**Figure 71**). It should turn smoothly. If the bearing turns roughly or if there is any noise or other damage, replace it. Refer to Chapter One for typical bearing replacement procedures.

4. Make sure the openings in the housing are clear. Refer to **Figure 72** and **Figure 73**. Clean out with solvent and compressed air if necessary.

5. Inspect the oil pump driveshaft (**Figure 63**) and the drive pin hole in the shaft for cracks or other damage.

> *NOTE*
> *Proceed with Step 6 only if the previous visual inspection confirms that all parts are good. If any component is worn or damaged, replace the oil pump as an assembly.*

6. Install the outer rotor into the housing. Measure the side clearance between the outer rotor and housing with a flat feeler gauge (**Figure 74**).

7. Install the inner rotor into the housing and outer rotor. Measure the tip clearance between the inner rotor tip and the outer rotor with a flat feeler gauge (**Figure 75**).

8. Remove the rotors from the housing.

9. Inspect the driven sprocket teeth (**Figure 76**) for damage.

STARTER CLUTCH

The starter clutch is mounted onto the back of the clutch housing. To service the starter clutch, refer to *Starter Clutch* in Chapter Six.

CRANKCASE

The crankcase is made of die-cast aluminum and the two halves are matched as a set. The mating of the halves is a precision fit with no gasket at the joint, only a thin layer of gasket sealer. Handle the crankcase carefully during all service procedures to avoid damaging the bearing and mating surfaces.

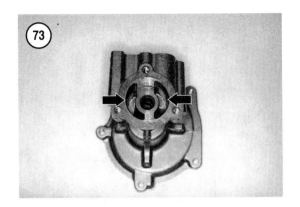

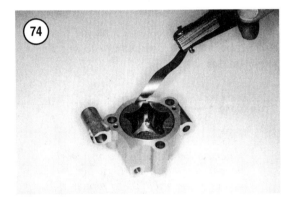

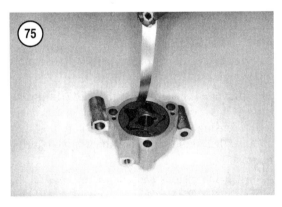

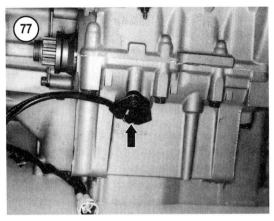

5

The cylinder block is an integral part of the upper crankcase. To remove the pistons, the engine must be removed from the frame and the crankcase halves split.

Crankcase Disassembly

1. While the engine is still in the frame, remove the following components as described in this and other related chapters:
   a. Camshafts.
   b. Clutch.
   c. Exterior gearshift mechanism.
   d. Alternator.
   e. Timing coil and rotor.
   f. Starter.
   g. Carburetor assembly or throttle body assembly.
   h. Oil cooler.
2. Remove the engine as described under *Engine* as described in this chapter.

> *CAUTION*
> *When servicing the engine on a workbench, support it on a rubber mat and/or wooden blocks to protect the gasket surfaces from damage.*

3. If still in place, unscrew and remove the speed sensor (**Figure 77**).
4. Remove the oil pan, oil strainer and pressure relief valve as described in this chapter.
5. Set the engine on the workbench so the lower crankcase half faces up.
6. Before removing the crankcase mounting bolts, draw an outline of each crankcase half on a piece of

thick cardboard. Then punch holes along the outline for the placement of each mounting bolt.

NOTE
*The number cast into the lower crankcase (**Figure 78**) indicates the bolt number used in Step 7.*

7. Follow the torque sequence in **Figure 79** starting with the largest number and decreasing to the lowest number. Loosen the bolts 1/4 turn at time in 3-4 stages until all bolts are loose.

8. Remove all of the bolts. Do not forget the washers on the ten main bearing bolts No. 1-10 shown in **Figure 79**.

9. Verify that all the lower crankcase bolts have been removed.

10. Tap the lower crankcase with a plastic mallet to help separate the case halves.

CAUTION
Do not pry the crankcase apart. The crankcase halves are machined as a set. If one is damaged, both will require replacement. If the halves will not separate, check for an unloosened bolt.

NOTE
When separating the crankcase halves, the crankshaft assembly, the transmission gear shafts, the shift drum and shift fork assembly will remain installed in the upper crankcase.

11. Lift the lower crankcase (**Figure 80**) off the upper crankcase. Turn the lower crankcase over immediately and be careful that the crankshaft main bearing inserts do not fall out. If any do, reinstall them immediately into their original position, if possible.

12. Remove the three dowel pins. Refer to **Figures 81-83**.

13. Remove the transmission shafts (A, **Figure 84**) as described in Chapter Seven.

14. Remove the internal shift mechanism as described in Chapter Seven.

15. Remove the crankshaft (B, **Figure 84**) as described under *Crankshaft* in this chapter.

16. Remove the main bearing inserts as described under *Crankshaft* in this chapter.

17. Remove the piston/connecting rod assemblies as described under *Piston and Connecting Rod Assembly* in this chapter.

Crankcase Assembly

CAUTION
When servicing the engine on a workbench, support it on a rubber mat and/or wooden blocks to protect the gasket surfaces from damage.

1. Clean and dry all of the crankcase mounting bolts.

2. Prior to assembly, coat all parts with assembly oil or engine oil.

3. If removed, install the crankshaft bearing inserts as described under *Crankshaft* in this chapter. If reusing old bearings, make sure that they are installed in the same location as noted during removal.

4. Install the pistons and connecting rods as described under *Piston/Connecting Rod Installation* in this chapter.

5. Install the crankshaft (B, **Figure 84**) as described under *Crankshaft* in this chapter.

6. Install the transmission shaft assemblies (A, **Figure 84**) as described under *Transmission* in Chapter Seven.

7. Install the internal shift mechanism as described in Chapter Seven.

8. Shift the transmission into neutral and spin the shafts by hand.

9. Install the three dowel pins. Refer to **Figures 81-83**.

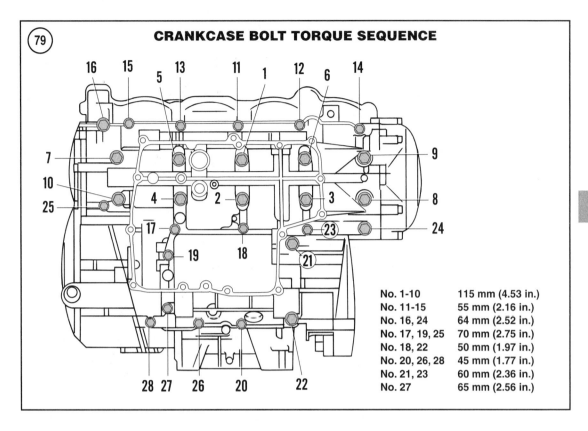

CRANKCASE BOLT TORQUE SEQUENCE

79

16 15 5 13 11 1 12 6 14

7

10

25

4 2 3 9

17 8

19 18 23 24

21

28 27 26 20 22

No. 1-10	115 mm (4.53 in.)
No. 11-15	55 mm (2.16 in.)
No. 16, 24	64 mm (2.52 in.)
No. 17, 19, 25	70 mm (2.75 in.)
No. 18, 22	50 mm (1.97 in.)
No. 20, 26, 28	45 mm (1.77 in.)
No. 21, 23	60 mm (2.36 in.)
No. 27	65 mm (2.56 in.)

80

82

81

83

10. Make sure both crankcase half sealing surfaces are clean and dry. Clean with aerosol contact cleaner and allow to dry.

> *NOTE*
> *Use a semi-drying liquid gasket sealer (ThreeBond Silicone Liquid Gasket 1207D or equivalent) to seal the crankcase. When selecting an equivalent, avoid thick and hard-setting materials.*

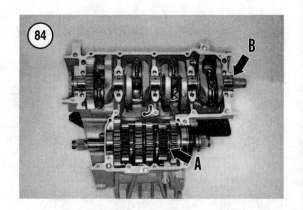

11. Apply a thin coating of gasket sealer to the lower crankcase sealing surfaces (**Figure 85**).

> *CAUTION*
> *Do not apply sealer to the curved bearing surfaces or oil passage areas, as it will restrict oil flow. Applying sealer to the bearing surfaces will change bearing clearance and cause crankshaft seizure.*

12. Position the lower crankcase (**Figure 80**) onto the upper crankcase. Set the front portion down first and lower the rear.

13. Join both halves and tap them together lightly with a plastic mallet. Check the gasket surface around the entire perimeter for any gaps.

14. If the crankcase halves do not fit together completely, note the following:

   a. Check that the transmission shafts are properly installed. Make sure the countershaft oil seal (**Figure 86**) is properly installed and seated.

   b. If the transmission is not the problem, separate the crankcase halves and investigate the cause of the interference.

> *CAUTION*
> *Crankcase halves should fit together without force. If the crankcase halves do not fit together completely, do not attempt to pull them together with the crankcase bolts. Do not risk damage by trying to force the halves together.*

> *NOTE*
> *Different size and length crankcase mounting bolts are used (**Figure 87**). When installing the mounting bolts, refer to the identification marks made during disassembly.*

15. Apply clean engine oil to the bolt threads and to the bolt head seating surfaces.

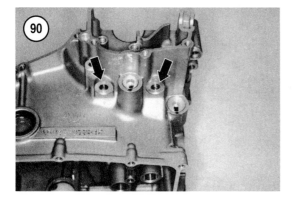

16A. On 1998-1999 models, install and tighten the 9-mm main journal bolts and washers (**Figure 88**) in two to three steps in a crisscross pattern. Start with the center two bolts, work to the outside and tighten to 32 N•m (23 ft.-lb.).

16B. On 2000-2003 models, perform the following:

    a. Install the 9-mm main journal bolts and washers (**Figure 88**).

    b. Tighten the ten bolts in two to three steps in a crisscross pattern. Start with the center two

bolts and work to the outside. Tighten to 15 N•m (133 in.-lb.).

    c. Loosen the bolts in reverse order of tightening.

    d. Tighten the ten bolts in two to three steps in a crisscross pattern. Start with the center two bolts and work to the outside and tighten to 15 N•m (133 in.-lb.).

    e. Use a torque angle gauge (**Figure 89**) and tighten the ten bolts an additional 45-50°, using the same crisscross pattern.

17. Refer to **Figure 79**, install the lower crankcase 6-mm and 8-mm bolts (**Figure 87**) and tighten finger-tight. Tighten these bolts in two to three steps and in a crisscross pattern to the following torque specifications:

    a. 6-mm shoulder bolts (No. 16, 24): 14 N•m (124 in.-lb.).

    b. 6-mm bolts (No. 11-15, 17-20, 23, 25-28): 12 N•m (106 in.-lb.).

    c. 8-mm bolts (No. 21, 22): 24 N•m (18 ft.-lb.).

18. Install a *new* O-ring on the speed sensor and apply engine oil to it.

19. Install the speed sensor (**Figure 77**) and tighten securely.

20. Install the oil strainer pressure relief valve and oil pan as described in this chapter.

21. Install the engine in the frame as described under *Engine* in this chapter.

Crankcase Cleaning

> *CAUTION*
> *Place the crankcase halves on wooden blocks or rubber mats and handle them carefully to avoid damaging the machined gasket surfaces.*

1. If still in place, unscrew and remove the speed sensor from the upper crankcase.

2. If still in place, unscrew and remove the neutral switch and washer from the upper crankcase.

3. Remove the main bearing inserts as described under *Crankshaft* in this chapter.

> *NOTE*
> *To ensure thorough cleaning of the crankcase, the oil passage sealing plugs must be removed.*

4. Remove the oil passageway sealing plugs and O-rings from each side of the lower crankcase. Refer to **Figure 90** and **Figure 91**.

5. Remove all sealer and gasket residue material from all crankcase gasket surfaces.

6. Check all bolts and threaded holes for stripping, cross-threading or deposit buildup. Clean out threaded holes with compressed air. Dirt buildup in the bottom of a hole may prevent the bolt from being accurately tightened to the correct torque specification. Replace damaged bolts and washers.

7. Inspect the crankcase threads for the oil cooler bolt (A, **Figure 92**) for damage.

8. Inspect machined surfaces for burrs, cracks or other damage. Repair minor damage with a fine-cut file or oilstone.

9. Inspect the crankcase oil cooler sealing surface (B, **Figure 92**) for burrs, cracks or other damage. This surface must provide a smooth surface for the oil cooler O-ring seal.

10. Inspect the oil filter mounting bolt threads (**Figure 93**) for damage. Replace the bolt if necessary.

11. Thoroughly clean the inside and outside of both crankcase halves and all oil passages with solvent. Refer to **Figure 94** and **Figure 95**.

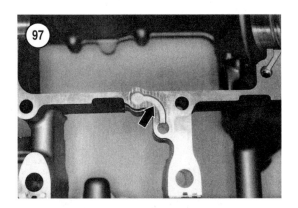

5

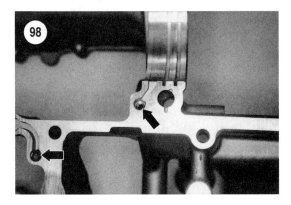

12. Make sure the oil pump openings (**Figure 96**) are clear.

13. Clean and dry the oil passages with compressed air. Refer to **Figure 97** and **Figure 98**. Make sure there is no sealer residue left in any of the oil passages. Use a small flashlight and visually check the oil passages for contamination.

14. Dry the case halves with compressed air. Make sure there is no solvent residue remaining in the cases, as it will contaminate the new engine oil.

15. Inspect the oil level gauge window (**Figure 99**) for signs of oil leakage. Replace if necessary.

16. Inspect both breather plates for damage and/or loose mounting bolts. Refer to **Figure 100** and **Figure 101**. Tighten the mounting bolts securely, if necessary.

17. Install a *new* O-ring seal (**Figure 102**) for the oil pump/water pump assembly receptacle.

18. Remove the oil delivery pipe (**Figure 103**) from the lower crankcase. Install three *new* O-rings and reinstall the pipe. Push it in and lock the tab into place in the crankcase notch (**Figure 104**).

19. Inspect the transmission mainshaft bearing (**Figure 105**). It should turn smoothly. If the bearing turns roughly or it there is any noise or other damage, replace it. Refer to Chapter One for typical bearing procedures.

20. Make sure the crankcase studs (**Figure 106**) are tight. Tighten securely if necessary.

21. Install a *new* O-ring onto the crankcase oil passage sealing plugs. Install the plugs into the lower crankcase and tighten securely. Refer to **Figure 90** and **Figure 91**.

22. Make sure the coolant passageways in the upper crankcase are clear. Refer to **Figure 107** and **Figure 108**. Clean out if necessary.

23. Apply a light coat of clean engine oil to the cylinder walls to prevent any rust formation.

Upper Crankcase/Cylinder Block Inspection

The cylinder block is an integral part of the upper crankcase half. When measuring the cylinder block, compare the actual measurements to the specifications in **Table 2**. Replace the crankcase assembly if the cylinder block if damaged or out of specification as described in this section. The cylinders cannot be bored. Yamaha does not offer oversize pistons for this engine.

1. Check the cylinder block mating surface for cracks and damage (A, **Figure 109**).

2. Check the top surface cylinder block for warp with a straightedge and flat feeler gauge (**Figure 110**). Check at different spots across the cylinder block.

NOTE
If the cylinder block is warped beyond the specification, refer service to a Yamaha dealership.

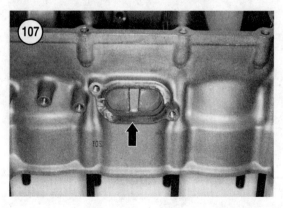

5

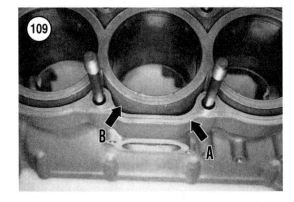

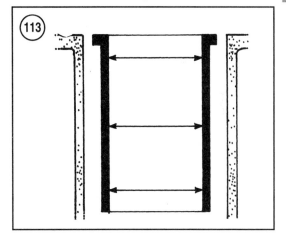

3. Check the cylinder walls (**Figure 111**) for deep scratches or signs of seizure or other damage.

4. Measure the cylinder bores with a bore gauge (**Figure 112**) or micrometer and telescoping gauge at the points shown in **Figure 113**. Measure in two axes-aligned with the piston pin and at 90° to the pin. If the bore diameter, taper or out-of-round for any cylinder exceeds the specifications, replace the crankcase assembly.

5. Make sure all of the coolant passages (B, **Figure 109**) surrounding the cylinders are clear. Clean out any debris or residue from the base of the coolant passages.

6. If the oil has been removed from the cylinder walls, lubricate each cylinder wall with clean engine oil to prevent the cylinder liners from rusting.

PISTON AND CONNECTING ROD ASSEMBLY

The crankcase must be separated to remove the pistons and connecting rods.

Piston/Connecting Rod Removal and Piston Ring Removal

The pistons, connecting rods and bearing inserts must be reinstalled in their original locations. Mark all parts as they are removed and store them in individual parts boxes or containers. Mark the parts with a 1, 2, 3 and 4 starting from the left side of the engine. The No. 1 cylinder is on the left side (**Figure 114**). The No. 1-4 marks relate to the left and right side of the engine as it sits in the frame, not as it sits on the workbench.

The pistons and connecting rods are removed as an assembly from the upper surface of the cylinder block.

1. Mark the cylinder number on the crown of each piston (**Figure 115**).

2. Measure the connecting rod big end side clearance. Insert a flat feeler gauge between a connecting rod big end and either crankshaft machined web. Record the clearance for each connecting rod and compare to the specification in **Table 2**. Note the following:

   a. If the clearance is greater than specified, replace the connecting rods and re-measure.

   b. If the clearance is greater than specified with the new connecting rods, replace the crankshaft.

3. Remove the connecting rod cap nuts (**Figure 116**).

> *CAUTION*
> *Keep each bearing insert in its original place in the crankcase, rod or rod cap. If reusing the original inserts, they must be installed exactly as removed to prevent rapid wear or bearing seizure.*

4. Remove the connecting rod caps (**Figure 117**) and bearing insert assemblies.

5. Place a piece of plastic tubing over the connecting rod bolts (A, **Figure 118**) to prevent the studs from damaging the cylinder bore surfaces when removing the piston/connecting rod assembly.

6. Lift the crankshaft (B, **Figure 118**) out of the upper crankcase half and remove it. Support the crankshaft on the workbench so that it cannot roll off.

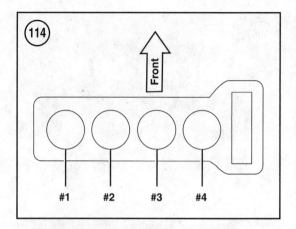

> *CAUTION*
> *Do **not** remove the connecting rod/piston assembly through the bottom of the cylinder. Doing so will allow the oil ring to expand into the gap between the cylinder liner and upper crankcase, which prevents piston removal without damaging the engine.*

7. Remove the piston and connecting rods out through the top of the cylinder block.

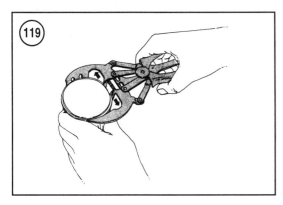

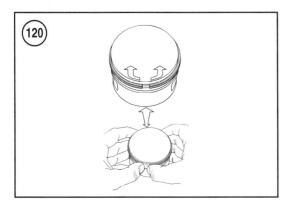

8. Remove the plastic tubing and reinstall the connecting rod caps and bearing inserts onto the connecting rods. Install the nuts and tighten finger-tight.

WARNING
The edges of the piston rings are very sharp. Be careful when handling them to avoid cutting fingers.

NOTE
*There are two ways to remove the rings: with a ring expander tool (**Figure 119**) or by hand (**Figure 120**). The ring expander tool is useful because it removes the rings without damaging them or scratching the piston. If this tool is not available, remove the rings by carefully spreading their end gaps with two thumbs and sliding them off the top of the piston.*

NOTE
The top and second rings have identification marks near their end gaps. These marks are not always visible on used rings. If the rings are going to be reused, mark them for location and direction during disassembly. On original equipment pistons and rings, the top ring is narrower than the second ring.

9. Remove the piston rings from the piston, starting with the top ring and working down.
10. Repeat to remove the remaining piston/connecting rod assemblies.

NOTE
If necessary, remove the pistons from the connecting rods as described in Steps 11-14.

11. Before removing the piston, hold the rod tightly and rock the piston. Any rocking motion (do not confuse with the normal sliding motion) indicates wear on the piston pin, rod bushing, pin bore or, more likely, a combination of all three.
12. Mark the piston, pin and connecting rod with its cylinder number so they will be reassembled into the same set.

WARNING
The piston pin clips are under spring tension and can fly out. Wear safety

glasses when removing them in the following step.

13. Remove the clip from each side of the piston pin bore (**Figure 121**) with a small screwdriver or small scribe. Hold a thumb over one edge of the clip when removing it to prevent the clip from springing out.

> *CAUTION*
> *Discard the piston clips. New clips must be installed during assembly.*

14. Push the piston pin out of the piston by hand. If the pin is tight, make the tool shown in **Figure 122** to remove it. Do not drive the piston pin out, as this may damage the piston pin, connecting rod or piston.
15. Lift the piston off the connecting rod.
16. Repeat Steps 12-15 for the remaining pistons.
17. Inspect the piston and connecting rod assemblies as described in this chapter.

Piston Inspection

When measuring the piston components, compare the actual measurements to the specifications in **Table 2**. Replace worn or damaged parts as described in this section.

1. Carefully clean the carbon from the piston crown (**Figure 123**) with a soft scraper or wire wheel. Large carbon accumulations reduce piston cooling and result in detonation and piston damage. Do not remove or damage the carbon ridge around the circumference of the piston above the top ring. If the pistons, rings and cylinders are found to be dimensionally correct and can be reused, removal of the carbon ring from the top of the piston or the carbon ridges from the cylinders will promote excessive oil consumption.

> *CAUTION*
> *Do not use a wire brush on piston skirts or ring lands. The wire brush removes aluminum and increases piston clearance. It also rounds the corners of the ring lands, which results in decreased support for the piston rings.*

> *CAUTION*
> *Make sure to renumber the piston crowns after performing Step 1. Used*

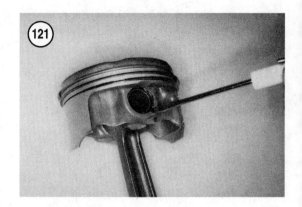

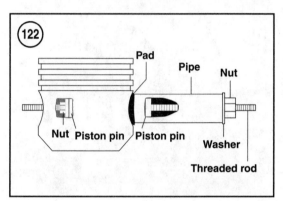

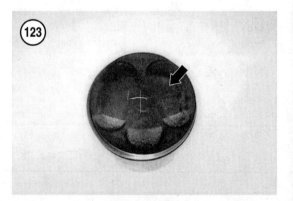

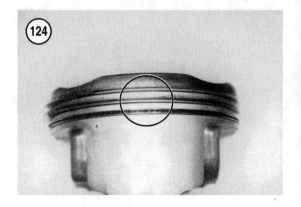

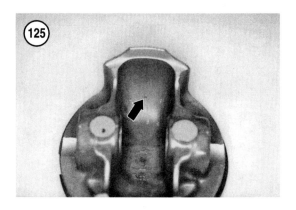

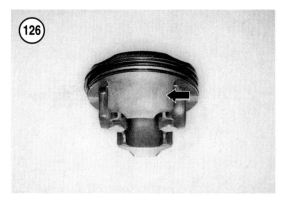

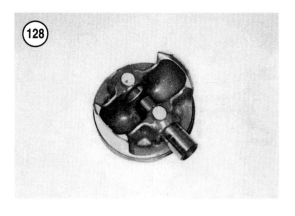

pistons must be reinstalled in their original cylinder.

2. After cleaning the piston, examine the crown. There should be no wear or damage. If the crown appears pecked or spongy-looking, also check the spark plug, valves and combustion chamber for aluminum deposits. If these deposits are found, the cylinder(s) is overheating due to a lean fuel mixture or preignition.

3. Examine each ring groove (**Figure 124**) for burrs, dented edges and excessive wear. Pay particular attention to the top compression ring groove, as it usually wears more than the other grooves. Because the oil rings are constantly exposed to oil, these rings and grooves wear little compared to compression rings and their grooves. If there is evidence of oil ring groove wear or if the oil ring assembly is tight and difficult to remove, the piston skirt may have collapsed due to excessive heat and is permanently deformed. Replace the pistons.

4. Check the oil control holes (**Figure 125**) in the piston for carbon or oil sludge buildup. Clean the holes by hand using a small diameter drill bit.

CAUTION
*The piston skirts have a special coating (**Figure 126**). Do not scrape or use any type of abrasive on this surface, as it will be damaged.*

5. Check the piston skirts (**Figure 126**) for cracks or other damage. If a piston(s) shows signs of partial seizure (bits of aluminum build-up on the piston skirts), replace the pistons and bore the cylinders, if necessary, to reduce the possibility of engine noise and further piston seizure.

NOTE
If the piston skirts are worn or scuffed unevenly from side to side, the connecting rod may be bent or twisted.

6. Inspect the piston pin clip grooves (**Figure 127**) in each piston for cracks, metal fatigue or other damage.

7. Insert the piston pin into the piston, rotate it (**Figure 128**) and check for ease of rotation.

8. Measure the piston-to-cylinder clearance as described under *Piston Clearance* in this section.

9. If damage or wear indicates piston replacement, select new pistons as described under *Piston Clearance* in this section.

Piston Pin Inspection

When measuring the piston pins, compare the actual measurements to the specifications in **Table 2**. Replace the piston pins if worn or damaged as described in this section.

1. Clean and dry the piston pins.

2. Inspect the piston pin for chrome flaking or cracks. Replace if necessary.

3. Measure the piston pin bore inside diameter (**Figure 129**) with a telescoping gauge.

4. Measure the piston pin outside diameter (**Figure 130**) with a micrometer.

5. Subtract the measurement made in Step 4 from the measurement made in Step 3 to determine piston pin oil clearance.

6. Repeat for each piston pin and piston.

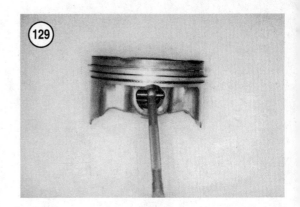

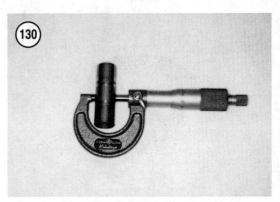

Piston Clearance

1. Make sure the piston and cylinder walls are clean and dry.

2. Measure the cylinder bore inside diameter as described under *Upper Crankcase/Cylinder Block Inspection* in this chapter. Record the largest bore diameter obtained.

3. Measure the piston outside diameter (**Figure 131**) at right angles to the piston pin with a micrometer. Measure at a distance 5 mm (0.20 in.) up from the bottom of the piston skirt.

4. Piston clearance is the difference between maximum piston diameter and minimum cylinder diameter. Subtract the largest piston diameter from the largest bore diameter to determine piston-to-cylinder clearance. If the piston clearance exceeds the service limit in **Table 2**, note the following:

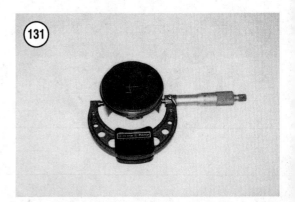

    a. If the bore diameter is still within specification, the pistons are worn. It may be possible to install new pistons (same size) to decrease the excessive piston-to-cylinder clearance. However, check carefully before deciding to use new pistons.

    b. If the bore diameter is out of specification, replace the crankcase assembly since the cylinders cannot be bored.

5. Repeat for the other pistons and cylinders.

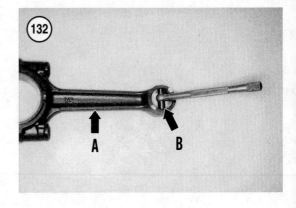

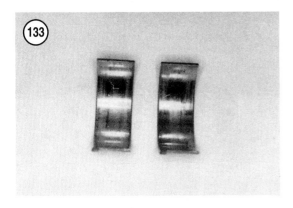

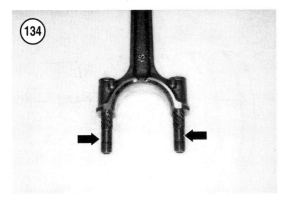

Connecting Rod Inspection

When measuring the connecting rods, compare the actual measurements to the specifications in **Table 2**. Replace connecting rods that are worn or damaged as described in this section.

1. Check each connecting rod (A, **Figure 132**) for obvious damage such as cracks and burns.

2. Check the piston pin bore for wear or scoring.

3. Measure the connecting rod piston pin bore inside diameter (B, **Figure 132**) with a snap gauge. Then measure the snap gauge with a micrometer and check against the service limit.

4. If the connecting rod straightness is in question, take the connecting rods to a Yamaha dealership or machine shop and have them checked for twisting and bending.

5. Examine the bearing inserts (**Figure 133**) for excessive wear, scoring or burning. They are reusable if in good condition. Make a note of the bearing color (if any) marked on the side of the insert if the bearing is to be discarded.

6. Remove the connecting rod bearing bolts (**Figure 134**) and check them for cracks or twisting. Replace bolts and nuts in pairs.

7. Check bearing clearance as described in this chapter.

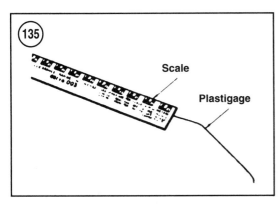

Connecting Rod Bearing Clearance Measurement

This section describes how to measure the connecting rod bearing clearance using Plastigage (**Figure 135**). Plastigage, available in different clearance ranges, is a material that flattens when pressure is applied to it. The marked bands on the envelope are then used to measure the width of the flattened Plastigage.

1. Clean and dry the crankshaft crankpins.

2. Before measuring the connecting rod bearing clearance, measure the outside diameter, taper and out-of-roundness of each crankpin with a micrometer (**Figure 136**). Note the following:

    a. To check for taper, measure at several places in a line along the crankpin. Record the measurements for each crankpin.

    b. To check for out-of-roundness, measure the crankpin diameter all the way around the crankpin. Record the measurements for each crankpin.

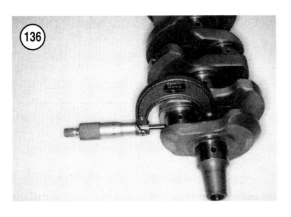

c. If the crankpins are tapered or out-of-round
   by more than 0.025 mm (0.001 in.), the crankshaft may have to be replaced. However, before doing so, consult with a Yamaha
   dealership on the appropriate service.

3. Install the crankshaft into the upper crankcase.
Turn the crankshaft so that none of the crankpin oil
holes face up.

4. Check each rod bearing insert (**Figure 137**) for
uneven wear, nicks, seizure and scoring. If the bearings do not show any visible wear, they can be used
with the Plastigage to check the bearing clearance.
If the crankpins are in good condition but the bearing inserts are too worn or damaged to be used with
the Plastigage, refer to *Connecting Rod Bearing Selection* in this section.

5. Clean the connecting rod and cap bearing surfaces and bearings inserts.

6. Install the rod bearing inserts in the connecting
rod and bearing cap. Make sure the anti-rotation
tabs on the bearing inserts lock into the rod and cap
notches correctly.

> *CAUTION*
> *Install the used bearing inserts in
> their original locations.*

7. Install all of the pistons and connecting rods as
described in this section.

8. Slide the piston down its bore and install the
connecting rod onto the crankshaft, being careful
not to damage the crankpin surface with the rod
bolts.

9. Place a piece of Plastigage (**Figure 135**) over the
connecting rod bearing journal parallel to the crankshaft (**Figure 138**). Do not place the Plastigage material over an oil hole in the crankshaft.

> *CAUTION*
> *Do not rotate the crankshaft while the
> Plastigage is in place. This will
> spread the Plastigage and cause an
> inaccurate reading.*

10. Match the identification code number on the
end of the cap with the mark on the rod and install
the cap.

> *CAUTION*
> *In Step 11A, if the tightening is inter-
> rupted between 20 N•m (15 ft.-lb.)
> and 36 N•m (25 ft.-lb.), stop and
> loosen the cap nuts to below 20 N•m,*

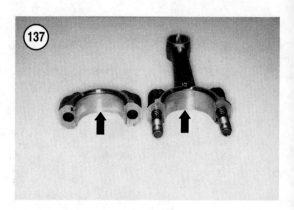

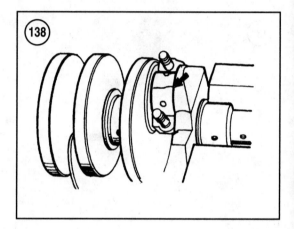

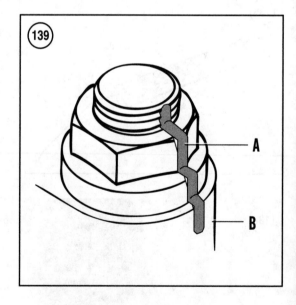

then start over until 36 N•m is
reached.

11A. On 1998-2001 models, apply a light coat of
oil to the connecting rod bolt threads and install the

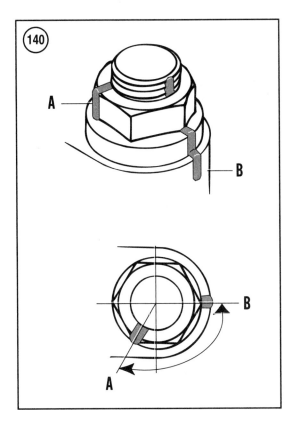

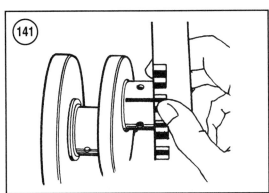

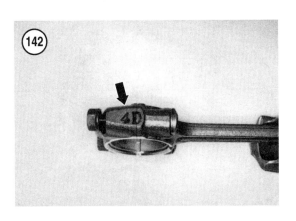

cap nuts. Tighten the cap nuts in one continuous motion to 36 N•m (27 ft.-lb.).

11B. On 2002-2003 models, perform the following:

    a. Apply a light coat of oil on the connecting rod bolt threads and install the cap nuts.

    b. Tighten the cap nuts in two to three stages to 20 N•m (15 ft.-lb.).

    c. Clean the connecting rod and nuts with an aerosol cleaner and dry.

    d. Make a straight-line mark on the connecting rod nut (A, **Figure 139**) and connecting rod (B).

    e. Use a torque angle gauge and tighten the connection rod nut an additional 120° as shown in **Figure 140**.

12. Loosen the nuts and carefully remove the cap from the connecting rod.

13. Place the envelope scale over the flattened Plastigage (**Figure 141**) to measure it. Compare the different marked bands on the envelope and find one that is closest to the width of the flattened Plastigage. The number adjacent to that band is the oil clearance indicated in millimeters or inches. Then measure the Plastigage at both ends of the strip. If the width of the Plastigage varies from one end to the other, the crankpin is tapered. Confirm with a micrometer. Refer to **Table 2** for the correct connecting rod bearing oil clearance. Record the clearance for each crankpin.

14. Remove the Plastigage strips from the main bearing journals with solvent or contact cleaner. Do not scrape the Plastigage off.

15. If the bearing oil clearance is greater than specified, select new bearings as described in the next section.

Connecting Rod Bearing Selection

Due to manufacturing tolerances, the connecting rod inside diameters (without bearing inserts) and the crankpin outside diameters are identified in four size groups. These size groups are listed in **Table 3**.

The connecting rod bearing journal inside diameter code number (1-5) is marked on the side of each connecting rod and cap (**Figure 142**).

The left side crankshaft web is marked with a series of numbers (1-5) that represents the outside diameter of each crankpin (Nos. 1-4) reading from left to right (**Figure 143**).

> *NOTE*
> *The letter on the left-hand end relates to the bearing insert in the left side (No. 1 cylinder) and so on, working across from left to right (**Figure 144**). Remember, the left side relates to the engine as it sits in the motorcycle's frame, not as it sits on the workbench. See **Figure 114** for cylinder numbers.*

1. To select new bearings, perform the following:
   a. Subtract the number on the crankshaft big end bearing journal number stamped on the crankshaft web (**Figure 145**) (No. 1) from the connecting rod number marked on the connecting rod (**Figure 142**) (No. 4).
   b. From the number achieved in sub-step a, subtract an additional 2.
   c. For *example*, 4-1-2=1, or a blue insert as listed in **Table 3**.
2. The connecting rod bearing inserts are color-coded on the side of the bearing insert (**Figure 146**).
3. Clean and oil the main bearing journals and insert faces.

Connecting Rod Selection

A numerical weight code (1-5) is marked on the side of the connecting rod and cap (**Figure 142**). When replacing a connecting rod, replace it with the same weight code as the original connecting rod.

Piston/Connecting Rod Assembly

1. Thoroughly clean the piston, piston pin and connecting rod assemblies. Dry with compressed air and place on a clean lint-free cloth until assembly.

> *CAUTION*
> *Do not install used piston pin clips during assembly. Piston pin clips are not designed to be reused. A weak clip that pops from its groove will cause severe cylinder damage.*

2. Install one piston pin clip in one piston pin bore groove of each piston. The pin clip ends must not

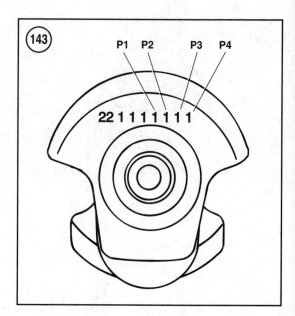

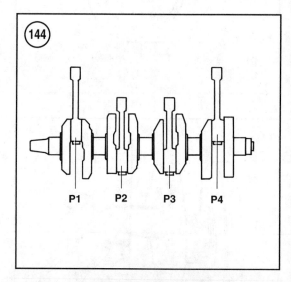

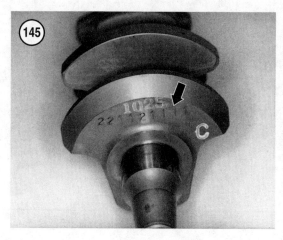

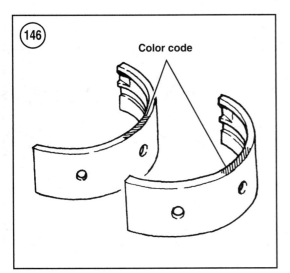

(146)

Color code

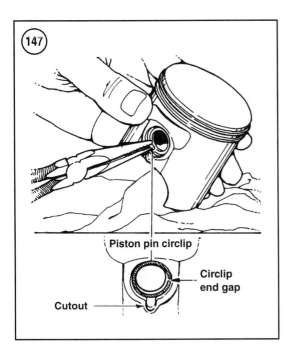

(147)

Piston pin circlip

Circlip end gap

Cutout

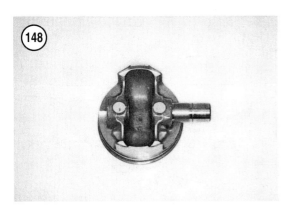

(148)

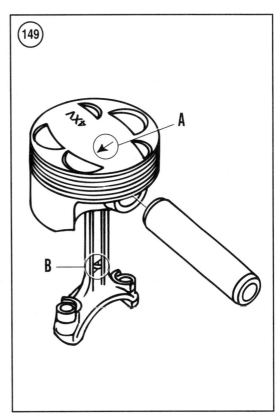

(149)

A

B

align with the cutout in the piston pin bore (**Figure 147**).

3. Apply molybdenum disulfide grease to the inside surface of the connecting rod's small end and to the piston pin outside surface.

4. Install the piston pin in the piston until its end extends slightly beyond the inside of the boss (**Figure 148**).

5. Install the pistons onto the connecting rods as follows:

   a. Refer to the reference numbers marked on the pistons and connecting rods during removal and install the pistons on their original connecting rods. If the cylinders were bored, match each piston with the correct cylinder.

   b. Install the pistons so the arrow mark (A, **Figure 149**) on each piston crown is on the same side as the *Y* mark on the side of the connecting rod (B, **Figure 149**).

   c. The *Y* mark will face toward the left side of the engine when the piston is properly installed in the cylinder block.

6. Line up the piston pin with the hole in the connecting rod. Push the piston pin into the connecting

rod (**Figure 150**). Do not use force during installation or damage may occur. Push the piston pin in until it clears the pin clip groove (**Figure 151**) or until it touches the clip on the other side of the piston.

7. After the piston is installed, recheck and make sure the piston and connecting rod are aligned as described in Step 5.

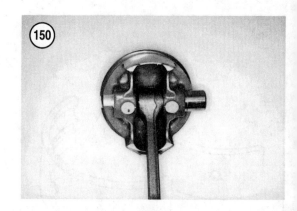

> *NOTE*
> *In the next step, install the second pin clip with the gap away from the notch in the piston. The first pin clip was installed during Step 2.*

8. Install the second piston pin clip (**Figure 152**) in the groove in the piston. Make sure both piston pin clips are correctly seated in the piston pin grooves.
9. Repeat Steps 1-8 for the remaining three pistons.
10. Install the piston rings as described in this chapter.
11. Install the piston/connecting rod assemblies as described in this chapter.

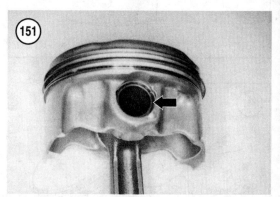

Piston Ring Inspection

> *WARNING*
> *The piston ring edges are sharp. Be careful when handling them.*

1. Carefully remove all carbon buildup from the ring grooves with a broken piston ring. Do not gouge the groove or remove any aluminum. Inspect the grooves carefully for burrs, nicks or broken and cracked lands. Replace the piston if necessary.

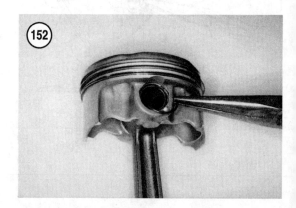

> *CAUTION*
> *Do not use a wire brush on piston skirts or ring lands. The wire brush removes aluminum and increases piston clearance. It also rounds the corners of the ring lands, which results in decreased support for the piston rings.*

2. Roll each ring around its piston groove as shown in **Figure 153** to check for binding. If there is any binding, check the ring groove and piston for damage.
3. Place each piston ring, one at a time, into the bottom of its cylinder, and square it in the bore with the piston. Measure the gap with a flat feeler gauge (**Figure 154**) and compare it to the specifications in

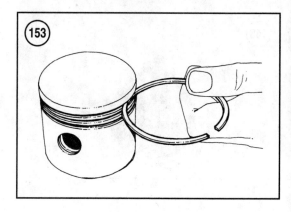

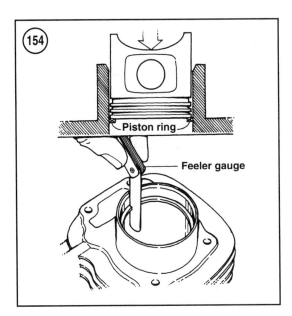

154

Piston ring

Feeler gauge

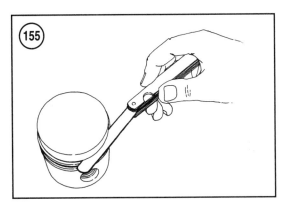

155

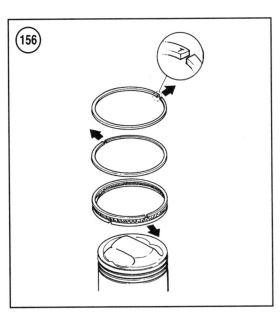

156

Table 2. If the gap is greater than specified, replace the piston rings.

NOTE
When checking the oil ring assembly, measure the end gap of the upper and lower side rails. Do not measure the oil spacer.

4. When installing new rings, measure their end gap as described in Step 3 and compare to the specifications in **Table 2**. If the end gap is greater than specified, the cylinder may be worn excessively. Check the cylinder inside diameter as described under *Cylinder Block Inspection* in this chapter.

5. Measure piston ring side clearance as follows:
   a. Install the top and second compression rings as described under *Piston Ring Installation* in this section.
   b. Push the ring until its outer surface is flush with the piston and measure the clearance with a flat feeler gauge (**Figure 155**).
   c. Compare the clearance to the specifications in **Table 2**. If the clearance is greater than specified, replace the piston rings.
   d. If using new rings, measure the side clearance of the rings and compare to the specifications in **Table 2**. If the clearance is greater than specified, the piston ring lands are worn excessively. Replace the pistons.
   e. Repeat for each piston and compression ring.

6. If new rings are installed, the cylinders must be very carefully honed (brush-type hone) for the new rings to seat. Refer this process to a Yamaha dealership or a motorcycle service shop. After completed, check the end gap of each ring (Step 3) and compare to the specifications in **Table 2**.

Piston Ring Installation

1. Thoroughly clean the pistons and piston rings and dry with compressed air.

2. When installing the piston rings, note the following:
   a. When installing the original piston rings, refer to the reference numbers marked on the piston rings during removal and install the piston rings in their original positions.
   b. When installing new piston rings, identify the rings as shown in **Figure 156**.

5

c. The top and second rings have identification marks near the end gap (**Figure 156**). These marks must face up when the rings are installed on the piston. On original equipment piston rings, the top ring is narrower than the second.

> *NOTE*
> *When installing aftermarket piston rings, follow the manufacturer's directions regarding ring identification and installation.*

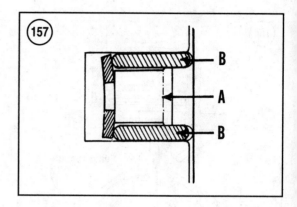

3. Install the oil spacer first (A, **Figure 157**), then both side rails (B). The original equipment oil ring side rails do not have top and bottom designations and can be installed either way. If reassembling used parts, install the side rails as they were removed.

> *NOTE*
> *There are two ways to install the rings: with a ring expander tool (**Figure 158**) or by hand (**Figure 159**). The ring expander tool is useful because it installs the rings without damaging them or scratching the piston. If this tool is not available, install the rings by carefully spreading their end gaps by hand and sliding them on the top of the piston.*

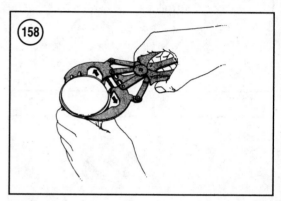

4. Install the second and top compression rings.

> *NOTE*
> *The top compression ring is narrower than the second compression ring.*

5. Make sure the rings are seated completely in their grooves all the way around the piston and that the end gaps are distributed around the piston, as shown in **Figure 160**. It is important that the ring gaps are not aligned with each other when installed to prevent compression pressures from escaping past them during initial start-up.

Piston/Connecting Rod Installation

The pistons, connecting rods and bearing inserts must be reinstalled in their original cylinder number locations. Refer to **Figure 161** for cylinder numbers.

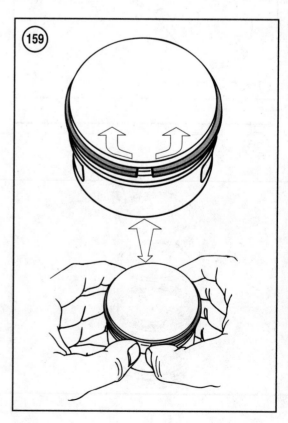

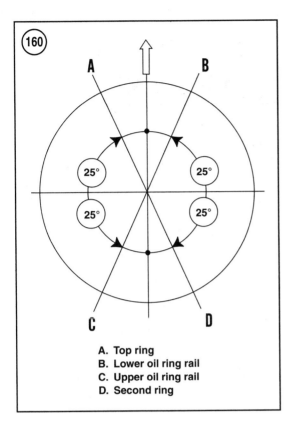

A. Top ring
B. Lower oil ring rail
C. Upper oil ring rail
D. Second ring

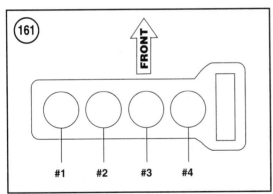

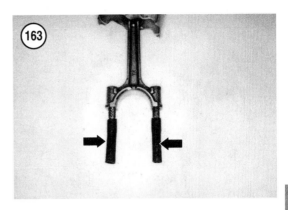

1. Install the piston rings onto the pistons as described in this chapter.

2. Clean the cylinder bores. Apply clean engine oil to the cylinder walls.

3. Place the upper crankcase on supports to allow room for the connecting rods to protrude through the bottom of the crankcase (**Figure 162**).

4. Clean and assemble the piston/connecting rod assemblies as described in this chapter.

5. Place a piece of plastic tubing over the connecting rod bolts (**Figure 163**) to prevent the studs from damaging the cylinder bore surfaces when installing the piston/connecting rod assembly.

CAUTION
Do not install the connecting rod/piston assembly through the bottom of the cylinder. Doing so will allow the oil ring to expand into the gap between the cylinder liner and upper crankcase, which prevents piston installation without damaging the engine.

6. Make sure the piston ring end gaps are not lined up with each other. They must be staggered, as shown in **Figure 160**.

7. Lightly oil the piston rings with clean engine oil.

8. Install the pistons as follows:

 a. Lubricate the piston and the inside of a piston ring compressor with engine oil.

NOTE
It does not matter in which order the pistons are installed. In the following steps, the No. 1 piston is installed first.

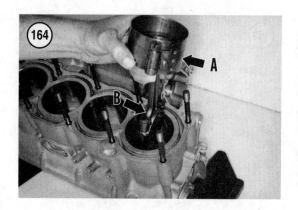

b. Align the piston assembly with the cylinder bore so the *Y* mark on the connecting rod faces toward the left side of the engine.

c. Install the piston ring compressor on the piston. Compress the piston rings (A, **Figure 164**) following the manufacturer's instructions.

d. Install the connecting rod and piston into the top of the cylinder bore (B, **Figure 164**).

CAUTION
The piston ring compressor must seat flush against the top surface of the upper crankcase bore when removing the piston through it. If there is a gap between the ring compressor and top surface, a ring will push out and catch on top of the cylinder. If the piston becomes tight when installing it, stop and inspect the piston rings. More than likely, one ring is caught between the ring compressor and cylinder block. If this happens, remove the piston assembly and reinstall the ring compressor onto it.

e. With the ring compressor located flush on top of the cylinder bore (**Figure 165**), slowly push the piston into the cylinder with a hammer handle until it is slightly below the top of the cylinder bore.

f. Remove the piston ring compressor and push the piston into the cylinder bore until it is flush with the top surface of the cylinder bore (**Figure 166**).

9. Repeat Step 8 for the remaining three pistons (**Figure 167**).

10. Turn the upper crankcase over and set it on the supports (**Figure 168**).

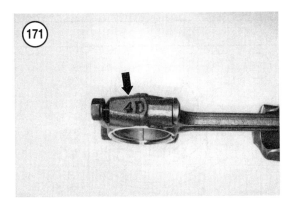

11. Apply a light, even coating of molybdenum disulfide grease to the connecting rod and cap bearing inserts and to the main bearing inserts (**Figure 169**) in the crankcase.

12. Move the No. 2 and No. 3 pistons to top dead center (TDC) (A, **Figure 170**).

13. Move the No. 1 and No. 4 pistons at bottom dead center (BDC).

14. Carefully install the crankshaft past the connecting rod bolts and into position in the upper crankcase (B, **Figure 170**).

15. Remove the pieces of hose from the connecting rod bolts.

16. Match the identification code number on the end of the cap with the mark on the rod (**Figure 171**) and install the caps (**Figure 172**).

17. Apply a light coat of oil to the connecting rod cap nut threads and seating surfaces and install the cap nuts (**Figure 173**).

18. Repeat Steps 16 and 17 for the remaining two connecting rods.

CAUTION
In Step 19A, if the tightening is interrupted between 20 N•m (15 ft.-lb.) and 36 N•m (25 ft.-lb.), stop and loosen the cap nuts to below 20 N•m, then start over until 36 N•m is reached.

19A. On 1998-1999 models, apply a light coat of oil to the connecting rod bolt threads and install the cap nuts. Tighten the cap nuts (**Figure 174**) in one continuous motion to 36 N•m (27 ft.-lb.).

19B. On 2000-2003 models, perform the following:

   a. Apply a light coat of oil on the connecting rod bolt threads and install the cap nuts.

5

b. Tighten the cap nuts in two to three stages to 20 N•m (15 ft.-lb.).

c. Clean the connecting rod and nuts with an aerosol cleaner and dry.

d. Make a straight-line mark on the connecting rod nut (A, **Figure 175**) and connecting rod (B).

e. Use a torque angle gauge and tighten the connection rod nut an additional 120° as shown in **Figure 176**.

20. When all the pistons and rods are installed and the nuts tightened to the specified torque, rotate the crankshaft several complete revolutions to make sure it turns smoothly.

21. Recheck the big end side clearance as described under *Piston/Connecting Rod Removal* in this section.

CRANKSHAFT

Crankshaft Removal

1. Disassemble the crankcase as described under *Crankcase* in this chapter.

> *CAUTION*
> *Keep each bearing insert in its original place in the crankcase, rod or rod cap. If the engine is reassembled with the original inserts, they must be installed exactly as removed to prevent rapid wear or engine seizure.*

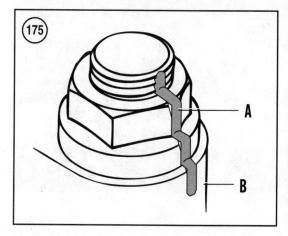

2. Remove the connecting rod cap nuts (**Figure 173**).

3. Remove the four connecting rod caps (**Figure 172**) and bearing inserts.

4. Install a piece of hose over the connecting rod bolts to prevent the rod bolts from damaging the crankshaft journal and cylinder bore surfaces when removing the crankshaft assembly. Repeat for each piston/rod assembly.

5. Lift the crankshaft (**Figure 177**) out of the upper crankcase half and remove it. Support the crankshaft on the workbench so that it cannot roll off.

6. If necessary, remove the pistons and connecting rods as described under *Piston and Connecting Rod Assembly* in this chapter.

> *NOTE*
> *In Step 7, the bearings are identified as Nos. 1-5 from left to right. The left*

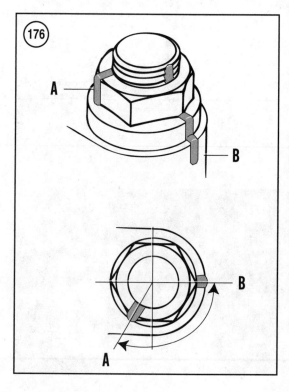

side of the engine refers to it as it sits in the frame, not as it sits on the workbench.

7. Remove the bearing inserts as follows:

    a. Remove the main bearing inserts from the upper (**Figure 178**) and lower (**Figure 179**) crankcase halves.

    b. Mark the backs of the bearing inserts from left to right with a 1, 2, 3, 4 or 5 and U (upper) or L (lower).

8. Inspect the crankshaft and main bearings as described in this chapter.

Crankshaft Installation

1. Clean the crankshaft in solvent and dry it thoroughly with compressed air. Make sure to remove all solvent residue from the oil holes.

2. Place the upper crankcase half upside down on a workbench.

> *CAUTION*
> *If the piston/connecting rod assemblies are installed, install a hose guide over each connecting rod bolt, or place a piece of duct tape on the rod bolt, to prevent them from damaging the crankpin journals.*

3. Install the upper (**Figure 178**) main bearing inserts in the upper crankcase case half. Make sure the anti-rotation tabs on the bearing inserts lock into the case notches correctly (**Figure 180**).

4. Install the lower (**Figure 179**) main bearing inserts in the lower crankcase case half. Make sure the anti-rotation tabs on the bearing inserts lock into the case notches correctly.

> *CAUTION*
> *Used bearing inserts must be installed in their original locations.*

5. Install the crankshaft (**Figure 177**) into the upper crankcase.

6. Install the connecting rods onto the crankshaft as described in this chapter.

7. Assemble the crankcase as described in this chapter.

Crankshaft Inspection

1. Clean the crankshaft (**Figure 181**) thoroughly with solvent. Clean the oil holes (A, **Figure 182**) with rifle cleaning brushes; flush thoroughly and dry with compressed air. Lightly oil all oil journal surfaces immediately to prevent rust.

2. Inspect each main bearing journal and crankpin journal (**Figure 183**) for scratches, ridges, scoring, nicks and other damage.

3. Inspect the primary drive gear teeth (**Figure 184**). If damaged, the crankshaft must be replaced. Also check the clutch outer housing gear teeth (**Figure 185**), as they may also be damaged.

4. Inspect the crankshaft flywheel taper (B, **Figure 182**) for scoring or damage.

5. Inspect the threaded hole (**Figure 186**) for the timing coil rotor mounting bolt for damage.

6. Check the crankshaft for bending. Mount the crankshaft in the crankcase and rotate it one full turn with a dial gauge contacting the center journal (**Figure 187**). Actual runout is half the reading shown on the gauge. If the runout exceeds the service limit in **Table 2**, replace the crankshaft.

Crankshaft Main Bearing
Clearance Measurement

This section describes how to measure crankshaft main bearing clearance using Plastigage. Plasti- gage, available in different clearance ranges, is a material that flattens when pressure is applied to it. The marked bands on the envelope are used to measure the width of the flattened Plastigage.

1. Clean and dry the crankshaft main bearing journals.

2. Before measuring the crankshaft main bearing clearance, measure the outside diameter, taper and out-of-roundness of each main bearing journal (**Figure 188**) with a micrometer. Note the following:

    a. To check the main bearing journal for wear, measure the journal at several places with a micrometer. Subtract the largest diameter from the standard diameter to determine the minimum amount of wear.

    b. To check for taper, measure at both ends of a main bearing journal. Do not measure where the radius connects the crank web to the main

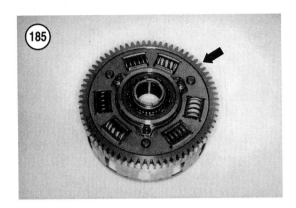

bearing journal. Subtract the smallest diameter from the largest diameter to obtain the maximum amount of taper. Record the measurements for each main bearing journal.

c. To check for out-of-roundness, measure the main bearing journal diameter at different places around the journal. Record the different measurements for each crankpin. Subtract the smallest diameter from the largest diameter to determine the maximum out-of-round.

d. If the main bearing journal is tapered or out-of-round by more than 0.025 mm (0.001 in.), the crankshaft may have to be replaced. However, before doing so, consult with a Yamaha dealership on the appropriate service.

3. Clean all of the bearing surfaces of the insert in the upper and lower crankcases.

4. Clean and dry each main bearing insert.

CAUTION
There must be no dirt, lint or other material on the bearing bores or bearing inserts. If these parts are not clean, an incorrect bearing clearance reading may be obtained. This may result in the installation of the incorrect size bearings, leading to bearing seizure and engine damage.

5. Check each main bearing insert for uneven wear, nicks, seizure and scoring. If the bearings do not show any visible wear, they can be used with the Plastigage to check the main bearing clearance. If the main bearing journals are in good condition but the bearing inserts are too worn to be used with the Plastigage, refer to *Crankshaft Main Bearing Selection* in this section.

NOTE
The bearing inserts must be installed in their original operating position.

6. Install the upper (**Figure 178**) and lower (**Figure 179**) main bearing inserts into the upper and lower crankcase halves. Make sure the anti-rotation tabs on the bearing inserts lock into the case notches correctly (**Figure 180**).

7. Place the upper and lower crankcase halves upside down on a workbench.

NOTE
If the piston/connecting rod assemblies are installed, make sure hose

guides are placed over the connecting rod bolts. The hose guides will prevent the connecting rod bolts from damaging the main bearing journals when installing the crankshaft.

8. Install the crankshaft (**Figure 177**) into the upper crankcase.

9. Place a piece of Plastigage over each main bearing journal parallel to the crankshaft (**Figure 189**). Do not place the Plastigage over an oil hole in the crankshaft.

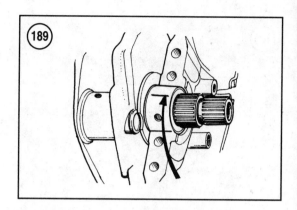

> *CAUTION*
> *Do not rotate the crankshaft while the Plastigage is in place. This will spread the Plastigage and cause an inaccurate reading (reduced oil clearance measurement).*

10. Position the lower crankcase onto the upper crankcase. Set the front portion down first and lower the rear. Join both halves and tap them together lightly with a plastic mallet. Do not use a metal hammer, as it will damage the case.

> *CAUTION*
> *Crankcase halves should fit together without force. If the crankcase halves do not fit together completely, do not attempt to pull them together with the crankcase bolts. Separate the crankcase halves and investigate the cause of the interference. Do not risk damage by trying to force the case together.*

11. Apply clean engine oil to the 9-mm bolt threads and to the bolt head seating surfaces.

12A. On 1998-1999 models, install and tighten the 9-mm main journal bolts and washers (**Figure 190**) in two to three steps in a crisscross pattern. Start with the center two bolts and work to the outside and tighten to 32 N•m (23 ft.-lb.).

12B. On 2000-2003 models, perform the following:

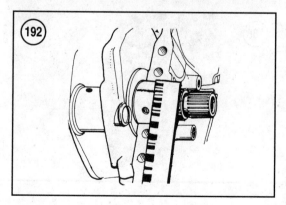

   a. Install the 9-mm main journal bolts and washers (**Figure 190**).

   b. Tighten the ten bolts in two to three steps in a crisscross pattern. Start with the center two bolts and work to the outside and tighten to 15 N•m (133 in.-lb.).

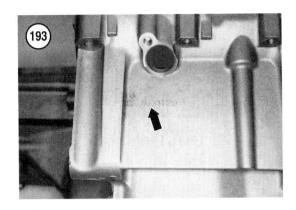

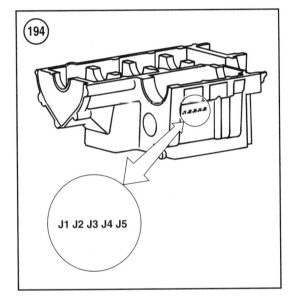

J1 J2 J3 J4 J5

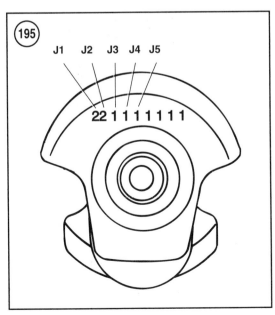

J1   J2   J3 J4 J5

22 1 1 1 1 1 1

c. Loosen the ten bolts in the reverse order of tightening.

d. Tighten the ten bolts in two to three steps in a crisscross pattern. Start with the center two bolts and work to the outside and tighten to 15 N•m (133 in.-lb.).

e. Use a torque angle gauge and tighten the ten bolts an additional 45-50° (**Figure 191**), using the same crisscross pattern.

13. Starting at the outside and working in, loosen the lower crankcase 9-mm bolts in two to three stages in a crisscross pattern. Then remove the bolts, starting from the inside and working out.

14. Carefully remove the lower crankcase half.

15. Place the envelope scale over the flattened Plastigage (**Figure 192**) and compare the different marked bands with the flattened Plastigage. Find the band that is closest to the width of the flattened Plastigage. The number adjacent to that band is the oil clearance. Then measure the Plastigage at both ends of the strip. If the width of the Plastigage varies from one end to the other, the main bearing journal is tapered. Confirm with a micrometer. Refer to **Table 2** for the main bearing oil clearance specification. Record the clearance for each journal.

16. Remove the Plastigage strips from the main bearing journals with solvent or contact cleaner. Do not scrape the Plastigage off.

17. If the bearing oil clearance is greater than specified, select new bearings as described in the next section.

Crankshaft Main Bearing Selection

The lower crankcase is marked with a series of numbers that represent the inside diameter of each crankcase main bearing bore (Nos. 1-5) from left to right. Refer to **Figure 193** and **Figure 194**. The first number of the five is for the left side journal (No. 1) and reading across from left to right (**Figure 194**).

The left side crankshaft web is marked with a series of five numbers (Nos. 1-5) that represents the outside diameter of each main crankpin (Nos. 1-5) reading across from left to right (**Figure 195**).

NOTE
The letter on the left-hand end relates to the main bearing insert in the left side (No. 1 cylinder) and so on, work-

ing across from left to right (Figure 196). Remember, the left side relates to the engine as it sits in the motorcycle's frame, not as it sits on the workbench. See Figure 197 for cylinder numbers.

1. To select new bearings, perform the following:
   a. Subtract the number on the crankshaft big end bearing journal number stamped on the crankshaft web (**Figure 198**) (No. 1) from the crankcase main bearing number marked on the lower crankcase (**Figure 194**).
   b. From the number achieved in substep a, subtract an additional 2.
   c. For *example*, 6-2-2=2, or the pink/black insert as listed in **Table 4**.
2. The main bearing inserts are color-coded on the side of the bearing insert (**Figure 199**).
3. Clean and oil the main bearing journals and insert faces.
4. After new bearings have been installed, recheck clearance by repeating this procedure. If a clearance is incorrect, measure the crankshaft journal with a micrometer. Replace the crankshaft if a crankshaft outside diameter dimension is beyond the specified range of the stamped number code. If the crankshaft is within specification, the crankcase is worn and requires replacement.
5. Clean and oil the main bearing journals and bearing inserts.

BREAK-IN PROCEDURE

If the rings were replaced, new pistons installed or major lower end work performed, break in the engine just as though it were new. The performance and service life of the engine depends greatly on a careful and sensible break-in.

For the first 600 miles (1000 km), engine rpm should not exceed 4000 rpm. Prolonged steady running at one speed, no matter how moderate, is to be avoided, as well as hard acceleration.

Increase engine speed by 1000 rpm between 600 miles (1000 km) and 1000 miles (1600 km). Engine speed should be frequently varied during this mileage interval. Do not exceed 5000 rpm.

At 1000 miles (1600 km), full throttle operation can be used. However, never exceed the tachometer redline zone at any time, as this may damage the engine.

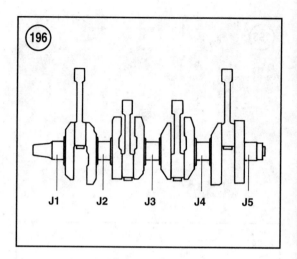

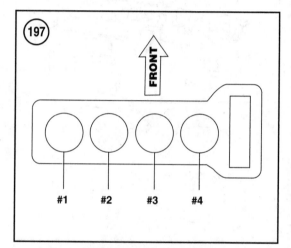

During engine break-in, oil consumption will be higher than normal. It is therefore important to frequently check and correct oil level. At no time during the break-in or later should the oil level be allowed to drop below the lower line on the oil level window. If the oil level is low, the oil will become

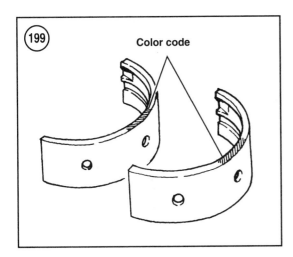

Color code

overheated, resulting in insufficient lubrication and increased wear.

600 Mile (1000 km) Service

It is essential that the oil and oil filter be changed after the first 600 miles (1000 km). In addition, it is a good ideal to change the oil and filter at the completion of the break-in (about 1500 miles [2414 km]) to ensure that all of the particles produced during the break-in are removed from the lubrication system. The minimal added expense may be considered a small investment that will pay off in increased engine life.

Table 1 OIL PUMP SERVICE SPECIFICATIONS

Item	Standard mm (in.)	Service limit mm (in.)
Side clearance	0.03-0.08 (0.001-0.003)	–
Tip clearance	0.09-0.15 (0.004-0.006)	–

Table 2 ENGINE LOWER END SPECIFICATIONS

Item	Standard mm (in.)	Service limit mm (in.)
Crankshaft		
Big end side clearance	0.160-0.262 (0.0063-0.0103)	–
Crankpin oil clearance	0.031-0.055 (0.0012-0.0022)	–
Journal taper and out-of-round	–	0.025 (0.001)
Main bearing oil clearance	0.029-0.053 (0.0011-0.0021)	–
Cylinder		
Bore	74.00-74.010 (2.9134-2.9138)	–
Taper	–	0.05 (0.0020)
Out of round	–	0.05 (0.0020)
Cylinder block top surface warp	–	Max. 0.1 (0.004)
Piston		
Outside diameter*	73.955-73.970 (2.9118-2.9122)	–
Piston-to-cylinder clearance	0.03-0.055 (0.001-0.002)	0.12 (0.005)
Piston-pin bore		
inside diameter	17.002-17.013 (0.6694-0.6698)	–
Piston pin outside diameter	16.991-17.000 (0.6689 0.6693)	–
Piston pin oil clearance	0.002-0.022 (0.00008-0.00087)	0.072 (0.0028)
Piston rings		
Ring-to-groove clearance		
Top	0.030-0.065 (0.0012-0.0026)	–
Second	0.015-0.050 (0.0006-0.0020)	0.08 (0.003)
Ring end gap (installed)		
Top		
1998-2001 models	0.19-0.31 (0.007-0.012)	–
2002-2003 models	0.32-0.44 (0.013-0.017)	–
(continued)		

Table 2 ENGINE LOWER END SPECIFICATIONS (continued)

Item	Standard mm (in.)	Service limit mm (in.)
Piston rings (continued)		
Ring end gap (installed) (continued)		
Second		
1998-2001 models	0.30-0.45 (0.012-0.018)	–
2002-2003 models	0.43-0.58 (0.017-0.023)	–
Oil ring side rail	0.10-0.35 (0.004-0.014)	–
Ring thickness		
Top	0.90 (0.035)	–
Second	0.80 (0.031)	–
* Measured at a point 5 mm (0.2 in.) from the bottom of the piston shirt. See text for information.		

Table 3 CONNECTING ROD BEARING SELECTION

Connecting rod bearing number	Bearing rod insert color
-1	Violet
0	White
1	Blue
2	Black

Table 4 CRANKSHAFT MAIN BEARING SELECTION

Connecting rod bearing number	Bearing rod insert color
-1	Pink/violet
0	Pink/white
1	Pink/blue
2	Pink/black
3	Pink/brown

Table 5 ENGINE LOWER END TORQUE SPECIFICATIONS

Item	N•m	in.-lb.	ft.-lb.
Engine mounting fasteners			
1998-2001 models			
Left side, upper front bolt	40	–	30
Right side			
Upper front bolt	55	–	41
Upper front pinch bolt	24	–	18
Lower rear through bolt nut	55	–	41
Pinch bolts	24	–	18
Upper rear through bolt nut	55	–	41
2002-2003 models			
Left side, upper front bolt	45	–	33
Right side			
Primary upper front bolt	45	–	33
Secondary upper front bolt	45	–	33
Upper front pinch bolts	24	–	18
Lower rear through bolt nut	50	–	37
Upper rear through bolt nut	50	–	37
(continued)			

Table 5 ENGINE LOWER END TORQUE SPECIFICATIONS (continued)

Item	N•m	in.-lb.	ft.-lb.
Connecting rod cap nut	Refer to text		
Crankcase bolts[1]			
9 mm main journal bolts			
(bolts No. 1-10[2])			
1998-1999 models	32	–	23
2000-2003 models	Refer to text		
6 mm shoulder bolts[2]			
(bolts No. 16, 24)	14	124	–
6 mm bolts[2]			
(bolts No. 11-15, 17-20, 23, 25-28)	12	106	–
8 mm bolts[2]			
(bolts No. 21, 22)	24	–	18
Drive sprocket nut	85	–	63
Gearshift drum bearing and			
shift shaft set bolt	12	106	–
Camshaft chain tensioner			
pivot bolt	10	88	–
Oil baffle plate	10	88	–
Oil cooler bolt	35	–	26
Oil delivery pipe bolts	10	88	
Oil drain plug	43	–	32
Oil filter bolt	70	–	52
Oil gallery plug			
1998-2001 models	20	–	15
2002-2003 models	10	88	–
Oil level switch bolt	10	88	–
Oil pan bolts[3]	10	88	–
Oil pipe bolts	10	88	–
Oil pump/water pump			
Oil pump housing bolt	10	88	–
Drive chain cover bolt	12	106	–
Drive chain guide bolt	12	106	–
Driven sprocket bolt[3]	15	133	–
Oil strainer bolts[3]	10	88	–
Oil/water pump housing bolts[2]	10	88	–
Timing coil rotor bolt	60	–	44
Transmission mainshaft bolts	12	106	–
Water pump outlet pipe bolt	10	88	–

1. Refer to the procedure for bolt number locations.
2. Lubricate fasteners, threads and head seating surface with engine oil.
3. Apply a medium strength threadlock to the designated fastener threads.

5

CHAPTER SIX

CLUTCH AND EXTERNAL SHIFT MECHANISM

This chapter contains service procedures for the following components:

1. Clutch cover.
2. Clutch assembly.
3. Clutch cable.
4. Starter clutch assembly.
5. External shift mechanism.

Specifications are in **Table 1** and **Table 2** at the end of the chapter.

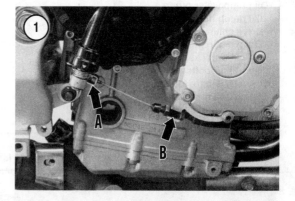

CLUTCH COVER

Removal/Installation

> *NOTE*
> *Some of the photos in this procedure are shown with the engine removed to better illustrate the steps.*

1. Remove the right side fairing panel and bottom cowl as described in Chapter Sixteen.

2. Drain the engine oil as described under *Engine Oil and Filter Change* in Chapter Three.

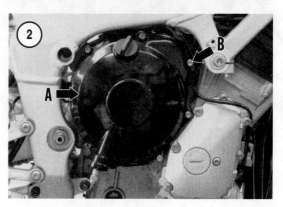

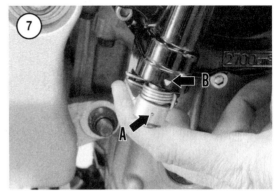

3. Disconnect the clutch cable from the clutch lifter lever (A, **Figure 1**) and the cable bracket (B) on the timing coil cover.

4. Using a crisscross pattern, loosen and then remove the bolts securing the clutch cover (A, **Figure 2**). Note the location of the timing coil electrical wire and clamp (B, **Figure 2**).

5. Remove the clutch cover and the gasket (**Figure 3**).

6. If loose, remove the two dowel pins (**Figure 4**).

7. Remove all gasket sealer residue from the crankcase and cover mating surfaces.

8. If removed, install the two dowel pins (**Figure 4**).

9. Make sure the teeth on the lifter piece are positioned correctly toward the rear (**Figure 5**) to ensure correct engagement with the clutch lifter arm gear (**Figure 6**).

10. Apply a light coat of gasket sealer to the entire perimeter of the clutch cover.

11. Install the *new* gasket (**Figure 3**).

12. Install the clutch cover while turning the clutch lifter arm clockwise to engage the lifter arm teeth with the lifter piece teeth.

13. Push the clutch cover (A, **Figure 2**) up against the crankcase until it bottoms.

14. Install all bolts securing the clutch cover and tighten securely. Install the timing coil electrical wire and clamp (B, **Figure 2**) in the location noted in Step 4.

15. Tighten the clutch cover bolts to 12 N•m (106 in.-lb.).

16. Push the pull lever forward and make sure the punch mark on the lever (A, **Figure 7**) is aligned with the arrow on the clutch cover (B). Realign if necessary.

17. Connect the clutch cable onto the clutch lifter lever (A, **Figure 1**). Install the clutch cable bracket

and mounting bolts. Note the location of the timing coil electrical wire and clamp (**Figure 1**).

> *CAUTION*
> *Debris generated by burnt clutch plates contaminates the engine oil. If the clutch plates are burnt or damaged, replace them and change the engine oil and filter. This step is important, even though the engine may be between oil changes, to remove contaminants from the lubrication system.*

18. Refill the engine with oil as described in Chapter Three.

19. Install the bottom cowl and the right side fairing panel as described in Chapter Sixteen.

Release Mechanism
Removal/Inspection/Installation

The clutch release mechanism (**Figure 8**) is located in the clutch cover.

1. Remove the snap ring and washer (A, **Figure 9**) from the outer end of the shaft.

2. Remove the pull lever and spring (B, **Figure 9**).

3. Remove the snap ring and washer (**Figure 10**) from the inner end of the shaft.

4. Withdraw the shaft (**Figure 11**) from the clutch cover.

5. Inspect all parts (**Figure 12**) for wear or damage. Check the splines in the shaft and pull lever (**Figure 13**) for damage.

6. Install the shaft (**Figure 11**) into the clutch cover.

7. At the inner end of the shaft, install the washer and the snap ring (**Figure 10**). Make sure the snap ring is completely seated in the shaft groove.

8. Position the pull lever with the UP mark facing up and install the pull lever (**Figure 14**) onto the shaft.

9. Install the washer (**Figure 15**) and snap ring (**Figure 16**). Make sure the snap ring is completely seated in the shaft groove.

Oil Seal Replacement

1. Inspect the clutch cover for cracks or damage.

2. Carefully pry the oil seal out of the cover (**Figure 17**) with a flat blade screwdriver.

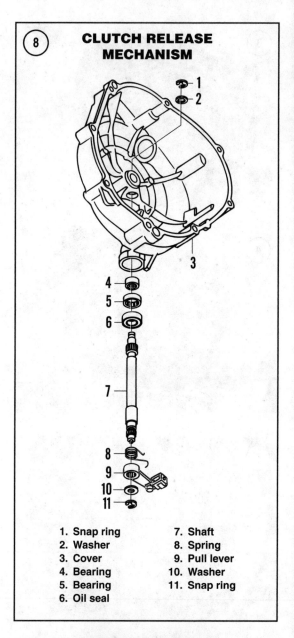

CLUTCH RELEASE MECHANISM

1. Snap ring	7. Shaft
2. Washer	8. Spring
3. Cover	9. Pull lever
4. Bearing	10. Washer
5. Bearing	11. Snap ring
6. Oil seal	

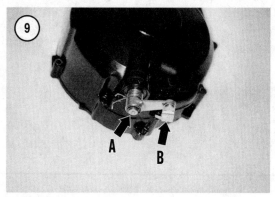

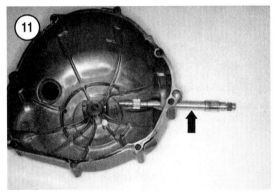

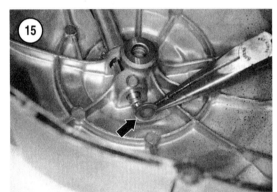

6

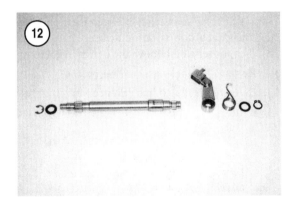

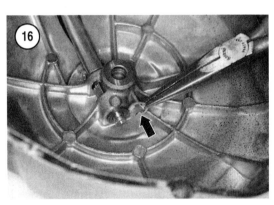

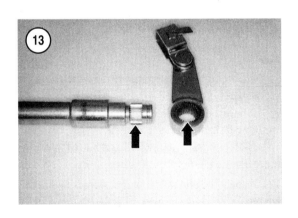

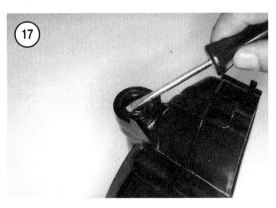

3. Inspect the bearing for damage. If necessary, re-place the bearing. Refer to Chapter One for typical bearing replacement.

4. Position the seal with the sealed side facing out.

5. Install the new bearing squarely in the cover opening. Select a driver or socket (**Figure 18**) with the outside diameter slightly smaller than the seal's outside diameter. Then drive the oil seal into the bore until it bottoms out.

CLUTCH

NOTE
These procedures are shown with the engine removed to better illustrate the steps.

Refer to **Figure 19**.

Removal

1. Remove the clutch cover as described in this chapter.

2. Remove the bolts securing the diaphragm spring retainer (**Figure 20**) and remove the retainer.

3. Remove the diaphragm spring (**Figure 21**).

4. Remove the diaphragm spring seat (**Figure 22**).

5. Remove the pressure plate (**Figure 23**) and clutch lifter piece. Remove the lifter piece (**Figure 24**) from the backside of the pressure plate.

CAUTION
The last friction discs A (next to the clutch hub) must be installed in the same location during assembly. Keep the parts in the order removed.

6. Remove the clutch plates and friction discs B (**Figure 25**) from the clutch hub.

7. Remove the wire retainer from the clutch hub as follows:

   a. Push up on the ends of the wire retainer (**Figure 26**) and release the ends from the hole in the clutch hub.

   b. Carefully remove the wire retainer from the clutch hub.

8. Remove the clutch disc and the friction disc A.

9. Remove the damper spring and the spring seat from the clutch hub.

10. Straighten the tab on the clutch nut lockwasher (**Figure 27**).

11A. If the engine is installed in the frame, shift the transmission into sixth gear. Have an assistant apply the rear brake.

CAUTION
When using the clutch holder in Step 11B, make sure to secure it squarely onto the clutch hub splines. If the clutch holder slips, release the pressure from the clutch locknut and repo-sition the clutch holder. If the clutch holder slips, it may damage the clutch hub splines.

11B. If the engine is removed from the frame, se-cure the clutch hub with a clutch holder (**Figure 28**), then loosen and remove the clutch locknut.

12. Remove the lockwasher (**Figure 29**).

13. Remove the clutch hub (**Figure 30**).

14. Remove the thrust washer (**Figure 31**) from the clutch housing.

CAUTION
In Step 15, after removing the clutch housing assembly, hold it with the starter clutch gear assembly facing up. If turned over the starter gear as-sembly will fall off of the backside of the clutch housing.

15. Pull straight out and remove the clutch housing assembly (**Figure 32**).

16. Remove the needle bearing (A, **Figure 33**) from the transmission shaft.

17. On 2002-2003 models, slide the washer off the transmission shaft.

18. Inspect the clutch assembly as described in this chapter.

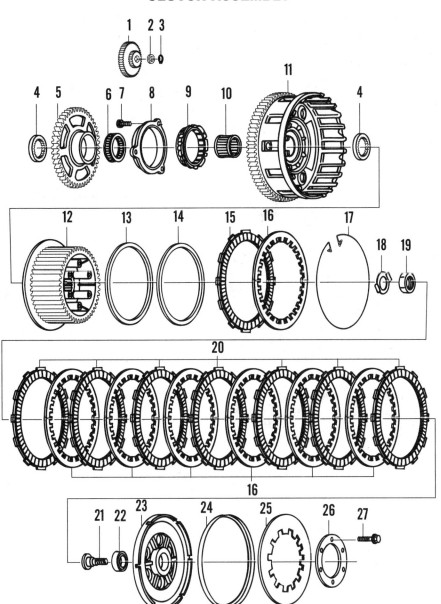

CLUTCH ASSEMBLY

6

1. Starter idle gear
2. Washer
3. Snap ring
4. Washer (2002-2003 models)
5. Starter gear
6. Needle bearing
7. Bolt
8. Retainer
9. Sprag clutch
10. Needle bearing
11. Clutch housing
12. Clutch hub
13. Damper spring seat
14. Damper spring
15. Friction disc A
16. Clutch plates
17. Wire retainer
18. Lockwasher
19. Nut
20. Friction discs B
21. Lifter piece
22. Bearing
23. Pressure plate and bearing
24. Diaphragm spring seat
25. Diaphragm spring
26. Diaphragm spring retainer
27. Bolt

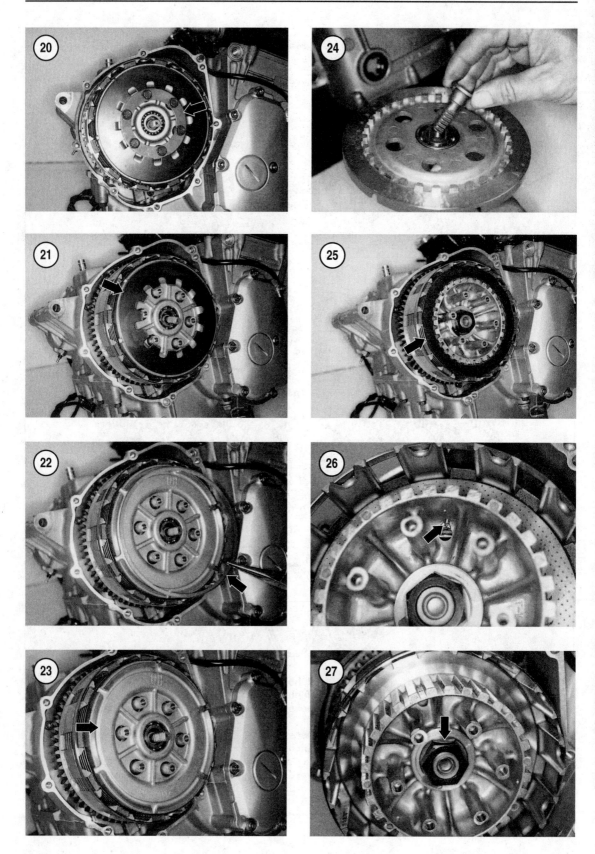

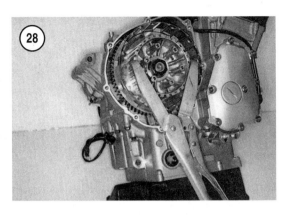

Installation

1. Coat clutch parts with engine oil before assembly.

2. If removed, install the starter gear assembly into the backside of the clutch housing (A, **Figure 34**).

3. On 2002-2003 models, install the washer onto the transmission shaft.

4. Install the needle bearing (A, **Figure 33**) onto the transmission shaft.

NOTE
Step 5 is necessary to ensure correct
engagement of the clutch outer hous-

*ing to the oil pump drive sprocket and
drive the oil pump/water pump.*

5. Install the clutch housing as follows:

  a. Rotate the oil pump drive sprocket so the raised bosses are located at the 12 and 6 o'clock positions as shown in B, **Figure 33**.

  b. Position the clutch outer housing so the two notches are also at the 12 and 6 o'clock positions as shown in B, **Figure 34**.

  c. Install the clutch housing over the mainshaft (**Figure 32**) and align the housing notches with the raised bosses on the oil pump drive sprocket.

  d. At the same time, mesh the clutch housing gear with the starter idle gear. Use a screwdriver and turn the starter idle gear to help align the gear with the clutch housing gear (**Figure 35**). Remove the screwdriver.

  e. Push the clutch housing on until it bottoms and both sets of gears are aligned (A, **Figure 36**). At this time, the clutch housing and oil pump drive sprocket also must be correctly aligned. If the oil pan is removed, slightly rotate the oil pump driven gear (B, **Figure 36**) to aid in alignment.

  f. The clutch housing inner surface must be flush with the raised flange and the mainshaft splines must be visible as shown in **Figure 37**. If the flange and splines are not visible as shown, the clutch housing has not bottomed out. Correct the problem at this time.

CAUTION
Make sure the clutch housing notches are engaged properly with the oil pump drive sprocket raised bosses. Rotate the clutch housing and listen for oil pump drive chain movement. The chain is not visible for viewing after the clutch housing is in place.

6. Install the spline washer (**Figure 38**). Push it on until it bottoms (**Figure 31**).

7. Install the clutch hub (**Figure 30**).

CAUTION
*The mainshaft splines must be visible (**Figure 39**) in order to accept the lockwasher. If the splines are not visible, the clutch housing was not installed correctly.*

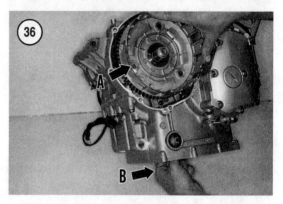

8. Install the *new* lockwasher (A, **Figure 40**) onto the mainshaft splines. Push it on until it is engaged with the mainshaft.

9. Position the clutch nut with the recessed side (B, **Figure 40**) going on first and install the clutch nut (**Figure 41**). Tighten finger-tight.

10A. If the engine is mounted in the frame, make sure the transmission is still in gear. Have an assistant apply the rear brake.

CAUTION
When using the clutch holder in Step 8B, make sure to secure it squarely onto the clutch hub splines. If the clutch holder starts to slip, stop tightening the clutch locknut and reposition the clutch holder. If the clutch holder slips, it may damage the clutch hub splines.

10B. If the engine is removed from the frame, hold the clutch hub with the same clutch holder tool (A, **Figure 42**) used during disassembly.

11. Tighten the clutch locknut (B, **Figure 42**) to the following:

    a. 1998-2001 models: 70 N•m (52 ft.-lb.).

    b. 2002-2003 models: 105 N•m (77 ft.-lb.).

    c. Remove the clutch holder tool.

NOTE
Check the clutch hub splines for any burrs caused by the clutch holder. Remove burrs with a file, and then clean the area of all aluminum debris.

12. Bend up one of the lockwasher tabs against the flat on the clutch locknut.

13. Install the damper spring seat (**Figure 43**) over the clutch hub.

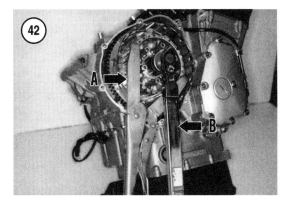

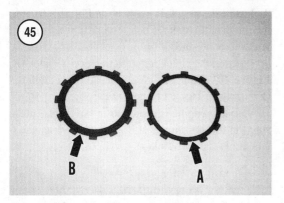

B   A

14. Position the damper spring with the OUTSIDE mark facing out and install it (**Figure 44**) over the clutch hub.

15. Push the damper spring seat and damper spring on and seat against the clutch hub shoulder.

16. Lubricate the friction discs and clutch plates with engine oil.

NOTE
*The friction disc A has a larger inside diameter (A, **Figure 45**) than the remaining friction discs B (B).*

17. Install friction disc A (**Figure 46**) over the damper spring seat and damper spring. Push it on until it is seated correctly.

18. Install a clutch plate (**Figure 47**) and push it on until it is completely seated against the friction disc A.

19. Install the wire retainer as follows:

   a. Insert one end of the wire retainer into the hole in the clutch hub (**Figure 48**). Push it through until it snaps into place.

6

b. Use needlenose pliers and pull the wire retainer around the circumference of the clutch hub (**Figure 49**).

c. Push the end of the wire retainer down with a narrow flat blade screwdriver (A, **Figure 50**) and pull the end through the hole in the clutch hub with a scribe (B).

d. Use a scribe and completely push the end of the wire retainer down though the hole in the clutch hub (**Figure 51**) until it snaps into place.

e. Ensure that both ends of the wire retainer (**Figure 52**) are correctly installed. Both ends must protrude though the hole in the clutch hub and are locked into place.

20. Install friction disc B (**Figure 53**), then a clutch plate (**Figure 54**).

21. Continue to alternately install a clutch plate and a friction disc B.

22. The last plate installed must be a friction disc (**Figure 55**).

23. If removed, install the bearing into the pressure plate.

24. Install the clutch lifter piece (**Figure 56**) through the backside of the pressure plate.

25. Align the pressure plate and clutch hub, then install the pressure plate (**Figure 57**) over the clutch hub. Make sure the pressure plate seats flush against the outer friction disc.

26. Install the diaphragm spring seat (**Figure 58**) and make sure it is correctly seated in the pressure plate (**Figure 59**).

27. Install the diaphragm spring (**Figure 60**) onto the diaphragm spring seat. Make sure it is correctly seated.

28. Install the diaphragm spring retainer (**Figure 61**) and install the bolts (**Figure 62**).

29. Using a crisscross pattern, tighten the clutch diaphragm spring bolts to 8 N•m (71 in.-lb.).

30. Install the clutch cover as described in this chapter.

31. Refill the engine with the correct type and quantity of oil (Chapter Three).

32. Shift the transmission into neutral and start the engine. After the engine warms up, pull the clutch in and shift the transmission into first gear. Note the following:

   a. If there is a loud grinding and spinning noise coming from the clutch immediately after starting the engine, the engine was not filled with oil or new clutch plates were installed and not lubricated with oil. Once the engine oil lubricates the new plates, the noise will stop.

   b. If the motorcycle jumps forward and stalls or creeps with the transmission in gear and the clutch pulled in, check for improper clutch cable adjustment. Refer to Chapter Three.

   c. For additional information, refer to *Clutch Troubleshooting* in Chapter Two.

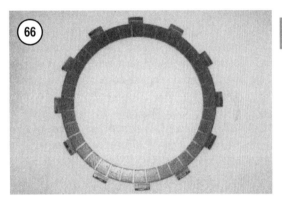

Inspection

When measuring the clutch components, compare the actual measurements to the specifications in **Table 1**. Replace worn or damaged parts as described in this section.

1. Clean and dry all parts.

2. Inspect the diaphragm spring (**Figure 63**) for cracks or damaged fingers.

3. Measure the diaphragm spring height at the tip if the fingers (**Figure 64**) with a vernier caliper.

4. Inspect the diaphragm spring retainer (**Figure 65**) for cracks or damage.

5. Inspect the friction discs (**Figure 66**) as follows:

> *NOTE*
> *If any friction disc is damaged or out of specification as described in the following steps, replace all of the friction discs as a set.*

a. The friction material used on the friction discs (**Figure 66**) is bonded onto an aluminum plate. Inspect the friction material for excessive or uneven wear, cracks and other

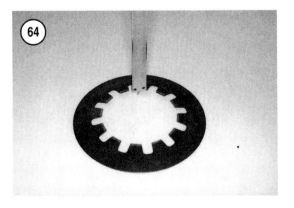

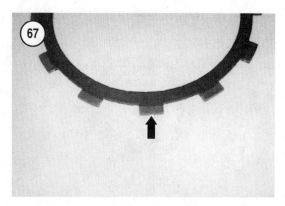

damage. Check the disc tangs (**Figure 67**) for surface damage. The sides of the disc tangs must be smooth where they contact the clutch housing fingers; otherwise, the discs cannot engage and disengage correctly.

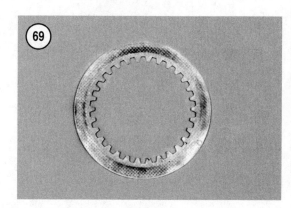

> *NOTE*
> *If the disc tangs are damaged, inspect the clutch housing fingers carefully as described in this section.*

   b. Measure the thickness of each friction disc with a vernier caliper (**Figure 68**). Measure at several places around the disc.

6. Inspect the steel clutch plates (**Figure 69**) as follows:

   a. Inspect the clutch plates for cracks, damage or color change. Overheated clutch plates will have a blue discoloration.

   b. Check the clutch plates for an oil glaze buildup. Remove buildup by lightly sanding both sides of each plate with 400 grit sandpaper placed on a surface plate or piece of glass.

   c. Place each clutch plate on a surface plate or piece of glass and check for warp with a feeler gauge (**Figure 70**). If the clutch plates are warped, compare the measurement to the service limit in **Table 1**. If any are warped beyond the specification, replace the entire set.

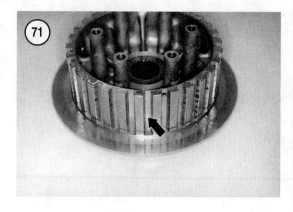

   d. The clutch plate inner teeth mesh with the clutch hub splines. Check the clutch plate teeth for any roughness or damage. The teeth contact surfaces must be smooth; otherwise, the plates cannot engage and disengage correctly.

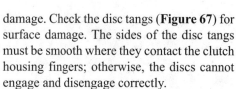

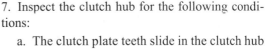

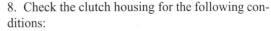

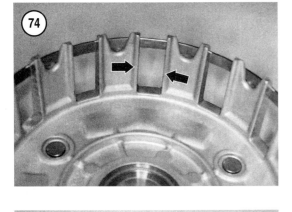

NOTE
If the clutch plate teeth are damaged, inspect the clutch hub splines carefully as described in this section.

7. Inspect the clutch hub for the following conditions:

   a. The clutch plate teeth slide in the clutch hub splines (**Figure 71**). Inspect the splines for rough spots, grooves or other damage. Repair minor damage with a file or oil stone. If the damage is excessive, replace the clutch hub.

   b. Damaged spring towers and threads (**Figure 72**).

   c. Inspect the inner splines (**Figure 73**) for damage.

8. Check the clutch housing for the following conditions:

   a. The friction disc tangs slide in the clutch housing grooves. Inspect the grooves (**Figure 74**) for cracks or galling. Repair minor damage with a file. If the damage is excessive, replace the clutch housing.

   b. Check the clutch housing gear (**Figure 75**) for excessive wear, pitting, chipped gear teeth or other damage.

NOTE
If the clutch housing gear is excessively worn or damaged, check the primary drive gear assembly for the same wear conditions.

   c. Check the support band (A, **Figure 76**) around the outer perimeter for damage. Make sure it is secure to each of the fingers (B, **Figure 76**).

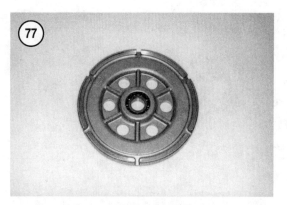

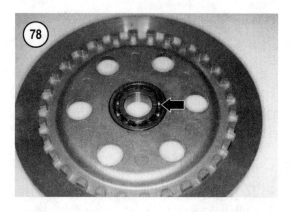

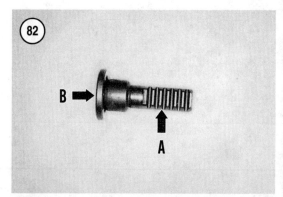

9. Inspect the pressure plate (**Figure 77**) for the following conditions:

    a. Inspect for cracks or other damage.

    b. Slowly turn the ball bearing (**Figure 78**) by hand. If any roughness or binding is noted, replace the bearing.

    c. Check the fingers (**Figure 79**) for damage.

    d. Inspect the diaphragm spring seat (A, **Figure 80**) and the pressure plate surface (B) where the seat rides for excessive wear or damage.

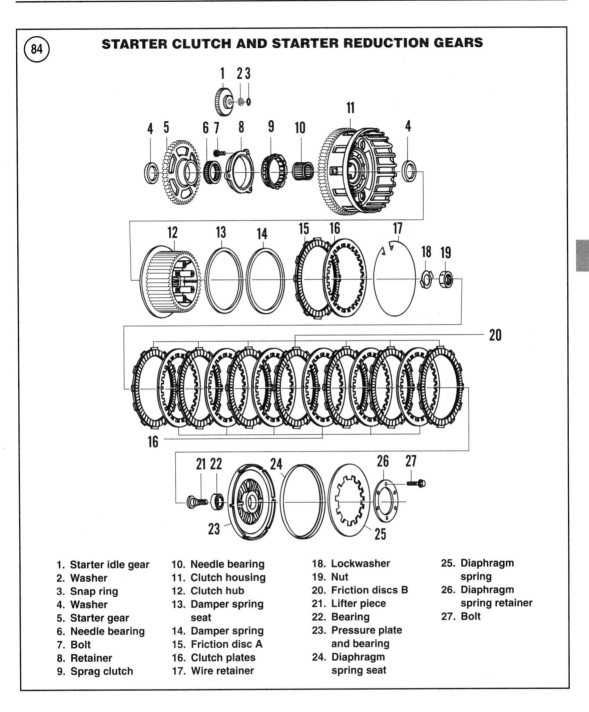

STARTER CLUTCH AND STARTER REDUCTION GEARS

1. Starter idle gear
2. Washer
3. Snap ring
4. Washer
5. Starter gear
6. Needle bearing
7. Bolt
8. Retainer
9. Sprag clutch
10. Needle bearing
11. Clutch housing
12. Clutch hub
13. Damper spring seat
14. Damper spring
15. Friction disc A
16. Clutch plates
17. Wire retainer
18. Lockwasher
19. Nut
20. Friction discs B
21. Lifter piece
22. Bearing
23. Pressure plate and bearing
24. Diaphragm spring seat
25. Diaphragm spring
26. Diaphragm spring retainer
27. Bolt

10. Inspect the diaphragm spring and the seat (**Figure 81**) for cracks, warp or other damage. Replace as a set even if only one requires replacement.

11. Check the lifter piece for straightness and damage. Inspect the teeth (A, **Figure 82**) and the end (B) where it contacts the lifter lever for abnormal wear.

12. Inspect the spline washer (**Figure 83**) for wear or damage.

STARTER CLUTCH AND STARTER REDUCTION GEARS

Removal/Installation

The starter clutch assembly (**Figure 84**) is removed during clutch removal as described in this chapter.

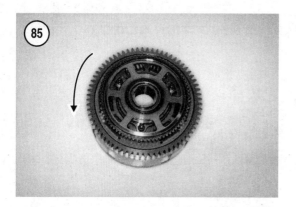

Starter Clutch Disassembly/Assembly

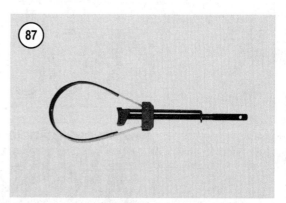

1. Hold the clutch housing with one hand, then turn the starter driven gear clockwise and counterclockwise. The gear should only turn *counterclockwise* (**Figure 85**). If the gear turns clockwise, replace the starter clutch assembly.

2. Hold the clutch housing with one hand, then turn the starter driven gear counterclockwise (**Figure 85**) and pull up at the same time to remove it.

3. To remove the starter clutch assembly, perform the following:

> *CAUTION*
> *Install the holding tool as close to the gear area (**Figure 86**) as possible. Do not install it toward the outer ends of the fingers as the fingers may be damaged.*

   a. Install an adjustable holding tool (**Figure 87**) onto the clutch outer housing next to the gear area.

   b. Use an impact driver and loosen the Allen bolts (A, **Figure 88**).

   c. Remove the bolts, then remove the retainer and sprag clutch (B, **Figure 88**).

4. Clean the sprag clutch, needle bearing and driven gear in solvent and dry with compressed air.

5. Remove all threadlocking compound from the Allen bolts.

6. Inspect the starter driven gear teeth (**Figure 89**) for damage.

7. Inspect the starter driven outer needle bearing (A, **Figure 90**) and the gear boss (B) where the outer needle bearing rides for wear or damage.

8. Inspect the starter driven outer needle bearing (A, **Figure 91**) and the bearing surface (B) on the

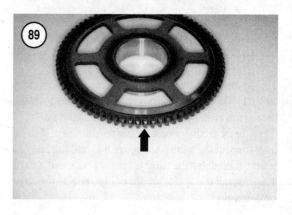

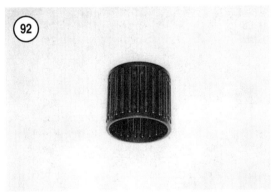

clutch outer housing where the needle bearing rides for wear or damage.

9. Inspect the inner needle bearing (**Figure 92**) and the inner surface of the clutch outer housing (**Figure 93**) where the inner needle bearing rides for wear or damage.

10. Install the starter clutch as follows:

   a. Lubricate the one-way sprag clutch with engine oil.

   b. Position the one-way sprag clutch with the flange side going on last and install it into the clutch outer housing.

   c. Install the retainer (B, **Figure 88**).

   d. Apply a medium strength threadlocking compound to the starter clutch Allen bolts and install them.

   e. Secure the clutch outer houing with the holding tool and tighten the Allen bolts (A, **Figure 88**) to 12 N•m (106 in.-lb.).

   f. Turn the starter driven gear counterclockwise and install it into the clutch housing.

   g. Recheck the one-way sprag clutch operation. Hold the clutch housing with one hand and turn the starter driven gear. The gear should turn counterclockwise (**Figure 85**) but not clockwise.

Starter Reduction Gear
Removal/Inspection/Installation

1. Remove the clutch assembly as described in this chapter.

2. Remove the snap ring and washer (A, **Figure 94**) and remove the starter reduction gear (B) from the pivot post on the crankcase.

3. Inspect the starter reduction gear teeth (**Figure 95**) for damage. If the gear teeth are damaged, also

check the starter splines (**Figure 96**) for possible damage.

4. Inspect the pivot post (**Figure 97**) for damage. If necessary, disassemble the crankcase (Chapter Five) and remove the bolt and washer securing it to the upper crankcase.

5. Install the starter reduction gear (A, **Figure 98**) on the crankcase pivot post. Push it on until it bottoms.

6. Install the washer (B, **Figure 98**), then install the snap ring (**Figure 99**) onto the post. Make sure the snap ring is correctly seated in the post groove.

7. Install the clutch assembly as described in this chapter.

EXTERNAL GEARSHIFT MECHANISM

The external gearshift mechanism consists of the shift shaft, shift drum cam and stopper arm assembly (**Figure 100**). The external shift mechanism can be serviced with the engine in the frame. Shift drum removal and installation procedures are covered in Chapter Seven.

If the motorcycle is experiencing shifting problems, refer to *Gearshift Linkage and Transmission* in Chapter Two before removing the shift mechanism in this section.

Removal

1. Remove the left side fairing panel and bottom cowl as described in Chapter Sixteen.

2. Shift the transmission into neutral.

3. Loosen the locknut at each end of the shift shaft (A, **Figure 101**).

> *NOTE*
> *The shift shaft has left-hand threads at one end. Turning the shift shaft in one*

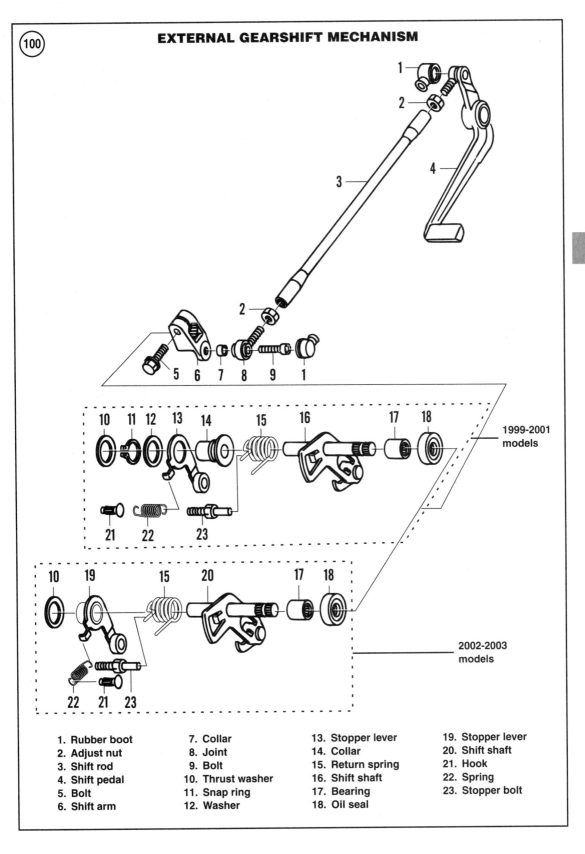

EXTERNAL GEARSHIFT MECHANISM

6

1999-2001 models

2002-2003 models

1. Rubber boot
2. Adjust nut
3. Shift rod
4. Shift pedal
5. Bolt
6. Shift arm
7. Collar
8. Joint
9. Bolt
10. Thrust washer
11. Snap ring
12. Washer
13. Stopper lever
14. Collar
15. Return spring
16. Shift shaft
17. Bearing
18. Oil seal
19. Stopper lever
20. Shift shaft
21. Hook
22. Spring
23. Stopper bolt

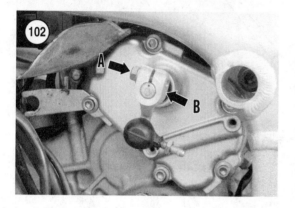

direction will unscrew it from both ends.

4. Unscrew the shift rod (B, **Figure 101**) from the joint at each end and remove it.

5. Remove the bolts securing the sprocket cover (C, **Figure 101**) and remove the cover.

6. Unscrew the clamp bolt (A, **Figure 102**) securing the shift arm to the shift shaft. Remove the shift arm (B, **Figure 102**) and reinstall the clamp bolt to avoid misplacing it.

7. Disengage the idle adjust control knob from the bracket.

8. Remove the bolts securing the shift shaft cover (A, **Figure 103**) and remove the cover and gasket. Note the location of the idle adjust control knob bracket (B, **Figure 103**).

9. If loose, remove the two locating dowels.

10. Unhook the spring (**Figure 104**) from the hook.

11. Withdraw the shift shaft (**Figure 105**) and the thrust washer.

12. Inspect all parts as described in this section.

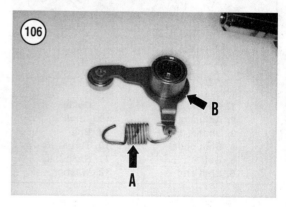

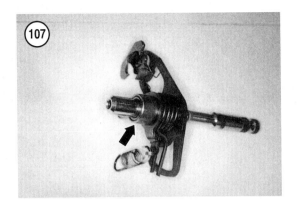

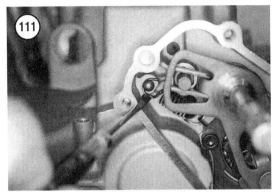

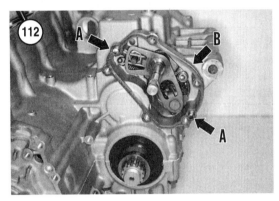

Installation

1. Hook the spring (A, **Figure 106**) onto the stopper lever (B).

2. Install the stopper lever (**Figure 107**) onto the shift shaft.

3. Install the thrust washer onto the shift shaft (**Figure 108**).

4. Install the shift shaft (**Figure 109**) as follows:

   a. Center the return spring on the shift spring with the pin in the crankcase (A, **Figure 110**).

   b. Engage the stopper lever roller onto the shift drum ramp (B, **Figure 110**).

   c. Push the shift shaft in until it bottoms.

5. Attach the spring (**Figure 111**) onto the hook.

6. If removed, install the two locating dowels (A, **Figure 112**).

7. Install a *new* gasket (B, **Figure 112**).

8. Install the shift shaft cover (A, **Figure 103**) and bolts. Make sure to install the idle adjust control knob bracket (B, **Figure 103**) in the location noted during removal. Tighten the bolts to 12 N•m (106 in.-lb.).

9. Install the idle adjust control knob onto the bracket.

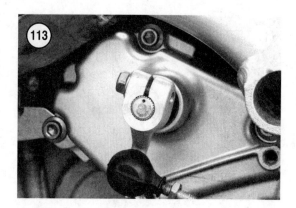

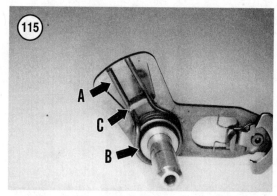

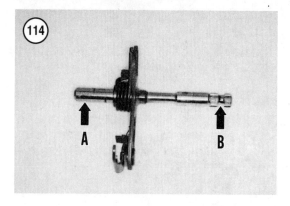

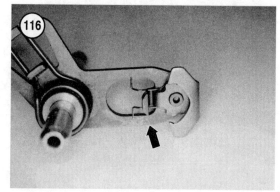

10. Align the slot in the gearshift lever arm with the alignment mark on the shift shaft (**Figure 113**) and install the lever arm onto the shift shaft. Tighten the clamp bolt to 10 N•m (88 in.-lb.).

11. Install the sprocket cover (C, **Figure 101**) and bolts and tighten securely.

12. Install the shift rod (B, **Figure 101**) onto the front joint and to the shift pedal. Rotate the shift rod and screw it into place.

13. Adjust the gearshift pedal height as described under *Gearshift Pedal Adjustment* in Chapter Three.

14. Install the bottom cowl and the left side fairing panel as described in Chapter Sixteen.

Inspection

Replace worn or damaged parts as described in this section.

1. Inspect the shift shaft for the following:
   a. Bent shaft (A, **Figure 114**).
   b. Damaged splines (B, **Figure 114**).
   c. Weak or damaged return spring (A, **Figure 115**).

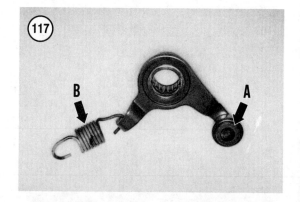

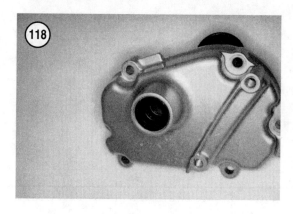

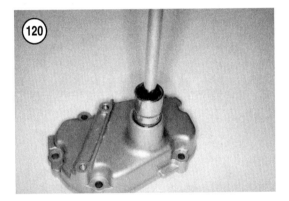

d. Stuck or damaged shift arm (**Figure 116**).

2. To replace the return spring, perform the following:

    a. Remove the washer (B, **Figure 115**) and snap ring.

    b. Remove the return spring (A, **Figure 115**).

    c. Slide on the new spring, then spread the spring arms and fit the spring over the shift shaft arm (C, **Figure 115**).

    d. Install the snap ring and washer.

3. Inspect the stopper lever assembly for:

    a. Damaged stopper lever arm. Check stopper arm for a damaged pivot hole or stuck or binding roller (A, **Figure 117**).

    b. Bent or damaged washer. A damaged washer can prevent the stopper arm from moving correctly.

    c. Weak or damaged return spring (B, **Figure 117**).

Cover Oil Seal Replacement

1. Inspect the cover (**Figure 118**) for cracks or damage.

2. Carefully pry the oil seal out of the cover (**Figure 119**) with a flat blade screwdriver.

3. Inspect the bearing for damage. If the bearing is damaged, replace it by following the typical bearing replacement procedures in Chapter One.

4. Position the seal with the sealed side facing out.

5. Install the new seal squarely in the cover opening. Select a driver or socket (**Figure 120**) with the outside diameter slightly smaller than the seal's outside diameter. Then drive the oil seal into the bore until it bottoms out.

6

Table 1 CLUTCH SPECIFICATIONS

Item	Standard mm (in.)	Service limit mm (in.)
Friction disc		
Quantity	8	–
Thickness	2.9-3.1 (0.114-0.122)	2.8 (0.110)
Clutch plate		
Quantity	7	–
Thickness	1.9-2.1 (0.075-0.083)	–
Warp	–	0.10 (0.004)
Diaphragm spring height	6.5 (0.256)	–

Table 2 CLUTCH TORQUE SPECIFICATIONS

Item	N•m	in.-lb.	ft.-lb.
Clutch cover bolts	12	106	–
Clutch hub lock nut			
1998-2001 models	70	–	52
2002-2003 models	105	–	77
Diaphragm spring bolts	8	71	–
Gearshift drum retainer	10	88	–
Gearshift stopper arm bolt	12	106	–
Shift arm clamp bolt	10	88	–
Shift shaft cover bolts	12	106	–
Starter clutch retainer Allen bolts*	12	106	–

*Apply a medium strength locking agent to fastener threads.

CHAPTER SEVEN

TRANSMISSION AND INTERNAL SHIFT MECHANISM

This chapter covers service for the transmission and internal shift mechanism. The external shift mechanism is covered in Chapter Six. Transmission and internal shift mechanism service requires crankcase disassembly as described in Chapter Five.

Transmission specifications are listed in **Table 1**. **Tables 1-3** are at the end of the chapter.

TRANSMISSION AND INTERNAL SHIFT MECHANISM

The transmission assemblies and internal shift mechanism (**Figure 1**) must be removed and installed at the same time.

All three assemblies are installed in the upper crankcase.

Removal

1. Remove the engine as described in Chapter Five.

2. Remove the bolts (A, **Figure 2**) securing the shift drum retainer (B) and remove the retainer.

3. Split the crankcase as described under *Crankcase Disassembly* in Chapter Five.

4. Remove the countershaft assembly (**Figure 3**) and the set-ring (A, **Figure 4**).

5. Withdraw the shift fork shaft and remove the right (B, **Figure 4**) and left (C) shift forks. Do not lose the spring in each end of the shaft.

6. Withdraw the shift fork shaft (A, **Figure 5**) and center shift fork (**Figure 6**). Do not lose the spring in each end of the shaft.

7. Withdraw the shift drum (B, **Figure 5**) from the upper crankcase.

8. Use an impact driver and loosen the T-30 Torx bolts (**Figure 7**). Remove the three bolts securing the bearing retainer.

9. Install two 6-mm bolts (**Figure 8**) into the bearing retainer. Tighten the bolts slowly and release the bearing retainer and bearing from the upper crankcase. Remove the two bolts.

10. Withdraw the countershaft assembly and bearing (**Figure 9**) from the upper crankcase.

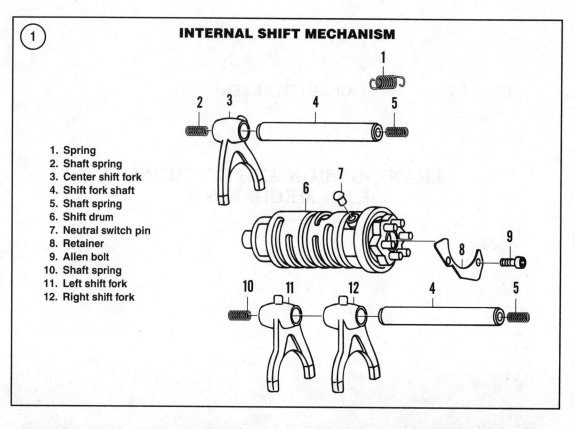

INTERNAL SHIFT MECHANISM

1. Spring
2. Shaft spring
3. Center shift fork
4. Shift fork shaft
5. Shaft spring
6. Shift drum
7. Neutral switch pin
8. Retainer
9. Allen bolt
10. Shaft spring
11. Left shift fork
12. Right shift fork

11. Perform the *Preliminary Inspection* prior to shaft disassembly. Perform this even though the shafts may not be intended for service.

12. If necessary, service the transmission shafts as described in this chapter.

13. Wrap the shafts in clean shop cloths and store in a box to avoid damage.

Installation

1. If necessary, replace the countershaft oil seal as follows:
   a. Slide the old seal off of the shaft and discard it.
   b. Pack the lips of the *new* oil seal with a water-proof bearing grease prior to installation.
   c. Position the *new* oil seal with the manufacturer's marks facing out and install the oil seal (**Figure 10**). Push it on until it bottoms.

2. Prior to installing any components, apply clean engine oil to all bearing surfaces.

3. Install the countershaft into the right side of the crankcase (**Figure 9**) and into the bearing receptacle (**Figure 11**) on the left side. If necessary, tap on

the end of the shaft to make sure it is properly seated.

4. Align the bearing retainer with the crankcase and make sure it locks the oil deliver pipe (**Figure 12**) in place.

5. Install *new* T-30 Torx bolts (**Figure 7**) and tighten to 12 N•m (106 in.-lb.).

6. Rotate the countershaft and make sure it rotates freely without any play or noise.

7. Install the shift drum (B, **Figure 5**) into the upper crankcase. Push it in until it bottoms.

> *NOTE*
> *The shift forks are marked with a R (right) L (left) and C (center) (**Figure 13**). These marks relate to the engine as it sits in the frame. These marks must face the clutch side of the engine.*

> *NOTE*
> *When installing the shift forks in the following steps, engage the pin on the fork with the corresponding groove in the shift drum.*

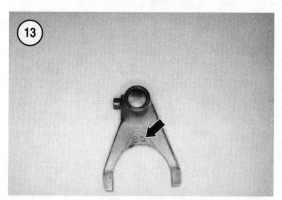

8. Install the center shift fork (**Figure 14**) into the transmission third/fourth combination gear groove. Index the pin into the shift drum groove.

9. Install the spring into each end of the shift fork. Make sure the springs do not fall out during installation.

10. Install the shift fork shaft (**Figure 15**) through the center shift fork (**Figure 16**). Install the shaft into the receptacle in the right side of the crankcase and push it in until it bottoms. Do not lose the spring in each end of the shaft.

11. Install the left shift fork (**Figure 17**) and shift fork shaft (A, **Figure 5**). Push the shaft through the left shift fork.

12. Install the right shift fork (**Figure 18**) and push the shaft through the right shift fork. Install the shaft into the receptacle in the right side of the crankcase and push it in until it bottoms. Do not lose the spring in each end of the shaft.

13. Install the set ring (A, **Figure 4**) into the crankcase groove.

14. Correctly position the left (B, **Figure 4**) and right (C) shift forks in the up position to accept the countershaft assembly.

15. Install the countershaft assembly (**Figure 3**) down onto the right and left shift forks.

16. Make sure the countershaft is seated correctly in the set ring (A, **Figure 19**). Also make sure the oil seal lip (B, **Figure 19**) is seated correctly in the groove.

17. Spin the countershaft (**Figure 3**) by hand. It must rotate freely without any play or noise.

18. Assemble the crankcase as described under *Crankcase Assembly* in Chapter Five.

19. Install the shift drum retainer (B, **Figure 2**) and the bolts (A). Tighten the bolts to 10 N•m (88 in.-lb.).

20. Install the spacer (**Figure 20**) onto the end of the countershaft.

21. Install the engine as described in Chapter Five.

Preliminary Inspection

1. Clean and inspect the assemblies prior to disassembling them. Place the assembled shaft into a large can or plastic bucket and thoroughly clean the assembly with a petroleum-based solvent, such as kerosene, and a stiff brush. Dry the assembly with compressed air or let it sit on rags to drip dry. Do this for both shaft assemblies.

2. Visually inspect the components for excessive wear. Check the gear teeth for chips, burrs or pitting. Clean up damage with an oilstone. Replace any components with damage that cannot be cleaned up.

> *NOTE*
> *Replace defective gears and their mating gear on the other shaft as well, even though it may not show as much wear or damage.*

3. Carefully check the engagement dogs. If any are chipped, worn, rounded or missing, the affected gear must be replaced.

7

4. Rotate the transmission bearings by hand. Refer to mainshaft bearing in **Figure 21** and countershaft bearings in **Figure 22**. Check for roughness, noise and radial play. Replace any bearing that is suspect.

5. If the transmission shafts are satisfactory and are not going to be disassembled, apply assembly oil or engine oil to all components and reinstall them into the crankcase as described in Chapter Five.

NOTE
If disassembling a used, high-mileage transmission for the first time, pay particular attention to any additional shims not shown in the illustrations or photographs. To compensate for wear, additional shims may have been installed during the previous repair. If the transmission is being reassembled with the old parts, install these shims in their original locations since the shims have developed a wear pattern. If new parts are being used, discard the additional shims.

Transmission Service Notes

1. Parts with two different sides, such as gears, snap rings and shift forks, can be installed backward. To maintain the correct alignment and position of the parts during disassembly, store each part in order and in a divided container (**Figure 23**).

2. The snap rings are a tight fit on the transmission shafts and will bend and twist during removal. Install new snap rings during transmission assembly.

3. To avoid bending and twisting the new snap rings during installation, use the following installation technique:

    a. Open the new snap ring with a pair of snap ring pliers while holding the back of the snap ring with a pair of pliers (**Figure 24**).

    b. Then slide the snap ring down the shaft and seat it into its correct transmission groove. Check the snap ring to make sure it seats in its groove completely.

4. When installing snap rings, align the snap ring opening with the shaft groove as shown in **Figure 25**.

5. Snap rings and flat washers have one sharp edge and one rounded edge (**Figure 26**). Install the snap rings with the sharp edge facing away from the gear producing the thrust.

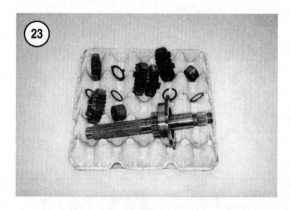

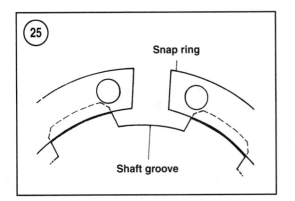

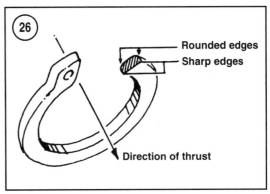

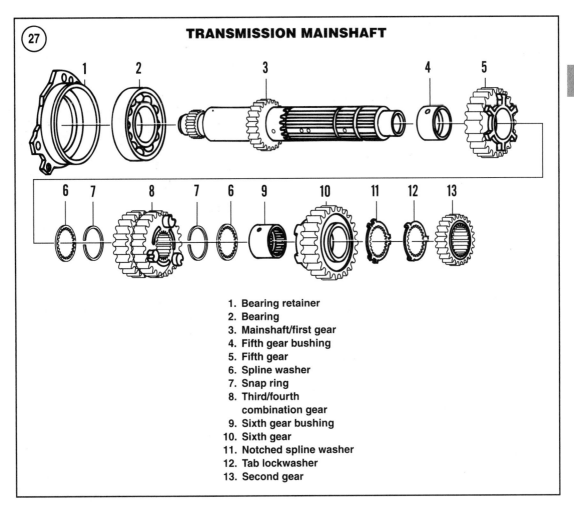

TRANSMISSION MAINSHAFT

1. Bearing retainer
2. Bearing
3. Mainshaft/first gear
4. Fifth gear bushing
5. Fifth gear
6. Spline washer
7. Snap ring
8. Third/fourth
   combination gear
9. Sixth gear bushing
10. Sixth gear
11. Notched spline washer
12. Tab lockwasher
13. Second gear

Mainshaft Disassembly

Refer to **Figure 27**.

1. Clean the assembled mainshaft in solvent, then dry with compressed air.

2. Slide off the second gear and tab lockwasher. Rotate the notched spline washer to clear the spline groove and remove it.

3. Slide off the sixth gear and sixth gear splined bushing.

4. Remove the snap ring and spline washer.

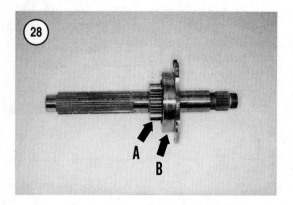

5. Slide off the third/fourth combination gear.
6. Remove the snap ring and spline washer.
7. Slide off the fifth gear and the fifth gear bushing.

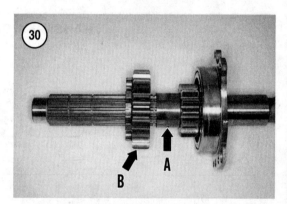

> *NOTE*
> *Mainshaft first gear (A, **Figure 28**) is an integral part of the mainshaft.*

> *NOTE*
> *Do not remove the bearing and retainer (B, **Figure 28**) unless they are going to be replaced.*

8. If necessary, press off the mainshaft ball bearing and retainer (B, **Figure 28**). Refer to *Bearing Replacement* in Chapter One for typical procedures.
9. Inspect the mainshaft assembly as described under *Transmission Inspection* in this chapter.

Mainshaft Assembly

Refer to **Figure 27**.
1. Prior to mainshaft assembly, note the following:
   a. The mainshaft uses two snap rings. These snap rings are identical, having the same part number.
   b. Install *new* snap rings.
   c. Install the snap rings and thrust washers with their chamfered edge facing away from the thrust load (**Figure 26**).
   d. Align the snap ring gap with the transmission shaft groove as shown in **Figure 25**.
2. If the mainshaft bearing (B, **Figure 28**) was removed, install the new bearing as follows:
   a. Being careful not to damage the first gear or the mainshaft splines, support the shaft and first gear with a bearing splitter in a press and press on the bearing. Use a tool that will apply force only to the mainshaft bearing's inner

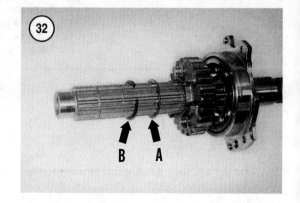

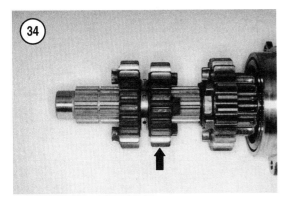

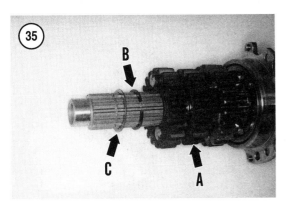

race. Refer to *Bearing Replacement* in Chapter One for typical procedures.

> *CAUTION*
> *If pressure is applied to the bearing's outer race, the bearing will be damaged.*

   b. Press the bearing (A, **Figure 28**) onto the mainshaft until it bottoms.

   c. Press the retainer (**Figure 29**) onto the bearing until it bottoms.

3. Apply a light coat of clean engine oil to all sliding surfaces prior to installing any parts.

4. Slide on the fifth gear bushing (A, **Figure 30**).

5. Position the fifth gear with the dog side going on last (**Figure 31**) and install the fifth gear (B, **Figure 30**) onto the bushing.

6. Install the spline washer (A, **Figure 32**).

7. Install a *new* snap ring (B, **Figure 32**). Make sure the snap ring is correctly seated in the groove (**Figure 33**).

8. Install third/fourth combination gear as follows:

   a. Position the third/fourth combination gear with the smaller third gear side (**Figure 34**) going on first.

   b. Slide on the third/fourth combination gear (A, **Figure 35**).

9. Install a *new* snap ring (B, **Figure 35**). Make sure the snap ring is correctly seated in the groove.

10. Install the spline washer (C, **Figure 35**) and push it against the snap ring.

11. Align the oil hole in the sixth gear bushing (**Figure 36**) with the mainshaft oil hole. Slide on the sixth gear bushing. Push it up against the spline washer.

12. Position the sixth gear with the dog side going on first and install the sixth gear onto the bushing (**Figure 37**).

13. Slide on the notched spline washer (**Figure 38**). This washer is symmetrical (both sides are flat). Slightly rotate the splined washer so it is locked in the mainshaft groove (**Figure 39**) and is held in place by the splines.

14. Position the tab lockwasher with the locking arms facing the notched spline washer installed in Step 13.

15. Slide on the tab lockwasher and insert the locking arms into the notches in the spline washer as shown in **Figure 40**.

16. Position the second gear with the small raised boss side (**Figure 41**) going on first and slide on the second gear (**Figure 42**).

17. Refer to **Figure 43** for the correct placement of the mainshaft gears. Make sure each gear engages properly to the adjoining gear where applicable.

Countershaft Disassembly

Refer to **Figure 44**.

1. Clean the assembled countershaft in solvent, then dry with compressed air.

2. Slide off the ball bearing and the thrust washer.

3. Slide off the first gear and first gear bushing.

4. Slide off the fifth gear.

5. Remove the snap ring.

6. Slide off the spline washer, the third gear and the third gear splined bushing.

7. Remove the tab lockwasher. Rotate the notched spline washer to clear the spline groove and remove it.

8. Slide off the fourth gear and fourth gear bushing.

9. Slide off the spline washer and remove the snap ring.

10. Slide off the sixth gear.

11. Remove the snap ring and slide off the spline washer.

12. Slide off the second gear and second gear bushing.

13. If still in place, remove the spacer from the other end of the shaft.

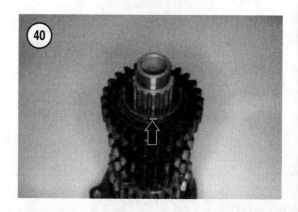

NOTE
Do not remove the bearing and spacer
unless they are going to be replaced.

14. If necessary, press off the countershaft ball bearing (A, **Figure 45**) and spacer (B). Refer to *Bearing Replacement* in Chapter One for typical procedures.

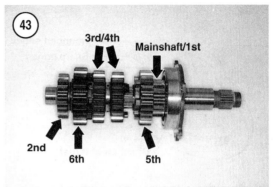

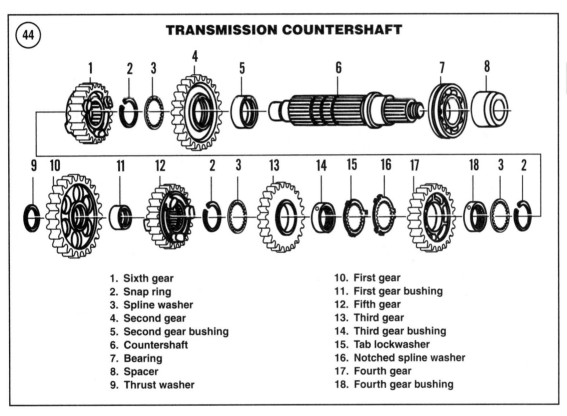

TRANSMISSION COUNTERSHAFT

1. Sixth gear
2. Snap ring
3. Spline washer
4. Second gear
5. Second gear bushing
6. Countershaft
7. Bearing
8. Spacer
9. Thrust washer
10. First gear
11. First gear bushing
12. Fifth gear
13. Third gear
14. Third gear bushing
15. Tab lockwasher
16. Notched spline washer
17. Fourth gear
18. Fourth gear bushing

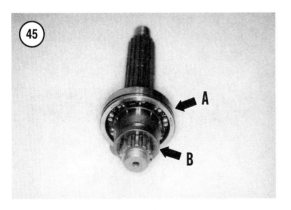

15. Inspect the countershaft assembly as described under *Transmission Inspection* in this chapter.

Countershaft Assembly

1. Prior to countershaft assembly, note the following:

    a. The countershaft uses three snap rings. Each snap ring is identical, having the same part number.

    b. Install new snap rings.

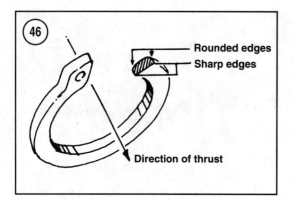

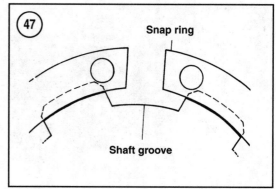

c. The countershaft uses three splined washers. Each washer is identical, having the same part number. When reusing the spline washers, install them in their original mounting position.

d. Install the snap rings and thrust washers with their chamfered edge facing away from the thrust load (**Figure 46**).

e. Align the snap ring gap with the transmission shaft groove as shown in **Figure 47**.

2. Apply a light coat of clean engine oil to all sliding surfaces prior to installing any parts.

3. If the countershaft spacer (B, **Figure 45**) and bearing (A) were removed, install the new bearing and spacers as follows:

a. The new bearing must be installed so that the groove in the outer race faces toward the outside of the shaft as shown in A, **Figure 48**.

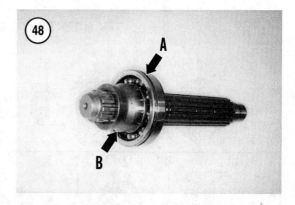

b. Support the shaft on the press bed and press on the bearing. Use a tool that will apply force only to the countershaft bearing's inner race. Refer to *Bearing Replacement* in Chapter One for typical procedures.

> *CAUTION*
> *If pressure is applied to the bearing's outer race, the bearing will be damaged.*

c. Press the bearing onto the countershaft until it bottoms on the shaft flange.

d. Position the spacer with the larger diameter (B, **Figure 48**) side going on first.

e. Press the spacer onto the shaft until it bottoms on the bearing's inner race.

f. Rotate the bearing by hand. The bearing must rotate freely, if not, one or both of the parts have been installed incorrectly. Correct the problem at this time.

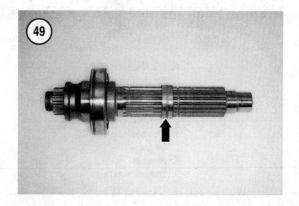

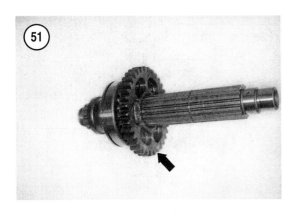

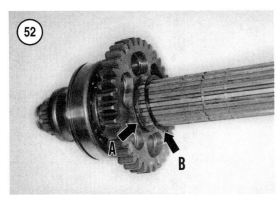

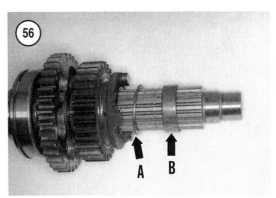

7

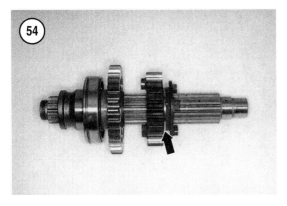

4. Slide on the second gear bushing (**Figure 49**).

5. Position the second gear with the smooth side going on first (**Figure 50**) and install the second gear onto the bushing (**Figure 51**).

6. Position the spline washer with the chamfered side going on first and install the spline washer (A, **Figure 52**).

7. Install a *new* snap ring (B, **Figure 52**). Make sure the snap ring is correctly seated in the groove (**Figure 53**).

8. Install the sixth gear as follows:
   a. Position the sixth gear with the shift fork groove side going on last (**Figure 54**).
   b. Align the oil hole in the gear with the countershaft oil hole.
   c. Slide on the sixth gear.

9. Install a *new* snap ring. Make sure the snap ring is correctly seated in the groove (**Figure 55**).

10. Position the spline washer with the chamfered side going on last. Install the spline washer (A, **Figure 56**).

11. Align the oil hole in the fourth gear bushing with the countershaft oil hole and slide on the fourth gear bushing (B, **Figure 56**).

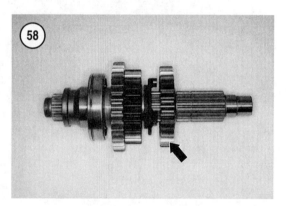

12. Position the fourth gear with the smooth side going on last (**Figure 57**) and slide the fourth gear onto the bushing (**Figure 58**).

13. Slide on the notched spline washer. This washer is symmetrical (both sides are flat). Slightly rotate the splined washer so it is locked in the countershaft groove and held in place by the splines (**Figure 59**).

14. Position the tab lockwasher with the locking arms facing toward the notched spline washer installed in Step 12.

15. Slide on the tab lockwasher (**Figure 60**) and insert the locking arms into the notches in the spline washer as shown in **Figure 61**.

16. Align the oil hole in the third gear bushing with the countershaft oil hole and slide on the third gear bushing (**Figure 62**).

17. Position the third gear with the shift dog side going on last (**Figure 63**) and install the third gear onto the bushing.

18. Position the spline washer with the chamfered side going on first. Install the spline washer (**Figure 64**).

19. Install a *new* snap ring (**Figure 65**). Make sure the snap ring is correctly seated in the groove (**Figure 66**).

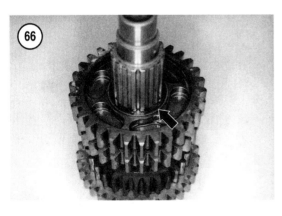

20. Install the fifth gear as follows:

   a. Position the fifth gear with the shift fork groove side going on first (**Figure 67**).

   b. Align the oil hole in the gear's shift fork groove with the countershaft oil hole.

   c. Slide on the fifth gear (A, **Figure 68**).

21. Install the first gear bushing (B, **Figure 68**).

22. Position the first gear with the smooth side going on last (**Figure 69**) and slide the first gear onto the first gear bushing.

23. Position the thrust washer with the chamfered side going on first and install the thrust washer (**Figure 70**).

24. Install the ball bearing (**Figure 71**).

25. Onto the other end of the countershaft, perform the following:

   a. Pack the lips of the *new* oil seal with a water-proof bearing grease prior to installation.

   b. Position the *new* oil seal with the manufacturer's marks facing out and install the oil seal (**Figure 72**). Push it on until it bottoms.

26. Refer to **Figure 73** for the correct placement of the countershaft gears. Make sure each gear engages properly to the adjoining gear where applicable.

27. After both transmission shafts have been assembled, mesh the two assemblies together in the correct position (**Figure 74**). Check that the gear engages properly with the adjoining gear where applicable. This is the last check prior to installing the shaft assemblies in the lower crankcase; make sure they are correctly assembled.

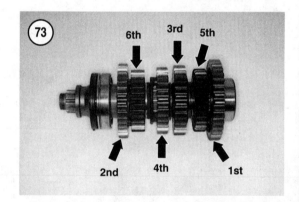

TRANSMISSION INSPECTION

When measuring the mainshaft and countershaft components, compare the actual measurements to the specifications in **Table 2**. Replace the shaft(s) if worn or damaged as described in this section.

Maintain the alignment of the mainshaft and the countershaft components when cleaning and inspecting the parts in this section.

> *NOTE*
> *When cleaning the transmission components, make sure to keep all of the parts in their exact order of disassembly.*

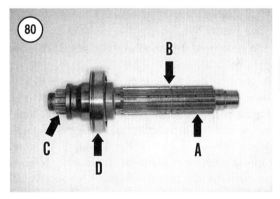

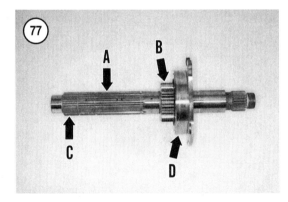

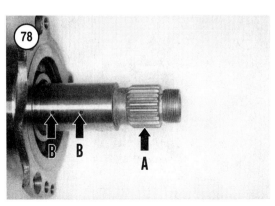

1. Clean the mainshaft and the countershaft bearing assembly in solvent and dry with compressed air.

2. Place each shaft assembly on V-blocks and dial indicator and check for shaft runout. Refer to **Figure 75** for the mainshaft and **Figure 76** for the countershaft.

3. Flush the oil control holes through each shaft assembly with compressed air.

4. Inspect the mainshaft for:

    a. Worn or damages splines (A, **Figure 77**).

    b. Missing, broken or chipped first gear teeth (B, **Figure 77**).

    c. Excessively worn or damaged bearing surfaces.

    d. Cracked or rounded-off snap ring grooves (C, **Figure 77**).

    e. Damaged clutch hub splines (A, **Figure 78**).

    f. Clogged oil holes (B, **Figure 78**).

5. Inspect the mainshaft bearing retainer (**Figure 79**) for cracks or mounting hole elongation.

6. Inspect the countershaft for:

    a. Worn or damages splines (A, **Figure 80**).

    b. Excessively worn or damaged bearing surfaces.

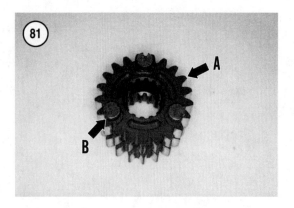

c. Cracked or rounded-off snap ring grooves (B, **Figure 80**).

d. Damaged drive sprocket splines (C, **Figure 80**).

7. Hold the shaft and turn the bearing outer race by hand. Refer to D, **Figure 77** for the mainshaft or D, **Figure 80** for the countershaft. The bearings should turn smoothly. Then check if the bearing is a tight fit on the respective shaft. If the bearing(s) is loose, turns roughly or is damaged, replace it. Refer to *Bearing Replacement* in Chapter One for typical procedures.

> *NOTE*
> *If the bearing(s) is a loose fit on the shaft, check the bearing's mounting position on the shaft carefully for any cracks, excessive wear or other damage. The shaft(s) may require replacement at the same time.*

8. Check each gear for:
   a. Missing, broken or chipped teeth (A, **Figure 81**).
   b. Worn, damaged, or rounded-off gear dogs (B, **Figure 81**).
   c. Worn, damaged, or rounded-off gear dog receptacles (**Figure 82**).
   d. Worn or damaged splines (**Figure 83**).
   e. Cracked or scored gear bore (**Figure 84**).
   f. Worn shift fork groove (A, **Figure 85**).
   g. Clear oil holes (B, **Figure 85**).
9. Check the bushings for:
   a. Severely worn or damaged bearing surface (**Figure 86**).
   b. Worn or damaged splines.
   c. Cracked or scored bore.

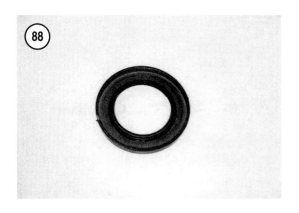

d. Insert the busing into the gear and rotate it (**Figure 87**). It must rotate smoothly without any binding or roughness.

10. Check the countershaft oil seal (**Figure 88**) for damage and deterioration.

11. Make sure each gear slides or turns on its respective shaft (**Figure 89**) without any binding or roughness.

12. Check the snap rings, tab lockwashers and notched spline washers for burn marks, excessive wear or other damage. Refer to **Figure 90** and **Figure 91**.

INTERNAL SHIFT MECHANISM INSPECTION

When measuring the shift fork shaft, compare the actual measurements to the specifications in **Table 2**. Replace worn or damaged parts as described in this section.

1. Clean and dry the shift forks and shaft (**Figure 92**).

2. Inspect each shift fork for signs of wear or damage. Examine the shift forks at the points

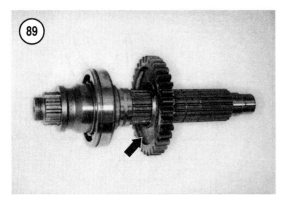

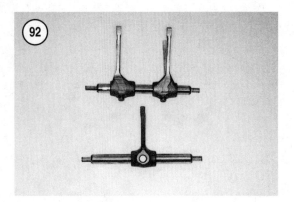

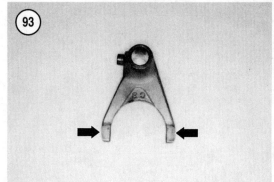

where they contact the slider gear (**Figure 93**). These surfaces must be smooth with no signs of wear, bending, cracks, heat discoloration or other damage.

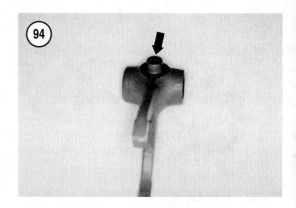

3. Check each shift fork pin (**Figure 94**) for cracks, excessive wear or other damage. If damage or wear is noted, check the corresponding shift drum groove.

4. Check the shift fork shaft (**Figure 95**) for bending or other damage. Roll the shift fork shaft on a surface plate or piece of glass and check for any clicking or other conditions that indicate a bent shaft. Install each shift fork on the shaft and slide it back and forth (**Figure 96**). Each shift fork should slide smoothly with no binding or tight spots. If binding is noticed with all three shift forks, inspect for a bent shaft. If a binding condition is noticed with one shift fork only, check that shift fork for a damaged bore.

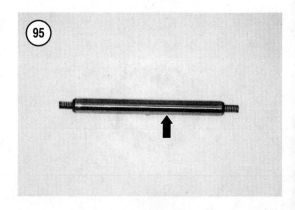

5. Check the spring (**Figure 97**) at each end of the shift fork for damage or sagging.

6. Clean and dry the shift drum.

7. Check the shift drum for:

  a. Severely worn or damaged cam grooves (**Figure 98**).

  b. Severely worn or damaged bearing surfaces.

8. Spin the shift drum bearing (**Figure 99**) by hand. The bearing should turn smoothly. If the bearing turns roughly or catches or there is other damage, replace it.

9. Check the ramps on the gearshift cam (**Figure 100**) for wear or damage.

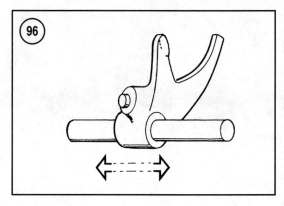

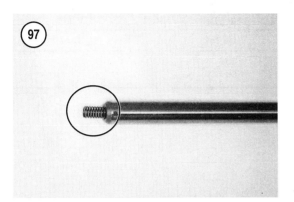

Table 1 TRANSMISSION SPECIFICATIONS

Transmission	Constant mesh, 6-speed
Shift pattern	1-N-2-3-4-5-6
Primary reduction ratio	1.581 (68/43)
Final reduction ratio	2.688 (43/16)
Transmission gear ratios	
First gear	
1998-1999 models	2.600 (39/15)
2000-2003 models	2.500 (35/14)
Second gear	1.842 (35/19)
Third gear	1.500 (30/20)
Fourth gear	1.333 (28/21)
Fifth gear	1.200 (30/25)
Sixth gear	1.115 (29/26)

Table 2 TRANSMISSION SPECIFICATIONS

Item	Standard mm (in.)	Service limit mm (in.)
Mainshaft runout	–	0.08 (0.003)
Countershaft runout	–	0.08 (0.003)
Shift fork shaft runout	–	0.10 (0.004)

Table 3 TRANSMISSION TORQUE SPECIFICATIONS

Item	N•m	in.-lb.	ft.-lb.
Countershaft bearing retainer	12	106	–
Shift drum retainer	10	88	–

CHAPTER EIGHT

FUEL, CARBURETORS, EMISSION CONTROL AND EXHAUST SYSTEMS

This chapter describes service procedures for the fuel system on carbureted models as well as the emission control systems for *both* the carbureted and fuel injected models. The exhaust and Exhaust Ultimate Power Valve (EXUP) systems are also covered. **Tables 1-3** are at the end of the chapter.

The 2000-2001 model is equipped with a diagnostic system to detect faults. The systems that feature a diagnostic capability and the chapter they are covered in are as follows:

1. EXUP System (this chapter).
2. Combination meter/speed sensor (Chapter Ten).
3. Fuel level warning light (Chapter Ten).
4. Throttle position sensor (TPS) (Chapter Ten).

FUEL TANK

Removal/Installation

Refer to **Figure 1**.

Read this procedure through before starting work. Make sure all of the necessary equipment is on hand to keep from damaging the fuel tank.

> *WARNING*
> *Some fuel may spill and fuel vapors will be present when removing the fuel tank. Because gasoline is extremely flammable, perform this procedure away from all open flames, including appliance pilot lights and sparks. Do not smoke or allow someone who is smoking in the work area, as an explosion and fire may occur. Always work in a well-ventilated area. Wipe up spills immediately.*

> *WARNING*
> *Gasoline is extremely flammable and must not be stored in an open container. Store gasoline in a sealed gasoline storage container, away from heat, sparks or flames.*

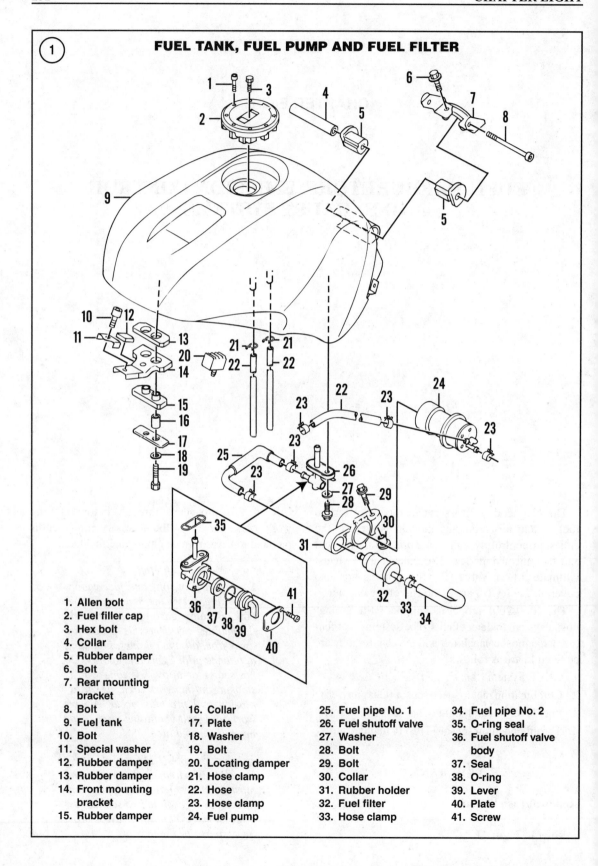

FUEL TANK, FUEL PUMP AND FUEL FILTER

1. Allen bolt
2. Fuel filler cap
3. Hex bolt
4. Collar
5. Rubber damper
6. Bolt
7. Rear mounting
   bracket
8. Bolt
9. Fuel tank
10. Bolt
11. Special washer
12. Rubber damper
13. Rubber damper
14. Front mounting
    bracket
15. Rubber damper
16. Collar
17. Plate
18. Washer
19. Bolt
20. Locating damper
21. Hose clamp
22. Hose
23. Hose clamp
24. Fuel pump
25. Fuel pipe No. 1
26. Fuel shutoff valve
27. Washer
28. Bolt
29. Bolt
30. Collar
31. Rubber holder
32. Fuel filter
33. Hose clamp
34. Fuel pipe No. 2
35. O-ring seal
36. Fuel shutoff valve
    body
37. Seal
38. O-ring
39. Lever
40. Plate
41. Screw

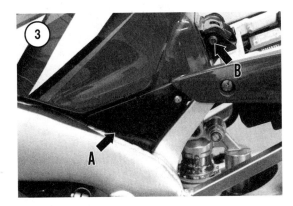

1. Remove the rider's seat as described in Chapter Sixteen.

2. Disconnect the battery negative cable as described in Chapter Ten.

3. If the fuel tank is more than one-quarter full, siphon the fuel into a container approved for gasoline storage. This reduces the weight of the tank before having to remove and turn the tank over when disconnecting the fuel hoses later in this procedure. To do this, perform the following:

   a. Open the fuel filler cap (**Figure 2**).

   b. Place a siphon hose into the fuel tank. Place the other end of the siphon hose into a fuel storage can.

   c. Operate the siphon to drain as much fuel from the tank as possible.

   d. When the siphon shuts off, remove it from the fuel tank and storage can. Close the fuel filler cap and place the storage can in a safe place, away from all flames and sparks. Drain the siphon of all gasoline before putting it away.

4. Remove the bolt securing the small trim panel (A, **Figure 3**) and remove the trim panel from each side of the fuel tank.

5. Remove the bolt and special washer (**Figure 4**) securing the front of the fuel tank.

6. Raise the front of the fuel tank and block it in this position with a piece of wood or soft face hammer (**Figure 5**).

7. Disconnect the electrical connector from the fuel level sensor (**Figure 6**).

WARNING
Place several shop cloths under the fuel hose to catch any fuel remaining in the hose. After the fuel hose is disconnected, plug the end. Properly discard the shop cloths.

8. Turn the fuel shutoff valve (A, **Figure 7**) off. Label, then disconnect, the following hoses from the valve:

   a. Fuel hose (B, **Figure 7**).

   b. Overflow hose (C, **Figure 7**).

   c. Breather hose (except California models) (D, **Figure 7**).

   d. Rollover valve-to-fuel tank hose (California models).

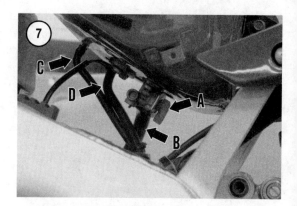

9. Remove the piece of wood or soft face hammer (**Figure 5**) installed in Step 6 and lower the fuel tank onto the frame.

10. On the left side, remove the bolt (B, **Figure 3**) securing the rear of the fuel tank, then remove the fuel tank.

11. Install the fuel tank by reversing these removal steps while noting the following:

   a. Turn the fuel shutoff valve on.

   b. Make sure the hoses are securely in place and that the clamps are tight.

   c. First tighten the front fuel tank mounting bolts securely, then tighten the rear mounting bolts (including the seat bracket) securely.

   d. Turn the ignition switch on and allow the fuel pump to pressurize the system. Check the fuel tank hoses for leaks.

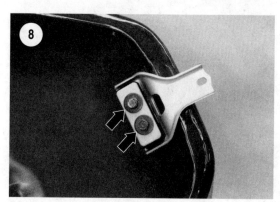

Inspection

1. Inspect all of the hoses for cracks, deterioration and other damage. Replace damaged hoses with the same Yamaha type and size materials. The hoses must be flexible and strong enough to withstand fuel pressure, engine heat and vibration.

2. Inspect the rear rubber dampers for deterioration or other damage. Replace if necessary. Make sure the metal collars are in place within the rubber grommets.

3. Check the mounting bracket for damage. Make sure the mounting bolts (**Figure 8**) are tight.

4. Make sure the locating dampers are in place. Check for deterioration or other damage.

5. Use the ignition key and open the fuel filler cap. Inspect the fuel filler cap gasket (**Figure 9**). If the gasket is damaged or starting to deteriorate, replace the filler cap assembly. Remove the inner hex bolt and the outer Allen bolts securing the filler cap (**Figure 10**) and remove the cap.

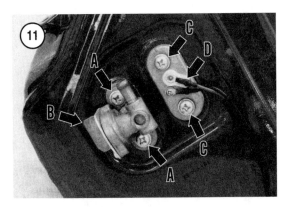

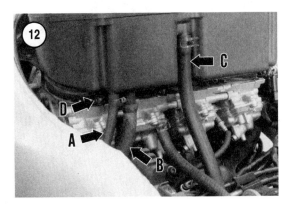

FUEL SHUTOFF VALVE

Removal/Installation

1. Remove the fuel tank as described in this chapter.

2. Place several heavy towels on the workbench to protect the fuel tank finish.

3. Turn the fuel tank on its side on the workbench.

4. Remove the mounting screws (A, **Figure 11**) and remove the shutoff valve (B) from the fuel tank.

5. Clean the filter of all dirt and debris. Replace the fuel shutoff valve filter and O-ring if worn or damaged.

6. Install by reversing these removal steps. Check for fuel leakage after the fuel tank is installed and the fuel pump has been turned on.

FUEL LEVEL SENDER

Removal/Installation

1. Remove the fuel tank as described in this chapter.

2. Place several heavy towels on the workbench to protect the fuel tank finish.

3. Turn the fuel tank on its side on the workbench.

4. Remove the mounting screws (C, **Figure 11**) and remove the fuel level sender (D) from the fuel tank.

5. Clean the filter of all dirt and debris. Replace the fuel shutoff valve filter and O-ring if worn or damaged.

6. Install by reversing these removal steps. Check for fuel leakage after the fuel tank is installed and the fuel pump has been turned on.

AIR FILTER HOUSING

Removal/Installation

1. Remove the fuel tank as described in this chapter.

2. Disconnect the following hoses from the air filter lower housing:

    a. Air filter housing breather hose (A, **Figure 12**).

    b. Air induction system hose (B, **Figure 12**) on models so equipped.

    c. Crankcase breather hose (C, **Figure 12**).

3. Use a long Phillips screwdriver and loosen the clamp screw (D, **Figure 12**) on the four clamps securing the housing to the carburetors.

4. Remove the bolt (**Figure 13**) securing the front of the air filter housing to the frame.

5. Cover each carburetor intake air funnel openings to prevent contamination or small parts from entering the throttle bores.

6. While the air filter housing is off the engine, visually check all of the exposed hoses for damage

that may have occurred when disconnecting them. Replace damaged hoses with the correct size replacement hose.

7. Install the air filter assembly by reversing these removal steps while noting the following:

a. Make sure the intake air funnels (**Figure 14**) are in place on the carburetors.

b. Inspect the housing and its gaskets; replace if necessary.

c. Route and connect all of the hoses correctly. Make sure all hose clamps, where used, are positioned correctly on the hose ends.

CARBURETOR

Operation

For proper operation, the engine must be supplied with air and fuel mixed in proper proportions by weight. A mixture with an excessive amount of fuel is said to be rich. A lean mixture is one that contains insufficient fuel. The properly adjusted carburetors supply the proper air/fuel mixture under all operating conditions.

Each carburetor consists of several major systems. A float and float valve mechanism maintain a constant fuel level in the float bowls. The pilot system supplies fuel at low speeds. The main fuel system supplies fuel at medium and high speeds. A starter (choke) system supplies the very rich mixture needed to start a cold engine.

Service

If poor engine performance, hesitation and little or no response to mixture adjustment are observed, and if all other factors that could affect performance are correct, remove the carburetors as described in this section and refer to *Carburetor Overhaul* in this chapter.

Removal/Installation

> *NOTE*
> *There are numerous vacuum hoses on the carburetor assembly. Mark each hose and fitting to aid in installation.*

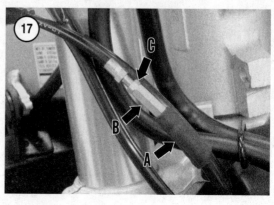

Remove all four carburetors as an assembled unit.

1. Remove the rider's seat as described in Chapter Sixteen.

2. Remove the left side fairing as described in Chapter Sixteen.

3. Remove the fuel tank as described in this chapter.

4. Remove the air filter housing as described in this chapter.

5. Remove the ignition coil plate assembly as described in Chapter Ten.

6. Carefully pull up on the rear of the rubber baffle (**Figure 15**) and move it forward off the carburetor assembly.

7. Loosen the clamp screw (A, **Figure 16**) and disconnect the starter (choke) cable from the cable holder and disconnect it from the starter control arm (B).

8. Provide slack in the throttle cables as follows:

   a. On the right side of the steering stem, slide back the rubber boot (A, **Figure 17**) on the in-line adjuster.

   b. Loosen the locknut (B, **Figure 17**) and turn the adjuster (C) in either direction until the correct amount of free play is obtained. Tighten the locknut.

9. On the right side, disconnect the throttle position sensor electrical connector (**Figure 18**). Move the wiring harness out of the way.

10. On the right side, disconnect the float chamber air vent hose (**Figure 19**).

11. On the left side, disconnect the throttle adjust knob (**Figure 20**) from the bracket. Carefully pull the throttle adjust knob and cable up through the frame.

12. On California models, perform the following:

   a. Disconnect the two hoses from the left side of the carburetor assembly.

   b. Disconnect the hose going to the EVAP purge control valve.

13. Use a Phillips screwdriver bit and ratchet and loosen the clamp screw on the four intake manifolds on the cylinder head (**Figure 21**).

14. Pull the carburetor assembly upward and disengage it from the intake manifolds.

NOTE
All models are equipped with two throttle cables. The decelerator (or

8

push) cable is located at the bottom of the throttle cable bracket (A, Figure 22). The accelerator (or pull) cable is located at the top of the throttle cable bracket (B, Figure 22). The carburetor assembly shown in this figure is placed upside down.

15. Loosen the locknuts on both throttle cables and disconnect them from the throttle wheel and the cable mounting bracket.

16. Cover the cylinder head intake openings with clean shop cloths (**Figure 23**).

17. Install by reversing these removal steps while noting the following:

   a. Make sure all four carburetors are fully seated downward in the intake manifolds on the cylinder head. A solid bottoming out will be felt when they are correctly seated.

   b. Make sure each carburetor clamp screw is tight to avoid a vacuum loss and possible valve damage due to a lean fuel mixture.

   c. Make sure all hoses are connected to the correct fittings.

   d. Adjust the throttle cables as described in Chapter Three.

CARBURETOR OVERHAUL

Alterations in jet size, throttle slide cutaway and jet needle position should only be attempted by those experienced in this type of tuning work. Do not adjust or modify the carburetors in an attempt to fix a drivability problem caused by another system.

Disassembly

Leave the carburetors assembled as a unit. If necessary, refer to *Separation* in this section. Disassemble only one carburetor at a time to prevent the accidental interchange of parts.

> *CAUTION*
> *The throttle position sensor is pre-set by the manufacturer. Do not remove the throttle position sensor (Figure 24) from the bracket unless it requires replacement. Removal of the sensor may cause the sensor to move out of position, resulting in improper ignition timing. Refer all testing and re-*

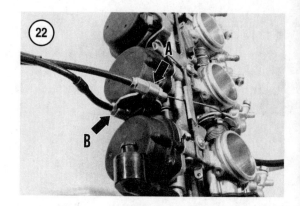

placement of the sensor to a Yamaha dealership.

Refer to **Figure 25**.

1. Pull straight up on each air funnel (**Figure 26**) and remove all four funnels.

2. Remove the mounting screws and the cover (**Figure 27**).

3. Remove the spring (A, **Figure 28**) and the diaphragm/piston valve assembly (B).

4. Disassemble the diaphragm/piston valve as follows:

CARBURETOR

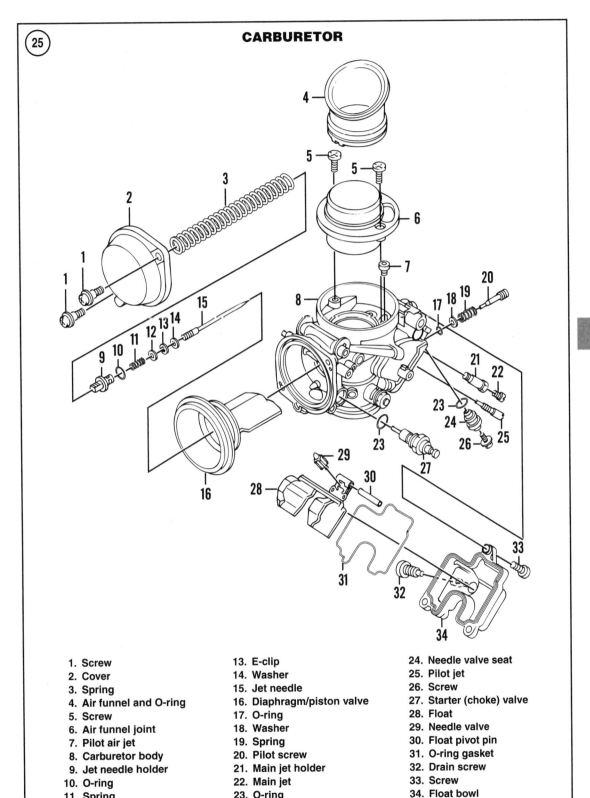

1. Screw	13. E-clip	24. Needle valve seat
2. Cover	14. Washer	25. Pilot jet
3. Spring	15. Jet needle	26. Screw
4. Air funnel and O-ring	16. Diaphragm/piston valve	27. Starter (choke) valve
5. Screw	17. O-ring	28. Float
6. Air funnel joint	18. Washer	29. Needle valve
7. Pilot air jet	19. Spring	30. Float pivot pin
8. Carburetor body	20. Pilot screw	31. O-ring gasket
9. Jet needle holder	21. Main jet holder	32. Drain screw
10. O-ring	22. Main jet	33. Screw
11. Spring	23. O-ring	34. Float bowl
12. Washer		

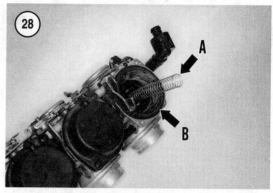

a. Use needlenose pliers and withdraw the jet needle holder (**Figure 29**).

b. Withdraw the spring, jet needle and washer.

5. Unscrew and remove the pilot air jet (**Figure 30**).

6. Remove the float bowl screws (A, **Figure 31**) and remove the float bowl (B).

7. Push out and remove the float pin (A, **Figure 32**).

8. Pull straight up and remove the float assembly (B, **Figure 32**). Do not lose the needle valve hanging on the float tang.

9. Unscrew and remove the main jet (C, **Figure 32**) from the end of the main jet holder.

10. Unscrew and remove the pilot jet (**Figure 33**).

11. Remove the screw (A, **Figure 34**) and remove the needle valve seat (B).

12. Slowly screw the pilot screw (**Figure 35**) in until it *lightly* seats while counting and recording the number of turns. The pilot screw must be reinstalled to this same position during assembly. Unscrew and remove the pilot screw, spring, washer and O-ring.

13. Unscrew and remove the main jet holder (**Figure 36**).

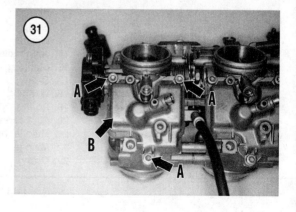

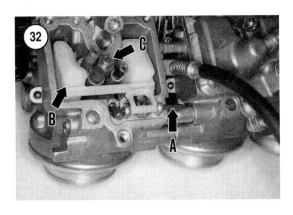

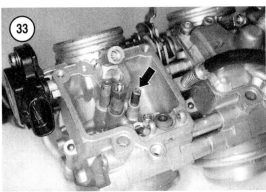

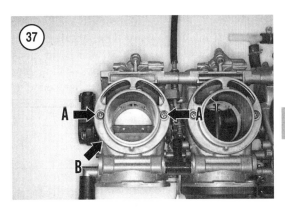

8

14. If necessary, remove the mounting screws (A, **Figure 37**) and remove the air funnel joint (B).

15. If necessary, remove the starter (choke) valves as follows:

    a. Remove the center screw (A, **Figure 38**) and the return spring (B) from the starter arm.

    b. Remove the remaining two screws and washers securing the starter arm and remove the starter arm (**Figure 39**).

    c. Unscrew the starter valve (**Figure 40**) from each carburetor body.

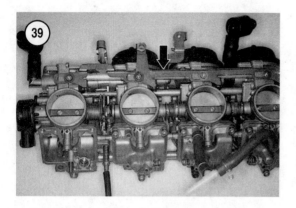

16. Do not remove the throttle position sensor (**Figure 24**) unless necessary. If the throttle position sensor is going to be removed, make and index mark adjacent to the mounting screws on the carburetor body. This will ensure correct alignment during installation.

> **CAUTION**
> *Further disassembly is neither necessary nor recommended. Do not remove the throttle shaft and butterfly assemblies (**Figure 41**). If these parts are damaged, the carburetor must be replaced, as these items are not available separately.*

17. Clean and inspect all parts as described in this chapter.

Assembly

1. If removed, install the throttle position sensor (**Figure 24**) in the exact same location noted during *Disassembly* Step 16. Tighten the screws securely.

2. If removed, install the starter (choke) valves as follows:

    a. Screw the starter valve (**Figure 40**) into the carburetor body and tighten securely.

    b. Connect the starter arm (**Figure 39**) to the starter valves.

    c. Install the center screw, washer (A, **Figure 38**) and the return spring (B) onto the starter arm.

    d. Install the remaining two washers and the screws securing the starter arm. Tighten the screws securely, but do not overtighten.

3. If removed, install the air funnel joint (B, **Figure 37**) and the mounting screws (A). Tighten the screws securely.

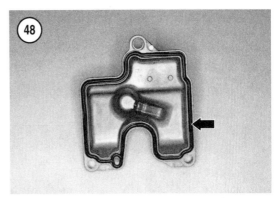

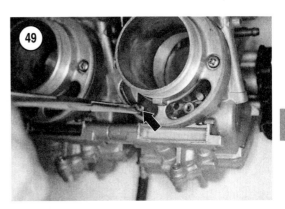

8

4. Install the main jet holder (**Figure 42**) and tighten securely.

5. Install the pilot screw (**Figure 43**) to the same position noted during *Removal* Step 12.

6. Install a *new* O-ring on the needle valve seat (**Figure 44**) and install the seat. Install the screw (A, **Figure 34**) and tighten securely.

7. Install the pilot jet (**Figure 45**) and tighten securely (**Figure 33**).

8. Install the main jet (**Figure 46**) into the end of the main jet holder and tighten securely (C, **Figure 32**).

9. Install the float valve (**Figure 47**) onto the float assembly.

10. Install the float (B, **Figure 32**) while indexing the needle valve into the housing.

11. Install the float pin (A, **Figure 32**) and push it in until it seats.

12. Install a *new* float bowl O-ring gasket (**Figure 48**).

13. Install the float bowl (B, **Figure 31**) and tighten the screws (A) securely.

14. Install the pilot air jet (**Figure 49**) and tighten securely (**Figure 30**).

15. Assemble the diaphragm/piston valve as follows:

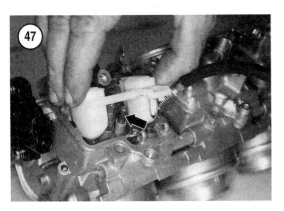

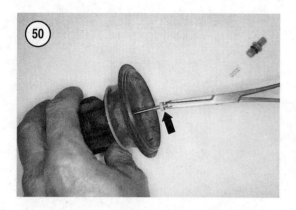

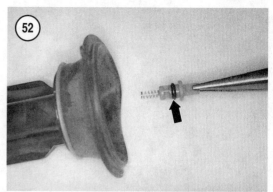

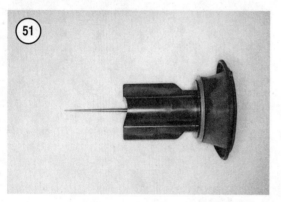

a. Use needlenose pliers and install the jet needle and washer (**Figure 50**). Push the assembly down until it bottoms (**Figure 51**).

b. Use needlenose pliers and install the jet needle holder and spring (**Figure 52**). Push the assembly down until it bottoms (**Figure 29**).

16. Turn the lip of the diaphragm down (**Figure 53**) and install the diaphragm/piston valve assembly into the carburetor body. Guide the jet needle into the opening in the venturi (**Figure 54**).

17. Make sure the diaphragm is seated correctly around the perimeter (**Figure 55**) and is correctly aligned with the vent hole (**Figure 56**).

NOTE
The piston valve spring is very long and is difficult to install while keeping it straight. Use the method listed in Step 18 to avoid having the spring getting misaligned within the top cover.

18. Install the top cover and spring as follows:

a. Insert the upper end of the spring (A, **Figure 57**) into the piston valve receptacle (B) and into the receptacle in the top cover.

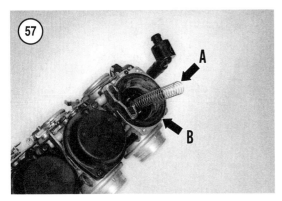

8

b. Hold onto the top cover with one hand, raise the piston valve with a finger, and correctly compress the spring between these two parts.

c. Hold the piston valve in the raised position and install the top cover (**Figure 58**) onto the top of the carburetor.

d. Lower the piston valve and temporarily install the top cover screws.

e. Insert a finger into the venturi area and move the piston valve up in the carburetor body (**Figure 59**). The piston valve should rise all the way up into the bore and slide back down immediately with no binding. If it binds or if the movement is sluggish, chances are the diaphragm did not seat correctly, or the spring is misaligned to one side or not centered within the top cover. If necessary, remove the top cover and reposition the spring.

f. If the spring is installed correctly, tighten the top cover screws securely.

19. Push the air funnel straight down onto the carburetor body and align the groove with the notch in the carburetor body (**Figure 60**). Install all four air funnels (**Figure 61**).

20. After the assembly and installation are completed, adjust the carburetors as described in this chapter and in Chapter Three.

Cleaning and Inspection

> *CAUTION*
> *The carburetor bodies are equipped with plastic parts that cannot be removed. Do not dip the carburetor body, O-rings, float assembly, needle valve or diaphragm/piston valve into carburetor cleaner or other harsh solutions that can damage these parts. Yamaha does not recommend the use of a caustic carburetor cleaning solvent. Instead, clean the carburetors and related parts in a petroleum-based solvent.*

1. Initially clean all parts in a mild petroleum-based cleaning solution. Wash the parts in hot soap and water and rinse them with cold water. Blow-dry the parts with compressed air.

> *CAUTION*
> *If compressed air is not available, allow the parts to air dry or use a clean lint-free cloth. Do not use a paper towel to dry carburetor parts. The small paper particles could plug openings in the carburetor housing or jets.*

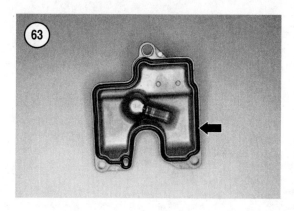

2. Allow the carburetor body and components to dry thoroughly before assembly. Blow out the jets and the needle jet holder with compressed air.

> *CAUTION*
> *Do not use wire or drill bits to clean jets. Even minor gouges in a jet can alter flow rate and alter the air/fuel mixture.*

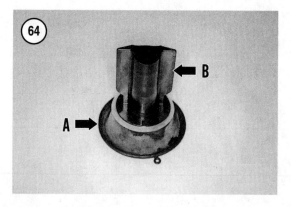

3. Make sure the float bowl drain screw (**Figure 62**) is in good condition and does not leak. Replace the drain screw if necessary.
4. Inspect the float bowl O-ring gasket (**Figure 63**) for hardness or deterioration. Replace as necessary.
5. Inspect the diaphragm (A, **Figure 64**) for cracks, deterioration or other damage. Check the sides of the piston valve (B, **Figure 64**) for excessive wear.

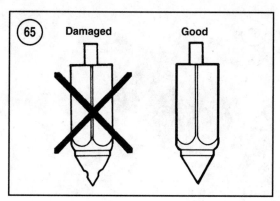

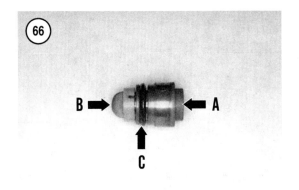

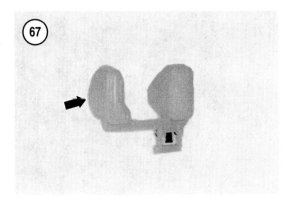

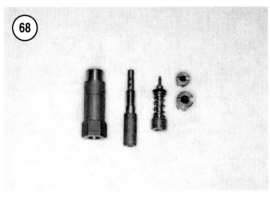

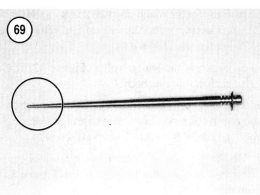

Install the piston valve into the carburetor body and move it up and down in the bore. The piston valve should move smoothly with no binding or excessive play. Replace the piston valve and/or carburetor body if necessary.

6. Inspect the tapered end of the needle valve for steps, uneven wear or damage (**Figure 65**).

7. Inspect the needle valve seat (A, **Figure 66**) for steps, uneven wear or other damage. Insert the needle valve into the valve seat, and slowly move it back and forth and check for smooth operation. If either part is worn or damaged, replace both parts as a set.

8. Inspect the filter end (B, **Figure 66**) and O-ring (C) for damage or deterioration.

9. Inspect the float (**Figure 67**) for deterioration or damage. Place the float in a container of water and push it down. If the float sinks or if bubbles appear (indicating a leak), replace the float.

10. Inspect all of the jets (**Figure 68**). Make sure all holes are open and no part is worn or damaged. Replace the worn or unserviceable parts.

11. Inspect the jet needle taper (**Figure 69**) for steps, uneven wear or other damage. Install a *new* O-ring on the holder.

12. If removed, inspect the pilot screw O-ring. Replace the O-ring if it has become hard or is starting to deteriorate.

13. Inspect the starter (choke) valve (**Figure 70**) for wear and make sure the spring has not sagged.

14. Inspect the air funnel joint for contamination.

15. Make sure all openings in the carburetor housing are clear. Refer to **Figure 71** and **Figure 72**. Clean them out if they are plugged in any way, then apply compressed air to all openings.

16. Check the top cover for cracks or damage and replace if necessary.

17. Inspect the air funnel for hardness or deterioration.

18. Make sure the throttle plate screws (**Figure 73**) are tight.

19. Inspect the carburetor body for internal or external damage. If damaged, replace the carburetor assembly. The body cannot be replaced separately.

20. Move the throttle wheel back and forth from stop to stop. The throttle lever should move smoothly and return under spring tension. Replace the carburetor if the throttle wheel does not move freely or if it sticks in any position.

Separation

Refer to **Figure 74**.

> *CAUTION*
> *The throttle position sensor is pre-set by the manufacturer. Do not remove the throttle position sensor (**Figure 75**) from the bracket unless it requires replacement. Removal of the sensor may cause the sensor to move out of position, resulting in improper ignition timing. Refer all testing and replacement to a Yamaha dealership.*

1. Remove the carburetor assembly as described in this chapter.

2. Remove the four air funnels (**Figure 76**).

3. Note the throttle lever (A, **Figure 77**) and return spring location (B) next to the No. 4 carburetor. The spring must be installed in the exact same location.

4. Note the location of all of the spacers (A, **Figure 78**) and the carburetor synchronization springs (B). Mark each spacer as it is removed as they are all of different lengths.

5. Remove the idle adjust knob and cable (A, **Figure 79**).

6. If still installed, remove all fuel, air and vacuum hoses (B, **Figure 79**) from the carburetors. Label each hose and fitting so the hoses can be reinstalled in their original locations during assembly.

7. Remove the starter (choke) valves as follows:

    a. Remove the center screw (A, **Figure 80**) and the return spring (B) from the starter arm.

    b. Remove the remaining two screws and washers securing the starter arm and remove the starter arm (**Figure 81**).

    c. Unscrew the starter valve (**Figure 82**) from each carburetor body.

8. Loosen the synchronization adjusting screws and remove the synchronization springs. Although only one screw is visible, loosen all screws.

9. On the left side of the carburetor assembly, unscrew and remove the through bolts (**Figure 83**) from the carburetors.

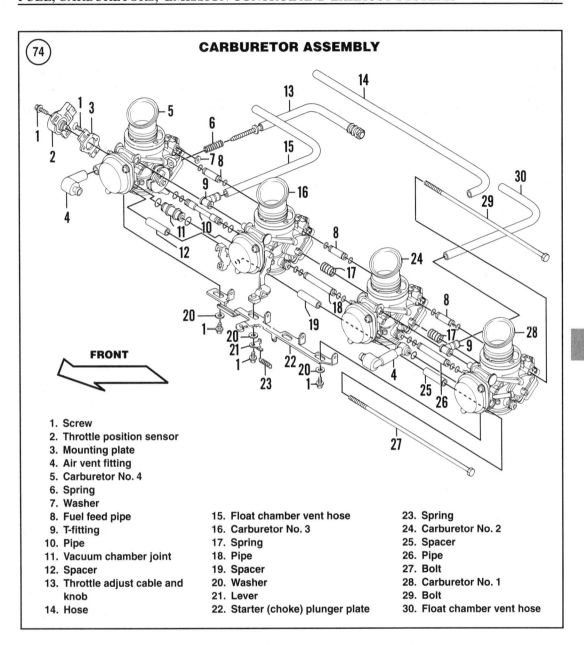

CARBURETOR ASSEMBLY

1. Screw
2. Throttle position sensor
3. Mounting plate
4. Air vent fitting
5. Carburetor No. 4
6. Spring
7. Washer
8. Fuel feed pipe
9. T-fitting
10. Pipe
11. Vacuum chamber joint
12. Spacer
13. Throttle adjust cable and knob
14. Hose

15. Float chamber vent hose
16. Carburetor No. 3
17. Spring
18. Pipe
19. Spacer
20. Washer
21. Lever
22. Starter (choke) plunger plate

23. Spring
24. Carburetor No. 2
25. Spacer
26. Pipe
27. Bolt
28. Carburetor No. 1
29. Bolt
30. Float chamber vent hose

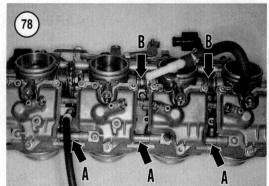

10. Carefully separate the No. 1 and No. 2 carburetors from the No. 3 and No. 4 carburetors.

11. Remove the fuel feed pipes, spacers and interconnecting vacuum pipes between the carburetors.

12. Assemble the carburetors by reversing these disassembly steps, noting the following:

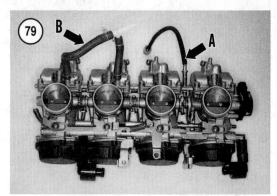

    a. Install *new* O-rings on the fuel feed pipes, vacuum chamber joint and air vent joints connecting the carburetors.

    b. Place the carburetor assembly on a piece of plate glass.

    c. Install the front and rear connecting bolts through all four carburetors.

    d. Install and tighten the connecting bolt nuts securely while pressing down on all four carburetors to maintain proper alignment between all four carburetors.

    e. Connect the air, fuel and vacuum hoses to the proper fittings as noted during disassembly.

    f. Push the air funnel straight down onto the carburetor body and align the groove with the notch in the carburetor body (**Figure 84**). Install all four air funnels (**Figure 76**).

CARBURETOR ADJUSTMENTS

Synchronization

Refer to *Carburetor Synchronization* in Chapter Three.

Fuel Level Inspection

A Yamaha fuel level gauge is required for this procedure. For U.S. and Canada models, use part No. YM-01312-A. For other models, use part No. 90890-1312.

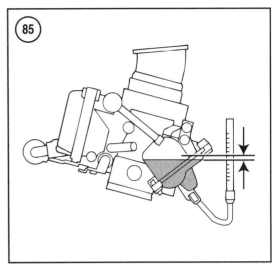

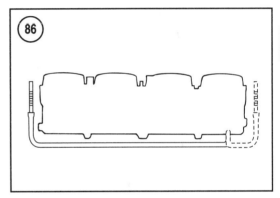

NOTE
A piece of clear plastic of the appropriate size can be substituted for the Yamaha tool.

1. Support the motorcycle on level ground with the front wheel off the ground. Refer to *Motorcycle Stands* in Chapter Twelve.

2. Remove the rider's seat as described in Chapter Sixteen.

3. Remove the fuel tank and air filter housing as described in this chapter.

4. Start with the No. 1 carburetor on the left side, then work across the carburetors in order. Note the fuel level dimension for each carburetor.

5. Install the tool into the fitting on the float bowl. Hold the tool vertically next to the carburetor being checked (**Figure 85**).

6. Slowly unscrew the drain screw and allow the fuel to enter the tool. The fuel in the tool will reach the same level as the fuel in the float chamber. Note the fuel level, then move the tool to the opposite side of the carburetor assembly (**Figure 86**). The level must be the same on both sides. The correct fuel level is listed in **Table 1** or **Table 2**.

7. Tighten the drain screw and disconnect the fuel level tool. Repeat Step 5 and Step 6 for the remaining three carburetors.

8. If the fuel level is incorrect in the carburetor(s), remove the carburetor assembly as described in this chapter.

9. To adjust the fuel level, perform the following:

a. Remove the float bowl screws (A, **Figure 87**) and remove the float bowl (B).

b. Push out and remove the float pin (A, **Figure 88**).

c. Pull straight up and remove the float assembly (B, **Figure 88**). Remove the needle valve from the float tang.

d. Carefully bend the float tang (**Figure 89**) a little at a time. Bending the tang up lowers the fuel level; bending it down raises the fuel level.

e. Install the float valve (**Figure 90**) onto the float assembly.

f. Install the float (B, **Figure 88**) while indexing the needle valve into the housing.

g. Install the float pin (A, **Figure 88**) and push it in until it seats.

h. Install the float bowl (B, **Figure 87**) and tighten the screws (A) securely.

10. Install the carburetor assembly and recheck the fuel level(s). Readjust if necessary.

11. Install the air filter housing and fuel tank as described in this chapter.

12. Install the rider's seat as described in Chapter Sixteen.

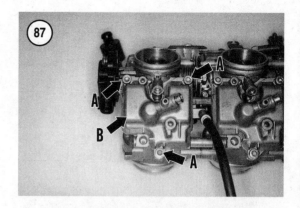

Needle Jet Adjustment

The needle jet is non-adjustable on all models.

Rejetting

1. Do not attempt to solve a poor engine running condition by rejetting the carburetors. Make sure all other systems are operating correctly before considering the carburetors as the source of the problem. If the following list of conditions hold true, carburetor rejetting is most likely not the problem.

a. The engine has held a good tune in the past with the standard jetting.

b. The engine has not been modified.

c. The motorcycle is being operated in the same geographical region under the same general climatic conditions as in the past.

d. The motorcycle was and is being ridden at average highway speeds.

2. The following are conditions under which carburetor rejetting may be required:

a. A non-standard air filter element is installed.

b. A non-standard exhaust system is installed.

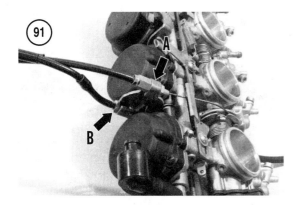

c. Any top end components (pistons, camshafts, valves, compression) have been modified.

d. The motorcycle is in use at considerably higher or lower elevation or in a considerably hotter or colder climate than in the past.

e. The motorcycle is operated at considerably higher speeds than before; a colder spark plug heat range does not solve the problem.

f. Someone has previously changed the carburetor jetting. Original equipment jet sizes are listed in **Table 1** and **Table 2**.

g. The motorcycle has never held a satisfactory engine tune.

3. If it is necessary to rejet the carburetors, check with a Yamaha dealership or motorcycle performance specialist for recommendations on the size of jets to install for specific conditions.

4. If the jets are going to be replaced, do so only one size at a time. After rejetting, test ride the motorcycle and inspect the spark plugs as described in Chapter Three.

THROTTLE CABLE REPLACEMENT

Always replace both throttle cables as a set.

1. Support the motorcycle on a swing arm safety stand. Block the front wheel so the motorcycle will not roll in either direction while on the safety stand.

2. Remove the right side fairing and the front fairing as described in Chapter Sixteen.

3. Perform Steps 1-14 of *Carburetor Removal/Installation* in this chapter and partially remove the carburetor assembly to gain access to the throttle wheel and bracket.

NOTE
All models are equipped with two throttle cables and they are different. Use masking tape to label the old cables before removing them. The decelerator (or push) cable is located at the bottom of the throttle cable bracket (A, Figure 91). The accelerator (or pull) cable is located at the top of the throttle cable bracket (B, Figure 91). The carburetor assembly shown in this figure is placed upside down.

4. Note the location of the throttle cables within the throttle wheel. They must be reinstalled in the correct location.

5. Loosen the locknuts on both throttle cables and disconnect them from the throttle wheel and the cable mounting bracket.

6. Make a drawing of the cable routing from the right hand throttle housing to the carburetor assembly. Record this information for proper cable routing and installation.

7. At the right handlebar, remove the throttle cable housing screws (**Figure 92**) and open the housing assembly.

8. Disconnect the throttle cables from the throttle grip (**Figure 93**).

8

9. Remove the cables from around the front of the right side fork tube (**Figure 94**) and over the steering head lower bracket (**Figure 95**). Note the position of any cable clamps for installation.

10. Compare the new and old cables.

11. If cables without nylon liners are used, lubricate them as described in Chapter Three.

12. Route the new cables through the same path as the old cables.

> *WARNING*
> *The throttle cables are the push/pull type and must not be interchanged. Attach the cables following the identification labels made on the old cables.*

13. Lightly grease the throttle cable ends and connect them to the throttle grip in the correct location as follows:

   a. Install the push cable (**Figure 96**) onto the receptacle in throttle grip, then slowly rotate the throttle grip.

   b. Slightly rotate the throttle grip, then install the pull cable (A, **Figure 97**) onto the receptacle in the throttle grip.

   c. Move the rear portion of the throttle cable housing (B, **Figure 97**) into position on the throttle grip.

   d. Install the front portion of the throttle cable housing into position on the throttle grip and install the screws (**Figure 92**). Tighten the screws securely.

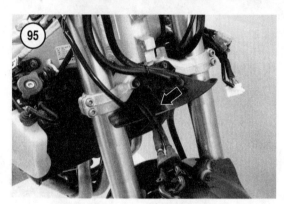

> *NOTE*
> ***Figure 91** is shown with the carburetor assembly placed upside down.*

14. Install the throttle cables onto the throttle cable bracket and throttle wheel as follows:

   a. Install the decelerator (or push) cable at the bottom of the throttle cable bracket (A, **Figure 91**) and onto the bottom portion of the throttle wheel (**Figure 98**).

   b. Install the accelerator (or pull) cable at the top of the throttle cable bracket (B, **Figure 91**) and onto the top portion of the throttle wheel.

15. Install the carburetor assembly as described under *Carburetor Removal/Installation* in this chapter.

16. Open the throttle and release it. The throttle should snap back smoothly. If operation is incorrect, carefully check that the cables are attached correctly and there are no tight bends in the cables. Repeat this

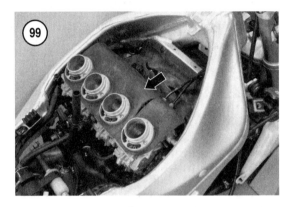

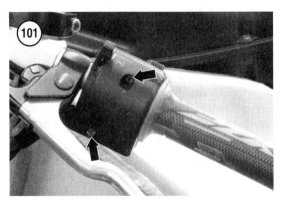

check with the front wheel pointing straight ahead and then with the wheel turned full left and full right.

17. Adjust the throttle cables as described in Chapter Three.

18. When the throttle is operating correctly, start the engine and run it at idle speed with the transmission in neutral. Turn the handlebar from side to side, making sure the idle speed does not increase. If it does, the throttle cables are improperly installed. If the idle speed did not increase, test ride the motorcycle slowly at first. If there is any problem with the throttle, stop the motorcycle and make the necessary repairs.

> *WARNING*
> *An improperly adjusted or incorrectly routed throttle cable can cause the throttle to stick in the open position. This could cause a loss of control. Do not ride the motorcycle until the throttle cable operation is correct.*

19. Install the front fairing and the right side fairing as described in Chapter Sixteen.

STARTER (CHOKE) CABLE REPLACEMENT

1. Support the motorcycle on a swing arm safety stand. Block the front wheel so the motorcycle will not roll in either direction while on the safety stand.

2. Remove the rider's seat (Chapter Sixteen).

3. Remove the left side fairing (Chapter Sixteen).

4. Remove the fuel tank as described in this chapter.

5. Remove the air filter housing as described in this chapter.

6. Remove the ignition coil plate assembly as described in Chapter Ten.

7. Carefully pull up on the rear of the rubber baffle (**Figure 99**) and move it forward off the carburetor assembly.

8. Loosen the clamp screw (A, **Figure 100**) and disconnect the starter (choke) cable from the cable holder and disconnect it from the starter control arm (B) on the carburetor assembly.

9. Make a drawing of the starter (choke) cable routing from the left side switch assembly to the carburetor assembly. Record this information for proper cable routing and installation.

10. At the left side handlebar, remove the screws (**Figure 101**) securing the switch housing and open the switch housing assembly.

11. Disconnect the starter (choke) cable from the lever (**Figure 102**).

12. Remove the cable from around the front of the left side fork tube and over the lower fork bridge (**Figure 103**). Note the position of any cable clamps for installation.

13. Compare the new and old cable.

14. If a cable is without a nylon liner, lubricate it as described in Chapter Three.

15. Route the new cable through the same path as the old cable.

16. Apply grease onto the exposed choke cable wire and connect the cable end onto the choke lever.

17. Install the choke lever into the switch housing (**Figure 102**) and onto the handlebar (**Figure 104**).

18. Install the left handlebar switch and align the switch projection with the hole in the handlebar. Install the screws and tighten securely.

19. Connect the starter (choke) cable onto the starter control arm (B, **Figure 100**) and tighten the clamp screw (A) on the carburetor assembly.

20. Operate the choke lever and make sure the carburetor linkage is operating correctly with no binding. If the cable operation is incorrect, check that the cable is attached correctly and that there are no tight bends in the cable.

21. Carefully move the rubber baffle back into position over the carburetor assembly.

22. Install the ignition coil plate assembly as described in Chapter Ten.

23. Install the air filter housing as described in this chapter.

24. Install the fuel tank as described in this chapter.

25. Install the left side fairing as described in Chapter Sixteen.

26. Install the rider's seat as described in Chapter Sixteen.

FUEL PUMP

Removal/Installation

1. Support the motorcycle on a swing arm safety stand. Block the front wheel so the motorcycle will not roll in either direction while on the safety stand.

2. Remove the rider's seat as described in Chapter Sixteen.

3. Disconnect the negative battery cable as described in Chapter Ten.

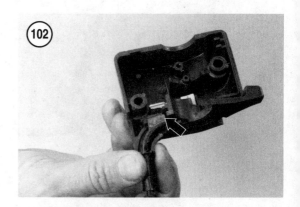

4. Remove the fuel tank as described in this chapter.

5. Remove the bolt (A, **Figure 105**) securing the fuel pump and fuel filter rubber mount to the frame. Do not lose the collar in the mounting hole.

6. On the right side, disconnect the 2-pin black electrical connector (black and blue/black wires) for the fuel pump.

> *WARNING*
> *Place several shop cloths under the fuel hose to catch any fuel remaining in the hose. After the fuel hose is disconnected, plug the end. Properly discard the shop cloths.*

7. Note the location of the two fuel hoses. The lower U-shaped hose (B, **Figure 105**) is on the lower fitting and it goes to the fuel filter. The upper straight hose (C, **Figure 105**) is the fuel feed hose that goes to the carburetor assembly.

8. Loosen the upper straight hose clamp and disconnect the upper straight hose (C, **Figure 105**) from the fuel pump. Loosen the lower hose clamp

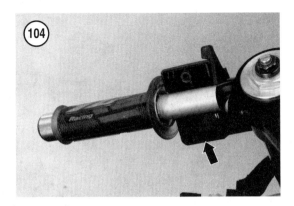

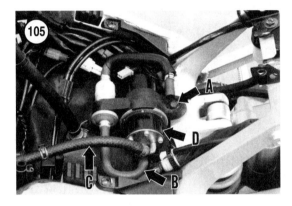

and disconnect the lower fuel hose (B, **Figure 105**) from the fuel pump. Plug the ends of both hoses.

9. Remove the fuel pump (D, **Figure 105**) from the rubber mount and remove the fuel pump.

10. Install by reversing these removal steps. Make sure the hoses are installed onto the correct fittings and the clamps are tight.

Fuel Pump Tests

Prior to checking the fuel pump, perform the *Fuel Pump Relay Test* in Chapter Ten.

Fuel flow test

> *NOTE*
> *Prior to running this test, make sure the fuel filter has been replaced recently. If in doubt, install a new filter at this time to ensure an accurate test.*

1. Support the motorcycle on a swing arm safety stand. Block the front wheel so the motorcycle will not roll in either direction while on the safety stand.

2. Remove the rider's seat as described in Chapter Sixteen.

3. Remove the fuel tank as described in this chapter.

4. Disconnect the upper straight fuel feed hose (C, **Figure 105**) that goes to the carburetor assembly. Place the hose over the side of the frame member.

5. Turn the fuel shut off valve on, then partially install the fuel tank onto the top of the frame.

6. Place the loose end of the fuel feed hose into a container.

7. Turn the engine stop switch to the RUN position.

8. Start the engine and check to see if fuel flows out of the fuel feed hose. Note the following:

    a. Fuel flows out of the fuel feed hose: fuel pump is good.

    b. Fuel does not flow out of the fuel feed hose: fuel pump is faulty.

9. Stop the engine and check to see if the fuel stops flowing.

    a. Fuel stops flowing out of the fuel feed hose: fuel pump is good.

    b. Fuel flows out of the fuel feed hose: fuel pump is faulty.

10. Turn the fuel shut off valve on.

11. Remove the fuel tank and discard the spent fuel correctly.

12. Connect the upper straight fuel feed hose (C, **Figure 105**) onto the carburetor assembly.

13. Install the fuel tank as described in this chapter.

14. Install the rider's seat as described in Chapter Sixteen.

Running test

1. Remove the rider's seat as described in Chapter Sixteen.

2. On the right side, disconnect the 2-pin black electrical connector (black and blue/black wires) for the fuel pump.

> *CAUTION*
> *Do not connect the battery jumper cables for more than 2-3 seconds or the fuel pump may be damaged.*

3. Connect 12-volt battery jumper cables to the following fuel pump terminals:

    a. Battery positive lead: blue/black wire.

    b. Battery negative lead: black.

4. The fuel pump should run. Replace the fuel pump if it fails this test.

5. Connect the fuel pump 2-pin electrical connector.

6. Install the rider's seat as described in Chapter Sixteen.

Resistance test

1. Remove the rider's seat as described in Chapter Sixteen.

2. On the right side, disconnect the 2-pin black electrical connector (black and blue/black wires) for the fuel pump.

3. Connect an ohmmeter to the following fuel pump terminals:

   a. Ohmmeter positive test lead: blue/black.

   b. Ohmmeter negative test lead: black.

4. The specified resistance is 4-30 ohms. Replace the fuel pump if it fails this test.

5. Connect the fuel pump 2-pin electrical connector.

6. Install the rider's seat as described in Chapter Sixteen.

FUEL FILTER

Removal/Installation

1. Support the motorcycle on a swing arm safety stand. Block the front wheel so the motorcycle will not roll in either direction while on the safety stand.

2. Remove the rider's seat as described in Chapter Sixteen.

3. Disconnect the negative battery cable as described in Chapter Ten.

4. Remove the fuel tank as described in this chapter.

> *WARNING*
> *Place several shop cloths under the fuel hose to catch any fuel remaining in the hose. After the fuel hose is disconnected, plug the end. Properly discard the shop cloths.*

5. Note the location of the two fuel hoses. The right side U-shaped hose (A, **Figure 106**) is the fuel feed hose that goes to the carburetor assembly. The left side U-shaped hose (B) goes from the fuel filter to the fuel pump.

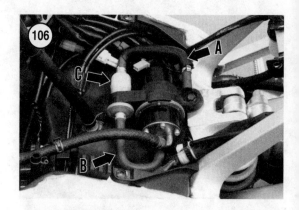

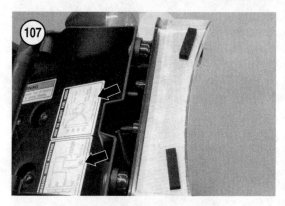

6. Loosen the hose clamp on both fuel hoses and disconnect the hoses from the fuel filter. Plug the ends of both hoses.

> *NOTE*
> *Note the direction of the fuel filter in the rubber mount. The flange side of the filter is on the left side with the fitting that goes to the fuel pump.*

7. Remove the fuel filter from the rubber mount (C, **Figure 106**) and remove the fuel filter.

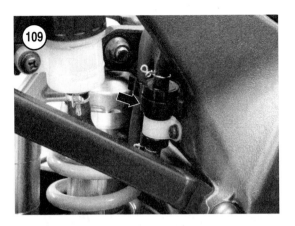

8. Install by reversing these removal steps. Make sure the hoses are installed onto the correct fittings and the clamps are tight.

EMISSION CONTROL SYSTEM LABELS

Emission control information labels are mounted on the rear fender under the passenger's seat (**Figure 107**, typical). On California models, a vacuum hose routing diagram label is also mounted on the rear fender.

On most models, the hoses and fittings are labeled with identification numbers that correspond with the numbers listed on the vacuum hose routing diagram label. If these identification numbers have deteriorated or are missing, mark the hoses and their fittings with a piece of masking tape for proper installation. There are many vacuum hoses on these models. Reconnecting them can be confusing if they are not properly identified.

CRANKCASE BREATHER SYSTEM

All models, and years, are equipped with a crankcase breather system. The system re-circulates crankcase vapors into the air filter housing (**Figure 108**) and then into air/fuel mixture so they can be burned.

EVAPORATIVE EMISSION CONTROL SYSTEM (CALIFORNIA MODELS)

An evaporative emission control system (EVAP) is installed on all models, and years, sold in California.

A vacuum hose routing diagram label is mounted on the rear fender under the passenger seat (**Figure 107**, typical). Fuel vapor from the fuel tank is routed through a rollover valve (**Figure 109**) and into a charcoal canister, where it is stored when the engine is not running. When the engine is running, these vapors are drawn into the EVAP purge control solenoid valve and through the carburetor assembly or the throttle body and into the engine to be burned. Make sure all hose clamps are tight. Check all hoses for deterioration and replace as necessary.

Charcoal Canister Removal/Installation

1. Support the motorcycle on a swing arm safety stand. Block the front wheel so the motorcycle will not roll in either direction while on the safety stand.
2. Remove both side fairing panels as described in Chapter Sixteen.
3. Remove the bolts securing the charcoal canister (**Figure 110**) to the frame cross member.
4. Label the hoses at the charcoal canister, then disconnect them.
5. Check all hoses for cuts, damage or soft spots. Replace any damaged hoses.
6. Install by reversing these removal steps. Make sure all hose fittings are tight.

AIR INDUCTION SYSTEM (AIS)

The air induction system (AIS) is installed on all 2000-2001 carbureted models and on all fuel injected models (**Figure 111**). The AIS system lowers emissions output by introducing fresh secondary air into the exhaust ports. The introduction of air raises

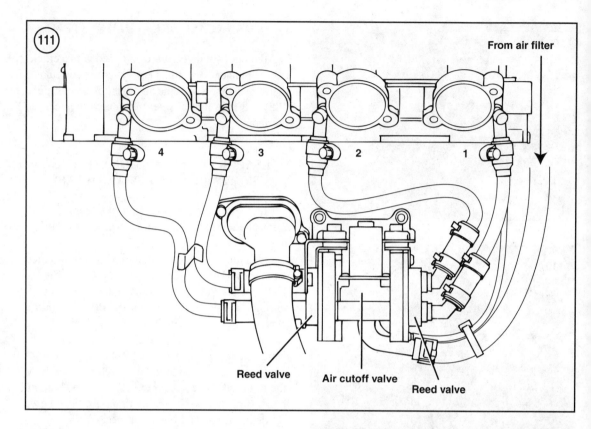

Reed valve   Air cutoff valve   Reed valve

the exhaust temperature, which consumes some of the unburned fuel in the exhaust.

When there is negative pressure in the exhaust port, the reed valves in the air cutoff valve assembly, open thus allowing fresh secondary air to flow into the exhaust port. The reed valves also close to prevent a reverse flow of air through the system to avoid backfiring during deceleration.

Preliminary Inspection

There are no test procedures for the AIS system. If the valve clearance is adjusted properly and the carburetors or fuel injector bodies have been synchronized correctly and the engine will not idle correctly, then there may be a problem within the AIS system.

1. Support the motorcycle on a swing arm safety stand. Block the front wheel so the motorcycle will not roll in either direction while on the safety stand.

2. Remove the rider's seat as described in Chapter Sixteen.

3. Remove both side fairing panels and bottom cowl as described in Chapter Sixteen.

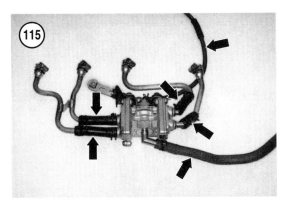

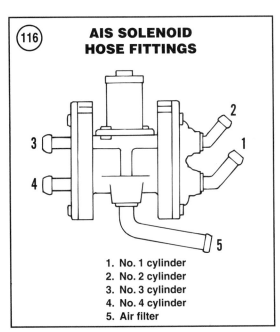

AIS SOLENOID HOSE FITTINGS

1. No. 1 cylinder
2. No. 2 cylinder
3. No. 3 cylinder
4. No. 4 cylinder
5. Air filter

4. Inspect the hoses (**Figure 112**) for hardness or deterioration. Replace as necessary.

5. Check the tightness of the fitting clamps at the cylinder head (**Figure 113**). Tighten if necessary.

6. If these preliminary inspections do not exhibit any problems, remove the assembly for further inspection as described in the following procedure.

7. Install the bottom cowl and both side fairing panels as described in Chapter Sixteen.

8. Install the seat as described in Chapter Sixteen.

Removal/Inspection/Installation

1. Support the motorcycle on a swing arm safety stand. Block the front wheel so the motorcycle will not roll in either direction while on the safety stand.

2. Remove the seat as described in Chapter Sixteen.

3. Remove both side fairing panels and bottom cowl as described in Chapter Sixteen.

4. Drain the cooling system as described in Chapter Three.

5. Remove the exhaust system as described in this chapter.

6. Remove the crankcase water jacket fitting assembly (A, **Figure 114**) as described in Chapter Eleven.

7. On 2002-2003 models, disconnect the 2-pin electrical connector (orange and green wires) from the solenoid.

8. Remove the bolts securing the solenoid housing (B, **Figure 114**) mounting bracket to the crankcase.

9. Loosen the fitting clamps at the cylinder head (**Figure 113**) and disconnect the fittings.

10. Remove the assembly from the crankcase.

11. Inspect the hoses (**Figure 115**) for hardness or deterioration. Refer to **Figure 116** for correct hose connections.

12. Inspect the solenoid housing (**Figure 117**) for cracks or damage.

13. On 2000-2001 models, inspect the vacuum solenoid portion (**Figure 118**) for damage.

14. On 2002-2003 models, inspect the electric solenoid (C, **Figure 114**) portion for damage.

NOTE
The reed valves must not be serviced or disassembled. Do not try to bend the stopper. If any part of the valve is defective, the entire solenoid housing must be replaced.

15. To inspect the reed valves, perform the following:

   a. Remove the screws (**Figure 119**) securing the reed valve covers and remove the cover from each side.

   b. Inspect the reed valves, reed valve seats and stopper plates for damage.

   c. Use a straightedge and flat feeler gauge and check the reed valve distortion. The maximum clearance between the reed and the holder is 0.4 mm (0.016 in.).

   d. Check the reed valve seats for foreign matter and heat distortion. If necessary, use an aerosol carburetor cleaner and remove any foreign matter.

   e. If either reed valve assembly is damaged, replace the solenoid housing since the reed valves are not sold separately.

16. Install a *new* muffler gasket into each cylinder head fitting.

17. Install by reversing these removal steps.

EXHAUST SYSTEM

The exhaust system (**Figure 120**) is vital to engine performance. Check the exhaust system for deep dents and fractures and repair or replace them immediately. Check the muffler-to-frame mounting flanges for fractures and loose bolts. Check the cylinder head mounting flanges for tightness. A loose exhaust pipe connection can reduce engine performance.

Removal

WARNING
Do not remove or service the exhaust system when it is hot.

1. Park the motorcycle on level ground. Support the motorcycle securely on a swing arm stand with the rear wheel off the ground.

2. Remove the rider's seat as described in Chapter Sixteen.

3. Remove the fuel tank as described in this chapter.

4. Remove both side fairing panels and bottom cowl as described in Chapter Sixteen.

5. Remove the bolts securing the EXUP pulley cover (**Figure 121**) and remove the cover.

6. Insert a punch into the pulley notch to keep it from rotating (A, **Figure 122**).

7. Loosen the bolt and washer (B, **Figure 122**) securing the cable pulley.

8. Remove the bolt and washer loosened in Step 7.

9. Note the location of the cables within the pulley (C, **Figure 122**) then remove the pulley from the shaft. They must be reinstalled in the correct location.

10. Disconnect the cables from the cable bracket (D, **Figure 122**).

11. Disconnect both cables from the pulley and remove the pulley.

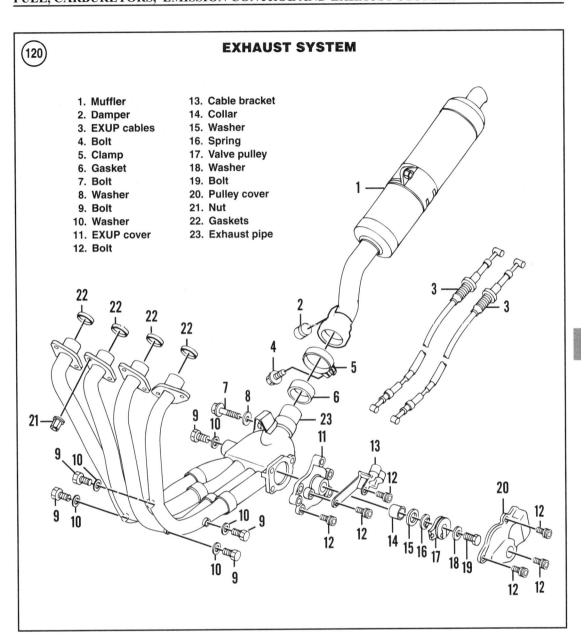

EXHAUST SYSTEM

(120)

1. Muffler
2. Damper
3. EXUP cables
4. Bolt
5. Clamp
6. Gasket
7. Bolt
8. Washer
9. Bolt
10. Washer
11. EXUP cover
12. Bolt
13. Cable bracket
14. Collar
15. Washer
16. Spring
17. Valve pulley
18. Washer
19. Bolt
20. Pulley cover
21. Nut
22. Gaskets
23. Exhaust pipe

8

(121)

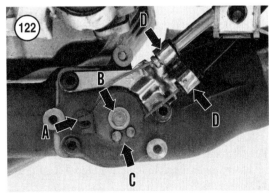

(122)

12. Loosen the muffler-to-exhaust pipe clamp bolts.

13. Remove the bolt (**Figure 123**) securing the muffler to the rear footpeg bracket.

14. Carefully pull the muffler free from the exhaust pipe assembly and remove the muffler.

15. Remove the radiator as described in Chapter Eleven.

16. Remove the bolt and washer securing the exhaust pipe to the frame mount.

17. Remove the front exhaust pipe nuts (**Figure 124**) at the cylinder head and remove the exhaust pipe assembly (**Figure 125**).

18. Remove the exhaust pipe gaskets (**Figure 126**) at each cylinder head exhaust port. Discard the gaskets.

Installation

1. Install *new* exhaust pipe gaskets (**Figure 126**) into each cylinder head exhaust port. Apply grease to the gaskets to prevent them from falling out of place.

2. Install the exhaust pipe assembly (**Figure 125**) onto the cylinder head and install the nuts. Tighten finger-tight at this time.

3. Install the bolt and washer securing the exhaust pipe to the frame mount. Tighten finger-tight at this time.

4. Install a new gasket (**Figure 127**) into the muffler inlet port.

5. Move the muffler into position and connect it onto the exhaust pipe.

6. Install the bolt (**Figure 123**) securing the muffler to the rear footpeg bracket. Tighten finger-tight at this time.

7. Push the muffler in until it bottoms. Tighten the muffler-to-exhaust pipe clamp bolts finger-tight at this time.

8. Tighten the exhaust pipe-to-cylinder head nuts to 20 N•m (15 ft.-lb.).

9. Install the exhaust pipe-to-frame bolt to 20 N•m (15 ft.-lb.).

10. Tighten the muffler-to-exhaust pipe clamp bolts to 20 N•m (15 ft.-lb.).

11. Tighten the muffler-to-rear footpeg bracket bolt to 38 N•m (28 ft.-lb.).

12. Connect both cables onto the pulley in the correct location as noted in *Removal* Step 9 (C, **Figure 122**).

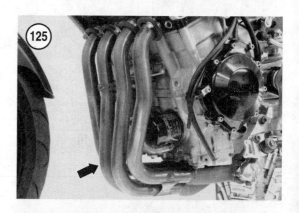

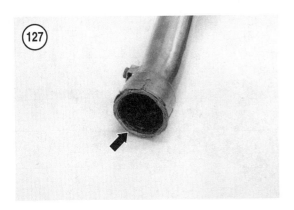

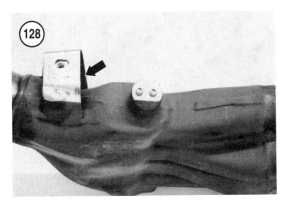

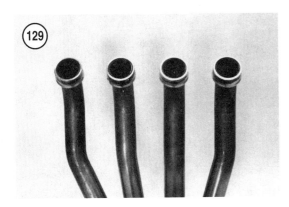

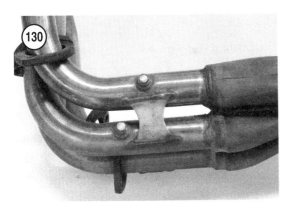

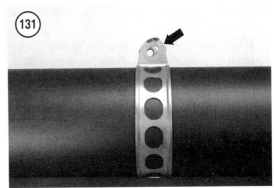

13. Connect the cables onto the cable bracket (D, **Figure 122**).

14. Install the pulley onto the shaft and install the bolt and washer (B, **Figure 122**) securing the cable pulley.

15. Insert a punch into the pulley notch to keep it from rotating (A, **Figure 122**) and tighten the bolt securely.

16. Install the EXUP pulley cover (**Figure 121**) and bolts and tighten securely.

17. After installation is complete, start the engine and make sure there are no exhaust leaks.

18. Adjust the EXUP cables as described in Chapter Three.

19. Install the radiator as described in Chapter Eleven.

20. Refill the cooling system as described in Chapter Three.

21. Install the bottom cowl and both side fairings as described in Chapter Sixteen.

22. Install the fuel tank as described in this chapter.

23. Install the rider's seat as described in Chapter Sixteen.

Inspection

1. Inspect the muffler mounting bracket (**Figure 128**) for cracks or damage.

2. Inspect the exhaust pipe-to-cylinder head flanges (**Figure 129**) for corrosion, burned areas or damage.

3. Inspect all welds (**Figure 130**) for leakage or corrosion.

4. Inspect the muffler mounting strap (**Figure 131**) for cracks or deterioration.

5. Check the muffler mounting rubber grommet and collar on the rear footpeg mounting bracket.

8

Replace the rubber grommet if it is starting to harden or deteriorate.

6. If the EXUP assembly was removed from the exhaust pipe, inspect the EXUP cover mating surface (**Figure 132**) for heat damage or warp.

7. Refer to the following procedure for the components relating to the EXUP system.

EXUP SYSTEM (1998-2001 MODELS)

The Exhaust Ultimate Power Valve (EXUP) system increases engine performance by regulating the opening of the exhaust pipe just ahead of the muffler. The system adjusts the exhaust opening with a valve controlled by the servomotor located under the left side of the fuel tank.

Cable Replacement

1. Park the motorcycle on level ground. Support the motorcycle securely on a swing arm stand with the rear wheel off the ground.

2. Remove the rider's seat as described in Chapter Sixteen.

3. Remove the fuel tank as described in this chapter.

4. Remove both side fairings and bottom cowl as described in Chapter Sixteen.

NOTE
Steps 5-11 are located at the EXUP valve on the exhaust pipe.

5. Remove the bolts securing the EXUP pulley cover (**Figure 121**) and remove the cover.

6. Insert a punch into the pulley notch to keep it from rotating (A, **Figure 122**).

7. Loosen the bolt and washer (B, **Figure 122**) securing the cable pulley.

8. Remove the bolt and washer loosened in Step 7.

9. Note the location of the cables within the pulley (C, **Figure 122**) then remove the pulley from the shaft. They must be reinstalled in the correct location.

10. Disconnect the cables from the cable bracket (D, **Figure 122**).

11. Disconnect both cables from the pulley and remove the pulley.

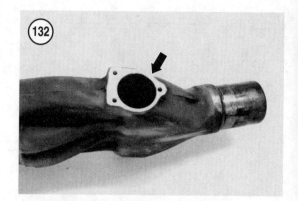

NOTE
Steps 12-17 are located at the servomotor under the seat.

12. To allow slack in both cables, loosen both locknuts (A, **Figure 133**) and turn both cable adjusters *clockwise* (B).

13. Carefully pull the servomotor up and out of the frame mounting tab and set it on its side.

14. Note the location of the cables within the pulley (A, **Figure 134**).

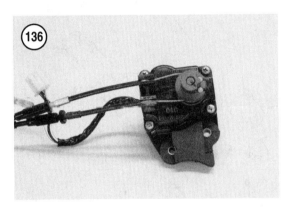

15. The EXUP cables are different and must be installed correctly. Label the cables with an A and B. Follow the cables up through the frame to the servo motor and label the opposite end of each cable with the appropriate A and B. This will ensure the correct installation of each cable at both components.

16. Disconnect the cables from the cable bracket (B, **Figure 134**).

17. Disconnect both cables from the pulley.

18. Make a drawing of the cable routing from the servomotor to the EXUP pulley at the exhaust pipe. Record this information for proper cable routing and installation.

19. Withdraw the cables from the frame.

20. Compare the new and old cables.

21. If cables without nylon liners are used, lubricate them as described in Chapter Three.

22. Route the new cables through the same path as the old cables.

23. Lightly grease the cable ends and connect them to the servomotor pulley (A, **Figure 134**).

24. Connect the cables onto the cable bracket (B, **Figure 134**).

25. Install the servomotor to the frame mount.

26. Lightly grease the opposite end of the cable ends.

27. At the exhaust pipe, connect both cables onto the pulley in the correct location as noted in *Removal* Step 9.

28. Connect the cables onto the cable bracket (D, **Figure 122**).

29. Install the pulley onto the shaft and install the bolt and washer (B, **Figure 122**) securing the cable pulley.

30. Insert a punch into the pulley notch to keep it from rotating (A, **Figure 122**) and tighten the bolt securely.

31. Install the EXUP pulley cover (**Figure 121**) and bolts and tighten securely.

32. After installation is complete, start the engine and make sure there are no exhaust leaks.

33. Adjust the EXUP cables as described in Chapter Three.

34. Install the bottom cowl and both side fairing panels as described in Chapter Sixteen

35. Install the fuel tank as described in this chapter.

36. Install the rider's seat as described in Chapter Sixteen.

Servo Motor Removal/Inspection/Installation

1. Remove the rider's seat as described in Chapter Sixteen.

2. Remove the fuel tank as described in this chapter.

3. On the right side of the area under the fuel tank, pull back the rubber boot (A, **Figure 135**), follow the wires (B), locate the EXUP servomotor 4-pin electrical connector and disconnect it.

4. To allow slack in both cables, loosen both locknuts (A, **Figure 133**) and turn both cable adjusters *clockwise* (B).

5. Carefully pull the servomotor up and of the frame mounting tab and set it on its side.

6. Note the location of the cables within the pulley (A, **Figure 134**).

7. The EXUP cables are different and must be installed correctly. Label the cables with an A and B. This will ensure the correct installation of each cable.

8. Disconnect the cables from the cable bracket (B, **Figure 134**).

9. Disconnect both cables from the pulley.

10. Remove the servomotor.

11. Inspect the servomotor (**Figure 136**) for wear or damage. Make sure the pulley moves freely with

8

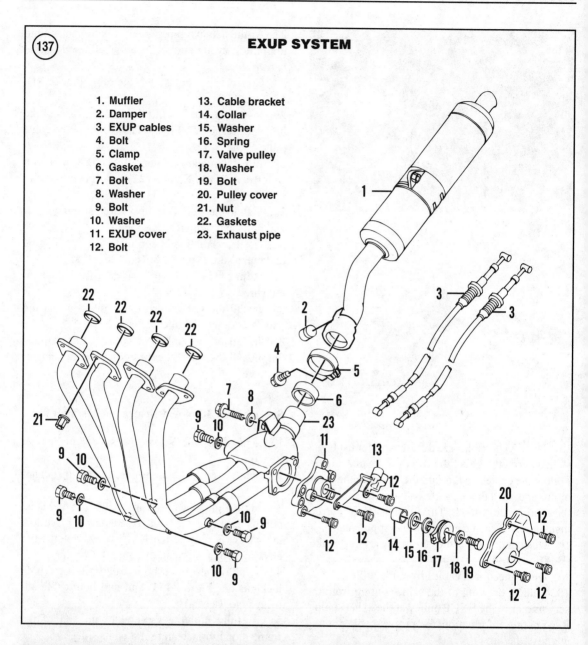

EXUP SYSTEM

137

1. Muffler
2. Damper
3. EXUP cables
4. Bolt
5. Clamp
6. Gasket
7. Bolt
8. Washer
9. Bolt
10. Washer
11. EXUP cover
12. Bolt
13. Cable bracket
14. Collar
15. Washer
16. Spring
17. Valve pulley
18. Washer
19. Bolt
20. Pulley cover
21. Nut
22. Gaskets
23. Exhaust pipe

138

139

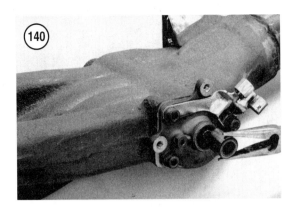

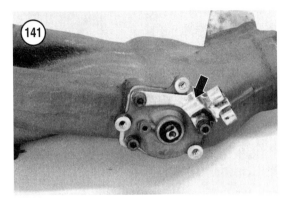

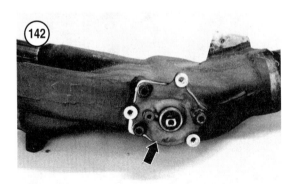

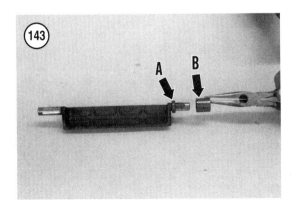

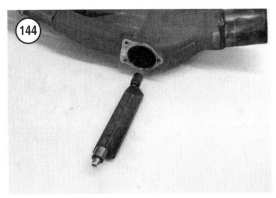

the cables. Electrical testing of the servomotor is covered in Chapter Ten.

12. Install by reversing these removal steps while noting the following:

    a. Install the cables onto the correct location within the pulley.

    b. Adjust the cables as described in Chapter Three.

Valve Disassembly/Assembly

The EXUP components (**Figure 137**) can be disassembled with the exhaust pipe in place. This procedure is shown with the exhaust pipe removed from the engine and frame to better illustrate the steps.

1. Remove the bolt and washer (A, **Figure 138**) securing the valve pulley and remove the valve pulley (B).

2. Remove the spring (A, **Figure 139**) and washer (B).

3. Remove the collar (**Figure 140**) from the end of the valve.

4. Remove the bolts securing the cable bracket (**Figure 141**) and remove the bracket.

5. Remove the bolts securing the EXUP cover (**Figure 142**) and remove the cover.

6. Remove the EXUP valve from the exhaust pipe receptacle. Do not lose the bushing and washer on the inner end of the valve.

7. Inspect the components as described in this chapter.

8. Install the washer (A, **Figure 143**) and bushing (B) onto the inner end of the valve.

9. Install the valve assembly into the exhaust pipe (**Figure 144**) and insert it into the receptacle on the

8

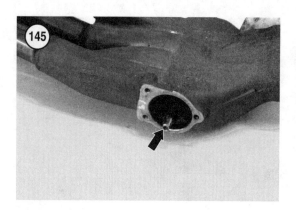

other side of the exhaust pipe. Push it in until it bottoms (**Figure 145**).

10. Rotate the valve until the wedge portion is located toward the top (**Figure 146**).

11. Install the EXUP cover (**Figure 142**) and the cable bracket (**Figure 141**) and install the screws. Tighten the screws securely.

12. Install the collar (**Figure 140**) and push it on until it bottoms.

13. Rotate the EXUP valve back and forth to make sure it rotates freely back and forth.

14. Install the washer (**Figure 147**).

15. Position the spring with the larger coil (**Figure 148**) going on first against the washer, then install the spring.

16. Position the valve pulley with the fork tab (**Figure 149**) facing toward the front of the exhaust pipe, then index it onto the valve and install the valve pulley (B, **Figure 138**).

17. Install the washer and bolt (A, **Figure 138**) and tighten the bolt securely.

18. Do not install the pulley cover at this time since the cables must be attached later.

Valve Inspection

1. Inspect the EXUP valve, washer and collars (**Figure 150**) for wear or damage.

2. Check the EXUP cover inner surface (**Figure 151**) and outer surface (**Figure 152**) for heat damage or warp.

3. Inspect the cable pulley (**Figure 153**) for damage.

4. Inspect the EXUP cover mating surface (**Figure 154**) on the exhaust pipe for damage or warp.

5. Make sure the screws are tight on the small cover plate (**Figure 155**). Tighten if necessary.

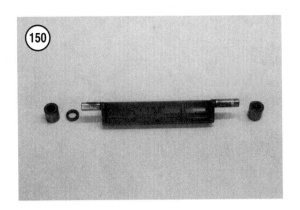

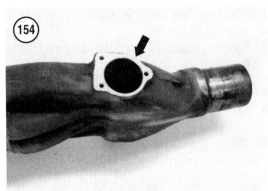

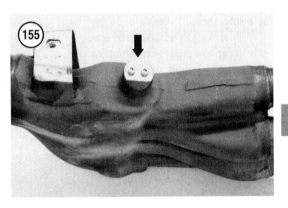

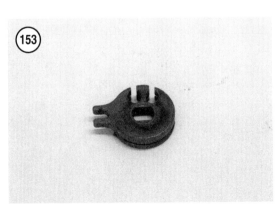

Diagnostics

The 2000-2001 models are equipped with a diagnostic system to detect faults in the EXUP system. If there is a fault within the system it will be indicated as follows. When the engine is turned on, the tachometer will first indicate zero rpm for three seconds, then indicate 7000 rpm for two and one-half seconds, then the actual engine speed for three seconds. The tachometer will repeat this sequence until the engine is turned off. The motorcycle can be ridden in this condition but lack of performance may be noticed. Test the system as described in the following procedure.

EXUP cable adjustment is covered in Chapter Three.

The 2002-2003 model diagnostic system is covered in Chapter Nine.

Testing

1. Remove the rider's seat as described in Chapter Sixteen.

2. Disconnect the cables from the servomotor as described in this chapter.

3. Start the engine and increase engine speed to 2000 rpm.

4. The pulley on the servomotor should rotate.

5. Turn the engine off.

6. Remove the fuel tank as described in this chapter.

7. On the right side of the area under the fuel tank, pull back the rubber boot (A, **Figure 156**), follow the wires (B), locate the EXUP servomotor 4-pin electrical connector and disconnect it.

8. Connect a voltmeter to the main harness side of the connectors as follows:

    a. Positive probe: black/red wire.

    b. Negative probe: black/yellow wire.

9. Turn the ignition switch to the on position and measure the voltage. There should be battery voltage.

10A. If there is no battery voltage, inspect the wiring to the connector.

10B. If there is battery voltage, proceed to Step 11.

CAUTION
In Step 11, do not leave the battery leads connected to the terminal for more than 2-3 seconds. If attached longer, the servomotor will be damaged.

11. Connect a fully charged 12-volt battery to the servo motor side of the electrical connectors as follows:

    a. Positive battery lead to the black/yellow terminal.

    b. Negative battery lead to the black/red terminal.

    c. The servomotor should rotate several times.

12A. If the servomotor does not rotate, replace it.

12B. If the servomotor rotates, proceed to Step 13.

13. Connect an ohmmeter to the servomotor side of the 4-pin electrical connector as follows:

    a. Positive test lead: white/black terminal.

    b. Negative test lead: yellow/blue.

    c. The specified resistance is 5.3-9.8 ohms. Proceed to Step 14.

14. Connect an ohmmeter to the servomotor side of the 4-pin electrical connector and single connector as follows:

    a. Positive test lead: white/black terminal.

    b. Negative test lead: white/red terminal.

    c. Slowly rotate the servomotor pulley by hand and measure the resistance. The specified resistance is 0 to approximately 7500 ohms.

15A. If the servomotor fails Step 13 and Step 14, the servomotor is faulty and must be replaced.

15B. If the servomotor passes Step 13 and Step 14, inspect the wiring to the servomotor. If the wiring is good, replace the ignitor unit.

16. Connect the servomotor 4-pin electrical connector.

17. Connect the cables to the servomotor as described in this chapter.

18. Install the rider's seat as described in Chapter Sixteen.

Table 1 CARBURETOR SPECIFICATIONS (U.S. AND CANADA MODELS)

Item	Specification
Model	Mikuni—BDSR40 × 4
Carburetor identification	
49-state and Canada	4XV4 20
California	4XV5 30
Main jet	130
Main air jet	
No. 1 and No. 4 carburetor	No. 60
No. 2 and No. 3 carburetor	No. 65
Jet needle	
1998-1999 models	6DEY5-53-3
2000-2001 models	6DEY8-53-1
Needle jet	
1998-1999 models	P-0
2000-2001 models	P-0M
Pilot air jet	120
Pilot outlet	1.0
Pilot jet	15
Bypass	
No. 1	0.8
No. 2	0.9
No. 3	0.8
Pilot screw	3 1/8 turns out
Valve seat size	1.5
Starter jet	
No. 1	35
No. 2	0.7
Butterfly valve size	100
Fuel level	4.1-5.1 mm (0.161-0.201 in.)
Idle speed	
1998-1999 models	1050-1150 rpm
2000-2001 models	1000-1100 rpm
Throttle cable free play	3-5 mm (0.12-0.20 in.)

8

Table 2 CARBURETOR SPECIFICATIONS (OTHER THAN U.S. AND CANADA MODELS)

Item	Specification
Model	Mikuni—BDSR40 × 4
Carburetor identification	
1998-1999 models	4XV1 00
2000-2001 models	5JJ1 00
Main jet	130
Main air jet	
No. 1 and No. 4 carburetor	No. 60
No. 2 and No. 3 carburetor	No. 65
Jet needle	6DEY5-53-3
Needle jet	
1998-1999 models	P-0
2000-2001 models	P-0M
Pilot air jet	120
Pilot outlet	1.0
Pilot jet	
1998-1999 models	17.5
2000-2001 models	15

(continued)

Table 2 CARBURETOR SPECIFICATIONS
(OTHER THAN U.S. AND CANADA MODELS) (continued)

Item	Specification
Bypass	
No. 1	0.8
No. 2	0.9
No. 3	0.8
Pilot screw	
1998-1999 models	2 1/2 turns out
2000-2001 models	3 1/4 turns out
Valve seat size	1.5
Fuel level	4.1-5.1 mm (0.161-0.201 in.)
Idle speed	
1998-1999 models	1050-1150 rpm
2000-2001 models	1000-1100 rpm
Throttle cable free play	3-5 mm (0.12-0.20 in.)

Table 3 EXHAUST TORQUE SPECIFICATIONS

Item	N•m	in.-lb.	ft.-lb.
Exhaust pipe-to-cylinder head nuts	20	–	15
Exhaust pipe-to-frame bolt	20	–	15
Muffler-to-exhaust pipe clamp bolts	20	–	15
Muffler-to-footpeg bolt	38	–	28

CHAPTER NINE

FUEL, ELECTRONIC FUEL INJECTION AND EXHAUST SYSTEMS

This chapter describes service procedures for the fuel injection system. Emission control systems for both carbureted and fuel injected models are covered in Chapter Eight.

Fuel injection system component locations are shown in **Figure 1**.

Specifications are in **Tables 1-4** at the end of the chapter.

FUEL INJECTION SYSTEM PRECAUTIONS

Servicing the fuel injection system (**Figure 2**) requires special precautions to prevent damage to the throttle body and the engine control unit (ECU). Service procedures acceptable on other motorcycles with different fuel and electrical systems may damage parts of this system.

1. The fuel system is pressurized. Wear eye protection whenever working on the fuel system, espe-cially when depressurizing the system. Refer to *Depressurizing the Fuel System* in this chapter.

2. Make sure the ignition switch is off before disconnecting any components. ECU damage may occur if electrical components are disconnected or connected with the ignition on.

3. Refer to *Electrical Component Replacement* and *Electrical Connectors* in Chapter Ten.

> *WARNING*
> *Always wear eye protection when working on the fuel system.*

> *WARNING*
> *Some fuel may spill and fuel vapors will be present when depressurizing the fuel system. Because gasoline is extremely flammable, perform this procedure away from all open flames, including appliance pilot lights and sparks. Do not smoke or allow some-one who is smoking in the work area, as an explosion and fire may occur.*

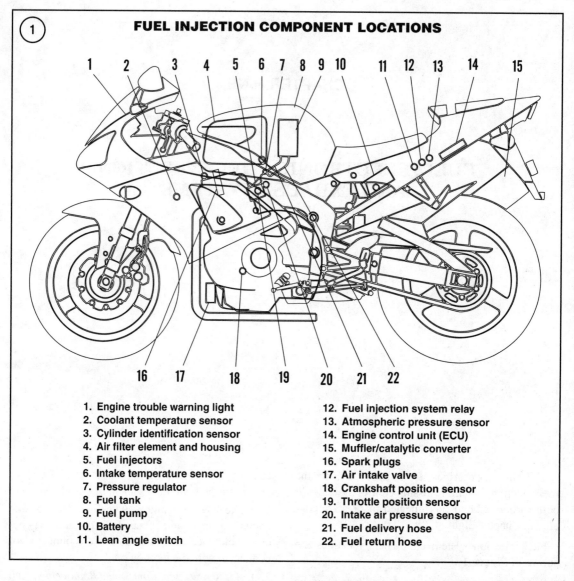

FUEL INJECTION COMPONENT LOCATIONS

1. Engine trouble warning light
2. Coolant temperature sensor
3. Cylinder identification sensor
4. Air filter element and housing
5. Fuel injectors
6. Intake temperature sensor
7. Pressure regulator
8. Fuel tank
9. Fuel pump
10. Battery
11. Lean angle switch
12. Fuel injection system relay
13. Atmospheric pressure sensor
14. Engine control unit (ECU)
15. Muffler/catalytic converter
16. Spark plugs
17. Air intake valve
18. Crankshaft position sensor
19. Throttle position sensor
20. Intake air pressure sensor
21. Fuel delivery hose
22. Fuel return hose

Always work in a well-ventilated area. Wipe up spills immediately.

market parts suppliers carry this kit, or similar equivalents.

HOSE AND WIRING HARNESS IDENTIFICATION

The fuel system uses a number of fuel and vacuum hoses. To allow easier assembly, develop a system to identify the hoses and connection points before disconnecting them. A vacuum hose identifier kit (Lisle part No. 74600) is used in the following procedures. This set consists of color-coded hose fittings in various sizes. Automotive and after-

DEPRESSURIZING THE FUEL SYSTEM

The fuel system is under pressure at all times, even when the engine is not operating. Whenever a fuel line or fitting is loosened or removed, gasoline will spray out unless the system is depressurized first. Before disconnecting any fuel line or fitting, refer to *Fuel Injection System Precautions* in this chapter, and perform the following steps.

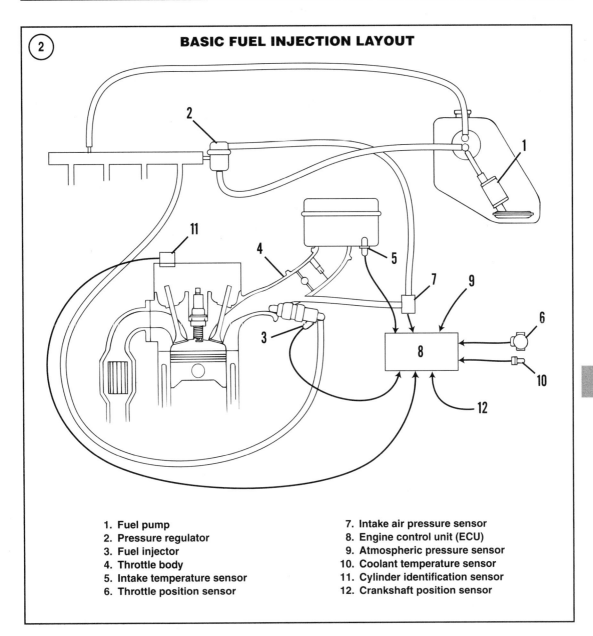

② **BASIC FUEL INJECTION LAYOUT**

1. Fuel pump
2. Pressure regulator
3. Fuel injector
4. Throttle body
5. Intake temperature sensor
6. Throttle position sensor
7. Intake air pressure sensor
8. Engine control unit (ECU)
9. Atmospheric pressure sensor
10. Coolant temperature sensor
11. Cylinder identification sensor
12. Crankshaft position sensor

9

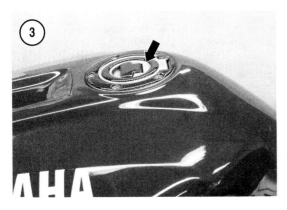

③

1. Siphon the fuel from the tank into a container approved for gasoline storage. To do this, perform the following:

    a. Open the fuel filler cap (**Figure 3**).

    b. Place a siphon hose into the fuel tank. Place the other end of the siphon hose into a fuel storage can.

    c. Operate the siphon to drain as much fuel from the tank as possible.

    d. When the siphon shuts off, remove it from the fuel tank and storage can. Close the fuel filler cap and place the storage can in a safe place,

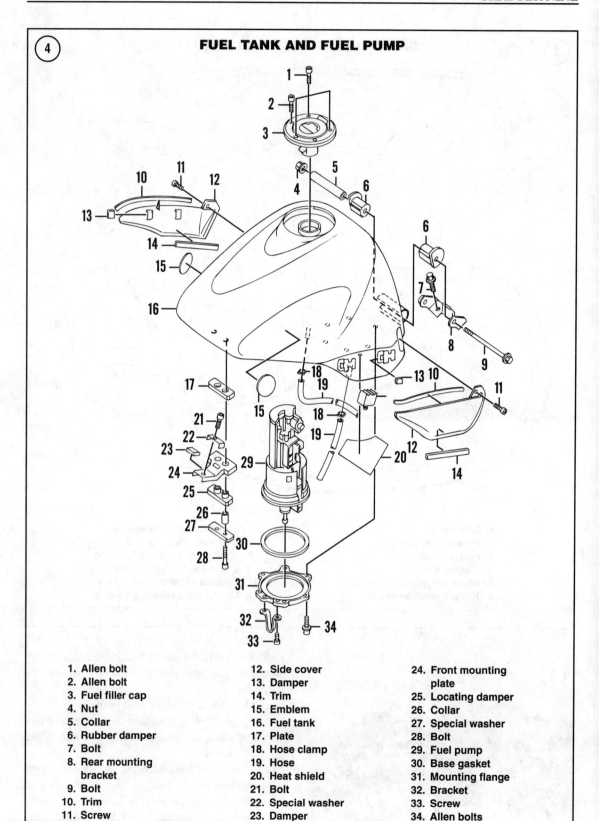

FUEL TANK AND FUEL PUMP

1. Allen bolt
2. Allen bolt
3. Fuel filler cap
4. Nut
5. Collar
6. Rubber damper
7. Bolt
8. Rear mounting
   bracket
9. Bolt
10. Trim
11. Screw

12. Side cover
13. Damper
14. Trim
15. Emblem
16. Fuel tank
17. Plate
18. Hose clamp
19. Hose
20. Heat shield
21. Bolt
22. Special washer
23. Damper

24. Front mounting
    plate
25. Locating damper
26. Collar
27. Special washer
28. Bolt
29. Fuel pump
30. Base gasket
31. Mounting flange
32. Bracket
33. Screw
34. Allen bolts

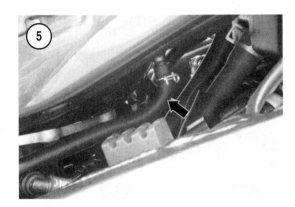

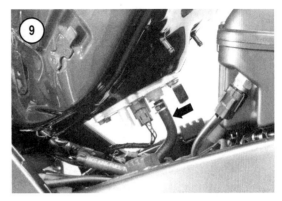

away from all flames and sparks. Drain the siphon of all gasoline before putting it away.

2. Start the engine and let it run until the remaining fuel is consumed from the fuel system.

3. Turn the ignition switch off.

FUEL TANK

Removal/Installation

Refer to **Figure 4**.

1. Refer to *Fuel Injection System Precautions* and *Depressurizing the Fuel System* in this chapter.

2. Remove the rider's seat as described in Chapter Sixteen.

3. Remove the bolt securing the front of the fuel tank to the frame.

4. Raise the front of the fuel tank up part way in order to perform Step 5.

5. On California models, on the right side, disconnect the hose (**Figure 5**) going to the charcoal canister rollover valve.

6. On the left side, disconnect the fuel tank breather hose (**Figure 6**).

7. Use needlenose pliers and disconnect the connector cover from the fuel feed hose (**Figure 7**).

> *NOTE*
> *Place several shop rags under the fuel hoses that are going to be disconnected to catch any residual fuel in the system.*

8. Disconnect the fuel feed hose (**Figure 8**). Plug the fuel hose end to prevent residual fuel from leaking out of the hose.

9. Disconnect the fuel return hose (**Figure 9**). Plug the fuel hose end to prevent residual fuel from leaking out of the hose.

10. Disconnect the fuel pump and the fuel level sender electrical connectors (**Figure 10**).

11. Lower the fuel tank.

12. On the right side, remove the self-locking nut (**Figure 11**) on the rear through bolt.

13. On the left side, withdraw the rear mounting bolt.

14. Pull straight back and release the front mounting bracket from the frame tab and remove the fuel tank.

15. Install the fuel tank by reversing these removal steps while noting the following:

    a. Make sure the fuel low-pressure hose is routed correctly with no sharp bends or where it may become crimped.

    b. Tighten the rear fuel tank mounting bolt and *new* self-locking nut to 10 N•m (88 in.-lb.).

    c. After reconnecting the fuel tank air vent and overflow hoses to the fuel tank, make sure to clamp the hoses securely in place.

    d. Make sure to install the connector cover onto the fuel feed hose (**Figure 7**) and push it on until it locks into place.

    e. Turn the ignition switch on and allow the fuel pump to pressurize the system. Check the fuel tank hoses for leaks.

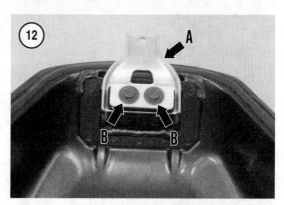

Inspection

1. Inspect all of the hoses for cracks, deterioration and other damage. Replace damaged hoses with the same Yamaha type and size materials. The hoses must be flexible and strong enough to withstand fuel pressure, engine heat and vibration.

2. Inspect the front, side and rear grommets for deterioration or other damage. Replace if necessary.

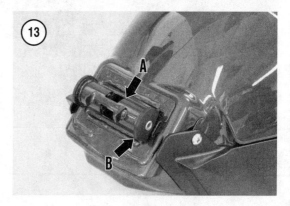

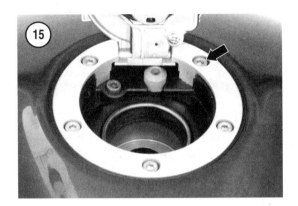

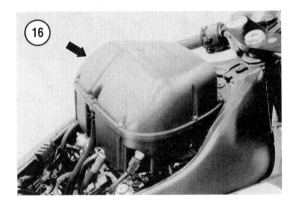

Make sure the metal collars are in place within the grommets.

3. Check the front mounting bracket for damage (A, **Figure 12**) and make sure the mounting bolts (B) are tight.

4. Check the rear mounting bracket for damage (A, **Figure 13**) and check the rubber dampers (B) for deterioration. Replace if necessary.

5. Use the ignition key and open the fuel filler cap. Inspect the fuel filler cap gasket (**Figure 14**). If damaged or starting to deteriorate, replace the filler cap assembly. Remove the inner hex bolt and the outer Allen bolts (**Figure 15**) securing the fuller cap and remove the filler cap.

AIR FILTER HOUSING

Removal/Installation

1. Remove the fuel tank as described in this chapter.

2. Remove the air filter housing cover screws and lift the cover (**Figure 16**) off the housing. Do not forget the center screw and the front screw (**Figure 17**).

3. Lift the air filter element (**Figure 18**) out of the housing.

4. On the right side, disconnect the intake temperature sensor electrical connector (**Figure 19**).

5. Disconnect the crankcase breather hose (A, **Figure 20**).

6. On the left side, disconnect the air filter housing breather hose (B, **Figure 20**).

7. Disconnect the Air Induction System hose (C, **Figure 20**).

8. Use a long Phillips screwdriver and loosen the clamp screw on the four clamps securing the housing to the throttle body assembly. Remove the housing.

9

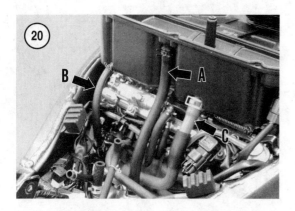

9. Cover each throttle body intake opening to prevent contamination or small parts from entering the throttle bores.

10. While the air filter housing is off the engine, visually check all of the exposed vacuum hoses for damage that may have occurred when disconnecting them. Replace damaged hoses with the correct size replacement hose.

11. Install the air filter assembly by reversing these removal steps while noting the following:

    a. Inspect the housing and its gaskets; replace if necessary.

    b. Route and connect all of the hoses correctly. Make sure all hose clamps, where used, are positioned correctly on the hose ends.

Inspection

1. Visually check all of the exposed vacuum hoses for damage that may have occurred when disconnecting them. Replace damaged hoses with the correct size replacement hose.

2. Inspect the four clamps (**Figure 21**) for damage at the base where the housing attaches to the throttle body.

3. Check that the intake temperature sensor (**Figure 22**) is secure in the housing.

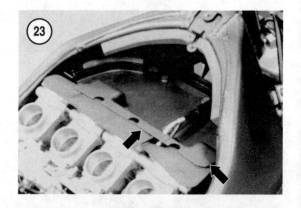

THROTTLE BODY

Removal

1. Refer to *Fuel Injection System Precautions* and *Depressurizing the Fuel System* in this chapter.

2. Remove both side fairing panels as described in Chapter Sixteen.

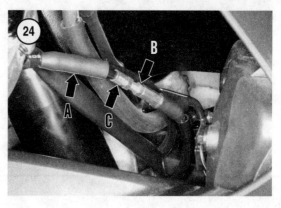

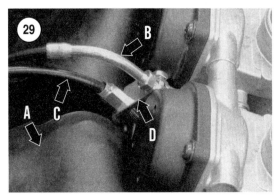

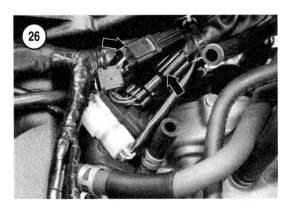

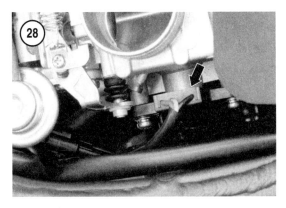

3. Remove the fuel tank and air filter housing as described in this chapter.

4. Drain the cooling system (Chapter Three).

5. Disconnect the thee trim clips securing the ignition coil plates and remove both plates (**Figure 23**).

6. To allow slack in the throttle cable, perform the following:

   a. On the right side of the steering stem, slide back the rubber boot (A, **Figure 24**) on the in-line adjuster.

   b. Loosen the locknut (B, **Figure 24**) and turn the adjuster (C) to allow maximum slack in the cable.

7. Disconnect the coolant hose (**Figure 25**) from the fast idle plunger assembly. Plug the end of the hose to prevent the loss of coolant.

8. On the left side, disconnect the 4-pin and 6-pin electrical connectors (**Figure 26**) from the throttle body sub-harness.

9. On the left side, disconnect the throttle idle adjust knob (**Figure 27**) from the frame bracket.

10. On the right side, disconnect the 3-pin electrical connector (**Figure 28**) from the throttle position sensor.

11. Use a long Phillips screwdriver and loosen the clamping bands on all intake manifolds.

12. Carefully pull the rubber dam (A, **Figure 29**) forward and off the throttle body assembly to expose the throttle cable ends.

13. Note the location of the throttle accelerator (B, **Figure 29**) and the decelerator (C) cables. Remove the throttle cables from the bracket (D, **Figure 29**).

14. Partially remove the throttle body assembly from the engine and turn it over to gain access to the throttle drum.

15. Note the location of the throttle accelerator and the decelerator cables on the throttle drum. Remove the throttle cables from the throttle drum.

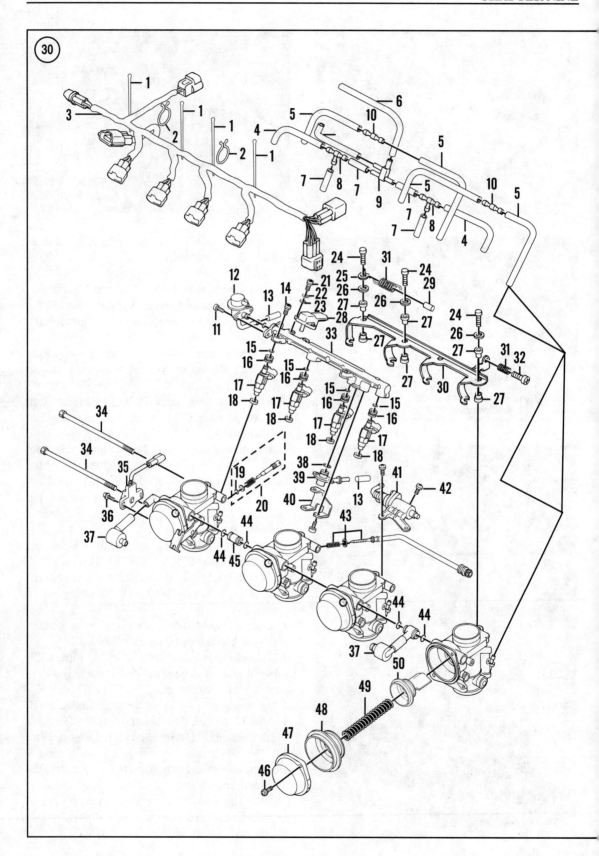

FUEL INJECTION COMPONENT ASSEMBLY

1. Tie wrap
2. Ring
3. Fuel injector wire harness
4. Vent hose
5. Synchronization hoses
6. Hose
7. Hose
8. T-fitting
9. Hose joint
10. Joint
11. Screw
12. Pressure regulator
13. Hose
14. Screw
15. O-ring
16. Cushion ring
17. Fuel injector
18. Seal ring
19. O-ring
20. Air screw set
21. Screw
22. Lockwasher
23. Washer
24. Screw
25. Lockwasher
26. Washer
27. Collar
28. Intake air pressure sensor
29. Spacer
30. Starter (choke) plunger plate
31. Spring
32. Screw
33. Distribution rail
34. Bolt
35. Throttle position sensor
36. Screw
37. Filter
38. O-ring
39. Fuel pipe
40. Mounting bracket
41. Fast idle plunger
42. Screw
43. Idle adjust cable and knob
44. O-ring
45. Joint
46. Screw
47. Cover
48. Diaphragm
49. Spring
50. Piston valve

16. Carefully pull the throttle adjust knob and cable up through the frame.

17. Remove the throttle body assembly from the engine and frame.

18. Tape or plug the intake ports to prevent debris from falling into the cylinder head.

Installation

1. Remove the tape or plugs covering the intake ports.

2. Place the throttle body assembly upside down above the intake manifolds to have access to the throttle drum.

3. Install the throttle accelerator and the decelerator cables onto the throttle drum in the correct location noted in *Removal* Step 15.

4. Align the throttle body and intake manifolds with the cylinder head ports and push the throttle body assembly down firmly until they bottom. Tighten the four intake manifold clamp screws securely. Reposition the throttle adjust cable and knob through the left side of the frame opening.

5. Install the throttle accelerator (B, **Figure 29**) and the decelerator (C) cables onto the cable bracket (D).

6. Carefully pull the rubber dam (A, **Figure 29**) back over the throttle body assembly.

7. On the left side, connect the throttle idle adjust knob (**Figure 27**) onto the frame bracket.

8. On the right side, connect the 3-pin electrical connector (**Figure 28**) onto the throttle position sensor.

9. On the left side, connect the 4-pin and 6-pin electrical connectors (**Figure 26**) onto the throttle body sub-harness.

10. Connect the coolant hose (**Figure 25**) onto the fast idle plunger assembly. Make sure the hose clamp is tight.

11. Install both ignition coil plates (**Figure 23**) and secure them with the three quick disconnect fasteners.

12. Install the air filter housing and the fuel tank as described in this chapter.

13. Install both side fairing panels as described in Chapter Sixteen.

FUEL INJECTORS

Removal

Refer to **Figure 30**.

9

1. Remove the throttle body assembly as described in this chapter.

2. Disconnect the fuel supply hose (**Figure 31**) from the fuel pipe.

3. If necessary, tag all hoses and fittings and remove the hose assembly (**Figure 32**) from the throttle body assembly.

4. Remove the screw securing the fast idle plunger unit (**Figure 33**).

5. Remove the screws securing the fuel distribution rail and fuel injector assembly (**Figure 34**).

6. Carefully pull the assembly away from the throttle body assembly (**Figure 35**).

> *NOTE*
> *Identify and label each fuel injector, starting with the No. 1 on the left end. The right end has the throttle position sensor and the fuel pressure regulator.*

7. Carefully remove the fuel injector (**Figure 36**) from the fuel distribution rail.

8. Remove the cushion ring (A, **Figure 37**) and O-ring (B) from the fuel injector. Remove the seal ring (**Figure 38**) from the throttle body assembly. All three parts must be replaced with *new* ones every time a fuel injector is removed from the fuel distribution rail.

9. Repeat for each fuel injector.

10. If necessary, remove the screws (**Figure 39**) securing the fuel pipe to the fuel distribution rail.

11. If necessary, remove the screws and brackct (A, **Figure 40**) securing the intake air pressure sensor (B) and remove it. Disconnect the electrical connector from the sensor.

12. If necessary to remove the throttle position sensor, perform the following:

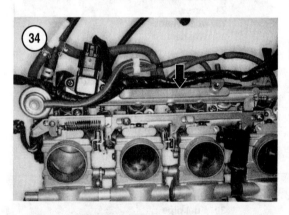

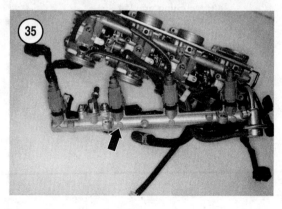

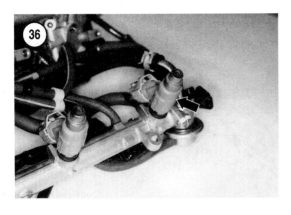

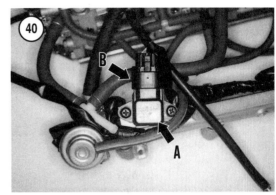

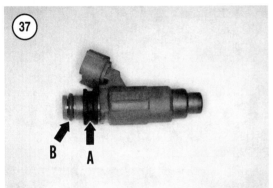

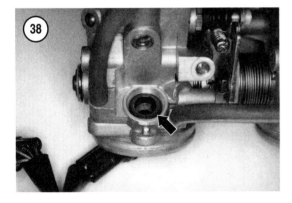

9

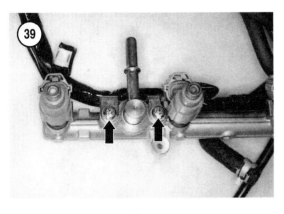

a. Make and index mark adjacent to the mounting screws on the throttle body. This will ensure correct alignment during installation.

b. Remove the screws (A, **Figure 41**) securing the throttle position sensor to the throttle body assembly and remove the sensor (B).

Installation

1. If the throttle position sensor was removed, install it as following:

a. Install the throttle body sensor onto the throttle body.

b. Align the index marks and install the screws. Tighten the screws securely.

c. Adjust the throttle position sensor as described in Chapter Ten.

2. If removed, connect the electrical connector to the air pressure sensor. Install the intake air pressure sensor (B, **Figure 40**), bracket (A) and screws. Tighten the screws securely.

3. If removed, install the fuel pipe to the fuel distribution rail and tighten the screws (**Figure 39**) securely.

4. Install a *new* seal ring (**Figure 38**) into each injector port in the throttle body assembly. Make sure it is properly seated.

5. Install a *new* cushion ring (A, **Figure 37**) onto the fuel injector. Make sure it is properly seated.

6. Apply a thin coat of clean engine oil to a *new* injector O-ring.

7. Install the O-ring (**Figure 42**) into the groove in the injector body.

> *CAUTION*
> *Be careful not to damage the **new** O-ring (**Figure 42**) when installing the fuel injector into the fuel distribution rail.*

8. Install each fuel injector (**Figure 36**) onto the fuel distribution rail in the correct location. Make sure each fuel injector is correctly seated in the fuel distribution rail and that the cushion ring is seated against both the fuel injector and the rail (**Figure 43**).

> *CAUTION*
> *Do not tear the seal ring when installing the fuel injectors into the throttle body.*

9. Push the fuel injector and fuel distribution assembly (**Figure 34**) evenly and straight into the throttle body to avoid damaging the seal ring. Do not turn the injectors during installation.

10. Check that the fuel distribution rail seats evenly over the throttle body.

> *CAUTION*
> *In Step 11, do not use the screws to align or center the fuel distribution rail and the fuel injectors over the throttle body. Make sure the fuel distribution rail seats evenly over each fuel injector before installing and tightening the screws.*

11. Install the screws securing the fuel distribution rail and fuel injector assembly.

12. Install the fast idle plunger unit (**Figure 33**) and tighten the screws securely.

13. If disconnected, install the hose assembly (**Figure 32**) onto the throttle body assembly. Be sure to connect the hoses to correct fittings as noted during removal.

14. Connect the fuel supply hose (**Figure 31**) onto the fuel pipe.

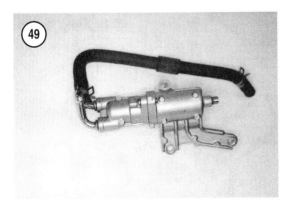

15. Install the throttle body assembly as described in this chapter.

Inspection

1. Visually inspect the fuel injectors for damage.

2. Check the electrical connector (**Figure 44**) on the fuel injector and wiring harness side (**Figure 45**) for corrosion or damage.

3. Inspect the spray nozzle (**Figure 46**) for carbon buildup or damage. Replace if necessary.

4. Repeat for each fuel injector.

5. Clean the fuel injector opening (**Figure 47**) in the fuel distribution rail.

6. Inspect the injector ports in the throttle body (**Figure 48**) for contamination.

7. Inspect the fast idle plunger unit (**Figure 49**) for damage and coolant leakage.

VACUUM SLIDE

Removal/Inspection/Installation

1. Remove the throttle body (this chapter).

2. Remove the mounting screws and cover (**Figure 50**).

3. Remove the spring (A, **Figure 51**) and the diaphragm/piston valve assembly (B).

4. Inspect the diaphragm (A, **Figure 52**) for cracks, deterioration or other damage. Check the sides of the piston valve (B) for excessive wear. Install the piston valve into the carburetor body and move it up and down in the bore. The piston valve should move smoothly with no binding or excessive play. Replace the piston valve and/or throttle body if necessary.

5. Install the diaphragm/piston valve assembly into the throttle body and make sure the diaphragm is seated correctly around its perimeter (**Figure 53**).

6. Install the cover and spring as follows:

    a. Install the lower end of the spring (A, **Figure 51**) into the piston valve receptacle (B).

    b. Install the cover onto the throttle body.

    c. Hold the cover with one hand, raise the piston valve with a finger, and correctly compress the spring between these two parts.

    d. Hold the piston valve in the raised position and install the cover screws (**Figure 50**).

    e. Lower the piston valve.

    f. Insert a finger into the venturi area and move the piston valve up in the throttle body (**Figure 54**). The piston valve should rise all the way up into the bore and slide back down immediately with no binding. If it binds or if the movement is sluggish, chances are the diaphragm did not seat correctly, or the spring is misaligned to one side or not centered within the cover. If necessary, remove the cover and reposition the spring.

    g. If the spring is installed correctly, tighten the top cover screws securely.

PRESSURE REGULATOR

Removal/Installation

1. Remove the throttle body (this chapter).

2. Partially remove the fuel injector assembly from the throttle body.

3. Disconnect the vacuum hose (A, **Figure 55**) from the pressure regulator.

4. Hold onto the fuel delivery pipe and remove the screws (B, **Figure 55**) securing the pressure regulator.

5. Remove the pressure regulator and O-ring (C, **Figure 55**).

6. Install a *new* O-ring onto the base of the pressure regulator.

7. Install the pressure regulator and mounting screws onto the fuel delivery pipe. Hold onto the fuel delivery pipe and tighten securely.

8. Connect the vacuum hose to the pressure regulator.

9. Install the fuel injector assembly on the throttle body.

10. Install the throttle body (this chapter).

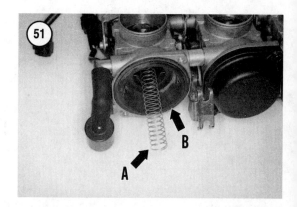

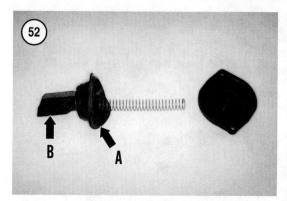

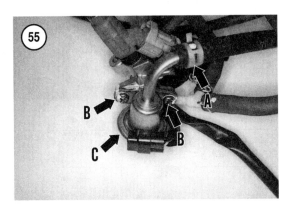

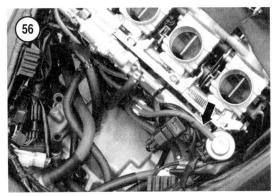

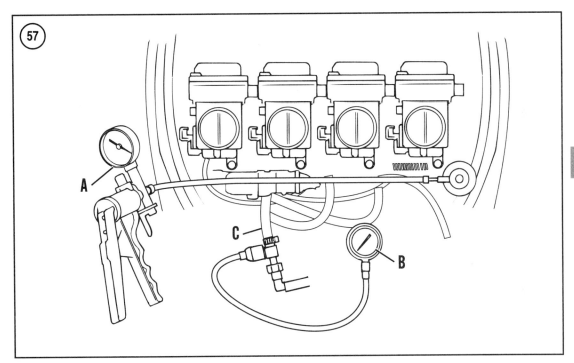

FUEL PRESSURE CHECK

The Yamaha fuel pressure gauge (U.S. part No. YU-03153, U.K. part No. 90890-03153), adapter (U.S. part No. YM-03176, U.K. part No. 90890-03176) and Mityvac are required for this procedure.

WARNING
Some fuel may spill and fuel vapors are present when measuring the fuel pressure. Because gasoline is extremely flammable, perform this procedure away from all open flames, including appliance pilot lights and sparks. Do not smoke or allow someone who is smoking in the work area, as an explosion and fire may occur. Always work in a well-ventilated area. Wipe up spills immediately.

1. Start the engine and allow it to warm up to normal operating temperature. Turn off the engine.
2. Disconnect the negative battery cable as described in Chapter Ten.
3. Remove the fuel tank and air filter housing as described in this chapter.
4. Disconnect the vacuum hose from the pressure regulator (**Figure 56**).
5. Connect the Mityvac to the pressure regulator (A, **Figure 57**).

6. Connect the adapter and fuel pressure gauge (B, **Figure 57**) to the fuel supply hose (C). Make sure the adapter is securely connected to the fuel supply hose.

7. Install the fuel tank as described in this chapter.

8. Start the engine and allow it to idle.

CAUTION
Do not exceed 100 kPa (14.5 psi) in Step 9 or the pressure regulator will be damaged.

9. Apply vacuum and observe the pressure gauge as follows:

    a. Increase vacuum pressure; the fuel pressure should decrease.

    b. Decrease the vacuum pressure; the fuel pressure should increase.

10. If the pressure regulator fails either of these tests, replace the pressure regulator as described in this chapter.

11. Turn off the engine.

12. Remove the fuel tank as described in this chapter.

13. Disconnect the Mityvac from the pressure regulator.

14. Disconnect the adapter and fuel pressure gauge from to the fuel supply hose.

15. Connect the vacuum hose to the pressure regulator (**Figure 56**).

16. Install the air filter housing and the fuel tank as described in this chapter.

17. Connect the negative battery cable as described in Chapter Ten.

FUEL PUMP

The fuel pump is mounted on the base of the fuel tank. The fuel filter is an integral part of the fuel pump and cannot be replaced separately.

Fuel Pump Tests

Prior to checking the fuel pump, perform the *Fuel Pump Relay Test* in Chapter Ten.

Running test

1. Turn the ignition switch on and listen for fuel pump operation. If the fuel pump does not operate for a few seconds, turn the ignition switch off and continue with Step 2.

2. Partially remove the fuel tank as described in this chapter to gain access to the fuel pump electrical connectors at the rear of the fuel tank.

NOTE
There are two electrical connectors at the rear of the fuel tank. One is for the fuel level gauge (black and green/white wires) and the other is for the fuel pump (black and red/blue wires).

3. Disconnect the fuel pump electrical connector (**Figure 58**) at the fuel pump.

4. Connect a voltmeter between the red/blue (+) and black (–) connector terminals on the wiring harness side.

5. Turn the ignition switch on while reading the voltmeter. It should read 13.0-13.2 volts (battery voltage) for a few seconds.

6. If there is battery voltage, replace the fuel pump.

7. If there is no battery voltage, check the following:

    a. 50 amp main fuse as described in Chapter Ten.

    b. 10 amp fuel injection system sub-fuse as described in Chapter Ten.

    c. Engine stop switch as described in Chapter Ten.

    d. Fuel cut-off relay as described in Chapter Ten.

8. Disconnect the voltmeter and connect the fuel pump electrical connector (**Figure 58**) at the fuel pump.

9. Lower and secure the fuel tank as described in this chapter.

Resistance test

1. Partially remove the fuel tank as described in this chapter to gain access to the fuel pump electrical connectors at the rear of the fuel tank.

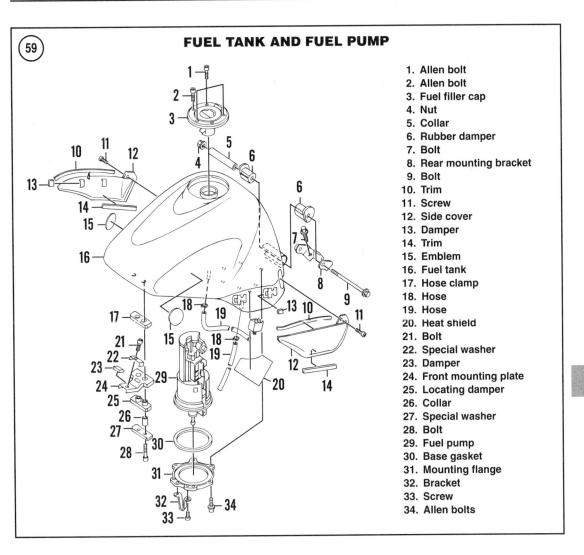

FUEL TANK AND FUEL PUMP

1. Allen bolt
2. Allen bolt
3. Fuel filler cap
4. Nut
5. Collar
6. Rubber damper
7. Bolt
8. Rear mounting bracket
9. Bolt
10. Trim
11. Screw
12. Side cover
13. Damper
14. Trim
15. Emblem
16. Fuel tank
17. Hose clamp
18. Hose
19. Hose
20. Heat shield
21. Bolt
22. Special washer
23. Damper
24. Front mounting plate
25. Locating damper
26. Collar
27. Special washer
28. Bolt
29. Fuel pump
30. Base gasket
31. Mounting flange
32. Bracket
33. Screw
34. Allen bolts

NOTE
There are two electrical connectors at the rear of the fuel tank. One is for the fuel level gauge (black and green/white wires) and the other is for the fuel pump (black and red/blue wires).

2. Disconnect the fuel pump electrical connector (**Figure 58**) at the fuel pump.
3. Connect a ohmmeter between the red/blue (+) and black (–) connector terminals on the fuel pump wiring harness side of the connector.
4. The specified resistance is 0.2-3.0 ohms.
5. If the resistance is not within specification, replace the fuel pump as described in this chapter.
6. Disconnect the ohmmeter and connect the fuel pump connector at the fuel pump.
7. Lower and secure the fuel tank (this chapter).

Removal/Installation

WARNING
Some fuel may spill and fuel vapors are present when removing and installing the fuel pump. Because gasoline is extremely flammable, perform this procedure away from all open flames, including appliance pilot lights and sparks. Do not smoke or allow someone who is smoking in the work area, as an explosion and fire may occur. Always work in a well-ventilated area. Wipe up spills immediately.

Refer to **Figure 59**.

1. Remove the fuel tank as described in this chapter.

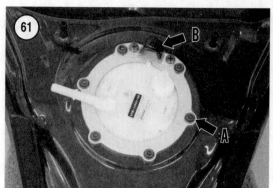

2. Place the fuel tank upside down on several towels or blanket (**Figure 60**) to protect the finish.

3. Remove the fuel pump mounting bolts and remove the fuel pump mounting flange (A, **Figure 61**).

4. Carefully remove the fuel pump (**Figure 62**) from the base of the fuel tank.

5. Inspect the O-ring gasket mating surface (**Figure 63**) on the fuel tank for corrosion or damage. Clean off any leaked fuel residue to ensure a leak-free sealing surface.

6. Make sure the base gasket (**Figure 64**) is in place and correctly seated in the base of the flange.

7. Carefully install the fuel pump assembly into the fuel tank (**Figure 62**), making sure not to damage the fuel sender. Move the fuel pump into the correct orientation within the fuel tank with the fuel pressure inlet fitting (**Figure 65**) directed to the right side (fuel tank installed) of the fuel tank.

8. Install the mounting flange (**Figure 66**) onto the fuel pump. Push it into position until it seats correctly against the fuel pump.

9. Install the mounting bolts (A, **Figure 61**) and tighten (**Figure 67**) to 4 N•m (35 in.-lb.).

10. Add about one gallon of fuel and check for leakage. If there is a problem, correct it at this time.

11. Install the fuel tank as described in this chapter.

12. Start the engine and once again check for any fuel leakage. If there is a problem, correct it at this time.

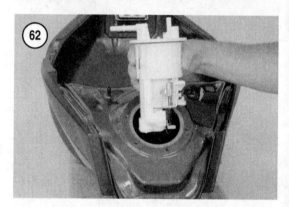

Inspection

The fuel pump cannot be disassembled as there are no replacement parts available.

1. Inspect the fuel pump (**Figure 68**) for corrosion and old gasoline residue.

2. Make sure the internal electrical connector (**Figure 69**) is attached correctly.

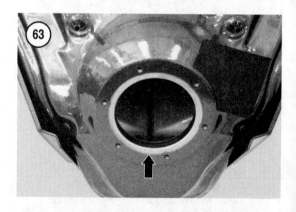

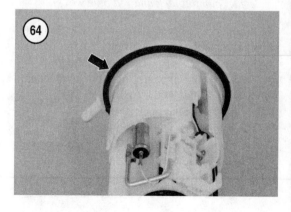

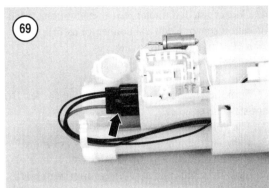

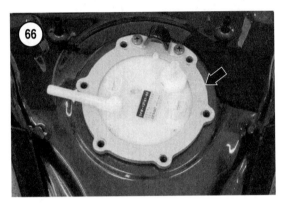

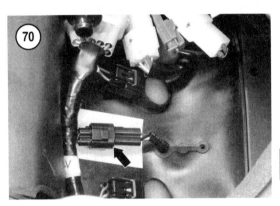

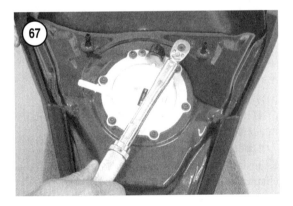

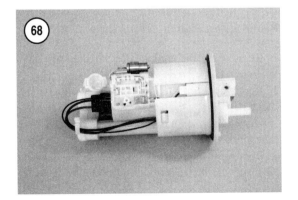

3. Do not remove the raised foot (B, **Figure 61**) from the mounting flange. This raised foot is used to protect the fuel pump plastic fittings when the fuel tank is set down right side up on a workbench. This raised foot makes contact with the workbench, not the fragile plastic fittings.

FUEL PUMP RELAY

The fuel pump relay is part of the relay unit that also consists of the starter circuit cutoff relay and is described in Chapter Ten.

CYLINDER IDENTIFICATION SENSOR

The cylinder identification sensor is located on top of the cylinder head cover.

Testing

1. Remove the fuel tank (this chapter).
2. Remove the air filter housing (this chapter).
3. Do *not* disconnect the cylinder identification sensor electrical connector (**Figure 70**).

4. Connect a voltmeter to the cylinder identification sensor electrical connector as follows:
   a. Positive test lead: white.
   b. Negative test lead: black/blue.
5. Turn the ignition switch on.
6. Turn the engine over *slowly* with the starter. Do not start the engine.
7. The voltmeter should read as follows:
   a. When the sensor is ON: 4.8 volts or more.
   b. When the sensor is OFF: 0.8 volt or less.
8. Stop the engine and turn the ignition switch off.
9. Disconnect the voltmeter.
10. Replace the sensor if it fails this test.
11. Install the air filter housing as described in this chapter.
12. Install the fuel tank as described in this chapter.

Removal/Installation

1. Remove the fuel tank as described in this chapter.
2. Remove the air filter housing as described in this chapter.
3. Disconnect the cylinder identification sensor electrical connector (**Figure 70**).
4. Carefully pull the rubber dam out of the way to gain access to the cylinder head cover.
5. Remove the screw and remove the sensor from the cylinder head cover.
6. Apply clean engine oil to the O-ring (**Figure 71**) and install the sensor onto the cylinder head cover. Tighten the screw.
7. Connect the cylinder identification sensor electrical connector (**Figure 70**).
8. Install the air filter housing as described in this chapter.
9. Install the fuel tank as described in this chapter.

INTAKE AIR PRESSURE SENSOR

The intake air pressure (IAP) sensor is located on the right side of the fuel distribution rail next to the pressure regulator.

Testing

1. Remove the fuel tank and air filter housing as described in this chapter.
2. Do *not* disconnect the intake air pressure sensor electrical connector (A, **Figure 72**).

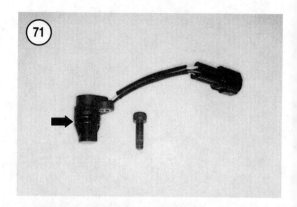

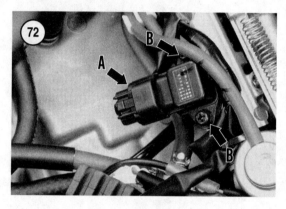

3. Connect a voltmeter to the intake air pressure sensor electrical connector as follows:
   a. Positive test lead: pink/white.
   b. Negative test lead: black/blue.
4. Turn the ignition switch on.
5. The voltmeter should read 3.75-4.24 volts.
6. If measurement does not meet specification, the intake air pressure sensor must be replaced.
7. Disconnect the voltmeter.
8. Install the air filter housing as described in this chapter.
9. Install the fuel tank as described in this chapter.

Removal/Installation

1. Remove the fuel tank as described in this chapter.
2. Remove the air filter housing as described in this chapter.
3. Disconnect the intake air pressure sensor electrical connector (A, **Figure 72**).
4. Remove the screws (B, **Figure 72**) securing the sensor to the fuel distribution rail and remove the sensor.

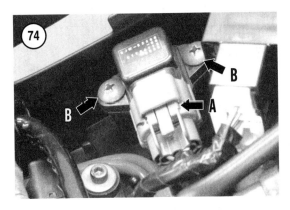

5. Install by reversing these removal steps.

INTAKE AIR TEMPERATURE SENSOR

The intake air temperature (IAT) sensor is located on the lower right side of the air filter housing.

Removal/Testing/Installation

1. Remove the fuel tank as described in this chapter.

2. Remove the air filter housing as described in this chapter.

3. Unscrew and remove the intake air temperature sensor (**Figure 73**) from the air filter housing.

4. Measure the sensor resistance as follows:
   a. Positive test lead: brown/white.
   b. Negative test lead: black/blue.

5. The specified resistance is 450-500 ohms.

6. If measurement does not meet specification, the intake air temperature sensor must be replaced.

7. Disconnect the ohmmeter.

8. If the sensor meets the requirement, install it into the air filter housing and tighten securely.

9. Install the air filter housing as described in this chapter.

10. Install the fuel tank as described in this chapter.

ATMOSPHERIC PRESSURE SENSOR

The atmospheric pressure (AP) sensor is mounted in the left side of the seat rail.

1. Remove both seats as described in Chapter Sixteen.

2. Remove the rear cowl as described in Chapter Sixteen.

3. Do *not* disconnect the 3-pin electrical connector (A, **Figure 74**).

4. Connect a voltmeter to the atmospheric pressure sensor electrical connector as follows:
   a. Positive test lead: blue.
   b. Negative test lead: black/blue.

5. Turn the ignition switch on.

6. The voltmeter should read 3.75-4.24 volts.

7. If measurement does not meet specification, the atmospheric pressure sensor must be replaced.

8. Disconnect the voltmeter.

9. Install the rear cowl as described in Chapter Sixteen.

10. Install the rider seat as described in Chapter Sixteen.

Removal/Installation

1. Remove both seats as described in Chapter Sixteen.

2. Remove the rear cowl as described in Chapter Sixteen.

3. Disconnect the 3-pin electrical connector (A, **Figure 74**).

4. Remove the screws (B, **Figure 74**) securing the sensor to the seat rail and remove the sensor.

5. Install by reversing these removal steps.

CRANKSHAFT POSITION SENSOR

The crankshaft position (CP) sensor is located on the right side of the engine under the pickup coil cover. The CP sensor uses the signals of the pickup coil to relay information to the ECU.

9

Testing

1. Remove the bottom cowl and right side fairing as described in Chapter Sixteen.

2. Remove the fuel tank and air filter housing as described in this chapter.

3. Follow the electrical cable (A, **Figure 75**) up from the pickup cover to the area ahead of the throttle body assembly.

4. Disconnect the crankshaft position sensor electrical connector (black and gray wires) from the main harness.

5. Measure the sensor resistance as follows:
   a. Positive test lead: gray.
   b. Negative test lead: black.

6. The specified resistance is 248-372 ohms.

7. If the measurement does not meet specification, the sensor must be replaced.

8. Disconnect the ohmmeter.

9. If the sensor meets the requirement, reconnect the electrical connector.

10. Install the air filter housing and the fuel tank as described in this chapter.

11. Install the right side fairing and the bottom cowl as described in Chapter Sixteen.

Removal/Installation

1. Remove the bottom cowl and right side fairing as described in Chapter Sixteen.

2. Remove the fuel tank and air filter housing as described in this chapter.

3. Follow the electrical cable (A, **Figure 75**) up from the pickup cover, through the frame and to the area ahead of the throttle body assembly.

4. Disconnect the crankshaft position sensor electrical connector (one gray, one black wire) from the main harness.

5. Disconnect the clutch cable (B, **Figure 75**) from the pickup coil rotor cover.

6. Remove the screws securing the pickup coil rotor cover (C, **Figure 75**) and remove the cover and gasket. Do not lose the locating dowels. Note the location of the clutch cable bracket (D, **Figure 75**) and the electrical cable locating tab (E).

7. Remove the Allen bolts (A, **Figure 76**) securing the crankshaft position sensor (B). Carefully pull the electrical cable and grommet (C, **Figure 76**) out of the notch in the crankcase. Remove the

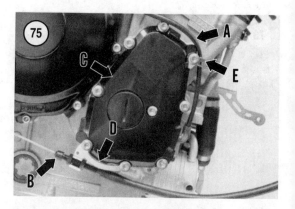

sensor and electrical cable from the engine and frame.

8. Install by reversing these removal steps while noting the following:
   a. Install and tighten the Allen bolts (A, **Figure 76**) to 10 N•m (88 in.-lb.).
   b. Apply a light coat of gasket sealer to the crankcase notch, then push the electrical cable and grommet (C, **Figure 76**) into the notch until it bottoms.
   c. If removed, install the locating dowels (A, **Figure 77**), then install the *new* gasket (B)

6. Do *not* disconnect the electrical connector (D, **Figure 78**) from the lean angle cut-off switch.

7. Connect a voltmeter to the lean angle cut-off switch electrical connector as follows:

    a. Positive test lead: blue.

    b. Negative test lead: yellow/green.

8. Turn the ignition switch on.

9. Rotate the lean angle cut-off switch 65° in both directions from its normal upright position.

10. The voltmeter should read 1.0-4.0 volts in both rotated directions.

11. If measurement does not meet specification, the lean angle cut-off switch must be replaced.

12. Turn the ignition switch off and disconnect the voltmeter.

13. If replacement is necessary, disconnect the electrical connector (D, **Figure 78**) from the lean angle cut-off switch, then install a new switch.

14. Install the rear cowl as described in Chapter Sixteen.

15. Install both seats as described in Chapter Sixteen.

EMISSION CONTROL SYSTEM

Refer to Chapter Eight.

THROTTLE CABLE REPLACEMENT

Always replace both throttle cables as a set.

1. Support the motorcycle on a swing arm safety stand. Block the front wheel so the motorcycle will not roll in either direction while on the safety stand.

2. Remove the front fairing as described in Chapter Sixteen.

3. Perform Steps 1-15 of *Throttle Body, Removal* in this chapter and partially remove the throttle body assembly to gain access to the throttle wheel and bracket.

4. Make a drawing of the cable routing from the right hand throttle housing to the carburetor assembly. Record this information for proper cable routing and installation.

5. At the right handlebar, remove the throttle cable housing screws (**Figure 79**) and open the housing assembly.

6. Disconnect the throttle cables from the throttle grip (**Figure 80**).

and the pickup coil rotor cover (A, **Figure 75**).

    d. Install the clutch cable bracket (D, **Figure 75**) and the electrical cable locating tab (E) in the correct locations and tighten the screws securely.

LEAN ANGLE CUT-OFF SWITCH

The lean angle cut-off switch is mounted on the right side of the frame behind the battery.

Removal/Testing/Installation

1. Remove both seats as described in Chapter Sixteen.

2. Remove the rear cowl as described in Chapter Sixteen.

3. Move the starter cable (A, **Figure 78**) out of the way.

4. Remove the screws (B, **Figure 78**) securing the lean angle cut-off switch (C).

5. Move the switch up out of the frame area so it can be rotated in Step 9.

7. Remove the cables from around the front of the right side fork tube (**Figure 81**) and the under steering head lower bracket. Note the position of any cable clamps for installation.

8. Compare the new and old cables.

9. If cables without nylon liners are used, lubricate them as described in Chapter Three.

10. Route the new cables through the same path as the old cables.

> *WARNING*
> *The throttle cables are the push/pull type and must not be interchanged. Attach the cables following the identification labels made on the old cables.*

11. Lightly grease the throttle cable ends and connect them to the throttle grip in the correct location as follows:

　a. Install the push cable (**Figure 82**) onto the receptacle in throttle grip, then slowly rotate the throttle grip.

　b. Slightly rotate the throttle grip, then install the pull cable (A, **Figure 83**) onto the receptacle in the throttle grip.

　c. Move the rear portion of the throttle cable housing (B, **Figure 83**) into position on the throttle grip.

　d. Install the front portion of the throttle cable housing into position on the throttle grip and install the screws (**Figure 79**). Tighten the screws securely.

12. Install the throttle body assembly as described under *Throttle Body, Installation* in this chapter.

13. Open the throttle and release it. The throttle should snap back smoothly. If operation is incorrect, carefully check that the cables are attached correctly and there are no tight bends in the cables. Repeat this check with the front wheel pointing straight ahead and then with the wheel turned full left and full right.

14. Adjust the throttle cables as described in Chapter Three.

15. When the throttle is operating correctly, start the engine and run it at idle speed with the transmission in neutral. Turn the handlebar from side to side, making sure the idle speed does not increase. If it does, the throttle cables are improperly installed. If the idle speed did not increase, test ride the motorcycle slowly at first. If there is any problem with the

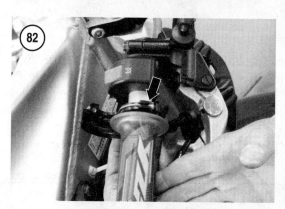

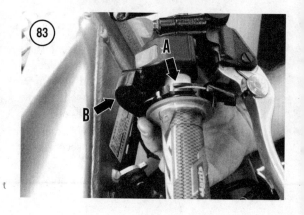

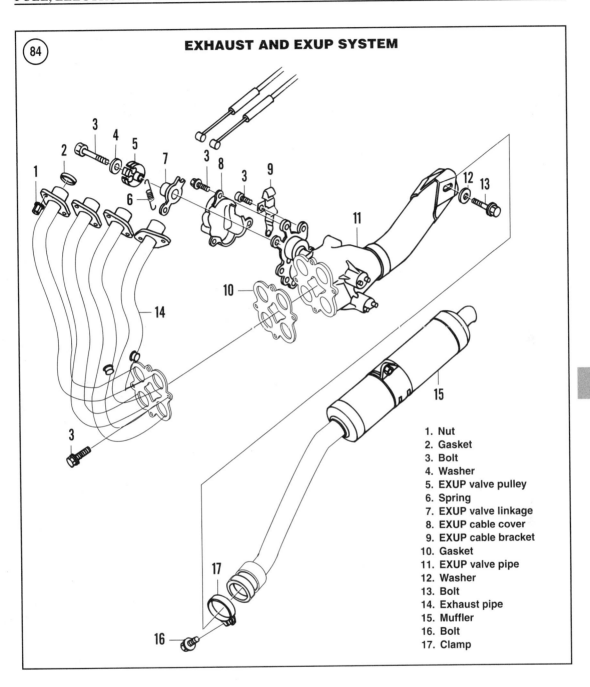

EXHAUST AND EXUP SYSTEM

(84)

1. Nut
2. Gasket
3. Bolt
4. Washer
5. EXUP valve pulley
6. Spring
7. EXUP valve linkage
8. EXUP cable cover
9. EXUP cable bracket
10. Gasket
11. EXUP valve pipe
12. Washer
13. Bolt
14. Exhaust pipe
15. Muffler
16. Bolt
17. Clamp

9

throttle, stop the motorcycle and make the necessary repairs.

> *WARNING*
> *An improperly adjusted or incorrectly routed throttle cable can cause the throttle to stick in the open position. This could cause a loss of control. Do not ride the motorcycle until the throttle cable operation is correct.*

16. Install the front fairing as described in Chapter Sixteen.

EXHAUST SYSTEM

The exhaust system (**Figure 84**) is vital to engine performance. Check the exhaust system for deep dents and fractures and repair or replace components immediately. Check the muffler-to-frame mounting flanges for fractures and loose bolts. Check the cylinder head mounting flanges for tightness. A loose exhaust pipe connection can reduce engine performance.

Removal

> *WARNING*
> *Do not remove or service the exhaust system when it is hot.*

1. Park the motorcycle on level ground. Support the motorcycle securely on a swing arm stand with the rear wheel off the ground.
2. Remove the rider's seat as described in Chapter Sixteen.
3. Remove the fuel tank as described in this chapter.
4. Remove both side fairing panels and bottom cowl as described in Chapter Sixteen.
5. Refer to *EXUP System* in this chapter and perform Steps 1-9 of *Cable Replacement*.
6. Loosen the muffler-to-exhaust pipe clamp bolt (**Figure 85**).
7. Remove the bolt (**Figure 86**) securing the muffler to the rear footpeg bracket.
8. Carefully pull the muffler free from the exhaust valve pipe assembly and remove the muffler.
9. Remove the radiator as described in Chapter Eleven.
10. Remove the bolt and washer (**Figure 87**) securing the exhaust pipe and EXUP valve pipe assembly to the frame mount.
11. Remove the front exhaust pipe nuts (**Figure 88**) at the cylinder head and remove the exhaust pipe and EXUP valve pipe assembly.
12. Remove the exhaust pipe gasket (**Figure 89**) at each cylinder head exhaust port. Discard the gaskets.

Installation

1. Install a *new* exhaust pipe gasket (**Figure 89**) into each cylinder head exhaust port. Apply grease to the gaskets to prevent them from falling out of place.
2. Install the exhaust pipe and exhaust valve pipe assembly onto the cylinder head and install the nuts. (**Figure 88**) Tighten finger-tight at this time.

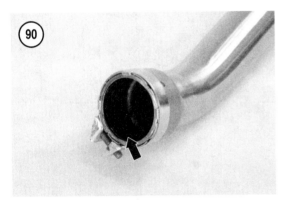

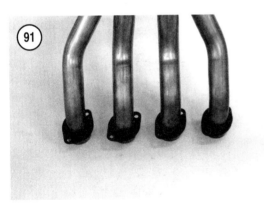

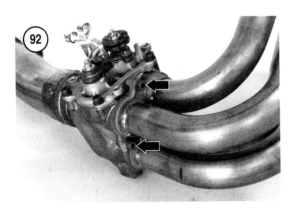

3. Install the bolt and washer (**Figure 87**) securing the exhaust pipe and exhaust valve pipe assembly to the frame mount. Tighten finger-tight at this time.

4. Install a new gasket (**Figure 90**) into the muffler inlet port.

5. Move the muffler into position and connect it onto the exhaust valve pipe.

6. Push the muffler in until it bottoms. Tighten the muffler-to-exhaust pipe clamp bolt (**Figure 85**) finger-tight at this time.

7. Install the bolt (**Figure 86**) securing the muffler to the rear footpeg bracket. Tighten finger-tight at this time.

8. Tighten the exhaust pipe-to-cylinder head nuts to 20 N•m (15 ft.-lb.).

9. Install the exhaust pipe and EXUP valve pipe-to-frame mount bolt to 20 N•m (15 ft.-lb.).

10. Tighten the muffler-to-EXUP valve pipe clamp bolts to 20 N•m (15 ft.-lb.).

11. Tighten the muffler to the rear footpeg bracket bolt to 38 N•m (28 ft.-lb.).

12. Refer to *EXUP System* in this chapter and perform Steps 20-29 of *Cable Replacement*.

13. After installation is complete, start the engine and make sure there are no exhaust leaks.

14. Install the radiator as described in Chapter Eleven.

15. Refill the cooling system as described in Chapter Three.

16. Install the bottom cowl and both side fairing panels as described in Chapter Sixteen.

17. Install the fuel tank as described in this chapter.

18. Install the rider's seat as described in Chapter Sixteen.

Inspection

1. Inspect the muffler mounting bracket for cracks or damage.

2. Inspect the exhaust pipe-to-cylinder head flanges (**Figure 91**) for corrosion, burned areas or damage.

3. Inspect all welds for leakage or corrosion.

4. Check the muffler mounting rubber grommet and collar on the rear footpeg mounting bracket. Replace the rubber grommet if it is starting to harden or deteriorate.

5. Inspect the four Allen bolts (**Figure 92**) securing the EXUP valve pipe to the exhaust pipe. Tighten if necessary. If there is an exhaust leak, remove the

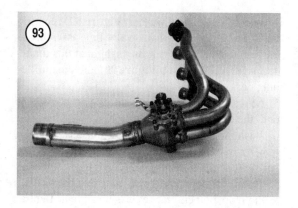

four Allen bolts and separate the EXUP valve pipe
from the exhaust pipe and replace the gasket.

6. Inspect the gasket (**Figure 90**) in the exhaust
pipe assembly for deterioration.

7. Inspect all welds on the exhaust pipe assembly
(**Figure 93**) for leakage or corrosion.

8. Refer to the following procedure for the components relating to the EXUP system.

EXUP SYSTEM (2002-2003 MODELS)

The Exhaust Ultimate Power Valve (EXUP) system boosts engine power by a valve assembly that
regulates the opening of the exhaust pipe just ahead
of the muffler. The system constantly adjusts the exhaust opening to achieve maximum performance.
The valve assembly is controlled by the servomotor
located under the right side frame inboard of the
front footpeg assembly.

Cable Replacement

NOTE
The EXUP cables are different and
must be installed correctly. Follow the
cables from the servomotor to the pul-
ley on the exhaust pipe. Label the op-
posite end of each cable also with the
appropriate A and B. The labels en-
sures the correct installation of each
cable at both components.

1. Park the motorcycle on level ground. Support
the motorcycle securely on a swing arm stand with
the rear wheel off the ground.

2. Remove the right side fairing panel and bottom
cowl as described in Chapter Sixteen.

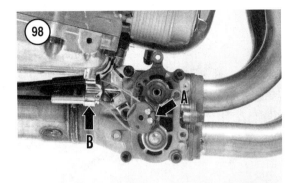

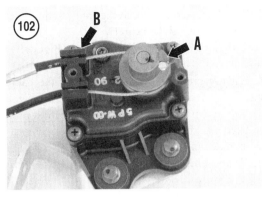

3. Remove the bolts securing the EXUP pulley cover (**Figure 94**) and remove the cover.

4. Remove the spring (**Figure 95**) from both pulleys.

5. To lock the pulley in place, insert a 4-mm long pin, or punch (A, **Figure 96**) through the notch in the EXUP pulley and into the hole in the EXUP valve cover (B).

6. Loosen, then remove, the bolt and washer (A, **Figure 97**) securing the cable pulley.

7. Remove the 4-mm long pin or punch from the EXUP pulley.

8. Note the location of the cables within the pulley (B, **Figure 97**) then remove the pulley from the shaft. The cables must be reinstalled in the correct location.

9. Disconnect the cables from the pulley (A, **Figure 98**) and the cable bracket (B).

10. On the right side of the frame, remove the bolts securing the EXUP servomotor cover (**Figure 99**) and remove the cover.

11. Remove the bolts (**Figure 100**) securing the servomotor to the frame. Lower the servomotor out of the frame. Disconnect the 6-pin electrical connector (**Figure 101**) from the servomotor and remove the servomotor.

12. Note the location of the cables within the pulley (A, **Figure 102**).

13. Disconnect both cables from the servomotor pulley and from the cable bracket (B, **Figure 102**).

14. Compare the new and old cables.

15. If cables without nylon liners are used, lubricate them as described in Chapter Three.

16. Route the new cables through the same path as the old cables.

17. Lightly grease the cable ends. Connect both cables onto the cable bracket (B, **Figure 102**) and the servomotor pulley (A).

18. Install the servomotor to the frame and tighten the bolts (**Figure 100**) securely.

19. Install the EXUP servomotor cover (**Figure 99**) and tighten the bolt securely.

20. Lightly grease the opposite end of the cable ends.

21. At the exhaust pipe, connect both cables onto the cable bracket (B, **Figure 98**) in the correct location as noted in *Removal* Step 8.

22. Connect the cables onto the pulley (A, **Figure 98**).

23. Install the pulley onto the shaft and push it on until it bottoms.

24. Install the bolt and washer (A, **Figure 97**) and tighten finger-tight.

25. To lock the pulley in place, insert a 4-mm long pin, or punch (A, **Figure 96**) through the notch in the EXUP pulley and into the hole in the EXUP valve cover (B). Tighten the bolt securely.

26. Remove the 4-mm long pin or punch from the EXUP pulley.

27. Install the spring as shown in **Figure 95** and hook it onto both pulleys.

28. Install the EXUP pulley cover (**Figure 94**) and bolts. Tighten the bolts securely.

29. Adjust the EXUP cables as described in Chapter Three.

30. After installation is complete, start the engine and make sure there are no exhaust leaks.

31. Install the bottom cowl and both side fairing panels as described in Chapter Sixteen.

Servomotor Removal/Installation

1. Park the motorcycle on level ground. Support the motorcycle securely on a swing arm stand with the rear wheel off the ground.

2. Remove the right side fairing panel and bottom cowl as described in Chapter Sixteen.

3. On the right side of the frame, remove the bolts securing the EXUP servomotor cover (**Figure 99**) and remove the cover.

4. Remove the bolts (**Figure 100**) securing the servomotor to the frame. Lower the servomotor out of the frame. Disconnect the 6-pin electrical connector (**Figure 101**) from the servomotor and remove it.

5. Note the location of the cables within the pulley (A, **Figure 102**).

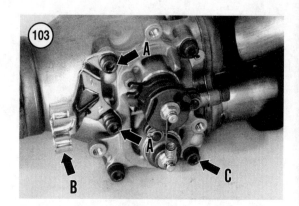

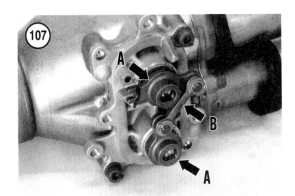

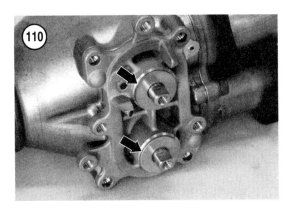

6. Disconnect both cables from the servomotor pulley and from the cable bracket (B, **Figure 102**).

7. Install by reversing these removal steps while noting the following:

   a. Install the cables onto the correct location within the pulley.

   b. Adjust the cables as described in Chapter Three.

Valve

Disassembly

1. Remove the exhaust pipe as described in this chapter.

2. Remove the bolts (A, **Figure 103**) securing the cable bracket (B) and remove the bracket. Remove the front lower bolt (C, **Figure 103**).

3. If still in place, unhook and remove the spring (**Figure 104**).

4. Remove the bolt (**Figure 105**) securing the lower pulley.

5. Remove the bolt (A, **Figure 106**) securing the cable upper pulley and remove the pulley (B).

6. Pull straight off and remove both valve pulleys (A, **Figure 107**) and the interconnecting link arm (B) assembly.

7. Remove the two remaining bolts (**Figure 108**) securing the valve cover.

8. Remove the spring (**Figure 109**) from both valve shafts.

9. Remove the washer (**Figure 110**) from both valve shafts.

10. Remove the outer bushing (**Figure 111**) from both valve shafts.

11. Pull straight off and remove the cover (**Figure 112**).

9

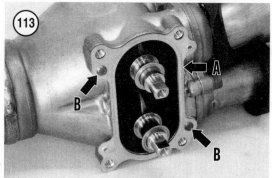

12. Remove the gasket (A, **Figure 113**) and both locating dowels (B).

13. Remove the washer (**Figure 114**) from each valve shaft.

14. Withdraw both valves (**Figure 115**) from the housing.

15. Use wide end type snap ring pliers (A, **Figure 116**) and extract both inner bushings (B) from within the housing.

16. Inspect the assembly as described in this chapter.

Assembly

1. Install both inner bushings (B, **Figure 116**) into the receptacles (**Figure 117**) in the housing. Make sure they are correctly seated and not cocked within the receptacles.

2. Position the valve vertically (**Figure 118**) and install it into the housing and into the inner bushing. Push it in until it bottoms in the inner bushing.

3. Repeat Step 2 for the other valve.

4. Install the washer (**Figure 114**) on each valve shaft.

5. Install the locating dowels (**Figure 119**) into the housing.

6. Install a *new* gasket (**Figure 120**).

7. Make sure both valves are *vertical*. The flats on the shaft ends must be *horizontal* in order to accept the valve pulleys in Step 14.

8. Install the cover (**Figure 112**) and push it on until it seats against the gasket.

9. Install the bushing (**Figure 111**) onto both valve shafts. Push them on until they bottom.

10. Install the washer (**Figure 110**) onto both valve shafts.

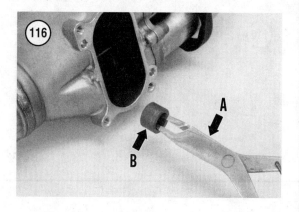

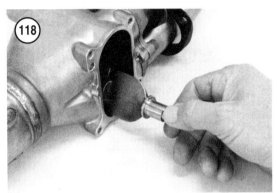

11. Position the spring with the larger coil (**Figure 121**) going on first against the washer. Install the spring (**Figure 109**) onto both valve shafts.

12. Install the two bolts (**Figure 108**) securing the valve cover. Tighten the bolts securely.

13. Make sure the flats on the shaft ends are still *horizontal*. Readjust if necessary.

14. Install the valve pulleys (A, **Figure 107**) and interconnecting link (B) assembly onto the valve shafts. The interconnecting link must be positioned as shown in **Figure 122**, otherwise the linkage will bind and not work properly.

15. Position the cable upper pulley with the cable end receptacles (**Figure 123**) toward the front and install the upper pulley (B, **Figure 106**) and bolt (A). Tighten the bolt securely.

16. Install the bolt (**Figure 105**) securing the lower pulley and tighten securely.

17. Install the spring onto both pulley bolt heads as shown in **Figure 104**.

18. Install the cable bracket (B, **Figure 103**) and bolts (A). Install the front lower bolt (C, **Figure 103**). Tighten the bolts securely.

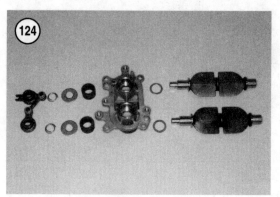

19. Operate the linkage and make sure both valves operate without binding. If there is a problem, correct it at this time.

20. Install the exhaust pipe as described in this chapter.

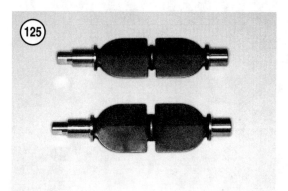

Inspection

Replace any component (**Figure 124**) that is worn or damaged. All parts can be replaced individually.

1. Clean all components in solvent and dry.

2. Inspect the valves (**Figure 125**) for wear, or heavy carbon buildup.

3. Check that the interconnecting link pivots freely on both pulleys (**Figure 126**). Clean off any corrosion from the pulley pivot points.

4. Check the springs (A, **Figure 127**), washers (B) and bushings (C) for wear or damage.

5. Inspect the cover (**Figure 128**) for cracks or warpage. Clean off the gasket sealing surface.

6. Inspect the valve operating area (A, **Figure 129**) within the EXUP chamber for corrosion, carbon buildup or damage.

7. Inspect the gasket sealing surface (B, **Figure 129**) on the EXUP chamber for corrosion and warp.

8. Check for exhaust leakage where the exhaust pipes are attached to the EXUP valve pipe (A, **Figure 130**). If leakage is present, remove the four Allen bolts (B, **Figure 130**) and separate the exhaust pipe assembly from the EXUP valve pipe. Install a new gasket and tighten the Allen bolts securely.

9. Inspect the servomotor housing and mounting bracket (**Figure 131**) for damage.

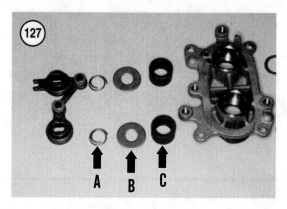

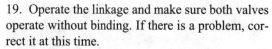

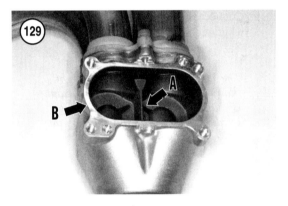

9

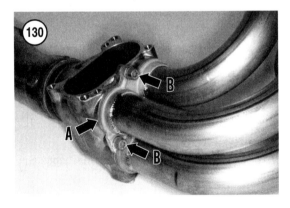

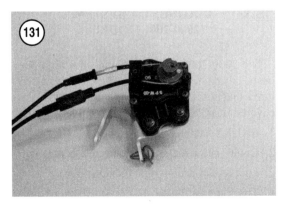

Testing

The EXUP system is part of the self-diagnosis system. If there is a fault with the system the respective code will be displayed on the tachometer face when the ignition is turned on and the engine started. Refer to *Diagnostic System (2002-2003 Models)* in this chapter.

EXUP servomotor is stuck

> *NOTE*
> *This test relates to the fuel injection trouble code No. 18.*

1. Disconnect the negative battery cable as described in Chapter Ten.
2. Remove the right side fairing panel and bottom cowl as described in Chapter Sixteen.
3. On the right side of the frame, remove the bolts securing the EXUP servomotor cover (**Figure 132**) and remove the cover.
4. Remove the bolts (**Figure 133**) securing the servomotor to the frame. Lower the servomotor out of the frame. Disconnect the 6-pin electrical connector

(**Figure 134**) from the servomotor and remove the servomotor.

> *CAUTION*
> *In Step 6, do not connect the battery to the electrical terminal connectors for more than a few seconds as the servomotor will be damaged.*

6. Connect a fully charged 12-volt battery to the EXUP servomotor side of the electrical connector as follows:

    a. Connect the positive battery terminal to the white/red wire terminal.

    b. Connect the negative battery terminal to the black/blue wire terminal.

7. The servomotor should rotate several times.

8. If the servomotor does not rotate it is defective and must be replaced.

9. Refer to *Electrical Connectors* in Chapter Ten and pack the connector with dielectric grease compound.

10. Install the fuel tank as described in this chapter.

11. Connect the negative battery cable as described in Chapter Ten.

12. Install the rider's seat described in Chapter Sixteen.

Servomotor potention circuit

> *NOTE*
> *This test relates to the fuel injection trouble code No. 17.*

1. Disconnect the negative battery cable as described in Chapter Ten.

2. Remove the right side fairing panel and bottom cowl as described in Chapter Sixteen.

3. On the right side of the frame, remove the bolts securing the EXUP servomotor cover (**Figure 132**) and remove the cover.

4. Remove the bolts (**Figure 133**) securing the servomotor to the frame. Lower the servomotor out of the frame. Disconnect the 6-pin electrical connector (**Figure 134**) from the servomotor and remove the servomotor.

5. Check the resistance as follows:

    a. Connect the ohmmeter positive test lead to the blue terminal on the servomotor side of the connector.

    b. Connect the ohmmeter negative lead to the white/red terminal on the connector.

> *NOTE*
> *The meter readings may differ slightly than those specified. More important is that the needle movement changes gradually and smoothly during the full range of movement.*

    c. Slowly rotate the EXUP servo motor pulley and measure the resistance. The resistance should be approximately 0 ohm.

    d. If not within specification, the servo motor is defective and must be replaced.

6. Refer to *Electrical Connectors* in Chapter Ten and pack the connector with dielectric grease compound.

7. Install the fuel tank as described in this chapter.

8. Connect the negative battery cable as described in Chapter Ten.

9. Install the rider's seat described in Chapter Sixteen.

DIAGNOSTIC SYSTEM (2000-2001 MODELS)

The 2000-2001 model is equipped with a diagnostic system to detect faults. The systems that feature a diagnostic capability and the chapter they are covered in are as follows:

1. EXUP System (Chapter Eight).

2. Combination meter/speed sensor (Chapter Ten).

3. Fuel level warning light (Chapter Ten).

4. Throttle position sensor (TPS) (Chapter Ten).

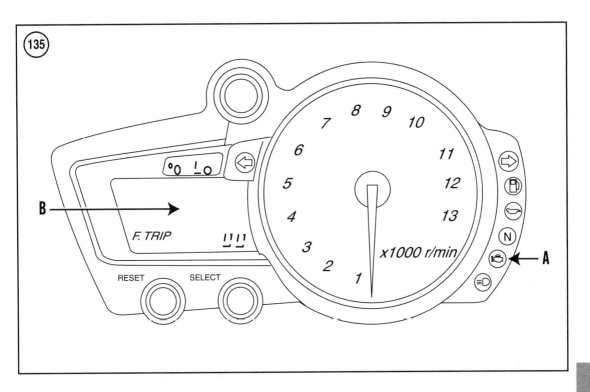

DIAGNOSTIC SYSTEM
(2002-2003 MODELS)

The fuel injection system is equipped with a diagnostic system to detect faults that may occur within the fuel injection system and the EXUP system. If an EXUP system fault is indicated, also refer to *EXUP System* in this chapter.

Under normal operating conditions, the instrument cluster engine trouble warning light (A, **Figure 135**) is illuminated for 1.4 seconds after the ignition switch is turned on. The light should blink while the start button is being pressed. If the warning light does not come on or blink as described, check for a blown bulb or other problem in the circuit.

If there is a problem with the fuel injection system, the trouble warning light will be illuminated and will either stay on continuously or will blink depending on the fault.

After the engine is stopped a digital number(s) representing the diagnostic trouble code(s) will appear on the clock LCD portion of the combination meter (B, **Figure 135**). Once the trouble code has been displayed, it remains stored in the engine control unit (ECU) memory until the deletion operation is performed to erase the code.

Read through the following sections before beginning diagnostic system troubleshooting. Refer to *Electrical Component Replacement* in Chapter Ten prior to replacing a component(s). If the procedures are not followed carefully an incorrect diagnosis may occur. Do not overlook the possibility that something as simple as a loose electrical connector or vacuum hose may be the source of a problem. If the source of a trouble code cannot be solved, take the motorcycle to a Yamaha dealership as soon as possible for troubleshooting and repair.

Trouble Codes and Diagnostic Codes

There are two different types of codes as follows:
1. *Trouble Codes*: If a problem occurs within the system, the rider is notified with a *trouble code* that is shown on the clock LCD portion of the combination meter. This trouble code will appear when the ignition switch is operated during starting and stopping of the engine. At this time the motorcycle may or may not be able to be started and ridden, depending on the type of the malfunction. Refer to **Table 5** for trouble codes.
2. *Diagnostic Codes*: After a trouble code is displayed, this can be cross referenced to the *diagnostic code*. Enter the diagnostic code into the combination

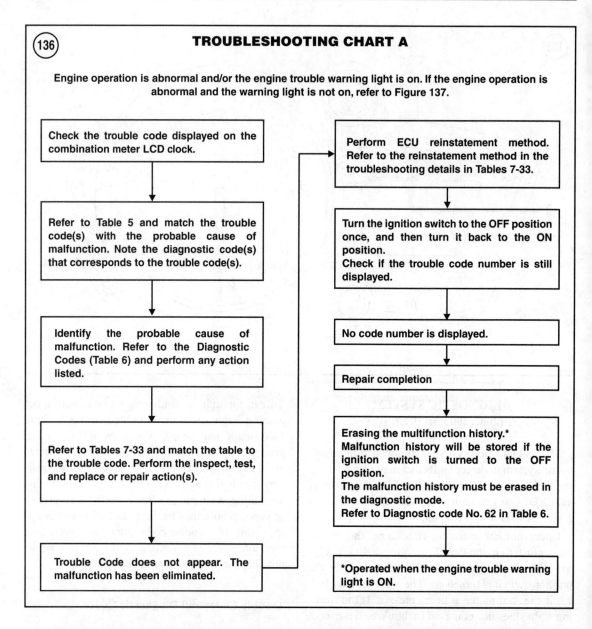

(136)   **TROUBLESHOOTING CHART A**

Engine operation is abnormal and/or the engine trouble warning light is on. If the engine operation is abnormal and the warning light is not on, refer to Figure 137.

Check the trouble code displayed on the combination meter LCD clock.

↓

Refer to Table 5 and match the trouble code(s) with the probable cause of malfunction. Note the diagnostic code(s) that corresponds to the trouble code(s).

↓

Identify the probable cause of malfunction. Refer to the Diagnostic Codes (Table 6) and perform any action listed.

↓

Refer to Tables 7-33 and match the table to the trouble code. Perform the inspect, test, and replace or repair action(s).

↓

Trouble Code does not appear. The malfunction has been eliminated.

Perform ECU reinstatement method. Refer to the reinstatement method in the troubleshooting details in Tables 7-33.

↓

Turn the ignition switch to the OFF position once, and then turn it back to the ON position.
Check if the trouble code number is still displayed.

↓

No code number is displayed.

Repair completion

Erasing the multifunction history.*
Malfunction history will be stored if the ignition switch is turned to the OFF position.
The malfunction history must be erased in the diagnostic mode.
Refer to Diagnostic code No. 62 in Table 6.

↓

*Operated when the engine trouble warning light is ON.

meter by following the *Setting the Diagnostic Mode* procedure described in this section. By entering the diagnostic code, specification data for that particular component/system will be displayed on the combination meter. Refer to **Table 6** for diagnostic codes.

**Substitute Operation With
Trouble Codes Present**

If the warning light *stays on* continuously, the motorcycle may or may not be able to be ridden, depending on the trouble code.

When a problem with a sensor/actuator is detected by the ECU, the ECU processes the information and enters a programmed specified value for the sensor/actuator. This *fail-safe action*, depending on the trouble code, may allow the motorcycle to be operated. Refer to the individual trouble code tables (**Tables 7-33**) for a description of the fail-safe action. It may be necessary to stop operation of the motorcycle, depending on what area(s) of the system is affected.

If the light is *blinking*, the motorcycle will cease to operate and it cannot be started or ridden. At this

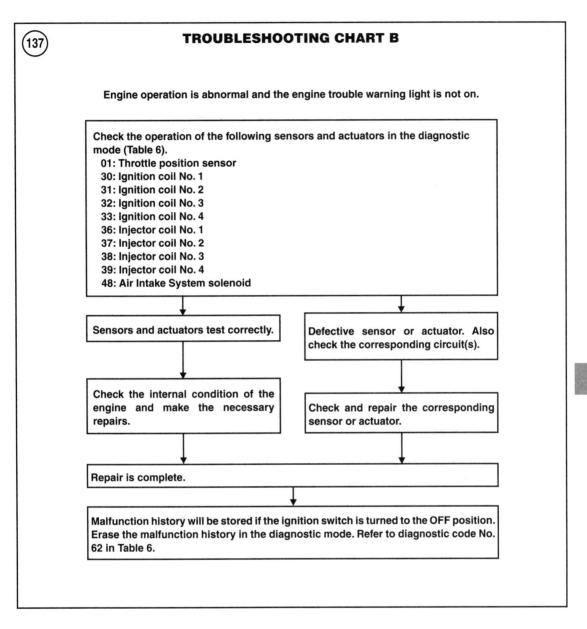

TROUBLESHOOTING CHART B

(137)

Engine operation is abnormal and the engine trouble warning light is not on.

Check the operation of the following sensors and actuators in the diagnostic mode (Table 6).
01: Throttle position sensor
30: Ignition coil No. 1
31: Ignition coil No. 2
32: Ignition coil No. 3
33: Ignition coil No. 4
36: Injector coil No. 1
37: Injector coil No. 2
38: Injector coil No. 3
39: Injector coil No. 4
48: Air Intake System solenoid

Sensors and actuators test correctly.

Defective sensor or actuator. Also check the corresponding circuit(s).

Check the internal condition of the engine and make the necessary repairs.

Check and repair the corresponding sensor or actuator.

Repair is complete.

Malfunction history will be stored if the ignition switch is turned to the OFF position. Erase the malfunction history in the diagnostic mode. Refer to diagnostic code No. 62 in Table 6.

time one of the following trouble codes will appear on the clock LCD:

1. No. 11: Cylinder identification sensor.

2. No. 12: Crankshaft position sensor.

3. No. 19: Side stand switch (open circuit in wire to ECU).

4. No. 30: Lean angle cut-off switch (latch up detected).

5. No. 41: Lean angle cut-off switch (open or short circuit).

6. No. 50: ECU internal malfunction (memory check error).

Troubleshooting

Refer to **Figure 136** and **Figure 137** for an outline of the diagnostic steps. Refer to **Figure 136** if a trouble code is present. Refer to **Figure 137** if an abnormal engine condition is occurring and no trouble code is present.

Use the trouble code information (**Table 5**) and, if appropriate, diagnostic code information (**Table 6**), along with the corresponding display data to diagnose the fault(s). Refer to **Tables 7-33** by specific individual trouble code for testing procedures.

Setting the diagnostic mode

1. Turn the ignition switch off and the engine stop switch to the ON position.

NOTE
In Step 2, all indications on the meter disappear except for the clock and trip indications.

2. Simultaneously depress both the SELECT and RESET buttons on the combination meter and turn the ignition switch on. Keep both buttons depressed for more than eight seconds. Release both buttons.

3. Depress the SELECT button and select the diagnostic mode that appears as *dIAG*. Do not use the CO adjustment mode.

4. After selecting the *dIAG* mode, simultaneously depress both the SELECT and RESET buttons for more than two seconds to execute the selection.

5. Raise the fuel tank as described in this chapter and disconnect the fuel pump electrical connector (**Figure 138**) from the fuel tank.

6. Turn the engine stop switch to the OFF position. If the diagnostic code numbers 03 and 09 are shown, turn the engine stop switch to the ON position.

7. Use either the SELECT or RESET button to select the diagnostic code that applies to the item that was verified with the trouble code. For example, if the diagnostic code is 21, use the SELECT button to scroll through the numbers from small to large (01—70). If the diagnostic code is 48, use the RESET button to scroll through the codes from large to small (70—01). Stop when the correct code is shown.

8. Refer to **Table 6** and verify the operation of the sensor/actuator by performing the intruction(s) in the action column.

9. Turn the ignition switch off to cancel the diagnostic mode process.

Table 1 FUEL SYSTEM ABBREVIATIONS

Name	Specification
Atmospheric pressure sensor	AP sensor
Coolant temperature sensor	CT sensor
Crankshaft position sensor	CP sensor
Engine control unit	ECU
Engine coolant temperature sensor	ECT sensor
Intake air pressure sensor	IAP sensor
Intake air temperature sensor	IAT sensor
Throttle position sensor	TP sensor

Table 2 FUEL SYSTEM GENERAL SPECIFICATIONS

Throttle body identification number	Mikuni × 4
U.S. and Canada	5PW1 00
California	5PW5 20
France	5PWZ 10
All other models	5PW1 00
Throttle body size	100

Table 3 FUEL SYSTEM TEST SPECIFICATIONS*

Item	Specification
Atmospheric pressure sensor output voltage	3.75-4.25 volts
Base throttle valve synchronization	No. 3 throttle body
Crankshaft position sensor	248-372 ohms
Cylinder identification sensor output voltage	
Sensor on	4.8 volts or more
Sensor off	0.8 volts or less
EXUP servomotor resistance	
When pulley is turned once	0 to approximately 7500 ohms
Fuel pressure	284 kPa (40.4 psi)
Fuel pump resistance	0.2-3.0 ohms
Idle speed	1000-1100 rpm
Intake air pressure sensor output voltage	3.75-4.24 volts
Intake air temperature resistance	450-550 ohms
Speed sensor	
Sensor on	4.8 volts or more
Sensor off	0.6 volts or less
Throttle grip free play	3-5 mm (0.12-0.20 in.)
Vacuum pressure at idle speed	25.3 kPa (190 mmHg/7.48 in.Hg)

*All voltage and resistance readings taken at 20° C (68° F)

Table 4 FUEL AND EXHAUST SYSTEM TORQUE SPECIFICATIONS

Item	N•m	in.-lb.	ft.-lb.
Atmospheric pressure sensor	7	62	–
Crankshaft position sensor	10	88	–
Exhaust system			
Exhaust pipe-to-cylinder head nuts	20	–	15
Exhaust pipe-to-exhaust valve pipe	20	–	15
Exhaust pipe-to-frame bolt	20	–	15
Muffler-to-footpeg bolt	38	–	28
Fuel pump mounting bolts	4	35	–
Fuel tank mounting bolt	10	88	–
Intake air temperature sensor	18	–	13
Speed sensor	10	88	–

Table 5 TROUBLE CODES

Trouble code number	Symptoms	Probable cause of malfunction	Diagnostic code number
11	Normal signals are not received from the cylinder identification sensor Engine unable to start Engine will continue to run based on inputs up to the point of last signal	Open or short circuit in wiring sub lead Open or short circuit in wiring harness Defective cylinder identification sensor Malfunction in the ECU Improperly installed sensor	–

(continued)

Table 5 TROUBLE CODES (continued)

Trouble code number	Symptoms	Probable cause of malfunction	Diagnostic code number
12	Normal signals are not received from the crankshaft position sensor Engine unable to start	Open or short in wiring harness Defective crankshaft position sensor Malfunction in timing pickup rotor Malfunction in the ECU Improperly installed sensor	–
13	Intake air pressure sensor open or short circuit detected Engine able to start	Open or short circuit in wiring sub lead Open or short circuit in wiring harness Defective intake air pressure sensor Malfunction in the ECU	03
14	Faulty intake air pressure sensor hose system, causing constant application of the atmospheric pressure sensor Engine able to start	Hose is detached, clogged or damaged Defective intake air pressure sensor Malfunction in the ECU	03
15	Throttle position sensor open or short circuit detected Engine able to start	Open or short circuit in wiring sub lead Open or short circuit in wiring harness Defective throttle position sensor Malfunction in the ECU Improperly installed throttle position sensor	01
16	Stuck throttle position sensor is detected Engine is able to start	Stuck throttle position sensor Malfunction in the ECU	01
17	EXUP servomotor potention circuit, open or short circuit is detected Engine is able to start	Open or short circuit in wiring sub lead Detected EXUP servomotor (potention circuit)	53
18	EXUP servomotor is stuck Engine is able to start	Open or short circuit in wiring sub lead Stuck EXUP servomotor (mechanism) Stuck EXUP servomotor (motor)	53
19	Open circuit in the input line from the sidestand switch to the ECU is detected when the start button is pressed Engine is unable to start.	Open or short circuit in wiring harness Malfunction in the ECU	20

(continued)

Table 5 TROUBLE CODES (continued)

Trouble code number	Symptoms	Probable cause of malfunction	Diagnostic code number
20	When the ignition switch is turned to the ON position, the atmospheric pressure sensor voltage and intake air pressure sensor voltage differ greatly Engine is able to start	Atmospheric pressure sensor hose is clogged Intake air pressure sensor hose is clogged, kinked or pinched Malfunction of the atmospheric pressure sensor in the intermediate electrical potential Malfunction of the intake air pressure sensor in the intermediate electrical potential Malfunction in the ECU	03, 02
21	Coolant temperature sensor, open or short circuit detected Engine is able to start	Open or short circuit in wiring harness Defective coolant temperature sensor Improperly installed sensor Malfunction in the ECU	06
22	Intake temperature sensor, open or short circuit detected Engine is able to start	Open or short circuit in wiring harness Defective intake temperature sensor Improperly installed sensor Malfunction in the ECU	05
23	Atmospheric pressure sensor, open or short circuit detected Engine is able to start	Open or short circuit in wiring sub lead Defective atmospheric pressure sensor Improperly installed sensor Malfunction in the ECU	02
30	The motorcycle has overturned Engine is unable to start	Motorcycle overturned Malfunction in the ECU	08
33	Open circuit is detected in the primary lead of the No. 1 direct ignition coil Engine able to start, depending on number of inoperative cylinders	Open or short circuit in wiring harness Malfunction in the direct ignition coil Malfunction in a component of the ignition cut off circuit system Malfunction in the ECU	30
34	Open circuit is detected in the primary lead of the No. 2 direct ignition coil Engine able to start, depending on number of inoperative cylinders	Open or short circuit in wiring harness Malfunction in the direct ignition coil Malfunction in a component of the ignition cut off circuit system Malfunction in the ECU	31

(continued)

9

Table 5 TROUBLE CODES (continued)

Trouble code number	Symptoms	Probable cause of malfunction	Diagnostic code number
35	Open circuit is detected in the primary lead of the No. 3 direct ignition coil Engine able to start, depending on number of inoperative cylinders	Open or short circuit in wiring harness Malfunction in the direct ignition coil Malfunction in a component of the ignition cut off circuit system Malfunction in the ECU	32
36	Open circuit is detected in the primary lead of the No. 4 direct ignition coil Engine able to start, depending on number of inoperative cylinders	Open or short circuit in wiring harness Malfunction in the direct ignition coil Malfunction in a component of the ignition cut off circuit system Malfunction in the ECU	33
41	Lean angle cut-off switch, open or short circuit detected Engine unable to start	Open or short circuit in wiring harness Defective lean angle cut-off switch Malfunction in the ECU	08
42	No signals are received from the speed sensor; or, an open or short circuit is detected in the neutral switch Engine able to start	Open or short circuit in wiring harness Defective speed sensor Malfunction in the vehicle speed sensor detected unit Defective neutral switch Malfunction in the engine side of the neutral switch Malfunction in the ECU	07, 21
43	The ECU is unable to monitor the battery voltage (an open circuit in the monitor line to the ECU unit) Engine able to start	Open circuit in wiring harness Malfunction in the ECU	09
44	An error is detected while reading or writing on E2PROM Engine able to start	Malfunction in the ECU	60
50	Faulty ECU memory; when this malfunction is detected, the trouble code number might not appear on the combination meter Engine unable to start	Malfunction in the ECU; the program and data are not properly written on or read from the internal memory	–
Er-1	No signals are received from the ECU	Open or short circuit in wiring sub-lead Malfunction in the combination meter Malfunction in the ECU	–

(continued)

Table 5 TROUBLE CODES (continued)

Trouble code number	Symptoms	Probable cause of malfunction	Diagnostic code number
Er-2	No signals are received from the ECU within the specified duration	Improper connection in wiring sub-lead Malfunction in the combination meter Malfunction in the ECU	–
Er-3	Data from the ECU cannot be received correctly	Improper connection in wiring sub-lead Malfunction in the combination meter Malfunction in the ECU	–
Er-4	Non-registered data has been received from the combination meter	Improper connection in wiring sub-lead Malfunction in the combination meter Malfunction in the ECU	–

Table 6 DIAGNOSTIC CODES

Diagnostic code	Component	Description of action	Data displayed on combination meter
01	Throttle angle	Displays the throttle angle: • Check with the throttle closed • Check with the throttle open	0-125° Fully closed position (15-17°) Fully open position (97-100°)
02	Atmospheric pressure	Displays the atmospheric pressure: • Use an atmospheric pressure gauge and check the atmospheric pressure	Compare to the value displayed on the combination meter
03	Pressure difference (atmospheric pressure-intake air pressure)	Displays the pressure difference (atmospheric pressure— intake air pressure). If a gauge is not available, use base value of 760 mm Hg (30 in. Hg).	10-200 mm Hg (0.4-7.9 in. Hg)
05	Intake temperature	Displays the intake air temperature: • Check the temperature in the air filter housing case as close to the sensor as possible	Compare to the value displayed on the combination meter
06	Coolant temperature	Displays the coolant temperature • Check the coolant temperature as close to the sensor on the thermostat housing as possible.	Compare it to the value displayed on the combination meter

(continued)

9

Table 6 DIAGNOSTIC CODES (continued)

Diagnostic code	Component	Description of action	Data displayed on combination meter
07	Vehicle speed pulse	Displays the accumulation of the vehicle pulses that are generated when the rear wheel is rotated	(0 to 999; resets to 0 after 999) Good if the numbers appear on the combination meter
08	Lean angle cut-off switch	Displays the lean angle cut-off switch values	Upright: 0.4 to 1.4 volts Overturned: 3.8 to 4.2 volts
09	Fuel system voltage (battery voltage)	Displays the fuel system voltage (battery voltage) Engine stop switch in on position	0 to 16.7 volts Normally, approximately 12 volts
20	Sidestand switch	Displays that the switch is on or off (when the transmission is in any gear other than neutral).	Sidestand raised: on Sidestand lowered: off
21	Neutral switch	Displays that the switch is on or off	Neutral: on In gear: off
30	Ignition coil No. 1	After one second has elapsed from the time the engine stop switch has been turned from the OFF to ON position, it actuates the ignition coil No. 1 for five times every second and illuminates the engine trouble warning light • Connect an ignition checker • If the engine stop switch is on, turn it off once and then turn it back on	Check the spark generated five times with the engine stop switch in the ON position
31	Ignition coil No. 2	After one second has elapsed from the time the engine stop switch has been turned from the off to on position, it actuates them ignition coil No. 1 for five times every second and illuminates the engine trouble warning light • Connect an ignition checker • If the engine stop switch is on, turn it off once and then turn it back on	Check the spark generated five times with the engine stop switch in the ON position
32	Ignition coil No. 3	After one second has elapsed from the time the engine stop switch has been turned from the off to on position, it actuates the ignition coil No. 1 for five times every second and illuminates the engine trouble warning light • Connect an ignition checker • If the engine stop switch is on, turn it off once and then turn it back on	Check the spark generated five times with the engine stop switch in the ON position
		(continued)	

Table 6 DIAGNOSTIC CODES (continued)

Diagnostic code	Component	Description of action	Data displayed on combination meter
33	Ignition coil No. 4	After one second has elapsed from the time the engine stop switch has been turned from the OFF to ON position, it actuates the ignition coil No. 1 for five times every second and illuminates the engine trouble warning light • Connect an ignition checker • If the engine stop switch is on, turn it off once and then turn it back on	Check the spark generated five times with the engine stop switch in the ON position
36	Fuel injector No. 1	After one second has elapsed from the time the engine stop switch has been turned from the OFF to ON position, it actuates the fuel injector No. 1 for five times every second and illuminates the engine trouble warning light • If the engine stop switch is on, turn it off once and then turn it back on	Check the operating sound of the fuel injector five times with the engine switch in the ON position
37	Fuel injector No. 2	After one second has elapsed from the time the engine stop switch has been turned from the OFF to ON position, it actuates the fuel injector for five times every second and illuminates the engine trouble warning light • If the engine stop switch is on, turn it off once and then turn it back on	Check the operating sound of the fuel injector five times with the engine switch in the ON position
38	Fuel injector No. 3	After one second has elapsed from the time the engine stop switch has been turned from the OFF to ON position, it actuates the fuel injector No. 3 for five times every second and illuminates the engine trouble warning light • If the engine stop switch is on, turn it off once and then turn it back on	Check the operating sound of the fuel injector five times with the engine switch in the ON position
39	Fuel injector No. 4	After one second has elapsed from the time the engine stop switch has been turned from the OFF to ON position, it actuates the fuel injector No. 4 for five times every second and illuminates the engine trouble warning light • If the engine stop switch is on, turn it off once and then turn it back on	Check the operating sound of the fuel injector five times with the engine switch in the ON position

(continued)

9

Table 6 DIAGNOSTIC CODES (continued)

Diagnostic code	Component	Description of action	Data displayed on combination meter
48	Air induction (AI) system solenoid	After one second has elapsed from the time the engine stop switch has been turned from the OFF to ON position, it actuates the AI system solenoid for five times every second and illuminates the engine trouble warning light • If the engine stop switch is on, turn it off once and then turn it back on	Check the operating sound of AI system solenoid five times with the engine switch in the ON position
50	Fuel injection system relay	After one second has elapsed from the time engine stop switch has been turned from the OFF to ON position, it actuates the fuel injection system relay for five times every five seconds and illuminates the engine trouble warning light (the warning light is off when the relay is on and the light is off when the relay is on • If the engine stop switch is on, turn it off once and then turn it back on	Check the fuel injection system relay operating sound five times with the engine switch in the ON position
51	Radiator cooling fan motor relay	After one second has elapsed from the time engine stop switch has been turned from the OFF to ON position, it actuates the radiator cooling fan relay for five times every five seconds and illuminates the engine trouble warning light (the warning light is on for two seconds then off for three seconds) • If the engine stop switch is on, turn it off once and then turn it back on	Check the radiator cooling fan motor relay operating sound five times with the engine switch in the ON position (at that time, the cooling fan motor rotates)
52	Headlight relay	After one second has elapsed from the time engine stop switch has been turned from the OFF to ON position, it actuates the headlight relay five times every five seconds and illuminates the engine trouble warning light (the warning light is on for two seconds then off for three seconds) • If the engine stop switch is on, turn it off once and then turn it back on	Check the headlight relay operating sound five times with the engine switch in the ON position (at that time the headlight turns on)

(continued)

Table 6 DIAGNOSTIC CODES (continued)

Diagnostic code	Component	Description of action	Data displayed on combination meter
53	EXUP servomotor	After one second has elapsed from the time engine stop switch has been turned from the OFF to ON position, it actuates the servomotor to turn to the open side at three seconds and to the closed side at three seconds • If the engine stop switch is on, turn it off once and then turn it back on	Turns on the engine trouble warning light while the servomotor is operating
60	E2PROM fault	Transmits the abnormal portion of the data in the E2PROM that has been detected as diagnostic fault code No. 44 • If multiple malfunctions have been detected, different codes are displayed at two-second intervals, and the process is repeated	(01 to 04) Displays the cylinder number (00) Displays when there is no malfunction
61	Malfunction history code display	Displays trouble code(s) of a malfunction that ocurred once and which has been corrected • If multiple malfunctions have been detected, different codes are displayed at two-second intervals, and the process is repeated	(11 to 50) (00) Displays when there is no history
62	Malfunction history code erasure	• Displays trouble code(s) of a malfunction that occurred once and which has been corrected • Erases the history codes only when the engine stop switch is turned from the OFF to the ON position. If the engine stop switch is on, turn it off once, and then turn it back to the on position	(00 to 21) (00) Displays when there is no history
70	Control number	Displays the program control number	(00 to 255)

Table 7 TROUBLE CODE 11: NORMAL SIGNALS ARE NOT RECEIVED FROM THE CYLINDER IDENTIFICATION SENSOR

Possible cause/fail-safe action	Inspect, test and replace or repair
Sensor installation	Check the sensor for correct installation within the cylinder head cover for looseness or pinching Tighten mounting screw if necessary
Cylinder identification sensor faulty	Test the cylinder identification sensor as described in Chapter Ten Replace if necessary If the sensor is good, proceed to the next steps

(continued)

Table 7 TROUBLE CODE 11: NORMAL SIGNALS ARE NOT RECEIVED FROM THE CYLINDER IDENTIFICATION SENSOR (continued)

Possible cause/fail-safe action	Inspect, test and replace or repair
Starter operation	Inspect and test the starter as described in Chapter Ten Replace starter if necessary

Open or short circuit detected in wiring harness and/or sub-lead	Repair or replace if there is an open or short in the sensor circuit
	Check continuity between the sensor coupler and the ECU coupler connectors as follows:
	  1. Blue to blue
	  2. White/black to white/black
	  3. Black/blue to black/blue

Electrical connector faulty	Inspect the electrical connector for any loose or pulled out pins Check the locking condition of the electrical connector Repair or replace the electrical connector(s) within the circuit if necessary
Fail-safe action	Continues to operate the engine based on the results of the cylinder identification that existed up to that point
Reinstatement method after sensor problem is completed	Start the engine and operate it at idle

Table 8 TROUBLE CODE 12: NORMAL SIGNALS ARE NOT RECEIVED FROM THE CRANKSHAFT POSITION SENSOR

Possible cause/fail-safe action	Inspect, test and replace or repair
Sensor installation	Check the sensor for correct installation within the crankcase for looseness or pinching Tighten the mounting screw if necessary
Crankshaft position sensor faulty	Test the crankshaft position sensor as described in Chapter Ten Replace if necessary If the sensor is good, proceed to the next steps

Open or short circuit detected in the wiring harness and/or sub-lead	Repair or replace if there is an open or short in the crankshaft position sensor circuit
	Check continuity between the sensor coupler and the ECU coupler connectors as follows:
	  1. Gray to gray
	  2. Black/blue to black/blue

Electrical connector faulty	Inspect the electrical connector for any loose or pulled out pins Check the locking condition of the electrical connector Repair or replace the electrical connector(s) within the circuit if necessary
Fail-safe action	Stops the engine (by stopping the injection and ignition)
Reinstatement method after sensor problem is completed	Start the engine and operate it at idle

Table 9 TROUBLE CODE 13: OPEN OR SHORT CIRCUIT DETECTED IN THE INTAKE AIR PRESSURE SENSOR (USE DIAGNOSTIC CODE NO. 03)

Possible cause/fail-safe action	Inspect, test and replace or repair
Sensor installation	Check the sensor for correct installation within the air filter housing for looseness or pinching
Defective intake air pressure sensor	Test the intake air pressure sensor as described in this chapter If the sensor is good, proceed to the next steps
Open or short circuit detected in the wiring harness and/or sub-lead	Repair or replace if there is an open or short in the sensor circuit Check continuity between the sensor coupler and the ECU coupler connectors as follows: 1. Black/blue to black/blue 2. Pink/white to pink/white 3. Blue to blue
Electrical connector faulty	Inspect the electrical connector for any loose or pulled out pins Check the locking condition of the electrical connector Repair or replace the electrical connector(s) within the circuit if necessary
Fail-safe action	Fixes the intake air pressure to 760 mm Hg
Reinstatement method after sensor problem is completed	Start the engine and operate it at idle

Table 10 TROUBLE CODE 14: CLOGGED OR DETACHED HOSE IN THE INTAKE AIR PRESSURE SENSOR (USE DIAGNOSTIC CODE NO. 03)

Possible cause/fail-safe action	inspect, test and replace or repair
Sensor installation	Check the sensor for correct installation within the air filter housing. Check for looseness or pinching
Defective intake air temperature sensor	Replace if defective Refer to trouble code No. 13 If sensor is good, proceed to the next steps
Intake air pressure sensor hose detached Sensor malfunction at intermediate electrical potential Atmospheric pressure sensor Malfunction at intermediate electrical potential	Repair or replace the sensor hose
Fail-safe action	Fixes the intake air pressure to 760 mm Hg
Reinstatement method after sensor problem is completed	Start the engine and operate it at idle

9

**Table 11 TROUBLE CODE 15: OPEN OR SHORT CIRCUIT DETECTED IN
THE THROTTLE POSITION SENSOR (USE DIAGNOSTIC CODE NO. 01)**

Possible cause/fail-safe action	Inspect, test and replace or repair
Sensor installation	Check the sensor for correct installation on the end of the throttle body housing for looseness as described in this chapter Check that the sensor is installed in the correct position on the throttle body as described in this chapter
Throttle position sensor defective	Replace the throttle position sensor as described in this chapter If sensor is good, proceed to the next steps
Open or short circuit detected in wiring harness and/or sub-lead	Repair or replace if there is an open or short in the sensor circuit Check continuity between the sensor coupler and the ECU coupler connectors as follows: 1. Black/blue to black/blue 2. Yellow to yellow 3. Blue to blue
Electrical connector faulty	Inspect the electrical connector for any loose or pulled out pins Check the locking condition of the electrical connector Repair or replace the electrical connector(s) within the circuit if necessary
Fail-safe action	Fixes the throttle position sensor to fully open
Reinstatement method after sensor problem is completed	Turn the ignition switch to the ON position

**Table 12 TROUBLE CODE 16: STUCK THROTTLE POSITION SENSOR
(USE DIAGNOSTIC CODE NO. 01)**

Possible cause/fail-safe action	Inspect, test and replace or repair
Sensor installation	Check the sensor for correct installation on the end of the throttle body housing for looseness as described in this chapter Tighten the screws if necessary Check that the sensor is installed in the correct position on the throttle body as described in this chapter Readjust if necessary
Throttle position sensor faulty	Replace the throttle position sensor as described in this chapter
Fail-safe action	Fixes the throttle position sensor to fully open
Reinstatement method after sensor problem is completed	Start the engine and operate it at idle, then rapidly increase engine speed

Table 13 TROUBLE CODE 17: OPEN OR SHORT CIRCUIT DETECTED IN THE EXUP SERVOMOTOR PROTECTION CIRCUIT (USE DIAGNOSTIC CODE NO. 53)

Possible cause/fail-safe action	Inspect, test and replace or repair
Defective EXUP servomotor potention circuit	Test the potention circuit as described in this chapter
Open or short circuit detected in the wiring harness and/or sub-lead	Repair or replace if there is an open or short in the sensor circuit Disconnect the EXUP servomotor coupler Check continuity between the sensor coupler and the ECU coupler connectors as follows: 1. Black/blue to black/blue 2. White/red to white/red 3. Blue to blue
Electrical connector faulty	Inspect the electrical connector for any loose or pulled out pins Check the locking condition of the electrical connector Repair or replace the electrical connector(s) within the circuit if necessary
Fail-safe action	Turn the EXUP servo motor toward the open side for 3 seconds and then stop It
Reinstatement method after sensor problem is completed	Turn the ignition switch to the ON position

9

Table 14 TROUBLE CODE 18: THE EXUP SERVOMOTOR IS STUCK (USE DIAGNOSTIC CODE NO. 53)

Possible cause/fail-safe action	Inspect, test and replace or repair
Defective servo motor	Test the EXUP servomotor for pulley rotation as described in this chapter Replace the servomotor if necessary
Open or short circuit detected in the wiring harness and/or sub-lead	Repair or replace if there is an open or short in the EXUP servomotor circuit Disconnect the EXUP servomotor coupler Check continuity between the sensor coupler and the ECU coupler connectors as follows: 1. Black/green to black/green 2. Black/red to black/red
Electrical connector faulty	Inspect the electrical connector for any loose or pulled out pins Check the locking condition of the electrical connector Repair or replace the electrical connector(s) within the circuit if necessary
Fail-safe action	Perform the preventive control against motor locking (perform the lock release operation twice every 100 seconds)
Reinstatement method after sensor problem is completed	Turn the ignition switch to the ON position It takes 120 seconds maximum before the servomotor can return to normal rotation

Table 15 TROUBLE CODE 19: OPEN CIRCUIT DETECTED IN THE INPUT LINE FROM THE SIDESTAND SWITCH TO THE ECU (USE DIAGNOSTIC CODE NO. 20)

Possible cause/fail-safe action	Inspect, test and replace or repair
Switch installation	Check for correct installation on the sidestand switch for looseness as described in Chapter Ten Tighten the mounting bolts if necessary
Sidestand switch defective	Test the sidestand switch as described in Chapter Ten If switch is faulty, replace it as described in Chapter Ten If the switch is good, proceed to the next steps
Open or short circuit detected in wiring harness and/or sub-lead	Repair or replace if there is an open or short in the switch circuit Check continuity between the switch coupler and the ECU coupler connector as follows: Blue/black to black
Electrical connector faulty	Inspect the electrical connector for any loose or pulled out pins Check the locking condition of the electrical connector Repair or replace the electrical connector
Fail-safe action	No start
Reinstatement method after switch problem is completed	Shift the transmission into any gear and raise the sidestand

Table 16 TROUBLE CODE 20: FAULTY ATMOSPHERIC PRESSURE SENSOR OR INTAKE AIR PRESSURE SENSOR (USE DIAGNOSTIC CODE NO. 03 AND NO. 02)

Possible cause/fail-safe action	Inspect, test and replace or repair
Sensor installation	Check the atmospheric pressure sensor for correct placement on the seat rail Check the intake air pressure sensor for correct installation on the fuel rail assembly Tighten the mounting screws if necessary
Intake air pressure sensor hose detached, clogged, kinked or pinched Atmospheric pressure sensor is clogged	Repair or replace the sensor hose(s) If hose(s) is good, proceed to the next step
Defective atmospheric pressure sensor or intake air pressure sensor	Replace if defective. Refer to trouble code No. 13 or 23
Fail-safe action	Fixes the intake air pressure and atmospheric pressure to 760 mm Hg
Reinstatement method after sensor problem is completed	Turn the ignition switch to the ON position

Table 17 TROUBLE CODE 21: OPEN OR SHORT CIRCUIT DETECTED IN THE COOLANT TEMPERATURE SENSOR (USE DIAGNOSTIC CODE NO. 06)

Possible cause/fail-safe action	Inspect, test and replace or repair
Sensor installation	Check the sensor for correct installation on the thermostat housing for looseness as described in Chapter Eleven
Coolant temperature sensor is defective	Test the coolant temperature sensor as described in Chapter Ten If faulty, replace the sensor If sensor is good, proceed to the next steps
Open or short circuit detected in wiring harness and/or sub-lead	Repair or replace if there is an open or short in the sensor circuit Check continuity between the sensor coupler and the ECU coupler connectors as follows: 1. Black/blue to black/blue 2. Green/white to green/white
Electrical connector faulty	Inspect the electrical connector for any loose or pulled out pins Check the locking condition of the electrical connector Repair or replace the electrical connector(s) within the circuit if necessary
Fail-safe action	Fixes the coolant temperature to 60° C (140° F)
Reinstatement method after sensor problem is completed	Turn the ignition switch to the ON position

Table 18 TROUBLE CODE 22: OPEN OR SHORT CIRCUIT DETECTED IN THE INTAKE TEMPERATURE SENSOR (USE DIAGNOSTIC CODE NO. 05)

Possible cause/fail-safe action	Inspect, test and replace or repair
Sensor installation	Check the sensor for correct installation within the air filter housing for looseness
Intake temperature sensor is defective	Test the intake temperature sensor as described in this chapter If faulty, replace the sensor If sensor is good, proceed to the next steps
Open or short circuit detected in wiring harness and/or sub-lead	Repair or replace if there is an open or short in the sensor circuit Check continuity between the sensor coupler and the ECU coupler connectors as follows: 1. Black/blue to black/blue 2. Brown/white to brown/white
Electrical connector faulty	Inspect the electrical connector for any loose or pulled out pins Check the locking condition of the electrical connector Repair or replace the electrical connector(s) within the circuit if necessary
Fail-safe action	Fixes the intake temperature to 20° C (68° F)
Reinstatement method after sensor problem is completed	Turn the ignition switch to the ON position

9

Table 19 TROUBLE CODE 23: OPEN OR SHORT CIRCUIT DETECTED IN THE ATMOSPHERIC PRESSURE SENSOR (USE DIAGNOSTIC CODE NO. 02)

Possible cause/fail-safe action	Inspect, test and replace or repair
Sensor installation	Check the sensor for correct installation on the seat rail for looseness Tighten the screws if necessary
Atmospheric pressure sensor is defective	Test the atmospheric pressure sensor as described in this chapter If faulty, replace the sensor if faulty If sensor is good, proceed to the next steps
Open or short circuit detected in wiring harness and/or sub-lead	Repair or replace if there is an open or short in the sensor circuit Check continuity between the sensor coupler and the ECU coupler connectors as follows: 1. Blue to blue 2. Black/blue to black/blue 3. Pink to pink
Electrical connector faulty	Inspect the electrical connector for any loose or pulled out pins Check the locking condition of the electrical connector Repair or replace the electrical connector(s) within the circuit if necessary
Fail-safe action	Fixes the atmospheric pressure to 760 mm Hg
Reinstatement method after sensor problem is completed	Turn the ignition switch to the ON position

Table 20 TROUBLE CODE 30: THE MOTORCYCLE HAS OVERTURNED (USE DIAGNOSTIC CODE NO. 08)

Possible cause/fail-safe action	Inspect, test and replace or repair
Switch installation	Check the switch for correct installation on the frame rail for looseness Tighten the screws if necessary
Lean angle cut-off switch is defective	Test the lean angle cut-off switch as described in this chapter If faulty, replace the switch If switch is good, proceed to the next steps
Electrical connector faulty	Inspect the electrical connector for any loose or pulled out pins Check the locking condition of the electrical connector Repair or replace the electrical connector(s) within the circuit if necessary
Fail-safe action	Turns off the fuel injection system relay of the fuel system
Reinstatement method after switch problem is completed	Turn the ignition switch first to the OFF, then to the ON position

Table 21 TROUBLE CODE 33: MALFUNCTION DETECTED IN THE PRIMARY LEAD OF THE NO. 1 IGNITION COIL (USE DIAGNOSTIC CODE NO. 30)

Possible cause/fail-safe action	Inspect, test and replace or repair
Ignition coil installation	Check the primary lead for correct installation on top of the No. 1 ignition coil
Ignition coil is defective	Test the No. 1 ignition coil primary and secondary circuits as described in Chapter Ten If faulty, replace the ignition coil If the ignition coil is good, proceed to the next steps
Open or short circuit detected in wiring harness and/or sub-lead	Repair or replace if there is an open or short in the No. 1 ignition coil circuit Check continuity between the No. 1 ignition coil coupler and the ECU coupler connector as follows: 1. Orange to orange 2. Red/black to red/black
Electrical connector faulty	Inspect the electrical connector for any loose or pulled out pins Check the locking condition of the electrical connector Repair or replace the electrical connector within the circuit if necessary
Fail-safe action	Fuel is cut off only to the cylinder in which a malfunction is detected
Reinstatement method after ignition coil problem is completed	Start the engine and operate at idle speed In the event of multiple ignition coil problems, turn the ignition switch to the ON and OFF positions between each start of the engine

Table 22 TROUBLE CODE 34: MALFUNCTION DECTED IN THE PRIMARY LEAD OF THE NO. 2 IGNITION COIL (USE DIAGNOSTIC CODE NO. 31)

Possible cause/fail-safe action	Inspect, test and replace or repair
Ignition coil installation	Check the primary lead for correct installation on top of the No. 2 ignition coil
Ignition coil is defective	Test the No. 2 ignition coil primary and secondary circuits as described in Chapter Ten If faulty, replace the ignition coil If the ignition coil is good, proceed to the next steps
Open or short circuit detected in wiring harness and/or sub-lead	Repair or replace if there is an open or short in the No. 2 ignition coil circuit Check continuity between the No. 2 ignition coil coupler and the ECU coupler connector as follows: 1. Gray/red to gray/red 2. Red/black to red/black
Electrical connector faulty	Inspect the electrical connector for any loose or pulled out pins Check the locking condition of the electrical connector Repair or replace the electrical connector within the circuit if necessary
Fail-safe action	Fuel is cut off only to the cylinder in which a malfunction is detected
Reinstatement method after ignition coil problem is completed	Start the engine and operate at idle speed In the event of multiple ignition coil problems, turn the ignition switch to the ON and OFF positions between each start of the engine

9

Table 23 TROUBLE CODE 35: MALFUNCTION DECTED IN THE PRIMARY LEAD OF THE NO. 3 IGNITION COIL (USE DIAGNOSTIC CODE NO. 32)

Possible cause/fail-safe action	Inspect, test and replace or repair
Ignition coil installation	Check the primary lead for correct installation on top of the No. 3 ignition coil
Ignition coil is defective	Test the No. 3 ignition coil primary and secondary circuits as described in Chapter Ten If faulty, replace the ignition coil If the ignition coil is good, proceed to the next steps
Open or short circuit detected in wiring harness and/or sub-lead	Repair or replace if there is an open or short in the No. 3 ignition coil circuit Check continuity between the No. 3 ignition coil coupler and the ECU coupler connector as follows: 1. Orange/green to orange/green 2. Red/black to red/black
Electrical connector faulty	Inspect the electrical connector for any loose or pulled out pins Check the locking condition of the electrical connector Repair or replace the electrical connector within the circuit if necessary
Fail-safe action	Fuel is cut off only to the cylinder in which a malfunction is detected
Reinstatement method after ignition coil problem is completed	Start the engine and operate at idle speed In the event of multiple ignition coil problems, turn the ignition switch to the ON and OFF positions between each start of the engine

Table 24 TROUBLE CODE 36: MALFUNCTION DECTED IN THE PRIMARY LEAD OF THE NO. 4 IGNITION COIL (USE DIAGNOSTIC CODE NO. 33)

Possible cause/fail-safe action	Inspect, test and replace or repair
Ignition coil installation	Check the primary lead for correct installation on top of the No. 4 ignition coil
Ignition coil is defective	Test the No. 4 ignition coil primary and secondary circuits as described in Chapter Ten If faulty, replace the ignition coil If the ignition coil is good, proceed to the next steps
Open or short circuit detected in wiring harness and/or sub-lead	Repair or replace if there is an open or short in the No. 4 ignition coil circuit Check continuity between the No. 1 ignition coil coupler and the ECU coupler connector as follows: 1. Gray/green to gray/green 2. Red/black to red/black
Electrical connector faulty	Inspect the electrical connector for any loose or pulled out pins Check the locking condition of the electrical connector Repair or replace the electrical connector within the circuit if necessary
Fail-safe action	Fuel is cut off only to the cylinder in which a malfunction is detected
Reinstatement method after ignition coil problem is completed	Start the engine and operate at idle speed In the event of multiple ignition coil problems, turn the ignition switch to the ON and OFF positions between each start of the engine

Table 25 TROUBLE CODE 41: OPEN OR SHORT CIRCUIT DETECTED IN THE LEAN ANGLE CUT-OFF SWITCH (USE DIAGNOSTIC CODE NO. 08)

Possible cause/fail-safe action	Inspect, test and replace or repair
Switch installation	Check the switch for correct installation on the frame rail for looseness Tighten the screws if necessary
Lean angle cut-off switch is defective	Test the lean angle cut-off switch as described in this chapter If faulty, replace the switch If switch is good, proceed to the next steps
Open or short circuit detected in wiring harness and/or sub-lead	Repair or replace if there is an open or short in the switch circuit Check continuity between the sensor coupler and the ECU coupler connectors as follows: 1. Black/blue to black/blue 2. Yellow/green to yellow/green 3. Blue to blue
Electrical connector faulty	Inspect the electrical connector for any loose or pulled out pins Check the locking condition of the electrical connector Repair or replace the electrical connector(s) within the circuit if necessary
Fail-safe action	Turns off the fuel injection system relay of the fuel system
Reinstatement method after sensor problem is completed	Turn the ignition switch to the ON position

Table 26 TROUBLE CODE 42: NORMAL SIGNALS ARE NOT RECEIVED FROM THE SPEED SENSOR. OPEN OR SHORT CIRCUIT DETECTED IN THE NEUTRAL SWITCH (USE DIAGNOSTIC CODE NO. 07 (SPEED SENSOR), NO. 21 (NEUTRAL SWITCH)

Possible cause/fail-safe action	Inspect, test and replace or repair
Speed sensor installation	Check the sensor for correct installation on the back surface of the crankcase for looseness Tighten mounting screw if necessary
Speed sensor faulty	Test the speed sensor as described in Chapter Ten Replace if necessary If the sensor is good, proceed to the next steps
Open or short circuit detected in speed sensor wiring harness and/or sub-lead	Repair or replace if there is an open or short in the sensor circuit Check continuity between the sensor coupler and the ECU coupler connectors as follows: 1. Blue to blue 2. White/yellow to white/yellow 3. Black/blue to black/blue
Defective gear related to the speed sensor	Replace the transmission gear as described in Chapter Seven

(continued)

**Table 26 TROUBLE CODE 42: NORMAL SIGNALS ARE NOT RECEIVED FROM THE SPEED SENSOR.
OPEN OR SHORT CIRCUIT DETECTED IN THE NEUTRAL SWITCH
(USE DIAGNOSTIC CODE NO. 07 (SPEED SENSOR), NO. 21 (NEUTRAL SWITCH) (continued)**

Possible cause/fail-safe action	Inspect, test and replace or repair
Electrical connector faulty	Inspect the electrical connector for any loose or pulled out pins Check the locking condition of the electrical connector Repair or replace the electrical connector(s) within the circuit if necessary
Neutral switch installation	Check the switch for correct installation on the back surface of the crankcase for looseness Tighten the switch if necessary
Neutral switch faulty	Test the neutral switch as described in Chapter Ten. Replace if necessary If the switch is good, proceed to the next steps
Open or short circuit detected in neutral switch wiring harness and/or sub-lead	Repair or replace if there is an open or short in the switch circuit Check continuity between the sensor coupler and the ECU coupler connector as follows: Sky blue to black/yellow
Faulty neutral location pin on the shift drum	Replace the neutral location pin as described in Chapter Seven
Electrical connector faulty	Inspect the electrical connector for any loose or pulled out pins Check the locking condition of the electrical connector Repair or replace the electrical connector(s) within the circuit if necessary
Fail-safe action	Fixes the gear to the top gear
Reinstatement method after sensor and/or switch problem is corrected	Start the engine and ride the motorcycle at a speed of 12-19 mph (20-30 km/h) to reset the speed sensor This also applies to the neutral switch

**Table 27 TROUBLE CODE 43: THE ECU IS UNABLE TO MONITOR THE
BATTERY VOLTAGE (USE DIAGNOSTIC CODE NO. 09)**

Possible cause/fail-safe action	Inspect, test and replace or repair
Malfunction in the ECU	The fuel injection system relay is on
Malfunction or open circuit in the fuel injection system relay	Test the relay unit as described under *Starting Circuit Cut-off Relay Unit (2002-2003 Models)— Starting Circuit* in Chapter Ten If the relay unit is good, proceed to the next steps
Open or short circuit detected in wiring harness and/or sub-lead	Repair or replace if there is an open or short in the sensor circuit Check continuity between the battery terminal and the ECU coupler connectors as follows: 1. Red to white 2. Red to blue/yellow (ignition switch and engine stop switch in the ON position) 3. Red to red/blue (fuel injection system relay is on)

(continued)

Table 27 TROUBLE CODE 43: THE ECU IS UNABLE TO MONITOR THE BATTERY VOLTAGE (USE DIAGNOSTIC CODE NO. 09) (continued)

Possible cause/fail-safe action	Inspect, test and replace or repair
Electrical connector faulty	Inspect the electrical connector for any loose or pulled out pins Check the locking condition of the electrical connector Repair or replace the electrical connector(s) within the circuit if necessary
Fail-safe action	Fixes the battery voltage to 12V
Reinstatement method after relay unit problem is completed	Start the engine and run it at idle

Table 28 TROUBLE CODE 44: ERROR CODE IS DETECTED WHILE READING OR WRITING ON E2PROM (IMPROPER CYLINDER IDENTIFICATION) (USE DIAGNOSTIC CODE NO. 60)

Possible cause	Inspect, test and replace or repair
Malfunction in the ECU	Execute diagnostic code No. 60 Check the faulty cylinder (if there are multiple cylinders, the number of the faulty cylinder appear alternately at two second intervals) Replace the ECU if defective
Reinstatement method after ECU problem is completed	Turn the ignition switch to the ON position

9

Table 29 TROUBLE CODE 50: FAULTY ECU MEMORY. WHEN THIS MALFUNCTION IS DETECTED IN THE ECU, THE TROUBLE CODE NUMBER MIGHT NOT APPEAR ON THE CLOCK LCD FACE

Possible cause	Inspect, test and replace or repair
Malfunction in the ECU Reinstatement method after ECU problem is completed	Replace the ECU Turn the ignition switch to the ON position

Table 30 TROUBLE CODE ER-1: NO SIGNALS ARE RECEIVED FROM THE ECU

Possible cause	Inspect, test and replace or repair
Open or short circuit detected in wiring harness and/or sub-lead	Repair or replace if there is an open or short in the ECU circuit Check continuity between the combination meter and the ECU coupler connectors
Electrical connector faulty	Inspect the electrical connector for any loose or pulled out pins Check the locking condition of the electrical connector Repair or replace the electrical connector(s) within the circuit if necessary
Malfunction in the combination meter	Replace the combination meter

(continued)

Table 30 TROUBLE CODE ER-1: NO SIGNALS ARE RECEIVED FROM THE ECU (continued)

Possible cause	Inspect, test and replace or repair
Malfunction in the ECU	Replace the ECU
Reinstatement method after combination meter and/or ECU problem is completed	Turn the ignition switch to the ON position

Table 31 TROUBLE CODE ER-2: NO SIGNALS ARE RECEIVED FROM THE ECU
WITHIN A SPECIFIED DURATION

Possible cause	Inspect, test and replace or repair
Open or short circuit detected in wiring harness and/or sub-lead	Repair or replace if there is an open or short in the ECU circuit Check continuity between the combination meter and the ECU coupler connectors
Electrical connector faulty	Inspect the electrical connector for any loose or pulled out pins Check the locking condition of the electrical connector Repair or replace the electrical connector(s) within the circuit if necessary
Malfunction in the combination meter	Replace the combination meter
Malfunction in the ECU	Replace the ECU
Reinstatement method after combination meter and/or ECU problem is completed	Turn the ignition switch to the ON position

Table 32 TROUBLE CODE ER-3: DATA FROM THE ECU CANNOT BE RECEIVED CORRECTLY

Possible cause	Inspect, test and replace or repair
Open or short circuit detected in wiring harness and/or sub-lead	Repair or replace if there is an open or short in the ECU circuit Check continuity between the combination meter and the ECU coupler connectors
Electrical connector faulty	Inspect the electrical connector for any loose or pulled out pins Check the locking condition of the electrical connector Repair or replace the electrical connector(s) within the circuit if necessary
Malfunction in the combination meter	Replace the combination meter
Malfunction in the ECU	Replace the ECU
Reinstatement method after combination meter and/or ECU problem is completed	Turn the ignition switch to the ON position

**Table 33 TROUBLE CODE ER-4: NON-REGISTERED DATA HAS BEEN
RECEIVED FROM THE COMBINATION METER**

Possible cause	Inspect, test and replace or repair
Open or short circuit detected in wiring harness and/or sub-lead	Repair or replace if there is an open or short in the ECU circuit Check continuity between the combination meter and the ECU coupler connectors
Electrical connector faulty	Inspect the electrical connector for any loose or pulled out pins Check the locking condition of the electrical connector Repair or replace the electrical connector(s) within the circuit if necessary
Malfunction in the combination meter	Replace the combination meter
Malfunction in the ECU	Replace the ECU
Reinstatement method after combination meter and/or ECU problem is completed	Turn the ignition switch to the ON position

9

ELECTRICAL SYSTEM

This chapter contains service and test procedures for the electrical systems/components.

Refer to **Tables 1-10** at the end of the chapter for specifications.

ELECTRICAL COMPONENT REPLACEMENT

Most motorcycle dealerships and parts suppliers will not accept the return of any electrical part. If you cannot determine the exact cause of any electrical system malfunction, have a Yamaha dealership retest that specific system to verify your test results. If you purchase a *new* electrical component(s), install it, and then find that the system still does not work properly, you will probably not be able to return the unit for a refund.

Consider any test results carefully before replacing a component that tests only slightly out of speci-

fication, especially resistance. A number of variables can affect test results dramatically. These include the testing meter's internal circuitry, ambient temperature and conditions under which the machine has been operated. All instructions and specifications have been checked for accuracy; however, successful test results depend to a great extent upon individual accuracy.

ELECTRICAL CONNECTORS

All models are equipped with numerous electrical components, connectors and wires. Corrosion-causing moisture can enter these electrical connectors and cause poor electrical connections, leading to component failure. Troubleshooting an electrical circuit with one or more corroded electrical connectors can be time-consuming and frustrating.

When reconnecting electrical connectors, pack them in a dielectric grease compound. Dielectric grease is specially formulated for sealing and waterproofing electrical connections without interfering with current flow. Use only this compound or an equivalent designed for this specific purpose. Do not use a substitute that may interfere with the current flow within the electrical connector. Do not use silicone sealant.

After cleaning both the male and female connectors, make sure they are thoroughly dry. Apply dielectric grease to the interior of one of the connectors prior to connecting the connector halves. For best results, the compound should fill the entire inner area of the connector. On multi-pin connectors, also pack the backside of both the male and female side with the compound to prevent moisture from entering the connector. After the connector is fully packed, wipe all excessive compound from the exterior.

Get into the practice of cleaning and sealing all electrical connectors every time they are disconnected. This may prevent a breakdown on the road and also save time when troubleshooting a circuit.

BATTERY

A sealed, maintenance-free battery is installed on all models. The battery electrolyte level cannot be serviced. When replacing the battery, use a sealed type; do not install a non-sealed battery. Never attempt to remove the sealing caps from the top of the battery. The battery does not require periodic electrolyte inspection or refilling. Refer to **Table 1** for battery specifications.

To prevent accidental shorts that could blow a fuse when working on the electrical system, always disconnect the negative battery cable from the battery.

WARNING
Even though the battery is a sealed type, protect eyes, skin and clothing; electrolyte is corrosive and can cause severe burns and permanent injury. The battery case may be cracked and leaking electrolyte. If electrolyte gets into the eyes, flush both eyes thoroughly with clean, running water and get immediate medical attention. Al-

ways wear safety goggles when servicing the battery.

WARNING
While batteries are being charged, highly explosive hydrogen gas forms in each cell. Some of this gas escapes through filler cap openings and may form an explosive atmosphere in and around the battery. This condition can persist for several hours. Sparks, an open flame or a lighted cigarette can ignite the gas, causing an internal battery explosion and possible serious personal injury.

NOTE
Recycle the old battery. When replacing the old battery, be sure to turn in the old battery at that time. The lead plates and the plastic case can be recycled. Most motorcycle dealerships accept old batteries in trade when purchasing a new one. Never place an old battery in household trash; it is illegal, in most states, to place any acid or lead (heavy metal) contents in landfills.

Safety Precautions

Take the following precautions to prevent an explosion:

1. Do not smoke or permit any open flame near any battery being charged or which has been recently charged.
2. Do not disconnect live circuits at the battery. A spark usually occurs when a live circuit is broken.
3. Take care when connecting or disconnecting a battery charger. Turn the power switch off before making or breaking connections. Poor connections are a common cause of electrical arcs, which cause explosions.
4. Keep children and pets away from the charging equipment and the battery.

Removal/Installation

The battery is installed horizontally in the box located underneath the rider's seat.

1. Refer to *Safety Precautions* in this section.
2. Turn the ignition switch off.

3. Remove the rider's seat as described in Chapter Sixteen.

4. Unhook the rubber strap (A, **Figure 1**).

5. First disconnect the negative battery cable (B, **Figure 1**), then the positive cable (C) from the battery terminals.

6. Grab the battery from the top and remove it from the battery box.

7. After the battery has been serviced or replaced, install it by reversing these removal steps while noting the following:

    a. Install the battery into the frame with the negative terminal on the left side of the frame.

    b. Always connect the positive battery cable first (C, **Figure 1**), then the negative cable (B).

CAUTION
Make sure the battery cables are connected to their proper terminals. Connecting the battery backward reverses the polarity and damages the rectifier and ignition system.

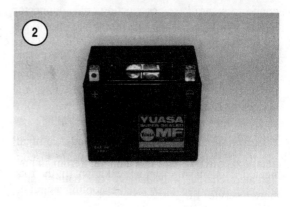

    c. Coat the battery leads with dielectric grease or petroleum jelly.

Cleaning/Inspection

The battery electrolyte level cannot be serviced. Never attempt to remove the sealing bar cap from the top of the battery. The battery does not require periodic electrolyte inspection or refilling.

1. Refer to *Safety Precautions* in this section.

2. Remove the battery from the motorcycle as described in the previous section. Do not clean the battery while it is mounted in the motorcycle.

3. Clean the battery case (**Figure 2**) with a solution of warm water and baking soda. Rinse thoroughly with clean water.

4. Inspect the physical condition of the battery. Look for bulges or cracks in the case, leaking electrolyte or corrosion buildup.

5. Check the battery terminal bolts, spacers and nuts for corrosion and damage. Clean parts with a solution of baking soda and water, and rinse thoroughly. Replace if damaged.

6. Check the battery cable clamps for corrosion and damage. If corrosion is minor, clean the battery cable clamps with a stiff brush. Replace excessively worn or damaged cables.

Testing

The maintenance-free battery can be tested while mounted in the motorcycle. A digital voltmeter is required for this procedure. See **Table 1** for battery voltage readings for the maintenance free battery.

1. Refer to *Safety Precautions* in this section.

NOTE
To prevent false test readings, do not test the battery if the battery terminals are corroded. Remove and clean the battery and terminals as described in this chapter, then reinstall it.

2. Connect a digital voltmeter between the battery negative and positive leads. Note the following:

    a. If the battery voltage is 13.0-13.2 volts (at 20° C [68° F]), the battery is fully charged. See **Table 3**.

    b. If the battery voltage is below 12.8 volts (at 20° C [68° F]), the battery is undercharged and requires charging. See **Table 3**.

3. If the battery is undercharged, recharge it as described in this chapter. Then test the charging system as described in Chapter Two.

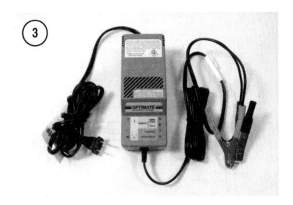

Charging

Refer to *Battery Initialization* in this chapter if the battery is new.

To recharge a maintenance-free battery, a digital voltmeter and a charger (**Figure 3**) with an adjustable or automatically variable amperage output are required. If this equipment is not available, have the battery charged by a shop with the proper equipment. Excessive voltage and amperage from an unregulated charger can damage the battery and shorten service life.

The battery should only self-discharge approximately one percent of its given capacity each day. If a battery not in use, without any loads connected, loses its charge within a week after charging, the battery is defective.

If the motorcycle is not used for long periods of time, an automatic battery charger with variable voltage and amperage outputs is recommended for optimum battery service life.

> *WARNING*
> *During the charging process, highly explosive hydrogen gas is released from the battery. Charge the battery only in a well-ventilated area away from any open flames (including pilot lights on home gas appliances). Do not allow any smoking in the area. Never check the charge of the battery by connecting screwdriver blades or other metal objects between the terminals; the resulting spark can ignite the hydrogen gas.*

> *CAUTION*
> *Always remove the battery from the motorcycle before connecting the battery charger. Never recharge a battery*

in the frame; corrosive gasses emitted during the charging process will damage surfaces.

1. Remove the battery as described in this chapter.
2. Connect the positive charger lead to the positive battery terminal and the negative charger lead to the negative battery terminal.
3. Set the charger at 12 volts and switch it on. Normally, a battery should be charged at a slow charge rate of 1/10 its given capacity. **Table 1** lists the battery capacity and charge rate for all models.
4. After the battery is charged, turn the charger off, disconnect the leads and check the battery with a digital voltmeter. It should be within 13.0-13.2 volts. If it is, and remains stable for one hour, the battery is charged.

Battery Initialization

A *new* battery must be fully charged before installation. Failure to do so reduces the life of the battery. Using a new battery without an initial charge causes permanent battery damage. That is, the battery will never be able to hold more than an 80% charge. Charging a new battery after it has been used will not bring its charge to 100%. When purchasing a new battery from a dealership or parts store, verify its charge status. If necessary, have them perform the initial or booster charge before accepting the battery.

10

CHARGING SYSTEM

The charging system consists of the battery, alternator and a voltage regulator/rectifier. A 30-amp (1998-2001 models) or 50-amp (2002-2003 models) main fuse protects the circuit. Refer to the wiring diagrams at the end of the manual.

Alternating current generated by the alternator is rectified to direct current. The voltage regulator maintains constant voltage to the battery and additional electrical loads (such as lights or ignition) despite variations in engine speed and load.

Troubleshooting

Refer to Chapter Two if the battery is discharging or overcharging.

Current Leakage (Draw) Test

Perform this test before performing the *Regulated Voltage Test.*
1. Turn the ignition switch off.
2. Disconnect the negative battery cable as described under *Battery, Removal/Installation* in this chapter.

> *CAUTION*
> *Before connecting the ammeter into the circuit in Step 5, set the meter to its highest amperage scale. This prevents a large current flow from damaging the meter or blowing the meter's fuse.*

3. Connect an ammeter between the negative battery cable and the negative battery terminal (**Figure 4**).
4. Switch the ammeter to its lowest scale and note the reading. The maximum current draw must not exceed the specification in **Table 1**.
5. Dirt and/or electrolyte on top of the battery or a crack in the battery case can create a path for battery current to flow. If an excessive current draw is noted, remove and clean the battery as described in this chapter, then repeat the test.
6. If the current draw is still excessive, consider the following probable causes:
   a. Faulty voltage regulator/rectifier.
   b. Damaged battery.
   c. Short circuit in the system.
   d. Loose, dirty or faulty electrical connectors in the charging circuit.
7. To find the short circuit that is causing the current draw, refer to the wiring diagrams at the end of this manual. Then continue to measure the current draw while disconnecting different connectors in the electrical system one by one. When the current draw returns to an acceptable level, the circuit is indicated. Test the circuit further to find the problem.
8. Disconnect the ammeter.
9. Reconnect the negative battery cable.
10. Reinstall the seat as described in Chapter Sixteen.

Regulated Voltage Test

This procedure tests charging system operation. It does not measure maximum charging system output. **Table 2** lists charging system test specifications.

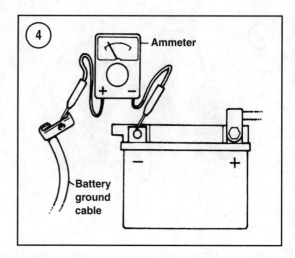

To obtain accurate test results, the battery must be fully charged (13.0 volts or higher).
1. Start and run the engine until it reaches normal operating temperature, then turn the engine off.
2. Connect a digital voltmeter to the battery terminals.

> *NOTE*
> *Do not disconnect either battery cable when making this test.*

3. Start the engine and allow it to idle. Turn the headlight switch to HI beam.
4. Gradually increase engine speed to 5000 rpm and read the voltage indicated on the voltmeter. Compare this with the regulated voltage reading in **Table 2**.

> *NOTE*
> *If the battery is often discharged but charging voltage tested normal during Step 4, the battery may be damaged.*

5. If the regulated voltage is too low, check for an open or short circuit in the charging system wiring harness, an open or short in the alternator or a damaged regulator/rectifier.
6. If the regulated voltage is too high, check for a poor regulator/rectifier ground, a damaged regulator/rectifier or a damaged battery.

Regulator/Rectifier Removal/Installation

1. Remove the rear cowl as described in Chapter Sixteen.

2. Disconnect the negative battery cable as described under *Battery, Removal/Installation* in this chapter.

3A. On 1998-2001 models, perform the following:

    a. Disconnect the regulator/rectifier 6-pin black electrical connector (A, **Figure 5**) on the right side.

    b. Remove the bolts securing the voltage regulator/rectifier (B, **Figure 5**) to the frame crossmember and remove it.

3B. On 2002-2003 models, perform the following:

    a. Disconnect the regulator/rectifier 3-pin black and 3-pin gray electrical connectors (A, **Figure 6**) located behind the fuel tank.

    b. Remove the bolts (B, **Figure 6**) securing the voltage regulator/rectifier to the frame crossmember and remove it.

4. Install by reversing these removal steps. Make sure all electrical connectors are secure and corrosion-free.

ALTERNATOR ROTOR AND STATOR

Stator Coil Resistance Test

The stator coil is mounted under the alternator cover on the left side of the engine. The stator coil can be tested while mounted on the engine.

1. Remove the right side fairing, bottom cowl and the rear cowl as described in Chapter Sixteen.

2. Disconnect the negative battery cable as described under *Battery, Removal/Installation* in this chapter.

3. Remove the fuel tank as described in Chapter Eight or Nine.

4. Follow the wiring harness from the alternator cover, through the left side of the frame. Disconnect the following:

    a. On 1998-2001 models, disconnect the stator coil 3-pin electrical connector (three white wires) (A, **Figure 5**) from the voltage regulator/rectifier.

    b. On 2002-2003 models, disconnect the lower 3-pin white electrical connector (three white wires) (A, **Figure 6**) from the voltage regulator.

5. Measure the resistance between each white wire on the alternator side of the connector. **Table 2** lists the specified stator coil resistance.

6. Replace the stator if the resistance is not as specified.

7. Check for continuity between each white stator wire and ground.

8. Replace the stator coil if continuity to ground is present in any wire. Continuity indicates a short within the stator coil winding.

NOTE
Before replacing the stator assembly, check the electrical wires to and within the electrical connector for any opens or poor connections.

9. If the stator coil fails either of these tests, replace it as described in this section.

10. Make sure the electrical connector is secure and corrosion-free.

11. Install the fuel tank as described in Chapter Eight or Chapter Nine.

12. Connect the negative battery cable.

13. Install the right side fairing, bottom cowl and rear cowl as described in Chapter Sixteen.

10

Rotor Removal

1. Remove the bottom cowl and the left side fairing as described in Chapter Sixteen.
2. Disconnect the negative battery cable as described under *Battery, Removal/Installation* in this chapter.
3. Place a clean drain pan underneath the alternator cover on the left side.

> *NOTE*
> *Some engine oil will drain when the alternator cover is removed.*

4. Remove the bolts and remove the alternator cover (**Figure 7**). Note the location of the cable clamp (**Figure 8**).
5. Remove the gasket and the dowel pins (if loose).
6. Hold the rotor with a rotor holder and loosen the bolt (**Figure 9**).
7. Remove the bolt and washer securing the rotor.
8. Screw the rotor puller (A, **Figure 10**) into the rotor.

> *CAUTION*
> *Do not try to remove the rotor without the correct puller. Any attempt to do so may damage the rotor and crankshaft.*

> *CAUTION*
> *If normal rotor removal attempts fail, do not force the puller. Excessive force will strip the flywheel threads, causing expensive damage. Take the engine to a dealership for rotor removal.*

9. Hold the rotor with the rotor holder (B, **Figure 10**) and gradually tighten the rotor puller until the rotor pops off the crankshaft taper.
10. Remove the rotor from the crankshaft.
11. Remove the puller from the rotor.

Rotor Installation

1. Degrease both the crankshaft taper and the rotor inner taper with aerosol parts cleaner. Allow both tapers to dry before installing the rotor.
2. Make sure there is no metal debris on the inner surface magnets of the rotor.

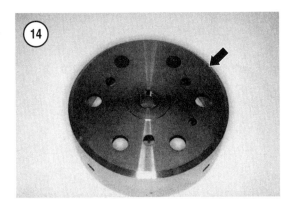

3. Install the rotor (**Figure 11**) onto the crankshaft taper. Push it on until it bottoms.

4. Lubricate the rotor bolt threads and *new* washer (**Figure 9**) with clean engine oil, then install and tighten finger-tight.

5A. On 1998-2001 models, hold the rotor with the rotor holder (A, **Figure 12**) and tighten the rotor bolt (B) to the following:

    a. 1998-1999 models: 95 N•m (70 ft.-lb.).

    b. 2000-2001 models: 65 N•m (48 ft.-lb.).

5B. On 2002-2003 models, hold the rotor with the rotor holder (A, **Figure 12**) and tighten the rotor bolt (B) as follows:

    a. Preliminary: 65 N•m (48 ft.-lb.).

    b. Final: an additional 60°.

6. Remove the torque wrench and rotor holder from the flywheel.

7. Install a *new* gasket (A, **Figure 13**) and two dowel pins (if removed) (B).

8. Install the alternator cover (**Figure 7**) and bolts. Tighten the bolts to 12 N•m (106 in.-lb.) in a criss-cross pattern. Install the cable clamp (**Figure 8**) as noted during removal.

9. Connect the negative battery cable as described in this chapter.

10. Install the left side fairing and bottom cowl as described in Chapter Sixteen.

11. Check the engine oil level as described in Chapter Three and add oil as required.

Rotor Inspection

1. Clean the rotor (**Figure 14**) in solvent and dry with compressed air.

2. Check the rotor for cracks or breaks.

> *WARNING*
> *Replace a cracked or chipped rotor. A damaged rotor can fly apart at high engine speeds, throwing metal fragments into the engine. Do not attempt to repair a damaged rotor.*

3. Check the rotor tapered bore and the crankshaft taper for damage.

4. Inspect the inside of the rotor (**Figure 15**) for metal debris picked up by the magnet. Remove all debris to avoid damage to the stator assembly.

10

Stator Coil Removal/Installation

1. Remove the alternator rotor as described in this section.

2. Follow the wiring harness from the alternator stator cover, through the opening on the left side of the frame. Disconnect the following:

    a. On 1998-2001 models, disconnect the stator coil 3-pin electrical connector (A, **Figure 5**) from the voltage regulator/rectifier.

    b. On 2002-2003 models, disconnect the lower 3-pin white electrical connector (A, **Figure 6**) from the voltage regulator.

3. Remove the wire harness bolt and clamp (A, **Figure 16**) and remove the clamp.

4. Remove the stator coil mounting bolts (**Figure 17**) and remove the stator coil.

5. Pull the wire harness grommet (B, **Figure 16**) out of the crankcase notch.

6. Do not clean the stator coils (**Figure 18**) in solvent. Wipe off with a clean rag.

7. Install the stator coil by reversing these steps, while noting the following:

    a. Apply Gasgacinch or an RTV sealer to the wiring harness rubber plug, then insert the plug into the crankcase notch (B, **Figure 16**).

    b. Apply a medium-strength threadlock onto the stator coil mounting bolts.

    c. Tighten the stator coil mounting bolts to 10 N•m (88 in.-lb.) on 1998-2001 models or 14 N•m (124 in.-lb.) on 2002-2003 models.

IGNITION SYSTEM

All models have an electronic ignition system.

The 1998-2001 models are equipped with separate ignition coils and secondary wires.

The 2002-2003 models use a direct ignition coil where the coil is integrated into the plug cap. This eliminates the secondary wire.

Refer to the wiring diagrams at the end of the manual.

Troubleshooting

Refer to Chapter Two.

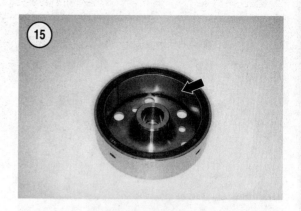

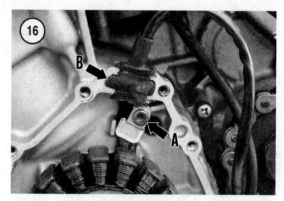

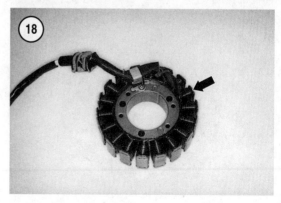

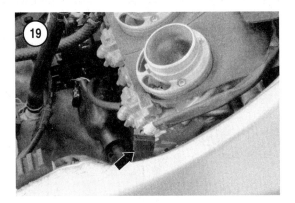

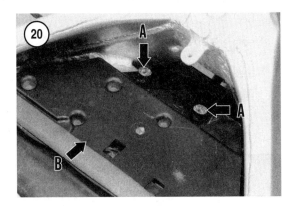

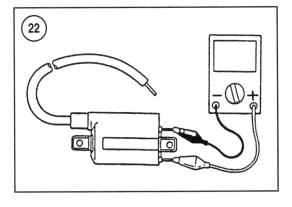

Ignition Coil Assembly
Removal/Installation (1998-2001)

1. Remove the rider's seat as described in Chapter Sixteen.

2. Remove the fuel tank and air filter housing as described in Chapter Eight.

> *NOTE*
> *Refer to **Body Panel Fasteners** in Chapter Sixteen for the correct procedure for releasing and installing the trim clips. These clips are also referred to as quick-disconnect fasteners.*

3. Disconnect the ignition coil 3-pin electrical connector (**Figure 19**).

4. Remove the two trim clips (A, **Figure 20**) securing the ignition coil plate.

5. Partially pull up on the ignition coil plate, then grasp the spark plug lead as near the spark plug as possible and pull the lead off the plug.

6. Disconnect all spark plug leads, then remove the ignition coil plate (B, **Figure 20**).

7. Reinstall the trim clips onto the ignition coil plate to avoid misplacing them.

8. Move the ignition coil plate into position and connect the spark plug leads. Push the leads down onto the spark plugs until they are completely seated. Repeat for each spark plug.

9. Install the ignition coil plate and secure it with the two trim clips (A, **Figure 20**).

10. Connect the ignition coil 3-pin electrical connector (**Figure 19**).

11. Install the fuel tank and air filter housing as described in Chapter Eight.

12. Install the rider's seat as described in Chapter Sixteen.

Ignition Coil Resistance Test
(1998-2001 Models)

1. Remove the ignition coil assembly as previously described.

2. Disconnect the primary terminal connectors (**Figure 21**).

3. Measure the primary coil resistance between the positive and the negative terminals (**Figure 22**). Record the measured resistance.

10

4. With the spark plug caps removed, measure the secondary coil resistance between both spark plug leads (**Figure 23**). Record the measured resistance.

5. If either measurement does not meet specification, the coil must be replaced. If the coil exhibits visible damage, replace it.

6. Repeat this procedure for the other ignition coil.

7. Install the ignition coil assembly as previously described.

Direct Ignition Coil Assembly
Removal/Installation (2002-2003 Models)

1. Remove the rider's seat as described in Chapter Sixteen.

2. Remove the fuel tank and air filter housing as described in Chapter Nine.

> *NOTE*
> *Refer to **Body Panel Fasteners** in Chapter Sixteen for the correct procedure for releasing and installing the trim clips. These clips are also referred to as quick-disconnect fasteners.*

3. Remove the trim clips securing the ignition coil plates and remove both plates (**Figure 24**). Install the trim clips to avoid misplacing them.

4. Carefully disconnect the 2-pin electrical connector from the top of each direct ignition coil (A, **Figure 25**).

5. Carefully pull straight up on the direct ignition coil and disengage it from the top of the spark plug. Remove it from the cylinder head cover and spark plug.

6. Disconnect the 3-pin electrical connector (**Figure 26**) from the cylinder identification sensor.

7. Move the rubber baffle (B, **Figure 25**) forward and out of the way.

8. Carefully pull straight up on the direct ignition coil and disengage it from the top of the spark plug. Remove it from the cylinder head cover and spark plug. Repeat for each spark plug.

9. Carefully push straight down on the direct ignition coil and engage it onto the top of the spark plug. Push it down until it seats completely on the spark plug and the cylinder head cover. Repeat for each spark plug.

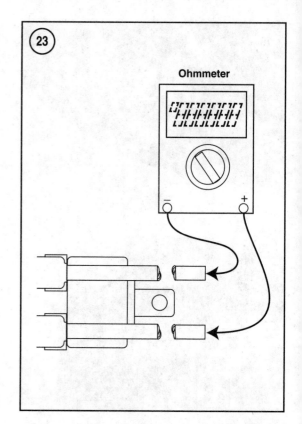

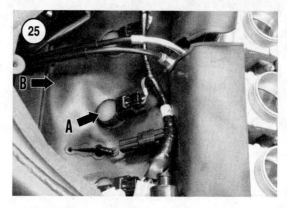

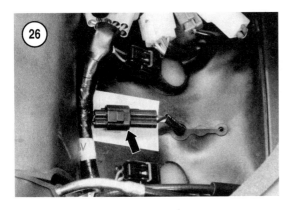

10. Move the rubber baffle back into position.

11. Connect the 3-pin electrical connector (**Figure 26**) onto the cylinder identification sensor.

12. Carefully connect the 2-pin electrical connector from the top of each direct ignition coil (A, **Figure 25**).

13. Install both ignition coil plates (**Figure 24**) and secure them with the three trim clips.

14. Install the air filter housing and fuel tank as described in Chapter Nine.

15. Install the rider's seat as described in Chapter Sixteen.

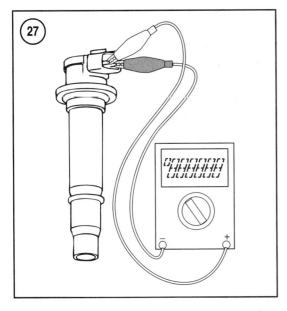

Direct Ignition Coil Resistance Test (2002-2003 Models)

1. Remove the direct ignition coil assembly as previously described.

2. Measure the primary coil resistance between the positive and the negative terminals on the top of the direct ignition coil (**Figure 27**). Record the measured resistance.

3. Measure the secondary coil resistance between the direct ignition coil terminal and the spark plug terminal (**Figure 28**). Record the measured resistance.

4. If either measurement does not meet specification (**Table 5**), the direct ignition coil must be replaced. If the coil exhibits visible damage, replace it.

5. Repeat this procedure for the other direct ignition coils.

6. Install the direct ignition coil assembly as previously described.

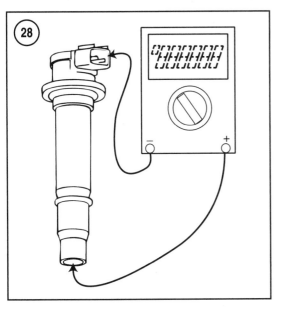

Timing Coil and Rotor (1998-2001 Models) or Crankshaft Position Sensor (2002-2003 Models) Removal/Installation

> *NOTE*
> *On 2002-2003 models, the timing coil is referred to as the Crankshaft Position (CP) sensor.*

1. Remove the bottom cowl and right side fairing as described in Chapter Sixteen.

2. Remove the fuel tank and air filter housing as described in this chapter.

3. Disconnect the negative battery cable as described under *Battery, Removal/Installation* in this chapter.

4. Follow the electrical cable (A, **Figure 29**) up from the timing cover, through the frame and to the area ahead of the carburetor or throttle body assembly.

5. Disconnect the timing coil electrical connector (gray and black wires) from the main harness.

6. Place a clean drain pan underneath the timing coil cover on the right side.

7. Disconnect the clutch cable (B, **Figure 29**) from the timing coil rotor cover.

8. Remove the screws securing the timing coil rotor cover (C, **Figure 29**) and remove the cover and gasket. Do not lose the locating dowels. Note the location of the clutch cable bracket (D, **Figure 29**) and the electrical cable locating tab (E).

9. Remove the screws (A, **Figure 30**) securing the timing coil sensor (B). Carefully pull the electrical cable and grommet (C, **Figure 30**) out of the notch in the crankcase. Remove the sensor and electrical cable from the engine and frame.

10. To keep the crankshaft from turning while loosening the bolt, hold the alternator rotor with a holder as described under *Rotor Removal* in this chapter.

11. Remove the bolt and washer (D, **Figure 30**) securing the timing coil rotor and remove the rotor (E).

NOTE
Figure 31 is shown with the engine removed to better illustrate the step.

12. Align the groove in the timing coil rotor with the raised pin on the crankshaft sprocket and install the rotor (**Figure 31**).

13. Install the bolt and washer (A, **Figure 32**) securing the timing coil rotor (B).

14. Use the same tool set-up used in Step 10 and tighten the bolt to 60 N•m (44 ft.-lb.).

15. Apply Gasgacinch or an RTV sealer to the wiring harness rubber plug, then insert the plug into the crankcase notch (C, **Figure 30**).

16. Apply a medium-strength threadlock onto the timing coil mounting Allen bolts.

17. Install and tighten the Allen bolts (A, **Figure 30**) to 10 N•m (88 in.-lb.).

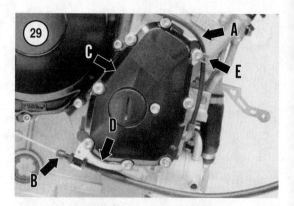

18. Install the two dowel pins (if removed) (A, **Figure 33**) and a *new* gasket (B).

19. Install the timing coil cover (C, **Figure 29**) and bolts. Install the timing coil cable clamp (E, **Figure 29**), the clutch cable bracket (D) and bolts in the correct locations. Tighten the bolts in a crisscross pattern to 12 N•m (106 in.-lb.).

20. Install the electrical cable (A, **Figure 29**) up from the timing cover, through the frame opening and to the area ahead of the carburetor or throttle body assembly.

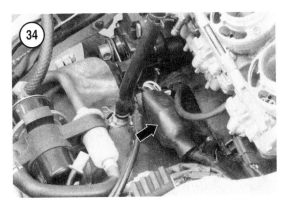

21. Connect the timing coil electrical connector onto the main harness.

22. Connect the negative battery cable as described in this chapter.

23. Install the right side fairing, bottom cowl and the rear cowl as described in Chapter Sixteen.

24. Check the engine oil level as described in Chapter Three and add oil as required.

25. Install the rider's seat as described in Chapter Sixteen.

Timing Coil Testing (1998-2001 Models)

NOTE
On 2002-2003 models, the timing coil is referred to as the Crankshaft Position (CP) sensor. Refer to Chapter Nine for testing.

1. Remove the rider's seat as described in Chapter Sixteen.
2. Remove the fuel tank as described in Chapter Eight.
3. Disconnect the negative battery cable as described in this chapter.
4. Follow the electrical cable (A, **Figure 29**) up from the timing cover, through the frame opening and to the area ahead of the carburetor assembly.
5. Pull back the rubber boot (**Figure 34**) and uncover the electrical connectors. Disconnect the timing coil sensor electrical connector (gray and black wires) from the main harness.
6. Measure the resistance on the timing coil side of the connector. Record the measured resistance.
7. If either measurement does not meet specification (**Table 4**), the timing coil must be replaced.
8. Connect the electrical connector and move the rubber boot back into position.
9. Connect the negative battery cable as described in this chapter.
10. Install the fuel tank as described in Chapter Eight.
11. Install the rider's seat as described in Chapter Sixteen.

Ignition Control Module (ICM)
Removal/Installation (1998-2001 Models)

1. Remove the rider's seat as described in Chapter Sixteen.
2. Disconnect the negative battery cable as described in this chapter.
3A. On 1998-1999 models, disconnect the two electrical connectors from the ICM.
3B. On 2000-2001 models, disconnect the one electrical connector (A, **Figure 35**) from the ICM.
4. Remove the screws securing the ICM (B, **Figure 35**) to the rear fender and remove the ICM (C).
5. Place the ICM in a reclosable plastic bag to keep it clean. Store it in a safe place to avoid damage to this expensive component.

10

6. Install by reversing these removal steps. Refer to *Electrical Connectors* at the beginning of this chapter and pack the connector(s) with dielectric grease compound.

Engine Control Unit (ECU) Removal/Installation (2002-2003 Models)

1. Remove the rider's seat and rear cowl as described in Chapter Sixteen.
2. Disconnect the negative battery cable as described in this chapter.
3. Disconnect the single large electrical connector (A, **Figure 36**) from the ECU.
4. Remove the screws securing the ECU (B, **Figure 36**) to the rear fender and remove the ECU.
5. Remove the ECU and place it in a reclosable plastic bag to keep it clean. Store it in a safe place to avoid damage to this expensive component.
6. Install by reversing these removal steps. Refer to *Electrical Connectors* at the beginning of this chapter and pack the connector with dielectric grease compound.

Engine Control Unit (ECU) Test (2002-2003 Models)

This test determines if the ECU is able to monitor the battery voltage and is performed on the starting circuit cut-off relay. Refer to Chapter Nine for additional ECU information.

1. Remove both seats and the rear cowl as described in Chapter Sixteen.
2. Disconnect the negative battery cable as described in this chapter.
3. Unhook the starting circuit cut-off relay (**Figure 37**) from the mounting tab on the rear fender.
4. Disconnect the connector (**Figure 38**) from the starting circuit cut-off relay.
5. Check the continuity as follows:
   a. Connect a fully charged 12-volt battery to the rely unit. Connect the positive battery terminal to the red/black wire terminal (**Figure 39**) and the negative battery terminal to the blue/yellow wire terminal.
   b. Connect the ohmmeter positive test lead to the red wire terminal on the relay unit and connect the negative lead to the red/blue wire terminal on the relay unit. The ohmmeter should show continuity.

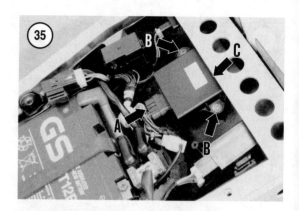

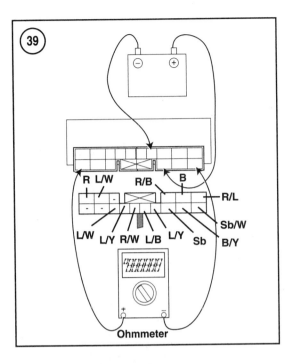

R L/W   R/B   B

R/L

L/W L/Y R/W L/B L/Y Sb Sb/W
                              B/Y

Ohmmeter

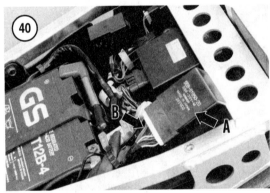

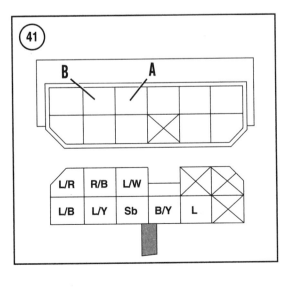

L/R	R/B	L/W		
L/B	L/Y	Sb	B/Y	L

c. Replace the relay unit if it fails this test.

6. Refer to *Electrical Connectors* at the beginning of this chapter and pack the connector with dielectric grease compound.

7. Connect the electrical connector (**Figure 38**) to the relay unit. Install the relay unit onto the mounting tab on the rear fender (**Figure 37**).

8. Connect the negative battery cable as described in this chapter.

9. Install the rear cowl and both seats as described in Chapter Sixteen.

RELAY UNIT (1998-2001 MODELS)– IGNITION CIRCUIT

The relay unit consists of the starter circuit cutoff relay and the fuel pump relay. The relay unit is designed to not allow current to the starter relay unless the transmission is in neutral or unless the clutch lever is pulled in and that the sidestand is in the raised position.

This test relates to the ignition circuit portion of the relay unit. There is an additional test later in this chapter for the starting circuit.

Removal/Installation

1. Remove both seats and the rear cowl as described in Chapter Sixteen.

2. Disconnect the negative battery cable as described in this chapter.

3. Unhook the relay unit (A, **Figure 40**) from the mounting tab on the rear fender.

4. Disconnect the connector (B, **Figure 40**) from the relay unit.

5. Install by reversing these removal steps. Refer to *Electrical Connectors* at the beginning of this chapter and pack the connector with dielectric grease compound.

Relay Unit Testing

1. Remove the relay unit as previously described.

2. Disconnect the electrical connector (B, **Figure 40**) from the relay unit and remove it.

3. Check the continuity as follows:
   a. Connect the positive test lead to the sky blue (A, **Figure 41**) terminal on the relay unit and connect the negative lead to the blue/yellow

(B, **Figure 41**) terminal on the relay unit. The ohmmeter should show continuity.

    b. Reverse the ohmmeter leads and check for continuity. The meter should now show no continuity.

    c. Replace the relay unit if it fails any part of this test.

4. Refer to *Electrical Connectors* at the beginning of this chapter and pack the connector with dielectric grease compound.

5. Install the relay unit as previously described.

STARTING CIRCUIT CUT-OFF RELAY (2002-2003 MODELS)–IGNITION CIRCUIT

The starting circuit cut-off relay unit consists of the starter circuit cut-off relay and the fuel pump relay. The relay unit is designed to not allow current to the starter relay unless the transmission is in neutral or unless the clutch lever is pulled in and the sidestand is in the raised position.

This test relates to the ignition circuit portion of the relay unit. There is an additional test later in this chapter for the starting circuit.

Removal/Installation

1. Remove both seats and the rear cowl as described in Chapter Sixteen.

2. Disconnect the negative battery cable as described in this chapter.

3. Unhook the starting circuit cut-off relay (**Figure 37**) from the mounting tab on the rear fender.

4. Disconnect the connector (**Figure 38**) from starting circuit cut-off relay.

5. Install by reversing these removal steps. Refer to *Electrical Connectors* at the beginning of this chapter and pack the connector with dielectric grease compound.

Relay Testing

1. Remove the relay unit as previously described.

2. Disconnect the electrical connector (**Figure 37**) from the relay unit and remove it.

3. Check the continuity as follows:

    a. Connect the positive test lead to the blue/yellow (A, **Figure 42**) terminal on the relay unit and connect the negative lead to the blue/black

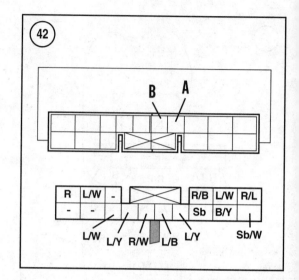

(B) terminal on the relay unit. The ohmmeter should show continuity.

    b. Reverse the ohmmeter leads and check for continuity. The meter should now show no continuity.

    c. Replace the relay unit if it fails any part of this test.

4. Refer to *Electrical Connectors* at the beginning of this chapter and pack the connector with dielectric grease compound.

5. Install the starting circuit cut-off relay unit as previously described.

STARTER

The starting system consists of the starter, starter gears, starter relay switch, various safety switches and the starter button.

Table 6 lists starter specifications.

> *CAUTION*
> *Do not operate the starter for more than five seconds at a time. Wait approximately ten seconds between starting attempts.*

Troubleshooting

Refer to Chapter Two.

Removal/Installation

1. Remove the rider's seat as described in Chapter Sixteen.

2. Remove the left side fairing panel as described in Chapter Sixteen.

3. Disconnect the negative battery cable as described in this chapter.

4. On 1998-2001 models, perform the following:
   a. Remove the EXUP servomotor (A, **Figure 43**) off the frame mount. Move the servomotor out of the way.
   b. Remove the fuel pump and filter assembly (B, **Figure 43**) as described in Chapter Eight.

5. Unhook the idle speed adjust knob (**Figure 44**) from the mounting bracket.

6. Move the rubber cap aside and disconnect the starter cable from the starter.

> *NOTE*
> *Figure 45 is shown with the engine removed from the frame to better illustrate the step.*

7. Remove the two starter mounting bolts (A, **Figure 45**). On 1998-1999 models, note the location of the ground cable (B, **Figure 45**) secured by the rear bolt.

8. Move the starter toward the left side and remove the starter (C, **Figure 45**).

9. Install by reversing these removal steps, plus the following:
   a. Lubricate the starter O-ring (**Figure 46**) with engine oil.
   b. Remove all corrosion from the starter cable.
   c. Tighten the starter mounting bolts securely. On 1998-1999 models, be sure to install the ground cable (B, **Figure 45**) under the rear bolt.

Disassembly (1998-1999 Models)

Refer to **Figure 47**.

> *NOTE*
> *Before disassembling the starter, locate the alignment marks on the starter housing and both end covers (**Figure 48**) for assembly. To maintain the correct alignment and position of the parts during disassembly, store*

10

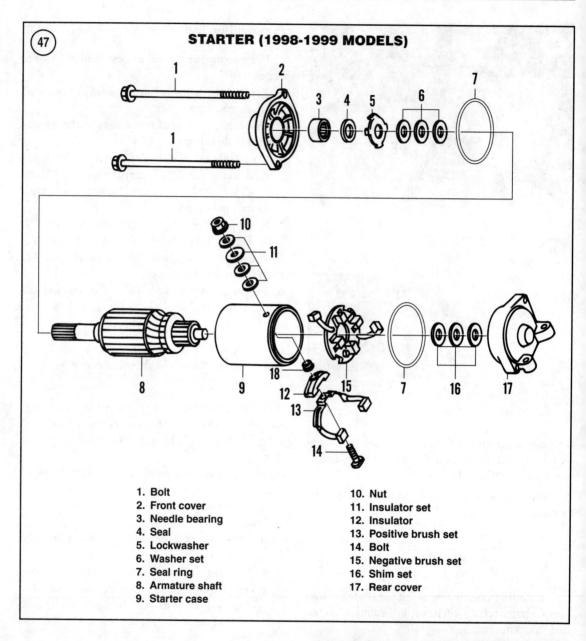

STARTER (1998-1999 MODELS)

1. Bolt
2. Front cover
3. Needle bearing
4. Seal
5. Lockwasher
6. Washer set
7. Seal ring
8. Armature shaft
9. Starter case
10. Nut
11. Insulator set
12. Insulator
13. Positive brush set
14. Bolt
15. Negative brush set
16. Shim set
17. Rear cover

each part in order and in a divided container.

1. Loosen the starter case through bolts (**Figure 49**) and remove them.

> *NOTE*
> *Record the number, type and thickness of the shims and washer used on both ends of the armature shaft. These shims and washer must be installed in their original order and positions.*

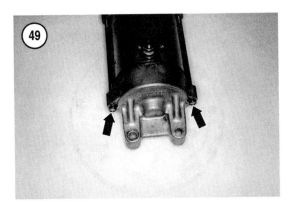

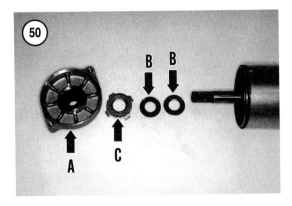

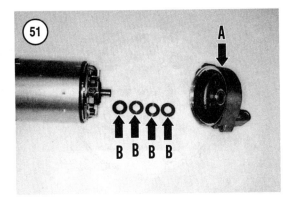

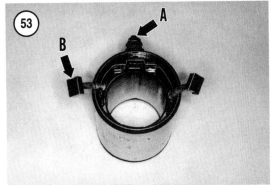

NOTE
The number of washers used in the starter varies.

2. Slide the front cover (A, **Figure 50**) off of the armature shaft, then remove the washers (B).
3. Remove the lockwasher (C, **Figure 50**) from the front cover.

NOTE
The number of shims used in the starter varies.

4. Slide the rear cover (A, **Figure 51**) off the armature shaft and remove the shims (B).
5. Slide the starter case off of the armature.
6. Remove the brush holder assembly (A, **Figure 52**).

NOTE
Before removing the nuts and washers in Step 7, record their description and their order. They must be reinstalled in the same order to insulate the positive brush set from the case.

7. Remove the nut and washers (A, **Figure 53**) securing the positive terminal bolt to the starter case.
8. Remove the terminal bolt, positive brush set (B, **Figure 53**), terminal bolt, insulator and O-ring.

CAUTION
Do not immerse the armature coil or starter case in solvent, as the insulation may be damaged. Wipe the windings with a cloth lightly moistened in solvent and dry with compressed air.

9. Clean all grease, dirt and carbon from the components.
10. Inspect the starter as described in this chapter.

10

Assembly (1998-1999 Models)

1. Install the positive brush set (B, **Figure 53**) as follows:

   a. Install the insulator on top of the positive brush set, then insert it into the starter case with the tab on the insulator facing toward the brush plate.

   b. Install the terminal bolt through the brush set, the insulator and starter case.

   c. Install the O-ring over the terminal bolt.

> *NOTE*
> *Reinstall all parts in the same order as noted during disassembly. This is essential in order to insulate this set of brushes from the starter case.*

   d. Install the two small insulated washers over the terminal bolt.

   e. Install the large insulated washer.

   f. Install the steel washer.

   g. Install the nut finger tight.

2. Install the negative brush plate onto the starter case, inserting the two positive brush wired through the plate as shown in B, **Figure 52**. Align the brush plate locating tab with the notch in the starter case (**Figure 54**).

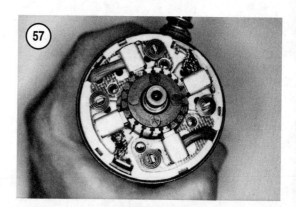

3. Install the brushes into their receptacles. Install a small shim between each spring and brush (**Figure 55**) to reduce spring pressure on the brushes.

4. Position the commutator end of the armature toward the negative brush plate and slowly insert the armature into the front of the starter case. Do not damage the brushes during this step.

5. Remove the shims (**Figure 56**) installed in Step 3.

6. Make sure that each brush seats squarely against the commutator (**Figure 57**).

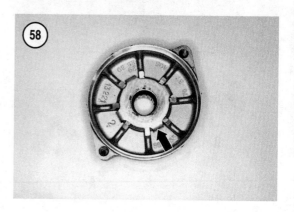

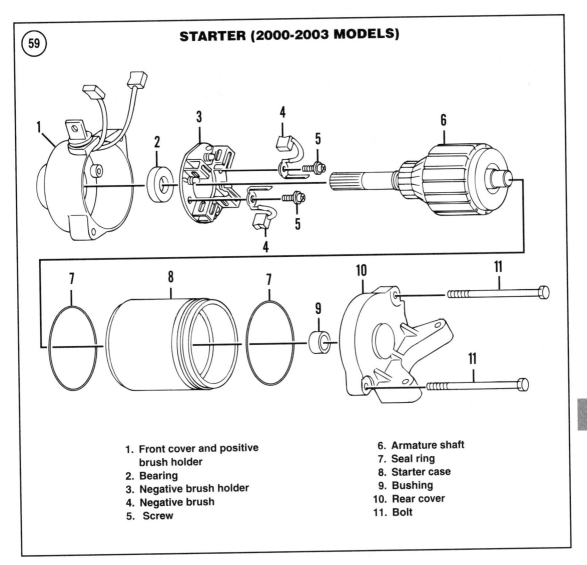

STARTER (2000-2003 MODELS)

1. Front cover and positive brush holder
2. Bearing
3. Negative brush holder
4. Negative brush
5. Screw
6. Armature shaft
7. Seal ring
8. Starter case
9. Bushing
10. Rear cover
11. Bolt

7. Install the shims (B, **Figure 51**) onto the commutator end of the shaft.

8. Install the seal ring into the rear case cover groove.

9. Check that the brush plate locating tab is still aligned with the notch in the starter case (**Figure 54**).

10. Install the shims (B, **Figure 50**) and insulated washer onto the front of the armature shaft.

11. Install the lockwasher (C, **Figure 50**) onto the front cover (**Figure 58**). Make sure it is correctly seated.

12. Install the seal ring into the front cover groove.

13. Install the front cover (A, **Figure 50**).

14. Align the index marks (**Figure 48**) on all three components.

15. Install the through bolts (**Figure 49**) and tighten securely.

NOTE
If the through bolt does not pass past the starter case and through the end covers, the components are installed incorrectly.

Disassembly (2000-2003 Models)

Refer to **Figure 59**.

NOTE
Before disassembling the starter, locate the index marks on the starter

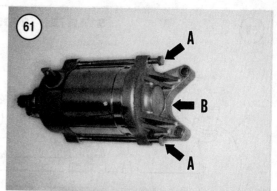

*housing and both end covers (**Figure 60**) for assembly. To maintain the correct alignment and position of the parts during disassembly, store each part in order and in a divided container.*

1. Loosen the starter case through bolts (A, **Figure 61**) and remove them.

2. Slide the rear cover (B, **Figure 61**) off of the armature shaft.

3. Slide the front cover (**Figure 62**) off the armature shaft and starter case.

4. Slide the starter case (A, **Figure 63**) off of the armature (B).

5. If necessary, remove the screws (A, **Figure 64**) securing the negative brushes to the brush holder and front cover. Remove the brushes.

6. If necessary, remove the positive brush assembly (B, **Figure 64**) from the brush holder and front cover.

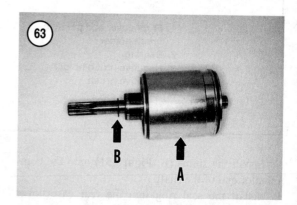

> **CAUTION**
> *Do not immerse the armature coil or starter case in solvent, as the insulation may be damaged. Wipe the windings with a cloth lightly moistened in solvent and dry with compressed air.*

7. Clean all grease, dirt and carbon from the components.

8. Inspect the starter as described in this chapter.

Assembly (2000-2003 Models)

1. Install the seal rings (**Figure 65**) into the case grooves.

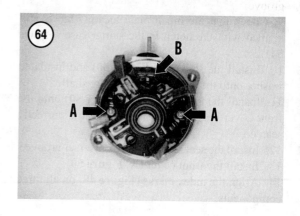

2. If removed, set the brushes onto the brush holder and end cover. Do not insert the brushes into their receptacles.

3. Move the brush coil spring out of the groove and onto the ledge of the brush receptacle (**Figure 66**). Repeat for all remaining springs.

4. Insert all four brushes into their receptacles (**Figure 67**). Make sure the coil springs do not release and exert pressure on the backside of the brushes.

5. Carefully install the front cover (A, **Figure 68**) onto the armature shaft.

NOTE
The hose clamp is used to keep the armature shaft locked securely into place within the front cover. If not securely held in place the armature will be pulled out of the front cover when the starter case is installed in Step 8.

6. Install a small hose clamp (B, **Figure 68**) onto the armature shaft to keep it installed into the front cover. Tighten the hose clamp securely.

7. Use a pick and release the four coil springs onto the backside of the four brushes bringing them into contact with the armature commutator. Make sure each brush is in contact with the commutator bars.

8. Install the starter case onto the armature shaft and the front cover and seat it against the front cover.

9. Align the index mark on the starter case with the front cover (A, **Figure 69**), then remove the hose clamp (B).

10. Install the rear cover (B, **Figure 61**) and seat it against the starter case.

11. Align the index marks (**Figure 60**) on all three components.

12. Install the through bolts (A, **Figure 61**) and tighten securely.

10

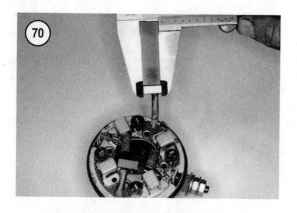

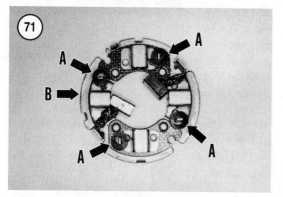

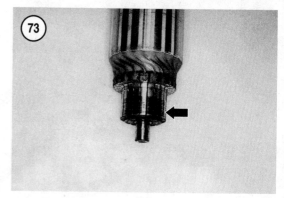

Inspection (All Models)

Check with a Yamaha dealership regarding replacement component availability for the starter. In most cases only the brush sets, O-ring and seal rings are available.

1. Measure the length of each brush (**Figure 70**) with a vernier caliper. If any brush is too short, replace both brush sets as part of the brush replacement parts set.

2A. On 1998-1999 models, inspect the brush springs (A, **Figure 71**) for fatigue, cracks or other damage. Replace the negative brush plate (B, **Figure 71**) if the springs (A) are severely worn or damaged. The positive brush plate is part of the brush replacement parts set.

2B. On 2000-2003 models, inspect the brush springs (A, **Figure 72**) for fatigue, cracks or other damage. If the springs are severely worn or damaged replace the starter.

3. Inspect the commutator (**Figure 73**) for abnormal wear or discoloration; neither condition can be repaired and requires replacement of the armature.

4. The mica in a good commutator is below the surface of the copper bars. On a worn commutator the

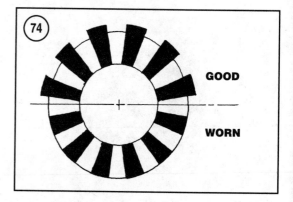

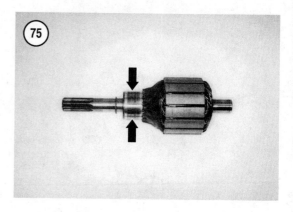

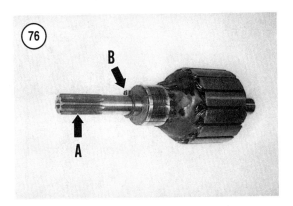

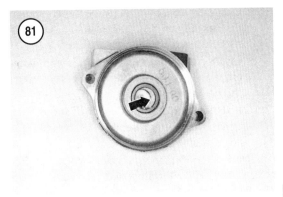

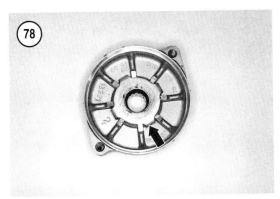

10

mica and copper bars may be worn to the same level (**Figure 74**). If necessary, undercut the mica between each pair of bars.

5. Measure the outside diameter of the commutator (**Figure 75**) and compare to the dimension in **Table 6**.

6. Check the armature shaft splines (A, **Figure 76**) for wear or damage. If worn or damaged, also inspect the starter reduction gear (**Figure 77**) for damage.

7. On 2000-2003 models, make sure the snap ring (B, **Figure 76**) is secure in the armature shaft groove.

8A. On 1998-1999 models, perform the following:

    a. Remove the lockwasher (**Figure 78**) from the front cover.

    b. Inspect the seal and needle bearing (**Figure 79**) for wear or damage.

    c. Inspect the bushing (**Figure 80**) in the rear cover for severe wear or damage.

8B. On 2000-2003 models, inspect the bushing in the front cover (B, **Figure 72**) and rear cover (**Figure 81**) for wear or damage.

9. Use an ohmmeter to make the following tests:

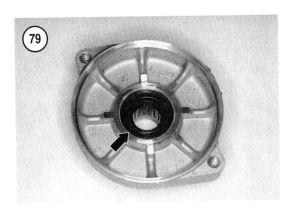

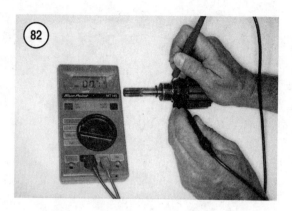

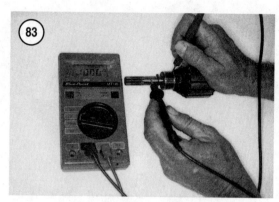

a. Check for continuity between the commutator bars (**Figure 82**); there should be continuity between pairs of bars.

b. Check for continuity between the commutator bars and the shaft (**Figure 83**); there should be no continuity.

c. If the commutator fails either of these tests, replace the starter assembly. The armature is not available separately.

10. On 1998-1999 models, check for continuity between the positive terminal and rear cover; there should be no continuity.

11. Replace the seal rings (**Figure 84**) if they are worn or damaged.

12. Check the magnets (**Figure 85**) bonded into the inner surface of the starter case. If damaged or loose, replace the starter assembly.

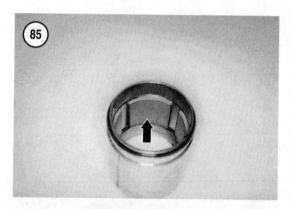

STARTER RELAY SWITCH

Testing

1. Remove the rider's seat as described in Chapter Sixteen.

2. Shift the transmission into neutral.

3. Turn the ignition switch on and press the starter button. The starter relay switch should click when the starter button is pressed. If a click is not heard, continue with Step 4.

4. Disconnect the 4-pin electrical connector (**Figure 86**) from the starter relay.

5. Check the continuity of the starter relay as follows:

a. Connect a fully charged 12-volt battery to the starter relay switch.

b. Connect the positive battery terminal to the red/white wire terminal and the negative bat-

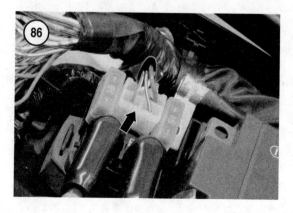

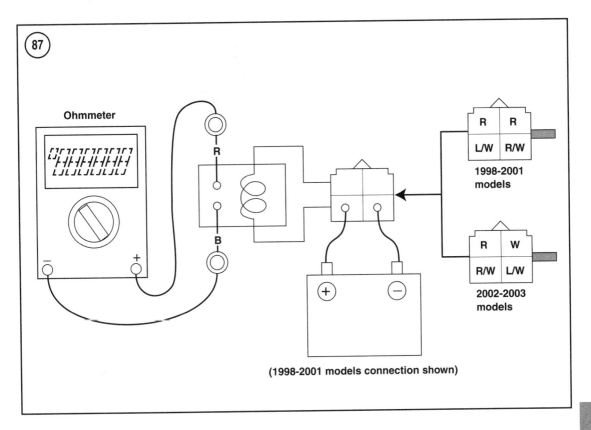

Ohmmeter

R

R

1998-2001
models

2002-2003
models

(1998-2001 models connection shown)

10

tery terminal to the blue/white terminal (**Figure 87**).

   c. The ohmmeter should now read continuity.

   d. Disconnect the battery and ohmmeter leads.

6. Replace the starter relay switch if it failed any part of this test.

7. Refer to *Electrical Connectors* at the beginning of this chapter and pack the connector with dielectric grease compound.

8. Reconnect the electrical connector at the starter relay switch.

9. Install the rider's seat as described in Chapter Sixteen.

Removal/Installation

1. Remove the rider's seat as described in Chapter Sixteen.

2. Disconnect the negative battery cable as described in this chapter.

3. Disconnect the starter relay switch electrical connector (A, **Figure 88**).

4. Slide the rubber boots (B, **Figure 88**) off the two large cable leads.

5. Disconnect the two large cable leads (C, **Figure 88**) at the starter relay switch.

6. Remove the starter relay switch from the frame.

7. Transfer the 30-amp (1998-2001 models) main fuse or 15-amp (2002-2003 models) fuel injection fuse and spare fuses to the *new* starter relay switch.

8. Install by reversing these removal steps. Refer to *Electrical Connectors* at the beginning of this chapter and pack the connector with dielectric grease compound.

RELAY UNIT (1998-2001 MODELS) OR STARTING CIRCUIT CUT-OFF RELAY UNIT (2002-2003 MODELS)– STARTING CIRCUIT

The relay unit, or starting circuit cut-off relay, is designed to not allow current to the starter relay unless the transmission is in neutral or unless the clutch lever is pulled in and the sidestand is in the raised position. The starting circuit cut-off relay is part of the relay unit.

This test relates to the starting circuit portion of both relay units. There is an additional test in this chapter that relates to the ignition circuit portion of the relay.

Testing

1. Remove both seats and the rear cowl as described in Chapter Sixteen.
2. Disconnect the negative battery cable as described in this chapter.
3A. On 1998-2001 models, perform the following:
   a. Unhook the relay unit (A, **Figure 89**) from the mounting tab on the rear fender.
   b. Disconnect the connector (B, **Figure 89**) from relay unit.
3B. On 2002-2003 models, perform the following:
   a. Unhook the starting circuit cut-off relay (**Figure 90**) from the mounting tab on the rear fender.
   b. Disconnect the connector (**Figure 91**) from starting circuit cut-off relay.
4A. On 1998-2001 models, check the continuity as follows:
   a. Connect a fully charged 12-volt battery to the rely unit. Connect the positive battery terminal to the red/black wire terminal (A, **Figure 92**) and the negative battery terminal to the black/yellow wire terminal (B).
   b. Connect the ohmmeter positive test lead to the blue/white (C, **Figure 92**) wire terminal on the relay unit and connect the negative lead to the blue (D) wire terminal on the relay unit. The ohmmeter should show continuity.
   c. Replace the relay unit if it fails this test.
4B. On 2002-2003 models, check the continuity as follows:
   a. Connect a fully charged 12-volt battery to the rely unit. Connect the positive battery termi-

nal to the red/black wire terminal (A, **Figure 93**) and the negative battery terminal to the black/yellow wire terminal (B).
   b. Connect the positive test lead to the blue/white (C, **Figure 93**) wire terminal on the relay unit and connect the negative lead to the other blue/white (D) wire terminal on the relay unit. The ohmmeter should show continuity.
   c. Replace the relay unit if it fails this test.

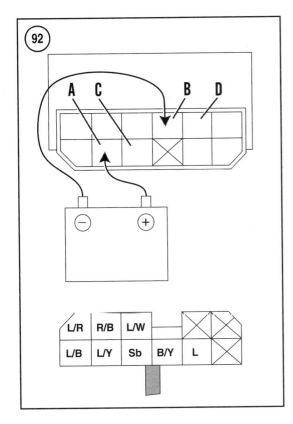

5. Refer to *Electrical Connectors* at the beginning of this chapter and pack the connector with dielectric grease compound.

6. Connect the electrical connector onto the relay unit.

7. Install the relay unit.

LIGHTING SYSTEM

The lighting system consists of a headlight, taillight, turn signals and indicator lights. **Table 7** lists replacement bulbs for these components.

Always use the correct wattage bulb listed in **Table 7**. Using the wrong size bulb gives a dim light or causes the bulb to burn out prematurely.

Headlight Bulb Replacement

> *WARNING*
> *If the headlight just burned out or it was just turned off, it will be hot! Do not touch the bulb until it cools off.*

> *CAUTION*
> *All models use a quartz-halogen bulbs. Traces of oil on this type of bulb reduce the life of the bulb. Do not touch the bulb glass. Clean any oil or other chemicals from the bulb with an alcohol-moistened cloth.*

> *NOTE*
> *This procedure is shown with the front fairing removed from both models to better illustrate the steps. There is sufficient room within the front suspension and front fairing (**Figure 94**) to replace the headlight bulb(s) with the front fairing in place.*

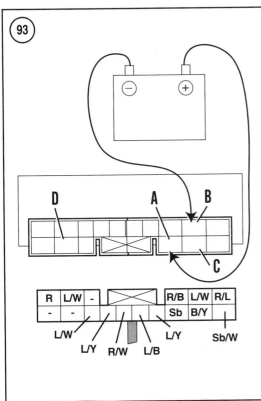

1. Disconnect the headlight bulb connector (**Figure 95**).

2. Remove the dust cover (A, **Figure 96**) from around the bulb.

3. Unhook the bulb retainer (A, **Figure 97**) and remove the bulb (**Figure 98**).

4. Check the connector for dirty or loose-fitting terminals.

5. Align the tabs on the *new* bulb with the notches in the bulb holder (B, **Figure 97**) and install the bulb. Secure the bulb with the bulb retainer.

6. Install the dust cover so its TOP mark (B, **Figure 96**) is at the top of the housing. Make sure the dust cover fits snugly around the bulb and the housing.

7. Plug the connector (**Figure 95**) into the back of the bulb. Press it on until it bottoms.

8. Repeat for the opposite side, if necessary.

9. Start the engine and check the headlight operation. If necessary, perform the *Headlight Adjustment* in this section.

Headlight Adjustment

Proper headlight beam adjustment is critical to both the rider and to oncoming drivers. Adjust the headlight horizontally and vertically according to local Department of Motor Vehicle regulations. If necessary, refer this adjustment to a Yamaha dealership.

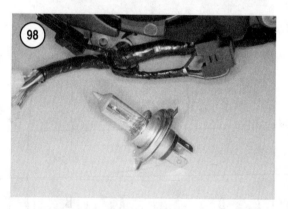

1. On 1998-2001 models, perform the following:

  a. To adjust the headlight horizontally, turn the upper inner screw(s) (A, **Figure 99**).

  b. To adjust the headlight vertically, turn the lower outer screw(s) (B, **Figure 99**).

2. On 2002-2003 models, perform the following:

  a. To adjust the headlight horizontally, turn the upper outer screw(s) (A, **Figure 100**).

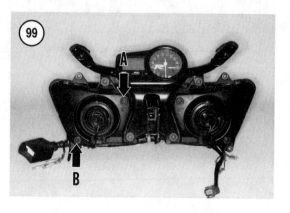

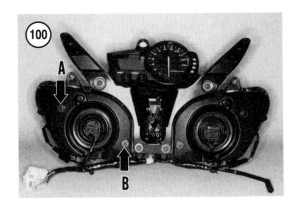

10

b. To adjust the headlight vertically, turn the lower inner screw(s) (B, **Figure 100**).

Headlight Housing Removal/Installation

1998-2001 models

1. Remove the front fairing (Chapter Sixteen).
2. On the left side, pull back the rubber sleeve (A, **Figure 101**) and disconnect the electrical connectors (B) for the headlight/combination meter assembly.
3. On the left side, remove the nuts (**Figure 102**) securing the front fairing mounting bracket to the steering head.
4. Have an assistant hold onto the headlight/meter assembly.
5. On the right side, remove the bracket (**Figure 103**) securing the front fairing mounting bracket to the steering head.
6. Remove the front fairing mounting bracket and headlight/meter assembly (**Figure 104**).
7. Disconnect the electrical connector from the backside of the combination meter.
8. Remove the two headlight housing upper mounting screws and washers (A, **Figure 105**).

9. Remove the two headlight housing lower mounting screws, washers (B, **Figure 105**) and carefully remove the headlight housing from the mounting bracket.

10. Install by reversing these removal steps.

11. Start the engine and check the headlight operation. If necessary, perform the *Headlight Adjustment* in this section.

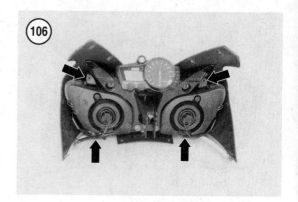

2002-2003 models

1. Remove the front fairing as described in Chapter Sixteen.

2. Remove the four mounting screws (**Figure 106**) securing the front fairing to the headlight, meter assembly and mounting bracket and remove the front fairing.

3. Disconnect the electrical connector (**Figure 107**) from the backside of the combination meter.

4. Remove the four headlight housing mounting screws (**Figure 108**) and carefully remove the headlight housing from the mounting bracket.

5. Install by reversing these removal steps.

6. Start the engine and check the headlight operation. If necessary, perform the *Headlight Adjustment* in this section.

Sidelight Bulb Replacement (1998-2001 U.K. Models)

1. Working under the front fairing, remove the rubber cover, then pull the bulb holder straight down and out of the headlight assembly.

2. Pull straight out and remove the bulb from the bulb socket.

3. Push a *new* bulb into the socket until it bottoms.

4. Install the bulb holder into the headlight assembly and the rubber cover. Make sure the rubber cover is seated correctly to keep out moisture.

Position Bulb Replacement (2002-2003 Models)

1. Pull straight out and remove the bulb and socket from the base of the headlight unit at the lower portion of the front fairing.

2. Remove the bulb from the socket and install a *new* bulb.

3. Insert the bulb and socket into the base of the headlight unit. Press it in until it bottoms.

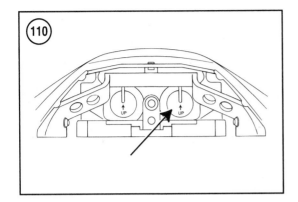

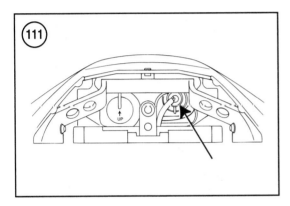

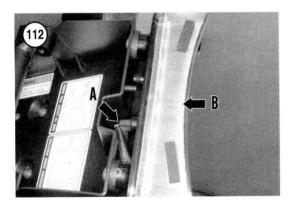

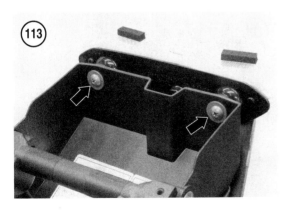

4. Connect the electrical connector to the bulb socket.

Front and Rear Turn Signal Light Replacement

1A. On 1998-2001 models, remove the side screw securing the lens and remove the lens.

1B. On 2002-2003 models, remove the lower screw securing the lens (**Figure 109**) and remove the lens.

2. Push the bulb and turn it counterclockwise to remove it.

3. Install the *new* bulb and lens by reversing these steps.

4. Turn the ignition switch on and check the turn signal light operation.

Taillight/Brake Light Bulb Replacement

1998-2001 models

1. Remove the passenger seat, as described in Chapter Sixteen.

2. Remove the cover(s) (**Figure 110**).

3. Turn the bulb socket (**Figure 111**) counterclockwise and remove it.

4. Pull straight out and remove the bulb from the bulb socket and remove it.

5. Push a *new* bulb into the socket until it bottoms.

6. Install the bulb socket into the taillight assembly and turn it clockwise until it locks into place.

7. Install the cover and push it in until it snaps into place.

8. Install the passenger seat (Chapter Sixteen).

9. Turn the ignition switch on and check the taillight and brake light operation.

2002-2003 models

The taillight/brake light assembly is an LED unit and must be replaced as an assembly if defective.

1. Remove the rear cowl (Chapter Sixteen).

2. Disconnect the electrical connector (A, **Figure 112**) from the backside of the assembly.

3. From the backside of the rear cowl hold onto the taillight assembly.

4. Remove the screws and washers (**Figure 113**) securing the assembly and remove the assembly (B, **Figure 112**).

10

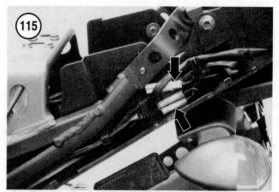

5. Install the new assembly and secure with the screws and washers. Tighten the screws securely.

6. Connect the electrical connector (A, **Figure 112**) onto the backside of the assembly.

7. Install the passenger seat (Chapter Sixteen).

8. Turn the ignition switch on and check the taillight and brake light operation.

Taillight/Brake Light Housing
Removal/Installation (1998-2001 Models)

1. Remove the rear cowl (Chapter Sixteen).

2. Release the wiring for the turn signals from the clip on each side of the taillight/brake light assembly backing plate.

3. Disconnect the 3-pin electrical connector for the taillight/brake light assembly.

4. Working under the rear fender, remove the bolt on each side securing the fender to the rear sub-frame.

5. Loosen the bolt securing the bungee hook.

6. Remove the two bolts securing the taillight/brake light assembly.

7. Release the three trim clips securing the taillight/brake light assembly. Refer to Chapter Sixteen for trim clip removal and installation.

8. Push down on the rear fender and remove the taillight/brake light assembly from the rear sub-frame.

9. Install by reversing these removal steps.

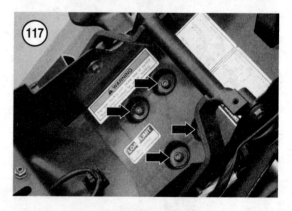

License Plate Light Replacement
(2002-2003 Models)

1. Remove the mounting screws (**Figure 114**) and lower the license plate light holder from the housing.

2. Pull straight out and remove the bulb from the bulb socket and remove it.

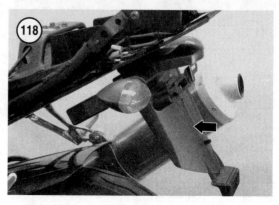

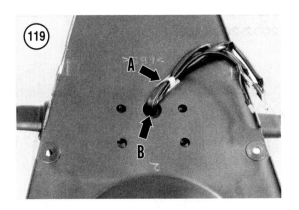

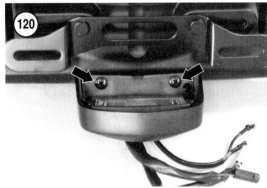

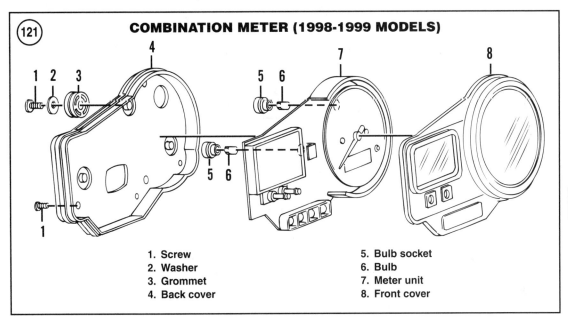

COMBINATION METER (1998-1999 MODELS)

1. Screw
2. Washer
3. Grommet
4. Back cover
5. Bulb socket
6. Bulb
7. Meter unit
8. Front cover

3. Push a *new* bulb into the socket until it bottoms.

4. Install the holder into the housing and secure it with the two screws (**Figure 114**).

License Plate Light Assembly Removal/Installation (2002-2003 Models)

1. Remove both seats as described in this chapter.

2. Remove the rear cowl (Chapter Sixteen).

3. Disconnect the three electrical connectors (**Figure 115**) for the license plate and rear turn signals.

4. Have an assistant hold onto the rear fender under panel assembly (**Figure 116**) containing the license plate light and rear turn signal assembly.

5. Remove the four screws (**Figure 117**) securing the rear fender under panel assembly. Lower the rear fender under panel assembly (**Figure 118**).

6. Unhook the electrical cables from the clip (A, **Figure 119**) and remove the cables down through the opening in the under panel (B).

7. Remove the screws (**Figure 120**) securing the license plate light assembly to the rear fender panel assembly. Remove the license plate light assembly.

8. Install by reversing these removal steps.

Combination Meter Illumination Light Bulb and Indicator Light Replacement

1998-1999 models

Refer to **Figure 121**.

NOTE
On 2000-2001 models, the illumination lights as well as the LED indica-

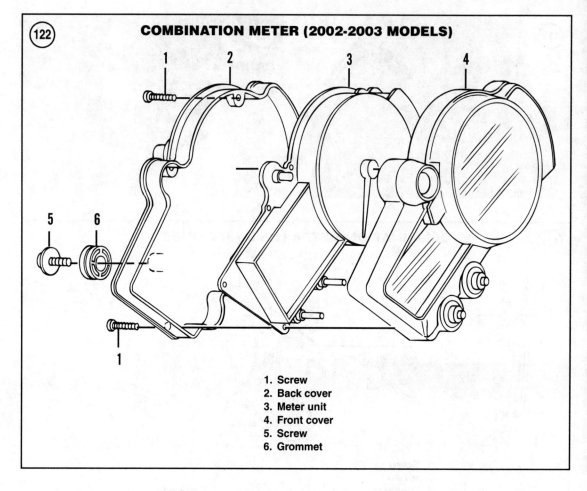

COMBINATION METER (2002-2003 MODELS)

1. Screw
2. Back cover
3. Meter unit
4. Front cover
5. Screw
6. Grommet

tor lights are part of the meter unit
*and cannot be replaced separately. If
the bulb(s) and/or LED's are defective
the entire combination meter must be
replaced as an assembly.*

NOTE
*Only the two illumination lights are
replaceable. If the LED's are defective, replace the combination meter
unit.*

1. Remove the combination meter as described in
this chapter.
2. Turn the combination meter upside down on
several shop cloths.
3. Remove the four screws and washers and lift off
the back cover.
4. Carefully rotate and pull up and remove the bulb
socket and bulb assembly from the meter unit.
5. Pull straight out and remove the bulb from the
bulb socket.

6. Push a *new* bulb into the socket until it bottoms.

7. Install the bulb socket and bulb assembly into
the meter unit. Rotate it to lock it into place.

8. Install the back cover and four screws and washers. Tighten the screws securely.

9. Install the combination meter as described in this
chapter.

10. Turn the ignition switch on and check the illumination light operation.

2002-2003 models

Refer to **Figure 122**.

The illumination lights, as well as the LED indicator lights, are part of the meter unit and cannot be
replaced separately. If the bulb(s) and/or LED's are
defective, the entire combination meter must be replaced as an assembly.

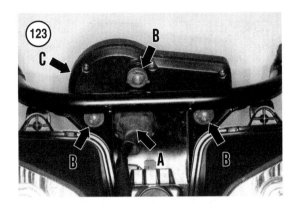

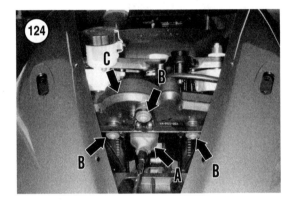

COMBINATION METER

The 2000-2001 model is equipped with a diagnostic system to detect faults within the speedometer speed sensor. If there is a fault within the system the following will occur. When the engine is turned on, the tachometer will first indicate zero rpm for three seconds, then indicate 4000 rpm for two and one-half seconds, then the actual engine speed for three seconds. The tachometer will repeat this sequence until the engine is turned off. The motorcycle can be ridden in this condition but inspect the speed sensor and related circuit as described in this chapter.

The 2002-2003 model is covered in Chapter Nine.

Removal/Installation

1998-2001 models

Refer to **Figure 121**.

1. Remove the seat and the front fairing as described in Chapter Sixteen.

2. Disconnect the negative battery cable as described in this chapter.

NOTE
Figure 123 is shown with the headlight and combination meter assembly removed from the frame to better illustrate the step.

3. Slide the rubber boot (A, **Figure 123**) back off the meter assembly.

4. Pull straight back and disconnect the electrical connector from the meter assembly.

5. Remove the three screws (B, **Figure 123**) securing the meter assembly to the front fairing mounting bracket and remove the meter assembly (C).

6. Install the combination meter by reversing these removal steps.

7. Start the engine and check the illumination and indicator lights and the gauge for proper operation.

2002-2003 models

Refer to **Figure 122**.

1. Disconnect the negative battery cable as described in this chapter.

2. Remove the windshield and rear view mirrors from the front fairing as described in Chapter Sixteen.

3. Slide the rubber boot (A, **Figure 124**) back off the meter assembly and electrical connector.

4. Pull straight back and disconnect the electrical connector from the meter assembly.

5. Remove the three screws (B, **Figure 124**) securing the meter assembly to the front fairing mounting bracket and remove the meter assembly (C).

6. Install the combination meter by reversing these removal steps.

7. Start the engine and check the illumination and indicator lights and the gauge for proper operation.

Disassembly/Assembly

1998-1999 and 2002-2003 models

Refer to **Figure 121** and **Figure 122**.

On the 1998-1999 and 2002-2003 models, only the front and rear covers can be replaced separately. If the meter unit is defective, the entire combination meter assembly must be replaced.

1. Remove the combination meter as described in this chapter.

2. Turn the combination meter upside down on several shop cloths.

10

3. Remove the four screws and washers and lift off the back cover.

4. Lift the meter unit out of the back cover.

5. Install the meter unit into the back cover, then install the front cover.

6. Install the four screws and washers securing the assembly together and tighten securely.

2000-2001 models

On the 2000-2001 models, the combination meter assembly is a sealed assembly and cannot be disassembled. If the meter unit is defective, the entire combination meter assembly must be replaced.

SPEED SENSOR

Removal/Installation

1. Support the motorcycle on level ground.

2. Block the front wheel so the motorcycle will not roll in either direction while the rear wheel is on the jack or swing arm stand.

3. Remove the tie wrap (**Figure 125**) securing the speed sensor wiring from any adjacent wiring. Disconnect the electrical connector from the main harness.

4. On the rear left side of the lower crankcase, remove the screw securing the speed sensor (**Figure 126**) and remove it from the lower crankcase.

> *NOTE*
> *The following steps are shown with the engine removed from the frame to better illustrate the steps.*

5. Apply clean engine oil to the O-ring seal (**Figure 127**) on the speed sensor.

6. Install the speed sensor and push it in until it bottoms. Install and tighten the screw securely.

Speed Sensor Test (2002-2003 Models)

> *NOTE*
> *There are no test procedures for the 1998-2001 models.*

1. Support the motorcycle on level ground.

2. Block the front wheel so the motorcycle will not roll in either direction while the rear wheel is on the jack or swing arm stand.

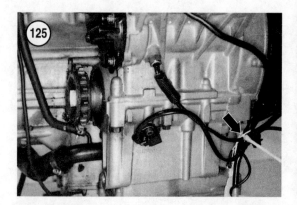

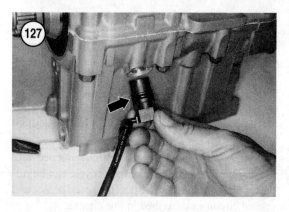

3. Remove the rider's seat as described in Chapter Sixteen.

4. Remove the fuel tank and air filter housing as described in Chapter Nine.

5. Follow the electrical wires from the speed sensor (**Figure 126**) on the lower left side of the crankcase to the 3-pin electrical connector (**Figure 128**) on the right side of the frame behind the throttle body assembly.

6. Connect a digital voltmeter as follows. On the harness side of the connector, connect the voltmeter

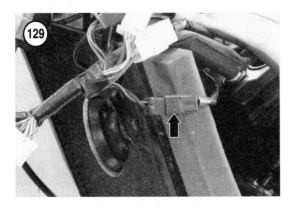

11. Turn the ignition switch off.

12. Disconnect the digital voltmeter.

13. Install the rider's seat as described in Chapter Sixteen.

14. Install the air filter housing and fuel tank as described in Chapter Nine.

15. Lower the rear of the motorcycle to the ground.

COOLING SYSTEM SWITCHES AND SENSORS

Radiator Fan Motor Testing (All Models)

1. Remove both side fairings as described in Chapter Sixteen.

2. Follow the wiring harness from the fan switch to the electrical connector at the main harness at the left side of the radiator. Disconnect the electrical connector. Refer to **Figure 129** for 1998-2001 models or **Figure 130** for 2002-2003 models.

3. Connect a fully charged 12-volt battery to the connector as follows:

    a. Positive battery lead to the blue terminal.

    b. Negative battery lead to the black terminal.

4. The fan motor should operate. If not, it is faulty and must be replaced as described in Chapter Eleven.

5. Reconnect the electrical connector to the main harness.

6. Install both side fairing panels as described in Chapter Sixteen.

Coolant Thermo Switch or Thermo Unit Testing (1998-2001 Models)

The coolant thermo switch (1998- 1999 models) or thermo unit (2000-2001 models) perform the same function.

1. Drain the cooling system as described in Chapter Eleven.

2. Remove the right side fairing as described in Chapter Sixteen.

3. Disconnect the electrical connector from the thermo switch or thermo unit.

4. Unscrew and remove the thermo switch or thermo unit (**Figure 131**) from the radiator.

NOTE
Make sure the switch terminals do not get wet.

positive test lead to the white/yellow terminal and connect the negative lead to the blue terminal on the connector.

7. Turn the ignition switch on.

8. Have an assistant rotate the rear wheel in the normal direction.

9. With each rotation of the rear wheel the voltage reading should read from 0.6 to 4.8 volts and then again from 0.6 to 4.8 volts.

10. If the speed sensor is not within specification, replace the sensor as previously described.

10

5. Place the switch in a pan filled with a 50:50 mixture of water and antifreeze (A, **Figure 132**). Support the switch so the threads are covered with the coolant and the sensor is away from the bottom of the pan.

6. Place a shop thermometer (B, **Figure 132**) in the pan. Use a thermometer that is rated higher than the test temperature.

7. Connect an ohmmeter to the two terminals on top of the switch.

8. Heat the coolant to the specified temperatures in **Table 8** and check the resistance between the terminal on the switch. Maintain the coolant at the specified temperature in **Table 8** for three minutes before testing.

9. If the resistance values do not match those listed in **Table 8**, replace the switch.

10. Install the thermo switch or thermo unit (**Figure 131**) onto the radiator and tighten to 23 N•m (17 ft.-lb.).

11. Connect the electrical connector onto the thermo switch or thermo unit.

12. Install the right side fairing as described in Chapter Sixteen.

13. Refill the cooling system as described in Chapter Eleven.

Coolant Sensor Testing (2002-2003 Models)

1. Drain the cooling system as described in Chapter Eleven.

2. Remove the fuel tank and air filter housing as described in Chapter Nine.

3. Partially remove the radiator to gain access to the thermostat housing at the front of the engine. Refer to Chapter Eleven.

4. Disconnect the electrical connector (**Figure 133**) from the coolant sensor.

5. Unscrew and remove the sensor from the thermostat housing.

NOTE
Make sure the sensor terminals do not get wet.

6. Place the switch in a pan filled with a 50:50 mixture of water and antifreeze (A, **Figure 134**). Support the sensor so that the threads are covered by the coolant and the sensor is away from the bottom of the pan.

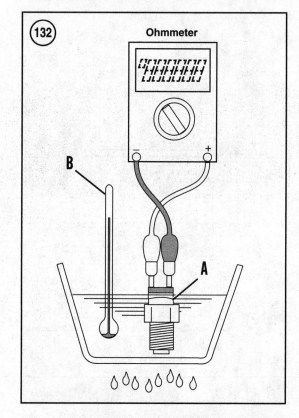

Ohmmeter

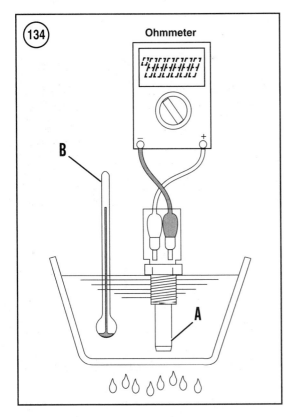

Ohmmeter

B

A

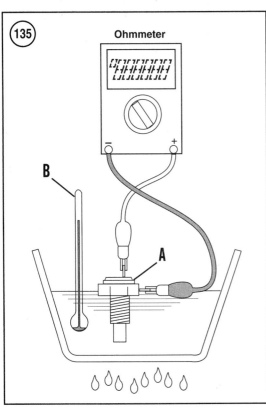

Ohmmeter

B

A

7. Place a shop thermometer (B, **Figure 134**) in the pan. Use a thermometer that is rated higher than the test temperature.

8. Connect an ohmmeter to the two terminals on top of the sensor.

9. Heat the coolant to the specified temperatures in **Table 8** and check the resistance between the terminal on the sensor. Maintain the coolant at the specified temperature in **Table 8** for three minutes before testing.

10. If the resistance values do not match those listed in **Table 8**, replace the sensor.

11. Install the sensor into the thermostat housing and tighten to 18 N•m (13 ft.-lb.).

12. Connect the electrical connector (**Figure 133**) onto the sensor.

13. Install the partially removed radiator. Refer to Chapter Eleven.

14. Install the air filter housing and the fuel tank as described in Chapter Nine.

15. Refill the cooling system as described in Chapter Eleven.

**Coolant Sender Testing
(1998-1999 Models)**

10

1. Drain the cooling system as described in Chapter Eleven.

2. Remove the right side fairing panel as described in Chapter Sixteen.

3. Disconnect the electrical connector from the coolant sender at the front right side of the radiator.

4. Unscrew and remove the sending unit from the radiator.

*NOTE
Make sure the switch terminals do not
get wet.*

5. Place the sender in a pan filled with a 50:50 mixture of water and antifreeze (A, **Figure 135**). Support the sender so that the threads are covered by the coolant and the sending unit is away from the bottom of the pan.

6. Place a shop thermometer (B, **Figure 135**) in the pan. Use a thermometer that is rated higher than the test temperature.

7. Connect an ohmmeter to the top terminal on top of the sender and to the threads.

8. Heat the coolant to the specified temperatures in **Table 8** and check the resistance between the terminal and the threads on the sender. Maintain the coolant at the specified temperature in **Table 8** for three minutes before testing.

9. If the resistance values do not match those listed in **Table 8**, the sender must be replaced.

10. Apply ThreeBond Sealock 10, or an equivalent to the sender threads.

11. Install the sender into the radiator and tighten to 15 N•m (133 in.-lb.).

12. Connect the electrical connector to the sender.

13. Install the right side fairing panel as described in Chapter Sixteen.

14. Refill the cooling system as described in Chapter Eleven.

Radiator Fan Motor Relay Testing (2000-2003 Models)

1. Remove the rider's seat as described in Chapter Sixteen.

2. Disconnect the 4-pin electrical connector (**Figure 136**) from the relay.

3A. On 2000-2001 models, check the continuity as follows:

   a. Connect a fully charged 12-volt battery to the rely unit. Connect the positive battery terminal to the brown wire terminal and the negative battery terminal to the green/black wire terminal.

   b. Connect the ohmmeter positive test lead to the brown wire terminal on the relay unit and connect the negative lead to the blue wire terminal on the relay unit. The ohmmeter should show continuity.

   c. Replace the relay unit if it fails this test.

3B. On 2002-2003 models, check the continuity as follows:

   a. Connect a fully charged 12-volt battery to the rely unit. Connect the positive battery terminal to the red/white wire terminal and the negative battery terminal to the green/yellow wire terminal.

   b. Connect the ohmmeter positive test lead to the brown/green wire terminal on the relay unit and connect the negative lead to the blue wire terminal on the relay unit. The ohmmeter should show continuity.

   c. Replace the relay unit if it fails this test.

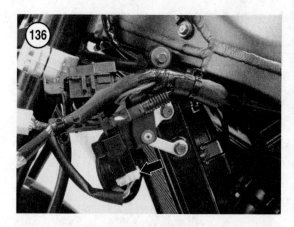

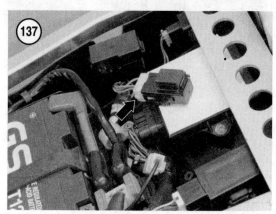

TURN SIGNAL RELAY

Testing

1. Before troubleshooting the turn signal system, perform the following:

   a. Check the battery to make sure it is fully charged and in good condition. Refer to *Battery* in this chapter.

   b. Check for a burned-out bulb. Clean the bulb sockets of any corrosion.

   c. Make sure the bulb is the correct type and wattage. Refer to **Table 7** for replacement bulbs.

   d. Check for a burned-out fuse.

   e. Check for loose connections in the circuit.

2. Remove the rider's seat as described in Chapter Sixteen.

3. Disconnect the 3-pin electrical connector from the turn signal relay. Refer to **Figure 137** for 1998-2001 models or **Figure 138** for 2002-2003 models.

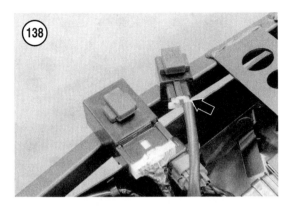

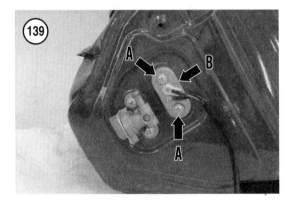

4. On the harness side of the electrical connector, connect the voltmeter positive test lead to the brown wire terminal and connect the negative lead to a bare metal ground.

5. Turn the ignition switch on.

6. There should be battery voltage.

7. If there is no battery voltage, inspect the wiring harness for an open circuit in the brown wire.

8. Connect the 3-pin white electrical connector to the turn signal relay.

9. Install the rider's seat as described in Chapter Sixteen.

FUEL LEVEL WARNING LIGHT SENDER (2000-2001 MODELS)

The 2000-2001 model is equipped with a diagnostic system to detect faults in the fuel level warning light. If there is a fault within the system the following will occur. When the engine is turned on, the tachometer will first indicate zero rpm for three seconds, then indicate 8000 rpm for two and one-half seconds, then the actual engine speed for three seconds. The tachometer will repeat this se-

quence until the engine is turned off. The motorcycle can be ridden in this condition, but inspect the fuel level warning light sender and related wiring as described in this chapter.

The 2002-2003 model diagnostic system is covered in Chapter Nine.

Testing

1. Remove the fuel tank as described in Chapter Eight or Chapter Nine.

2. Place the fuel tank on the workbench in the upright position.

3. Connect one of the ohmmeter test leads to the black terminal and the other test lead to the green terminal on the sender. The ohmmeter should show continuity.

4. If necessary, replace the fuel sensor.

5. Install the fuel tank as described in Chapter Eight or Chapter Nine.

Removal/Installation

1. Remove the fuel tank as described in Chapter Eight or Chapter Nine.

2. Place several heavy towels on the workbench to protect the fuel tank finish.

3. Turn the fuel tank on its side on the workbench.

4. Remove the sensor mounting screws (A, **Figure 139**) and remove the sensor (B) from the fuel tank.

5. Install by reversing these removal steps. Check for fuel leakage after the fuel tank is installed and the fuel pump has been turned on.

FUEL PUMP RELAY

The fuel pump relay is part of the relay unit. Whenever the ignition switch is turned on, the fuel pump relay energizes the fuel pump. If the relay is defective, the fuel pump will not operate.

Testing

1. Remove both seats and the rear cowl as described in Chapter Sixteen.

2. Disconnect the negative battery cable as described in this chapter.

10

3. Unhook the relay unit (A, **Figure 140**) from the mounting tab on the rear fender.

4. Disconnect the connector (B, **Figure 140**) from relay unit.

5A. On 1998-2001 models, check the continuity as follows:

   a. Connect a fully charged 12-volt battery to the rely unit. Connect the positive battery terminal to the red/black (A, **Figure 141**) and the negative battery terminal to the blue/red (B).

   b. Connect the ohmmeter positive test lead to the red/black (A, **Figure 141**) terminal on the relay unit and connect the negative lead to the blue/black (C) terminal on the relay unit. The ohmmeter should show continuity.

   c. Replace the relay unit if it fails this test.

5B. On 2002-2003 models, check the continuity as follows:

   a. Connect a fully charged 12-volt battery to the rely unit. Connect the positive battery terminal to the red/black (A, **Figure 142**) and the negative battery terminal to the blue/yellow (B).

   b. Connect the positive test lead to the red (C, **Figure 142**) terminal on the relay unit and connect the negative lead to the red/blue (D) terminal on the relay unit. The ohmmeter should show continuity.

   c. Replace the relay unit if it fails this test.

6. Refer to *Electrical Connectors* at the beginning of this chapter and pack the connector with dielectric grease compound.

7. Connect the electrical connector (B, **Figure 140**) onto the relay unit.

8. Attach the relay unit onto the mounting tab on the rear fender.

9. Install the relay unit as previously described in this chapter.

10. Connect the negative battery cable as described in this chapter.

11. Install the rear cowl and both seats as described in Chapter Sixteen.

THROTTLE POSITION SENSOR

The 2000-2001 model is equipped with a diagnosis system to detect faults within the throttle position sensor (TPS). If there is a fault, the following will occur. When the engine is turned on, the tachometer will first indicate zero rpm for three sec-

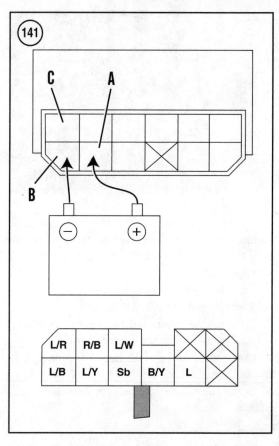

onds, then indicate 3000 rpm for two and one-half seconds, then the actual engine speed for three seconds. The tachometer will repeat this sequence until the engine is turned off. The motorcycle can be ridden in this condition with a slight difference in performance. Inspect the throttle position sensor and related wiring as described in this chapter.

The 2002-2003 model diagnostic system is covered in Chapter Nine. Throttle position sensor testing is covered in this chapter.

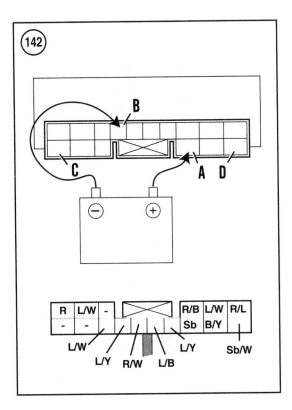

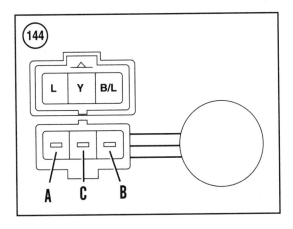

Test (1998-2001 Models)

1. Remove the rider's seat as described in Chapter Sixteen.

2. Disconnect the negative battery cable as described in this chapter.

3. Remove the fuel tank and air filter housing as described in Chapter Eight.

4. Disconnect the throttle position sensor electrical connector (**Figure 143**).

5. Check the continuity as follows:

   a. Connect the ohmmeter positive test lead to the blue (A, **Figure 144**) terminal on the sensor and connect the negative lead to the black/blue (B) terminal on the sensor.

   b. The ohmmeter should show 4000-6000 ohms.

   c. Connect the ohmmeter positive test lead to the yellow (C, **Figure 144**) terminal on the sensor and connect the negative lead to the black/blue (B) terminal on the sensor.

   NOTE
   The meter readings may differ slightly than those specified. The important factor is that the needle movement changes gradually and smoothly during the full range of movement.

   d. Slowly open the throttle from the closed to the wide-open position and note the needle movement. The resistance should change gradually from 0-5 or 6 ohms.

   e. If the movement is erratic or not within specification, the sensor is defective and must be replaced.

6. Refer to *Electrical Connectors* at the beginning of this chapter and pack the connector with dielectric grease compound.

7. Connect the throttle position sensor electrical connector (**Figure 143**).

8. Install the fuel tank as described in Chapter Eight.

9. Connect the negative battery cable as described in this chapter.

10. Install the rider's seat as described in Chapter Sixteen.

Adjustment (1998-2001 Models)

1. Remove the rider's seat as described in Chapter Sixteen.

2. Remove the fuel tank and air filter housing as described in Chapter Eight.

3. Turn the ignition switch on.

NOTE
Disconnecting, then reconnecting the throttle position sensor connector switches the tachometer to the throttle position sensor adjust mode.

4. Disconnect the electrical connector (**Figure 143**) from the throttle position sensor then reconnect it.

NOTE
Figure 145 is shown with the carburetor assembly removed to better illustrate the step.

5. Use a 90° screwdriver and loosen the mounting screws (A, **Figure 145**) and slowly rotate the throttle position sensor (B) until the tachometer needle is pointing to the 5000 mark.

6. Tighten the mounting screws securely.

7. Turn the ignition switch off or start the engine to exit the adjust mode.

8. Refer to *Electrical Connectors* at the beginning of this chapter and pack the connector with dielectric grease compound.

9. Install the fuel tank as described in Chapter Eight.

10. Install the rider's seat as described in Chapter Sixteen.

Test (2002-2003 Models)

1. Remove the rider's seat as described in Chapter Sixteen.

2. Disconnect the negative battery cable as described in this chapter.

3. Remove the fuel tank and air filter housing as described in Chapter Nine.

4. Refer to Chapter Nine and partially remove the throttle body assembly to gain access to the throttle position sensor (**Figure 146**).

5. Make an index mark adjacent to the mounting screws on the throttle body. This will ensure correct alignment during installation.

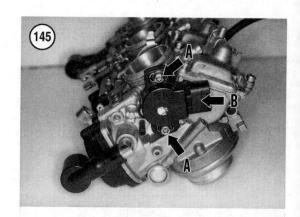

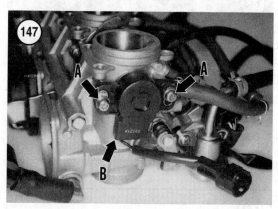

NOTE
The following steps are shown with the throttle body assembly removed to better illustrate the steps.

6. Remove the screws (A, **Figure 147**) securing the throttle position sensor to the throttle body assembly. Remove the sensor (B, **Figure 147**).

7. Check the continuity as follows:
   a. Connect the ohmmeter positive test lead to the blue (A, **Figure 148**) terminal on the sen-

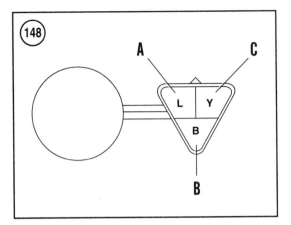

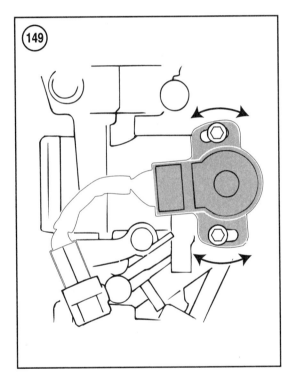

changes gradually and smoothly during the full range of movement.

   d. Slowly open the throttle from the closed to the wide-open position and note the needle movement. The resistance should change gradually from 0-5 or 6 ohms.

   e. If the movement is erratic or not within specification, the sensor is defective and must be replaced.

8. Refer to *Electrical Connectors* at the beginning of this chapter and pack the connector with dielectric grease compound.

9. Reinstall the throttle body as described in Chapter Nine.

10. Install the air filter housing and fuel tank as described in Chapter Nine.

11. Connect the negative battery cable as described in this chapter.

12. Install the rider's seat as described in Chapter Sixteen.

Adjustment (2002-2003 Models)

1. Remove the rider's seat as described in Chapter Sixteen.

2. Remove the fuel tank and air filter housing as described in Chapter Nine.

3. Turn the ignition switch on.

4. Connect a digital voltmeter as follows:

   a. Connect the voltmeter positive test lead to the blue (A, **Figure 148**) terminal on the sensor and connect the negative lead to the yellow (C) terminal on the sensor.

   b. The specified voltage is 0.63-0.73 volt.

   c. If the voltage is not within specification, perform Step 5.

5. Loosen the mounting screws and slowly rotate the throttle position sensor (**Figure 149**) until the voltage reading is within specification.

6. Tighten the mounting screws securely.

7. Turn the ignition switch off.

8. Install the fuel tank as described in Chapter Nine.

9. Install the rider's seat as described in Chapter Sixteen.

sor and connect the negative lead to the black (B) terminal on the sensor.

   b. The ohmmeter should show 3500-6500 ohms.

   c. Connect the ohmmeter positive test lead to the yellow (C, **Figure 148**) terminal on the sensor and connect the negative lead to the black (B) terminal on the sensor.

NOTE
The meter readings may differ slightly than those specified. The important factor is that the needle movement

10

OIL LEVEL SENSOR AND RELAY

Sensor Testing

1998-2001 models

1. Drain the engine oil as described in Chapter Three.

NOTE
Figure 150 is shown with the oil pan removed to better illustrate the step.

2. Remove the screws (A, **Figure 150**) securing the oil level sensor and remove the sensor (B) from the oil pan.
3. Hold the sensor in its normal orientation within the oil pan with the flange side down.
4. Check for continuity by connecting either test lead to the sensor's electrical connector and the other test lead to the sensor base. The ohmmeter should show continuity.
5. Turn the sensor upside down with the flange side up.
6. Check for continuity by connecting either test lead to the sensor's electrical connector and the other test lead to the sensor base. The ohmmeter should show no continuity.
7. Replace the sensor if it fails this test.
8. Inspect the O-ring seal on the sensor and replace if necessary.
9. Install the sensor into the oil pan and tighten the screws securely.
10. Refill the engine oil as described in Chapter Three.

2002-2003 models

1. Drain the engine oil (Chapter Three).
2. Remove the screws (A, **Figure 150**) securing the oil level sensor and remove the sensor (B) from the oil pan.
3. Hold the sensor in its normal orientation within the oil pan with the flange side down.
4. Check the resistance by connecting either test lead to the sensor's electrical connector and the other test lead to the sensor base. The specified resistance is 108-132 ohms.
5. Turn the sensor upside down with the flange side up.
6. Check the resistance by connecting either test lead to the sensor's electrical connector and the

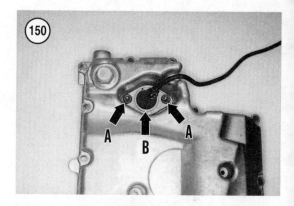

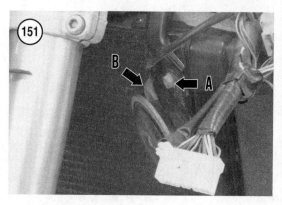

other test lead to the center finger of the base. The specified resistance is 526-624 ohms.
7. Replace the sensor if it fails this test.
8. Inspect the O-ring seal on the sensor and replace if necessary.
9. Install the sensor into the oil pan and tighten the screws securely.
10. Refill the engine oil as described in Chapter Three.

Relay Testing (1998-1999 Models)

NOTE
2000-2003 models are not equipped with the oil level sensor relay.

1. Remove the rider's seat as described in Chapter Sixteen.
2. Disconnect the negative battery cable as described in this chapter.
3. Lift the relay from the holder on the frame rail.
4. Disconnect the 4-pin electrical connector from the relay.
5. Check the continuity as follows.

a. Connect a fully charged 12-volt battery to the rely unit. Connect the positive battery terminal to the brown terminal and the negative battery terminal to the white terminal.

b. Connect the ohmmeter positive test lead to the red/blue terminal on the relay unit and connect the negative lead to the black terminal on the relay unit. The ohmmeter should show continuity.

c. Replace the relay unit if it fails this test.

6. Refer to *Electrical Connectors* at the beginning of this chapter and pack the connector with dielectric grease compound.

7. Connect the negative battery cable as described in this chapter.

8. Install the rider's seat as described in Chapter Sixteen.

HORN

Testing

1. Remove the left side fairing as described in Chapter Sixteen.

2. Disconnect the electrical connectors from the horn.

3. Connect a 12-volt battery across the horn terminals. The horn must sound loudly.

4. Replace the horn if it did not sound loudly in Step 3.

Removal/Installation

1. Remove the left side fairing as described in Chapter Sixteen.

2A. On 1998-2001 models, perform the following:
   a. Remove the bolt (A, **Figure 151**) securing the horn to the radiator mounting bracket.
   b. Disconnect the electrical connectors (B, **Figure 151**) from the horn and remove the horn.

2B. On 2002-2003 models, perform the following:
   a. Remove the bolts (**Figure 152**) securing the radiator mounting bracket.
   b. Move the bracket away from the radiator.
   c. Remove the nut (**Figure 153**) securing the horn to the bracket.
   d. Remove the horn from the bracket and disconnect the electrical connectors and remove the horn.

3. Install by reversing these removal steps. Make sure the electrical connections are secure and corrosion-free.

4. Check the horn operation. If the horn does not work properly, perform the *Horn Testing* procedure in this section.

> *WARNING*
> *Do not ride the motorcycle until the horn is working properly.*

SWITCHES

Testing

Test the switches for continuity using an ohmmeter (see Chapter One). Operate the switch in each of its operating positions and compare the results with the switch continuity diagrams included with the wiring diagrams at the end of the manual. For example, **Figure 154** shows the continuity diagram for the horn switch. When the horn button is pressed, there should be continuity between the brown and pink terminals. The line joining the two terminals shows continuity (**Figure 154**). An ohmmeter connected between these two terminals should indicate continu-

10

ity or a test light should illuminate. When the horn button is free, there should be no continuity between the same terminals.

1. Check the fuse as described under *Fuse* in this chapter.

2. Check the battery as described under *Battery* in this chapter. Charge the battery to the correct state of charge, if required.

3. Disconnect the negative battery cable at the battery if the switch connectors are not disconnected from the circuit.

> *CAUTION*
> *Do not attempt to start the engine with the battery disconnected.*

4. When separating two connectors, pull on the connector housings and not the wires.

5. After locating a defective circuit, check the connectors to make sure they are clean and properly connected. Check all wires going into a connector housing to make sure each wire is properly positioned and that the wire end is not loose.

6. Before disconnecting two connectors, check them for any locking tabs or arms that must be pushed or opened. If two connectors are difficult to separate, do not force them, as damage may occur.

7. When reconnecting electrical connector halves, push them together until they click or snap into place.

8. If the switch is operating erratically, chances are the contacts are oily, dirty or corroded. Disassemble the switch housing as described in this section to access the switch contacts. Clean the contacts as required.

9. If a switch or button does not perform properly, replace the switch as described in its appropriate section.

Left Handlebar Switch Housing Replacement

The left handlebar switch housing contains the dimmer, passing (U.K. models), horn and turn signal switches.

> *NOTE*
> *Iindividual switches are not available separately. If one switch is damaged, replace the switch housing assembly. On some models, the clutch interlock switch wires may be included in the wiring harness for the left handlebar*

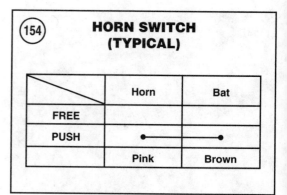

	Horn	Bat
FREE		
PUSH	•————————•	
	Pink	Brown

HORN SWITCH (TYPICAL)

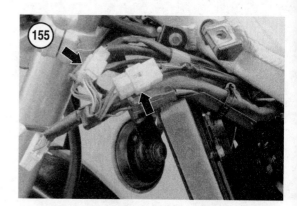

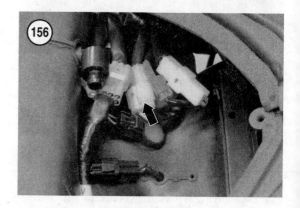

switch. If necessary, disconnect them from the clutch interlock switch.

1A. On 1998-2001 models, remove the left side faring as described in Chapter Sixteen.

1B. On 2002-2003 models, remove the fuel tank and air filter housing as described in Chapter Nine.

2A. On 1998-2001 U.S. and Canada models, follow the wire harness from the left handlebar switch to the left side of the frame rail. Locate the 4-pin and 6-pin electrical connectors (**Figure 155**) and disconnect them.

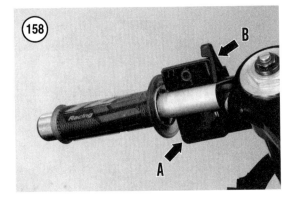

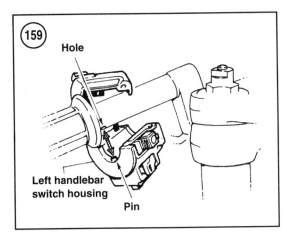

Hole

Left handlebar
switch housing

Pin

2B. On 1998-2001, other than U.S. and Canada models, follow the wire harness from the left handlebar switch to the front of the steering stem. Locate the electrical connectors (**Figure 155**) and disconnect them.

2C. On 2002-2003 U.S. and Canada models, follow the wire harness from the left handlebar switch to the front left side of the throttle body assembly. Locate the 9-pin electrical connector (**Figure 156**) and disconnect it.

2D. On 2002-2003, other than U.S. and Canada models, follow the wire harness from the left handlebar switch to the front left side of the throttle body assembly. Locate the 10-pin electrical connector (**Figure 156**) and disconnect it.

3. Remove or cut any clamps securing the switch wiring harness. Do not cut the wiring harness.

4. Remove the handlebar switch housing screws (**Figure 157**) and open the switch assembly (A, **Figure 158**). On 1998-2001 models, disconnect the choke cable end from the choke lever (B, **Figure 158**).

5. Remove the switch assembly from the handlebar.

6. Remove the wiring harness through the frame, then remove the switch housing from the handlebar.

7. Install the *new* switch housing, making sure to route the wiring harness along its original path.

8. Mount the left side handlebar switch housing onto the handlebar as follows:

    a. Install the left handlebar switch and align the switch projection with the hole in the handlebar. Install the screws and tighten securely.

    b. On 1998-2001 models, install the switch housing over the choke lever.

    c. Insert the pin on the switch housing into the hole in the handlebar (**Figure 159**). Try to twist the switch; it must not turn.

9. Install the rear switch housing screws and tighten both screws securely.

10. Reconnect the switch housing electrical connectors.

11. Start the engine and check the operation of each switch.

12A. On 1998-2001 models, install the left side faring as described in Chapter Sixteen.

12B. On 2002-2003 models, install the air filter housing and fuel tank as described in Chapter Nine.

WARNING
Do not ride the motorcycle until each switch function is working properly.

Right Handlebar Switch Housing Replacement

The right handlebar switch housing contains the starter button, engine stop, and on U.K. models, the lighting switch.

NOTE
The individual switches are not available separately. If one switch is dam-

10

aged, replace the switch housing assembly. On some models, the front brake light switch wires may be included in the wiring harness for the right handlebar switch. If necessary, disconnect them from the brake lever switch.

1. Remove the fuel tank and air filter housing as described in Chapter Eight or Chapter Nine.

NOTE
Figure 160 *is shown with the carburetor assembly removed to better illustrate the step.*

2A. On 1998-2001 U.S. and Canada models, follow the wire harness from the right handlebar switch to the front right side of the carburetor assembly. Locate the 6-pin electrical connector (**Figure 160**) and disconnect it.

2B. On 1998-2001, other than U.S. and Canada models, follow the wire harness from the right handlebar switch to the front right side of the carburetor assembly. Locate the 6-pin and 3-pin electrical connectors and disconnect them.

NOTE
Figure 161 *does not point directly to the electrical connector, but to the electrical connector's location on the inside surface of the frame rail.*

2C. On 2002-2003 U.S. and Canada models, follow the wire harness from the right handlebar switch to the front right side of the throttle body assembly. Locate the 6-pin electrical connector (**Figure 161**) and disconnect it.

2D. On 2002-2003, other than U.S. and Canada models, follow the wire harness from the right handlebar switch to the front right side of the throttle body assembly. Locate the 8-pin electrical connector (**Figure 161**) and disconnect it.

3. Disconnect the brake switch wire connector (**Figure 162**) at the brake light switch.

4. Remove or cut any clamps securing the switch wiring harness to the handlebar. Do not cut the wiring harness.

5. Remove the handlebar switch housing screws (A, **Figure 163**) and separate the switch housing (B) from around the handlebar and throttle grip.

6. Remove the wiring harness through the frame then remove the switch housing from the handlebar.

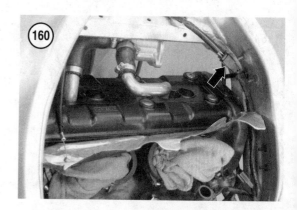

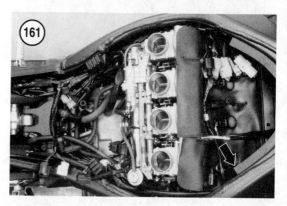

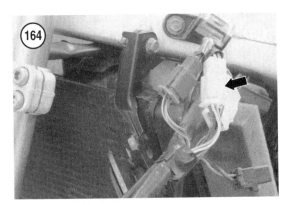

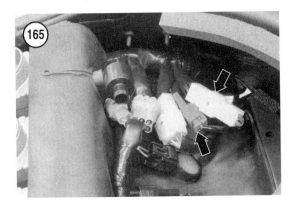

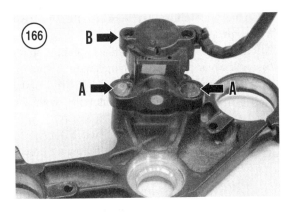

halves around the handlebar. Try to twist the switch; it must not turn.

b. Install the front and rear switch housing screws and tighten securely.

9. Reconnect the switch housing electrical connectors.

10. Install the air filter housing and fuel tank as described in Chapter Eight or Chapter Nine.

11. Start the engine and check the operation of each switch.

WARNING
Do not ride the motorcycle until each switch and both throttle cables are working properly.

Ignition Switch Replacement

1. Remove the left side faring and front fairing as described in Chapter Sixteen.

2. On 2002-2003 models, remove the fuel tank and air filter housing as described in Chapter Nine.

3A. On 1999-2001 models, disconnect the ignition switch 4-pin electrical connector (**Figure 164**) from the main harness.

3B. On 2002-2003 models, disconnect the two 2-pin electrical connectors (**Figure 165**) from the main harness.

4. Remove the upper fork bridge as described under *Steering Head And Stem* in Chapter Thirteen.

5. Drill out and remove the shear bolts (A, **Figure 166**) securing the ignition switch (B) to the bottom surface of the upper fork bridge.

6. Remove the ignition switch and wiring harness.

7. Install *new* shear bolts securing the ignition switch. Tighten the bolts until the heads shear off.

8. Install the upper fork bridge as described in Chapter Thirteen.

9. Check the operation of the ignition switch.

7. Install the *new* switch housing, making sure to route the wiring harness along its original path.

NOTE
There must be 2 mm (0.08 in.) clearance between the front master cylinder assembly and the switch housing.

8. Install the right side handlebar switch housing as follows:

a. Align the switch housing locating pin with the hole in the handlebar and close the switch

Clutch Interlock Switch Testing/Replacement

The clutch interlock switch is mounted in the clutch lever mounting bracket.

1. Disconnect the two electrical connectors (**Figure 167**) at the clutch interlock switch.

2. Connect an ohmmeter across the two clutch interlock switch terminals.

3. Read the ohmmeter scale while pulling in and then releasing the clutch lever. Note the following:

a. There must be continuity with the clutch lever pulled in and no continuity with the lever released.

b. Replace the clutch interlock switch if it fails to operate as described.

4. Remove the clutch interlock switch mounting screw and clutch switch.

5. Install a *new* clutch interlock switch by reversing these removal steps.

Front Brake Light Switch Testing/Replacement

The front brake switch (**Figure 162**) is mounted on the front master cylinder assembly.

1. Disconnect the two electrical connectors at the front brake light switch.

2. Connect an ohmmeter across the two front brake light switch terminals.

3. Read the ohmmeter scale while pulling in and releasing the front brake lever. Note the following:

a. There must be continuity with the front brake lever pulled in and no continuity with the lever released.

b. Replace the front brake light switch if it fails to operate as described.

4. Remove the brake switch mounting screw and brake switch.

5. Reconnect the two electrical connectors at the front brake light switch.

6. Turn on the ignition switch and apply the front brake lever. Make sure the brake light illuminates.

WARNING
Do not ride the motorcycle until the rear brake light and front brake light switch work correctly.

Rear Brake Light Switch

Testing

The rear brake switch is mounted on the rear brake pedal assembly.

1. Remove the seat and the rear cowl as described in Chapter Sixteen.

2. Remove the fuel tank as described in Chapter Eight or Chapter Nine.

3. Follow the rear brake light switch wires from the switch to the 2-pin brown electrical connector (yellow and brown wires) on the right side of the frame. Disconnect the connector (**Figure 168**, typical).

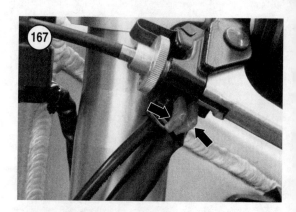

4. Connect an ohmmeter between the two rear brake light switch terminals.

5. Read the ohmmeter scale while applying and releasing the rear brake pedal. Note the following:

a. There must be continuity with the rear brake pedal applied and no continuity with the pedal released.

b. Replace the rear brake light switch if it fails to operate as described in the following procedure.

WARNING
Do not ride the motorcycle until the rear brake light and switch work correctly.

6. Install the fuel tank as described in Chapter Eight or Chapter Nine.

7. Install the rear cowl and seat as described in Chapter Sixteen.

Replacement

1. Remove the seat and the rear cowl as described in Chapter Sixteen.

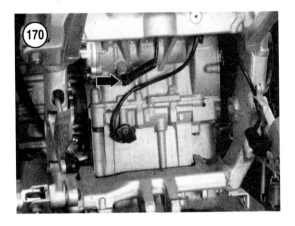

Neutral Switch

Testing

The neutral switch is mounted on the back surface of the upper crankcase directly above the speed sensor.

1. Support the motorcycle on level ground.

2. Block the front wheel so the motorcycle will not roll in either direction while the rear wheel is off the ground on the jack or swing arm stand.

3. Shift the transmission into neutral.

4. On the left side of the lower crankcase, disconnect the electrical connector (**Figure 170**) from the neutral switch.

5. Connect an ohmmeter to the neutral switch terminal and to a good engine ground.

6. Read the ohmmeter scale with the transmission in neutral, and then in gear. Note the following:

   a. The ohmmeter must read continuity with the transmission in neutral.

   b. The ohmmeter must read infinity with the transmission in gear.

   c. If either reading is incorrect, check the wiring harness for damage or dirty or loose-fitting terminals. If the wiring harness is good, replace the neutral switch.

7. Reconnect the wire onto the switch.

8. Start the engine and check the operation of the neutral switch indicator light with the transmission in neutral and in gear.

Replacement

1. Support the motorcycle on level ground.

2. Block the front wheel so the motorcycle will not roll in either direction while the rear wheel is off ground on the jack or swing arm stand.

3. Shift the transmission into neutral.

4. On the left side of the lower crankcase, disconnect the electrical connector (**Figure 170**) from the neutral switch.

NOTE
The following steps are shown with the engine removed from the frame to better illustrate the steps.

5. Unscrew the neutral switch and washer (**Figure 171**) from the lower crankcase.

6. Make sure the sealing washer (**Figure 172**) is installed on the neutral switch. Install the neutral

2. Remove the fuel tank as described in Chapter Eight or Chapter Nine.

3. Follow the rear brake light switch wires from the switch to the 2-pin brown electrical connector (yellow and brown wires) on the right side of the frame. Disconnect the connector (**Figure 168**, typical).

4. Refer to Chapter Fifteen and partially remove the rear brake pedal to gain access to the backside of the brake pedal assembly.

5. Disconnect the return spring (A, **Figure 169**) from the rear brake light switch and remove the switch (B) from its mounting bracket.

6. Install a new switch onto the bracket.

7. Reconnect the spring and the rear brake light switch electrical connector.

8. Adjust the rear brake light switch as described in Chapter Three.

9. Turn the ignition switch on and apply the rear brake pedal. Make sure the rear brake light operates correctly.

10

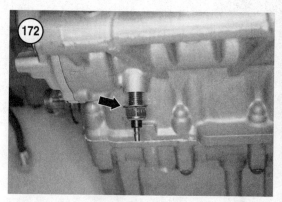

switch into the lower crankcase and tighten to 20 N•m (15 ft.-lbs.).

7. Install the electrical connector (**Figure 170**) onto the neutral switch. Push it on and make sure it is seated correctly.

Sidestand Switch Testing/Replacement

The sidestand switch is mounted on the outer surface of the sidestand.

1. Support the motorcycle on level ground.

2. Block the front wheel so the motorcycle will not roll in either direction while on the jack or swing arm stand.

3. Remove the fuel tank as described in Chapter Eight or Chapter Nine.

4. Trace the sidestand switch wire from the switch to the blue 2-pin connector. Disconnect the connector.

5. Connect an ohmmeter across the sidestand switch terminals in the connector.

6. Operate the sidestand in its up and down positions while reading the ohmmeter scale. Note the following:

   a. The ohmmeter must read continuity with the sidestand up.

   b. The ohmmeter must read infinity with the sidestand down.

   c. If either reading is incorrect, check the wiring harness for damage or dirty or loose-fitting terminals. If the wiring harness is good, replace the sidestand switch.

7. Release the sidestand switch wiring harness from the frame hooks.

8. Remove the bolts (**Figure 173**) securing the switch to the sidestand assembly. Remove the switch from the frame.

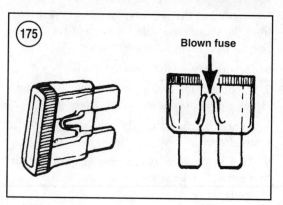

Blown fuse

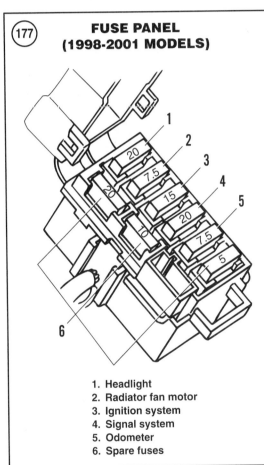

**FUSE PANEL
(1998-2001 MODELS)**

1. Headlight
2. Radiator fan motor
3. Ignition system
4. Signal system
5. Odometer
6. Spare fuses

9. Clean the switch mounting area on the sidestand.

10. Align the switch pin with the hole in the sidestand and install the sidestand switch. Tighten the bolts securely.

11. Install the sidestand assembly and tighten the mounting bolts securely.

12. Install the fuel tank as described in Chapter Eight or Chapter Nine.

FUSES

Whenever a fuse blows, determine the cause before replacing it. Usually, the trouble is a short circuit in the wiring. Worn-through insulation or a short to ground from a disconnected wire may cause this.

CAUTION
If replacing a fuse, make sure the ignition switch is turned off. This lessens the chance of a short circuit.

CAUTION
Never substitute any metal object for a fuse. Never use a higher amperage fuse than specified. An overload could cause a fire and the complete loss of the motorcycle.

Main Fuse

On 1998-2001 models, the 30-amp main fuse is mounted on the starter relay switch located underneath the seat. On 2002-2003 models, the main 50-amp fuse is located next to the battery positive terminal.

To check or replace the main fuse, perform the following:

1. Turn the ignition switch off.

2. Remove the rider's seat as described in Chapter Sixteen.

3A. On 1998-2001 models, perform the following:
   a. Remove the cover (**Figure 174**) from the front main fuse. The rear fuse is a spare main fuse.
   b. Remove the main fuse and inspect it. Replace the fuse if it has blown (**Figure 175**).

3B. On 2002-2003 models, perform the following:
   a. Remove the cover from the fuse.
   b. Remove the main fuse (**Figure 176**) and inspect it. Replace the fuse if it has blown (**Figure 175**).

4. Install the *new* main fuse and cover.

5. Reinstall the rider's seat as described in Chapter Sixteen.

Fuse Box

Refer to **Figure 177** and **Figure 178**.

10

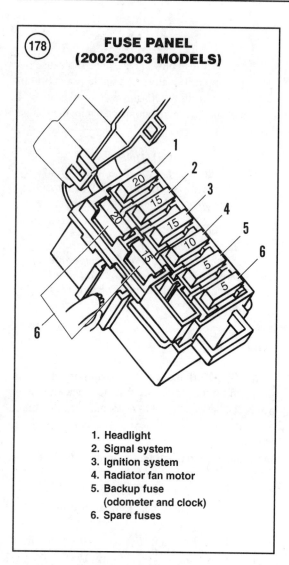

**FUSE PANEL
(2002-2003 MODELS)**

1. Headlight
2. Signal system
3. Ignition system
4. Radiator fan motor
5. Backup fuse
   (odometer and clock)
6. Spare fuses

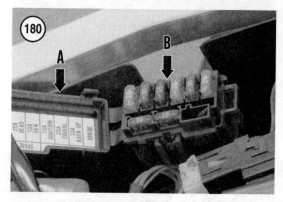

On 1998-2001 models, the fuse box is mounted underneath the rider's seat. On 2002-2003 models, the fuse box is located under the left side fairing inner panel (**Figure 179**), as well as the fuel injection fuse mounted on the starter relay switch.

To identify an individual fuse and its amperage, refer to the decal mounted on the underside of the fuse box cover and the wiring diagram at the end of this manual.

If a fuse blows, perform the following:

1. Turn the ignition switch off.

2A. On 1998-2001 models, perform the following:

  a. Remove the seat as described in Chapter Sixteen.

  b. Open the fuse box cover (A, **Figure 180**).

  c. Remove and inspect the fuse (B, **Figure 180**). Replace the fuse if it has blown (**Figure 175**).

2B. On 2002-2003 models, perform the following:

  a. Remove the seat and the left side fairing inner panel as described in Chapter Sixteen.

  b. Open the fuse box cover (**Figure 181**).

  c. Remove and inspect the fuse (**Figure 182**).

  d. To remove the fuel injection fuse, remove the cover from the fuse then remove the front fuse and inspect it. The rear fuse is a spare fuse.

  e. Replace the fuse if it has blown (**Figure 175**).

NOTE
There are spare fuses stored in the fuse box.

3. Close the fuse box cover.

4. Install the seat and the left side fairing inner panel as described in Chapter Sixteen.

WIRING DIAGRAMS

Color wiring diagrams for all models are located at the end of this manual.

Table 1 BATTERY SPECIFICATIONS

Type	Maintenance free (sealed)*
Capacity	12 volt 10 amp hour
Voltage (@ 68° F/20° C)	
Fully charged	13.0-13.2 volts
Need charging	Below 12.8 volts
Charging current	
Normal	0.9 amps at 5-10 hours
Quick	4.0 amps at 1 hour
Maximum current draw	Less than 0.1 mA

* A maintenance free battery is installed on all models. Because this type of battery requires a high-voltage charging system, do not install a standard type battery.

10

Table 2 ALTERNATOR AND CHARGING SYSTEM SPECIFICATIONS

Alternator	
Type	AC magneto
Model number	
1998-2001 models	F4T361 (Mitsubishi)
2002-2003 models	F4T471 (Mitsubishi)
Normal output	
1998-1999 models	14 volts/23.5 amps @ 5000 rpm
2000-2001 models	14 volts/365 watts @ 5000 rpm
2002-2003 models	14 volts/32 amps @ 5000 rpm
Stator coil resistance	
1998-2001 models	0.45-0.55 ohm*
2002-2003 models	0.19-0.23 ohm*
Voltage regulator/rectifier	
Model number	
1998-2001 models	SH650A-12
2002-2003 models	FH001
Regulator no-load regulated voltage	14.1-14.9 volts
Rectifier capacity	
1998-2001 models	18 amps
2002-2003 models	35 amps
Rectifier withstand voltage	200 volts

* Test must be made at an ambient temperature of 20° C (68° F). Do not test when the engine or component is hot.

Table 3 MAINTENANCE-FREE BATTERY VOLTAGE READINGS

State of charge	Voltage reading
100%	13.0-13.2
75%	12.8
50%	12.5
25%	12.2
0%	12.0 volts or less

Table 4 IGNITION SYSTEM SPECIFICATIONS (1998-2001 MODELS)

Type	Transistorized coil ignition
Ignition timing	
1998-1999 models	5° BTDC @ 1100 rpm
2000-2001 models	5° BTDC @ 1050 rpm
Timing coil resistance	248-372 ohms
Transistorized coil ignition unit	
1998-1999 models	
49-state and Canada	TNDF49 (Denso)
California	TNDF50 (Denso)
2000-2001 models	
49-state and Canada	TNDF58 (Denso)
California	TNDF57 (Denso)
Spark plug cap resistance	10,000 ohms
Ignition coil	
Model number	J0313 (Denso)
Primary resistance	1.87-2.53 ohms
Secondary resistance	12,000-18,000 ohms

Table 5 IGNITION SYSTEM SPECIFICATIONS (2002-2003 MODELS)

Type	Transistorized coil ignition (digital)
Ignition timing	5° BTDC @ 1050 rpm
Crankshaft position sensor resistance	248-372 ohms
Transistorized coil ignition unit	
49-state and Canada	F8T917 (Mitsubishi)
California	F8T918 (Mitsubishi)
Ignition coil	
Model number	F6T558 (Mitsubishi)
Primary resistance	1.19-1.61 ohms
Secondary resistance	8500-11,500 ohms

Table 6 STARTER SPECIFICATIONS

Item	New mm (in.)	Service limit mm (in.)
Starter model number		
1998-1999 models	SM-13 (Mitsuba)	
2000-2003 models	5JJ (Yamaha)	
Starter brush length		
1998-1999 models	10 (0.40)	5 (0.20)
2000-2003 models	9.8 (0.39)	3.65 (0.14)
Commutator outer diameter		
1998-1999 models	28 (1.10)	27 (1.06)
2000-2003 models	24.5 (0.96)	23.5 (0.93)
Mica under cut		
1998-1999 models	0.7 (0.03)	—
2000-2003 models	1.5 (0.06)	—

Table 7 REPLACEMENT BULBS

Item	Watt, quantity
Headlight-halogen (high/low beam)	60/55W (2)
Position light (2000-2003 models)	5 W (2)
Front turn signal (running light)	
U.S. and Canada	27/8 W (2)
U.K.	21 W (2)
Rear turn signal	
U.S. and Canada	27 W (2)
U.K.	21 W (2)
Tail/brake light	5/21 W
Instrument illumination light	
1998-1999 models	1.4 W (2)
License plate light (2002-2003 models)	5 W

Table 8 SENSOR TEST READINGS

Item	Test readings
Throttle position sensor	
1998-2001 models (standard resistance)	4000-6000 ohms
2002-2003 models	
Standard resistance	0 to 3500-6500 ohms
Maximum resistance	3500-6500 ohms
Coolant sender (1998-1999 models)	
At 176° F (80° C)	47.5-56.8 ohms
At 239° F (115° C)	16.5-20.5 ohms
Coolant sensor (2002-2003 models)	
At 32° F (0° C)	5210-6370 ohms
At 176° F (80° C)	2900-3500 ohms
Coolant thermo switch (1998-1999 models)	
0-208.4° F (0-98° C)	No continuity
208.4-221° F (98-105° C)	Continuity
Coolant thermo unit (2000-2001 models)	
122° F (50° C)	9700-11,400 ohms
176° F (80° C)	3400-4000 ohms
221° F (105° C)	1600-1900 ohms
248° F (120° C)	1100-1200 ohms

10

Table 9 FUSE SPECIFICATIONS

Main fuse	
1998-2001 models	30 amp
2002-2003 models	50 amp
Fuel injection system fuse (2002-2003 models)	15 amp
Sub-fuse (1998-1999 models)	
Headlight	20 amp
Signal system	20 amp
Ignition system	15 amp
Radiator fan	7.5 amp
Backup (odometer)	7.5 amp

(continued)

Table 9 FUSE SPECIFICATIONS (continued)

Sub-fuse (2000-2001 models)	
Headlight	20 amp
Signal system	20 amp
Ignition system	15 amp
Radiator fan	10 amp
Backup (odometer)	10 amp
Sub-fuse (2002-2003 models)	
Headlight	20 amp
Signal system	15 amp
Ignition system	15 amp
Radiator fan	10 amp
Backup (odometer and clock)	5 amp

Table 10 ELECTRICAL SYSTEM TORQUE SPECIFICATIONS

Item	N•m	in.-lb.	ft.-lb.
Alternator			
Rotor bolt			
1998-1999 models	95	–	68
2000-2001 models	65	–	47
2002-2003 models	Refer to text procedure		
Stator bolts			
1998-2001 models	10	88	–
2002-2003 models	14	124	
Cover bolts	12	106	–
Clutch cable bracket bolts	12	106	
Coolant sensor* (2002-2003 models)	18	–	13
Coolant sender* (1998-1999 models)	15	133	–
Coolant thermo switch*			
(1998-1999 models)	23	–	17
Coolant thermo unit			
(2000-2001 models)	23	–	17
Cooling fan motor screws	9	80	–
Ignition switch bolts	25	–	18
Neutral switch	20	–	15
Oil level sensor screws	10	88	–
Timing coil			
Rotor bolt	60	–	44
Cover bolts	12	106	–
Coil Allen bolts	10	88	–
Timing mark inspection bolt	15	133	–

*Apply sealant to sensor threads.

COOLING SYSTEM

This chapter describes the repair and replacement of cooling system components. **Table 1** and **Table 2** at the end of the chapter list cooling system specifications. For electrical test procedures, refer to Chapter Ten. For routine cooling system maintenance, refer to Chapter Three.

COOLING SYSTEM INSPECTION

The cooling system consists of the radiator, water pump, radiator cap, thermostat, electric cooling fan and coolant reserve tank.

> *WARNING*
> *Do not remove the radiator cap (Figure 1) when the engine is hot. The coolant is very hot and is under pressure. Severe scalding could result if the coolant contacts skin.*

> *WARNING*
> *The radiator fan and fan switch are connected directly to the battery. Whenever the engine is warm or hot, the fan may start even with the ignition switch turned OFF. Never work around the fan or touch the fan until the engine is completely cool.*

> *CAUTION*
> *Drain and flush the cooling system at the interval listed in Chapter Three. Refill with a mixture of ethylene glycol antifreeze (formulated for aluminum engines) and distilled water. Do not reuse the old coolant, as it deteriorates with use. Do not operate the cooling system with only distilled water, even in climates where antifreeze protection is not required; doing so will promote internal engine corro-*

sion. Refer to **Coolant Change** *in Chapter Three.*

> *NOTE*
> *Waste antifreeze is toxic and may never be discharged into storm sewers, septic systems, or onto the ground. Place used antifreeze in the original container and dispose of it according to local regulations. Do not store coolant where it is accessible to children or pets.*

It is important to keep the coolant level to the FULL mark on the coolant reserve tank. Refer to **Figure 2** for 1998-2001 models or A, **Figure 3** for 2002-2003 models.

1. Check the level with the engine at normal operating temperature and the motorcycle held upright.

2. If the level is low, remove the reservoir tank cap and add coolant to the reserve tank, not to the radiator. Refer to **Figure 4** for 1998-2001 models or **Figure 5** for 2002-2003 models.

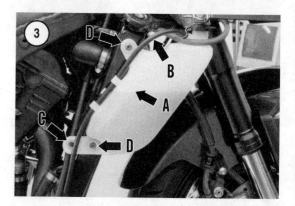

3. Check the coolant hoses and clamps for looseness or damage.

4. Start the engine and allow it to idle. If steam is observed at the muffler, a head gasket might be damaged. If enough coolant leaks into the cylinder, the cylinder could hydrolock, thus preventing the engine from being cranked. Coolant may also be present in the engine oil. If the oil on the dipstick is foamy or milky-looking, there is coolant in the oil. If so, correct the problem before returning the motorcycle to service.

> *CAUTION*
> *If the engine oil is contaminated with coolant, change the oil and filter after performing the repair.*

5. Check the radiator for clogged or damaged fins. Refer radiator repair to a Yamaha dealership or a radiator repair shop.

6. Check all coolant hoses for cracks or damage. Replace all questionable parts. Make sure the hose clamps are tight, but not so tight that they cut the hoses. Refer to *Hoses and Hose Clamps* in this chapter.

7. When troubleshooting the cooling system for loss of coolant, pressure test the system as described in Chapter Three.

HOSES AND HOSE CLAMPS

Hoses deteriorate with age. Replace them periodically or whenever they show signs of cracking or leakage. To be safe, replace the hoses every two years. The spray of hot coolant from a cracked hose can injure the rider and passenger. Loss of coolant can also cause the engine to overheat and cause damage.

Whenever any component of the cooling system is removed, inspect the hoses and clamps to determine if replacement is necessary.

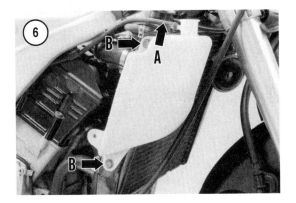

Inspection

1. With the engine cool, check the cooling hoses for brittleness, hardness or cracks. Replace hoses in this condition.

2. With the engine hot, examine the hoses for swelling along the entire hose length. Replace hoses that show signs of swelling.

3. Check the area around each hose clamp. Signs of rust around clamps indicate possible hose leakage from a damaged or over-tightened clamp.

Replacement

Perform hose replacement when the engine is cool.

1. Drain the cooling system as described under *Coolant Change* in Chapter Three.

2. Loosen the hose clamps from the hose to be replaced. Slide the clamps along the hose and out of the way.

3. Twist the hose end to break the seal and remove it from the connecting joint. If the hose has been on for some time, it may have become fused to the joint. If so, insert a small screwdriver or pick tool

between the hose and joint. While working the tool around the joint, carefully pry the hose loose with a thin screwdriver.

> *CAUTION*
> *Do not apply excessive force to a hose when attempting to remove it. Many of the hose connectors are fragile and can be easily damaged.*

4. Examine the connecting joint for cracks or other damage. Repair or replace parts as required. Remove rust and corrosion with a wire brush.

5. Inspect the hose clamps; replace if necessary. The hose clamps are as important as the hoses. If they do not hold the hose in place tightly, coolant will leak.

6. Slide the hose clamp over the outside of the hose and then install the hose over its connecting joint. Make sure the hose clears all obstructions and is routed properly.

> *NOTE*
> *If it is difficult to install a hose on a joint, apply antifreeze to the end of the hose where it seats onto its connecting joint. This usually aids installation.*

7. With the hose positioned correctly on the joint, position the clamp back away from end of the hose slightly. Tighten the clamp securely, but not so much that the hose is damaged.

> *NOTE*
> *If installing coolant hoses onto the engine while it is removed from the frame, check the position of the hose clamp(s) to make sure it can be loosened when installed in the frame.*

8. Refill the cooling system as described under *Coolant Change* in Chapter Three. Start the engine; check for leaks. Retighten hose clamps as necessary.

COOLANT RESERVE TANK

Removal/Installation (1998-2001 Models)

1. Park the motorcycle on level ground.

2. Remove the right side fairing (Chapter Sixteen).

3. Remove the reserve tank cap (**Figure 4**) and siphon tube.

4. Disconnect the breather hose (A, **Figure 6**) from the reserve tank.

11

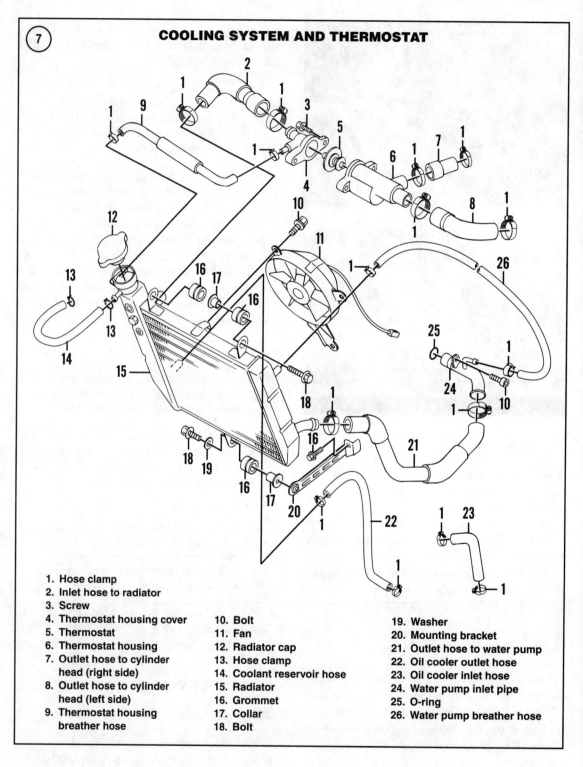

COOLING SYSTEM AND THERMOSTAT

1. Hose clamp
2. Inlet hose to radiator
3. Screw
4. Thermostat housing cover
5. Thermostat
6. Thermostat housing
7. Outlet hose to cylinder head (right side)
8. Outlet hose to cylinder head (left side)
9. Thermostat housing breather hose
10. Bolt
11. Fan
12. Radiator cap
13. Hose clamp
14. Coolant reservoir hose
15. Radiator
16. Grommet
17. Collar
18. Bolt
19. Washer
20. Mounting bracket
21. Outlet hose to water pump
22. Oil cooler outlet hose
23. Oil cooler inlet hose
24. Water pump inlet pipe
25. O-ring
26. Water pump breather hose

5. Remove the reserve tank mounting bolts (B, **Figure 6**).

6. Drain the coolant from the reserve tank into the drain pan.

7. Rinse the inside of the coolant reserve tank with water and allow it to drain.

8. Install the coolant reserve tank by reversing these removal steps while noting the following:

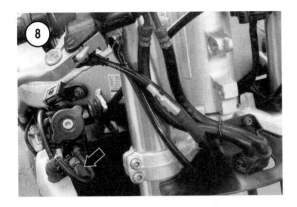

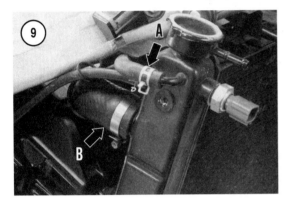

a. Install the mounting bolt. Do not overtighten.

b. Refill the coolant reserve tank with a 50:50 mixture of antifreeze and distilled water as described in Chapter Three.

c. Check the hoses for leaks.

Removal/Installation (2002-2003 Models)

1. Park the motorcycle on level ground.

2. Remove the right side fairing as described in Chapter Sixteen.

3. Remove the reserve tank cap (**Figure 5**) and siphon tube.

4. Disconnect the breather hose (B, **Figure 3**) from the reserve tank.

5. Unhook the clutch cable from the reserve tank tab (C, **Figure 3**).

6. Remove the reserve tank mounting bolts (D, **Figure 3**) and remove the tank.

7. Drain the coolant from the reserve tank into the drain pan.

8. Rinse the inside of the coolant reserve tank with water and allow it to drain.

9. Install the coolant reserve tank by reversing these removal steps while noting the following:

a. Install the mounting bolt. Do not overtighten.

b. Refill the coolant reserve tank with a 50:50 mixture of antifreeze and distilled water as described in Chapter Three.

c. Check the hoses for leaks.

RADIATOR

WARNING
The radiator fan and fan switch are connected to the battery. Whenever the engine is warm or hot, the fan may start with the ignition switch turned off. Never work around the fan or touch the fan until the engine is completely cool. If work is required in the fan area when the engine is hot, disconnect the negative battery cable.

Removal/Installation

The radiator and fan are removed as an assembly. Refer to **Figure 7**.

1. Park the motorcycle on level ground. Support the rear of the motorcycle securely on a swing arm motorcycle stand.

2. Disconnect the negative battery cable at the battery as described in Chapter Ten.

3. Remove the fuel tank as described in Chapter Eight or Chapter Nine.

4. Remove both side fairings and the bottom cowl as described in Chapter Sixteen.

5. Drain the cooling system as described in Chapter Three.

6. On 1998-1999 models, on the front right side, disconnect the electrical connector from the temperature sender. Also remove the screw and disconnect the ground lead.

7. On 1998-2001 models, on the front right side, disconnect the electrical connector from the thermo switch/unit (**Figure 8**). Also remove the screw and disconnect the ground lead.

8. Remove the coolant reserve tank as described in this chapter.

9. On the right side, perform the following:

a. Disconnect the thermostat housing breather hose (A, **Figure 9**).

b. Disconnect the upper hose (B, **Figure 9**) from the radiator.

11

c. Disconnect the oil cooler outlet hose (**Figure 10**) from the lower fitting on the radiator.

10. On the left side, perform the following:

a. Disconnect the water pump breather hose (**Figure 11**) from the radiator.

b. Disconnect the lower hose (**Figure 12**) from the radiator.

c. Disconnect the radiator fan electrical connector. Refer to **Figure 13** for 1998-2001 models or **Figure 14** for 2002-2003 models.

11. On the right side, remove the lower bolt and washer (**Figure 15**) securing the bottom of the radiator to the lower mounting bracket. Do not lose the collar within the rubber bushing in the radiator mount.

12A. On 1998-2001 models, perform the following:

a. Remove the upper bolt and washer (A, **Figure 16**) securing the top of the radiator and the horn bracket to the frame mount.

b. Move the horn (B, **Figure 16**) and electrical connectors out of the way.

12B. On 2002-2003 models, perform the following:

a. Remove the bolts (**Figure 17**) securing the electrical connector assembly to the side of the radiator. Move the assembly out of the way to gain access to the bolt.

b. Remove the upper bolt and washer (**Figure 18**) securing the top of the radiator to the frame mount.

13. Carefully move the radiator toward the right side and disengage it from the upper mounting lug (**Figure 19**) on the right side.

14. Carefully remove the radiator down and out of the frame. Do not make contact with the lower frame bracket. Remove the radiator.

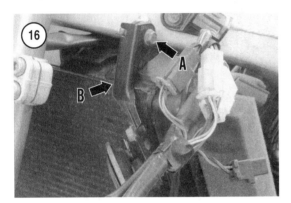

15. Install by reversing these removal steps, plus the following:

    a. Make sure the rubber grommets and flange collars are in place in the radiator mounting brackets. These help to prevent road shocks and vibration from damaging the mounting brackets.

    b. When installing the radiator, align the grommet on top of the radiator with the mounting boss on the right side of the frame.

    c. On 1998-2001 models, secure the lower hose to the oil cooler with a tie-wrap (**Figure 20**) to keep the hose away from the exhaust pipe.

    d. Make sure all electrical connectors are free of corrosion, then reconnect.

    e. Refill the cooling system with the recommended type and quantity of coolant as described in Chapter Three.

    f. Check the hoses for leaks.

Inspection

1. Inspect the radiator cap top and bottom seals (**Figure 21**) for deterioration or damage. Check the

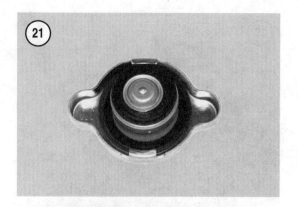

spring for damage. Pressure test the radiator cap as described under *Cooling System Inspection* in Chapter Three. Replace the radiator cap if necessary.

2. Flush off the exterior of the radiator with a water hose on low pressure. Spray both the front and the back to remove all dirt and debris. Carefully use a whiskbroom or stiff paintbrush to remove any stubborn debris.

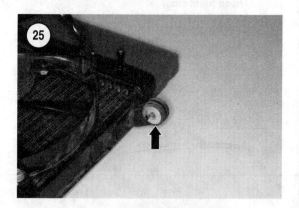

> *CAUTION*
> *Do not press too hard on the cooling fins and tubes, as they may be damaged and cause a leak.*

3. Carefully straighten out any bent cooling fins with a broad-tipped screwdriver.

4. Check for cracks or coolant leakage (usually a moss-green colored residue) at the filler neck (**Figure 22**), the various hose fittings (**Figure 23**) and both side tank seams (**Figure 24**).

5. Check the mounting bracket (**Figure 25**) and locating tab for cracks or damage.

6. To prevent oxidation to the radiator, touch up any area where the black paint is worn off. Use

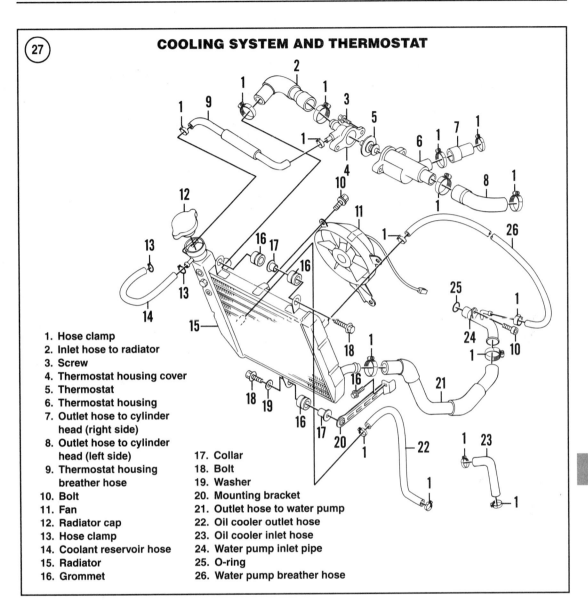

COOLING SYSTEM AND THERMOSTAT

27

1. Hose clamp
2. Inlet hose to radiator
3. Screw
4. Thermostat housing cover
5. Thermostat
6. Thermostat housing
7. Outlet hose to cylinder head (right side)
8. Outlet hose to cylinder head (left side)
9. Thermostat housing breather hose
10. Bolt
11. Fan
12. Radiator cap
13. Hose clamp
14. Coolant reservoir hose
15. Radiator
16. Grommet
17. Collar
18. Bolt
19. Washer
20. Mounting bracket
21. Outlet hose to water pump
22. Oil cooler outlet hose
23. Oil cooler inlet hose
24. Water pump inlet pipe
25. O-ring
26. Water pump breather hose

good-quality spray paint. Do not apply heavy coats, as this cuts down on the cooling efficiency of the radiator.

COOLING FAN

The cooling fan is mounted on the backside of the radiator.

Testing

To test the fan motor and switch, refer to *Cooling System Switches and Sensors* in Chapter Ten.

Removal/Installation

Refer to **Figure 7**.

1. Remove the radiator as described in this chapter.
2. Remove the screws (**Figure 26**) and then remove the fan assembly from the radiator.
3. Install by reversing these removal steps.

THERMOSTAT

Removal/Installation

Refer to **Figure 27**.

1. Drain the cooling system as described under *Coolant Change* in Chapter Three.

2A. On 1998-2001 models, remove the carburetor assembly as described in Chapter Eight.

2B. On 2002-2003 models, remove the throttle body assembly as described in Chapter Nine.

> *NOTE*
> *If necessary, loosen the hose clamp and disconnect the hose from the thermostat housing cover. The radiator is removed in this procedure to better illustrate the steps.*

3. Remove the bolts securing the thermostat housing cover (**Figure 28**). Lift off and remove the thermostat housing cover from the housing.

4. Remove the thermostat and the rubber seal (A, **Figure 29**).

5. If necessary, test the thermostat as described in this chapter.

6. Install a *new* rubber seal onto the thermostat.

7. Install the thermostat and rubber seal into the thermostat housing. Align the thermostat with the air bleed hole (B, **Figure 29**) facing upward.

8. Install the thermostat housing cover onto the thermostat housing. Tighten the bolts to 10 N•m (88 in.-lb.).

9. Refill the cooling system with the recommended type and quantity of coolant as described under *Coolant Change* in Chapter Three.

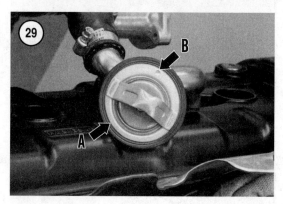

Inspection

Test the thermostat to ensure proper operation as follows:

> *NOTE*
> *Do not allow the thermometer or thermostat to touch the sides or bottom of the pan, or a false reading will result.*

1. Suspend the thermostat in a pan of water (**Figure 30**) and place a thermometer in the pan of water. Use a thermometer that is rated higher than the test temperature.

2. Gradually heat the water and continue to gently stir the water until it reaches the temperature specified in **Table 1**. At this temperature, the thermostat should start to open.

3. Replace the thermostat if it remains open at normal room temperature or stays closed after the spec-

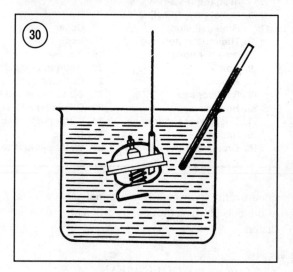

ified temperature has been reached during the test procedure. Make sure the replacement thermostat has the same temperature rating.

> *NOTE*
> *After the specified temperature is reached, it may take three to five minutes for the valve to open completely.*

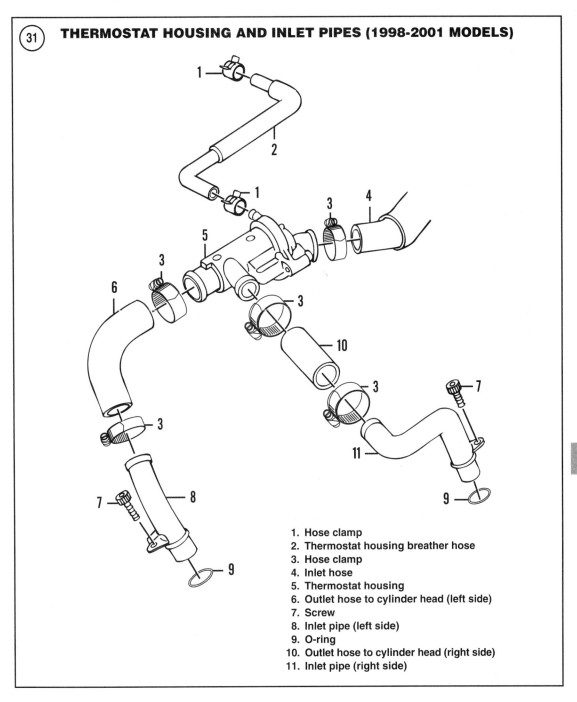

THERMOSTAT HOUSING AND INLET PIPES (1998-2001 MODELS)

(31)

1. Hose clamp
2. Thermostat housing breather hose
3. Hose clamp
4. Inlet hose
5. Thermostat housing
6. Outlet hose to cylinder head (left side)
7. Screw
8. Inlet pipe (left side)
9. O-ring
10. Outlet hose to cylinder head (right side)
11. Inlet pipe (right side)

11

THERMOSTAT HOUSING AND INLET PIPES

Removal/Installation

Refer to **Figure 31** and **Figure 32**.

1. Drain the cooling system as described under *Coolant Change* in Chapter Three.

2A. On 1998-2001 models, perform the following:

  a. Remove the carburetor assembly as described in Chapter Eight.

  b. Remove the ignition coil plate assembly as described in Chapter Ten.

2B. On 2002-2003 models, remove the throttle body assembly as described in Chapter Nine.

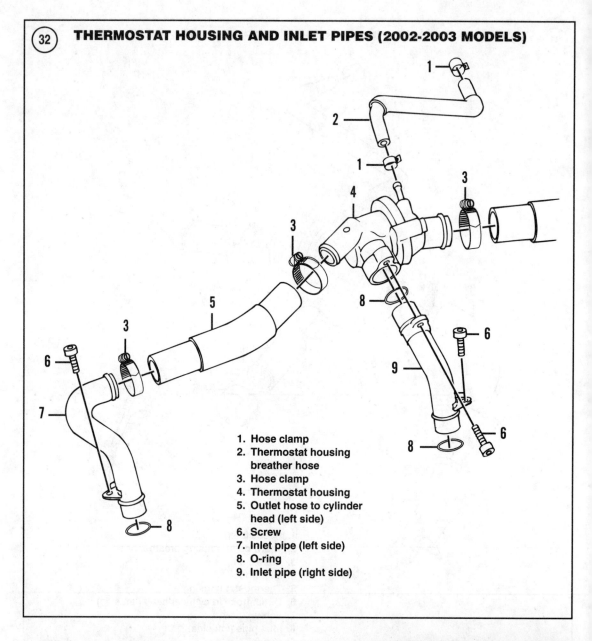

THERMOSTAT HOUSING AND INLET PIPES (2002-2003 MODELS)

1. Hose clamp
2. Thermostat housing breather hose
3. Hose clamp
4. Thermostat housing
5. Outlet hose to cylinder head (left side)
6. Screw
7. Inlet pipe (left side)
8. O-ring
9. Inlet pipe (right side)

3. Disconnect the breather hose (A, **Figure 33**) from the front of the radiator.

4. Loosen the hose clamp and disconnect the upper hose (B, **Figure 33**) from the radiator.

5. On 2002-2003 models, disconnect the coolant temperature sensor connector from the thermostat housing.

CAUTION
Make sure the spark plugs are still in place in the cylinder head. Some residual coolant will drain out of the

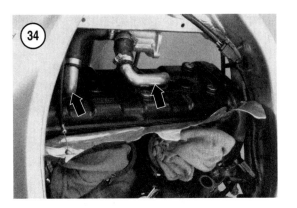

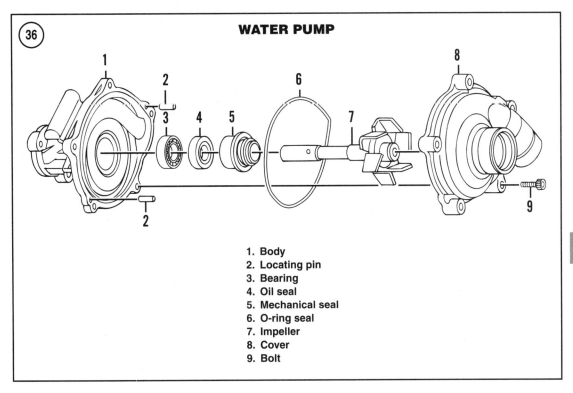

WATER PUMP

1. Body
2. Locating pin
3. Bearing
4. Oil seal
5. Mechanical seal
6. O-ring seal
7. Impeller
8. Cover
9. Bolt

thermostat housing as it is removed. Do not allow any coolant to enter the cylinder head.

6. Remove the 6-mm Allen screw securing each inlet pipe (**Figure 34**) to the cylinder head.

7. Pull the thermostat housing and inlet pipes straight up and out of the cylinder head and remove the assembly.

8. Inspect the thermostat housing and hoses (**Figure 35**) for damage and deterioration.

9. Install by reversing these removal steps while noting the following:

a. Use compressed air and blow away any coolant that may have drained into the spark plug receptacles.

b. Install a *new* O-ring onto the end of both inlet pipes and apply a light coat of lithium soap base grease to the O-rings.

c. Install the inlet pipes and tighten the screws to 10 N•m (88 in.-lb.).

WATER PUMP

The water pump/oil pump assembly (**Figure 36**) is mounted in the lower crankcase. The water pump

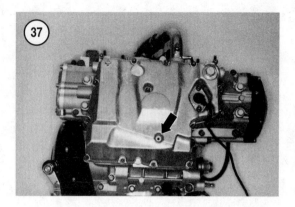

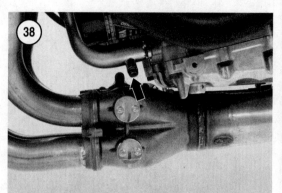

is an integral part of the oil pump and is removed as an assembly. The procedures in this section cover the water pump specific portion of the assembly. The oil pump, including removal and installation, is covered in Chapter Five.

Pre-inspection

There are two different seals within the water pump assembly. The mechanical seal rides against the impeller and seals the coolant portion of the pump, while the oil seal provides protection for the oil pump side of the assembly.

> *NOTE*
> *The pre-inspection step can be per-formed with the water pump installed on the engine.*

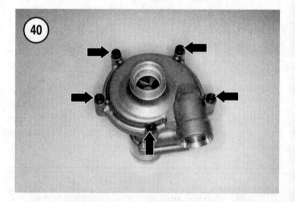

Check the water pump drain hole (**Figure 37**) in the base of the oil pan for leakage. If coolant leaks from the drain hole, the internal mechanical seal is damaged; replace the water pump mechanical seal. If there is no indication of coolant leakage from the inspection hole, pressure test the cooling system as described under *Cooling System Inspection* in Chapter Three.

Remove the bottom cowl as described in Chapter Sixteen. Check the drain bolt and sealing washer (**Figure 38**) on the coolant pipe at the front of the engine for leakage. If necessary, replace the sealing washer and tighten the bolt securely.

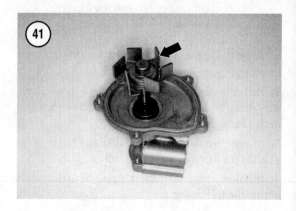

Removal/Installation

Refer to *Oil Pump/Water Pump* in Chapter Five.

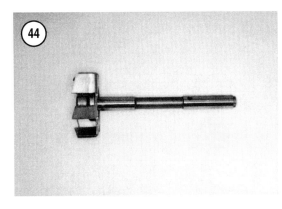

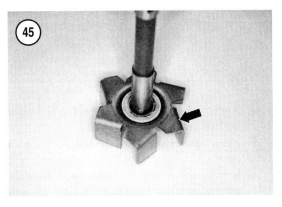

Disassembly/Inspection/Assembly

Replace all parts that exhibit wear. There are no specifications for the water pump components.

1. Remove the oil pump/water pump assembly as described in Chapter Five.

2. Check the weep hole (**Figure 39**) for indications of coolant leakage past the mechanical seal.

NOTE
The oil pump portion must be removed in order to remove the impeller from the body.

3. Disassemble the oil pump portion of the assembly as described in Chapter Five.

4. Remove the bolts (**Figure 40**) securing the cover and remove the cover and O-ring. Do not lose the two locating pins.

5. Pull straight up and remove the impeller and shaft (**Figure 41**) from the body.

6. Inspect the mechanical seal (**Figure 42**) for damage. If damaged, replace the seal as described in the following procedure.

NOTE
The mechanical seal must be removed to inspect the oil seal.

7. Inspect the oil seal (**Figure 43**) for damage. If damaged, replace the seal as described in this chapter.

8. Inspect the impeller and shaft (**Figure 44**) for wear or corrosion.

9. Check the impeller blades (**Figure 45**) for corrosion or damage. If corrosion is minor, clean the blades. Replace the impeller assembly, if corrosion is severe or if the blades are cracked or broken.

10. Inspect the water pump cover (**Figure 46**) for corrosion and damage. Remove any corrosion from

11

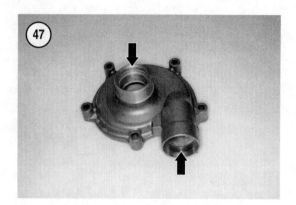

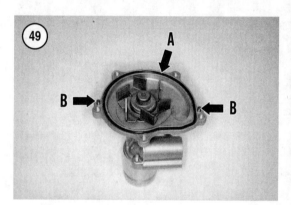

the cover. Make sure the inlet and outlet fittings are clear (**Figure 47**).

11. Apply a light coat of clean engine oil, or waterproof grease, to the oil seal and mechanical seal lips.

12. Install the impeller shaft into the mechanical and oil seals while slowly rotating the impeller into the body (**Figure 41**). Push the impeller down until it is completely seated in the body (**Figure 48**). Rotate the impeller to make sure it rotates freely.

13. Install a *new* O-ring seal (A, **Figure 49**) into the body. Make sure it is correctly seated in the groove.

14. If removed, install the locating pins (B, **Figure 49**).

15. Install the cover and bolts (**Figure 40**) and tighten to 10 N•m (88 in.-lb.).

16. Once again, rotate the impeller shaft and make sure the impeller and shaft rotate freely without touching the cover. If the impeller makes contact with the cover, it has not been installed correctly within the body. Correct the problem at this time.

Mechanical Seal, Oil Seal and Bearing Replacement

1. Carefully tap the mechanical seal (A, **Figure 50**) out of the body from the opposite side of the body.

2. Carefully tap the oil seal (**Figure 43**) out of the body from the opposite side.

3. Use a long drift from the opposite side and tap the bearing (B, **Figure 50**) out of the body working in a circle around the bearing inner race.

4. Clean and dry the inner bore of the body.

5. Make sure the weep holes in the body are clear. Refer to **Figure 51** and **Figure 52**. Install the bearing as follows:

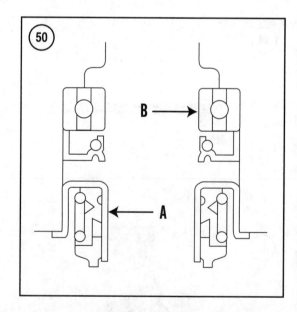

a. Apply a light coat of engine oil to the outer surface of the bearing.

b. Place the bearing squarely against the bore opening.

c. Select a driver or socket with the outside diameter slightly smaller than the bearing's out-

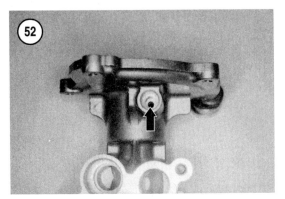

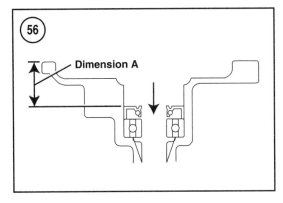

Dimension A

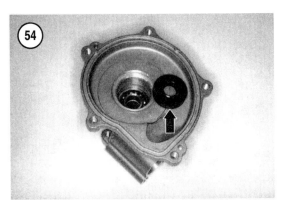

side diameter. Then drive the bearing into the bore until it bottoms out (**Figure 53**).

6. Install the oil seal as follows:

   a. Apply tap water or coolant to the outer surface of the oil seal.

   b. Position the oil seal with the closed side going in last (**Figure 54**).

   c. Place the oil seal squarely against the bore opening (**Figure 43**).

   d. Select a driver or socket with the outside diameter slightly smaller than the oil seal's outside diameter. Drive the oil seal into the bore (**Figure 55**) until dimension A is 21.2 mm (0.835 in.) from the top of the outer sealing surface of the body (**Figure 56**).

7. Install the mechanical seal as follows:

CAUTION
Do not lubricate the outer surface of the mechanical seal with oil or grease.

   a. Apply a light coat of Yamaha bond No. 1215 or Quick Gasket ACC-11001-05-01 to the mechanical seal's seating surface of the body.

11

b. Place the mechanical seal onto a socket of the appropriate size (**Figure 57**).

c. Place the mechanical seal squarely against the bore opening (**Figure 58**).

d. Drive the mechanical seal into the bore opening until it bottoms out (**Figure 59**).

OIL COOLER AND CRANKCASE WATER JACKET FITTING

Removal/Installation

Refer to **Figure 60**.

1. Remove the radiator as described in this chapter.

2. Remove the exhaust system as described in Chapter Eight or Chapter Nine.

3. To remove the oil cooler, perform the following:

a. Place drain pan under the oil cooler.

b. Disconnect the hose from the inlet (A, **Figure 61**) and outlet (B) fittings on the oil cooler.

c. Straighten the tab on the lockwasher and loosen the bolt (A, **Figure 62**) securing the oil cooler to the lower crankcase.

d. Secure the oil cooler, remove the bolt and remove the oil cooler. Drain out any residual coolant and engine oil.

4. Remove the bolt securing the water pump outlet pipe (B, **Figure 62**) to the crankcase.

5. Remove the bolts securing the crankcase water jacket fitting (C, **Figure 62**) to the crankcase.

6. Pull straight out and remove the outlet pipe from the crankcase. Remove the outlet pipe, hose and water jacket fitting as an assembly.

7. Install by reversing these removal steps while noting the following:

a. Install a *new* O-ring onto the water jacket fitting (**Figure 63**) and onto the oil cooler. Lubricate the O-rings with a lithium base grease.

b. Apply a medium-strength threadlocking compound to the water pump outlet pipe and crankcase water jacket fitting bolts, then tighten to 10 N•m (88 in.-lb.).

c. Install the oil cooler onto the crankcase and align the boss on the oil cooler with the locating slot in the crankcase.

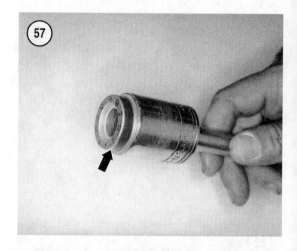

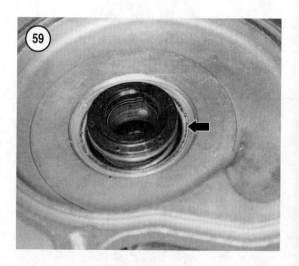

d. Install a *new* lockwasher and bolt. Tighten the bolt to 35 N•m (26 ft.-lb.).

e. Bend the lockwasher tab up against one flat on the bolt.

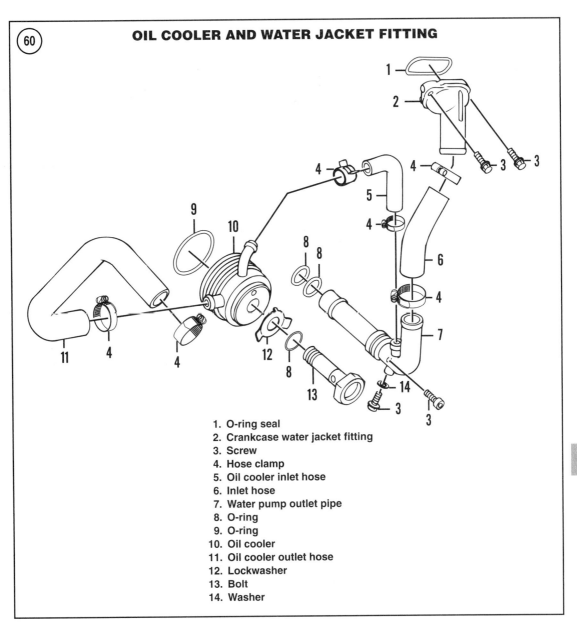

OIL COOLER AND WATER JACKET FITTING

60

1. O-ring seal
2. Crankcase water jacket fitting
3. Screw
4. Hose clamp
5. Oil cooler inlet hose
6. Inlet hose
7. Water pump outlet pipe
8. O-ring
9. O-ring
10. Oil cooler
11. Oil cooler outlet hose
12. Lockwasher
13. Bolt
14. Washer

11

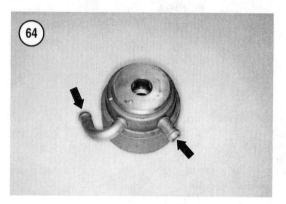

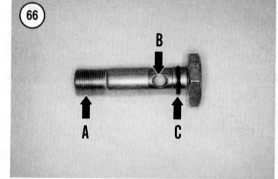

Inspection

1. Make sure the oil cooler inlet and outlet fittings (**Figure 64**) are clear. Clean out with low-pressure air if necessary.

2. Check the O-ring seal groove (**Figure 65**) for corrosion and damage.

3. Inspect the bolt threads (A, **Figure 66**) for damage. Clean out if necessary.

4. Make sure the bolt opening (B, **Figure 66**) is clear.

5. Remove and discard the O-ring seal (C, **Figure 66**).

6. Inspect the crankcase inlet fitting and hoses (**Figure 67**) for damage or deterioration.

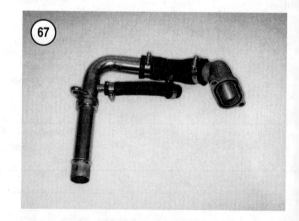

Table 1 COOLING SYSTEM SPECIFICATIONS

Coolant type	High-quality ethylene glycol*
Standard concentration	50% mixture coolant and purified water
Coolant capacity	
1998-2001 models	
Radiator and engine	2.55 L (2.7 U.S. qt.)
Reserve tank	0.45 L (0.48 U.S. qt.)
2002-2003 models	
Radiator and engine	2.45 L (2.6 U.S. qt.)
Reserve tank	0.24 L (0.25 U.S. qt.)
Radiator cap pressure relief	95-125 kPa (13.8-18.1 psi)
Thermostat—begins to open	71-85° C (160-185 F°)

*Use a high quality ethylene glycol coolant containing corrosion inhibitors for aluminum engines. See text for further information.

Table 2 COOLING SYSTEM TORQUE SPECIFICATIONS

Item	N•m	in.-lb.	ft.-lb.
Coolant inlet fitting			
On cylinder block	10	88	–
Pipe screws	10	88	–
Coolant sensor* (2002-2003 models)	18	–	13
Coolant sender* (1998-1999 models)	15	133	–
Coolant thermo switch*			
(1998-1999 models)	23	–	17
Coolant thermo unit			
(2000-2001 models)	23	–	17
Cooling fan mounting bolt	9	80	–
Oil cooler mounting bolt	35	–	26
Radiator mounting bolts	10	88	–
Thermostat housing cover bolt	10	88	–
Water pump cover bolt	10	88	–
Water jacket fitting bolt	10	88	–
Water pump outlet bolts	10	88	–

*Apply sealant to sensor threads.

11

CHAPTER TWELVE

WHEELS, TIRES AND DRIVE CHAIN

This chapter describes service procedures for the wheels, wheel bearings, tires, drive chain and sprockets.

Tire, wheel and drive train specifications are in **Tables 1-3** at the end of the chapter.

MOTORCYCLE STANDS

Many procedures in this chapter require the front or rear wheel to be lifted off the ground. A motorcycle front end stand (**Figure 1**) is required to lift the front wheel. Before purchasing and using a front wheel stand, check the manufacturer's instructions to make sure the stand will work with the model being worked on. If any adjustments or accessories are required for the motorcycle and/or stand, perform the necessary adjustment or install the correct parts before lifting the front wheel. When using a front wheel stand, have an assistant standing by to help. After lifting the front wheel and supporting the motorcycle on a stand, make sure the motorcy-

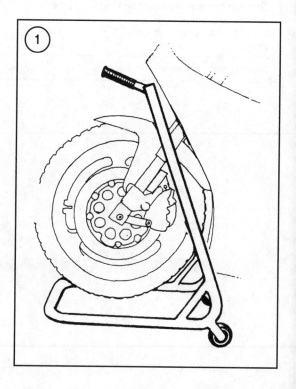

cle is properly supported before walking away from it.

To lift the rear wheels, use a suitable size jack under the engine or use a swing arm safety stand.

FRONT WHEEL

Removal

1. Support the motorcycle with the front wheel off the ground. Refer to *Motorcycle Stands* in this chapter.

2. Remove both the right and left side brake calipers as follows:

    a. Push the brake caliper in (toward the wheel) by hand. Doing so pushes the caliper pistons into the caliper to provide additional brake pad clearance when reinstalling the caliper.

    b. Remove both brake calipers as described in Chapter Fifteen.

NOTE
Insert a spacer in the calipers to hold the brake pads in place. Then, if the brake lever is inadvertently squeezed, the pistons will not be forced out of the calipers. If this does happen, the calipers must be disassembled to reseat the pistons and the system will have to be bled.

3A. On 1998-2001 models, perform the following:

    a. Remove the axle pinch bolt on the right side (**Figure 2**).

    b. On the right side, loosen the axle from the left fork leg (**Figure 3**).

3B. On 2002-2003 models, perform the following:

    a. Loosen the axle pinch bolts on the left side.

    b. Remove the plug from the right side end of the front axle.

    c. Hold the front axle and loosen the axle bolt on the left side (**Figure 4**).

    d. Loosen the axle pinch bolts on the right side (A, **Figure 5**).

NOTE
Before removing the front wheel, note the direction of the rim and tire rotation arrows. The wheel must be reinstalled so the arrows point in the direction of forward rotation. The

12

wheel can be installed in either direction.

NOTE
The dust seals and wheel collars on the right and left sides are identical (same part No.). It is suggested that the dust seals and collars be installed on the same side during installation as they will have a wear pattern. Identify the collars before removing them and mark them after wheel removal.

4. Withdraw the front axle (B, **Figure 5**) from the right side and lower the wheel to the ground.
5. Remove the collar and dust seal (**Figure 6**) from the right and left side of the hub.

CAUTION
Do not set the wheel down on the disc surface, as it may be damaged.

Installation

1. Make sure the axle bearing surfaces of the fork sliders and axle are free from burrs and nicks.
2. Lightly coat the axle with bearing lithium base grease and set aside until installation.
3. Lubricate the oil seal lips (**Figure 7**), on each side, with waterproof lithium base grease.

NOTE
In Step 4, install the collars in their original mounting positions and facing in the same direction.

4. Install the collar (A, **Figure 8**) into the dust seal (B) with the flange toward the outside.
5. Install the dust seal and collar into the right and left side of the hub (**Figure 6**).
6. Install the wheel between the fork tubes with the wheel's rim and tire arrow marks facing in the direction of forward rotation.

WARNING
The front wheel can be installed in either rotational direction. Make sure to install it correctly as noted in Step 6.

7. Position the front wheel between the fork sliders. Raise the wheel assembly up and align it with the front axle holes in both fork sliders.
8A. On 1998-2001 models, perform the following:

a. Install the axle from the right side (**Figure 3**) and push it through until it contacts the left side slider.
b. Screw the axle into the left side slider and tighten it to 72 N•m (53 ft.-lb.).
c. Install the axle pinch bolt and tighten it finger tight.
8B. On 2002-2003 models, perform the following:
a. Install the axle (B, **Figure 5**) from the right side and push it through until it bottoms in the left side slider.

9. Check that both the right side and left side axle collars and dust seals are correctly in place.

10. Install both the right and left side brake caliper as described in Chapter Fifteen. Spin the front wheel and apply the front brake to reposition the brake pads in both calipers.

11. Remove the stand from the motorcycle so both wheels are on the ground. Then apply the front brake and pump the fork several times to seat the axle.

12A. On 1998-2001 models, tighten the axle pinch bolt (**Figure 2**) to 23 N•m (17 ft.-lb.).

12B. On 2002-2003 models, tighten the right side axle pinch bolts (A, **Figure 5**) to 18 N•m (13 ft.-lb.).

13. Apply the front brake and push down hard on the handlebars several time of check for proper fork operation.

Inspection

Replace worn or damaged parts as described in this section.

1. If still in place, remove the collar and dust seal (**Figure 6**) from each side of the hub.

2. Clean the axle, collars and dust seals to remove all lithium base grease and dirt.

3. Remove any corrosion on the front axle and collars with a piece of fine emery cloth.

4. Check the axle surface for any cracks or other damage. Check the axle operating areas for any nicks or grooves that can cut and damage the seals.

5. Check the axle runout with a set of V-blocks and a dial indicator (**Figure 9**). If the axle is bent, replace it. The manufacturer does not provide a wear limit specification for the axle.

6. Check the axle bolt and axle threads for damage. Replace the axle and axle bolt if their corners are damaged.

7. Check the disc brake bolts (**Figure 10**) for tightness. Tighten the bolts to 18 N•m (13 ft.-lb.) if necessary. To service the brake disc, refer to Chapter Fifteen.

8. Clean the oil seals with a rag. Then inspect the oil seals (A, **Figure 11**) for wear, hardness, cracks or other damage. If necessary, replace the seals as described under *Front and Rear Hubs* in this chapter.

9. Turn each bearing inner race (B, **Figure 11**) by hand. The bearing must turn smoothly. Some axial play (side to side) is normal, but radial play (up and

b. Install the axle bolt on the left side.

c. Hold the front axle and tighten the axle bolt (B, **Figure 4**) to 90 N•m (66 ft.-lb.).

d. Install the plug into the end of the front axle.

e. Tighten the left side axle pinch bolts to 18 N•m (13 ft.-lb.).

f. Use a soft-faced mallet and tap on the outer side of the right fork slider to align it with the end of the front axle.

12

down) must be negligible. See **Figure 12**. If one bearing is damaged, replace both bearings as a set. Refer to *Front Hub* in this chapter.

10. Check wheel runout as described in this chapter.

REAR WHEEL

Removal

NOTE
This procedure is shown with the drive chain removed to better illustrate the steps.

1. Support the motorcycle on level ground.
2. Block the front wheel so the motorcycle will not roll in either direction while the rear wheel is off ground on the jack or swing arm stand.
3. Remove the screws securing the drive chain guard. This allows for easy removal of the drive chain from the driven sprocket.

WARNING
If the motorcycle has just been run, the muffler will be very HOT. If possible, wait for the muffler to cool down. If not, wear heavy gloves.

4. Have an assistant apply the rear brake, then loosen the rear axle nut. Refer to A, **Figure 13** for 1998-2001 models, or **Figure 14** for 2002-2003 models.
5. Loosen the drive chain adjust bolt locknut (B, **Figure 13**) and adjust bolt (C) on both sides of the swing arm to provide the maximum amount of slack in the drive chain.

CAUTION
If using a jack, place a piece of wood on the jack pad to protect the crankcase.

6A. If using a jack, perform the following:
  a. Remove the bottom cowl as described in Chapter Sixteen.
  b. If necessary, place a suitable size jack or wooden blocks under the crankcase to support the motorcycle securely with the rear wheel off the ground.
6B. Raise the rear of the motorcycle with a safety stand.

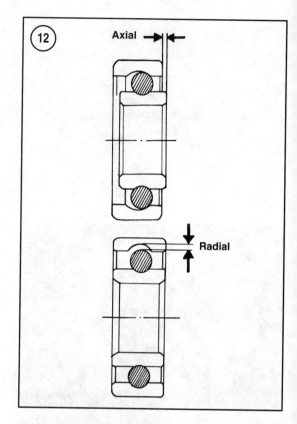

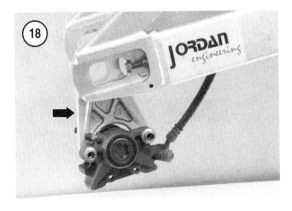

7. Remove the rear axle nut (A, **Figure 13**), washer (**Figure 15**) and the drive chain adjusting block (**Figure 16**).

8. Push the wheel forward and derail the drive chain from the rear sprocket.

9. Withdraw the rear axle (A, **Figure 17**) from the left side, then remove the drive chain adjusting block (B).

10. Pull the wheel rearward and remove it from the swing arm. Secure the rear caliper to the swing arm (**Figure 18**).

NOTE
The wheel collars on the right and left sides are different. Identify the collars before removing them and mark them after wheel removal.

11. Remove the dust seal and collar from the right the left side of the wheel hub and driven flange.

CAUTION
Do not set the wheel down on the disc surface, as it may be damaged.

NOTE
Place a plastic or wooden spacer between the brake pads in place of the disc. Then, if the brake pedal is inadvertently pressed, the piston will not be forced out of the caliper. If this occurs, disassemble the caliper to reseat the piston.

12. Inspect the wheel as described in this chapter.

Installation

1. Make sure all contact surfaces on the axle, swing arm, drive chain adjuster plates and spacers are free of dirt and burrs.

2. Apply a light coat of lithium base grease to the axle, bearings, spacers and seals.

3. If removed, install the caliper assembly into place on the swing arm guide (**Figure 18**).

4. Partially position the wheel into place and roll it forward.

5. Install the dust seal and collar into the right side (**Figure 19**) of the hub and the left side (**Figure 20**) of the driven flange.

6. Move the wheel forward and onto the caliper assembly, being careful not to damage the leading edge of the brake pads.

12

7. Install the drive chain onto the rear sprocket.

8. Raise the rear wheel up and into alignment with the swing arm.

9. Position the left side adjusting block with the raised bars side facing out (A, **Figure 21**) toward the axle flange and install it onto the rear axle (B).

10. Push the rear axle through adjusting block, the swing arm, the wheel, the caliper bracket and through the other side of the swing arm. Push the rear axle in until it bottoms making sure the adjusting block is positioned correctly within the swing arm and within the recess in the adjusting block.

11. Position the right side adjusting block with the tapered side facing the swing arm and install it onto the rear axle and positioned correctly within the swing arm (**Figure 16**).

12. Install the washer (**Figure 15**) onto the rear axle and install the rear axle nut. Refer to **Figure 13** for 1998-2001 models or **Figure 14** for 2002-2003 models. Finger-tighten the nut at this time.

13. Adjust the drive chain as described in Chapter Three.

14. Tighten the rear axle nut to 150 N•m (111 ft.-lb.).

15. If used, remove the jack or wooden block(s) from under the crankcase. Remove the blocks from the front wheel.

16. If removed, install the bottom cowl as described in Chapter Sixteen.

17. Roll the motorcycle back and forth several times. Apply the rear brake as many times as necessary to make sure the brake pads are against the brake disc correctly.

Inspection

> *NOTE*
> *The rear wheel hub is equipped with a single oil seal that is located on the right side of the hub. The other seal is located in the driven flange assembly on the left side.*

1. If still in place, remove the collar and dust seal from the right and the left side of the hub.

2. Clean the axle and spacers in solvent to remove all old lithium base grease and dirt. Make sure all axle contact surfaces are clean and free of dirt and old lithium base grease prior to installation. If these

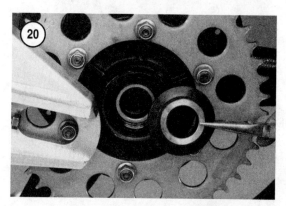

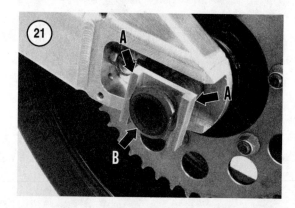

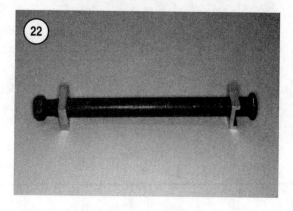

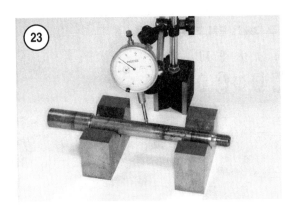

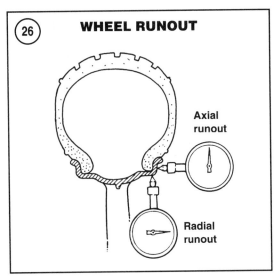

WHEEL RUNOUT

Axial
runout

Radial
runout

place it. The manufacturer does not provide a wear limit specification for the axle.

6. Check the axle bolt and axle threads for damage. Replace the axle and axle bolt if their corners are damaged.

7. Check the disc brake bolts (**Figure 24**) for tightness. Tighten the bolts to 18 N•m (13 ft.-lb.) if necessary.

8. Check the rear sprocket self-locking nuts (**Figure 25**) for tightness. If necessary, tighten the nuts to the following:

    a. 1998-2001 models: 69 N•m (51 ft.-lb.).

    b. 2002-2003 models: 100 N•m (74 ft.-lb.).

9. Check rim runout as follows:

    a. Measure the radial (up and down) runout of the wheel with a dial indicator (**Figure 26**). If runout exceeds the limit specification, check the wheel bearings.

    b. Measure the axial (side to side) runout of the wheel with a dial indicator (**Figure 26**). If runout exceeds the limit specification, check the wheel bearings.

    c. If necessary, replace the rear wheel and/or rear coupling bearings as described in *Front and Rear Hubs* in this chapter.

10. Inspect the wheel for dents, bending or cracks. Check the wheel and tire sealing surface for scratches that are deeper than 0.5 mm (0.01 in.). If any of these conditions are present, replace the wheel.

11. Since the rear caliper is off the disc at this time, check the brake pads for wear. Refer to Chapter Fifteen.

surfaces are not cleaned, the axle may be difficult to remove later on.

3. Remove any corrosion on the rear axle and spacers with a piece of fine emery cloth.

4. Check the axle surface (**Figure 22**) for cracks or other damage. Check the axle operating areas for any nicks or grooves that can cut and damage the seals.

5. Check the axle runout with a set of V-blocks and a dial indicator (**Figure 23**). If the axle is bent, re-

12

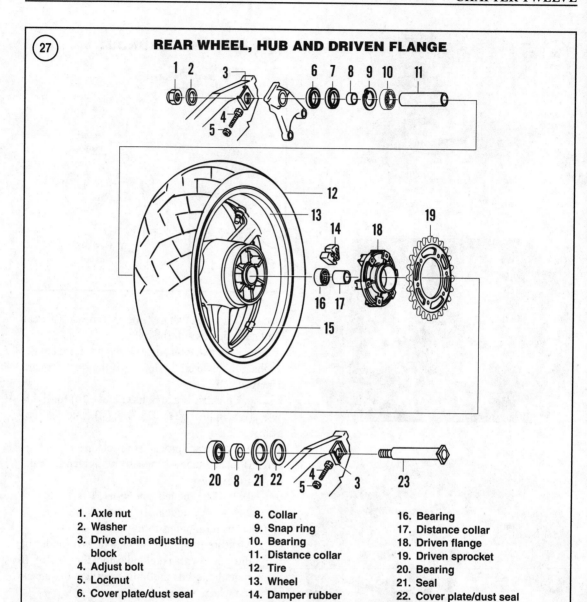

REAR WHEEL, HUB AND DRIVEN FLANGE

1. Axle nut
2. Washer
3. Drive chain adjusting block
4. Adjust bolt
5. Locknut
6. Cover plate/dust seal
7. Seal
8. Collar
9. Snap ring
10. Bearing
11. Distance collar
12. Tire
13. Wheel
14. Damper rubber
15. Balance weight
16. Bearing
17. Distance collar
18. Driven flange
19. Driven sprocket
20. Bearing
21. Seal
22. Cover plate/dust seal
23. Rear axle

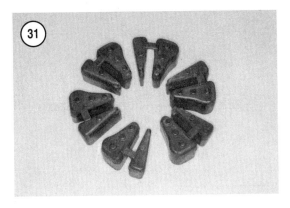

**REAR COUPLING AND
REAR SPROCKET**

Removal/Disassembly/Assembly

Refer to **Figure 27**.

1. Remove the rear wheel as described in this chapter.

2. If still in place, remove the left side collar and dust seal.

3. If the rear sprocket is going to be removed, loosen and remove the self-locking nuts (**Figure** 25) securing the rear sprocket to the rear driven flange at this time.

NOTE
If the rear coupling assembly is difficult to remove from the hub, tap on the backside of the sprocket (from the opposite side of the wheel through the wheel spokes) with the wooden handle of a hammer. Tap evenly around the perimeter of the sprocket until the coupling assembly is free of the hub and the rubber dampers.

4. Pull straight up and remove the rear coupling assembly from the rear hub.

5. Remove the distance collar (A, **Figure 28**) from the rear hub.

6. Inspect the rear sprocket-to-driven flange area as described in this chapter.

7. Install by reversing these removal steps while noting the following:

    a. Align the driven flange bosses (**Figure 29**) with the receptacles between the rubber damper (B, **Figure 28**) and install the driven flange. Press it down until it bottoms.

CAUTION
On a new motorcycle or after a new rear sprocket has been installed, check the torque on the rear sprocket nuts after ten minutes of riding and after each ten-minute riding period until the nuts have seated and remain tight. Failure to keep the sprocket nuts correctly tightened will damage the rear hub.

    b. Tighten the rear sprocket self-locking nuts on 1998-2001 models to 69 N•m (50 ft.-lb.) and on 2002-2003 models to 100 N•m (74 ft.-lb.) after the assembly has been reinstalled in the rear wheel.

Inspection

1. Remove the rubber dampers (**Figure 30**) and inspect them (**Figure 31**) for signs of damage or deterioration. If damaged, replace as a complete set.

2. Inspect the raised webs (**Figure 32**) in the rear hub. Check for cracks or wear. If any damage is visible, replace the rear wheel.

12

3. Inspect the driven flange assembly (**Figure 33**) for cracks or damage, replace if necessary.

4. Inspect the rear sprocket teeth (**Figure 34**). If the teeth are visibly worn or undercut (**Figure 35**), replace the rear sprocket as described in this chapter.

> *CAUTION*
> *If the rear sprocket requires replacement, also replace the engine drive sprocket and the drive chain (Figure 36). Never install a new drive chain over worn sprockets or a worn drive chain over new sprockets. The old parts will wear out the new part prematurely.*

5. If the rear sprocket requires replacement, also inspect the drive chain as described in Chapter Three and the engine sprocket as described in Chapter Seven. They also may be worn and need replacing.

6. Inspect the rear hub bearing (**Figure 37**) and driven flange bearing (**Figure 38**) for excessive axial play and radial play (**Figure 39**). Replace the bearing if it has an excess amount of free play.

7. On a non-sealed bearing, check the balls for evidence of wear, pitting or excessive heat (bluish tint). Turn the inner race by hand. The bearing must turn smoothly without excessive play or noise. Replace questionable bearings. Ensure a perfect match by comparing the old bearing to the new one.

> *NOTE*
> *Fully sealed bearings are available from many bearing specialty shops. Fully sealed bearings provide better protection from dirt and moisture that passes through worn or damaged seals.*

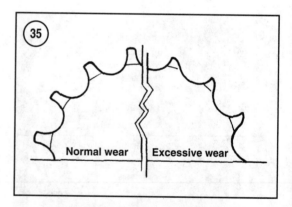

Normal wear　Excessive wear

FRONT AND REAR HUBS

Pre-inspection

Inspect each wheel bearing as follows:

1. Support the motorcycle with either the front or rear wheel off the ground. Make sure the axle is tightened securely.

   a. Hold the wheel along its sides (180° apart) and try to rock it back and forth. If there is any noticeable play at the axle, the wheel bearings are worn or damaged and require replacement. Have an assistant apply the front or rear brake

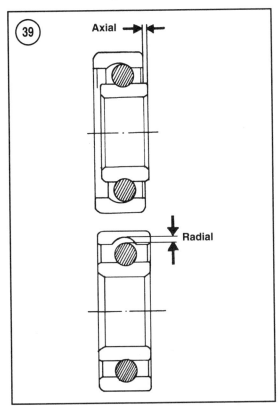

while rocking the wheel again. On severely worn bearings, play is detected at the bearings even though the wheel is locked in position.

b. Push the front caliper(s) in by hand to move the brake pads away from the brake disc. This makes it easier to spin the wheel when performing substep c.

c. Spin the wheel and listen for excessive wheel bearing noise. A grinding or catching noise indicates worn bearings.

d. Apply the front or rear brake several times to reposition the brake pads in the calipers.

e. To check any questionable bearing, continue with Step 2.

CAUTION
Do not remove the wheel bearings for inspection purposes, as they may be damaged during removal. Remove the wheel bearings only if they require replacement.

2A. Remove the front wheel (this chapter).

2B. Remove the rear wheel (this chapter).

CAUTION
When handling the wheel assembly in the following steps, do not lay the wheel down where it is supported by the brake disc, as this could damage the disc. Support the wheel on wooden blocks.

3. Pry the seals out of the hub (**Figure 40**). Support the tool with a rag to avoid damaging the hub or brake disc.

NOTE
If a seal is hard to remove, do not damage the mounting bore by trying

to force it out. Remove the seal with a seal removal tool as described in Chapter One.

4. Remove any burrs created during seal removal. Use emery cloth to smooth the mounting bore. Do not enlarge the mounting bore.

> *NOTE*
> *Before removing the wheel bearings, check the tightness of the bearings in the hub by pulling the bearing up and then from side to side. The outer bearing race should be a tight fit in the hub with no movement. If the outer bearing race is loose and wobbles, the bearing bore in the hub may be cracked or damaged. Remove the bearings as described in this procedure and check the hub bore carefully. If any cracks or damage are found, replace the wheel. It cannot be repaired.*

5. Turn each bearing inner race by hand. The bearing must turn smoothly with no roughness, catching, binding or excessive noise. Some axial play (side to side) is normal, but radial play (up and down) must be negligible (**Figure 39**).

6. Check the bearing's outer seal (**Figure 41**) for buckling or other damage that would allow dirt to enter the bearing.

7A. On the front wheel, if one bearing is damaged, replace both bearings as a set.

7B. On the rear wheel, if the one bearing is damaged, also replace the bearing in the rear coupling as a set.

Disassembly

This section describes removal of the wheel bearings from the front and rear hub. Refer to **Figure 42** and **Figure 43**. If the bearings are intact, one of the removal methods described in this section can be used. To remove a bearing where the inner race assembly has fallen out, refer to *Removing Damaged Bearings* in this section.

> *CAUTION*
> *When handling the wheel assembly in the following steps, do not lay the wheel down where it is supported by the brake disc because this could*

damage the disc. Support the wheel on two wooden blocks.

1. If still in place, remove the dust seal and collar from each side of the hub.

2. Pry the seal(s) out of the hub (**Figure 40**). Support the tool with a rag to avoid damaging the hub or brake disc.

> *NOTE*
> *If a seal is hard to remove, do not damage the mounting bore by trying to force the seal out. Remove the seal with a seal removal tool as described under **Seals** in Chapter One.*

3. Remove any burrs created during seal removal. Use emery cloth to smooth the mounting bore. Do not enlarge the mounting bore.

4. Examine the wheel bearings (**Figure 37**) for excessive damage, especially the inner race. If the inner race of one bearing is damaged, remove the other bearing first. If both bearings are damaged, try to remove the bearing with the least amount of damage first. On rusted and damaged bearings, applying pressure against the inner race may cause the race to pop out, leaving the outer race in the hub.

> *WARNING*
> *Safety glasses must be worn when removing the bearings in the following steps.*

> *NOTE*
> *Step 5 describes two methods of removing the wheel bearings. Step 5A requires the use of the Kowa Seiki Wheel Bearing Remover set. Step 5B*

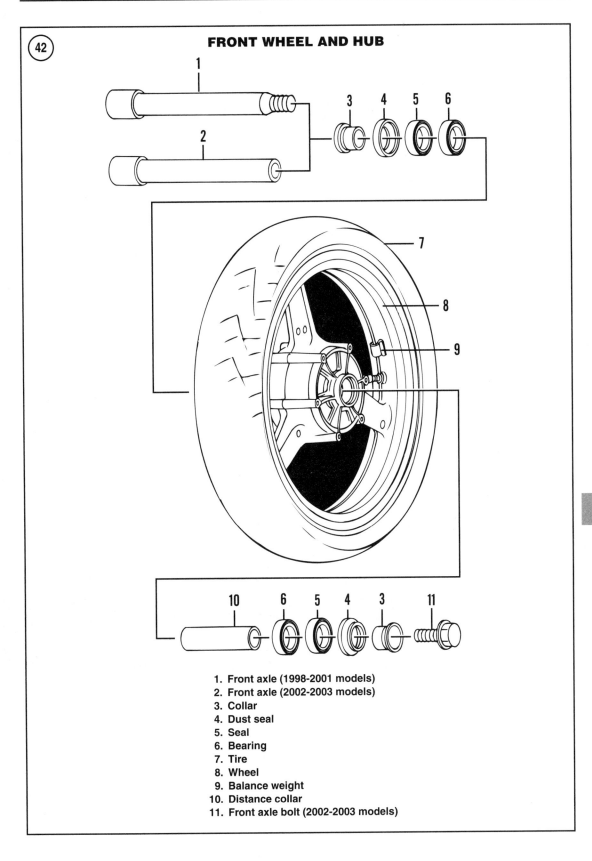

FRONT WHEEL AND HUB

1. Front axle (1998-2001 models)
2. Front axle (2002-2003 models)
3. Collar
4. Dust seal
5. Seal
6. Bearing
7. Tire
8. Wheel
9. Balance weight
10. Distance collar
11. Front axle bolt (2002-2003 models)

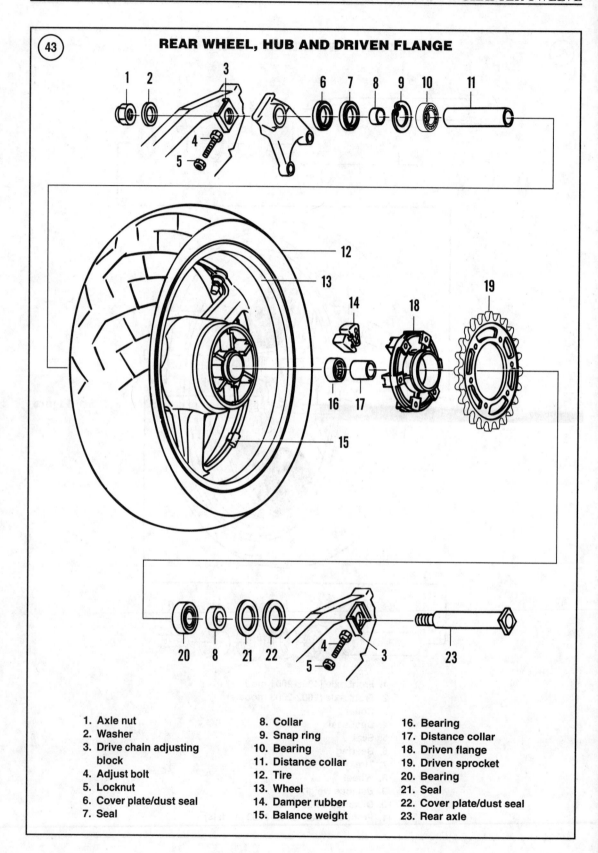

REAR WHEEL, HUB AND DRIVEN FLANGE

43

1. Axle nut
2. Washer
3. Drive chain adjusting
   block
4. Adjust bolt
5. Locknut
6. Cover plate/dust seal
7. Seal

8. Collar
9. Snap ring
10. Bearing
11. Distance collar
12. Tire
13. Wheel
14. Damper rubber
15. Balance weight

16. Bearing
17. Distance collar
18. Driven flange
19. Driven sprocket
20. Bearing
21. Seal
22. Cover plate/dust seal
23. Rear axle

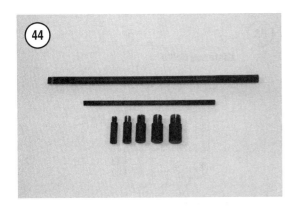

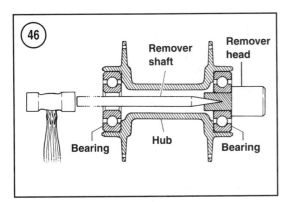

describes how to remove the bearings without special tools.

NOTE
The wheel bearing set consists of two remover shafts and a number of remover heads (expanding collets). The Kowa Seiki Wheel Bearing Remover set shown in Figure 44 can be ordered through a Yamaha dealership from K & L Supply Co. in Santa Clara, CA.

5. On the rear hub, remove the snap ring.

6A. To remove the wheel bearings with the Kowa Seiki Wheel Bearing Remover set:

   a. Select the correct size remover head tool and insert it into one of the bearings (**Figure 45**).

   b. From the opposite side of the hub, insert the remover shaft into the slot in the backside of the remover head (**Figure 46**). Then position the hub with the remover head tool resting against a solid surface and strike the remover shaft to force it into the slit in the remover head. This wedges the remover head tool against the inner bearing race. See **Figure 46**.

   c. Position the hub and strike the end of the remover shaft with a hammer to drive the bearing from the hub (**Figure 47**). Remove the bearing and tool. Release the remover head from the bearing.

   d. Remove the distance collar from the hub.

   e. Remove the opposite bearing the same way.

6B. To remove the wheel bearings without special tools:

CAUTION
The hub and bearings will be hot after heating them with a torch. Make sure to wear welding gloves when handling the parts.

NOTE
Clean the hub of all chemical residue before heating it with a torch in this procedure.

   a. Heat one side of the hub with a propane torch. Work the torch in a circular motion around the hub, making sure not to hold the torch in one area. Then turn the wheel over and remove the bearing as described in the next step.

12

b. Using a long drift, tilt the distance collar away from one side of the bearing (**Figure 48**).

> *NOTE*
> *Do not damage the distance collar when removing the bearing. If necessary, grind a clearance groove in the drift to enable it to contact the bearing while clearing the distance collar.*

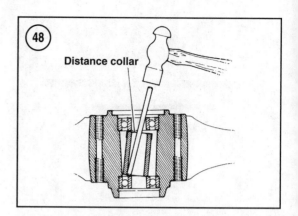

c. Tap the bearing out of the hub with a hammer, working in a circle around the bearing inner race.

d. Remove the distance collar from the hub.

e. Turn the hub over and heat the opposite side.

f. Drive out the opposite bearing, using a suitable driver.

g. Inspect the distance collar for burrs or dents created during removal.

7. Clean and dry the hub and distance collar.

Assembly

1. Before installing the new bearings and seals, note the following:

a. Install both bearings with their closed side facing out. If a bearing is sealed on both sides, install the bearing with its manufacturer's marks facing out.

b. Install the seals with their closed side facing out.

c. When lithium base grease is specified in the following steps, use water-resistant bearing lithium base grease.

2. Remove any dirt or debris from the hub before installing the bearings.

3. Pack the open side of each bearing with lithium base grease.

> *NOTE*
> *When installing the bearings, install the right side bearing first, then the left side bearing.*

4. Place the right side bearing squarely against the bore opening with its closed side facing out. Select a driver or socket (**Figure 49**) with an outside diameter slightly smaller than the bearing's outside diameter, then drive the bearing into the bore until it bottoms out.

5. Turn the wheel over and install the distance collar (**Figure 50**). Center it against the first bearing's inner race.

6. Place the left side bearing squarely against the bore opening with its closed side facing out. Using the same driver, drive the bearing partway into the bearing bore, then stop and make sure the distance collar is centered in the hub. If not, install the axle through the hub to align the distance collar with the bearing, then remove the axle and continue installing the bearing until it bottoms in the hub.

the ends appear compressed or damaged, replace the distance collar. Do not try to repair the distance collar by cutting or grinding its end surfaces, as this shortens the distance collar.

CAUTION
The distance collar operates against the wheel bearing inner races to prevent them from moving inward when the axle is tightened. If the ends of the distance collar are damaged, shortened, or if it is not installed in the hub, the inner bearing races move inward and bind as the axle is tightened, causing bearing damage and seizure.

3. Inspect the dust seals and collars (**Figure 52**) for hardness or deterioration. Replace as necessary.

Removing Damaged Bearings

When worn and rusted wheel bearings are used too long, the inner race can break apart and fall out of the bearing, leaving the outer race pressed in the hub. Because the outer race seats against a shoulder inside the hub, its removal is difficult because only a small part of the race is accessible above the hub's shoulder. This presents a small and difficult target to drive against. To remove a bearing's outer race under these conditions, first heat the hub evenly with a propane torch, then drive out the outer race with a drift and hammer. Grind a clearance tip on the end of the drift, if necessary, to avoid damaging the hub's mounting bore. Check this before heating the hub. When removing the race, apply force at opposite points around the race to prevent it from rocking and binding in the mounting bore once it starts to move. After removing the race, inspect the hub mounting bore carefully for cracks or other damage.

7. On the rear hub, install the snap ring.
8. Insert the axle through the hub and turn it by hand. Check for any roughness or binding, indicating bearing damage.

CAUTION
If the axle will not go in, the distance collar is not aligned correctly with one of the bearings.

9. Pack the lip of each seal (**Figure 51**) with lithium-base grease.
10. Place a seal squarely against one of the bore openings with its closed side facing out, then drive the seal in the bore until it is flush with the outside of the hub's mounting bore.
11. On the front hub, repeat Step 9 for the other seal.

Inspection

1. Check the hub mounting bore for cracks or other damage. If one bearing is a loose fit, the mounting bore is damaged. Replace the hub.
2. Inspect the distance collar for cracks, corrosion or other damage. Check the distance collar ends. If

WHEEL RUNOUT AND BALANCE

Proper wheel inspection includes visual inspection, checking rim runout and wheel balance. Checking runout and wheel balance requires a truing or wheel balancing stand. If these tools are not available, refer the service to a Yamaha dealership.

Replace the wheel if it is dented or damaged in any way. While a new wheel is not cheap, its cost does not compare to the personal injury that could

12

occur if a damaged wheel becomes unstable or fails while riding. If there is any doubt as to wheel condition, take it to a Yamaha dealership or sport motorcycle specialist and have them inspect the wheel. It is also a good idea to have a specialist inspect any used wheels that may be considered for purchase.

Wheel Runout Inspection

1. Clean the wheel to remove all road grit, chain lube and other debris. Any material left on the wheel affects the runout measurement. This includes any surface roughness caused by peeled or uneven paint and corrosion.

2. Inspect the wheel for dents, bending or cracks. Check the wheel and tire sealing surface for scratches that could cause the tire to leak air.

NOTE
The runout check can be performed
with the tire mounted on the wheel.

3. Mount the wheel on a truing stand. See **Figure 53** for the dial indicator inspection points.

4. Spin the wheel slowly by hand and measure the radial (up and down) runout with a dial indicator as shown in **Figure 53**. If the runout is excessive (**Table 2**), go to Step 6.

5. Spin the wheel slowly by hand and measure the axial (side to side) runout with a dial indicator as shown in **Figure 53**. If the runout is excessive (**Table 2**), go to Step 6.

6. If the runout is excessive, remove the wheel from the truing stand and turn each bearing inner race by hand. If necessary, remove the seal (A, **Figure 54**) to check the bearings closely. Each bearing (B, **Figure 54**) must turn smoothly and be a tight fit in its mounting bore. Some axial play (side to side) is normal, but radial play (up and down) must be negligible. Check the bearing for visual damage. If a bearing turns roughly, replace both bearings as a set. If a bearing is loose in its mounting bore, the hub is probably damaged. Remove the bearings and check the mounting bore for any cracks, gouges or other damage.

7. If the wheel bearings and hub are in good condition but the runout is out of specification, replace the damaged wheel.

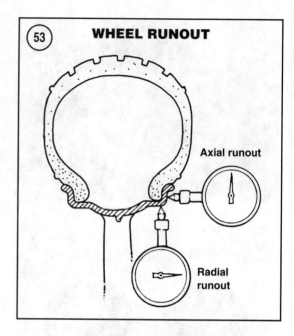

Wheel Balance Inspection

A wheel that is not balanced is unsafe because it seriously affects the steering and handling of the motorcycle. Depending on the degree of unbalance and the speed of the motorcycle, anything from a mild vibration to a violent shimmy may occur, which may result in loss of control. An imbalanced wheel also causes abnormal tire wear.

Motorcycle wheels can be checked for balance either statically or dynamically with spin balancing. This section describes how to static balance the wheels using a wheel inspection stand. To obtain a higher degree of accuracy, take both wheels to a dealership and have them balanced with a dynamic wheel balancer. This machine spins the wheel to accurately detect any imbalance.

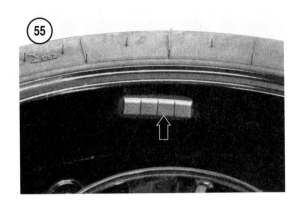

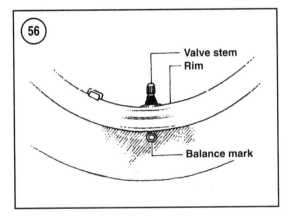

Balance weights are used to balance the wheel and are attached to the rim. Weight kits are available from motorcycle dealerships. Purchase the adhesive type that can be attached to the flat portion of the rim (**Figure 55**).

The wheel must be able to rotate freely when checking wheel balance. Because excessively worn or damaged wheel bearings affect the accuracy of this procedure, check the front wheel bearings as described in this chapter. Check the wheel hub for cracks and other damage. Also confirm that the tire

balance mark, a balance mark on the tire, is aligned with the valve stem (**Figure 56**). If not, break the tire loose from the rim and align the balance mark with the valve stem. Refer to *Tire Changing* in this chapter.

NOTE
When balancing the wheel, leave the brake disc(s) attached to the wheel.

1. Remove the wheel as described in this chapter.
2. Clean the seals and inspect the wheel bearings as described in this chapter.
3. Clean the tire and rim. Remove any stones or pebbles stuck in the tire tread.
4. Mount the wheel on an inspection stand (**Figure 57**, typical).

NOTE
To check the original balance of the wheel, leave the existing weights in place on the wheel.

5. Spin the wheel by hand and let it coast to a stop. Mark the tire at its bottom point with chalk.
6. Spin the wheel several more times. If the same spot on the tire stops at the bottom each time, the wheel is out of balance. This is the heaviest part of the tire. When an unbalanced wheel is spun, it always comes to rest with the heaviest spot at the bottom.
7. Attach a test weight to the wheel at the point opposite the heaviest spot and spin the wheel again.
8. Experiment with different weights until the wheel, when spun, comes to rest at a different position each time. When a wheel is correctly balanced, the weight of the tire and wheel assembly is distributed equally around the wheel.
9. Remove the test weight and install the correct size weight to the rim. Make sure it is secured properly to the rim's surface (**Figure 55**).
10. Record the number and position of weights on the wheel. Then, if the motorcycle experiences a handling or vibration problem at a later time, first check for any missing weights.
11. Install the wheel as described in this chapter.

TIRE CHANGING

Tire changing is an important part of the motorcycle's safety and operation. Changing sportbike tires, due to the size of the tire and tight bead/rim seal, can

12

be extremely difficult. Incorrect installation due to a lack of patience, skill or equipment can damage both the tire and the wheel. Many experienced owners who do most or all of their own maintenance and service choose to have their tires changed by a professional technician with specialized tire changing equipment designed for alloy wheels.

The following procedure is provided for those who choose to do the work.

Tools

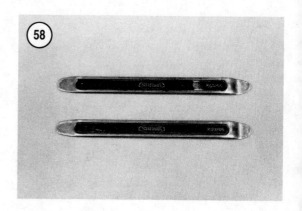

NOTE
Before purchasing a bead breaker, make sure it will work on the YZF-R1 tire sizes.

To change the tires, the following tools are required:
1. A set of tire levers or flat-handled tire irons with rounded ends (**Figure 58**).
2. Bead breaker.
3. Spray bottle filled with soapy water.
4. Plastic rim protectors for each tire iron.

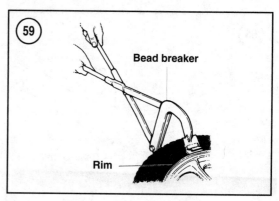

Removal

WARNING
The original equipment cast wheels are designed for use with tubeless tires. Do not install a tube inside of a tubeless tire, as excessive heat may build up in the tire and cause the tube to burst.

WARNING
The wheels can be damaged easily during tire removal. Work carefully to avoid damaging the tire beads, the inner liner of the tire or the wheel rim flange that form the sealing surfaces. As described in the text, insert the rim protectors between the tire irons and rim to protect the rim from damage.

NOTE
Tires are harder to replace when the rubber is hard and cold. If the weather is hot, place the wheels and new tires in the sun or in a closed automobile. The heat helps soften the rubber, easing removal and installation. If the weather is cold, place the

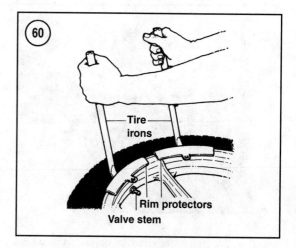

tires and wheels inside a warm building.

NOTE
It is easier to replace tires when the wheel is mounted on some type of raised platform. A popular item used by many home mechanics is a metal drum. Before placing the wheel on a drum, cover the drum edge with a

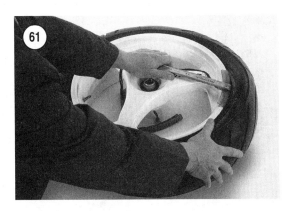

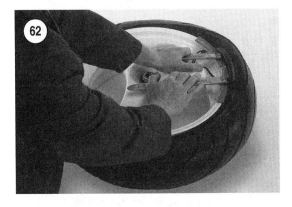

length of garden or heater hose, split lengthwise and secured in place with plastic ties. When changing a tire at ground level, support the wheel on two wooden blocks to prevent the brake disc from contacting the floor.

1. If the tire is going to be reused, mark the valve stem location on the tire (**Figure 56**) so the tire can be installed in the same position for easier balancing.

2. Remove the valve core to deflate the tire.

CAUTION
The inner rim and tire bead areas are sealing surfaces on a tubeless tire. Do not scratch the inside of the rim or damage the tire bead. Do not attempt to force the bead off the rim with any type of leverage, such as a long tire iron. It is very easy to damage the tire bead surface on the tire and rim. It is also possible to crack or break the alloy wheel. Removing tubeless tires from their rims can be difficult because of the exceptionally tight bead and rim seal. If unable to break the tire bead with a bead breaker, take the wheel to a motorcycle dealership and have them change the tire.

3. Use a bead breaker and break the bead all the way around the tire (**Figure 59**). Do not try to force the bead with tire irons. Make sure that both beads are clear of the rim beads.

4. Lubricate the tire beads with soapy water on the side to be removed first.

CAUTION
*Always use rim protectors (**Figure 60**) between the tire irons and the rim to protect the rim from damage.*

5. Insert the tire iron under the bead (**Figure 61**). Force the bead on the opposite side of the tire into the center of the rim and pry the bead over the rim with the tire iron.

6. Insert a second tire iron next to the first (no more than 20.3 cm [8 in.] apart) to hold the bead over the rim. Work around the tire with the first tool, prying the bead over the rim (**Figure 62**). Work slowly by taking small bites with the tire irons. Taking large bites or using excessive force can damage the tire bead or rim.

NOTE
If the tire is tight and hard to pry over the rim, use a third tire iron and a rim protector. Use one hand and arm to hold the first two tire irons, then use the other hand to operate the third tire iron when prying the tire over the rim.

7. Turn the wheel over. Insert a tire iron between the second bead and the same side of the rim that the first bead was pried over (**Figure 63**). Force the bead on the opposite side from the tool into the cen-

12

ter of the rim. Pry the second bead off the rim, working around the wheel with the two rim protectors and tire irons.

8. Remove the valve stem and discard it. Remove all rubber residue from the valve stem hole and inspect the hole for cracks and other damage.

9. Remove old balance weights from the rim surface.

10. Carefully clean the rim bead with a brush; do not use excessive force or damage the rim sealing surface. Inspect the sealing surface for any cracks, corrosion or other damage.

> *WARNING*
> *If there is any doubt as to wheel condition, take it to a Yamaha dealership or sport motorcycle specialist for a thorough inspection.*

Installation

1A. If installing the original tire, carefully inspect the tire for any damage.

1B. If installing a new tire, remove all stickers from the tire tread.

2. Lubricate both beads of the tire with soapy water.

3. Make sure the correct tire, either front or rear, is installed on the correct wheel and that the direction arrow on the tire faces in the direction of wheel rotation.

4. Align the balance spot (**Figure 56**) near the bead indicating the lightest point of the tire with the valve stem.

5. Place the backside of the tire into the center of the rim. The lower bead should go into the center of the rim and the upper bead outside (**Figure 64**). Use both hands to push the backside of the tire into the rim as far as possible. Use tire irons when it becomes difficult to install the tire by hand (**Figure 65**).

6. Press the upper bead into the rim opposite the valve. Pry the bead into the rim on both sides of the initial point with a tire tool, working around the rim to the valve (**Figure 66**).

7. Check the bead on both sides of the tire for an even fit around the rim.

8. Lubricate both sides of the tire with soapy water.

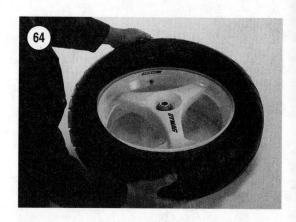

> *WARNING*
> *Always wear eye protection when seating the tire beads on the rim. Never exceed 386 kPa (56 psi) inflation pressure, as the tire could burst, causing severe injury. Never stand directly over the tire while inflating it.*

9. Inflate the tire until the beads seat into place. A loud pop should be heard as each bead seats against its side of the rim.

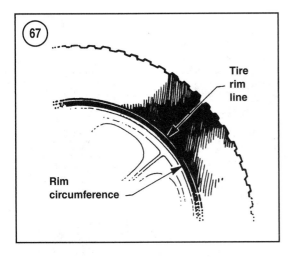

Tire rim line

Rim circumference

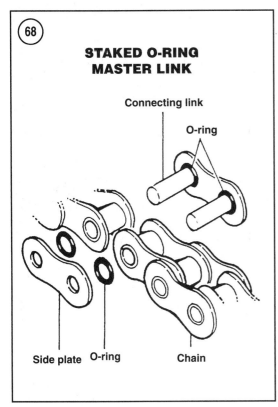

STAKED O-RING MASTER LINK

Connecting link

O-ring

Side plate   O-ring   Chain

10. After inflating the tire, check to see that the beads are fully seated and the tire rim lines (**Figure 67**) are the same distance from the rim all the way around the tire. If one or both beads do not seat, deflate the tire, re-lubricate the rim and beads with soapy water and re-inflate the tire.

11. Inflate the tire to the required pressure listed in **Table 1**. Screw on the valve stem cap.

12. Balance the wheel as described in this chapter.

NOTE
After installing new tires, follow the tire manufacturer's instructions for breaking-in (scuffing) the tire.

TIRE REPAIRS

Only use tire plugs as an emergency repair. Refer to the manufacturer's instructions to install and note the motorcycle weight and speed restrictions. After performing an emergency tire repair with a plug, consider the repair temporary and replace the tire at the earliest opportunity.

Refer all tire repairs to a Yamaha dealership or other qualified motorcycle technician.

DRIVE CHAIN

Refer to **Table 2** for drive chain specifications. Refer to *Drive Chain* in Chapter Three for routine drive chain inspection and lubrication procedures.

This section describes how to replace the drive chain with the swing arm mounted on the motorcycle.

Replacement

All models are originally equipped with a DID 50 chain with a ZJ connecting master link that must be staked during installation (**Figure 68**). On these models, the chain can be replaced with the swing arm mounted on the motorcycle. The following section describes chain replacement using an aftermarket drive chain tool and following its operating instructions. Use the following steps to supplement the instructions provided with the chain tool.

NOTE
DID recommends using the KM500 Cutting and Riveting tool for the removal and installation of the master link on their chains. If installing a chain other than DID, follow that chain manufacturer's instructions.

1. Support the motorcycle on level ground.

2. Block the front wheel so the motorcycle will not roll in either direction while the rear wheel is off ground on the jack or swing arm stand.

12

3. Remove the screws securing the drive chain guard. This allows for easy removal of the drive chain from the driven sprocket.

4. Have an assistant apply the rear brake, then loosen the rear axle nut. Refer to A, **Figure 69** for 1998-2001 models, or **Figure 70** for 2002-2003 models.

5. Loosen the drive chain adjust bolt locknut (B, **Figure 69**) and adjust bolt (C) on both sides of the swing arm to provide the maximum amount of slack in the drive chain.

> *CAUTION*
> *If using a jack, place a piece of wood on the jack pad to protect the oil pan.*

6A. If using a jack, perform the following:

  a. Remove the bottom cowl as described in Chapter Sixteen.

  b. If necessary, place a suitable size jack or wooden blocks under the oil pan to support the motorcycle securely with the rear wheel off the ground.

6B. Raise the rear of the motorcycle with a safety stand.

7. Rotate the rear wheel and chain to locate the crimped pin ends on the master link. Break the chain at this point.

8. Assemble the chain tool, following the manufacturer's instructions.

9. Install the chain tool across the master link, then operate the tool and push the connecting link out of the side plate to break the chain. Remove the side plate, connecting link and O-rings.

> *WARNING*
> *Never reuse the connecting link, side plate and O-rings, as they could break and cause the chain to separate. Reusing a master link may cause the chain to come apart and lock the rear wheel and cause a serious accident.*

10. Remove the drive chain.

11. If installing a new drive chain, count the links of the new chain, and if necessary, cut the chain to length as described under *Cutting a Drive Chain to Length* in this section. See **Table 2** for the original equipment chain sizes and link length.

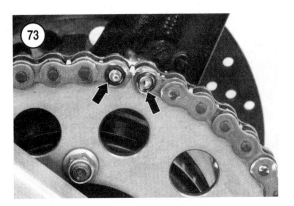

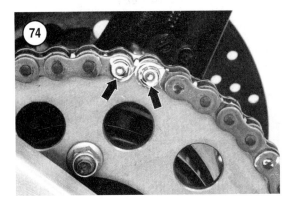

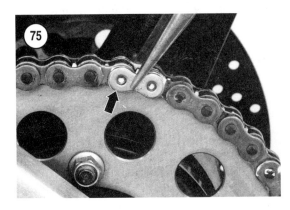

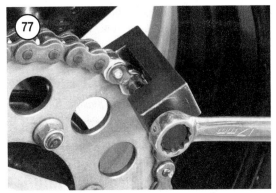

NOTE
Always install the drive chain through the swing arm before connecting and staking the master link.

12. Install the drive chain through the swing arm and around the drive sprocket with both link ends located at the top of the sprocket (**Figure 71**).

13. Assemble the new master link as follows:

    a. Install a *new* O-ring on each connecting link pin (**Figure 72**) and apply the lubrication supplied with the new master link kit.

    b. Insert the connecting link through the inside of the chain and connect both chain ends together.

    c. Install the remaining two *new* O-rings (**Figure 73**) onto the connecting link pins and apply additional lubricant (**Figure 74**).

    d. Install the side plate with its identification mark facing out (away from the chain) and crimp it into place with needlenose pliers (**Figure 75**).

14. Stake each connecting link pin as following the chain manufacturer's instructions. Assemble the chain tool onto the master link and carefully stake each connecting link pin end, following the manufacturer's instructions. Refer to **Figure 76** and **Figure 77**.

15. Remove the chain tool and inspect the master link for any cracks or other damage. Check the staked area for cracks (**Figure 78**), then make sure the master link O-rings were not crushed. If there are any cracks on the staked link surfaces or other damage, remove the master link and install a new one.

16. If there are no cracks, pivot the chain ends where they hook onto the master link. Each chain end must pivot freely. Compare by pivoting other

links of the chain. If one or both drive chain ends cannot pivot on the master link, the chain is too tight. Remove and install a *new* master link assembly.

> *WARNING*
> *An incorrectly installed master link may cause the chain to come apart and lock the rear wheel, causing a serious accident. If the tools to safely rivet the chain together are not available, take it to a Yamaha dealership. Do not ride the motorcycle unless absolutely certain the master link is installed correctly.*

17. Rotate the rear wheel and chain to make sure the chain is traveling over both sprockets without any binding.

18. Adjust the drive chain and tighten the rear axle nut as described in Chapter Three.

Cutting a Drive Chain to Length

Table 2 lists the correct number of chain links required for original equipment gearing. If the replacement drive chain is too long, cut it to length as follows:

1. Stretch the new chain on a workbench. Set the master link aside for now.

2. If installing a new chain over original equipment gearing, refer to **Table 2** for the correct number of links for the new chain. If sprocket sizes were changed, install the new chain over both sprockets, with the rear wheel moved forward, to determine the correct number of links to remove. Make a chalk mark on the two chain pins to be cut. Count the chain links one more time or check the chain length before cutting.

> *WARNING*
> *Using a hand or bench grinder as described in Step 3 will cause flying par-*

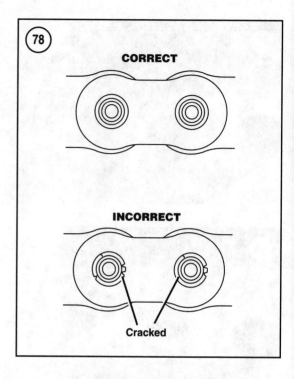

ticles. Do not operate a grinding tool without proper eye protection.

3A. If using the DID KM500 tool, use it to break the drive chain.

3B. If not using a chain tool, cut the chain as follows:

  a. Grind the head of two pins flush with the face of the side plate with a grinder or suitable grinding tool.

  b. Press the side plate out of the chain with a chain breaker; support the chain carefully while doing this. If the pins are still tight, grind more material from the end of the pins and then try again.

  c. Remove the side plate and push out the connecting link.

4. Install the new drive chain as described in this chapter.

Table 1 TIRE AND WHEEL SPECIFICATIONS

Item	Front	Rear
Tire type	Tubeless	Tubeless
Size		
1998-2001 models	120/70 ZR17 (58W)	180/55 ZR17 (73W)
2002-2003 models	120/70 ZR17 (58W)	190/55 ZR17 M/C (73W)
Manufacturer		
1998-1999 models	D207FN (Dunlop)	D207L (Dunlop)
2000-2001 models	MEZ3Y (Metzeler) or D207FQ (Dunlop)	MEZ3Y (Metzeler) or D207N (Dunlop)
2002-2003 models	Pilot Sport E (Michelin) or D2008FL (Dunlop)	Pilot Sport (Michelin) or D208L (Dunlop)
Minimum tread depth		
1998-1999 models	1.6 mm (0.06 in.)	1.6 mm (0.06 in.)
2000-2001 models	0.8 mm (0.03 in.)	0.8 mm (0.03 in.)
2002-2003 models	1.6 mm (0.06 in.)	1.6 mm (0.06 in.)
Inflation pressure (cold)[1]	250 kPa (36 psi)	250 kPa (36 psi)
		290 kPa (42 psi)[2]
Wheel runout limit		
Axial	0.50 mm (0.02 in.)	0.50 mm (0.02 in.)
Radial	1.0 mm (0.04 in.)	1.0 mm (0.04 in.)

1. Tire inflation pressure is for original equipment tires. Aftermarket tires may require different inflation pressure. The use of tires other than those specified by Yamaha may cause instability.
2. Tire pressure for maximum load of 90 kg (198 lbs.).

Table 2 DRIVE CHAIN AND SPROCKET SPECIFICATIONS

Item	Specification
Drive chain	
1998-2001 models	50ZVM (DID) (114 links)
2001-2003 models	50ZA8 (DID) (114 links)
Chain slack	40-50 mm (1.57-1.97 in.)
Drive chain maximum length (10 links)	150.1 mm (5.91 in.)
Sprocket sizes	
Drive (front)	16 teeth
Driven (rear)	43 teeth

12

Table 3 WHEEL TORQUE SPECIFICATIONS

Item	N•m	in.-lb.	ft.-lb.
Brake caliper mounting bolts	40	–	30
Brake disc bolts	18	–	13
Driven sprocket nuts			
1998-2001 models	69	–	51
2002-2003 models	100	–	74
Front axle (1998-2001 models)	72	–	53
Front axle bolt (2002-2003 models)	90	–	66
Front axle pinch bolt			
1998-2001 models	23	–	17
2002-2003 models	18	–	13
Rear axle nut	150	–	111

CHAPTER THIRTEEN

FRONT SUSPENSION AND STEERING

This chapter describes procedures for the repair and maintenance of the handlebar, front fork and steering components. Refer to Chapter Twelve for front wheel and tire service. Front suspension and steering specifications are listed in **Tables 1-3** at the end of the chapter.

> *WARNING*
> *Replace all fasteners used on the front suspension and steering components with parts of the same type. Do not use a replacement part of lesser quality or substitute design; this may affect the performance of the system or result in failure of the part that leads to loss of motorcycle control. Careful attention to the torque specifications during installation is required to ensure proper retention of these parts.*

HANDLEBAR ASSEMBLIES

All models are equipped with separate handlebar assemblies that slip over the top of the fork tubes and are located just below the upper fork bridge.

> *NOTE*
> *Before removing a handlebar, make a drawing of the appropriate control ca-*

bles from the handlebar and through the frame. This information is helpful when reinstalling the handlebars and cables.

Handlebar Removal/Installation (With All Components Still Attached)

> *NOTE*
> *If the fuel tank is still in place, cover it with a heavy towel or blanket to protect the finish during this procedure.*

1. Park the motorcycle on level ground on the sidestand.
2. Remove the front fairing (Chapter Sixteen).

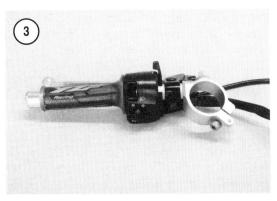

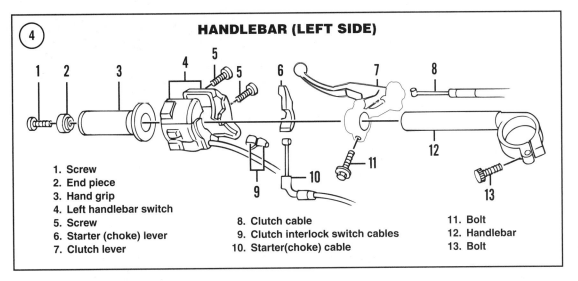

HANDLEBAR (LEFT SIDE)

1. Screw
2. End piece
3. Hand grip
4. Left handlebar switch
5. Screw
6. Starter (choke) lever
7. Clutch lever
8. Clutch cable
9. Clutch interlock switch cables
10. Starter(choke) cable
11. Bolt
12. Handlebar
13. Bolt

3. Remove the trim cap, then remove the handlebar locating bolt (**Figure 1**) securing the handlebar to the upper fork bridge.

4. Remove the upper fork bridge (A, **Figure 2**) as described in this chapter.

5. Loosen the clamp bolt (B, **Figure 2**) on the handlebar.

NOTE
On the right handlebar, do not disconnect the brake hydraulic line(s) from the master cylinder.

6. Carefully slide the handlebar assembly up off the front fork tube and remove it.

7. Secure the handlebar to the frame.

8. On the right handlebar, keep the front master cylinder upright to prevent the entry of air into the system.

9. Inspect the handlebar assembly (**Figure 3**, typical) for wear or damage.

10. Install the handlebar assembly onto the front fork tube and slide it down past its final location.

11. Install the upper fork bridge (A, **Figure 2**) as described in this chapter.

12. Move the left handlebar up into position under the upper fork bridge.

13. Correctly align the handlebar to the locating bolt hole in the upper fork bridge. Hold the handlebar in position and install the locating bolt (**Figure 1**). Tighten the bolt to 13 N•m (115 in.-lb.) and install the trim cap.

14. Tighten the handlebar clamp bolt (B, **Figure 2**) to 17 N•m (13 ft.-lb.).

15. Install the front fairing (Chapter Sixteen).

Left Side Handlebar Removal (Components Removed)

This section describes the removal of the components from the left handlebar (**Figure 4**) and then the handlebar from the left fork tube. If it is only necessary to remove the handlebar with all components intact, refer to the prior procedure.

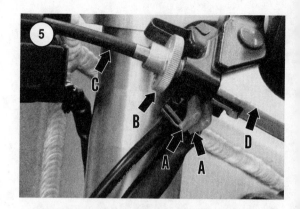

CAUTION
If the fuel tank is still in place, cover it with a heavy towel or blanket to protect the finish during this procedure.

1. Park the motorcycle on level ground on the sidestand.

2. Remove the front fairing as described in Chapter Sixteen.

3. Disconnect the electrical connectors (A, **Figure 5**) from the clutch interlock switch.

4. Screw the clutch cable adjuster (B, **Figure 5**) in to obtain maximum slack in the clutch cable. Disconnect the clutch cable (C, **Figure 5**) from the clutch lever.

5A. On 1998-2001 models, perform the following:
   a. Remove the screws (**Figure 6**) securing the left handlebar switch and separate the switch. Disconnect the choke lever from the switch housing (**Figure 7**).
   b. Remove the remainder of the switch housing (A, **Figure 8**) from the handlebar.

5B. On 2002-2003 models, remove the screws (**Figure 6**) securing the left handlebar switch and separate the switch. Remove the switch housing from the handlebar.

6. Remove the screw and the end piece (B, **Figure 8**) and remove it from the handlebar.

7. Remove the left grip end (C, **Figure 8**) as described in this chapter.

8. Remove the clutch lever bracket clamp bolt and slide the clutch lever assembly (D, **Figure 5**) off the handlebar.

9. Remove the upper fork bridge (A, **Figure 9**) as described in this chapter.

10. Loosen the clamp bolt (B, **Figure 9**) on the handlebar and slide the handlebar up and off the fork tube.

Left Side Handlebar Installation (Components Removed)

1. Install the left handlebar over the fork tube. Slide it down beyond its final location.

2. Install the upper fork bridge (A, **Figure 9**) as described in this chapter.

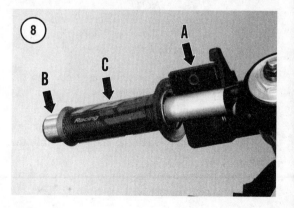

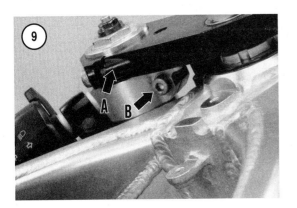

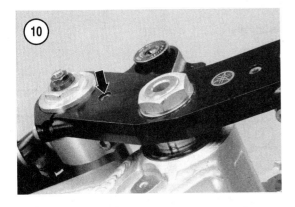

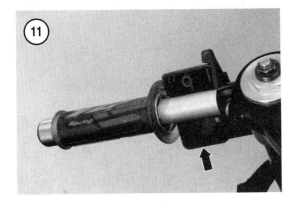

7. Slide the clutch lever assembly (D, **Figure 5**) onto the handlebar. Align the slit in the clutch lever holder with the handlebar punch mark.

8. Install and tighten the clutch lever bracket clamp bolt securely.

9. Install the left grip end as described in this chapter.

10. Install the end piece and screw (B, **Figure 8**) onto the end of the handlebar. Tighten the screw securely.

11A. On 1998-2001 models, perform the following:

  a. Apply grease to the exposed choke cable wire and connect the cable end to the choke lever.

  b. Install the choke lever into the switch housing (**Figure 7**) and onto the handlebar (**Figure 11**).

  c. Install the left handlebar switch and align the switch projection with the hole in the handlebar. Install the screws (**Figure 6**) and tighten securely.

11B. On 2002-2003 models, install the left handlebar switch and align the switch projection with the hole in the handlebar. Install the screws (**Figure 6**) and tighten securely.

12. Connect the clutch cable (C, **Figure 5**) onto the clutch lever. Screw the clutch cable adjuster (B, **Figure 5**) out to secure the clutch cable.

13. Connect the electrical connectors (A, **Figure 5**) onto the clutch interlock switch.

14. Adjust the clutch as described in Chapter Three.

13

Right Side Handlebar Removal (Components Removed)

This section describes the removal of the components from the right handlebar (**Figure 12**) and then the handlebar from the left fork tube. If it is only necessary to remove the handlebar with all components intact, refer to the prior procedure.

CAUTION
Cover the fuel tank with a heavy cloth or plastic tarp to protect it from brake fluid spills. Brake fluid damages plastic, painted and plated surfaces. Wash off spilled brake fluid immediately.

3. Move the left handlebar up into position under the upper fork bridge.

4. Correctly align the handlebar to the locating bolt hole in the upper fork bridge. Hold the handlebar in position and install the locating bolt (**Figure 10**). Tighten the bolt to 13 N•m (115 in.-lb.) and install the trim cap.

5. Tighten the handlebar clamp bolt (B, **Figure 9**) to 17 N•m (13 ft.-lb.).

6. Remove the bolt securing the clutch lever bracket.

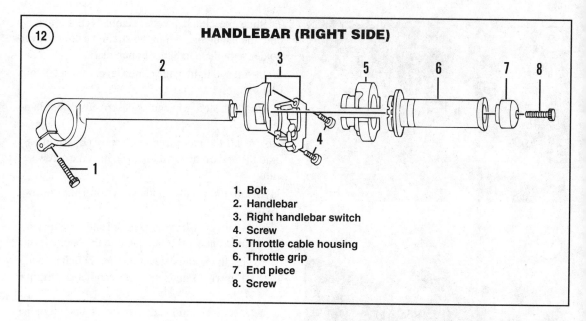

HANDLEBAR (RIGHT SIDE)

1. Bolt
2. Handlebar
3. Right handlebar switch
4. Screw
5. Throttle cable housing
6. Throttle grip
7. End piece
8. Screw

1. Park the motorcycle on level ground on the sidestand.

2. Remove the front fairing as described in Chapter Sixteen.

3. Disconnect the brake switch wire connector (**Figure 13**) at the brake light switch.

4. Remove the throttle cable housing screws (**Figure 14**) and open the housing assembly. Disconnect the throttle cables as described under *Throttle Cable Replacement* in Chapter Eight or Chapter Nine.

5. Remove the right handlebar switch housing screws (A, **Figure 15**). Open the switch assembly and remove it from the handlebar.

6. Remove the screw (**Figure 16**) securing the front master cylinder reservoir to the upper fork bridge.

NOTE
Do not disconnect the brake hydraulic line(s) from the master cylinder.

7. Remove the bolts (B, **Figure 15**) securing the front master cylinder assembly. Remove the clamp and move the front master cylinder assembly from the handlebar. Secure the brake lever and master cylinder to the frame with a bungee cord. Make sure the front master cylinder is in an upright position.

8. Remove the trim cap and remove the handlebar locating bolt (**Figure 17**).

9. Remove the upper fork bridge (A, **Figure 18**) as described in this chapter.

10. Loosen the handlebar pinch bolt (B, **Figure 18**). Carefully slide the handlebar up off the front fork tube and remove it.

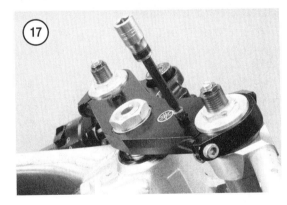

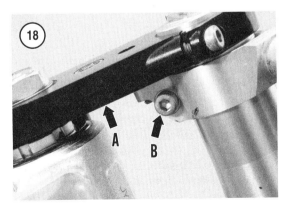

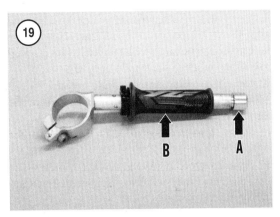

11. Remove the end piece (A, **Figure 19**) and throttle grip (B).

12. Inspect the right handlebar (**Figure 19**) or wear or damage.

Right Side Handlebar Installation (Components Removed)

1. Install the left handlebar over the fork tube. Slide it down beyond its final location.

2. Install the upper fork bridge (A, **Figure 18**) as described in this chapter.

3. Move the left handlebar up into position under the upper fork bridge.

4. Correctly align the handlebar to the locating bolt hole in the upper fork bridge. Hold the handlebar in position and install the locating bolt (**Figure 17**). Tighten the bolt to 13 N•m (115 in.-lb.) and install the trim cap.

5. Tighten the handlebar clamp bolt (B, **Figure 18**) to 17 N•m (13 ft.-lb.).

6. Install the front master cylinder assembly onto the handlebar. Position the clamp with the UP mark facing up and install it and the bolts (B, **Figure 15**). Tighten the bolts while aligning the mating surfaces with the handlebar punch mark. Tighten the bolts to the following:

    a. 1998-2001 models: 13 N•m (115 in.-lb.).

    b. 2002-2003 models: 9 N•m (80 in.-lb.).

7. Install the front master cylinder reservoir to the upper fork bridge. Install and tighten the screw securely (**Figure 16**).

> *NOTE*
> *There must be 2 mm (0.08 in.) clearance between the front master cylinder assembly and the switch housing.*

13

8. Install the right handlebar switch housing and align the switch projection (A, **Figure 20**) with the hole in the handlebar (B). Install the switch (A, **Figure 15**) and tighten the screws securely.

9. Clean the throttle grip of all old grease.

10. Lightly grease the right handlebar where the throttle grip operates.

11. Install the throttle grip (A, **Figure 21**) over the right handlebar.

12. Install the end piece and screw (B, **Figure 21**) onto the end of the handlebar. Tighten the screw securely.

13. Connect the throttle cables as described under *Throttle Cable Replacement* in Chapter Eight or Nine. Install the throttle cable housing and tighten the screws (**Figure 14**) securely.

14. Open and release the throttle grip. Make sure it opens and closes (snaps back) without any binding or roughness, then support the motorcycle on a stand and turn the handlebar from side to side, checking throttle operation at both steering lock positions.

> ### WARNING
> *An improperly installed throttle grip assembly may cause the throttle to stick open. Failure to properly assemble and adjust the throttle cables and throttle grip could cause a loss of steering control. Do not start or ride the motorcycle until the throttle grip is correctly installed and snaps back when released.*

15. Adjust the throttle cable as described in Chapter Three.

Left Hand Grip Replacement

1. Remove the screw and the end cap (A, **Figure 22**) from the handlebar end.

> ### NOTE
> *If reusing the hand grip, remove it carefully to avoid puncturing or tearing it.*

2. Carefully insert a thin flat-blade screwdriver between the handlebar and grip (B, **Figure 22**).

3. Spray electrical contact cleaner into the space created by the screwdriver. Then remove the screwdriver and quickly twist the grip back and forth to

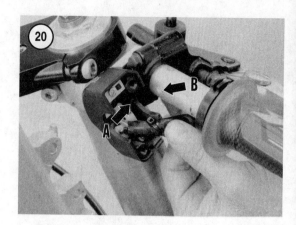

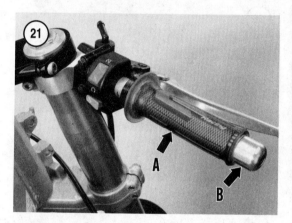

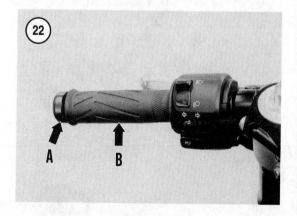

break the cement bond between the hand grip and handlebar.

4. Slide the hand grip off the handlebar.

> ### NOTE
> *Step 4 describes how to cement the hand grip. When using a hand grip cement (ThreeBond 1501C Griplock, or an equivalent), follow the manufacturer's instructions carefully.*

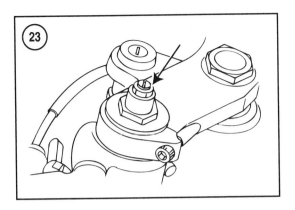

7. Apply the grip cement to the left handlebar and inside of the hand grip.

8. Install the hand grip (B, **Figure 22**) over the handlebar. Make sure there is clearance between the end of the grip and the switch housing. Remove all excess grip cement from the end of the hand grip.

9. Install the end cap and screw (A, **Figure 22**) on the handlebar end. Tighten the screw securely.

10. Follow the hand grip cement manufacturer's instructions regarding drying time before operating the motorcycle.

WARNING
Loose or damaged hand grips can slide off and cause loss of steering control. Make sure the hand grips are correctly installed and cemented in place before operating the motorcycle.

FRONT FORK

The following sections describe complete adjustment and service for the front fork. To prevent damaging the fork during service, note the following:

1. To avoid rounding off the shoulders on the fork caps, use a 30-mm 6-point socket when loosening and tightening the fork caps.

2. Do not overtighten the handlebar and fork bridge clamp bolts, as this can damage the fork bridge threads and fork tubes. Always refer to the torque specifications.

3. The fork sliders are easily scratched. Handle them carefully during all service procedures.

4. When holding the fork tubes in a vise, protect the tubes with soft jaws and do not overtighten.

13

Spring Preload Adjustment

Adjust the spring preload by turning the adjuster (**Figure 23**) in the top of each fork cap with a 14-mm open end wrench. The adjuster is marked with equally spaced alignment marks to ensure that both fork springs are adjusted equally.

The standard position is set when the distance from the upper alignment groove to the top of the fork cap (hexagon surface) is No. 6 as shown in **Figure 24**.

Turn the spring adjuster (A, **Figure 25**) clockwise to increase spring preload or counterclockwise

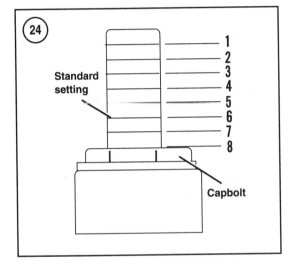

Standard setting

1 2 3 4 5 6 7 8

Capbolt

5. Clean and dry the hand grip area of the handlebar surface.

6. If reusing the hand grip, use a contact cleaner to remove all old glue residue from inside the hand grip.

NOTE
If the original hand grip is torn or damaged, install a new hand grip.

to decrease preload. Make certain that the preload is equal on both springs.

> *WARNING*
> *Both fork springs must be adjusted to the same setting. If the springs are set on different settings, it affects the motorcycle's handling and may cause a loss of steering control.*

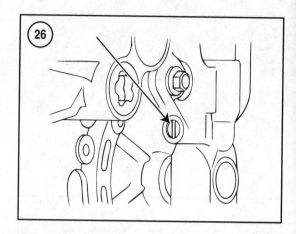

Compression Adjustment

Adjust the spring compression by turning the adjuster screw (**Figure 26**) in the adjuster at the base of the fork slider (**Figure 27**) with a screwdriver.

1. Turn the compression adjuster clockwise until it *lightly* seats and no longer turns. This is the full hard setting.

2. Turn the compression adjuster counterclockwise five clicks to the standard position.

3. To reduce compression damping, turn the adjuster counterclockwise nine clicks to the soft position.

> *WARNING*
> *Both fork springs must be adjusted to the same setting. If the springs are set on different settings, it affects the motorcycle's handling and may cause a loss of steering control.*

Rebound Adjustment

Adjust the spring rebound by turning the adjuster screw (**Figure 28**) in the top of each fork cap with a screwdriver.

1. Turn the adjuster (B, **Figure 25**) clockwise until it *lightly* seats and no longer turns. This is the full hard setting.

2. Turn the rebound adjuster counterclockwise five clicks to the standard position.

3. To reduce rebound damping, turn the adjuster counterclockwise 11 clicks to the soft position.

> *WARNING*
> *Both fork springs must be adjusted to the same setting. If the springs are set on different settings, it affects the motorcycle's handling and may cause a loss of steering control.*

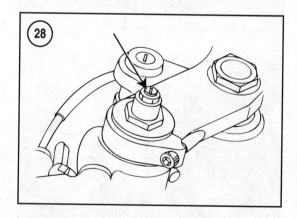

Removal/Installation

1. Remove the front fairing and both side fairings as described in Chapter Sixteen.

2. Remove the front wheel as described in Chapter Twelve.

3. Remove the front fender as described in Chapter Sixteen.

4. If the fork is going to be serviced, perform the following:

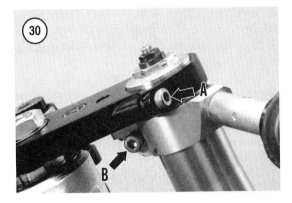

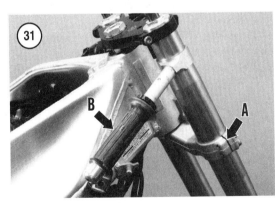

a. On 1998-2001 models, to gain access to the Allen bolt, remove the front axle pinch bolt from the right fork leg.

b. On 2002-2003 models, to gain access to the Allen bolt, remove both front axle pinch bolts from each fork leg.

c. Place a drain pan under the fork slider to catch the fork oil.

d. Use an 8-mm Allen wrench and impact driver and loosen the fork damper 8-mm Allen bolt at the base of the slider. Do not lose the copper washer on the Allen bolt.

e. Allow the fork oil to drain.

f. Reinstall the Allen bolt and washer to keep residual oil in the fork.

g. Repeat for the other fork assembly.

h. Reinstall the pinch bolt(s) to avoid misplacing them.

5. If both fork tube assemblies are going to be removed, mark them with an R (right side) and L (left side) so the assemblies will be reinstalled on the correct side.

6. Remove the trim cap and remove the handlebar locating bolt (**Figure 29**).

7. Loosen the upper fork bridge pinch bolt (A, **Figure 30**).

8. Loosen the handlebar clamp bolt (B, **Figure 30**).

CAUTION
Make sure to use a 30-mm 6-point socket to avoid cosmetic damage to the cap bolt. By using the incorrect size socket, the surface can be easily damaged.

9. If the fork is going to be serviced, use a 30-mm 6-point socket and loosen the cap bolt.

CAUTION
*Make sure the lower fork bridge clamp bolts are very loose in Step 10. If the fork tube does not want to slide out easily, use a large flat blade screwdriver and carefully open the gap on the lower fork bridge (A, **Figure 31**). The fork tubes have a colored anodized surface that can be easily scratched.*

10. Loosen the lower fork bridge clamp bolts (**Figure 32**) then carefully slide the fork assembly down and out for both fork bridges and the handlebar. It may be necessary to rotate the fork tube slightly

13

while pulling it down and out. Remove the fork assembly and take it to the workbench for service.

11. Remove the handlebar assembly (B, **Figure 31**) from the upper fork bridge if the components are still attached to the handlebar, secure the handlebar to the frame.

12. Repeat for the other fork assembly.

13. Install a fork tube through the lower fork bridge and the handlebar (A, **Figure 33**). Continue to push the fork tube up through the upper fork bridge until the top surface of the fork tube is flush with the top surface of the upper fork bridge (B, **Figure 33**).

14. Tighten the lower clamp bolts (**Figure 32**) to 23 N•m (17 ft.-lb.).

15. If the fork was serviced, tighten the 30-mm cap bolt (C, **Figure 33**) to 23 N•m (17 ft.-lb.).

16. Tighten the handlebar clamp bolt (B, **Figure 30**) to 17 N•m (13 ft.-lb.).

17. Tighten the upper clamp bolt (A, **Figure 30**) to 23 N•m (17 ft.-lb.).

18. Install the handlebar locating bolt (**Figure 29**) and tighten securely. Install the trim cap.

19. Install the front fender as described in Chapter Sixteen.

20. Install the front wheel as described in Chapter Twelve.

21. Install the front fairing and both side fairings as described in Chapter Sixteen.

Disassembly

This section describes complete disassembly of the front fork (**Figure 34**). If only changing the fork oil and/or setting the oil level, perform Steps 1-9.

NOTE
The fork spring cannot be compressed enough by hand to remove the cap bolt. A spring compressor tool is required. This type of tool is available from motorcycle dealerships and motorcycle parts/tool suppliers.

1. Hold the fork in a vertical position and unscrew the fork cap from the fork tube. The fork cap cannot be completely removed at this time as it is still attached to the fork damper.

2. Turn the fork assembly upside down and drain the residual fork oil into a suitable container. Pump

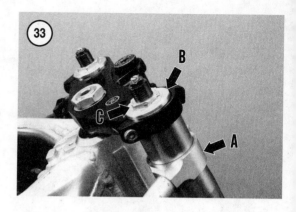

the fork several times by hand to expel most of the oil. Dispose of the fork oil properly.

3. Slide the fork tube down into the fork slider to expose the spring collar.

4. Install the lower portion of the fork slider in the spring compressor tool (**Figure 35**), following the manufacturer's instructions.

5. Install the upper portion of the spring compressor pins into the holes in the spacer (**Figure 36**) and tighten securely.

6. Secure the cap bolt (A, **Figure 37**) and loosen the nut (B).

7. Completely unscrew the cap bolt from the damper rod cartridge.

8. Gradually release the fork spring compressor and remove it from the fork assembly.

9. Remove the spring seat (A, **Figure 38**) and withdraw the fork spring (B).

NOTE
If only changing fork oil, proceed to
***Fork Oil Adjustment** in this chapter.*

10. Withdraw the damper adjust rod (A, **Figure 39**) from the damper rod, then remove the damper rod (B).

11. Carefully remove the dust seal (**Figure 40**) from the fork tube and slide it up on the slider.

12. Remove the stopper ring (**Figure 41**).

13. Withdraw the fork tube from the slider.

14. Use a flat blade screwdriver and carefully remove the oil seal. Be careful not to scratch the inner surface of the fork tube. Remove the washer.

NOTE
Do not remove the fork tube bushing(s) unless it is going to be replaced. Inspect as described in this chapter.

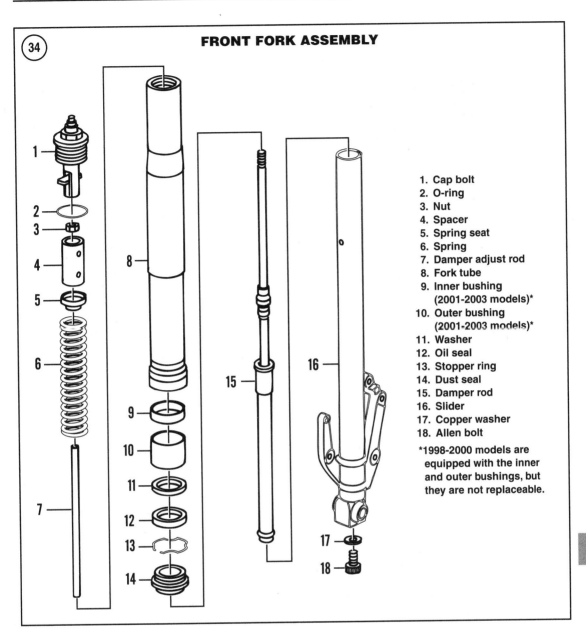

FRONT FORK ASSEMBLY

1. Cap bolt
2. O-ring
3. Nut
4. Spacer
5. Spring seat
6. Spring
7. Damper adjust rod
8. Fork tube
9. Inner bushing
   (2001-2003 models)*
10. Outer bushing
    (2001-2003 models)*
11. Washer
12. Oil seal
13. Stopper ring
14. Dust seal
15. Damper rod
16. Slider
17. Copper washer
18. Allen bolt

*1998-2000 models are
equipped with the inner
and outer bushings, but
they are not replaceable.

13

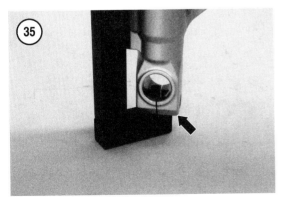

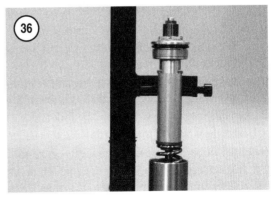

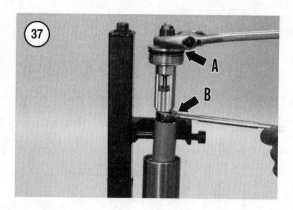

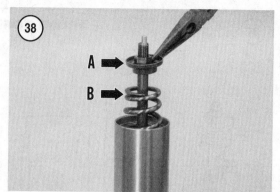

15. Inspect the components as described in this chapter.

Assembly

1. Before assembling the parts, make sure there is no solvent residue remaining in the slider or on any component.

2. If removed, install the fork tube bushing(s).

3. Install *new* O-rings where necessary. Then lubricate each O-ring with fresh fork oil.

4. Coat all parts with fresh fork oil prior to installation.

5. Install the dust seal (A, **Figure 42**) and the stopper ring (B) onto the fork slider.

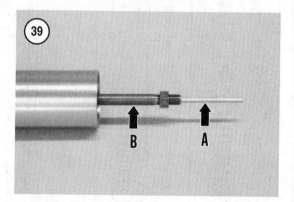

> *CAUTION*
> *Place a clinging type of plastic wrap (A, **Figure 43**) over the end of the fork slider and coat it with fork oil. This will prevent damage to the dust seal and oil seal lips when installing them over the top of the fork slider. These parts can then be carefully slid over the fork slider and plastic wrap without damaging the seals.*

6. Install a *new* fork seal onto the slider as follows:
   a. Lubricate the seal lips with fork oil or a light coat of lithium grease.
   b. Position the seal with the spring side (**Figure 44**) facing out and install it (B, **Figure 43**).

7. Remove the plastic wrap from the fork slider.

8. Install the washer (**Figure 45**) onto the fork slider.

9. Install the damper rod into the slider (**Figure 46**).

10. Install a *new* copper washer onto the 8-mm Allen bolt securing the damper rod to the slider.

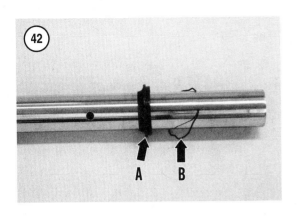

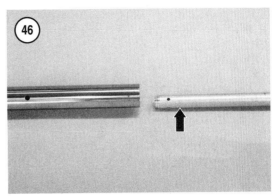

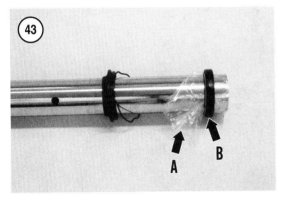

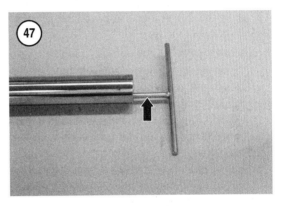

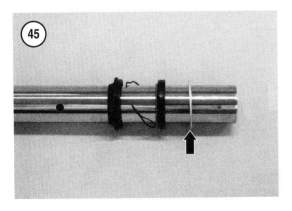

NOTE
The following step is necessary to keep the damper rod from rotating while tightening the 8-mm Allen bolt.

11A. Install the Yamaha special tool (part No. YM-1423) down into the fork tube. Index it into the top of the damper rod (**Figure 47**) and hold it in place. Remove the special tool after tightening the Allen bolt in Step 12.

11B. If the special tool is not used, temporarily install the fork spring, spring seat, spacer and fork cap to secure the damper rod. During this step, it is unnecessary to thread the fork cap onto the damper rod. Instead, push the damper rod down and bottom it out of the way. Installing these parts applies pressure against the damper rod and prevents it from turning. Remove these parts after tightening the Allen bolt in Step 12.

12. Apply a medium-strength threadlocking compound to the Allen bolt threads (**Figure 48**). Then thread the 8-mm Allen bolt into the bottom of the damper rod and tighten it to 40 N•m (30 ft.-lb.) (**Figure 49**).

13. Install the slider into the fork tube (**Figure 50**).

13

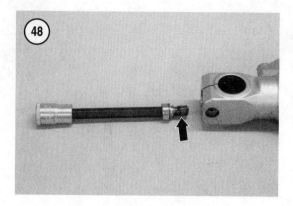

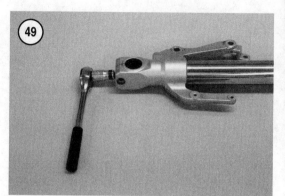

14. Move the dust seal and stopper ring up on the fork slider out of the way.

15. Install the washer and oil seal as follows:

    a. Slide the washer down into the fork tube bore. Make sure it is correctly seated otherwise the oil seal will not seat correctly.

    b. Slide the oil seal down the fork slider (A, **Figure 51**) and rest it on the washer in the fork tube bore.

    c. Use a fork oil seal driver (B, **Figure 51**) and drive the oil seal into the fork tube. Continue to install the seal until the groove in the fork tube can be seen above the top surface of the seal (**Figure 52**). Remove the oil seal driver.

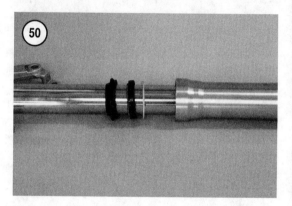

NOTE
Fork oil seal drivers can be purchased from aftermarket suppliers. To select a driver, first measure the outside diameter of one fork tube and the inside diameter of the oil seal area of the tube.

16. Install the stopper ring (**Figure 41**) and install it into the groove in the fork tube. Make sure the stopper ring is completely seated in the tube groove.

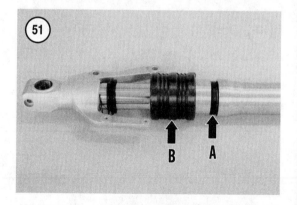

NOTE
If the stopper ring cannot seat completely into the slider groove, the oil seal has not been installed far enough into the slider.

17. Slide the dust seal down the fork tube and seat it into the fork tube (**Figure 40**).

CAUTION
In the following steps, hold the fork tube and fork slider together. They are not attached to each other at this time.

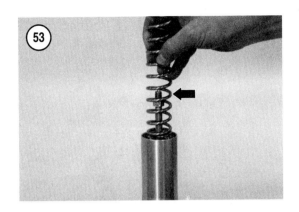

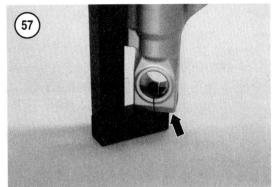

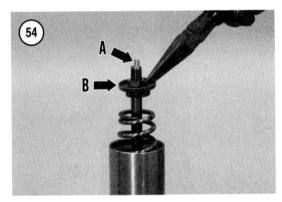

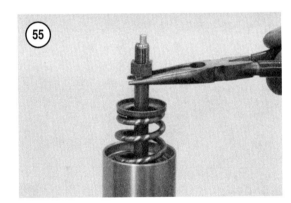

18. Hold the fork tube and the fork slider together and place the fork slider in a vise with soft jaws.

19. Fill the fork with oil, set the oil level as described under *Fork Oil Adjustment* in this section.

NOTE
In the following steps, keep the fork assembly vertical to avoid the loss of fork oil.

20. Install the fork spring with the closer wound coils going in last (**Figure 53**).

21. Install the damper adjust rod (A, **Figure 54**) into the damper rod.

22. Install the spring seat (B, **Figure 54**) onto the top of the fork spring.

NOTE
Fabricate a special rod holder tool to assist in the following steps and for bleeding the fork oil. Make an adapter 2 inches long with an inner metric thread of 12 × 1.0 mm. Attach a piece of rod onto the end of the adapter.

23. Pull the damper rod up (**Figure 55**), install and secure the special rod holder tool onto the top of the damper rod.

24. Install the spacer and index it into the top of the spring seat (**Figure 56**).

25. Install the fork slider in the spring compressor tool (**Figure 57**) following the manufacturer's instructions.

26. Install the fork spring compressor pins on the holes on the spacer (A, **Figure 58**). Tighten securely.

27. Pull up on the special tool (B, **Figure 58**) installed in Step 23, then compress the spring with the spring compressor tool until the top of the damper rod is visible above the spacer (A, **Figure 59**).

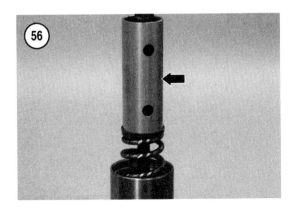

13

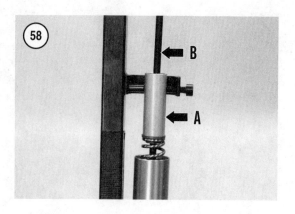

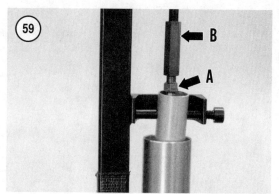

28. Unscrew and remove the rod holder special tool (B, **Figure 59**) from the damper rod.

29. Use a vernier caliper and check the position of the damper rod nut. It must be threaded down so there are 14 mm (0.55 in.) of threads exposed above the nut (**Figure 60**). Adjust the nut if necessary.

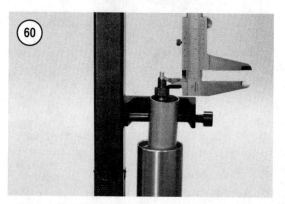

30. On the cap bolt, turn the spring preload adjuster *counterclockwise* (**Figure 61**) all the way out until it stops. This decreases pressure on the spring during final assembly.

> *CAUTION*
> *The following adjustment must be made to the rebound adjuster. If positioned incorrectly in the fork cap, the rebound adjuster cannot be adjusted after the fork has been assembled.*

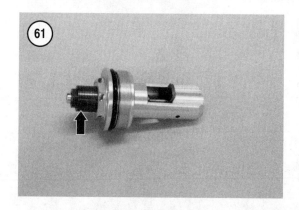

31. Reposition the rebound adjuster within the cap bolt as follows:

   a. Use a small narrow blade screwdriver and turn the adjuster (**Figure 62**) counterclockwise until it *lightly* seats.

   b. Turn the adjuster clockwise three complete turns, then stop.

32. Screw the cap bolt assembly onto the fork damper until it seats against the damper rod, not against the locknut.

33. Secure the cap bolt (A, **Figure 63**) and install a 14-mm open end wrench on the damper rod locknut (B). Tighten the locknut securely, then remove the 14-mm wrench.

34. Release the spring compressor and guide the top cap down through the spacer (**Figure 64**).

35. Keep the fork assembly vertical and remove the spring compressor.

36. Pull the fork tube up against the fork cap, screw the fork cap into the fork tube and tighten securely. Do not tighten to the correct torque at this time.

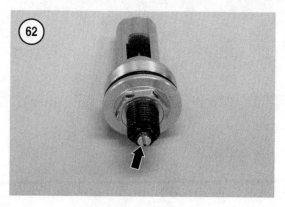

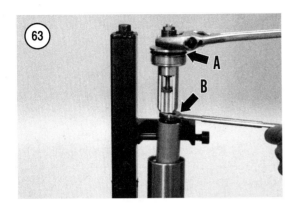

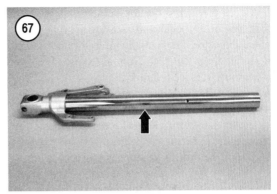

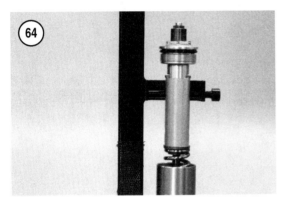

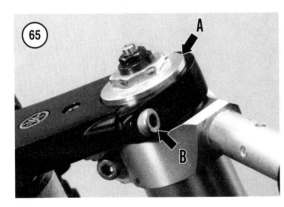

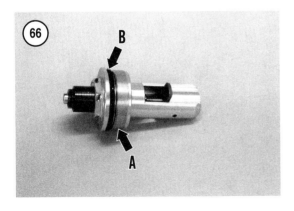

37. Install the fork assemblies as described in this chapter and perform the following:

    a. Tighten the cap bolt (A, **Figure 65**) to 23 N•m (17 ft.-lb.).

    b. Tighten the upper clamp bolt (B, **Figure 65**) to 23 N•m (17 ft.-lb.).

Inspection

Replace any damaged or excessively worn components. Repair damaged threads with an appropriate size metric tap or die. Simply cleaning and reinstalling unserviceable components will not improve performance of the front suspension.

1. Thoroughly clean the parts, except the fork damper, in solvent and dry them. Check the fork tube for signs of wear or scratches.

> *NOTE*
> *Cleaning the fork damper in solvent allows it to absorb some of the solvent that is difficult to remove. Solvent left in the fork damper will contaminate the fork oil. Instead, wipe the fork damper off with a clean cloth and set it aside for inspection and assembly.*

> *NOTE*
> *Do not disassemble the cap bolt as it is an integral assembly. If faulty, replace the cap bolt as an assembly.*

2. Inspect the cap bolt threads (A, **Figure 66**) for wear or damage.

3. Install a *new* O-ring (B, **Figure 66**) on the cap bolt.

4. Check the fork slider (**Figure 67**) for severe wear or scratches. Check for chrome flaking or other damage that could damage the oil seal.

13

5. Check the fork slider for straightness. Place the fork tube on V-blocks and measure the runout with a dial indicator. The manufacturer does not specify a service limit, but if the runout exceeds 0.20 mm (0.008 in.), replace the fork slider.

6. Inspect the cap bolt threads in the fork tube (**Figure 68**) for wear or damage.

7. Make sure the oil hole (**Figure 69**) in the fork slider is clear. Clean out if necessary.

8. Check the fork slider stopper ring and its groove (A, **Figure 70**) for wear or damage. Replace the stopper ring if stretched or damaged.

9. Inspect the oil seal seating area (B, **Figure 70**) in the fork tube for damage or burrs.

10. Check the slider for dents or exterior damage that may cause the upper fork tube to stick.

11. Inspect the brake caliper mounting bosses (A, **Figure 71**) on the slider for cracks or other damage.

12. Check the front axle bore (B, **Figure 71**) in the slider for burrs or damage.

13. Check the front axle clamp bolt(s) for thread damage.

14. Check the compression damping adjuster (**Figure 62**). Make sure it can be turned from one stop to the other.

15. Check the spring preload adjuster (**Figure 61**). Make sure it can be turned from one stop to the other.

16. The fork tube bushings vary among the different years as follows:

   a. 1998-2000 models: there are two bushings and neither is replaceable (no replacement parts available).

   b. 2001 models: there are two bushings and both are replaceable.

   c. 2002-2003 models: there are two bushings and only the lower one is replaceable.

NOTE
The fork tube inner bushing is positioned deep within the fork tube and is not easily accessible. Yamaha does not offer a removal and installation tool for the bushing replacement. If necessary, have the bushing(s) replaced by a Yamaha dealership or suspension specialist.

17. Inspect the fork tube outer (C, **Figure 70**) and inner bushings for scoring, excessive wear or damage. Check for discoloration and material coating damage. Replace the bushings if they are available.

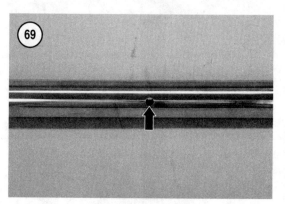

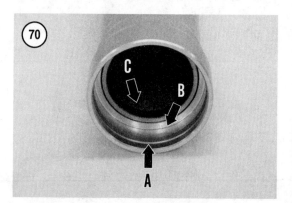

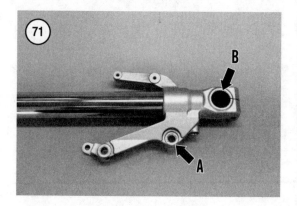

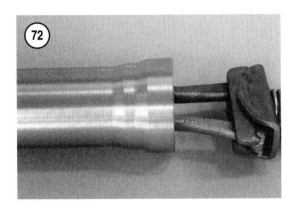

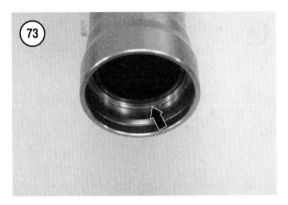

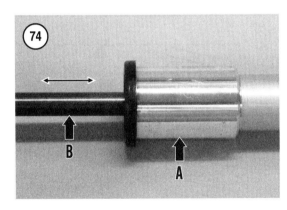

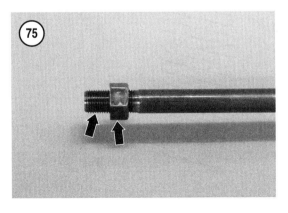

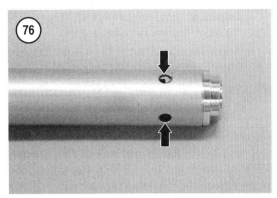

18. To replace the outer bushing, perform the following:

    a. Position the jaws on a 2-jaw pressure screw puller so the jaw fingers are pointing outward.

    b. Install the puller into the fork tube (**Figure 72**) and expand it to grab the underside of the outer bushing.

    c. Attach a slide hammer to the puller and, using in and out strokes, withdraw the bushing from the fork tube.

    d. Apply clean fork oil to the outer surface of the new bushing and to the walls of the fork tube.

    e. Use a socket of the appropriate size and install the new fork bushing into the fork tube. Tap the bushing into the fork tube until it is flush with the fork tube shoulder as shown in **Figure 73**.

> *NOTE*
> *Do not disassemble the damper rod as it is an integral assembly. If bent or faulty, replace the damper rod as an assembly.*

19. Inspect the fork damper assembly as follows:

    a. Check the fork damper housing for straightness.

    b. Hold the fork damper (A, **Figure 74**) and operate the piston rod (B) by hand. Make sure there is no binding or roughness, which indicates a bent piston rod or damaged fork damper.

    c. Check the threads and the nut (**Figure 75**) at the top of the fork damper for damage.

    d. Make sure the oil holes (**Figure 76**) are clear. Clean out if necessary.

13

e. Inspect the fork damper threads (**Figure 77**) for the Allen bolt for wear or damage.

f. Make sure the Allen bolt oil holes (**Figure 78**) are clear. Clean out if necessary.

20. Check the spring seat stopper and spring seat for cracks or distortion.

21. Measure the uncompressed length of the fork spring as shown in **Figure 79**. Replace the spring (**Figure 80**) if it has sagged to less than the new length specification. Replace both the right and left side springs if they are unequal in length.

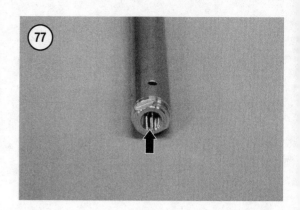

Fork Oil Adjustment

This section describes steps on filling the fork with oil and setting the oil level. Refer to **Table 1** for the recommended type of fork oil.

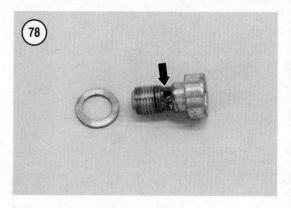

> *NOTE*
> *Steps 1-7 describe how to bleed the fork leg and set the oil level.*

1. Perform Steps 1-19 of *Assembly* in the prior procedure.

2. Push the fork tube down and bottom out against the slider.

3. Position the fork vertically and slowly pour the recommended type and quantity of fork oil into the fork (**Table 1**).

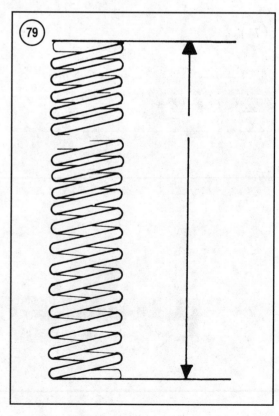

> *NOTE*
> *As oil replaces air during the bleeding procedure (Steps 4-5), the oil level in the fork drops. Continue to add oil to maintain a high oil level in the fork. When bleeding the fork tube, do not be concerned with maintaining or achieving the proper oil capacity. Setting the oil level (Step 9) determines the actual amount of oil used in each fork tube.*

4. Slowly pump the damper rod until fork oil flows out from the hole in the top of the damper rod hole. Continue to pump until all trapped air is expelled.

5. Hold the slider with one hand and slowly extend the fork tube. Repeat this until the fork tube moves smoothly with the same amount of tension through the compression and rebound travel strokes. Then stop with the fork tube bottomed out.

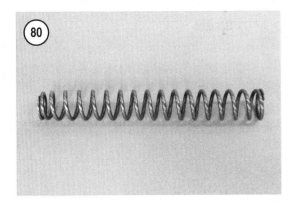

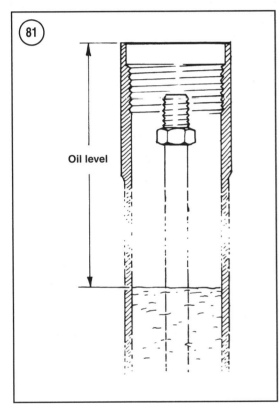

Oil level

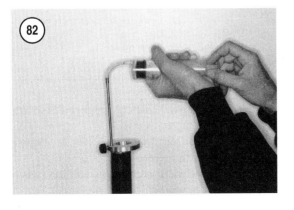

6. Set the fork tube aside for approximately five minutes to allow any suspended air bubbles in the oil to surface.

7. Set the oil level (**Figure 81**) as follows:

   a. Make sure the fork tube is bottomed against the slider and placed in a vertical position.

   b. Use an oil level gauge (**Figure 82**) or vernier caliper and set the oil level to the specification in **Table 1**.

NOTE
If no oil is drawn out when setting the oil level, there is not enough oil in the fork tube. Add more oil and reset the level.

   c. If used, remove the oil level gauge.

8. Perform Steps 20-37 of *Assembly*.

STEERING HEAD AND STEM

The steering head assembly (**Figure 83**) uses retainer-type steel ball bearings. Each bearing consists of three pieces: upper race, lower race and ball bearing. The bearings can be lifted out of their operating positions after removing the steering stem. Do not remove the lower inner race that is pressed onto the steering stem or the bearing races that are pressed into the frame steering head unless they are to be replaced.

Regular maintenance consists of steering inspection, adjustment and bearing lubrication. When the steering cannot be adjusted correctly, the bearings may require replacement. However, to determine bearing condition, the steering assembly must be removed and inspected. Inspect the steering adjustment and lubricate the bearings at the intervals listed in the maintenance schedule in **Table 1** of Chapter Three.

This section describes complete service and adjustment procedures for the steering head assembly.

Removal

Refer to **Figure 83**.

1. Remove the fuel tank as described in Chapter Eight or Chapter Nine.

2. Remove the front wheel as described in Chapter Twelve.

13

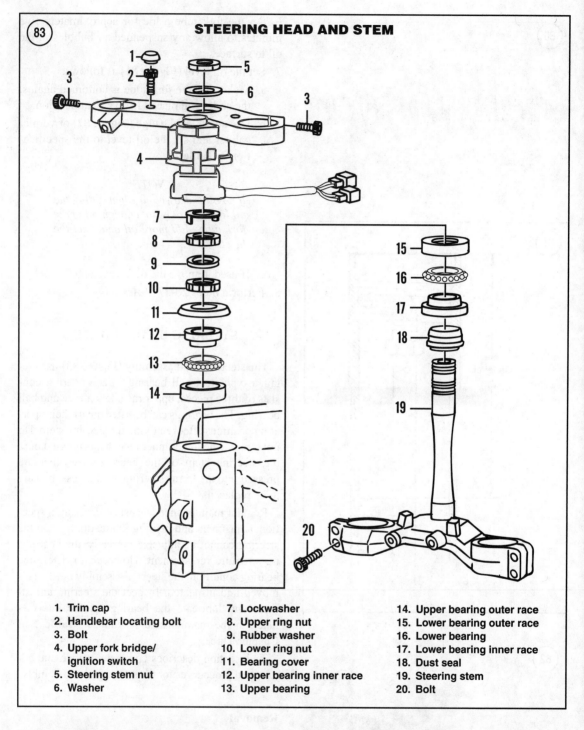

STEERING HEAD AND STEM

1. Trim cap
2. Handlebar locating bolt
3. Bolt
4. Upper fork bridge/
   ignition switch
5. Steering stem nut
6. Washer
7. Lockwasher
8. Upper ring nut
9. Rubber washer
10. Lower ring nut
11. Bearing cover
12. Upper bearing inner race
13. Upper bearing
14. Upper bearing outer race
15. Lower bearing outer race
16. Lower bearing
17. Lower bearing inner race
18. Dust seal
19. Steering stem
20. Bolt

3. Remove the front fender, both side fairings and the front fairing assembly as described in Chapter Sixteen.

4. Remove the bolts (A, **Figure 84**) securing the front brake hose and lower panel (B) to the steering stem. Move the panel out of the way.

5. Remove both handlebars (A, **Figure 85**) as described in this chapter.

6. Remove both front fork assemblies (B, **Figure 85**) as described in this chapter.

7. If still connected, disconnect the ignition switch electrical connector as described in Chapter Ten.

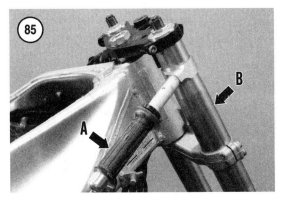

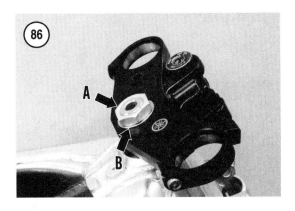

13

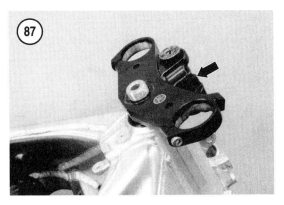

8. Remove the steering stem nut (A, **Figure 86**) and washer (B).

9. Remove the upper fork bridge (**Figure 87**).

10. Slide up and remove the lockwasher (**Figure 88**).

11. Remove the upper ring nut (**Figure 89**) from the steering stem and the rubber washer (**Figure 90**).

12. Loosen the lower ring nut with a spanner wrench (**Figure 91**).

13. Hold the lower end of the steering stem against the frame and remove the lower ring nut (**Figure**

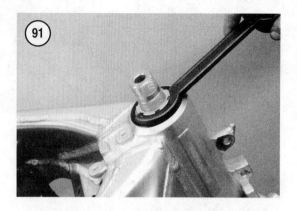

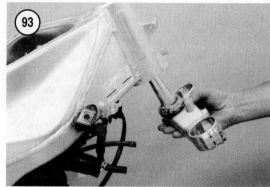

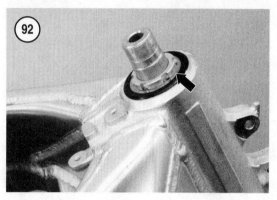

92), then lower the steering stem down (**Figure 93**) and out of the steering head.

14. Remove the bearing cover and the upper bearing and inner race.

15. Remove the lower bearing and inner race from its race on the steering stem.

16. Remove the dust seal (**Figure 94**).

> *NOTE*
> *The upper outer race, lower outer race and lower inner race are installed with a press fit. Only remove these parts when replacing the bearing assembly.*

Steering Stem Assembly and Steering Adjustment

1. Make sure the upper and lower bearing races are properly seated in the steering head. Then lubricate each bearing race with bearing grease (**Figure 95**).

2. Install the *new* dust seal (**Figure 94**) on the steering stem. Press it down until it is correctly seated.

3. Thoroughly lubricate each bearing with bearing grease.

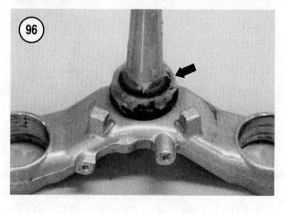

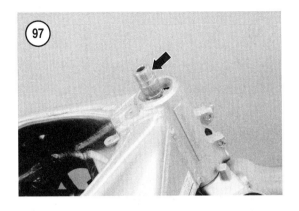

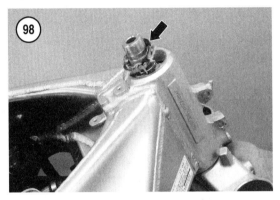

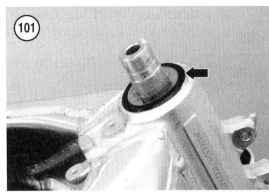

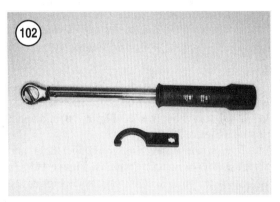

4. Install the lower steering bearing (**Figure 96**) onto the lower bearing inner race.

NOTE
Before installing the steering stem in Step 5, make sure the threads on the stem are clean. Any dirt, grease or other residue on the threads affects the steering stem tightening torque and adjustment.

5. Install the steering stem into the steering head and hold it in place (**Figure 97**). Make sure the lower bearing is centered inside the lower outer race.

6. Install the upper bearing (**Figure 98**) and seat it into its outer race.

7. Install the upper inner race (**Figure 99**) and seat it into the bearing (**Figure 100**).

8. Install the bearing cover (**Figure 101**) and seat it over the upper bearing assembly.

9. Apply oil to the lower ring nut threads and thread it onto the steering stem (**Figure 92**). Tighten finger-tight.

10. Tighten the lower ring nut as follows:

    a. Use a spanner wrench and torque wrench (**Figure 102**) to seat the bearing (A, **Figure**

13

103) in the following steps. Position the spanner wrench (B) at a right angle (90°) to the torque wrench (C).

b. Tighten the lower ring nut (**Figure 104**) to 28 N•m (21 ft.-lb.).

c. Turn the steering stem from lock to lock several times to seat the bearings. The steering stem must pivot smoothly.

d. Loosen the lower ring and retighten to 9 N•m (80 in.-lb.).

NOTE
If the steering stem does not pivot smoothly, one or both bearing assemblies may be damaged. Remove the steering stem and inspect the bearings.

e. Turn the steering stem from lock to lock to recheck bearing play.

11. Install the rubber washer (**Figure 90**) and upper ring nut (**Figure 89**).

12. Tighten the upper ring nut finger-tight and align the slots of both ring nuts (A, **Figure 105**).

13. Align the tabs of a new lockwasher (**Figure 88**) with the grooves in the steering stem adjust nut and install the lockwasher (B, **Figure 105**).

14. Turn the steering stem from lock to lock several times to check for smooth operation.

NOTE
Do not continue with Step 15 until the steering stem turns correctly. If there is excessive play or roughness, recheck the steering adjustment.

15. Install the upper fork bridge (**Figure 87**), the washer (**Figure 106**) and the steering stem head nut (A, **Figure 86**). Tighten the nut finger-tight at this time.

16. Install both handlebars (A, **Figure 85**) and both fork tubes (B) as described in this chapter. Tighten the lower fork bridge clamp bolts to 23 N•m (17 ft.-lb.).

17. Tighten the steering stem head nut (**Figure 107**) to 115 N•m (85 ft.-lb.).

18. Turn the steering stem from lock to lock. Make sure it moves smoothly.

NOTE
If the steering stem is too tight after tightening the steering stem head nut, the bearings may be damaged or the

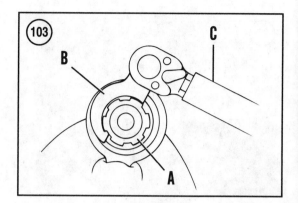

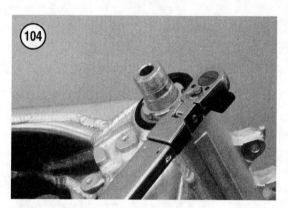

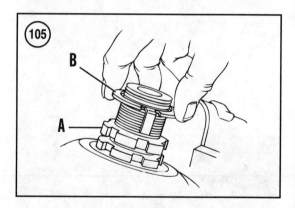

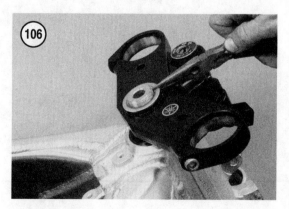

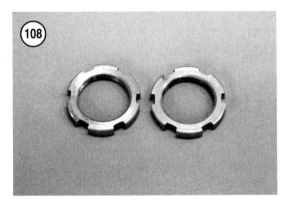

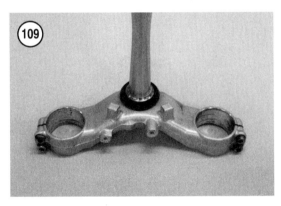

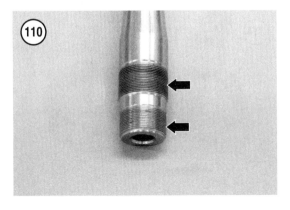

steering stem lower nut was tightened incorrectly. If the steering stem is too loose, the steering will become unstable.

19. Move the front brake hose and lower panel (B, **Figure 84**) onto position on the steering stem and install the bolts (A). Tighten the bolts securely.

20. Connect the ignition switch electrical connector as described in Chapter Ten.

21. Install the front wheel as described in Chapter Twelve.

22. Install both side fairing assemblies and the front fairing as described in Chapter Sixteen.

23. Install the fuel tank as described in Chapter Eight or Chapter Nine.

24. Check that the front brake works properly.

> *WARNING*
> *Do not ride the motorcycle until the horn, control cables and front brake all work properly.*

Inspection

Replace parts that show excessive wear or damage as described in this section.

> *WARNING*
> *The improper repair of damaged frame and steering components can cause the loss of steering control. If there is apparent frame, steering stem or fork bridge damage, consult with a Yamaha dealership or qualified frame shop.*

1. Clean and dry all parts.

2. Check the frame for cracks and fractures.

3. Inspect the steering stem nut, upper and lower nuts (**Figure 108**) for excessive wear or damage.

4. Inspect the rubber washer for tearing, deterioration or other damage.

5. Check the steering stem for (**Figure 109**):
   a. Cracked or bent stem.
   b. Damaged lower bridge.
   c. Damaged upper threads (**Figure 110**).

6. Check the upper fork bridge for cracks or other damage. Replace if necessary.

7. Inspect the bearing assemblies as follows:
   a. Inspect the bearing inner races for severe wear, pitting, cracks or other damage. To re-

13

place the lower inner bearing race (**Figure 111**) and the outer bearing races (**Figure 112**), refer to the procedures in this chapter.

b. Inspect the upper and lower bearings (**Figure 113**) for pitting, excessive wear, corrosion, retainer damage or discoloration.

c. Even if only one set is defective, replace the upper and lower bearing assemblies at the same time.

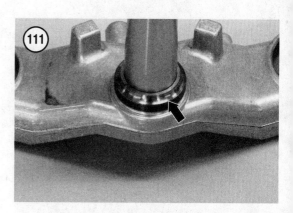

NOTE
*Each bearing assembly consists of the bearing and an inner and outer race (**Figure 114**). Always replace the bearings in upper and lower sets.*

8. When reusing bearings, clean them thoroughly with a bearing degreaser and dry thoroughly. Repack each bearing with grease.

STEERING HEAD BEARING RACES

The upper and lower bearing outer races must not be removed unless they are going to be replaced. These races are pressed into place and are damaged during removal. If removed, replace both the outer race along with the bearings at the same time. Never reuse an outer race that has been removed. It is no longer true and will damage the bearings if reused.

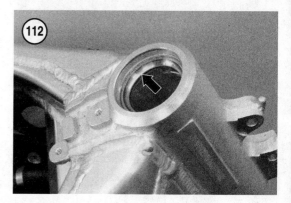

Do not remove the upper and lower outer bearing races unless they are going to be replaced. The bearing/race assembly must be replaced in sets.

CAUTION
If any binding is observed when removing or installing the bearing races, stop and release all tension from the bearing race. Check the tool alignment to make sure the bearing race is moving evenly in its mounting bore. Otherwise, the bearing race may gouge the frame mounting bore and cause permanent damage.

NOTE
The following procedure describes simple home techniques to remove the bearing races used on these models. If removal is difficult, do not chance damage to the steering head portion of the frame or new bearing races. Have a Yamaha dealership perform this procedure.

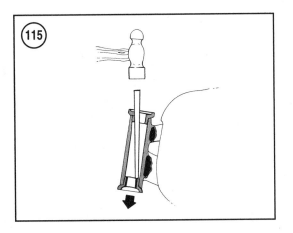

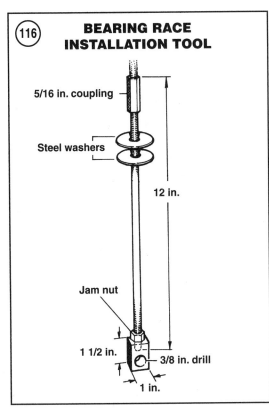

BEARING RACE INSTALLATION TOOL

5/16 in. coupling

Steel washers

12 in.

Jam nut

1 1/2 in.

3/8 in. drill

1 in.

1. Remove the steering stem (this chapter).

2. Insert an aluminum drift into the steering head using the cutouts in frame for the drift. Carefully tap the lower race out from the steering head (**Figure 115**). Repeat this procedure for the upper race.

3. Chill the new bearing outer races in a freezer for a few hours to shrink the outer diameter of the race as much as possible.

4. Clean the race seats in the steering head. Check for cracks or other damage.

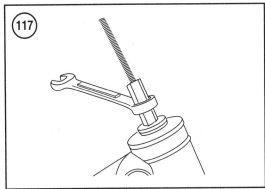

5. Insert the new race into the steering head with the cupped side facing out and square the race with the race bore.

> *CAUTION*
> *To avoid damaging the races and the race seats in the steering head, install the races as described in the following.*

6. Assemble a puller tool (**Figure 116**). The block mounted at the bottom of the threaded rod is used as a T-handle to hold the stationary when the bearing race is being installed from the opposite end. If the handle is not available, hold the bottom of the rod with two nuts locked together. The hole drilled through the block must be large enough to accept a suitable rod for a T-handle. Two or more *thick* washers are also required. The outer diameter of the washers must be greater than the outer diameter of the bearing races.

> *CAUTION*
> *When installing the bearing outer races with the threaded rod or similar tool, do not let the rod or tool contact the face of the bearing race. It could damage the race.*

7. To install the upper race, insert the puller through the bottom of the steering head. Seat the lower washer or plate against the steering head.

8. At the top of the steering stem, slide the large washer down. Seat it squarely on top of the bearing race. Install the required washers and coupling nut on the rod.

9. Hand-tighten the coupling nut and center the washer on the upper bearing race.

10. Hold the threaded rod to prevent it from turning and tighten the coupling nut with a wrench (**Figure 117**). Continue to tighten the coupling until the race

13

is completely drawn into the steering head. Remove the puller assembly and inspect the bearing race. It should be bottomed in the steering head as shown in **Figure 112**.

11. Turn the special tool over and repeat this procedure for the lower bearing race.

STEERING STEM BEARING REPLACEMENT

Do not remove the steering stem lower bearing outer race unless it is going to be replaced. The lower bearing outer race can be difficult to remove. If it cannot be removed as described in this procedure, have a Yamaha dealership perform this procedure.

Never reinstall a lower bearing outer race, which has been removed. It is no longer true and will damage the rest of the bearing assembly if reused.

1. Install the steering stem nut onto the top of the steering stem to protect the threads.

2. Loosen the lower bearing assembly, or lower bearing outer race, from the shoulder at the base of the steering stem with a chisel as shown in **Figure 118**. Slide the lower race off the steering stem. Discard the lower race.

3. Clean the steering stem with solvent and dry it thoroughly.

4. Position the lower bearing outer race onto the steering stem until it stops on the raised shoulder.

5. Align the lower bearing outer race with the machined shoulder on the steering stem.

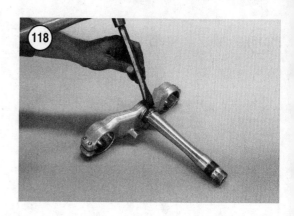

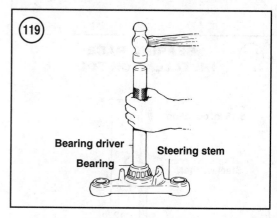

Bearing driver — Steering stem
Bearing

6. Slide a piece of pipe (**Figure 119**) over the steering stem until it seats against the inner portion of the lower bearing race.

7. Drive the lower bearing onto the steering stem until it bottoms.

8. Pack the bearing outer race with lithium grease.

Table 1 FRONT SUSPENSION SPECIFICATIONS

Item	Specification	Service limit
Front fork travel		
1998-2001 models	135 mm (5.31 in.)	–
2002-2003 models	120 mm (4.72 in.)	–
Fork oil (1998-1999 models)		
Type	Suspension oil *01* or an equivalent	
Capacity	477 ml (16.1 U.S. oz.)	
Oil level	78 mm (3.07 in.)	
Fork oil (2000-2001 models)		
Type	Suspension oil *01* or an equivalent	
Capacity	482 ml (16.3 U.S. oz.)	
Oil level	74 mm (2.91 in.)	
	(continued)	

Table 1 FRONT SUSPENSION SPECIFICATIONS (continued)

Item	Specification	Service limit
Fork oil (2002-2003 models)		
Type	Suspension oil *01* or an equivalent	
Capacity	543 ml (18.37 U.S. oz.)	
Oil level	74 mm (2.91 in.)	
Fork spring free length		
1998-2001 models	255 mm (10.00 in.)	–
2002-2003 models	251 mm (9.88 in.)	246 mm (9.69 in.)
Fork spring spacer length		
1998-2001 models	85 mm (3.35 in.)	–
2002-2003 models	74 mm (2.91 in.)	–

Table 2 FRONT FORK ADJUSTMENT SPECIFICATIONS

Spring preload adjusting positions	
Minimum	8
Standard	6
Maximum	1
Rebound damping adjusting positions	
1998-1999 models	
Minimum	13
Standard	5
Maximum	1
2000-2001 models	
Minimum	11
Standard	5
Maximum	1
2002-2003 models	
Minimum	26
Standard	13
Maximum	1
Compression damping adjusting positions*	
1998-1999 models	
Minimum	11
Standard	5
Maximum	1
2000-2001 models	
Minimum	9
Standard	5
Maximum	1
2002-2003 models	
Minimum	20
Standard	13
Maximum	1

*Number of turns from the fully turned-in position.

Table 3 FRONT SUSPENSION AND STEERING TORQUE SPECIFICATIONS

Item	N•m	in.-lb.	ft.-lb.
Damper rod Allen bolt*	40	–	30
Fork bridge			
Upper clamp bolt	23	–	17
Lower clamp bolts	23	–	17
		(continued)	

13

Table 3 FRONT SUSPENSION AND STEERING TORQUE SPECIFICATIONS (continued)

Item	N•m	in.-lb.	ft.-lb.
Front caliper mounting bolt	40	–	30
Front fork cap bolt	23	–	17
Front master cylinder clamp bolts			
1998-2001 models	13	115	–
2002-2003 models	9	80	–
Handlebar locating bolt	13	115	–
Handlebar clamp bolt	17	–	13
Handlebar weight mounting screw	4	35	–
Steering stem lower ring nut			
Initial tightening	28	–	21
Final tightening	9	80	–
Steering stem head nut	115	–	85

*Apply a medium strength threadlock to the threads.

CHAPTER FOURTEEN

REAR SUSPENSION

This chapter describes repair and replacement procedures for the rear suspension components. Refer to Chapter Eleven for rear wheel, driven flange and rear axle.

Rear suspension specifications are in **Table 1** and **Table 2** at the end of this chapter.

> *WARNING*
> *Replace all rear suspension fasteners with parts of the same type. Do not use a replacement part of lesser quality or substitute design, as this may affect the performance of the system or result in failure of the part, leading to loss of motorcycle control. The torque specifications listed must be used during installation to ensure proper component retention.*

SHOCK LINKAGE

Removal

Refer to **Figure 1**.

1. Support the motorcycle on level ground.

2. If a jack is going to be used in Step 4A, remove the bottom cowl as described in Chapter Sixteen.

3. Block the front wheel so the motorcycle will not roll in either direction while on the jack or safety stand.

> *CAUTION*
> *If using a jack, place a piece of wood on the jack pad to protect the oil pan.*

4A. If necessary, place a suitable size jack or wooden blocks under the crankcase to support the motorcycle with the rear wheel off the ground.

4B. Raise the rear of the motorcycle with a swing arm safety stand.

> *WARNING*
> *Do not service the suspension linkage when the exhaust system is hot.*

5. Remove the rear wheel as described in Chapter Twelve.

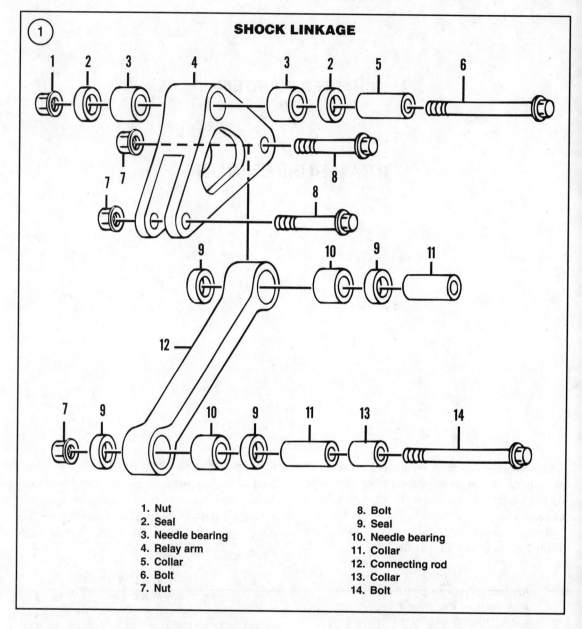

SHOCK LINKAGE

1. Nut
2. Seal
3. Needle bearing
4. Relay arm
5. Collar
6. Bolt
7. Nut
8. Bolt
9. Seal
10. Needle bearing
11. Collar
12. Connecting rod
13. Collar
14. Bolt

6. Remove the bolt and self-locking nut (**Figure 2**) securing the shock absorber to the relay arm.

7. Remove the bolt and self-locking nut (A, **Figure 3**) securing the relay arm to the connecting rod.

8. Lower the connecting rod (B, **Figure 3**).

9. Remove the bolt and self-locking nut (C, **Figure 3**) securing the relay arm to the swing arm. Remove the relay arm (D, **Figure 3**).

10. Remove the bolt (A, **Figure 4**) and collar (B) securing the connecting rod to the frame. Remove the connecting rod (C, **Figure 4**).

11. Inspect the shock linkage as described in this chapter.

Installation

Refer to **Figure 1**.

> *WARNING*
> *Replace all self-locking nuts as they are removed, since they lose some of their locking ability every time they are removed.*

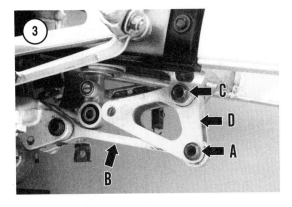

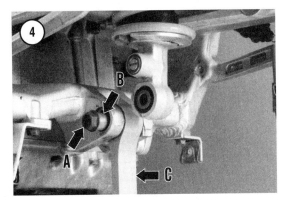

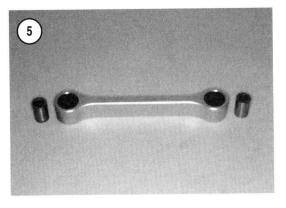

CAUTION
All mounting bolts are of a different length and must be installed in the correct location as shown in Figure 1. Install all bolts from the left side.

1. Apply a light coat of lithium grease to all of the shock linkage mounting bolts. Do not apply grease to the mounting bolt threads or nuts. These must be tightened with dry threads.

NOTE
The connecting rod is symmetrical and can be installed in either direction.

2. Install the connecting rod (C, **Figure 4**) onto the frame mount. Install the bolt (A, **Figure 4**) and collar (B) from the left side. Install a *new* self-locking nut and tighten finger-tight.

3. Correctly position the relay arm onto the swing arm (D, **Figure 3**).

4. Install the bolt from the left side (C, **Figure 3**). Install a *new* self-locking nut and tighten finger-tight.

5. Move the connecting rod (B, **Figure 3**) into position on the relay arm.

6. Install the bolt from the left side (A, **Figure 3**). Install a *new* self-locking nut and tighten finger-tight.

7. Move the lower portion of the shock absorber into position on the relay arm.

8. Install the bolt from the left side (**Figure 2**). Install a *new* self-locking nut and tighten finger-tight.

9. Tighten all linkage bolts and self-locking nuts and tighten to the following:
   a. 1998-2001: 40 N•m (30 ft.-lb.).
   b. 2002-2003: 45 N•m (33 ft.-lb.).

10. Install the rear wheel as described in Chapter Twelve.

11. Install the bottom cowl as described in Chapter Sixteen.

14

Inspection

Replace worn or damaged parts as described in this chapter. The pivot collars, oil seals and needle bearings are identical (same part number) for both pivot areas.

1. Remove both pivot collars (**Figure 5**) from the connecting rod.

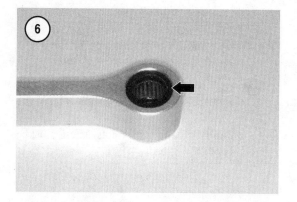

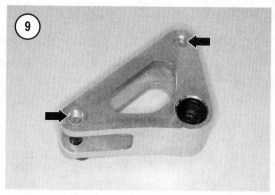

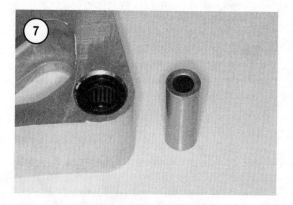

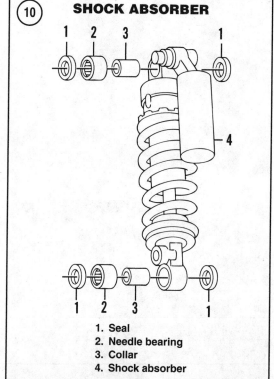

SHOCK ABSORBER

1. Seal
2. Needle bearing
3. Collar
4. Shock absorber

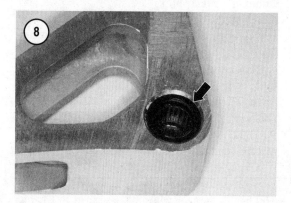

2. If necessary, pry the seals (**Figure 6**) out of both pivot areas of the connecting rod.

3. Remove the pivot collar (**Figure 7**) from the relay arm.

4. If necessary, pry the seals (**Figure 8**) out of the pivot area of the relay arm.

5. Clean and dry all mounting bolts and nuts. Replace all self-locking nuts.

6. Clean the connecting rod pivot collars and check for wear.

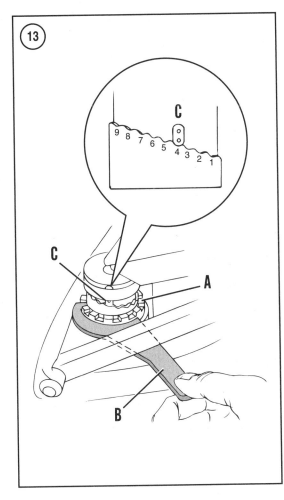

9. Inspect the relay arm pivot areas (**Figure 9**) for wear and elongation.

> *CAUTION*
> *If the needle bearings do not require replacement, do not remove them for inspection or lubrication, as they may be damaged during removal and reinstallation.*

10. Clean the bearings once again in solvent and thoroughly dry them with compressed air.

11. Pack the bearings with lithium grease.

12. Pack the lips of the new seals with the same grease and install into position on the connecting rod (**Figure 6**) and relay arm (**Figure 8**). Install the seals with the closed side facing out. Push them into place by hand.

13. Apply a thin film of the same grease to the outside of each collar and install the collars into their original mounting position. Center them in their bearings.

SHOCK ABSORBER

A single rear shock absorber (**Figure 10**) with adjustable preload, compression and rebound is used on all models. **Table 1** lists the standard, minimum and maximum settings for all three adjustments.

Spring Preload Adjustment

Set the spring preload by adjusting the notched cam collar. Refer to **Figure 11** for 1998-2001 models or **Figure 12** for 2002-2003 models. Use the pin spanner tool provided in the motorcycle tool kit. Turn the spring adjusting ring (A, **Figure 13**) with the pin spanner (B) so a notch sets against the index tab on the shock absorber housing (C). The cam positions are numbered 1 (softest) through 9 (heaviest). Turn the spring adjusting ring clockwise to decrease spring preload or counterclockwise to increase preload.

If necessary, use a drift and hammer to adjust the cam collar.

Rebound Damping Adjustment

The rear shock absorber is equipped with a rebound damping adjuster (**Figure 14**) on the bottom

7. Check each needle bearing for cracks, rust and other damage. Replace damaged bearings as described under *Bearing Replacement* in this chapter.

8. Inspect the pivot collars for excessive wear, rust or damage. Check the collars for burrs or nicks that may damage the seals. Remove burrs or nicks with sandpaper or a fine cut file.

14

left side of the shock housing. Turn the rebound adjuster screw with a screwdriver (**Figure 15**).

> *CAUTION*
> *Do not turn the rebound damping adjuster past the point where it stops at its full clockwise or counterclockwise positions. Doing so damages the adjuster screw and requires replacement of the shock absorber.*

1. To set the rebound damping adjuster to the maximum rebound position, turn the rebound adjuster clockwise until it stops. Then turn it back one click. This is the maximum hard position.
2. To set the rebound damping adjustment to the standard position, turn the adjuster counterclockwise 15 clicks from the maximum setting.
3. To set the rebound damping adjustment to the softest position, turn the adjuster counterclockwise 20 clicks from the maximum setting.

Compression Damping Adjustment

The rear shock absorber is equipped with a compression damping adjuster (**Figure 16**) on the upper end of the shock reservoir. Turn the compression adjuster screw with a screwdriver (**Figure 17**).

> *CAUTION*
> *Do not turn the compression damping adjuster past the point where it stops at its full clockwise or counterclockwise positions. Doing so damages the adjuster screw and requires replacement of the shock absorber.*

1. To set the compression damping adjuster to the maximum compression position, turn the rebound adjuster clockwise until it stops. Then turn it back one click. This is the maximum hard position.
2. To set the compression damping adjustment to the standard position, turn the adjuster counterclockwise 15 clicks from the maximum setting.
3. To set the compression damping adjustment to the softest position, turn the adjuster counterclockwise 20 clicks from the maximum setting.

Removal/Installation

Refer to **Figure 10**.
1. Support the motorcycle on level ground.

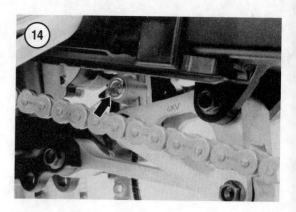

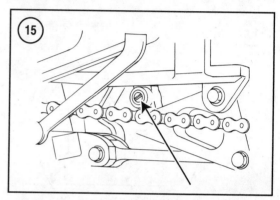

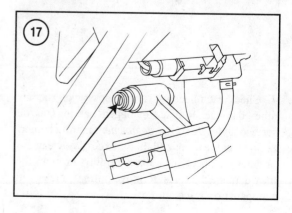

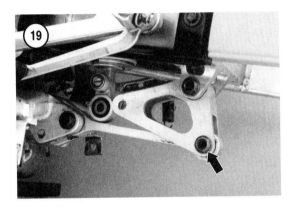

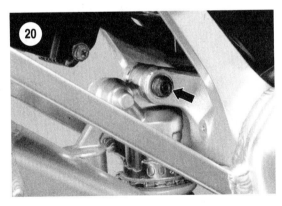

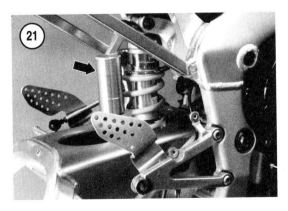

2. If a jack is going to be used in Step 4A, remove the bottom cowl as described in Chapter Sixteen.

3. Block the front wheel so the motorcycle will not roll either direction while on the jack or safety stand.

CAUTION
If using a jack, place a piece of wood on the jack pad to protect the oil pan.

4A. If necessary, place a suitable size jack or wooden blocks under the crankcase to support the motorcycle with the rear wheel off the ground.

4B. Raise the rear of the motorcycle with a swing arm safety stand.

WARNING
Do not service the shock absorber when the exhaust system is hot.

5. Remove the bolt and self-locking nut (**Figure 18**) securing the shock absorber to the relay arm.

6. Remove the bolt and self-locking nut (**Figure 19**) securing the relay arm to the connecting rod.

7. Lower the relay arm and connecting rod.

8. Remove the bolt, collar and self-locking nut (**Figure 20**) securing the upper portion of the shock absorber to the frame mount.

9. Carefully guide the shock absorber assembly down through the swing arm opening and remove the shock absorber assembly.

10. Apply a light coat of lithium grease to the shock absorber mounting bolts. Do not apply grease to the mounting bolt threads or nuts. These fasteners must be tightened with dry threads.

11. Install the shock absorber assembly into the frame with the reservoir (**Figure 21**) facing the rear.

12. Install the upper mounting bolt and collar (**Figure 22**) from the left side. Install a *new* self-locking nut (**Figure 20**) and tighten finger-tight.

14

13. Raise the relay arm and connecting rod up into position. Install the lower mounting bolt (**Figure 19**) from the left side, then install a *new* self-locking nut and tighten finger-tight.

14. Move the lower end of the shock absorber into position on the relay arm. Install the lower mounting bolt (**Figure 18**) from the left side, then install a *new* self-locking nut and tighten finger-tight.

15. Tighten all mounting bolts and self-locking nuts to the following:

    a. 1998-2001: 40 N•m (30 ft.-lb.).

    b. 2002-on: 45 N•m (33 ft.-lb.).

Inspection

Replace the shock absorber if it is leaking oil or shows damage as described in this section.

> *WARNING*
> *The shock absorber housing contains high-pressure nitrogen gas. Do not tamper with or attempt to open the shock housing. Do not place it near an open flame or other extreme heat. Do not dispose of the shock assembly. Take it to a dealership where it can be deactivated and disposed of properly.*

> *CAUTION*
> *The shock absorber is not serviceable. The only replacement parts available for the shocks are the collars and seals. Do not disassemble the shock absorber.*

1. Check the shock housing (A, **Figure 23**) for dents, damage or oil leakage.

2. Check the spring (B, **Figure 23**) for cracks or other damage. Check the spring seats for damage. The spring is not removable. If damaged, replace the shock absorber.

3. Inspect the rubber stopper (**Figure 24**) for wear or deterioration.

4. Push the collars (**Figure 25**) out of the upper and lower mounts.

5. Inspect the collars for scoring or excessive wear.

6. Pry the seals (A, **Figure 26**) out of the upper and lower mounts. The seals are easy to remove and can be reused if not damaged.

7. Check the needle bearings (B, **Figure 26**) for rust, excessive wear or damage. The needle bear-

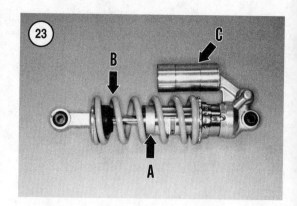

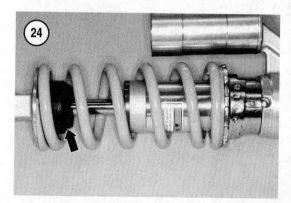

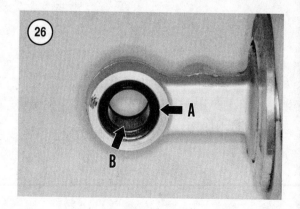

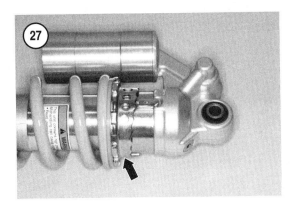

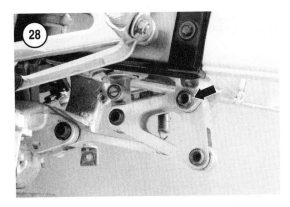

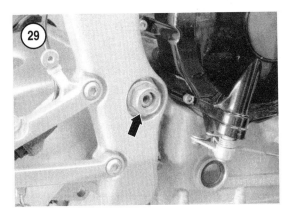

SWING ARM

Preliminary Inspection

The condition of the swing arm bearings can greatly affect the handling of the motorcycle. Worn bearings will cause wheel hop, pulling to one side under acceleration and pulling to the other side during braking. To check the condition of the swing arm bearings, perform the following procedure.

1. Remove the rear wheel (Chapter Twelve).
2. Remove the bolt and nut (**Figure 28**) securing the relay arm to the swing arm. Lower the relay arm and connecting rod.
3. The swing arm is now free to move under its own weight.
4. On the right side of the frame, make sure the swing arm pivot nut (**Figure 29**) is tight.

NOTE
Have an assistant steady the motorcycle when performing Step 5 and Step 6.

5. Grasp both ends of the swing arm and attempt to move it from side to side in a horizontal arc. If more than a slight amount of movement is felt, the bearings are worn and must be replaced.
6. Grasp both ends of the swing arm and move it up and down. The swing arm should move smoothly with no binding or abnormal noise from the bearings. If there is binding or noise, the bearings are worn and must be replaced.
7. Move the swing arm and relay arm into position. Install the bolt (**Figure 28**) from the left side and install a *new* self-locking nut. Tighten the bolt and nut to the following:
   a. 1999-2001 models: 40 N•m (30 ft.-lb.).
   b. 2002-2003 models: 45 N•m (33 ft.-lb.).
8. Install the rear wheel (Chapter Twelve).

Removal

Refer to **Figure 30**.

NOTE
On 2002-2003 models, a Yamaha special tool (U.S. part No. YM-01471, U.K. part No. 90890-01471) is required to tighten the pivot shaft adjusting bolt during the installation procedure.

ings are not replaceable and if damaged, replace the shock absorber.

8. Replace the seals (A, **Figure 26**) if excessively worn or damaged. Pack the lip of each seal with lithium grease prior to installation. Install the seals with their closed side facing out.
9. Inspect the reservoir (C, **Figure 23**) for leakage or damage. If any parts are damaged, replace the shock absorber assembly.
10. Check that the spring preload adjuster (**Figure 27**, typical) rotates freely with the spanner wrench.

14

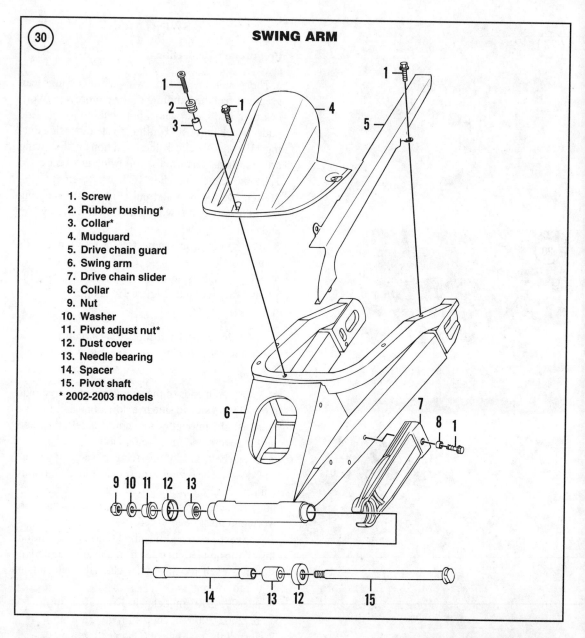

SWING ARM

30

1. Screw
2. Rubber bushing*
3. Collar*
4. Mudguard
5. Drive chain guard
6. Swing arm
7. Drive chain slider
8. Collar
9. Nut
10. Washer
11. Pivot adjust nut*
12. Dust cover
13. Needle bearing
14. Spacer
15. Pivot shaft
* 2002-2003 models

1. Remove the muffler as described in Chapter Eight or Chapter Nine. Wrap a plastic bag around the exhaust pipe opening to keep out debris.

2. Remove the screws securing the mudguard (**Figure 31**, typical) and remove the mudguard from the top of the swing arm. On 2002-2003 models, do not lose the collars located within the rubber grommets at the mounting holes.

3. Remove the drive sprocket cover as described in Chapter Six.

4. Remove the screws securing the drive chain guard and remove the guard from the swing arm.

31

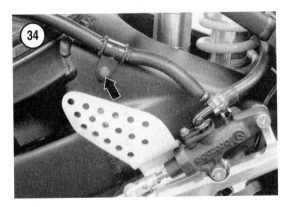

5. Remove the rear wheel (A, **Figure 32**) as described in Chapter Twelve.

6. Remove the drive chain as described in Chapter Twelve.

7. Remove the shock absorber and shock linkage as described in this chapter.

8A. On 1998-2001 models, perform the following:

    a. Remove the bolt and clamp (A, **Figure 33**) securing the front portion of the rear brake hose to the top of the swing arm. Unhook the lower portion of the hose from the underside of the swing arm (B, **Figure 33**).

    b. Remove the bolt and clamp securing the rear portion of the rear brake hose to the bottom of the swing arm.

    c. Move the caliper out through the right side of the swing arm and tie the caliper up to the frame.

8B. On 2002-2003 models, remove the bolt on the front clamp (**Figure 34**) and the rear bolt and bracket (B, **Figure 32**) securing the rear brake hose to the swing arm. Move the caliper out through the right side of the swing arm and tie the caliper up to the frame.

9. On the right side, loosen and remove the pivot shaft nut (**Figure 29**) and washer (**Figure 35**).

10. Lower the swing arm and rest it on the ground (A, **Figure 36**).

11. Carefully tap the pivot shaft into the right side of the frame and then pull the shaft (B, **Figure 36**) from the left side of the frame.

12. Remove the swing arm from the frame. Be careful not to damage the rear brake light switch. On 2002-2003 models, do not lose the adjust bolt on the right side.

13. If the swing arm bearings are not going to be serviced, place a strip of duct tape over each pivot

14

area. This will protect the bearing assemblies and prevent the loss of any small parts.

14. Inspect the swing arm as described in this chapter. Lubricate all bearings as described in this chapter.

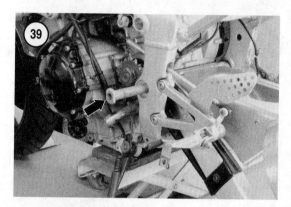

Installation

> *NOTE*
> *Have an assistant available before starting swing arm installation. The swing arm can be installed by one person, but the job is much easier with two.*

> *NOTE*
> *On 2002-2003 models, a pivot shaft wrench (part No. YM-01471) is required to tighten the pivot shaft adjusting bolt.*

1. If used, remove the duct tape from each pivot area of the swing arm. Make sure the dust cover (**Figure 37**) is in place on each side of the pivot area.

2. If removed, install the drive chain slider (**Figure 38**) onto the swing arm and tighten the bolt securely.

3. Lubricate the swing arm pivot shaft and needle bearings with lithium grease prior to installation.

4. If still in place, engage the drive chain with the swing arm and locate it over the pivot left side shaft area.

5. Carefully position the swing arm into position. Be careful not to damage the rear brake light switch.

6. From the left side of the motorcycle, install the swing arm pivot shaft (**Figure 39**) from the left side of the frame, through the swing arm pivot area and the right side of the frame. Correctly position the

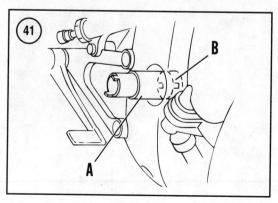

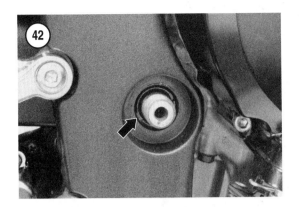

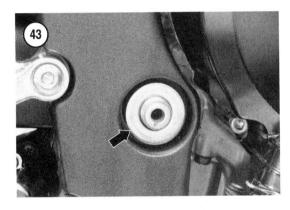

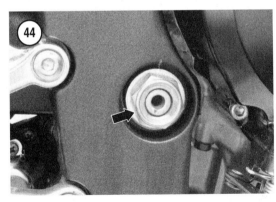

flats of the pivot shaft into the frame receptacle as shown in **Figure 40** to lock the pivot shaft in place.

7. On 2002-2003 models, on the right side use the special tool (A, **Figure 41**) and tighten the pivot adjust bolt (B) to 5 N•m (44 in.-lb.). Refer to **Figure 42**.

8. On the right side, install the washer (**Figure 43**) and pivot nut (**Figure 44**) onto the end of the pivot shaft and tighten finger-tight at this time.

9. Engage the drive chain with the engine sprocket.

10. Grab the end of each arm and raise and lower the swing arm. The swing arm should pivot smoothly with no binding.

11. Secure the pivot shaft and tighten the pivot shaft nut (**Figure 45**) to the following:

    a. 1998-2001 models: 125 N•m (92 ft.-lb.).

    b. 2002-2003 models: 105 N•m (77 ft.-lb.).

12. Install the caliper in through the right side of the swing arm and into position on the swing arm (**Figure 46**).

13A. On 1998-2001 models, perform the following:

    a. Install the bolt and clamp (A, **Figure 33**) securing the front portion of the rear brake hose to the top of the swing arm. Tighten the bolt securely.

    b. Install the bolt and clamp (B, **Figure 33**) securing the rear portion of the rear brake hose to the bottom of the swing arm. Tighten the bolt securely.

13B. On 2002-2003 models, install the bolt on the front clamp (**Figure 34**) and the rear bolt and bracket (B, **Figure 32**) securing the rear brake hose to the swing arm. Tighten the bolts securely.

14. Install the mudguard (**Figure 31**, typical) and the screws onto the top of the swing arm. Tighten the screws securely. On 2002-2003 models, make sure the three collars are installed within the rubber grommets.

14

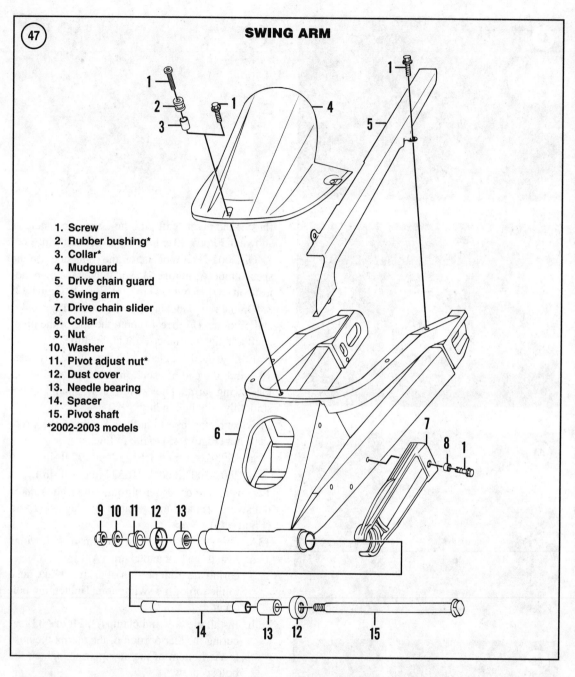

SWING ARM ㊼

1. Screw
2. Rubber bushing*
3. Collar*
4. Mudguard
5. Drive chain guard
6. Swing arm
7. Drive chain slider
8. Collar
9. Nut
10. Washer
11. Pivot adjust nut*
12. Dust cover
13. Needle bearing
14. Spacer
15. Pivot shaft
*2002-2003 models

15. Install the drive chain guard and screws and tighten securely.

16. Install the shock absorber and shock linkage as described in this chapter.

17. Install the rear wheel as described in Chapter Twelve.

18. Install the drive sprocket cover and tighten the bolts securely.

19. Remove the plastic bag from the exhaust pipe and install the muffler as described in Chapter Four.

20. Adjust the chain as described in Chapter Three.

Disassembly

Refer to **Figure 47**.

1. Remove the swing arm as described in this chapter.

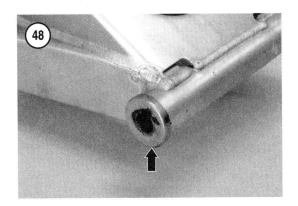

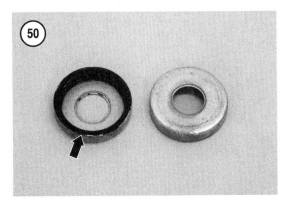

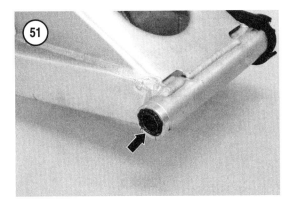

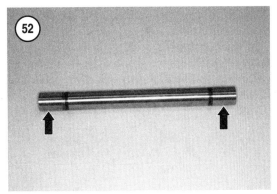

2. Remove the screw and collar securing the chain slider (**Figure 31**, typical) and remove it from the swing arm.

3. Remove the dust seal (**Figure 48**) from each side of the pivot area.

4. Withdraw the spacer (**Figure 49**) from the pivot area.

5. Inspect the swing arm as described in this chapter.

Assembly

1. Lubricate the needle bearings and the pivot collar with lithium grease.

2. Lubricate the spacer ends where they ride on the needle bearings with lithium grease.

3. Apply a light coat of lithium grease to the seals (**Figure 50**) within the dust seals and to the pivot ends of the swing arm (**Figure 51**).

4. Install the dust seal (**Figure 48**) onto each side of the pivot area. Press them on until completely seated.

5. Install the chain slider (**Figure 31**) onto the left side of the swing arm. Install the collar and screw and tighten the screw securely.

6. Install the swing arm assembly as described in this chapter.

Inspection

Replace parts that show excessive wear or damage as described in this section.

1. Clean and dry all parts.

2. Inspect the spacer for excessive wear, rust or other damage. If the spacer outer surface (**Figure 52**) is excessively worn or damaged, the needle bearings are probably damaged.

14

3. Inspect the swing arm needle bearings (**Figure 53**) for overheating, rust, or broken or dented needles. Then check the bearing fit in its mounting bore. The bearing(s) must be a tight fit. If the pivot collar was damaged, replace the pivot collar and needle bearings as a set at the same time.

NOTE
*Replace damaged bearings as described under **Bearing Replacement** in this section.*

4. Check the swing arm for cracks (**Figure 54**) or fractures and broken welds (**Figure 55**).

5. Check the pivot shaft runout with a set of V-blocks and a dial indicator (**Figure 56**). If the pivot shaft is bent, replace it. The manufacturer does not provide a wear limit specification for the pivot shaft.

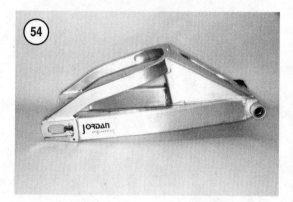

6. Inspect the drive chain slider (**Figure 38**) for wear, cracks or other signs of damage.

7. Inspect the relay arm attachment pivot points (**Figure 57**) for wear or elongation.

8. Check the drive chain adjuster bolt and locknut (**Figure 58**) for damage. Make sure there is no thread damage in the swing arm for the adjuster bolt. Clean out with a metric tap if necessary.

BEARING REPLACEMENT

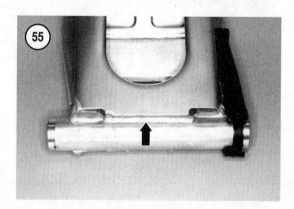

NOTE
*For general information on bearing replacement, refer to **Bearing Replacement** in Chapter One.*

Swing Arm Bearings

Do not remove the swing arm needle bearings unless they must be replaced. The needle bearings are pressed onto the swing arm and a blind bearing puller is required to remove them. The needle bearings can be installed with a homemade tool.

NOTE
If the needle bearings are replaced, replace the pivot collars at the same time. These parts should always be replaced as a set.

1. If still installed, remove the dust seals (**Figure 48**) and the spacer (**Figure 49**) from the needle bearings.

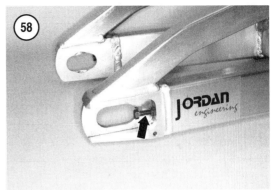

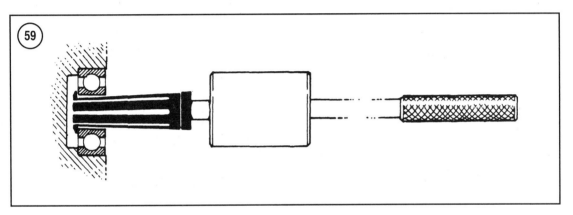

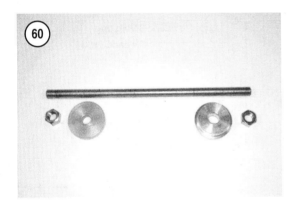

6. Withdraw the spacer located between the bearings in the swing arm pivot bore.

7. Repeat Steps 3-5 for the bearing on the other side.

8. Thoroughly clean out the inside of the pivot bore with solvent and dry it with compressed air.

9. Apply a light coat of lithium grease to the exterior of the new bearings, the spacer and to the inner circumference of the pivot bore. This will make bearing installation easier.

NOTE
Install one needle bearing at a time.
Make sure the bearing enters the pivot
boss squarely, otherwise the bearing
and the pivot boss may be damaged.

10. Position the bearing with the manufacturer's marks facing out.

NOTE
The bearing can be installed by using
a homemade tool consisting of a piece
of threaded rod, two thick washers
*and two nuts (**Figure 60**).*

2. Prior to removing the bearing, measure the location of the outer surface of the bearing in relation to the outer surface of the swing arm pivot bore (**Figure 53**). Note this dimension as it will be used during installation.

3. Insert the blind bearing puller through the needle bearing and expand it behind the bearing.

4. Using sharp strokes of the slide hammer (**Figure 59**), withdraw the needle bearing from the pivot boss.

5. Remove the bearing puller and the bearing.

14

11. Locate and square the new bearing in the pivot bore. Assemble the homemade tool through the pivot bore so the large washer presses against the bearing (**Figure 61**).

12. Hold the nut next to the bearing being installed. Tighten the nut on the opposite side and slowly pull the bearing into the pivot bore (**Figure 62**) until the bearing is in the same location as noted in Step 2.

13. Disassemble the tool.

14. Install the spacer into the swing arm pivot bore and against the just installed bearing.

15. Install the spacer into the pivot bore.

16. Reinstall the tool on the opposite side and then repeat Steps 9-14 and install the other bearing.

17. Make sure the bearings are properly seated. Turn each bearing by hand. It should turn smoothly.

18. Lubricate the new bearings with lithium grease.

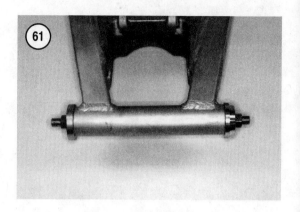

Relay Arm Bearings

Do not remove the needle bearings unless they must be replaced. The needle bearings are pressed onto the relay arm and a blind bearing puller is required to remove them. The needle bearings can be installed with a press or suitable size socket.

> *NOTE*
> *If the needle bearings are replaced, replace the pivot collars at the same time. These parts should always be replaced as a set.*

1. Remove the pivot collar (**Figure 63**) from the relay arm.

2. Pry the seals (**Figure 64**) out of the pivot area of the relay arm.

> *NOTE*
> *If the needle bearings are replaced, replace the pivot collar at the same time. These parts should always be replaced as a set.*

3. Prior to removing the bearing, measure the location of the outer surface of the bearing in relation to the outer surface of the relay arm pivot bore. Note this dimension; it will be used during installation.

4. Insert the blind bearing puller through the needle bearing and expand it behind the bearing.

5. Using sharp strokes of the slide hammer (**Figure 59**), withdraw the needle bearing from the pivot boss.

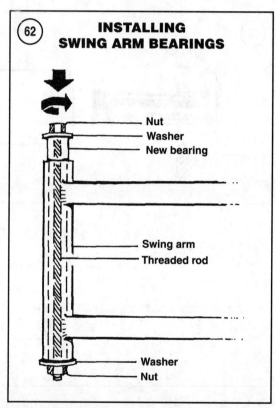

INSTALLING
SWING ARM BEARINGS

Nut
Washer
New bearing

Swing arm
Threaded rod

Washer
Nut

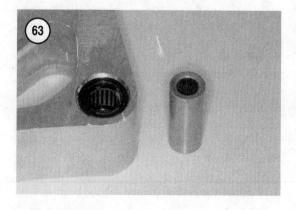

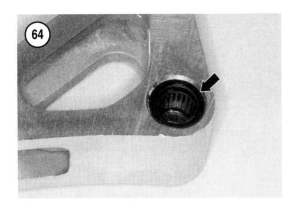

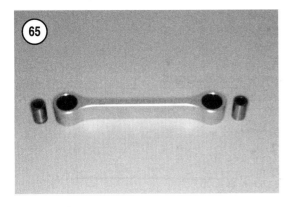

*boss squarely, otherwise the bearing
and the pivot boss may be damaged.*

  b. Position the bearing with the manufacturer's marks facing out.

  c. Locate and square the new bearing in the pivot bore.

  d. Place socket of the appropriate size above the bearing and tap the bearing squarely into the bore. Tap the bearing in until it is in the same location as noted in Step 4.

  e. Turn the relay arm over and repeat this step for the other bearing.

  f. Make sure the bearings are properly seated. Turn each bearing by hand. It should turn smoothly.

  g. Lubricate new bearings with lithium grease.

11B. To install the bearings with a press, perform the following:

  a. Support the relay arm in a press and press the bearing in until it is in the same location as noted in Step 4.

  b. Turn the relay arm over and repeat for the other bearing.

12. Pack the new bearings with lithium grease.

13. Install a *new* seal (**Figure 64**) onto each side of the pivot area of the relay arm.

14. Install the pivot collar (**Figure 63**) into the relay arm.

Connecting Arm Bearings

Do not remove the needle bearings unless they must be replaced. The needle bearings are pressed onto the connecting arm and they must be removed with a hydraulic press.

NOTE
If the needle bearings are replaced, replace the pivot collars at the same time. These parts should always be replaced as a set.

1. Remove both pivot collars (**Figure 65**) from the connecting rod.

2. If still installed, remove the dust seal (**Figure 66**) from each side of the needle bearings.

3. Support the connecting arm in a press and press out the needle bearing.

4. Repeat for the remaining bearing.

5. Clean the connecting arm in solvent and dry.

6. Remove the bearing puller and the bearing.

7. Repeat Steps 4-6 for the bearing on the other side.

8. Clean the relay arm in solvent and dry.

9. Inspect the mounting bore for cracks or other damage.

10. Apply a light coat of lithium grease to the exterior of the new bearings, the spacer and to the inner circumference of the pivot bore. This will make bearing installation easier.

NOTE
Install one needle bearing at a time. Make sure the bearing enters the pivot boss squarely, otherwise the bearing and the pivot boss may be damaged.

11A. To install the bearings without a press, perform the following:

  a. Apply a light coat of lithium grease to the exterior of the new bearings and to the inner circumference of the pivot bore. This will make bearing installation easier.

NOTE
Install one needle bearing at a time. Make sure the bearing enters the pivot

14

6. Inspect the mounting bore for cracks or other damage.

7. Apply a light coat of lithium grease to the exterior of the new bearings and the inner circumference of the pivot bore. This makes bearing installation easier.

8. Support the relay arm in a press. Press the bearing in until it is centered within the relay arm bore.

9. Repeat for the remaining bearing.

10. Pack the new bearing with lithium grease.

11. Install the *new* dust seals (**Figure 66**) onto each side of the needle bearings.

12. Install both pivot collars (**Figure 65**) into the connecting rod.

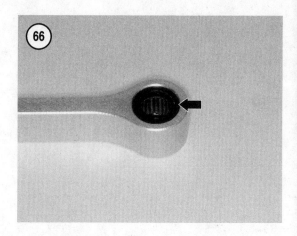

Table 1 REAR SUSPENSION SPECIFICATIONS

Item	Specification
Swing arm with link suspension	
Rear wheel travel	130 mm (5.12 in.)
Shock absorber	
Travel	65 mm (2.56 in.)
Spring free length	176 mm (6.93 in.)
Spring installed length	162.5 mm (6.40 in.)
Spring preload adjusting positions	
Minimum	1
Standard	4
Maximum	9
Rebound damping adjusting positions	
1998-1999 models	
Minimum	12
Standard	6
Maximum	1
2000-2001 models	
Minimum	11
Standard	7
Maximum	1
2002-2003 models	
Minimum	20
Standard	15
Maximum	1
Compression damping adjusting positions*	
1998-1999 models	
Minimum	12
Standard	8
Maximum	1
2000-2001 models	
Minimum	11
Standard	9
Maximum	1
2002-2003 models	
Minimum	20
Standard	15
Maximum	1
*Number of turns from the fully turned-in position.	

Table 2 REAR SUSPENSION TORQUE SPECIFICATIONS

Item	N•m	in.-lb.	ft.-lb.
Connecting arms			
1998-2001 models			
To frame bracket bolt and nut	40	–	30
To relay arm bolt and nut	40	–	30
2002-2003 models			
To frame bracket bolt and nut	45	–	33
To relay arm bolt and nut	45	–	33
Drive chain slider bolt	7	62	–
Relay arm			
1998-2001 models			
To swing arm bolt and nut	40	–	30
To shock absorber bolt and nut	40	–	30
2002-2003 models			
To swing arm bolt and nut	45	–	33
To shock absorber bolt and nut	45	–	33
Shock absorber			
1998-2001 models			
Upper bolt and nut	40	–	30
2002-2003 models			
Upper bolt and nut	45	–	33
Swing arm			
Pivot shaft bolt and nut			
1998-2001 models	125	–	92
2002-2003 models	105	–	77
Adjust bolt (2002-2003 models)	5	44	–

14

CHAPTER FIFTEEN

BRAKES

This chapter describes service procedures for the front and rear disc brakes. **Table 1** and **Table 2** at the end of the chapter list front and rear brake specifications.

BRAKE FLUID SELECTION

When adding brake fluid, use DOT 4 brake fluid from a sealed container.

Brake fluid is glycol-based and draws moisture, which greatly reduces its ability to perform correctly. Purchase brake fluid in small containers and discard any small leftover quantities. Do not store a container of brake fluid with less than 1/4 of the fluid remaining.

Periodically drain the brake fluid as described in this chapter. Refer to the maintenance schedule in Chapter Three for the interval recommendation.

> *CAUTION*
> *Do not intermix DOT 5 (silicone-based) brake fluid, as this can cause brake system failure.*

PREVENTING BRAKE FLUID DAMAGE

Many of the procedures in this chapter require handling brake fluid. Be careful not to spill any fluid, as it stains or damages most surfaces. To prevent brake fluid damage, note the following:

1. Before performing any procedure in which there is the possibility of brake fluid contacting the motorcycle, cover the work area with a large piece of plastic. It only takes a few drops of brake fluid to damage the surface of an expensive part.

2. Before handling brake fluid or working on the brake system, fill a bucket with soap and water and keep it close to the motorcycle while working. If brake fluid contacts the motorcycle, clean the area and rinse it thoroughly.

3. To help control the flow of brake fluid when filling the reservoirs, punch a small hole into the seal of a new container next to the edge of the pour spout.

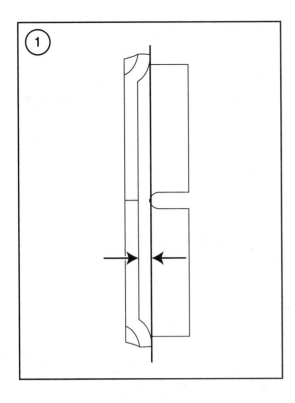

BRAKE SERVICE

WARNING
When working on the brake system, do not inhale brake dust. It may contain asbestos, which is a known carcinogen. Do not use compressed air to blow off brake dust. Use an aerosol brake cleaner. Wear a facemask and wash thoroughly after completing the work.

The disc brake system transmits hydraulic pressure from the master cylinders to the brake calipers. This pressure is transmitted from the calipers to the brake pads, which grip both sides of the brake discs and slow the motorcycle. As the pads wear, the pistons move out of the caliper bores to automatically compensate for wear. As this occurs, the fluid level in the master cylinder reservoir goes down. This must be compensated for by occasionally adding fluid.

The proper operation of this system depends on a supply of clean brake fluid (DOT 4) and a clean work environment when any service is being performed. Any tiny particle of debris that enters the system can damage the components and cause poor brake performance.

Brake fluid is hygroscopic (easily absorbs moisture) and moisture in the system will reduce brake performance. Purchase brake fluid in small containers and properly discard any small quantities that remain. Small quantities of fluid will quickly absorb the moisture in the container. Use only fluid clearly marked DOT 4. If possible, use the same brand of fluid. Do not replace the fluid with a silicone (DOT 5) fluid. It is not possible to remove all of the old fluid. Other types are not compatible with DOT 5. Do not reuse drained fluid and discard old fluid properly. Do not combine brake fluid with fluids for recycling.

Perform brake service procedures carefully. Do not use any sharp tools inside the master cylinders or calipers or on the pistons. Damage of these components could cause a loss of hydraulic system pressure. If there is any doubt about the ability to correctly and safely service the brake system, have a professional technician perform the task.

Consider the following when servicing the brake system:

1. The hydraulic components rarely require disassembly. Make sure it is necessary.

2. Keep the reservoir covers in place to prevent the entry of moisture and debris.

3. Clean parts with an aerosol brake parts cleaner or isopropyl alcohol. Never use petroleum-based solvents on internal brake system components. They will cause seals to swell and distort.

4. Do not allow brake fluid to contact plastic, painted or plated parts. It will damage the surface.

5. Dispose of brake fluid properly.

6. If the hydraulic system, not including the reservoir cover, has been opened, bleed the system to remove air from the system. Refer to *Brake Bleeding* in this chapter.

FRONT BRAKE PADS

There is no recommended mileage interval for changing the front brake pads. Pad wear depends greatly on riding habits and the condition of the brake system. Inspect the front brake pads for uneven wear, scoring, oil contamination or other damage. As the brake pads wear, the brake fluid level drops in the reservoir and automatically adjusts for wear. Replace the brake pads if the pad wear limit groove is worn away (**Figure 1**).

15

Always replace the front brake pads in sets by servicing both front calipers at the same time. Never use one new brake pad with a used brake pad in a caliper. Never replace the brake pads in one brake caliper without replacing them in the other caliper. Doing so results in an unbalanced braking condition.

> *CAUTION*
> *Due to the amount of pad material remaining after the wear limit grooves (**Figure 1**) are worn away, check the brake pads frequently. If pad wear is uneven, the backing plate may contact the disc and damage it.*

Replacement

> *NOTE*
> *Make sure to order the correct set of brake pads for the model year being worked on. There are different Yamaha part numbers for the various models.*

1. Read the information listed under *Brake Service* in this chapter.

2. Wipe clean the front master cylinder cap. Loosen the screw and release the cap stopper (A, **Figure 2**).

3. Unscrew the cap (B, **Figure 2**) and remove the diaphragm holder and diaphragm. Use a large syringe to remove and discard about 50 percent of the fluid from the reservoir. This prevents the master cylinder from overflowing when the caliper pistons are compressed for brake pad reinstallation. Do not drain the entire reservoir or air will enter the system.

4. Remove the front caliper from the fork slider as follows:

    a. Remove the bolt and nut (**Figure 3**) securing the brake hose mounting bracket.

    b. Remove the caliper upper and lower mounting bolts (**Figure 4**). On U.S. and Canada models, remove the side reflex reflector.

    c. Slide the caliper up and off the brake disc.

5. Hold onto the caliper assembly and insert a large flat bladed screwdriver or tire iron between the brake pads. Lever the brake pads and pistons back into the caliper bores. This will allow room for the new brake pads.

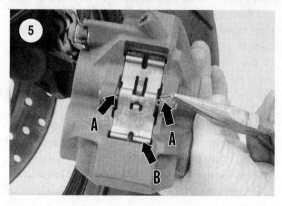

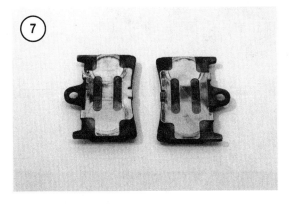

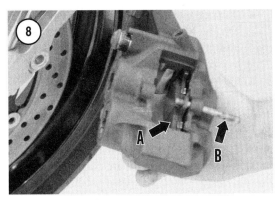

WARNING
The pistons should move smoothly when compressing them in Step 5. If not, check the caliper for sticking pistons or damaged caliper bores, pistons and seals. Repair requires overhaul of the brake caliper assembly.

CAUTION
Do not allow the master cylinder reservoir to overflow when performing Step 5. Brake fluid damages most surfaces it contacts.

6. Remove both clips (A, **Figure 5**) from the pad pin.

7. Withdraw the pan pin and remove the pad spring (B, **Figure 5**).

8. Remove both brake pads.

9. Inspect the pad pin for excessive wear, corrosion or damage. Use a wire-wheel to remove corrosion and dirt from the pad pin surface. A dirty or damaged pad pin surface prevents the brake pads from sliding properly and results in brake drag and overheating of the brake disc.

10. Inspect the brake pads (**Figure 6**) as follows:

   a. Inspect the friction material for light surface dirt, grease and oil contamination. Remove light contamination with sandpaper. If the contamination has penetrated the surface, replace the brake pads.

   b. Inspect the brake pads for excessive wear or damage. Replace the brake pads if the wear limit groove (**Figure 1**) is no longer visible.

   c. Inspect the brake pads for uneven wear. If one pad has worn more than the other, the brake caliper may not be working correctly. Refer to *Front Brake Caliper* in this chapter.

   d. Inspect the metal shims (**Figure 7**) on the backside of each pad for corrosion, tightness and damage.

WARNING
If brake fluid is leaking from around the pistons, overhaul the brake caliper as described in this chapter.

11. Service the brake disc as follows:

   a. Use brake cleaner and a fine-grade emery cloth to remove road debris and brake pad residue and any rust from the brake disc. Clean both sides of the disc.

CAUTION
Cleaning the brake disc is especially important if changing brake pad compounds. Many compounds are not compatible with each other.

   b. Check the brake disc for wear as described in this chapter.

12. Make sure the metal shims (**Figure 7**) are in place on the backside of each brake pad.

13. Install the inboard brake pad (A, **Figure 8**) into the caliper and partially install the pad pin (B) through the brake pad.

15

14. Install the outboard brake pad (**Figure 9**) into the caliper.

15. Position the pad spring (A, **Figure 10**) into the caliper with the arrow mark facing up.

16. Install and push the pad pin through the outboard pad, the spring's upper and lower (B, **Figure 10**) interlocking legs then through the inboard pad. This secures both brake pads and the spring into place. Push the pad pin all the way in (C, **Figure 10**) until it bottoms.

17. Install both clips into the pad pin and push them down until they *click* into place on the pad pin (**Figure 11**).

18. Install the front caliper onto the fork slider as follows:

   a. Install the brake caliper onto the brake disc and into position on the fork slider. Be careful not to damage the leading edge of the brake pads.

   b. Install the caliper upper and lower mounting bolts (**Figure 4**). On U.S. and Canada models, install the side reflex reflector. Tighten the bolts and nuts to 40 N•m (30 ft.-lb.).

   c. Move the brake hose mounting bracket into place and install the bolt and nut (**Figure 3**). Tighten the bolt and nut to 6 N•m (53 in.-lb.).

19. Repeat for the opposite brake assembly.

20. Operate the front brake lever to seat the pads against the disc, then check the brake fluid level in the reservoir (C, **Figure 2**). If necessary, add new DOT 4 brake fluid as described in Chapter Three.

> *WARNING*
> *Do not ride the motorcycle until the front brakes operate correctly with full hydraulic advantage. If necessary, bleed the front brakes as described in this chapter.*

FRONT BRAKE CALIPER

Removal/Installation

1. Remove the bolt and nut (**Figure 3**) securing the brake hose mounting bracket.

2. If the caliper is going to be removed and serviced, perform the following:

   a. Drain the brake fluid from the front master cylinder as described under *Brake Fluid Draining* in this chapter.

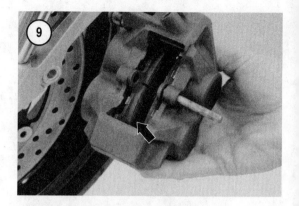

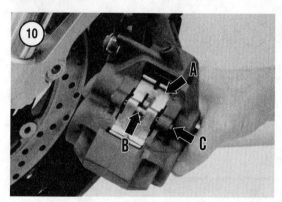

   b. Remove the brake hose banjo bolt and washers (A, **Figure 12**) at the caliper. Plug the hose, then place it in a reclosable plastic bag to prevent leakage and contamination.

3. Remove the caliper upper and lower mounting bolts (B, **Figure 12**).

4. On U.S. and Canada models, remove the side reflex reflector from the caliper.

5. Slide the caliper (C, **Figure 12**) up and off the brake disc. If the brake pads are not going to be removed, insert a block between the brake pads to keep them separated.

> *NOTE*
> *The spacer block prevents the pistons from being forced out of the caliper if the front brake lever is accidentally applied while the brake caliper is removed from the brake disc.*

6. Remove the brake pads as described in this chapter.

7. Inspect the caliper as described in this section.

8. Install the brake pads as described in this chapter.

9. If the brake caliper was not removed from the motorcycle, remove the spacer block from between the brake pads.

10. Install the brake caliper onto the brake disc and into position on the fork slider. Be careful not to damage the leading edge of the brake pads.

11. On U.S. and Canada models, correctly position the side reflex reflector on the caliper.

12. Install the caliper upper and lower mounting bolts (B, **Figure 12**). Tighten the bolts and nuts to 40 N•m (30 ft.-lb.).

13. If the caliper was serviced, perform the following:

   a. Remove the plastic bag from the brake hose.

   b. Place a *new* washer on each side of the brake hose. Then thread the banjo bolt (A, **Figure 12**) onto the caliper and tighten to 30 N•m (22 ft.-lb.).

   c. Refill the master cylinder and bleed the brake system as described in this chapter.

14. Move the brake hose mounting bracket into position and install the bolt and nut (**Figure 3**). Tighten the bolt and nut to 6 N•m (53 in.-lb.).

15. Repeat for the opposite brake caliper assembly.

16. Roll the motorcycle back and forth and apply the front brake several times to reposition the brake pads in both calipers.

> *WARNING*
> *Do not ride the motorcycle until both front brake calipers operate correctly with full hydraulic advantage.*

Disassembly

Brake caliper service involves removing the pistons. An air compressor is required during the disassembly procedure.

Refer to **Figure 13**.

1. Remove the brake caliper as described in this chapter.

2. Remove the brake pads as described in this chapter.

3. Remove the pistons as follows:

> *WARNING*
> *Compressed air forces the pistons out of the caliper under considerable force. Do not cushion the pistons by hand, as injury could result.*

   a. Two different size pistons are used.

   b. Place a thick towel or shop cloth between the two sets of pistons.

   c. Direct compressed air through the brake line port (**Figure 14**) to remove the outboard pistons.

   d. Remove the cloth and remove the outboard set of pistons.

   e. Remove the bleed valve.

   f. Place the thick towel or shop cloth back into the caliper below the remaining set of inboard pistons.

   g. Seal off the brake line port (A, **Figure 15**) to keep the air from escaping.

   h. Direct compressed air through the bleed valve port (B, **Figure 15**) to remove the inboard pistons.

   i. Remove the cloth and remove the inboard set of pistons.

4. Use a small tool to carefully pry the dust and piston seals from the grooves in the cylinder bore. Repeat for each bore.

15

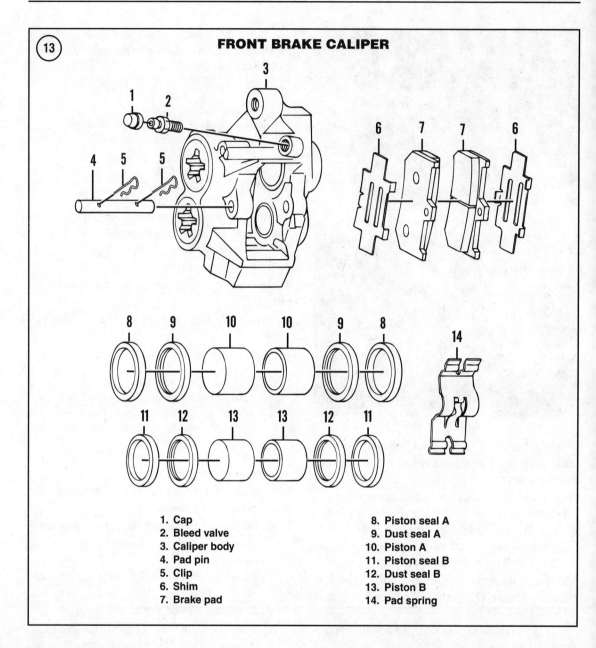

FRONT BRAKE CALIPER

1. Cap
2. Bleed valve
3. Caliper body
4. Pad pin
5. Clip
6. Shim
7. Brake pad
8. Piston seal A
9. Dust seal A
10. Piston A
11. Piston seal B
12. Dust seal B
13. Piston B
14. Pad spring

Assembly

Refer to **Figure 13**.

Use new DOT 4 brake fluid when lubricating the parts in the following steps.

> *NOTE*
> *Before soaking the new piston and dust seals in brake fluid, compare them to the old parts, determine their sizes and match them to their respective bores. Two different size seals are used. Refer to the brake caliper cylin-*

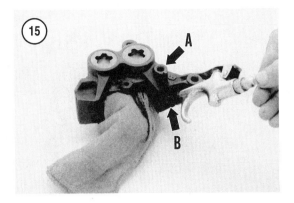

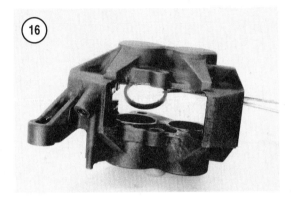

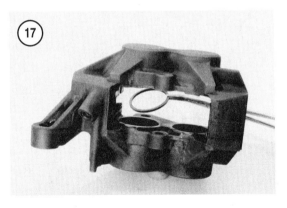

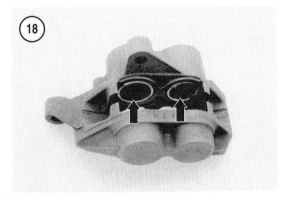

*der upper and lower bore measure-
ments in* **Table 1**.

1. Soak the *new* piston and dust seals in brake fluid.
2. Lubricate the pistons and cylinder bores with brake fluid.

NOTE
The piston seals are thicker than the dust seals.

3. Install a *new* piston seal (**Figure 16**) into each cylinder bore rear groove.
4. Install a *new* dust seal (**Figure 17**) into each cylinder bore front groove.

NOTE
Check that each seal fits squarely into its respective cylinder bore groove.

5. Install each inboard piston into its respective caliper bore with its open side facing out. To prevent the pistons from damaging the seals, turn them into the bore by hand. Install the pistons until they bottom.
6. Install each outboard piston into its respective caliper bore with its open side facing out. To prevent the pistons from damaging the seals, turn them into the bore by hand. Install the pistons until they bottom (**Figure 18**).
7. Install the bleed valve and tighten to 6 N·m (53 in.-lb.).
8. Install the brake pads as described in this chapter.
9. Install the brake caliper as described in this chapter.
10. Repeat for the other brake caliper.

Inspection

When measuring the brake caliper components, compare the actual measurements to the specifications in **Table 1**. Replace worn or damaged parts as described in this section.
1. Clean and dry the caliper assembly as follows:
   a. Handle the brake components carefully when servicing them.
   b. Use only DOT 4 brake fluid or isopropyl alcohol to wash rubber parts in the brake system. Never allow any petroleum-based

15

cleaner to contact the rubber parts. These chemicals cause the rubber to swell, requiring their replacement.

c. Clean the dust and piston seal grooves carefully to avoid damaging the caliper bore. Use a small pick or brush to clean the grooves. If a hard varnish residue has built up in the grooves, soak the caliper body halves in solvent to help soften the residue. Then wash the caliper halves in soapy water and rinse completely.

d. If alcohol or solvent was used to clean the caliper, blow dry with compressed air.

e. Check the fluid passages to make sure they are clean and dry.

f. After cleaning the parts, place them on a clean lint-free cloth until assembly.

CAUTION
Do not get any oil or grease onto any of the brake caliper components. These chemicals cause the rubber parts in the brake system to swell, permanently damaging them.

2. Check each cylinder bore for corrosion, deep scratches and other wear marks. Do not hone the cylinder bores.

NOTE
*The caliper uses two different bore diameters. The upper piston and bore have the larger diameter of the two (adjacent to the bleed valve). Refer to the upper and lower piston and caliper diameter specifications in **Table 1** when measuring the parts in the following steps.*

3. Measure each caliper cylinder diameter bore (**Figure 19**) with a small telescoping gauge.

4. Inspect the pistons (**Figure 20**) for pitting, corrosion, cracks or other damage.

5. Inspect the bleed valve (**Figure 21**) and the banjo bolt threads for wear or damage.

6. Clean the bleed valve with compressed air. Make sure the hole is clear. Replace the dust cap if missing or damaged.

7. Clean the banjo bolts with compressed air.

8. Inspect the pad pin and clips for wear or damage.

9. Inspect the pad spring (**Figure 22**) for cracks or damage.

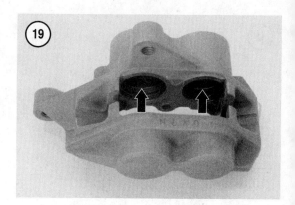

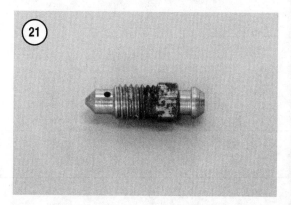

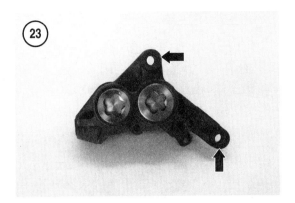

10. Check the caliper mounting brackets (**Figure 23**) for cracks or damage.

FRONT MASTER CYLINDER

Read the information listed under *Brake Service* in this chapter before servicing the front master cylinder.

Removal

1. Support the motorcycle on level ground.

2. Block the front wheel so the motorcycle will not roll in either direction while on the swing arm stand.

3. Remove the front fairing as described in Chapter Sixteen.

4. Cover the fuel tank with a heavy cloth or plastic tarp to protect them from accidental brake fluid spills.

> *CAUTION*
> *Wash brake fluid off any surface immediately, as it damages the finish. Use soapy water and rinse completely.*

5. Drain the front brake lever line as described under *Brake Fluid Draining* in this chapter.

6. Remove the banjo bolt and washers securing the brake hose(s) to the master cylinder. Refer to **Figure 24** (1998-2001 models) or **Figure 25** (2002-2003 models). Place the loose end of the brake hose(s) in a reclosable plastic bag to prevent leakage and hose contamination. Tie the loose end of the hose(s) to the handlebar.

7. Plug the bolt opening in the master cylinder to prevent leakage when removing the master cylinder in the following steps.

8. Disconnect the brake switch wire connector (**Figure 26**) at the brake light switch.

9. Remove the screw (**Figure 27**) securing the reservoir to the handlebar.

10. Disconnect the short hose (A, **Figure 28**) securing the reservoir to the master cylinder hose joint. Remove the reservoir (B, **Figure 28**).

11. Remove the brake master cylinder holder mounting bolts (**Figure 29**) and clamp, then remove the brake master cylinder and reservoir from the handlebar.

15

Installation

1. If necessary, service the master cylinder as described in this chapter.

2. Clean the handlebar, master cylinder and clamp mating surfaces.

3. Mount the master cylinder onto the handlebar and align the end of the master cylinder and clamp mating surfaces with the punch mark on the handlebar.

4. Install the master cylinder holder and its mounting bolts (**Figure 29**). Install the holder with its UP arrow facing up while aligning the with the handlebar punch mark.

5. Tighten the upper master cylinder clamp bolt first, then the lower bolt. Tighten both bolts to the following:

    a. 1998-2001 models: 13 N•m (115 in.-lb.).

    b. 2002-2003 models: 9 N•m (80 in.-lb.).

NOTE
When the master cylinder clamp is correctly installed, the upper edge of the clamp touches the master cylinder, leaving a gap at the bottom.

6. Install the reservoir and connect the short hose (A, **Figure 28**) securing the reservoir to the master cylinder hose joint. Tighten the hose clamp securely.

7. Install the screw (**Figure 27**) securing the reservoir to the handlebar and tighten securely.

8. Reconnect the front brake light switch connectors at the switch (**Figure 26**).

9. Secure the brake hose(s) to the master cylinder with the banjo bolt and *new* washers on each side of the brake hose(s). Refer to **Figure 24** (1998-2001 models) or **Figure 25** (2002-2003 models). Position the hose(s) so they are pointing directly down inline with the mating surfaces of the master cylinder and holder (**Figure 30**). Tighten the banjo bolt to 30 N•m (22 ft.-lb.).

10. Bleed the front brakes as described under *Brake Bleeding* in this chapter.

11. After bleeding the brakes and before riding the motorcycle, turn the ignition switch on and make sure the rear brake light comes on when operating the front brake lever. If not, check the front brake light switch and connectors.

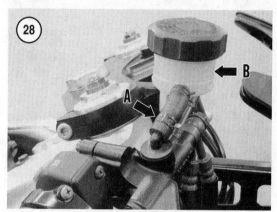

WARNING
Do not ride the motorcycle until the front and rear brakes and brake light operate properly.

Disassembly

Refer to **Figure 31** and **Figure 32**.

1. Remove the master cylinder as described in this section.

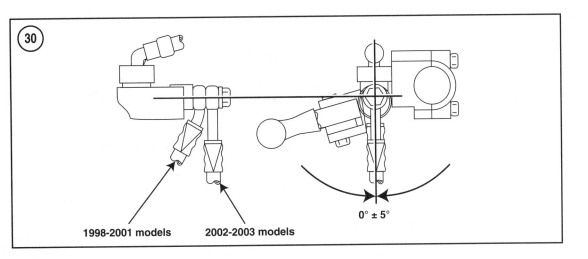

1998-2001 models   2002-2003 models

0° ± 5°

FRONT MASTER CYLINDER

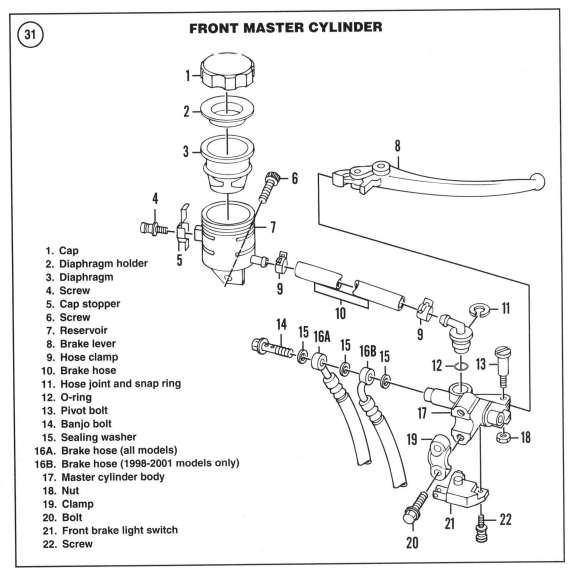

1. Cap
2. Diaphragm holder
3. Diaphragm
4. Screw
5. Cap stopper
6. Screw
7. Reservoir
8. Brake lever
9. Hose clamp
10. Brake hose
11. Hose joint and snap ring
12. O-ring
13. Pivot bolt
14. Banjo bolt
15. Sealing washer
16A. Brake hose (all models)
16B. Brake hose (1998-2001 models only)
17. Master cylinder body
18. Nut
19. Clamp
20. Bolt
21. Front brake light switch
22. Screw

15

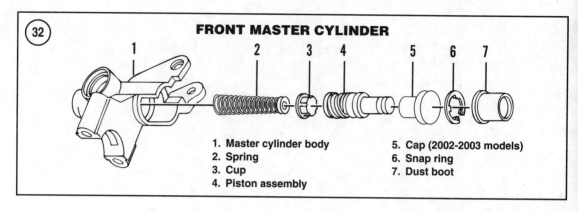

FRONT MASTER CYLINDER

1. Master cylinder body
2. Spring
3. Cup
4. Piston assembly
5. Cap (2002-2003 models)
6. Snap ring
7. Dust boot

2. Remove the nut and pivot bolt (A, **Figure 33**), then remove the brake lever and its adjuster assembly (B).

3. Remove the screw (A, **Figure 34**) and remove the front brake light switch (B).

4. Remove the rubber boot (**Figure 35**) from the hose joint.

5. Remove the snap ring (**Figure 36**) from the groove in the master cylinder, then remove the hose joint (**Figure 37**).

6. Remove the O-ring (**Figure 38**) from the hose joint receptacle.

7. Remove the rubber boot (**Figure 39**) from the groove in the end of the piston.

> *WARNING*
> *If brake fluid is leaking from the piston bore, the piston cups are worn or damaged. Replace the piston assembly.*

8. Compress the piston and remove the snap ring (**Figure 40**) from the groove in the master cylinder.

9. Remove the piston assembly and spring (**Figure 41**) from the master cylinder bore. Do not remove the primary and secondary cups from the piston.

Assembly

1. If installing a new piston assembly, assemble it as described under *Inspection* in this section.

2. Lubricate the piston assembly and cylinder bore with DOT 4 brake fluid.

3. Correctly position the spring with the large end going in first.

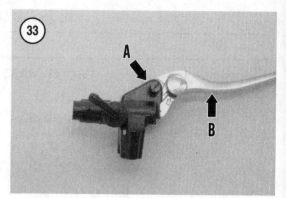

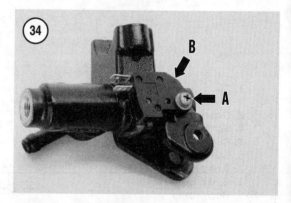

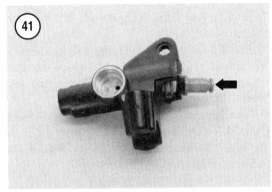

15

WARNING
Do not allow the piston cups to tear or turn inside out when installing the piston into the master cylinder bore. Both cups are larger than the bore. To ease installation, lubricate the cups and piston with DOT 4 brake fluid.

4. Insert the spring and primary piston assembly into the master cylinder bore (**Figure 42**). Push it in, then install the piston assembly into the master cylinder bore (**Figure 41**).

5. Compress the piston assembly and install the snap ring (**Figure 43**) into the master cylinder bore groove.

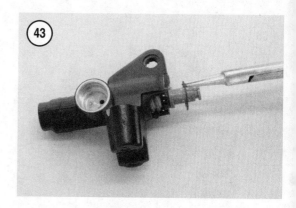

> *WARNING*
> *The snap ring must seat in the master cylinder groove completely (**Figure 40**). Push and release the piston a few times to make sure it moves smoothly and the snap ring does not pop out.*

6. Slide the rubber boot over the piston. Seat the outer dust cover lip into the groove in the end of the piston (**Figure 39**).

7. Install a *new* O-ring (**Figure 44**) into the hose joint receptacle.

8. Install the hose joint (**Figure 37**) and secure it with a snap ring (**Figure 45**). Make sure the snap ring is seated correctly in the hose joint receptacle groove (**Figure 36**).

9. Install the rubber boot (**Figure 35**) onto the hose joint. Push it down until it is seated correctly.

10. Install the front brake switch (B, **Figure 34**) and tighten the screw (A) securely.

11. Install the brake lever assembly as follows:

   a. Lubricate the pivot bolt with lithium base grease.

   b. Install the brake lever and adjuster assembly (B, **Figure 33**).

   c. Install the brake lever pivot bolt and tighten the nut brake lever pivot bolt securely. Check that the brake lever moves freely. If there is any binding or roughness, remove the pivot bolt and brake lever and inspect the parts.

   d. Hold the pivot bolt, then install and tighten the brake lever pivot nut (**Figure 46**) securely. Check that the brake lever moves freely.

Inspection

When measuring the front master cylinder components, compare the actual measurements to the specifications in **Table 1**. Replace worn or damaged parts as described in this section.

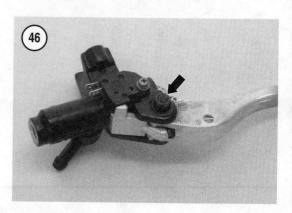

> *NOTE*
> *The dust boot, snap ring, piston assembly and spring are all included in the rebuild kit. Install all of these components regardless of condition of some of the original components.*

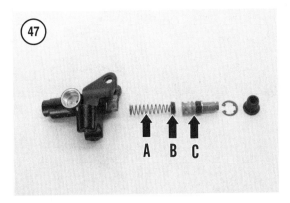

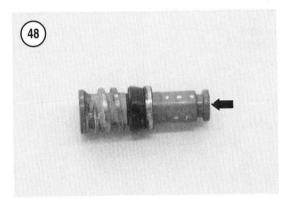

1. Clean and dry the master cylinder assembly as follows:
   a. Handle the brake components carefully when servicing them.
   b. Use only DOT 4 brake fluid or isopropyl alcohol to wash rubber parts (rubber boot and piston assembly) in the brake system. Never allow any petroleum-based cleaner to contact the rubber parts. These chemicals cause the rubber to swell, requiring their replacement.
   c. Clean the master cylinder piston snap ring groove carefully. Use a small pick or brush to clean the groove. If a hard varnish residue has built up, soak the master cylinder in solvent to help soften the residue. Wash the master cylinder in soapy water and rinse completely.
   d. Dry the master cylinder with compressed air.
   e. Place cleaned parts on a clean lint-free cloth until assembly.

> *WARNING*
> *Do not get any oil or grease on any of the master cylinder components. These chemicals cause the rubber parts in the brake system to swell, permanently damaging them.*

> *WARNING*
> *Do not remove the primary and secondary cups from the piston assembly for cleaning or inspection purposes.*

2. Check the piston assembly for the following:
   a. Broken, distorted or collapsed piston spring (A, **Figure 47**).
   b. Worn, cracked, damaged or swollen primary (B, **Figure 47**) and secondary cups (C).
   c. Scratched, scored or damaged piston (**Figure 48**).
   d. Corroded, weak or damaged snap ring.
   e. Worn or damaged rubber boot.
   f. If any of these parts are worn or damaged, replace the piston assembly with a rebuild kit.

3. Inspect the master cylinder bore (**Figure 49**). Replace the master cylinder if its bore is corroded, cracked or damaged. Do not hone the master cylinder bore to remove scratches or other damage.

4. Measure the master cylinder bore (**Figure 49**) with a small telescoping gauge.

5. Check for plugged supply and relief ports (**Figure 50**) in the base of the master cylinder. Clean with compressed air.

15

6. Check the banjo bolt threads (**Figure 51**) for damage.

7. Check the brake lever assembly for the following defects:

    a. Damaged brake lever.

    b. Excessively worn or damaged pivot bolt.

    c. Damaged adjuster arm assembly.

REAR BRAKE PADS

There is no recommended mileage interval for changing brake pads in the rear brake caliper. Pad wear depends on personal riding habits and brake system condition. Inspect the rear brake pads for uneven wear, scoring, oil contamination or other damage. Replace the brake pads if the wear limit grooves are not visible. Refer to **Figure 52** (1998-2001 models) or **Figure 53** (2002-2003 models). To maintain even brake pressure on the rear disc, replace both brake pads at the same time. Never use one new brake pad with a used brake pad in the caliper.

> *CAUTION*
> *Due to the amount of pad material remaining after the wear limit grooves are worn away, check the brake pads frequently. If pad wear is uneven, the backing plate may contact the disc and damage it.*

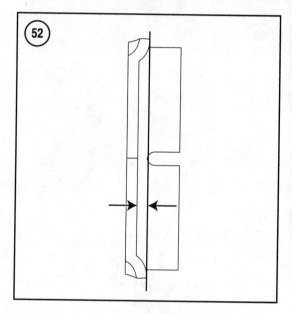

Replacement

1998-2001 models

> *NOTE*
> *The brake pads can be removed with the brake caliper mounted on the motorcycle, but it is easier if the caliper is removed and turned upside down. To inspect the piston and seals for leakage or damage, remove the brake caliper as described in this chapter.*

1. Read the information listed under *Brake Service* in this chapter.

2. Support the motorcycle on level ground.

3. Block the front wheel so the motorcycle will not roll in either direction while on the swing arm stand.

4. Remove the muffler (Chapter Eight).

5. On 1998-1999 models, remove the screw securing the master cylinder reservoir cap retainer and remove the retainer.

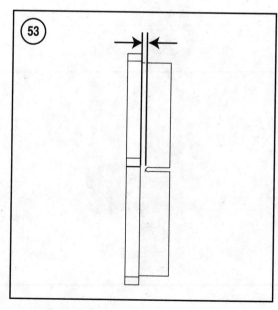

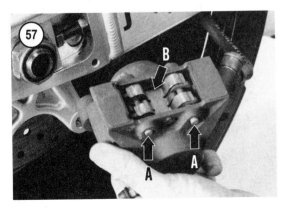

6. Remove the reservoir cap (**Figure 54**), diaphragm holder and diaphragm.

7. Use a large syringe to remove and discard about 50 percent of the fluid from the reservoir. This prevents the master cylinder from overflowing when the caliper pistons are compressed for reinstallation. Do not drain the entire reservoir, or air will enter the system. Reinstall the diaphragm, diaphragm holder and cap and tighten securely.

CAUTION
Do not allow the master cylinder reservoir to overflow when performing Step 9. Brake fluid damages most surfaces it contacts.

8. Remove the caliper mounting bolts (A, **Figure 55**).

9. Take hold of the caliper body (from the outside) and push it toward its brake disc (B, **Figure 55**), then pull it toward the disc. This pushes the pistons into the caliper body to make room for the new brake pads.

10. Pull the caliper down and off the brake disc.

11. Remove all four clips (**Figure 56**) from the pad pins.

12. Withdraw both pad pins (A, **Figure 57**) and the pad spring (B).

13. Remove both brake pads.

14. Inspect the pad pins for excessive wear, corrosion or damage. Use a wire-wheel to remove corrosion and dirt from the pad pin surface. A dirty or damaged pad pin surface prevents the brake pads from sliding properly and results in brake drag and overheating of the brake disc.

15. Inspect the brake pads as follows:

a. Inspect the friction material (**Figure 58**) for light surface dirt, grease and oil contamina-

15

tion. Remove light contamination with sand-paper. If the contamination has penetrated the surface, replace the brake pads.

b. Inspect the brake pads for excessive wear or damage. Replace the brake pads when the friction material is worn down to the wear indicator line.

c. Inspect the brake pads for uneven wear. If one pad is worn more than the other, the brake caliper may not be working correctly. Refer to *Rear Brake Caliper* in this chapter.

> *NOTE*
> *If brake fluid is leaking from around the piston, overhaul the brake caliper as described in this chapter.*

d. Inspect the metal shim (**Figure 59**) on the backside of each pad for corrosion, tightness and damage.

16. Service the brake disc as follows:

a. Use brake cleaner and a fine grade emery cloth to remove all brake pad residue and any rust from the brake disc. Clean both sides of the disc.

> *CAUTION*
> *A thorough cleaning of the brake disc is especially important when changing brake pad compounds. Many compounds are not compatible with each other.*

b. Check the brake disc for wear as described in this chapter.

17. Install the outboard brake pad (**Figure 60**) into the caliper.

> *NOTE*
> *Correctly position the holes in the pad pins so the clips can be installed in Step 23.*

18. Insert both pad pins through the caliper and the outboard brake pad (**Figure 61**).

19. Install the inboard brake pad (**Figure 62**) into the caliper.

20. Push one of the pad pins through the inboard brake pad (**Figure 63**) and into the other side of the caliper.

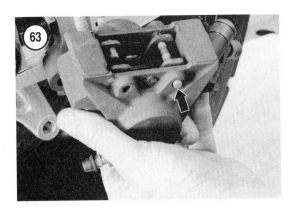

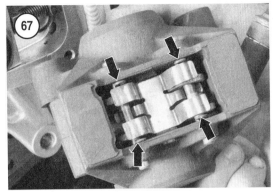

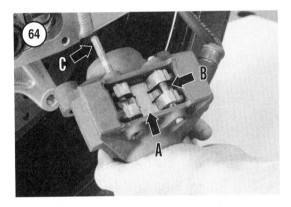

NOTE
In the following steps, make sure both pad pins are correctly positioned within the pad spring to correctly exert pressure on both pads.

21. Install the pad spring (A, **Figure 64**) on top of both brake pads and insert one end under the pad pin (B).

22. Push the remaining pad pin (C, **Figure 64**) through both brake pads and the pad spring. Push the pad pins in until they bottom (**Figure 65**).

23. Install the four clips (**Figure 66**) through the pad pins. Make sure all four pad clips are locked into place (**Figure 67**).

24. Install the brake caliper onto the brake disc and into position on the mounting bracket. Be careful not to damage the leading edge of the brake pads.

25. Install the caliper mounting bolts (A, **Figure 55**) and tighten to 40 N•m (30 ft.-lb.).

26. Operate the rear brake pedal several times to seat the pads against the disc, then check the brake fluid level in the reservoir. If necessary, add new DOT 4 brake fluid.

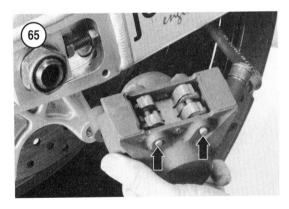

WARNING
Do not ride the motorcycle until the front and rear brakes operate correctly with full hydraulic advantage. If necessary, bleed the brakes as described in this chapter.

2002-2003 models

NOTE
This procedure is shown with the hydraulic brake hose removed from the caliper. It is not necessary to remove the brake hose for this procedure.

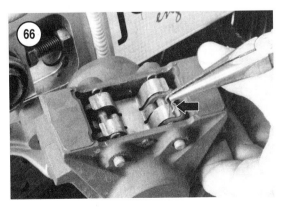

15

1. Read the information listed under *Brake Service* in this chapter.

2. Support the motorcycle on level ground.

3. Block the front wheel so the motorcycle will not roll in either direction while on the swing arm stand.

4. Remove the muffler as described in Chapter Nine.

5. Remove the rear master cylinder cap, diaphragm holder and diaphragm (**Figure 68**).

6. Use a large syringe to remove and discard about 50 percent of the fluid from the reservoir. This prevents the master cylinder from overflowing when the caliper pistons are compressed for reinstallation. Do not drain the entire reservoir, or air will enter the system. Reinstall the diaphragm, diaphragm holder and cap and tighten securely.

7. Remove both caliper pin bolts (A, **Figure 69**).

> *CAUTION*
> *Do not allow the master cylinder reservoir to overflow when performing Step 8. Brake fluid damages most surfaces it contacts.*

8. Take hold of the caliper body (from the outside) (B, **Figure 69**) and push it toward its brake disc. This pushes the pistons into the caliper to make room for the new brake pads.

9. Lift the caliper up and off the brake disc (**Figure 70**) and brake pads. Secure the caliper to the frame.

10. Remove both sets of brake pads and shims.

11. Do not remove the pad supports (**Figure 71**) from the caliper bracket, but make sure they are in good condition. Replace the pad supports if they appear weak or damaged.

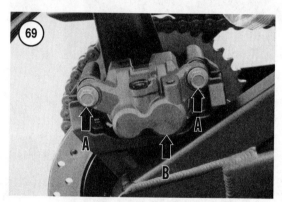

12. Inspect the pad pin bolts for excessive wear, corrosion or damage. Use a wire-wheel to remove corrosion and dirt from the pad pin surface. A dirty or damaged pad pin surface prevents the brake pads from sliding properly and results in brake drag and overheating of the brake disc.

13. Inspect the rubber boots (**Figure 72**) on the caliper bracket for wear or deterioration.

14. Inspect the brake pads as follows:

   a. Inspect the friction material (**Figure 73**) for light surface dirt, grease and oil contamination. Remove light contamination with sandpaper. If the contamination has penetrated the surface, replace the brake pads.

   b. Inspect the brake pads for excessive wear or damage. Replace the brake pads when the

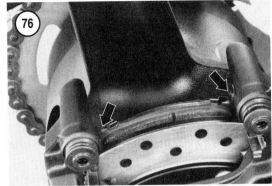

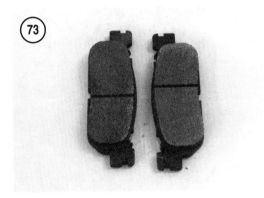

friction material is worn down to the wear indicator line.

c. Inspect the brake pads for uneven wear. If one
pad is worn more than the other, the brake caliper may not be working correctly. Refer to
Brake Caliper in this chapter.

NOTE
*If brake fluid is leaking from around
the piston, overhaul the brake caliper
as described in this chapter.*

d. Inspect the metal shims (**Figure 74**) on the
backside of each pad for corrosion, tightness
and damage. There are two shims on each
brake pad.

15. Service the brake disc as follows:

a. Use brake cleaner and a fine grade emery
cloth to remove all brake pad residue and any
rust from the brake disc. Clean both sides of
the disc.

NOTE
*A thorough cleaning of the brake disc
is especially important when changing brake pad compounds. Many
compounds are not compatible with
each other.*

15

b. Check the brake disc for wear as described in
this chapter.

16. Make sure both shims are in place on the backside or both brake pads.

17. Make sure both pad supports (**Figure 71**) are in
place on the caliper mounting bracket.

18. Install the inboard brake pad (**Figure 75**) into
the caliper mounting bracket. Insert the extended
arm on the end of each pad onto the pad supports in
the caliper bracket (**Figure 76**).

19. Install the outboard brake pad (**Figure 77**) into the caliper mounting bracket. Insert the extended arm on the end of each pad onto the pad supports in the caliper bracket (**Figure 78**).

20. Install the caliper onto the brake disc (**Figure 70**) and brake pads.

21. Install both caliper pin bolts (**Figure 79**) and tighten to 27 N•m (20 ft.-lb.).

22. Install the muffler as described in Chapter Nine.

23. Operate the rear brake pedal several times to seat the pads against the disc, then check the brake fluid level in the reservoir. If necessary, add new DOT 4 brake fluid.

> *WARNING*
> *Do not ride the motorcycle until the front and rear brakes operate correctly with full hydraulic advantage. If necessary, bleed the brakes as described in this chapter.*

REAR BRAKE CALIPER
(1998-2001 MODELS)

Removal/Installation

1. Support the motorcycle on level ground.

2. Block the front wheel so the motorcycle will not roll in either direction while on the swing arm stand.

3. Remove the muffler as described in Chapter Eight.

4. If the caliper is going to be removed and serviced, perform the following:

   a. Drain the brake fluid from the rear master cylinder as described under *Brake Fluid Draining* in this chapter.

   b. Remove the brake pads as previously described.

   c. Remove the brake hose banjo bolt and washers (A, **Figure 80**) at the caliper. Plug the hose, then place it in a reclosable plastic bag to prevent leakage and hose contamination.

5. Remove the caliper mounting bolts (B, **Figure 80**).

6. Pull the caliper down and off the brake disc.

7. If the brake hose was not disconnected at the caliper, insert a spacer block between the brake pads and support the caliper with a wire hook.

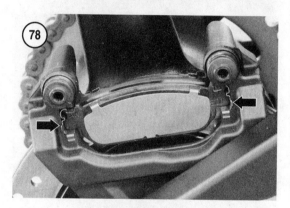

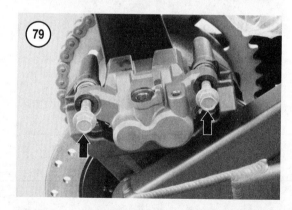

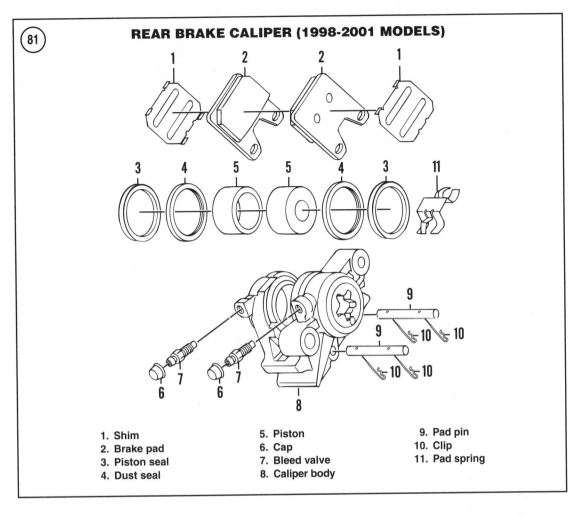

REAR BRAKE CALIPER (1998-2001 MODELS)

1. Shim
2. Brake pad
3. Piston seal
4. Dust seal
5. Piston
6. Cap
7. Bleed valve
8. Caliper body
9. Pad pin
10. Clip
11. Pad spring

NOTE
The spacer block prevents the piston from being forced out of the caliper if the rear brake pedal is accidentally applied while the brake caliper is removed from the brake disc.

8. If necessary, service the brake caliper as described in this chapter.

9. Check that the brake pads were not contaminated with brake fluid. If so, replace the brake pads as described in this chapter.

10. If the brake caliper was not completely removed from the motorcycle, remove the spacer block from between the brake pads.

11. Install the brake caliper onto the brake disc and into position on the mounting bracket. Be careful not to damage the leading edge of the brake pads.

12. Tighten the caliper mounting bolts (B, **Figure 80**) and tighten to 40 N•m (30 ft.-lb.).

13. If removed, place a new sealing washer on each side of the brake hose. Then thread the banjo bolt (A, **Figure 80**) into the caliper and tighten to 30 N•m (22 ft.-lb.).

14. Refill the master cylinder with new DOT 4 brake fluid.

15. Bleed the brake pedal lines as described in this chapter.

16. Operate the rear brake pedal to seat the pads against the brake disc.

WARNING
Do not ride the motorcycle until the rear brake operates with full hydraulic advantage.

Disassembly

Refer to **Figure 81**.

15

1. Remove the brake caliper as described in this section.

2. If still in place, remove the brake pads as described in this chapter.

3. Remove the inboard piston as follows:

> *WARNING*
> *Compressed air forces the piston out of the caliper under considerable force. Do not cushion the piston by hand, as injury could result.*

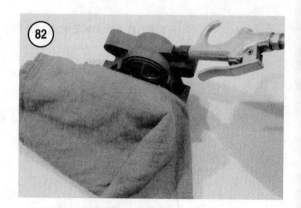

   a. Remove the inboard bleed valve.

   b. Place a thick towel, or shop cloth, between the piston and caliper. Make sure there is enough space underneath the caliper for the piston to be removed completely.

   c. Direct compressed air through the bleed valve port (**Figure 82**) and force the piston out of the caliper.

4. Remove the outboard piston as follows:

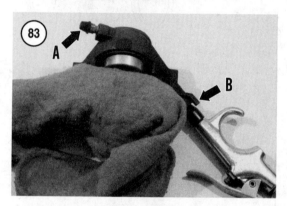

> *WARNING*
> *Compressed air forces the piston out of the caliper under considerable force. Do not cushion the piston by hand, as injury could result.*

   a. Do *not* remove the outboard bleed valve (A, **Figure 83**).

   b. Place a thick towel between the piston and workbench. Make sure there is enough space underneath the caliper for the piston to be removed completely.

   c. Direct compressed air through the brake line port (B, **Figure 83**) and force the piston out of the caliper.

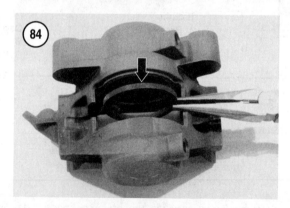

5. Use a small pick tool to carefully pry the dust and piston seals from the grooves in both cylinder bores.

6. Inspect the caliper as described in this section.

Assembly

1. Install the inboard bleed valve and cover into the caliper. Tighten finger-tight.

2. Soak the new piston and dust seals in DOT 4 brake fluid.

3. Lubricate the piston and cylinder bore with brake fluid.

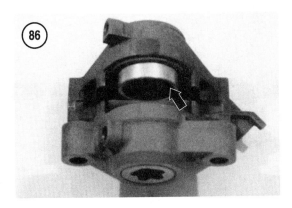

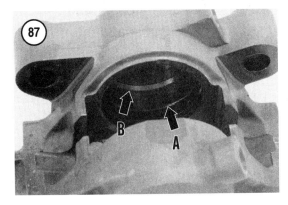

NOTE
The piston seal is thicker than the dust seal.

4. Install a new piston seal (**Figure 84**) into the lower groove of the cylinder bore.

5. Install a new dust seal (**Figure 85**) into the upper groove of the cylinder bore.

NOTE
Check that each seal fits squarely into its respective cylinder bore groove.

6. Install the piston into the caliper bore with its open side facing out (**Figure 86**). To prevent the piston from damaging the seals, turn them into the bore by hand. Install the piston until it bottoms out.

7. Repeat Steps 4-6 for the other piston seals and piston.

8. Install the brake pads.

9. Install the brake caliper.

Inspection

When measuring the brake caliper components, compare the actual measurements to the specifications in **Table 1**. Replace worn or damaged parts as described in this section.

1. Clean and dry the caliper assembly as follows:
   a. Handle the brake components carefully when servicing them.
   b. Use only DOT 4 brake fluid or isopropyl alcohol to wash rubber parts in the brake system. Never allow any petroleum-based cleaner to contact the rubber parts. These chemicals cause the rubber to swell, requiring their replacement.
   c. Clean the dust and piston seal grooves (A, **Figure 87**) carefully to avoid damaging the caliper bore. Use a small pick or brush to clean the grooves. If a hard varnish residue has built up in the grooves, soak the caliper body in solvent to help soften the residue, then wash the caliper in soapy water and rinse completely.
   d. If alcohol or solvent was used to clean the caliper, blow dry with compressed air.
   e. Check the fluid passages to make sure they are clean and dry.
   f. After cleaning the parts, place them on a clean lint-free cloth until assembly.

CAUTION
Do not get any oil or grease on any of the brake caliper components. These chemicals cause the rubber parts in the brake system to swell, permanently damaging them.

2. Check the cylinder bore (B, **Figure 87**) for corrosion, deep scratches and other wear marks. Do not hone the cylinder bore.

3. Measure the caliper cylinder bore diameter.

4. Inspect the pistons (**Figure 88**) for pitting, corrosion, cracks or other damage.

15

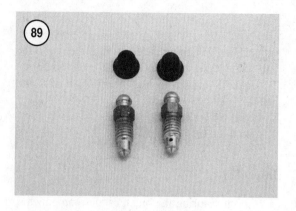

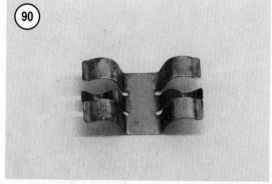

5. Clean the bleed valves (**Figure 89**) with compressed air. Check the valve threads for damage. Replace damaged dust cover.

6. Clean the banjo bolt with compressed air.

7. Inspect the pad spring (**Figure 90**) for damage.

8. Inspect the caliper pad pins for rust or corrosion.

9. Check the banjo bolt threads (**Figure 91**) for damage.

10. Check the bleed screw threads (**Figure 92**) for damage.

11. Inspect the pad pin holes (**Figure 93**) for damage or elongation.

12. If removed, inspect the caliper bracket (**Figure 94**) for cracks or damage.

REAR BRAKE CALIPER
(2002-2003 MODELS)

Removal/Installation

1. Support the motorcycle on level ground.

2. Block the front wheel so the motorcycle will not roll in either direction while on the swing arm stand.

3. Remove the muffler as described in Chapter Four.

4. If the caliper is going to be removed and serviced, perform the following:

    a. Drain the brake fluid from the rear master cylinder as described under *Brake Fluid Draining* in this chapter.

    b. Remove the brake pads as previously described.

    c. Remove the brake hose banjo bolt and washers at the caliper (**Figure 95**). Plug the hose, then place it in a reclosable plastic bag (**Figure 96**) to prevent leakage and hose contamination.

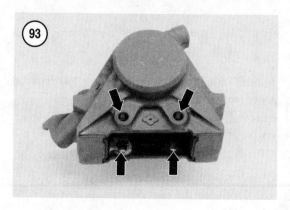

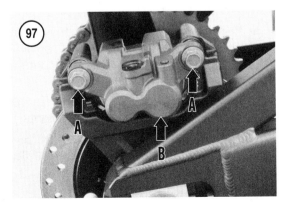

5. Remove both caliper mounting pin bolts (A, **Figure 97**).

6. Pull the caliper up and off the brake disc (B, **Figure 97**).

7. If the brake hose was not disconnected at the caliper, insert a spacer block between the brake pads and support the caliper with a wire hook.

NOTE
The spacer block prevents the piston from being forced out of the caliper if the rear brake pedal is accidentally applied while the brake caliper is removed from the brake disc.

8. If necessary, service the brake caliper as described in this chapter.

9. Check that the brake pads were not contaminated with brake fluid. If so, replace the brake pads as described in this chapter.

10. If the brake caliper was not completely removed from the motorcycle, remove the spacer block from between the brake pads.

11. Install the caliper assembly (B, **Figure 97**) over the brake disc. Be careful not to damage the leading edge of the pads.

12. Install both caliper mounting pin bolts (A, **Figure 97**) and tighten to 27 N•m (20 ft.-lb.).

13. If removed, place a new sealing washer on each side of the brake hose fitting (**Figure 98**). Then thread the banjo bolt (**Figure 95**) into the caliper and tighten to 30 N•m (22 ft.-lb.).

14. Refill the master cylinder with new DOT 4 brake fluid.

15. Bleed the brake pedal lines as described in this chapter.

16. Operate the rear brake pedal to seat the pads against the brake disc.

15

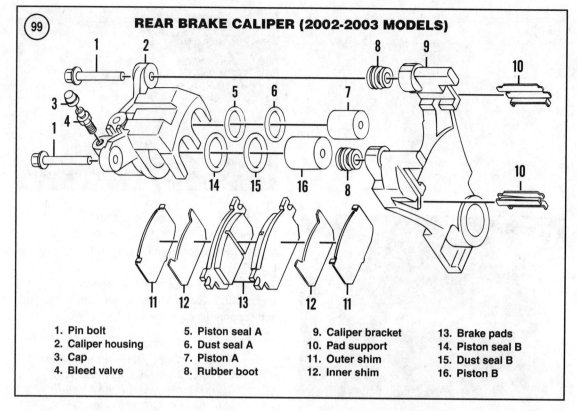

REAR BRAKE CALIPER (2002-2003 MODELS)

1. Pin bolt
2. Caliper housing
3. Cap
4. Bleed valve
5. Piston seal A
6. Dust seal A
7. Piston A
8. Rubber boot
9. Caliper bracket
10. Pad support
11. Outer shim
12. Inner shim
13. Brake pads
14. Piston seal B
15. Dust seal B
16. Piston B

17. Bleed the brake lever and brake pedal lines as described in this chapter.

18. Operate the rear brake pedal to seat the pads against the brake disc.

> *WARNING*
> *Do not ride the motorcycle until the rear brake operates with full hydraulic advantage.*

Disassembly

Refer to **Figure 99**.

1. Remove the brake caliper as described in this chapter.

2. If necessary, the brake pads can remain in place on the caliper bracket.

3. Do *not* remove the bleed valve and cap (A, **Figure 100**).

4. Remove the pistons as follows:

> *WARNING*
> *Compressed air forces the pistons out of the caliper under considerable force. Do not cushion the pistons by hand, as injury could result.*

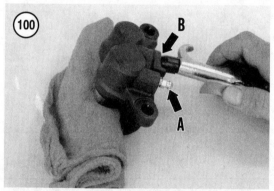

a. Two different size pistons are used.

b. Place a thick towel, or shop cloth, between the pistons and workbench. Make sure there is enough space underneath the caliper for the pistons to be removed completely.

c. Direct compressed air through the brake line port (B, **Figure 100**) to remove the pistons.

5. Use a small pick tool to carefully pry the dust and piston seals from the grooves in the cylinder bore. Repeat for each bore.

6. Repeat for the other caliper half.

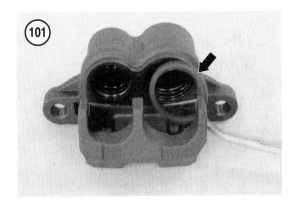

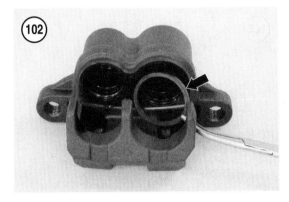

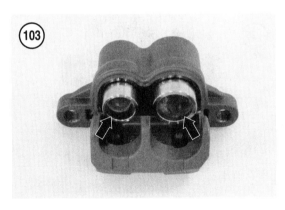

7. If still in place, remove the bleed valve and its cover from the outboard caliper half.

Assembly

Refer to **Figure 99**.

Use new DOT 4 brake fluid when lubricating the parts in the following steps.

NOTE
Before soaking the new piston and dust seals in brake fluid, compare

them to the old parts, determine their sizes and match them to their respective bores. Two different size seals are used. Refer to the brake caliper cylinder front and rear bore measurements in **Table 1**.

1. Soak the new piston and dust seals in brake fluid.
2. Lubricate the pistons and cylinder bores with brake fluid.

NOTE
The piston seals are thicker than the dust seals.

3. Install a new piston seal (**Figure 101**) into each cylinder bore rear groove.
4. Install a new dust seal (**Figure 102**) into each cylinder bore front groove.

NOTE
Check that each seal fits squarely into its respective cylinder bore groove.

5. Install each piston into its respective caliper bore with its open side facing out (**Figure 103**). To prevent pistons from damaging seals, turn them into the bore by hand. Install the pistons until they bottom.
6. If removed, install the bleed valve and cap (A, **Figure 100**).
7. If removed, install the brake pads onto the mounting bracket as described in this chapter.
8. Install the brake caliper.

Inspection

When measuring the brake caliper components, compare the actual measurements to the specifications in **Table 1**. Replace worn or damaged parts as described in this section.

1. Clean and dry the caliper assembly as follows:
   a. Handle the brake components carefully when servicing them.
   b. Remove all threadlocking compound residue from the brake caliper body halves and their mounting bolt threads.
   c. Use only DOT 4 brake fluid or isopropyl alcohol to wash rubber parts in the brake system. Never allow any petroleum-based cleaner to contact the rubber parts. These chemicals cause the rubber to swell, requiring their replacement.

15

d. Clean the dust and piston seal grooves (**Figure 104**) carefully to avoid damaging the caliper bore. Use a small pick or brush to clean the grooves. If a hard varnish residue has built up in the grooves, soak the caliper body halves in solvent to help soften the residue. Then wash the caliper halves in soapy water and rinse completely.

e. If alcohol or solvent was used to clean the caliper, blow dry with compressed air.

f. Check the fluid passages to make sure they are clean and dry.

g. After cleaning the parts, place them on a clean lint-free cloth until assembly.

CAUTION
Do not get any oil or grease onto any of the brake caliper components. These chemicals cause the rubber parts in the brake system to swell, permanently damaging them.

2. Check each cylinder bore (**Figure 105**) for corrosion, deep scratches and other wear marks. Do not hone the cylinder bores.

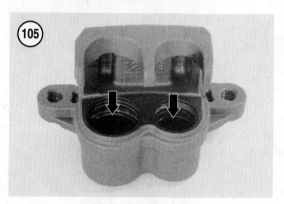

NOTE
The caliper uses two different bore diameters. The front piston and bore have the larger diameter of the two (adjacent to the bleed valve). Refer to the front (A, Figure 106) and rear (B) piston and caliper diameter specifications in Table 1 when measuring the parts in the following steps.

3. Measure each caliper cylinder diameter (**Figure 105**).

4. Inspect the pistons (**Figure 107**) for pitting, corrosion, cracks or other damage.

5. Inspect the bleed valve and the banjo bolt threads for wear or damage.

6. Clean the bleed valve with compressed air. Check the valve threads for damage. Replace the dust caps if missing or damaged.

7. Clean the banjo bolt with compressed air.

8. Inspect the threads in the caliper for the bleed valve (A, **Figure 108**) and the banjo bolt (B) for wear or damage.

9. Inspect the pad supports (**Figure 109**) for cracks or damage.

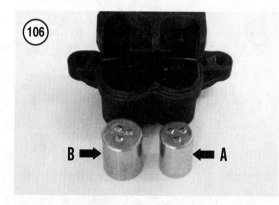

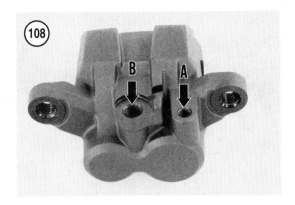

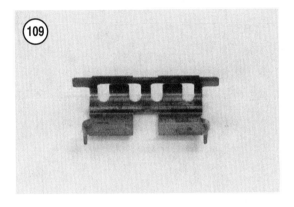

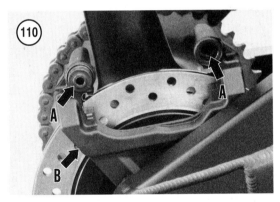

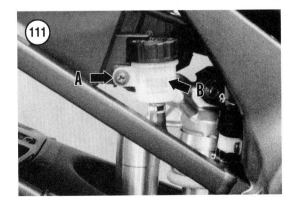

> *WARNING*
> *A floating caliper is used on these models. The caliper pad pin bolts go through the rubber boot on the caliper bracket. These two components allow the brake caliper to slide or float during piston movement. The rubber boot installed over the mounting bracket helps control caliper movement by preventing excessive vibration and play, and prevents dirt from damaging the pad pin bolts operating surfaces. If the pad pin bolts are excessively worn or damaged, the caliper cannot slide smoothly. This condition causes uneven brake pad wear, resulting in brake drag and overheating. The caliper pad pin bolts and rubber boots are an important part of the brake caliper and must be maintained to provide proper brake operation.*

10. Inspect the pad pin bolts for excessive wear, uneven wear (steps) and other damage.

11. Inspect the rubber boots (A, **Figure 110**) for damage or deterioration.

12. Inspect the caliper bracket (B, **Figure 110**) for cracks or damage.

REAR MASTER CYLINDER

Read the information listed under *Brake Service* in this chapter before servicing the rear master cylinder.

Removal

1. Support the motorcycle on level ground.

2. Block the front wheel so the motorcycle will not roll in either direction while on the swing arm stand.

3. Remove the seat, rear cowl and the right fairing panel as described in Chapter Sixteen.

> *CAUTION*
> *Wipe up any spilled brake fluid immediately, as it damages the finish of most plastic and metal surfaces. Use soapy water and rinse thoroughly.*

4. Drain the brake pedal line as described under *Brake Fluid Draining* in this chapter.

5. Remove the screw (A, **Figure 111**) securing the master cylinder reservoir to the rear fender inner

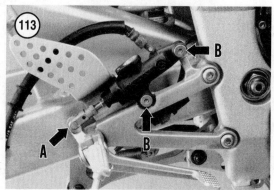

panel. Pull the master cylinder (B, **Figure 111**) away from the seat rail.

6. Remove the screw securing the reservoir hose joint (**Figure 112**) and disconnect it from the master cylinder. Remove the O-ring seal.

7. Remove the cotter pin and washer and the brake pedal joint pin (A, **Figure 113**). Discard the cotter pin.

8. Loosen, but do not remove, the bolts (B, **Figure 113**) securing the master cylinder to the footpeg bracket.

9. Remove the bolts (A, **Figure 114**) securing the rear brake pedal/footrest assembly (B) to the frame and move it away from the frame.

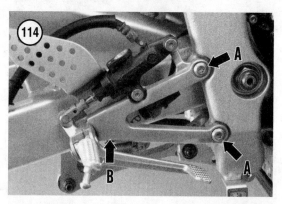

10. Turn the rear brake pedal/footrest assembly around to gain access to the master cylinder banjo bolt.

11. Remove the banjo bolt (**Figure 115**) and washers securing the rear brake hose to the backside of the master cylinder. Plug the brake hose and place the end in a reclosable plastic bag to prevent brake fluid from leaking out.

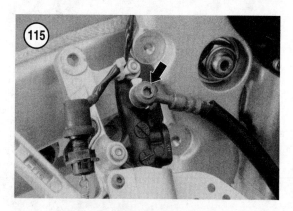

12. Remove the bolts (B, **Figure 113**) loosened in Step 8 and remove the master cylinder from the brake pedal.

Installation

1. Install the master cylinder into position on the footpeg bracket and install the bolts securely.

2. Remove the plastic bag and plug from the rear brake hose. Move the rear brake hose into position onto the backside of the master cylinder.

3. Secure the brake hose to the master cylinder with the banjo bolt and two *new* washers. Position the brake hose against the holder on the master cylinder

REAR MASTER CYLINDER

1. Cap retainer (1998-1999 models)
2. Cap
3. Diaphragm holder
4. Screw
5. Diaphragm
6. Reservoir
7. Hose clamp
8. Reservoir hose
9. Banjo bolt
10. Sealing washer
11. Caliper hose
12. Screw
13. Hose joint
14. O-ring
15. Master cylinder body
16. Bolt
17. Cotter pin or clip
18. Washer
19. Joint pin
20. Bolt

and tighten the banjo bolt (**Figure 115**) to 30 N•m (22 ft.-lb.).

4. Install the rear brake pedal/footrest assembly (B, **Figure 114**) onto the frame and install the bolts (A). Tighten the bolts to 28 N•m (21 ft.-lb.).

5. Tighten the master cylinder mounting bolts (B, **Figure 113**) to 23 N•m (17 ft.-lb.).

6. Connect the master cylinder onto the brake pedal. Insert the joint pin (A, **Figure 113**) from the outside and install a washer and a *new* cotter pin and bend the ends over completely.

7. Install a *new* O-ring seal (**Figure 116**) into the reservoir hose joint receptacle. Make sure it is seated correctly.

8. Move the reservoir hose and hose joint into position and connect it to the master cylinder (**Figure 112**). Tighten the screw securely.

9. Install the master cylinder reservoir onto the rear fender inner panel and tighten the screw securely.

10. Bleed the brakes as described in this chapter.

11. Adjust the rear brake pedal height as described in Chapter Three.

12. Turn the ignition switch on and check that the rear brake light comes on when the rear brake pedal is depressed.

> *WARNING*
> *Do not ride the motorcycle until the front and rear brakes and brake light work properly.*

Disassembly

Refer to **Figure 117** and **Figure 118**.

1. Slide the rubber boot (**Figure 119**) out of the master cylinder bore and away from the master cylinder body (A, **Figure 120**).

> *WARNING*
> *If brake fluid is leaking from the master cylinder bore, the piston cups are excessively worn or damaged. Replace the piston assembly.*

> *NOTE*
> *To aid in the removal/installation of the piston snap ring, thread a bolt and nut into the master cylinder and secure the nut and bolt in a vise.*

2. Compress the piston and remove the snap ring (B, **Figure 120**) from the groove in the master cyl-

15

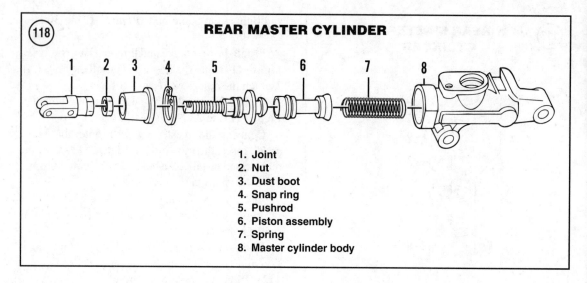

REAR MASTER CYLINDER

1. Joint
2. Nut
3. Dust boot
4. Snap ring
5. Pushrod
6. Piston assembly
7. Spring
8. Master cylinder body

inder, then remove the pushrod assembly (**Figure 121**).

3. Remove the piston assembly (A, **Figure 122**) and spring (B).

4. Inspect all components as described in this chapter.

Assembly

1. If installing a new piston assembly, assemble it as shown in **Figure 118**.

2. Lubricate the piston assembly and cylinder bore with DOT 4 brake fluid.

3. Install the spring into the master cylinder bore as shown in B, **Figure 122**.

CAUTION
Do not allow the piston cups to tear or turn inside out when installing the piston into the master cylinder bore. Both cups are larger than the bore. To ease installation, lubricate the cups and piston with brake fluid.

4. Insert the piston assembly (A, **Figure 122**) into the master cylinder bore and against the spring. Push the piston in until it bottoms (**Figure 123**).

5. Use silicone brake grease to lubricate the end of the pushrod that contacts the piston.

6. Install the pushrod into the master cylinder bore and seat it against the piston (**Figure 121**).

7. Push the pushrod to compress the piston assembly and position the washer below the snap ring

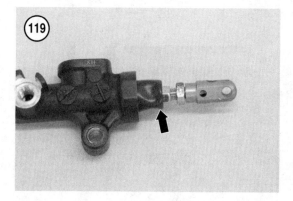

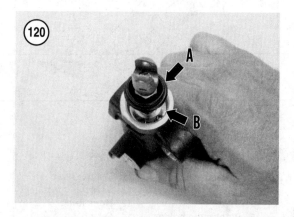

groove, then install the snap ring (B, **Figure 120**) into the master cylinder groove.

WARNING
The snap ring must seat in the master cylinder groove completely. Push and release the piston a few times to make

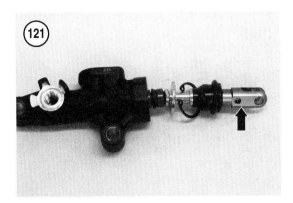

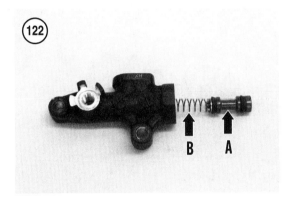

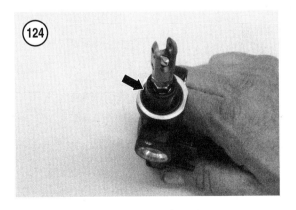

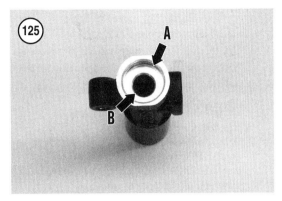

sure it moves smoothly and that the snap ring does not pop out.

8. Slide the dust boot (**Figure 124**) down the pushrod and seat it against the snap ring. Seat the outer end of the boot onto the pushrod (**Figure 119**).

9. Install the master cylinder as described in this chapter.

Inspection

When measuring the master cylinder components, compare the actual measurements to the specifications in **Table 1**. Replace worn or damaged parts as described in this section.

> *NOTE*
> *The dust boot, snap ring, pushrod, piston assembly and spring are all included in the rebuild kit. Install all of these components, regardless of the condition of the original components.*

1. Clean and dry the master cylinder assembly as follows:

    a. Handle the brake components carefully when servicing them.

    b. Use only DOT 4 brake fluid or isopropyl alcohol to wash rubber parts in the brake system. Never allow any petroleum-based cleaner to contact the rubber parts. These chemicals cause the rubber to swell, requiring their replacement.

    c. Clean the master cylinder snap ring groove (A, **Figure 125**) carefully. Use a small pick or brush to clean the groove. If a hard varnish residue has built up in the groove, soak the master cylinder in solvent to help soften the

15

residue. Wash the master cylinder in soapy water and rinse completely.

   d. Dry the master cylinder with compressed air.

   e. After cleaning parts, place them on a clean lint-free cloth until assembly.

> *WARNING*
> *Do not get any oil or grease on any of the brake master cylinder components. These chemicals cause the rubber parts in the brake system to swell, permanently damaging them.*

> *WARNING*
> *Do not remove the primary and secondary cups from the piston assembly for cleaning or inspection purposes.*

2. Check the piston assembly for the following defects:

   a. Broken, distorted or collapsed piston spring (A, **Figure 126**).

   b. Worn, cracked, damaged or swollen primary (B, **Figure 126**) and secondary cups (C).

   c. Scratched, scored or damaged piston (D, **Figure 126**).

   d. Corroded, weak or damaged snap ring.

   e. Worn or damaged rubber dust boot.

   f. If any of these parts are worn or damaged, replace the piston assembly.

3. Inspect the master cylinder bore (B, **Figure 125**). Replace the master cylinder if its bore is pitted, corroded, cracked or damaged in any way. Do not hone the master cylinder bore to remove scratches or other damage.

4. Measure the master cylinder bore inside diameter (B, **Figure 125**).

5. Check for plugged supply and relief ports (**Figure 127**) in the master cylinder. Clean with compressed air.

6. Check the pushrod assembly (**Figure 128**) for the following defects:

   a. Corroded or damaged pushrod.

   b. Damaged pushrod joint.

7. Inspect the banjo bolt threads (**Figure 129**) in the master cylinder for damage.

BRAKE HOSE REPLACEMENT

Check the brake hoses at the brake inspection intervals listed in Chapter Three. Replace the brake

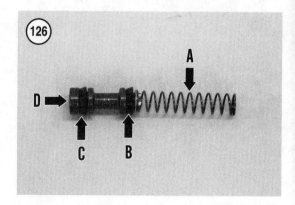

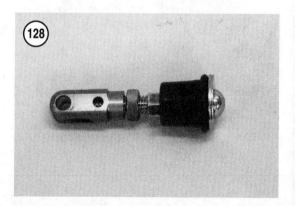

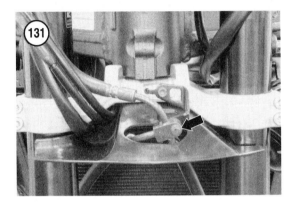

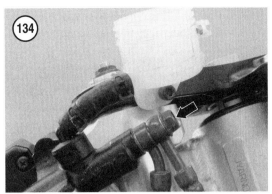

hoses if they show signs of wear or damage, or if they have bulges or signs of chafing.

To replace a brake hose, perform the following:

1. Drain the brake system as described under *Brake Fluid Draining* in this chapter.

2. Use a plastic drop cloth to cover areas that could be damaged by spilled brake fluid.

3. When removing a brake hose or brake line, note the following:

    a. Record the hose or line routing on a piece of paper.

    b. Remove any bolts or brackets securing the brake hose(s) to the frame or suspension component. Refer to **Figure 130** and **Figure 131** for the front and **Figure 132** and **Figure 133** for the rear.

    c. Before removing the banjo bolts (**Figure 134**), note how the end of the brake hose(s) is installed or indexed against the part it is threaded into. The hose(s) must be installed facing in the original position.

4. Replace banjo bolts with damaged hex-heads.

5. Always install *new* washers with the banjo bolts.

6. Reverse these steps to install the new brake hoses, while noting the following:

    a. Compare the new and old hoses to make sure they are the same.

    b. Clean the new washers, banjo bolts and hose ends to remove any contamination.

    c. Referring to the notes made during removal, route the brake hose along its original path.

    d. Install a *new* banjo bolt washer on each side of the brake hose.

    e. Tighten banjo bolts to 30 N•m (22 ft.-lb.).

    f. After replacing a front brake hose(s), turn the handlebars from side to side to make sure the hose does not rub against any part or pull away from its brake unit.

15

g. Refill the master cylinders and bleed the brakes as described in this chapter.

> *WARNING*
> *Do not ride the motorcycle until the front and rear brakes operate correctly with full hydraulic advantage and the brake light works properly.*

BRAKE DISC

Inspection

The front and rear brake discs can be inspected while installed on or removed from the motorcycle. Small marks on the disc are not important, but deep scratches or other marks may reduce braking effectiveness and increase brake pad wear. If these grooves are evident and the brake pads are wearing rapidly, replace the brake disc.

The minimum (MIN) disc thickness is stamped on the disc. Refer to **Table 1** for disc specifications.

1. Support the motorcycle on level ground.

2. Block the front wheel so the motorcycle will not roll in either direction while on the swing arm stand.

3. Measure the thickness around the disc at several locations with a micrometer (**Figure 135**). Replace the disc if its thickness at any point is less than the marked MIN thickness on the disc. Also refer to the service limit specified in **Table 1**.

4. Install a dial indicator and position its stem against the brake disc (**Figure 136**). Then zero the dial gauge. Slowly turn the front wheel or rear axle/brake disc and measure runout. If the runout exceeds the service limit in **Table 1**, check the following:

   a. Loose brake disc mounting bolts (**Figure 137**).

   b. Damaged wheel bearings or rear axle driven flange bearings (Chapter Twelve).

   c. Damaged brake disc mounting surface.

   d. If the bearings and disc mounting surfaces are in good condition, replace the brake disc.

5. Clean the disc of any rust or corrosion and wipe clean with brake cleaner. Never use an oil-based solvent that may leave an oil residue on the disc.

6. On the front wheel, check the floating disc fasteners (**Figure 138**) for damage or looseness. If any are damaged, replace the disc.

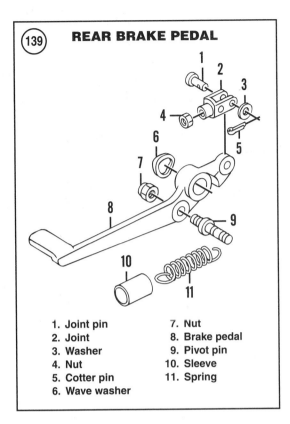

REAR BRAKE PEDAL (139)

1. Joint pin
2. Joint
3. Washer
4. Nut
5. Cotter pin
6. Wave washer
7. Nut
8. Brake pedal
9. Pivot pin
10. Sleeve
11. Spring

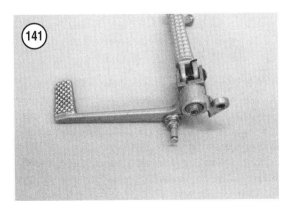

Removal/Installation

1A. Remove the front wheel as described in Chapter Twelve.

1B. Remove the rear wheel as described in Chapter Twelve.

2. Remove the bolts (**Figure 137**) securing the brake disc to the wheel and remove the disc.

3. Perform any necessary service to the front hub (wheel bearing or tire replacement) before installing the brake discs.

4. Clean the brake disc threaded holes in the hub.

5. Clean the brake disc mounting surface on the hub.

6. Install the brake disc with its directional arrow facing toward the wheel's normal rotating direction.

WARNING
The bolts securing the brake disc must be replaced every time they are removed.

7. Install new brake disc mounting bolts and tighten to 18 N•m (13 ft.-lb.).

8. Clean the disc of any rust or corrosion and spray clean with brake cleaner. Never use an oil-based solvent that may leave an oil residue on the disc.

9. Install the front or rear wheel as described in Chapter Twelve.

REAR BRAKE PEDAL

Removal

Refer to **Figure 139**.

1. Remove the right rear footpeg bracket assembly as described under *Rear Master Cylinder Removal* in this chapter.

2. Disconnect the brake light switch spring and brake pedal return spring (A, **Figure 140**) from the brake pedal.

3. Remove the bolt (B, **Figure 140**) securing the brake pedal and footpeg assembly to the footpeg bracket.

4. Clean the brake pedal and footpeg assembly pivot surfaces on the footpeg bracket.

5. Inspect the brake pedal assembly (**Figure 141**) and replace worn or damaged parts.

15

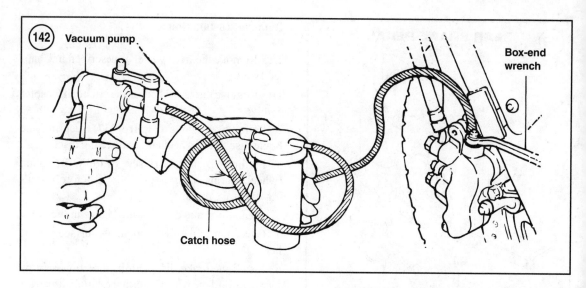

Vacuum pump. Box-end wrench. Catch hose.

Installation

1. Apply a water-resistant grease onto the brake pedal and footpeg pivot surfaces.
2. Install the rear brake pedal and footpeg assembly onto the footpeg bracket.
3. Install the bolt (B, **Figure 140**) and tighten securely.
4. Reconnect the brake light switch spring and brake pedal return spring (A, **Figure 140**).
5. Install the right footpeg holder assembly as described under *Rear Master Cylinder Installation* in this chapter.
6. Operate the rear brake pedal, making sure it moves without any binding or roughness.
7. Adjust the rear brake light switch as described in Chapter Three.

> *WARNING*
> *Do not ride the motorcycle until the rear brake, brake pedal and brake light work properly.*

BRAKE BLEEDING

Bleeding the brakes removes air from the brake system. Air in the brake system increases brake lever or pedal travel while causing it to feel spongy and less responsive. Under extreme braking (heat) conditions, it can cause complete loss of brake action.

The brake system can be bled manually or with the use of a vacuum pump. Both methods are described in this section. Refer to *Brake Fluid Selec-*

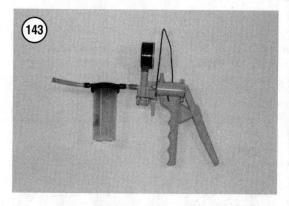

tion, *Preventing Brake Fluid Damage* and *Brake Service* at the beginning of this chapter.

General Bleeding Tips

> *NOTE*
> *When bleeding the brakes, check the fluid level in the front and rear master cylinders frequently to prevent them from running dry, especially when using a vacuum pump. If air enters the system it must be bled again.*

When bleeding the brakes, note the following:
1. Make sure the brake hoses and lines are tight.
2. Clean the bleed valves and the area around the valves of all dirt and debris. Make sure the passageway in the end of the valve is open and clear.
3. Use a box-end wrench to open and close the bleed valves. This prevents damage to the hex-head, especially if the valve is rusted in place.

4. Install the box-end wrench (**Figure 142**) on the bleed valve before installing the catch hose. This allows operation of the wrench without having to disconnect the hose.

NOTE
*The catch hose (**Figure 142**) is the hose installed between the bleed valve and catch bottle.*

5. Replace bleed valves that have damaged hex-head surfaces. If rounded off, the valves cannot be tightened fully and are also difficult to loosen.

6. Use a clear catch hose to allow visible inspection of the brake fluid as it leaves the caliper. Air bubbles visible in the catch hose indicate that there still may be air trapped in the brake system.

7. Depending on the play of the bleed valve when it is loosened, it is possible to see air exiting through the catch hose even through there is no air in the brake system. A loose or damaged catch hose also causes air leaks. In both cases, air is being introduced into the bleed system at the bleed valve threads and catch hose connection, and not from within the brake system itself. This condition can be

misleading and cause excessive brake bleeding when there is no air in the system.

8. Open the bleed valve just enough to allow fluid to pass through the valve and into the catch bottle. The farther the bleed valve is opened, the looser the valve becomes. This allows air to be drawn into the system from around the valve threads.

WARNING
Do not apply an excessive amount of grease to the bleed valve threads. This can block the bleed valve passageway and contaminate the brake fluid.

9. If air is suspected of entering the bleed system from around the bleed valve threads, remove the bleed valve and apply silicone brake grease to the valve's threads to prevent air from passing by them. Then reinstall the bleed valve into the brake caliper.

10. If the system is difficult to bleed, tap the banjo bolt on the master cylinder as well as the brake caliper and connecting hoses a few times. It is not uncommon for air bubbles to become trapped in the hose connection where the brake fluid exits the master cylinder and caliper. When a number of bubbles appear in the master cylinder reservoir after tapping the banjo bolt, air was trapped in this area. Also, tap the other hole and line connection points at the calipers and other brake units.

Brake Bleeder Procedure

This one-person procedure uses the Mityvac hydraulic brake bleeding kit (**Figure 143**). This tool and equivalents are available from automotive or motorcycle supply stores.

1. Support the motorcycle on level ground.

2. Block the front wheel so the motorcycle will not roll in either direction while on the swing arm stand.

3. To bleed the rear caliper, remove the muffler as described in Chapter Eight or Chapter Nine.

4. Remove the dust cap (**Figure 144**) from the caliper bleed valve.

5. Place a clean shop cloth over the caliper to protect it from accidental brake fluid spills.

6. Assemble the Mityvac tool according to its manufacturer's instructions. Secure it to the caliper bleed valve (**Figure 145**).

7. Clean the top of the master cylinder reservoir of all debris.

15

8. Turn the handlebars to level the front master cylinder and remove the reservoir cap (**Figure 146**), diaphragm holder and diaphragm.

9. Fill the reservoir almost to the top with DOT 4 brake fluid and reinstall the diaphragm holder, diaphragm and cap. Leave the cap in place during this procedure to prevent the entry of dirt.

10. Operate the pump several times to create a vacuum in the line. Brake fluid will quickly draw from the caliper into the pump's reservoir. Open the bleed valve and then tighten the caliper bleed valve before the fluid stops flowing through the hose. To prevent air from being drawn through the master cylinder, add fluid to maintain its level at the top of the reservoir.

> *NOTE*
> *Do not allow the master cylinder reservoir to empty during the bleeding operation or more air will enter the system. If this occurs, the procedure must be repeated.*

11. Continue the bleeding process until the fluid drawn from the caliper is bubble free. If bubbles are withdrawn with the brake fluid, more air is trapped in the line. Repeat Step 10, making sure to refill the master cylinder to prevent air from being drawn into the system.

12. When the brake fluid is free of bubbles, tighten the bleed valve and remove the brake bleeder assembly. Reinstall the bleed valve dust cap.

> *WARNING*
> *Dispose of the brake fluid expelled during the bleeding process. Do not reuse the brake fluid.*

13. If necessary, add fluid to correct the level in the master cylinder reservoir. When topping off the front master cylinder, turn the handlebar until the reservoir is level; add fluid until it is level with the reservoir gasket surface. The fluid level in the rear master cylinder must be slightly below the upper gasket surface.

14. On front brakes, repeat Steps 1-9 for the other caliper.

15. Reinstall the reservoir diaphragm, diaphragm holder and cap (**Figure 146**). Tighten the cap securely.

16. Test the feel of the brake lever or pedal. It must be firm and offer the same resistance each time it is

operated. If it feels spongy, it is likely that there is still air in the system and it must be bled again. After bleeding the system, check for leaks and tighten all fittings and connections as necessary.

> *WARNING*
> *Do not ride the motorcycle until the front and/or rear brake are operating correctly with full hydraulic advantage.*

17. Test ride the motorcycle, slowly at first, to make sure that the brakes are operating properly.

Manual Procedure

1. Support the motorcycle on level ground.

2. Block the front wheel so the motorcycle will not roll in either direction while on the swing arm stand.

3. To bleed the rear caliper, remove the muffler as described in Chapter Eight or Chapter Nine.

4. Remove the dust cap (**Figure 144**) from the caliper bleed valve.

5. Place a clean shop cloth over the caliper to protect it from accidental brake fluid spills.

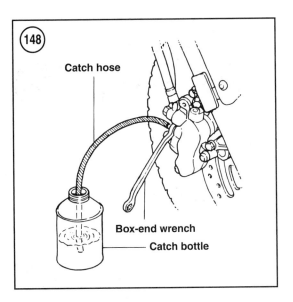

Catch hose

Box-end wrench

Catch bottle

6. Clean the top of the master cylinder reservoir of all dirt and foreign matter.

7. Turn the handlebars to level the front master cylinder and remove the reservoir cap (**Figure 146**), diaphragm holder and diaphragm.

8. Connect a length of clear tubing to the bleed valve on the caliper (**Figure 147**). Place the other end of the tube into a clean container (**Figure 148**). Fill the container with enough fresh DOT 4 brake fluid to keep the end of the tube submerged. The tube must be long enough so that a loop can be made higher than the bleeder valve to prevent air from being drawn into the caliper during bleeding.

9. Clean the top of the master cylinder reservoir of all dirt and foreign matter.

10. Turn the handlebars to level the front master cylinder and remove the reservoir cap (**Figure 146**), diaphragm holder and diaphragm.

11. Fill the reservoir almost to the top with DOT 4 brake fluid and reinstall the diaphragm holder, diaphragm and cap. Leave the cap in place during this procedure to prevent the entry of dirt.

NOTE
During this procedure, it is important to check the fluid level in the master cylinder reservoir often. If the reservoir runs dry, more air will enter the system.

12. Slowly apply the brake lever several times. Hold the lever in the applied position and open the bleed valve about 1/2 turn. Allow the lever to travel

to its limit. When the limit is reached, tighten the bleed valve, then release the brake lever. As the brake fluid enters the system, the level will drop in the master cylinder reservoir. Maintain the level at the top of the reservoir to prevent air from being drawn into the system.

13. Continue the bleeding process until the fluid emerging from the hose is completely free of air bubbles. If the fluid is being replaced, continue until the fluid emerging from the hose is clean.

NOTE
If bleeding is difficult, allowing the fluid to stabilize for a few hours. Repeat the bleeding procedure when the tiny bubbles in the system settle out.

14. Hold the lever in the applied position and tighten the bleed valve. Remove the bleed tube and install the bleed valve dust cap.

WARNING
Dispose of the brake fluid expelled during the bleeding process. Do not reuse the brake fluid.

15. If necessary, add fluid to correct the level in the master cylinder reservoir. When topping off the front master cylinder, turn the handlebar until the reservoir is level; add fluid until it is level with the reservoir gasket surface. The fluid level in the rear master cylinder must be slightly below the upper gasket surface.

16. On front brakes, repeat Steps 11-15 for the other caliper.

17. Install the diaphragm holder, diaphragm and cap. Tighten the cap securely.

18. Test the feel of the brake lever or pedal. It must be firm and offer the same resistance each time it is operated. If it feels spongy, it is likely that there is still air in the system and it must be bled again. After bleeding the system, check for leaks and tighten all fittings and connections as necessary.

WARNING
Do not ride the motorcycle until the front and/or rear brake are operating correctly with full hydraulic advantage.

19. Test ride the motorcycle, slowly at first, to make sure that the brakes are operating properly.

15

Brake Fluid Draining

Before disconnecting a brake hose from the front or rear brake, drain the brake fluid as described in this section. Doing so reduces the amount of brake fluid that can spill out when disconnecting the brake hoses and lines from the system.

Front brake lever line

1. Read the information listed under *Brake Bleeding* in this chapter.
2. Support the motorcycle on level ground.
3. Block the front wheel so the motorcycle will not roll in either direction while on the swing arm stand.
4. Turn the handlebars to level the front master cylinder and remove the reservoir cap (**Figure 146**), diaphragm holder and diaphragm.
5. Connect a brake bleeder to the front brake caliper bleed valve (**Figure 145**) as described in this section. Operate the bleeder tool to remove as much brake fluid from the system as possible.
6. Close the bleed valve and disconnect the brake bleeder tool.
7. Repeat for the other caliper.
8. Service the brake components as described in this chapter.

Rear brake pedal line

1. Read the information listed under *Brake Bleeding* in this chapter.
2. Support the motorcycle on level ground.
3. Block the front wheel so the motorcycle will not roll in either direction while on the swing arm stand.
4. Remove the reservoir cap (**Figure 149**), diaphragm holder and diaphragm.
5. Connect a brake bleeder to the rear brake caliper bleed valve (**Figure 150**) as described in this section. Operate the bleeder tool to remove as much brake fluid from the system as possible.

> *CAUTION*
> *Wipe up any spilled brake fluid immediately, as it damages the finish of most plastic and metal surfaces. Use soapy water and rinse thoroughly.*

6. Disconnect the brake bleeder and remove it from the brake caliper.

7. Service the brake components as described in this chapter.

Flushing The Brake System

When flushing the brake system, use DOT 4 brake fluid as a flushing fluid. Flushing consists of pulling new brake fluid through the system until the new fluid appears at the caliper and without the presence of any air bubbles. To flush the brake system, follow one of the bleeding procedures described in this section.

> *WARNING*
> *Never reuse old brake fluid. Properly discard all brake fluid flushed from the system.*

Table 1 BRAKE SPECIFICATIONS

Item	Standard mm (in.)	Service limit mm (in.)
Brake fluid	DOT 4	
Brake disc runout	–	0.10 (0.004)
Brake disc thickness	5.0 (0.20)	4.5 (0.18)
Brake pedal height		
Top of brake pedal below		
footrest bracket		
1998-2001 models	35-40 (1.38-1.57)	
2002-2003 models	38-42 (1.50-1.65)	
Brake pad thickness		
Front brake		
1998-2001 models	5.5 (0.22)	0.5 (0.02)
2002-2003 models	4.5 (0.18)	0.5 (0.02)
Rear brake		
1998-2001 models	5.5 (0.22)	0.5 (0.02)
2002-2003 models	5.1 (0.20)	0.8 (0.03)
Front master cylinder		
Cylinder bore	14.0 (0.55)	–
Front caliper		
Cylinder bore		
Upper bore A	30.2 (1.19)	–
Lower bore B	27.0 (1.06)	–
Rear master cylinder		
Cylinder bore	12.7 (0.5)	–
Rear caliper		
Cylinder bore		
1998-2001 models	38.2 (1.50)	–
2002-2003 models		
Front bore A	22.2 (0.87)	–
Rear bore B	27.0 (1.06)	–

Table 2 BRAKE TORQUE SPECIFICATIONS

Item	N•m	in.-lb.	ft.-lb.
Brake disc bolt (front and rear)	18	–	13
Brake hose banjo bolt	30	–	22
Brake hose mounting bracket bolt	6	53	–
Caliper bleed valve	6	53	–
Front caliper mounting bolt	40	–	30
Front master cylinder mounting bolt			
1998-2001 models	13	115	–
2002-2003 models	9	80	–
Rear brake pedal/footpeg bolts	28	–	21
Rear caliper			
Mounting bolt (1998-2001 models)	40	–	30
Mounting pin bolt (2002-2003 models)	27	–	20
Rear master cylinder mounting bolts	23	–	17
Pushrod joint nut	16	–	12

15

BODY PANELS

This chapter contains removal and installation procedures for the fairing components.

As soon as a body panel is removed from the frame, reinstall the mounting hardware onto the removed panel. If working on a used machine, some of the fasteners may be missing, incorrectly installed or of a different design from the original equipment.

The plastic body panels are expensive. After each panel is removed from the frame, wrap it in a towel or blanket and store it in a safe area where it will not be damaged.

BODY PANEL FASTENERS

There are several different types of quick-release fasteners used to attach the body panels to each other and to the frame. The one used most frequently is the plastic quick-release trim clip that can be reused. Another type is the quarter turn quick-release metal screw. Observe the type of fastener used prior to trying to release them from the body panel. The body panels are expensive and can be damaged if trying to release a fastener the incorrect way.

Quick-Release Trim Clips

The plastic quick-release trim clips degenerate with heat, age and use. Refer to A, **Figure 1** for a new trim clip and to B, **Figure 1** for a worn trim clip. It is very difficult, or sometimes impossible, to install a worn trim clip through the mounting hole(s). The ends may break off, or get distorted so they will not close down sufficiently to allow insertion into the body panel mounting holes.

These trim clips are inexpensive and should be replaced as necessary. Purchase approximately a dozen if all of the body panels are going to be removed.

To release the trim clips, push the center in with a Phillips screwdriver (A, **Figure 2**) to release the inner lock. The center portion will pop out, then with-

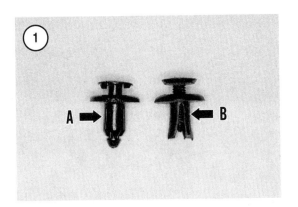

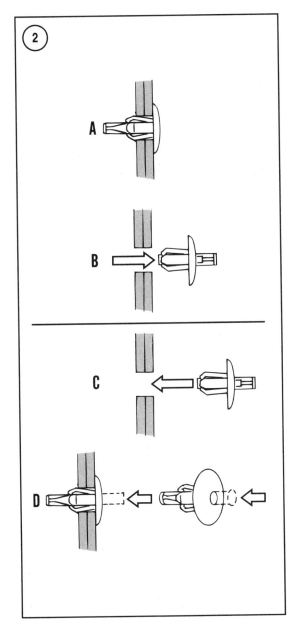

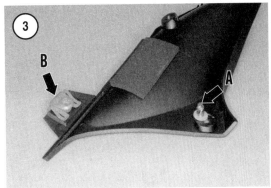

draw the trim clip (B, **Figure 2**) from the plastic panels.

To install the trim clips, press the clip into the opening in the plastic panel (C, **Figure 2**), then push the center portion in (D) to lock it into place.

Quick Fastener Screw and Special Nuts

The quarter turn quick-fastener screws (A, **Figure 3**) are used mainly to secure one body panel to one another. Use an Allen wrench and turn the fastener 1/4 turn (A, **Figure 4**) counterclockwise to release it from the adjacent body panel. The screw will usually stay with the outer body panel, as it is held in place with a plastic washer (A, **Figure 3**). This screw can be reused many times.

The special nuts (Tinnerman clips) are U-shaped metal clips (B, **Figure 3**) that are pushed onto the edge of a body panel and will usually remain secured to the body panel during removal. If one falls off, slightly crimp it together and push it back into place on the panel.

16

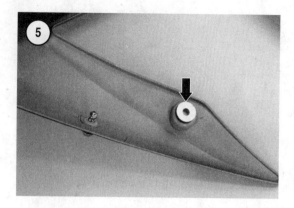

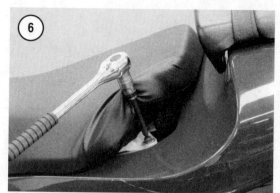

In some locations, a collar and rubber bushing are used in conjunction with a typical metal screw. Refer to **Figure 5** and B, **Figure 4**.

RIDER'S SEAT

Removal/Installation

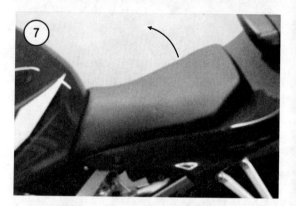

1. Pull the rear corner of the seat up and remove the mounting bolt (**Figure 6**).

2. Repeat for the other side, then pull the seat back up (**Figure 7**) while disconnecting the front seat hook from the fuel tank bracket.

3. Inspect the front hook (A, **Figure 8**) and both rear mounting tabs (B) for damage. Replace the seat if necessary.

4. To install, push the front of the seat down and lock it into the fuel tank bracket. Push the rear of the seat down and install both mounting bolts. Tighten the bolts securely.

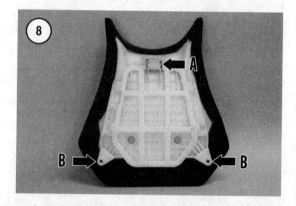

> **WARNING**
> *After the seat is installed, pull up on it firmly and move it from side to side to make sure it is securely mounted in place. If the seat is improperly installed, it could lead to loss of control and a possible accident.*

PASSENGER SEAT

Removal/Installation

1. Use the ignition key and unlock the seat lock (**Figure 9**) on the right side.

2. Slide the seat forward (**Figure 10**) to release the rear projection and remove the seat.

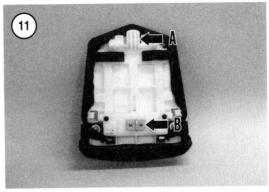

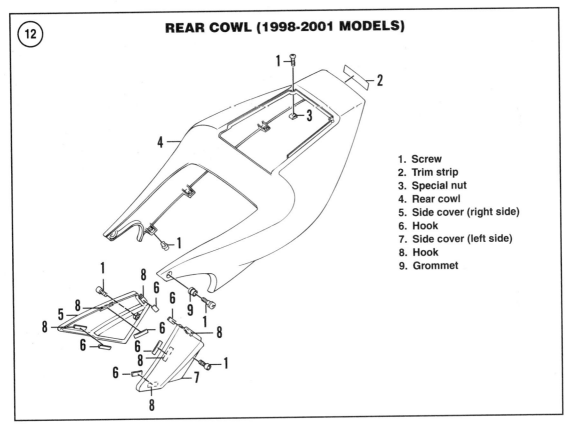

REAR COWL (1998-2001 MODELS)

1. Screw
2. Trim strip
3. Special nut
4. Rear cowl
5. Side cover (right side)
6. Hook
7. Side cover (left side)
8. Hook
9. Grommet

3. Inspect the rear hook (A, **Figure 11**) and the front mounting bracket (B) for damage. Replace the seat if necessary.

4. To install, hook the seat rear projection onto the seat holder, pivot the front down and lock the seat in place.

WARNING
After the seat is installed, pull up on it firmly and move it from side to side to make sure it is securely mounted in

place. If the seat is improperly installed, it could lead to the passenger sliding to one side and a possible accident.

REAR COWL (1998-2001 MODELS)

Removal/Installation

Refer to **Figure 12**.

1. Remove both seats as described in this chapter.

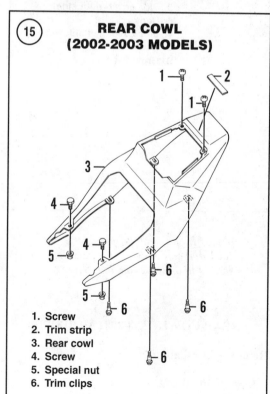

**REAR COWL
(2002-2003 MODELS)**

1. Screw
2. Trim strip
3. Rear cowl
4. Screw
5. Special nut
6. Trim clips

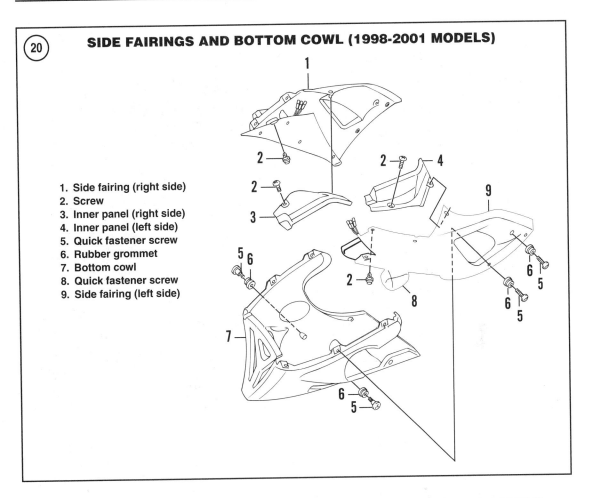

20 **SIDE FAIRINGS AND BOTTOM COWL (1998-2001 MODELS)**

1. Side fairing (right side)
2. Screw
3. Inner panel (right side)
4. Inner panel (left side)
5. Quick fastener screw
6. Rubber grommet
7. Bottom cowl
8. Quick fastener screw
9. Side fairing (left side)

2. Remove the top screw(s) (A, **Figure 13**) at the rear of the cowl.

3A. On 1998-1999 models, remove the three trim clips (B, **Figure 13**) on each side of the cowl (total of six).

3B. On 2000-2001 models, remove the four trim clips (B, **Figure 13**) on each side of the cowl (total of eight).

4. Remove the screw and rubber grommet (**Figure 14**) on each side of the cowl.

5. Carefully pull out on the front of the rear cowl, then pull it straight back and off the tail/brake light unit attached to the seat rail. Remove the rear cowl.

6. Install by reversing these removal steps while noting the following:

   a. Push the rear cowl mating surfaces against the seat rail prior to installing and tightening the mounting bolts, screws and trim clips.

   b. Tighten the screws securely.

REAR COWL (2002-2003 MODELS)

Removal/Installation

Refer to **Figure 15**.

1. Remove both seats as described in this chapter.
2. Remove the trim clips securing the panel (**Figure 16**) to the under side of the rear cowl.
3. Remove the trim clips (**Figure 17**) securing the front of the rear cowl to the seat rail.
4. Remove the two screws (**Figure 18**) securing the rear of the rear cowl to the seat rail.
5. Pull out on the sides, then move toward the rear (**Figure 19**) and remove the rear cowl.
6. Install by reversing these removal steps.

BOTTOM COWL

Removal/Installation

Refer to **Figure 20**.

16

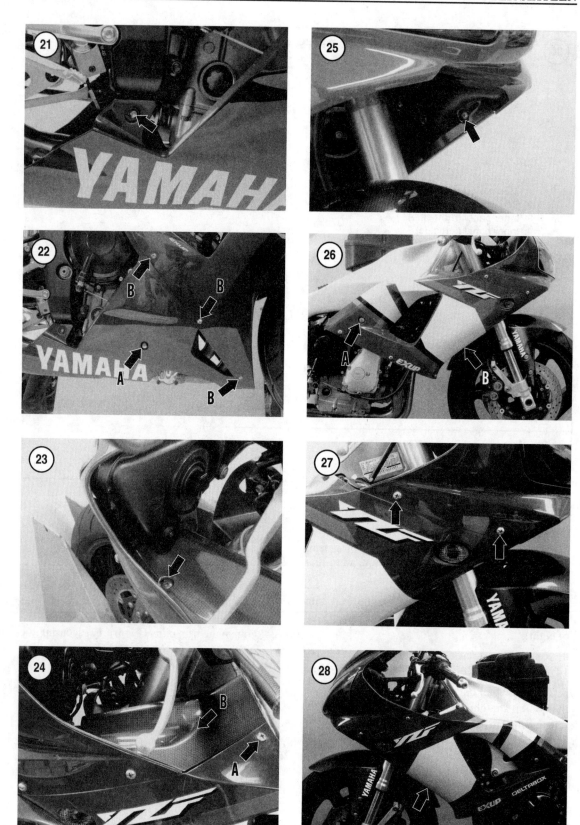

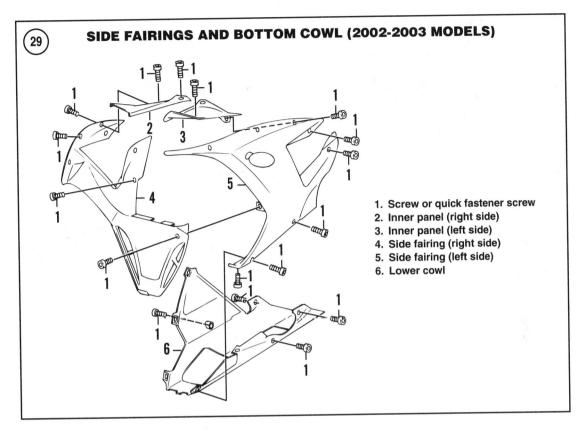

SIDE FAIRINGS AND BOTTOM COWL (2002-2003 MODELS)

29

1. Screw or quick fastener screw
2. Inner panel (right side)
3. Inner panel (left side)
4. Side fairing (right side)
5. Side fairing (left side)
6. Lower cowl

1. Place a cardboard box under the bottom cowl to support it after the fasteners have been removed from one side.

2. Remove the two quick fastener screws securing the lower portion of the bottom cowl to the frame. Refer to **Figure 21** and A, **Figure 22**.

3. Remove the three quick fastener screws (B, **Figure 22**) securing the upper portion of the bottom cowl to the side fairing.

4. Repeat Step 2 and Step 3 for the fasteners on the other side of the bottom cowl.

5. Remove the bottom cowl.

6. Install by reversing these removal steps.

SIDE FAIRING (1998-2001 MODELS)

Removal/Installation

Refer to **Figure 20**.

1. Remove both seats as described in this chapter.

2. Remove the bottom cowl as described in this chapter.

3. Remove the fuel tank as described in Chapter Eight.

4. Remove the screw (**Figure 23**) and the quick fastener screw (A, **Figure 24**) securing the inner panel (B). Remove the inner panel.

5. Remove the trim clip (**Figure 25**) securing the front inner portion of side fairing to the front fairing.

6. Disconnect the electrical connector from the front turn signal assembly.

7. Remove the screw (A, **Figure 26**) securing the rear portion of the side fairing to the frame.

8. Remove the two fastener screws (**Figure 27**) securing the front portion of side fairing to the front fairing.

9. Remove the side fairing (B, **Figure 26**) from the frame.

10. Repeat for side fairing (**Figure 28**) on the other side if necessary.

11. Install by reversing these removal steps.

SIDE FAIRING (2002-2003 MODELS)

Removal/Installation

Refer to **Figure 29**.

16

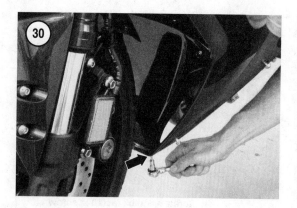

1. Remove both seats as described in this chapter.

2. Remove the bottom cowl as described in this chapter.

3. Remove the fuel tank as described in Chapter Nine.

4. On the lower left side, remove the screw (**Figure 30**) securing the portion of both panels together.

5. On the right side fairing panel, remove the screw (**Figure 31**) securing the left side of the front portion of the panel to the frame.

6. Remove the two screws (A, **Figure 32**) and one quick release fastener (B) securing the inner panel (C). Remove the inner panel.

7. Remove the two screws (**Figure 33**) securing the rear portion of the side fairing to the frame.

8. Remove the two fastener screws (A, **Figure 34**) securing the front portion of side fairing to the front fairing.

9. Slide the side fairing toward the rear to disengage the front tab (**Figure 35**) from the front fairing.

10. Lower the side fairing and disconnect the electrical connector (**Figure 36**) from the front turn signal assembly.

11. Remove the side fairing (B, **Figure 34**) from the frame.

12. Repeat for the other side if necessary.

13. Install by reversing these removal steps.

MIRRORS

Removal/Installation

1. Working inside the front fairing, remove the two nuts and the rubber cushion securing the mirror to the front fairing and mounting bracket.

2. Pull the mirror (**Figure 37**) straight up and off the front fairing.

3. Repeat for the other side if necessary.

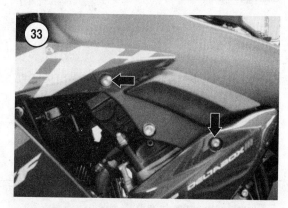

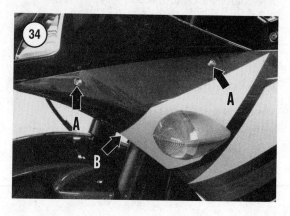

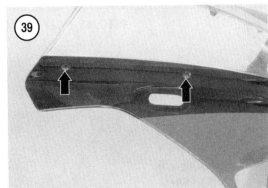

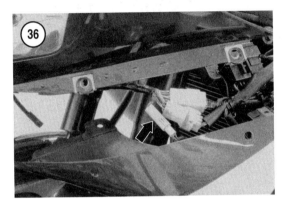

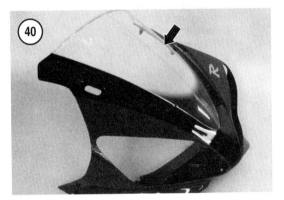

4. Install the mirror(s) and tighten the nuts securely.

5. Sit on the seat and readjust the mirrors before riding the motorcycle.

WINDSHIELD

Removal/Installation

1. Remove the left and right side mirrors as described in this chapter.

2. Remove the screws and washers (**Figure 38**) securing the windshield to the front fairing.

3. Carefully remove the windshield from the front faring.

4. Inspect the plastic nuts (**Figure 39**) for damage or deterioration.

5. Install by reversing these steps.

Cleaning

1. Never use a petroleum-based product to clean the windshield (**Figure 40**). This will damage the surface.

16

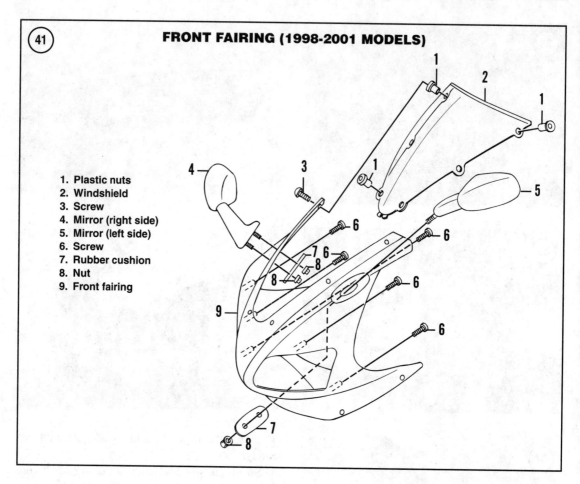

FRONT FAIRING (1998-2001 MODELS)

1. Plastic nuts
2. Windshield
3. Screw
4. Mirror (right side)
5. Mirror (left side)
6. Screw
7. Rubber cushion
8. Nut
9. Front fairing

2. Some commercially available glass cleaners can cause hazing to the windshield surface and may damage the hard coating. Avoid using them.

3. Some anti-fog windshield products can damage the windshield if not used properly. Do not apply in bright sunlight or allow it to dry on the windshield surface. If applied incorrectly, it will produce smears or hazing immediately after application.

4. To remove dried bugs, bird droppings or road dirt, wet a paper towel with water and apply it to the affected area of the windshield. Allow it to set for a few minutes to soften the debris. Remove the paper towel and *gently* wipe away the debris. This process also works very well to remove debris from the body panels and the fuel tank.

FRONT FAIRING (1998-2001 MODELS)

Removal/Installation

Refer to **Figure 41**.

1. Remove the fuel tank as described in Chapter Eight.

2. Remove the left and right side fairing panels as described in this chapter.

3. Place several heavy towels on the front fender to protect the finish on both the fender and the front fairing.

4. Remove the mirrors as described in this chapter.

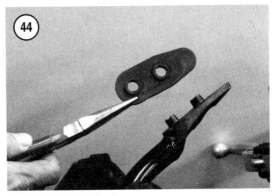

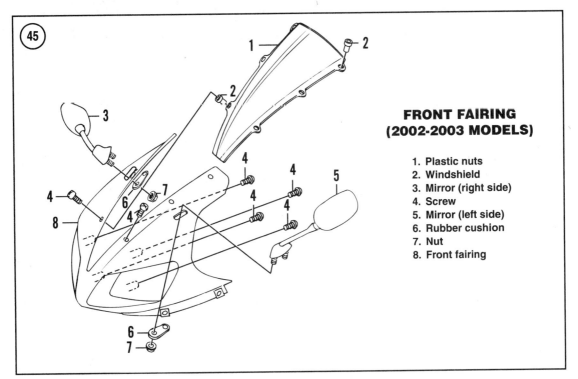

**FRONT FAIRING
(2002-2003 MODELS)**

1. Plastic nuts
2. Windshield
3. Mirror (right side)
4. Screw
5. Mirror (left side)
6. Rubber cushion
7. Nut
8. Front fairing

5. Remove the two screws (**Figure 42**) on each side securing the front fairing to the front fairing mounting bracket.

6. Pull out slightly on each side to release the fairing from the mirror mounts (A, **Figure 43**) on the mounting bracket. Remove the front fairing assembly (B, **Figure 43**). Do not lose the mirror rubber cushion (**Figure 44**) on the mounting bracket.

7. Install by reversing these removal steps while noting the following:

   a. Install the mirror rubber cushion (**Figure 44**) on the mounting bracket on both sides.

   b. Align the front faring mounting bosses with the rubber grommets on the fairing mounting grommets and push the fairing into place.

   c. Tighten the four screws securely.

FRONT FAIRING (2002-2003 MODELS)

Removal/Installation

Refer to **Figure 45**.

CAUTION
*The headlight and meter assembly
must be removed along with the front*

16

fairing. This is necessary to gain access to the front fairing center mounting screw located between the headlight units. If the front fairing is removed without first removing the center screw, the mounting post will be broken off.

1. Remove the fuel tank (Chapter Nine).

2. Remove the left and right side fairing panels as described in this chapter.

3. Remove the mirrors as described in this chapter.

4. On the left side, disconnect the two multi-pin electrical connectors (**Figure 46**) for the headlights and meter assembly.

5. Place several towels on the front fender to protect the finish on both the fender and the front fairing.

6. On the left side, remove the two nuts (**Figure 47**) securing the U-shaped mounting bracket to the frame.

7. Have an assistant hold onto the front fairing.

8. On the right side, remove the U-shaped mounting bracket (**Figure 48**) from the frame boss.

9. Pull out slightly on each side to release the fairing from the mirror mounts (**Figure 49**), then carefully pull the front fairing assembly straight forward and off the frame.

10. To remove the front fairing from the headlight and meter assembly, remove the four mounting screws (**Figure 50**). Remove the front fairing.

11. Use a long screwdriver and remove the center mounting screw (**Figure 51**) between the headlight units.

12. Separate the front fairing from the headlight and meter assembly.

13. Install by reversing these removal steps.

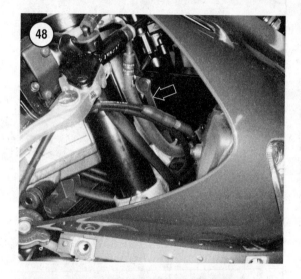

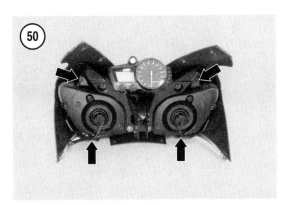

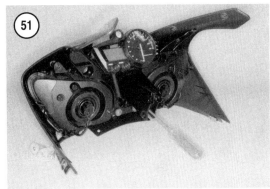

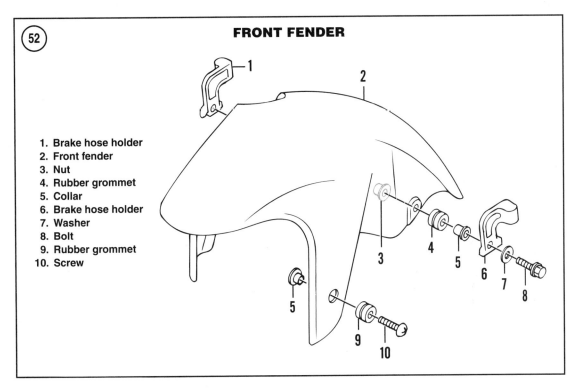

FRONT FENDER

1. Brake hose holder
2. Front fender
3. Nut
4. Rubber grommet
5. Collar
6. Brake hose holder
7. Washer
8. Bolt
9. Rubber grommet
10. Screw

FRONT FENDER

Removal/Installation

Refer to **Figure 52**.

1. Remove the bolt and brake line bracket (A, **Figure 53**) to the fender and brake caliper mounting bracket on each side.

2. Remove the two bolts (B, **Figure 53**) on each side securing the front fender to the fork mounting bracket on each side.

3. Pull the front fender (C, **Figure 53**) forward and remove it.

4. Install by reversing these removal steps.

16

INDEX

17

17

17

NOTES

NOTES

NOTES

NOTES

WIRING DIAGRAMS

1998-1999 YZF-R1 (U.S. AND CANADA MODELS)

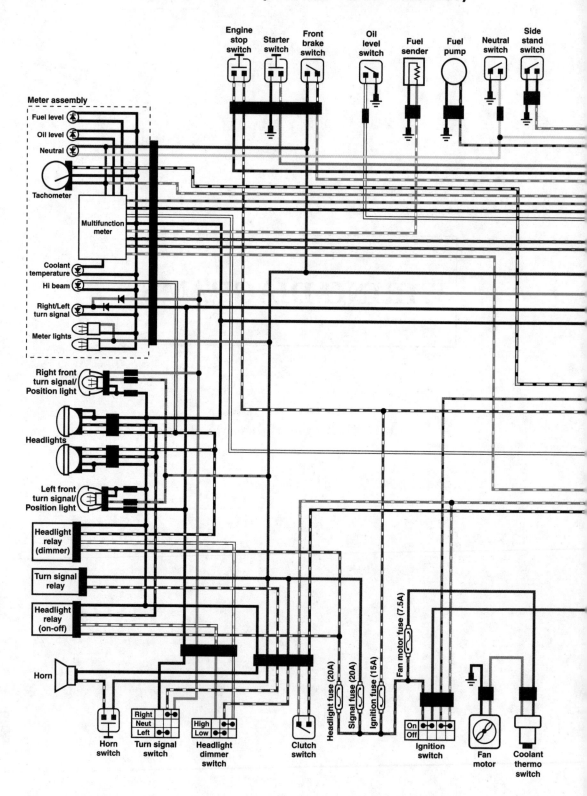

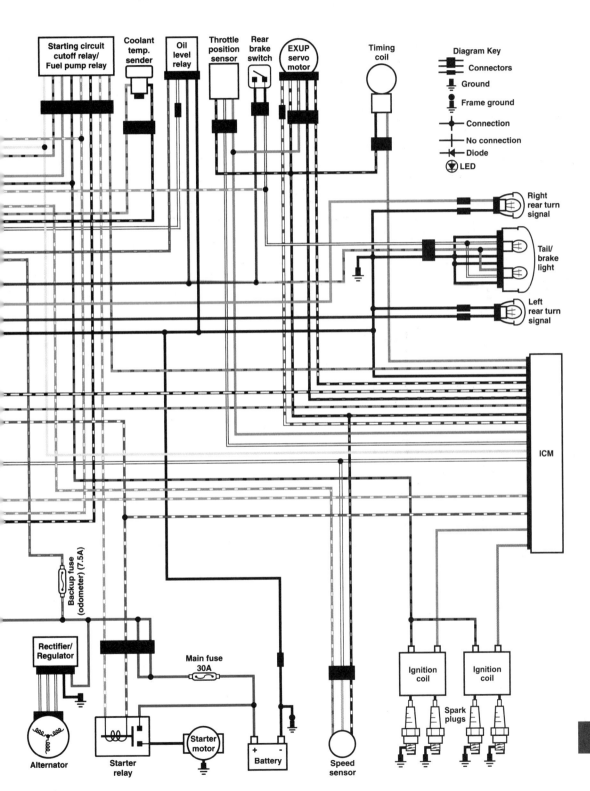

1998-1999 YZF-R1 (OTHER THAN U.S. AND CANADA MODELS)

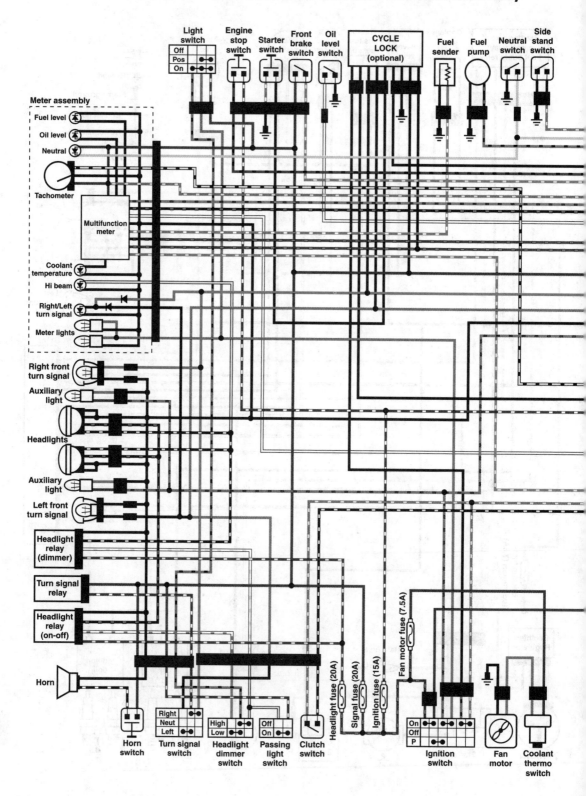

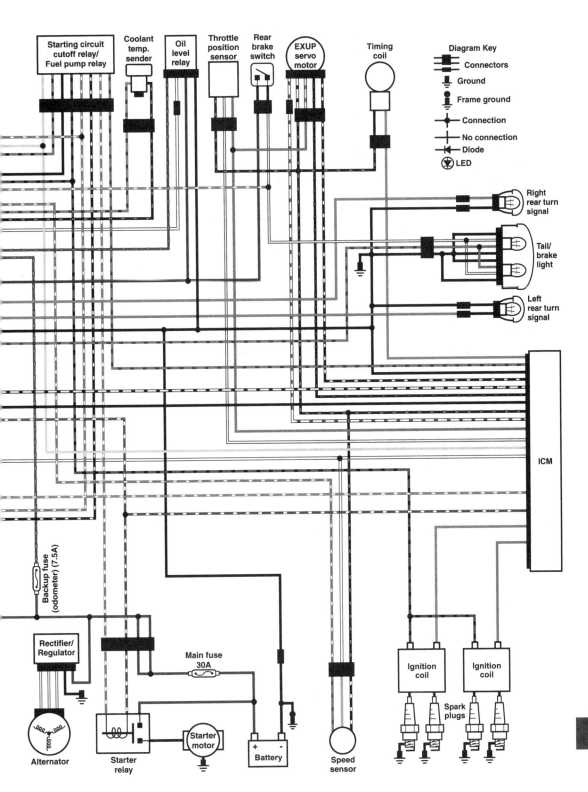

2000-2001 YZF-R1 (U.S. AND CANADA MODELS)

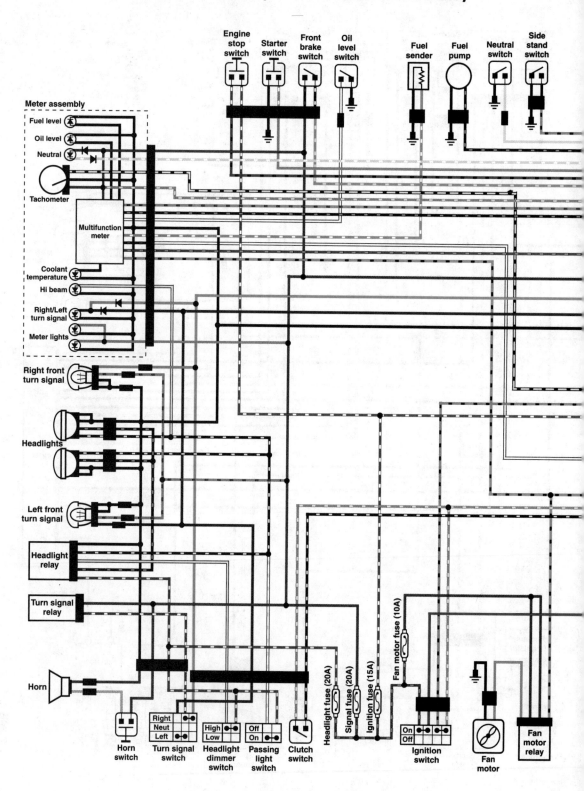

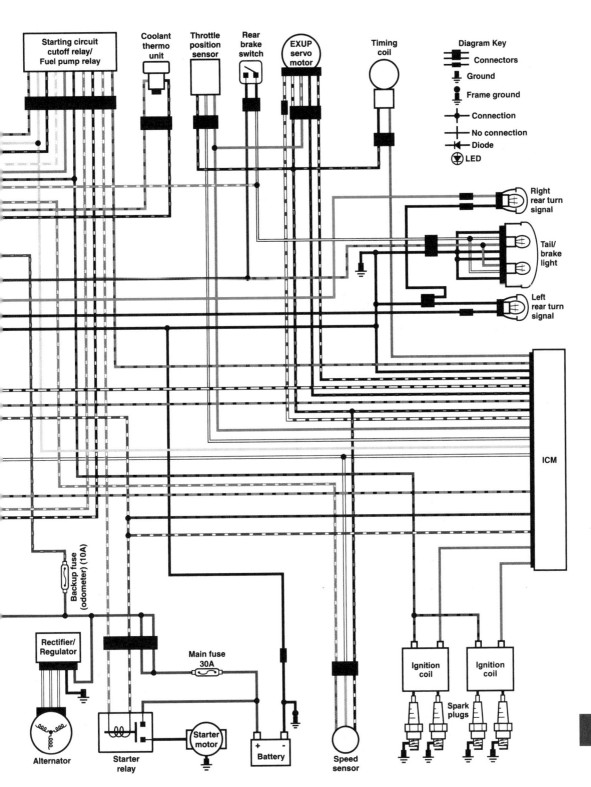

2000-2001 YZF-R1 (OTHER THAN U.S. AND CANADA MODELS)

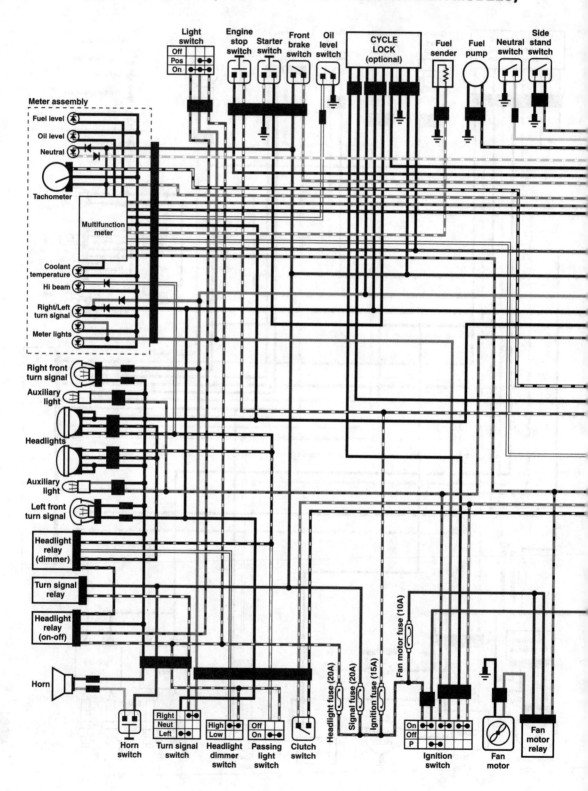

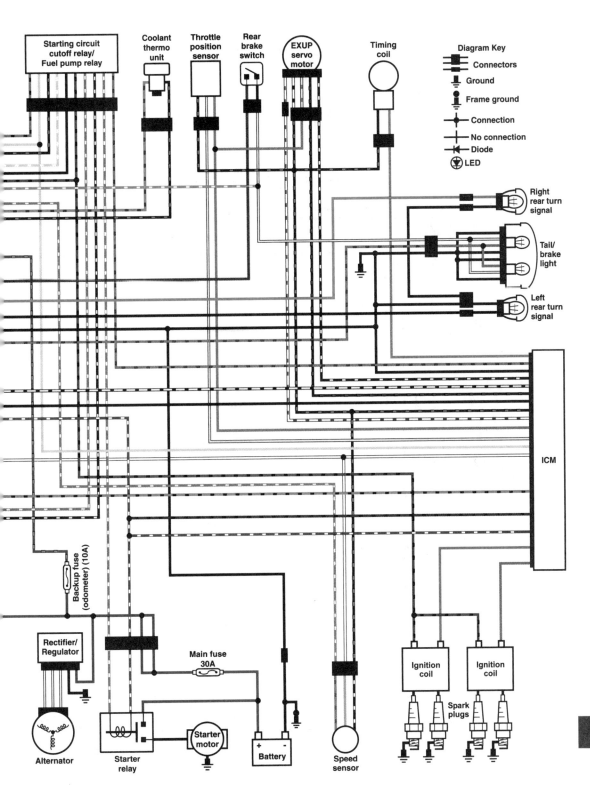

18

2002-2003 YZF-R1 (U.S. AND CANADA MODELS)

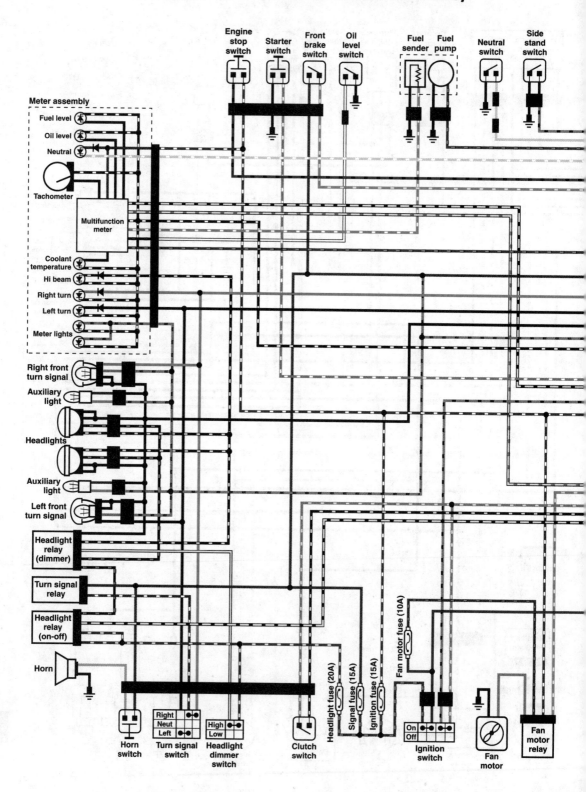

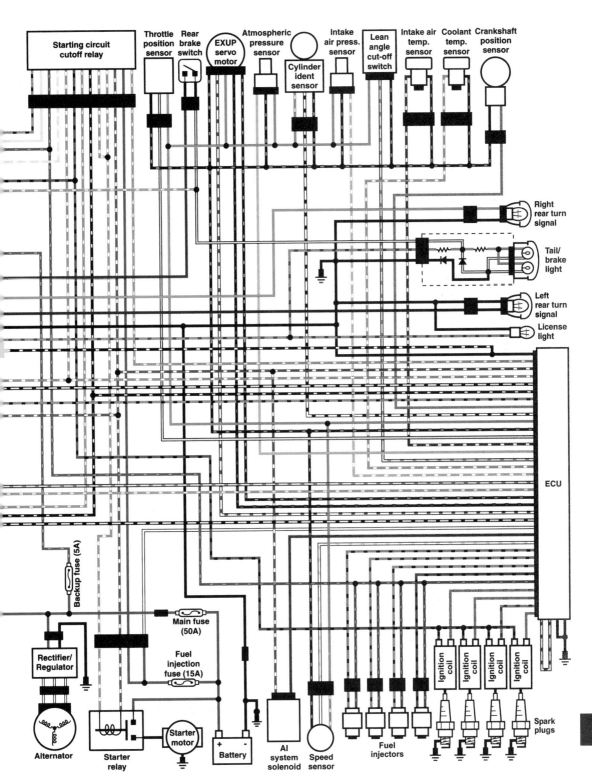

Starting circuit cutoff relay

Throttle position sensor

Rear brake switch

EXUP servo motor

Atmospheric pressure sensor

Cylinder ident sensor

Intake air press. sensor

Lean angle cut-off switch

Intake air temp. sensor

Coolant temp. sensor

Crankshaft position sensor

Right rear turn signal

Tail/ brake light

Left rear turn signal

License light

ECU

Backup fuse (5A)

Main fuse (50A)

Fuel injection fuse (15A)

Rectifier/ Regulator

Ignition coil

Spark plugs

Alternator

Starter relay

Starter motor

+ − Battery

AI system solenoid

Speed sensor

Fuel injectors

18

2002-2003 YZF-R1 (OTHER THAN U.S. AND CANADA MODELS)

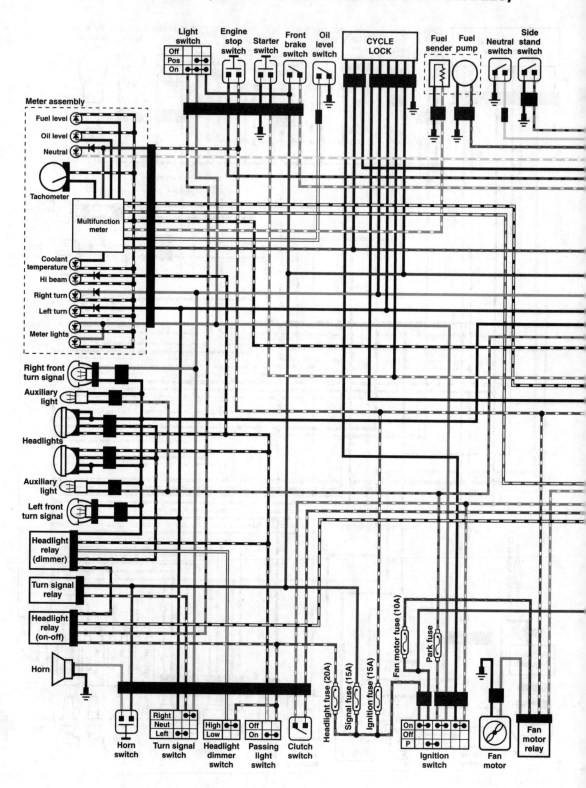

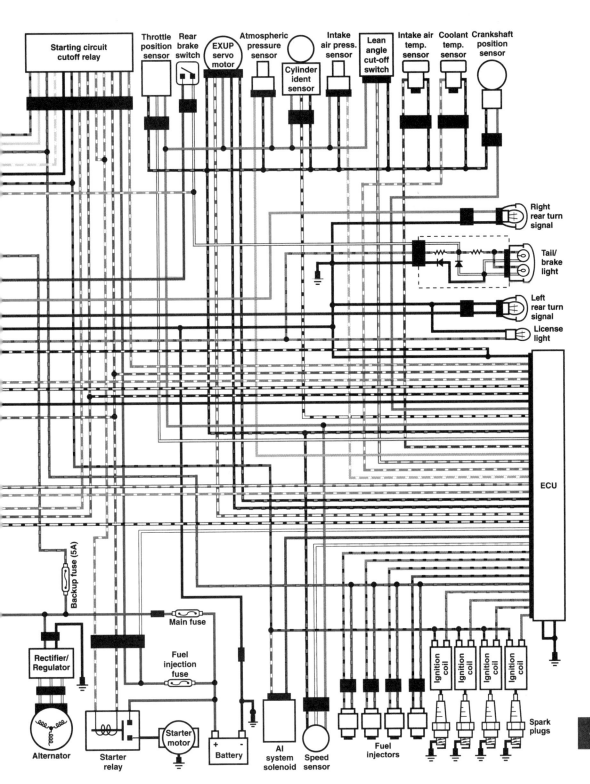

NOTES

MAINTENANCE LOG

Date	Miles	Type of Service

BMW

M308	500 & 600cc Twins, 55-69
M309	F650, 1994-2000
M500-3	BMW K-Series, 85-97
M501	K1200RS, GT & LT, 98-05
M502-3	BMW R50/5-R100GS PD, 70-96
M503-3	R850, R1100, R1150 and R1200C, 93-05

HARLEY-DAVIDSON

M419	Sportsters, 59-85
M429-5	XL/XLH Sportster, 86-03
M427-1	XL Sportster, 04-06
M418	Panheads, 48-65
M420	Shovelheads, 66-84
M421-3	FLS/FXS Evolution, 84-99
M423-2	FLS/FXS Twin Cam, 00-05
M422-3	FLH/FLT/FXR Evolution, 84-98
M430-4	FLH/FLT Twin Cam, 99-05
M424-2	FXD Evolution, 91-98
M425-3	FXD Twin Cam, 99-05
M426	VRSC Series, 02-07

HONDA

ATVs

M316	Odyssey FL250, 77-84
M311	ATC, TRX & Fourtrax 70-125, 70-87
M433	Fourtrax 90, 93-00
M326	ATC185 & 200, 80-86
M347	ATC200X & Fourtrax 200SX, 86-88
M455	ATC250 & Fourtrax 200/250, 84-87
M342	ATC250R, 81-84
M348	TRX250R/Fourtrax 250R & ATC250R, 85-89
M456-3	TRX250X 87-92; TRX300EX 93-04
M215	TRX250EX, 01-05
M446-3	TRX250 Recon & Recon ES, 97-07
M346-3	TRX300/Fourtrax 300 & TRX300FW/Fourtrax 4x4, 88-00
M200-2	TRX350 Rancher, 00-06
M459-3	TRX400 Foreman 95-03
M454-3	TRX400EX 99-05
M205	TRX450 Foreman, 98-04
M210	TRX500 Rubicon, 01-04

Singles

M310-13	50-110cc OHC Singles, 65-99
M319-2	XR50R, CRF50F, XR70R & CRF70F, 97-05
M315	100-350cc OHC, 69-82
M317	125-250cc Elsinore, 73-80
M442	CR60-125R Pro-Link, 81-88
M431-2	CR80R, 89-95, CR125R, 89-91
M435	CR80R, 96-02
M457-2	CR125R & CR250R, 92-97
M464	CR125R, 1998-2002
M443	CR250R-500R Pro-Link, 81-87
M432-3	CR250R, 88-91 & CR500R, 88-01
M437	CR250R, 97-01
M352	CRF250R, CRF250X, CRF450R & CRF450X, 02-05
M312-13	XL/XR75-100, 75-03
M318-4	XL/XR/TLR 125-200, 79-03
M328-4	XL/XR250, 78-00; XL/XR350R 83-85; XR200R, 84-85; XR250L, 91-96
M320-2	XR400R, 96-04
M339-8	XL/XR 500-600, 79-90
M221	XR600R & XR650L, 91-07
M225	XR650R, 00-07

Twins

M321	125-200cc Twins, 65-78
M322	250-350cc Twins, 64-74
M323	250-360cc Twins, 74-77
M324-5	Twinstar, Rebel 250 & Nighthawk 250, 78-03
M334	400-450cc Twins, 78-87
M333	450 & 500cc Twins, 65-76
M335	CX & GL500/650, 78-83
M344	VT500, 83-88
M313	VT700 & 750, 83-87
M314-3	VT750 Shadow Chain Drive, 98-06
M440	VT1100C Shadow, 85-96
M460-4	VT1100 Series, 95-07
M230	VTX1800 Series, 02-08

Fours

M332	CB350-550, SOHC, 71-78
M345	CB550 & 650, 83-85
M336	CB650, 79-82
M341	CB750 SOHC, 69-78
M337	CB750 DOHC, 79-82
M436	CB750 Nighthawk, 91-93 & 95-99
M325	CB900, 1000 & 1100, 80-83
M439	600 Hurricane, 87-90
M441-2	CBR600F2 & F3, 91-98
M445-2	CBR600F4, 99-06
M220	CBR600RR, 03-06
M434-2	CBR900RR Fireblade, 93-99
M329	500cc V-Fours, 84-86
M438	VFR800 Interceptor, 98-00
M349	700-1000 Interceptor, 83-85
M458-2	VFR700F-750F, 86-97
M327	700-1100cc V-Fours, 82-88
M340	GL1000 & 1100, 75-83
M504	GL1200, 84-87
M508	ST1100/Pan European, 90-02

Sixes

M505	GL1500 Gold Wing, 88-92
M506-2	GL1500 Gold Wing, 93-00
M507-2	GL1800 Gold Wing, 01-05
M462-2	GL1500C Valkyrie, 97-03

KAWASAKI

ATVs

M465-2	Bayou KLF220 & KLF250, 88-03
M466-4	Bayou KLF300, 86-04
M467	Bayou KLF400, 93-99
M470	Lakota KEF300, 95-99
M385-2	Mojave KSF250, 87-04

Singles

M350-9	80-350cc Rotary Valve, 66-01
M444-2	KX60, 83-02; KX80 83-90
M448	KX80/85/100, 89-03
M351	KDX200, 83-88
M447-3	KX125 & KX250, 82-91 KX500, 83-04
M472-2	KX125, 92-00
M473-2	KX250, 92-00
M474-2	KLR650, 87-06

Twins

M355	KZ400, KZ/Z440, EN450 & EN500, 74-95
M360-3	EX500, GPZ500S, Ninja 500 R, 87-02
M356-5	Vulcan 700 & 750, 85-06
M354-3	Vulcan 800 & Vulcan 800 Classic, 95-05
M357-2	Vulcan 1500, 87-99
M471-3	Vulcan 1500 Series, 96-08

Fours

M449	KZ500/550 & ZX550, 79-85
M450	KZ, Z & ZX750, 80-85
M358	KZ650, 77-83
M359-3	Z & KZ 900-1000cc, 73-81
M451-3	KZ, ZX & ZN 1000 &1100cc, 81-02
M452-3	ZX500 & Ninja ZX600, 85-97
M468-2	Ninja ZX-6, 90-04
M469	Ninja ZX-7, 91-98
M453-3	Ninja ZX900, ZX1000 & ZX1100, 84-01
M409	Concours, 86-04

POLARIS

ATVs

M496	3-, 4- and 6-Wheel Models w/250-425cc Engines, 85-95
M362	Magnum and Big Boss, 96-98
M363	Scrambler 500 4X4, 97-00
M365-2	Sportsman/Xplorer, 96-03

SUZUKI

ATVs

M381	ALT/LT 125 & 185, 83-87
M475	LT230 & LT250, 85-90
M380-2	LT250R Quad Racer, 85-92
M270	LT-Z400, 03-07
M343	LTF500F Quadrunner, 98-00
M483-2	King Quad/ Quad Runner 250, 87-98

Singles

M371	RM50-400 Twin Shock, 75-81
M369	125-400cc 64-81
M379	RM125-500 Single Shock, 81-88
M476	DR250-350, 90-94
M477	DR-Z400, 00-06
M384-4	LS650 Savage/S40, 86-07
M386	RM80-250, 89-95
M400	RM125, 96-00
M401	RM250, 96-02

Twins

M372	GS400-450 Chain Drive, 77-87
M481-5	VS700-800 Intruder, 85-07
M260	Volusia/Boulevard C50, 01-06
M482-2	VS1400 Intruder, 87-03
M261	1500 Intruder/C90, 98-07
M484-3	GS500E Twins, 89-02
M361	SV650, 1999-2002

Triple

M368	GT380, GT550 & GT750, 72-77

Fours

M373	GS550, 77-86
M364	GS650, 81-83
M370	GS750, 77-82
M376	GS850-1100 Shaft Drive, 79-84
M378	GS1100 Chain Drive, 80-81
M383-3	Katana 600, 88-96 GSX-R750-1100, 86-87
M331	GSX-R600, 97-00
M264	GSX-R600, 01-05
M478-2	GSX-R750, 88-92
	GSX750F Katana, 89-96
M485	GSX-R750, 96-99
M377	GSX-R1000, 01-04
M266	GSX-R1000, 05-06
M265	GSX1300R Hayabusa, 99-07
M338	Bandit 600, 95-00
M353	GSF1200 Bandit, 96-03

YAMAHA

ATVs

M499	YFM80 Badger, 85-88 & 92-01
M394	YTM200, 250 & YFM200, 83-86
M488-5	Blaster, 88-05
M489-2	Timberwolf, 89-00
M487-5	Warrior, 87-04
M486-6	Banshee, 87-06
M490-3	Moto-4 & Big Bear, 87-04
M493	Kodiak, 93-98
M280-2	Raptor 660R, 01-05
M285	Grizzly 660, 02-07

Singles

M492-2	PW50 & PW80, BW80 Big Wheel 80, 81-02
M410	80-175 Piston Port, 68-76
M415	250-400 Piston Port, 68-76
M412	DT & MX 100-400, 77-83
M414	IT125-490, 76-86
M393	YZ50-80 Monoshock, 78-90
M413	YZ100-490 Monoshock, 76-84
M390	YZ125-250, 85-87 YZ490, 85-90
M391	YZ125-250, 88-93 & WR250Z, 91-93
M497-2	YZ125, 94-01
M498	YZ250, 94-98 WR250Z, 94-97
M406	YZ250F & WR250F, 01-03
M491-2	YZ400F, YZ426F, WR400F WR426F, 98-02
M417	XT125-250, 80-84
M480-3	XT/TT 350, 85-00
M405	XT/TT 500, 76-81
M416	XT/TT 600, 83-89

Twins

M403	XS1, XS2, XS650 & TX650, 70-82
M395-10	XV535-1100 Virago, 81-03
M495-5	V-Star 650, 98-07
M281-3	V-Star 1100, 99-07
M282	Road Star, 99-05

Triple

M404	XS750 & XS850, 77-81

Fours

M387	XJ550, XJ600 & FJ600, 81-92
M494	XJ600 Seca II/Diversion, 92-98
M388	YX600 Radian & FZ600, 86-90
M396	FZR600, 89-93
M392	FZ700-750 & Fazer, 85-87
M411	XS1100, 78-81
M397	FJ1100 & 1200, 84-93
M375	V-Max, 85-03
M374	Royal Star, 96-03
M461	YZF-R6, 99-04
M398	YZF-R1, 98-03
M399	FZ1, 01-05

VINTAGE MOTORCYCLES

Clymer® Collection Series

M330	Vintage British Street Bikes, BSA, 500–650cc Unit Twins; Norton, 750 & 850cc Commandos; Triumph, 500-750cc Twins
M300	Vintage Dirt Bikes, V. 1 Bultaco, 125-370cc Singles; Montesa, 123-360cc Singles; Ossa, 125-250cc Singles
M305	Vintage Japanese Street Bikes Honda, 250 & 305cc Twins; Kawasaki, 250-750cc Triples; Kawasaki, 900 & 1000cc Fours